D0405659

ISABELLA OF CASTILE

ISABELLA

OF CASTILE

*The First
Renaissance
Queen*

NATIONAL UNIVERSITY
LIBRARY SAN DIEGO C.1

NANCY RUBIN

ST. MARTIN'S PRESS   NEW YORK

TO PETER

A WORD ABOUT MONEY

It is very difficult to compare the value of coins of the late fifteenth century with modern ones. Not only did their monetary value fluctuate during Isabella and Ferdinand's era, but the buying power of money was considerably different than it is today. During Isabella's era, the *maravedi* was the standard unit of account. By 1480, the *dobla,* a 19-carat gold coin, was worth 445 *maravedís* and the Aragonese *florin* 265 *maravedís.*

In 1497 the Castilian monarchs introduced and standardized other currencies. Foremost among these was the gold *excelente* which was roughly equivalent to the Florentine *florin* and the Venetian *ducat.* In Castile, the *excelente* was equivalent to 375 *maravedís,* the silver *real* worth 34 *maravedís,* and the copper *blanca,* whose value was 1/2 a *maravedi.* How much would a *maravedi* buy? In the late fifteenth century, a common laborer would earn 15 to 20 *maravedís* a day, a carpenter or mason about 40 *maravedís* for the same day's work.

ISABELLA OF CASTILE: THE FIRST RENAISSANCE QUEEN. Copyright © 1991 by Nancy Rubin. All rights reserved. Printed in the United States of America. No part of this book may be used or reproduced in any manner whatsoever without written permission except in the case of brief quotations embodied in critical articles or reviews. For information, address St. Martin's Press, 175 Fifth Avenue, New York, N.Y. 10010.

Production Editor: David Stanford Burr

Design by Judith Dannecker

Library of Congress Cataloging-in-Publication Data

Rubin, Nancy.
     Isabella of Castile / Nancy Rubin.
         p.   cm.
     ISBN 0-312-05878-0
     1. Isabella I, Queen of Spain, 1451–1504. 2. Spain—History—
Ferdinand and Isabella, 1479–1516. 3. Spain—Kings and rulers—
Biography.   I. Title.
DP163.R83   1991
946'03'092—dc20
[B]
                       90-27079
                       CIP

First Edition: October 1991

10 9 8 7 6 5 4 3 2 1

CONTENTS

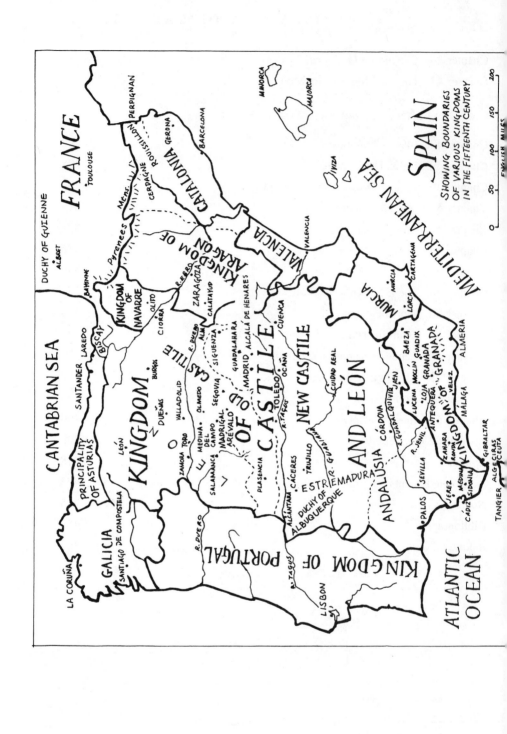

SPAIN

SHOWING BOUNDARIES
OF VARIOUS KINGDOMS
IN THE FIFTEENTH CENTURY

ENGLISH MILES
0   50   100   150   200

FRANCE

DUCHY OF GUIENNE

CANTABRIAN SEA

ATLANTIC OCEAN

MEDITERRANEAN SEA

KINGDOM OF NAVARRE

KINGDOM OF ARAGON

CATALONIA

VALENCIA

MURCIA

KINGDOM OF CASTILE

OLD CASTILE

NEW CASTILE

AND LEÓN

ANDALUSIA

KINGDOM OF GRANADA

ESTRIEMADURA

DUCHY OF ALBUQUERQUE

KINGDOM OF PORTUGAL

GALICIA

PRINCIPALITY OF ASTURIAS

Pyrenees

CERDAGNE   ROUSSILLON

Mtns.

PERPIGNAN

GERONA

BARCELONA

TOULOUSE

ALBRET

BAYONNE

BISCAY

SANTANDER   LAREDO

LA CORUÑA

SANTIAGO DE COMPOSTELA

LEÓN

ZAMORA   TORO

SALAMANCA

PLASENCIA

DUEÑAS

VALLADOLID

MEDINA DEL CAMPO

MADRIGAL   ARÉVALO

OLMEDO

SEGOVIA

BURGOS

OLITO

C.TORRA

R.EBRO

ZARAGOZA

CALÁTAYUD

R.DUERO

SIGUENZA

ALM

GUADALAJARA

ALCALÁ DE HENARES

MADRID

CUENCA

TOLEDO   OCAÑA

R.TAGUS

CÁCERES

TRUJILLO

ALCÁNTARA

CUIDAD REAL

CÓRDOVA

R.GUADIANA

R.GUADALQUIVIR

JAÉN

LUCENA   MOCLIN

LOJA   GRANADA

ANTEQUERA

VÉLEZ

MÁLAGA

BAEZA

GUADIX

ALMERÍA

SEVILLA

R.JENIL

ZAHARA   RONDA

JEREZ

MÉDINA SIDONIA

CÁDIZ

PALOS

GIBRALTAR

ALGECIRAS   CEUTA

TANGIER

IVIZA

MINORCA

MAJORCA

LISBON

R.TAGUS

R.DUERO

VALENCIA

MURCIA

LORCA   CARTAGENA

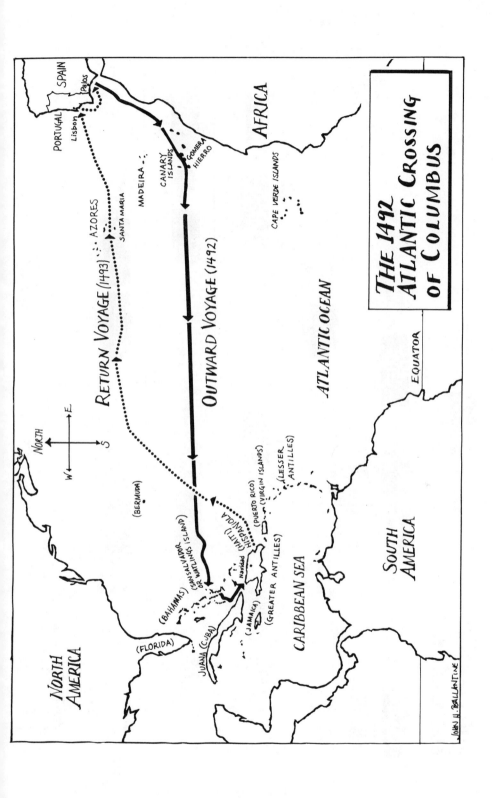

THE 1492
ATLANTIC CROSSING
OF COLUMBUS

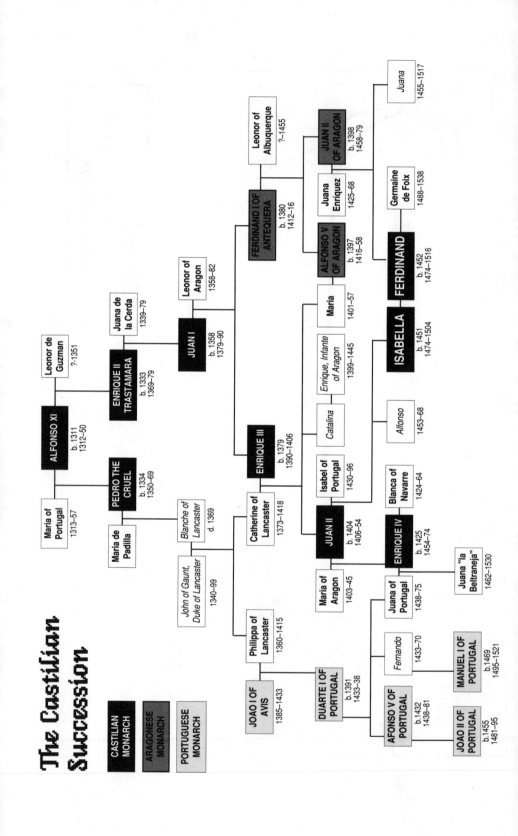

The Castilian Succession

CASTILIAN MONARCH

ARAGONESE MONARCH

PORTUGUESE MONARCH

Maria of Portugal 1313–57

ALFONSO XI b.1311 1312–50

Leonor de Guzman ?–1351

Juana de la Cerda 1339–79

Leonor of Aragon 1358–82

Leonor of Albuquerque ?–1455

Pedro the Cruel b.1334 1350–69

Maria de Padilla

ENRIQUE II TRASTAMARA b.1333 1369–79

JUAN I b.1358 1379–90

FERDINAND I OF ANTEQUERA b.1380 1412–16

Blanche of Lancaster d. 1369

John of Gaunt, Duke of Lancaster 1340–99

Catherine of Lancaster 1373–1418

ENRIQUE III b.1379 1390–1406

Catalina

Enrique, Infante of Aragon 1399–1445

Maria 1401–57

Juana Enriquez 1425–68

ALFONSO V OF ARAGON b.1397 1416–58

JUAN II OF ARAGON b.1398 1458–79

Juana 1455–1517

Philippa of Lancaster 1360–1415

Maria of Aragon 1403–45

JUAN II b.1404 1406–54

Isabel of Portugal 1430–96

Alfonso 1453–68

Blanca of Navarre 1424–64

ENRIQUE IV b.1425 1454–74

ISABELLA b.1451 1474–1504

FERDINAND b.1452 1474–1516

Germaine de Foix 1488–1538

JOAO I OF AVIS 1385–1433

DUARTE I OF PORTUGAL b.1391 1433–38

Juana of Portugal 1438–75

Fernando 1433–70

AFONSO V OF PORTUGAL b.1432 1438–81

Juana "la Beltraneja" 1462–1530

MANUEL I OF PORTUGAL b.1469 1495–1521

JOAO II OF PORTUGAL b.1455 1481–95

The Aragonese Succession

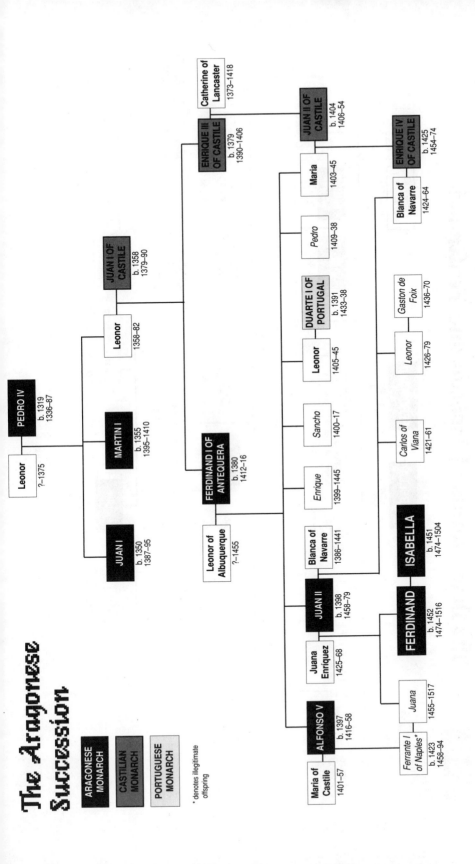

ARAGONESE MONARCH

CASTILIAN MONARCH

PORTUGUESE MONARCH

* denotes illegitimate offspring

Leonor
?–1375

PEDRO IV
b. 1319
1336–87

JUAN I
b. 1350
1387–95

MARTIN I
b. 1355
1395–1410

Leonor
1358–82

JUAN I OF CASTILE
b. 1358
1379–90

ENRIQUE III OF CASTILE
b. 1379
1390–1406

Catherine of Lancaster
1373–1418

JUAN II OF CASTILE
b. 1404
1406–54

Maria
1403–45

ENRIQUE IV OF CASTILE
b. 1425
1454–74

Blanca of Navarre
1424–64

Pedro
1409–38

DUARTE I OF PORTUGAL
b. 1391
1433–38

Leonor
1405–45

Sancho
1400–17

Enrique
1399–1445

Gaston de Foix
1436–70

Leonor
1426–79

Carlos of Viana
1421–61

Leonor of Albuquerque
?–1455

FERDINAND I OF ANTEQUERA
b. 1380
1412–16

Blanca of Navarre
1386–1441

JUAN II
b. 1398
1458–79

Juana Enriquez
1425–68

ALFONSO V
b. 1397
1416–58

Maria of Castile
1401–57

Juana
1455–1517

FERDINAND
b. 1452
1474–1516

ISABELLA
b. 1451
1474–1504

Ferrante I of Naples*
b. 1423
1458–94

The Descendants of Isabella and Ferdinand

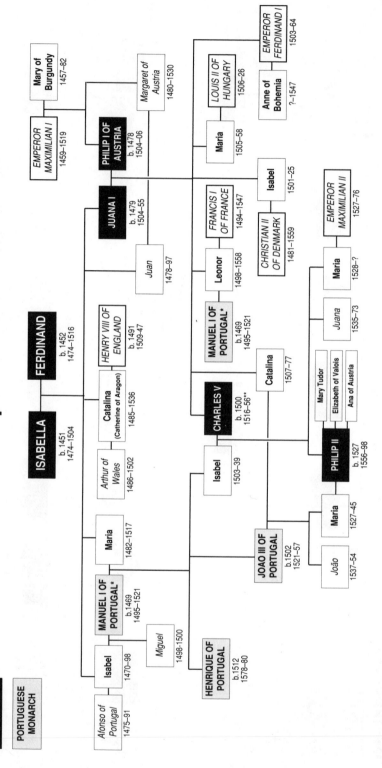

SPANISH MONARCH

PORTUGUESE MONARCH

* Manuel I of Portugal married three descendants of Isabella and Ferdinand.
** Charles I, king of Spain (1516–56), and Charles V, Holy Roman Emperor (1519–58)

PART ONE

An Embattled Princess
1451–1468

CHAPTER ONE

Doña Isabel, Queen Proprietress of Castile

O n Tuesday afternoon, December 13, 1474, thirty nobles assembled outside the turreted castle of Segovia to await Princess Isabella of Castile. The finely spun gold threads of their jerkins glittered in the winter light, and high fur collars and black broad-brimmed hats protected their clean-shaven faces from the cold.

A few hundred feet away Segovian artisans, merchants, and peasants began to gather in small groups. They too waited patiently, for rumors had swirled through the bustling wool-trade town for two days since King Enrique IV's death—rumors made all the more credible by the constant clatter of horses pounding over the castle's wooden drawbridge—that Isabella, Princess of Asturias, was about to be crowned the new Queen of Castile.

Above the human panorama loomed the eleventh-century alcázar—castle—with its azure turrets and massive ocher keep, poised 328 feet above the confluence of the Eresma and Clamores rivers. For nearly three centuries since feudal warriors wrested Segovia from Moorish rule and reconquered Castile for Christianity, guards sat in its watchtowers to scan the surrounding plains and wheat fields beneath its rocky edge. From the highest tower one guard could see that nearly the entire Segovian population had emptied onto the streets in anticipation of Isabella's appearance. Grimy-faced blacksmiths, aproned tanners, brightly dressed bawds, cripples, tonsured monks, young matrons and their children, Jewish merchants, even millers and shepherds from far ends of the city had ceased their work and now choked the city's streets. In their haste they had scattered the chickens, pigs, and goats that wandered the maze of hilly roads and muddy ditches just beyond the alcázar.

In contrast to the buzzing crowds of commoners, the nobles clustered silently around the castle entrance like a shield, their solemn dignity as remarkable as their splendid clothes. These *grandees*, or *ricos hombres*, as Spain's most ancient aristocrats were called, welcomed the russet-haired, twenty-three-year-old princess who was now within the alcázar making final preparations for the coronation. With her crowning, years of intrigue, civil strife, and bloodshed were about to be resolved.

At the appointed hour, Isabella appeared at the castle entrance in a rich *brial*, an elegant gown shimmering with jewels that swept to her ankles. Around her neck was a gold necklace set with gems and pearls. A large dark ruby glittered in its center. Isabella moved gracefully toward a richly harnessed horse, her steady and dignified gait revealing little of the tumultuous emotions that had gripped her in the thirty-six hours since her half brother, King Enrique IV of Castile, had died.

Foreign ambassadors and court observers of the day considered Isabella a beautiful woman. Like her Visigoth ancestors who had invaded Spain from the northern German territories a thousand years earlier, Isabella was a strawberry blonde—coloring especially admired in Castile because of its relative rarity.

Isabella's finely chiseled face and lively expression gave her a "comely aspect" that was not soon forgotten.[1] One courtier even remarked that she was "the handsomest lady I ever beheld."[2] According to her court secretary and historian of her reign, Fernando del Pulgar, Isabella was of medium height, "well formed in her person and the proportion of her limbs . . . very fair and blond: her eyes between green and blue, her look gracious and honest . . . her well-shaped face . . . beautiful and happy."[3]

While such accolades sound like court flattery, all commentators agree that Isabella was "the most gracious in her manners."[4] Whether beautiful or not, Isabella's youthful vitality, gentleness, and personal charisma made her extremely attractive to all who beheld her.

A day and a half earlier—on December 11—King Enrique, Isabella's fifty-year-old half brother, had died suddenly a few minutes before midnight. Two days before, with stubborn disregard for his doctors' orders, the ailing king had gone hunting in his private woods near Madrid. After his collapse he was rushed back to the Madrid palace. Although Enrique had suffered a stomach illness for months, his death came as a cruel shock to the Castilians because he had failed to name an heir to the throne. His ministers had begged the dying king to name either his twelve-year-old daughter, Juana, or his half sister, Isabella, as his successor. Later, there were rumors that Enrique told his secretary, Juan González, that Princess Juana should be his heir and left a will to that effect. But González's claim was mistrusted and the will never found. Such indecision was typical of Enrique. The King had hedged his bets for the last five years of his life, partly out of ambivalence, partly out of genuine fear, hoping to quell the seething aristocratic factions that threatened to tear Castile apart.

Perhaps Enrique did not believe he would die and planned to settle the question of the succession later. Or perhaps, sickened as much by the harrowing events of his reign as from the pains that tore at his belly, he now avenged himself upon Castile by dying silent. In either case Enrique's death left Castile shaken, its political integrity threatened, and its citizens unnerved by roaming packs of bandits, inflated bread and wine prices, and the likelihood of a new civil war. Castile was ripe for a political change, be it for better or for worse.

Isabella's allies lost no time in seizing the initiative. For nearly a year the princess had been living in Segovia with her childhood friend, Beatriz de Bobadilla, whose capable husband Andrés de Cabrera was governor of Segovia's alcázar. Respected by Enrique and sympathetic to Isabella's cause, Cabrera was entrusted with the Castilian treasury, which was housed within the formidable Segovian fortress.

Clearly, Isabella's location at the time of Enrique's death and Cabrera's friendship were indisputable advantages to her ascension. And so was Isabella's popularity with many of Castile's most powerful *grandees* and its common citizens. When Enrique's death was announced, Isabella's supporters urged her to assume the throne immediately. A hasty coronation was essential, they insisted.

Politically, the advice of Isabella's counselors made sense. If she could be enthroned quickly, horseback couriers would immediately ride to Castile's major cities and towns announcing her ascension as the new Queen of Castile and León. It was anticipated that the towns would express their approval by return courier. Later, when the *Cortes*, or parliament of Castile's cities, convened, Isabella would be formally recognized as queen. By the time Princess Juana's allies rallied and attempted to raise her to the throne, Isabella's coronation would have been long accepted by Castile's aristocrats, clergy, and commoners.

Although Isabella was not King Enrique's daughter, her claim as legitimate successor to the Castilian throne was theoretically justifiable. In 1469 Enrique had formally sworn Isabella as heir to the crown. Although later, with typical vacillation, the king had retracted that promise, many Castilians considered his oath inviolate.

On December 13, 1474, after attending a funeral mass for Enrique, the princess thus exchanged her dark mourning clothes for the rich dress in which she would be presented to the world as the new Queen of Castile and León, the first woman and sixth monarch to reign those ancient kingdoms in the Trastámara line.

For her, the coronation was the culmination of seven difficult years of waiting. From bitter experience she knew that a coronation, even one at Segovia with the royal crown of St. Ferdinand, did not necessarily guarantee that she would remain Queen of Castile. For most of those years Isabella had expected to inherit the throne from Enrique through a peaceable succession, but now the king's indecision and precipitous death made it likely that advocates of Isabella's twelve-year-old rival, Juana, would attempt to overrule her claim. Therefore, Isabella agreed that the coronation should take place immediately. The most disturbing aspect, however, was that she had no time to summon her husband, Ferdinand, Prince of Aragón and King of Sicily, from Zaragoza so that he could be crowned with her as king consort.

Thus it was that Isabella alone stepped beyond the heavy wooden doors of the Segovian alcázar. As she mounted the jennet, or small Moorish horse, whose golden reins were held by two Segovian city officials, the aristocrats raised a rich brocade canopy above her. The moment must have been magical, the canopy billowing above her before settling upon its poles, transforming the young princess into a royal figure who commanded the respect of Castilian nobility and symbolized the majesty of the kingdom's ancient laws. The procession slowly approached Segovia's central square, where only that morning carpenters had hastily constructed a broad platform.

The entourage was led by Gutierre de Cárdenas, one of Isabella's most faithful counselors. Mounted on a horse, he carried an unsheathed sword aloft, its tip pointed toward the heavens, to symbolize Castile's ancient sovereignty. Never before in Castile's recorded history had the naked sword been raised for a royal princess or a queen. Solemnly Isabella dismounted, approached the platform, climbed its rude steps, and walked toward the raised throne. Near her sat nobles, judges, and members of the Segovian clergy. Silence descended on the crowd.

Suddenly there was a fanfare of trumpets and horns. A herald's voice rang out, "Castile, Castile, for the Queen and our Proprietress the Queen Doña Isabella, and for the King Don Ferdinand, her legitimate husband!"[5]

Simultaneously Castile's royal banners were unfurled, church bells rang, and cannons were discharged from Segovia's alcázar in recognition of Isabella's coronation. Then the red-mantled Alfonso Carrillo de Acuña, the Archbishop of Toledo and Isabella's childhood mentor, placed a silver crown upon the princess's head. In the earnest manner that was to characterize the nearly thirty years of her reign, Isabella swore homage to Castile's ancient laws and privileges, vowing to respect them and the inhabitants of its kingdom. The *grandees* then rose and walked toward her. As each man knelt and kissed her hand, he acknowledged her as his queen proprietress and legitimate sovereign and swore an oath of lifelong homage as her vassal.

Surrounding Isabella were trusted friends and counselors including Cardinal Pedro González de Mendoza, the archbishop Alfonso Carrillo de Acuña, Admiral Fadrique Enríquez, and others faithful to her cause. Several important faces were missing—that of her younger brother Alfonso, now dead six years, who would have been Castile's next king, and that of her beautiful but deranged mother, Isabel of Portugal, Queen Widow of Castile, who was lost in hallucinations and cloistered in the nearby castle of Arévalo. And most conspicuous of all was the absence of Isabella's husband, Ferdinand, hundreds of miles away presiding over the Aragonese parliament in Zaragoza and still unaware of King Enrique's death.

After Isabella descended the platform, the royal procession moved slowly through the crowd toward Segovia's church of San Miguel. Within its hushed walls, the new queen and her court sang "Te Deum Laudamus." Isabella prostrated herself before the main altar to offer prayers of thanksgiving for the high honor she had received and for guidance and wisdom as a ruler.

Although it was customary in fifteenth-century Castile for rulers to exhibit such piety, Isabella's prayers were not empty rituals. From childhood, religious observance had been woven into every aspect of her life, instilled by her mother during their early years together in Arévalo.

When Isabella first arrived at King Enrique's intrigue-filled court, an observer noted that the ten- or eleven-year-old girl had simple country tastes and was a "sedate" child with a cheerful disposition. Others who watched the princess's behavior over the years knew that she could often be found in the royal chapel at her prayers rather than at cards, at her toilette, or at the banquet table.

Characteristically, during times of crises it was to prayers, fasting, and repentance that Isabella turned for solace, rather than to those around her.

Prayer, devotion, charity, humility—these were qualities that eventually won even the most jaded Castilian countryman to the young queen's side and helped her sway even the haughtiest *grandees* to royal obedience.

Besides her beauty and integrity, Isabella had made a judicious marriage. Her wedding five years earlier to Ferdinand of Aragón had been a coup that elicited enthusiasm from the Castilian towns and some important *grandees* and ecclesiastics. Although the prince came from the smaller, war-torn kingdom of Aragón, Ferdinand's blood relationship, youth, common language, and military prowess made him a far more popular choice as Isabella's husband than the suitors from Portugal, England, and France Enrique had tried to marry her to. In a 1471 circular to Castilian towns, Isabella explained that she had married Ferdinand because "he is so closely linked to these kingdoms, that should God plan anything adverse for me, the right of succession should belong to him."[6]

Nevertheless, Isabella's 1469 marriage to Ferdinand had been an act of rebellion against King Enrique, and she had never received his blessings.

Despite such acts of defiance, discretion was one of Isabella's strongest traits. She had clearly demonstrated it in her first meeting with her bridegroom. Isabella's counselors had demanded that Ferdinand bend and kiss the princess's hand to symbolize Aragón's lesser status. But the eighteen-year-old Isabella had refused to allow it. She would, she told her skeptical advisors, meet Ferdinand face to face as an equal, as befit husband and wife regardless of the size or wealth of their kingdoms. This sensitivity to male pride bore dividends. Love, even passion, bloomed between the young couple in the early years of their marriage, binding Ferdinand to Castile for reasons that were as personally compelling as politically self-aggrandizing.

Yet Isabella's popularity and her young husband's military prowess still would not assure her a bloodless succession to the throne. Sharp dissensions would arise over Isabella's coronation in Castile with old allies defecting from her cause and a second civil war erupting. But once Isabella settled into her role as Queen of Castile, the trust she inspired among her subjects would become the cornerstone of a new national identity—one enabling her to consolidate royal power, codify the Castilian laws, administer justice, conquer the Moors, and support visionaries such as Christopher Columbus, who in 1474 was still an obscure Genoese seafaring merchant. Over time, Isabella's personal vision and political policies would spread beyond Spain into Italy, Africa, and the New World where she would be remembered as the "Mother of the Americas."

But the dark side of her reign would overshadow these achievements. The impact of Isabella's religious piety would release twin fonts of devotional fanaticism. One stream scoured the Spanish church of corrupt practices, inspired a national reform of monastic orders, and strengthened the Spanish Catholic church so that it would survive the next century's Protestant Reformation. The other headwater, in the form of the Inquisition, would leave a dark stain of oppression, bigotry, and anti-intellectualism on the face of Western Europe for several centuries and contribute to Spain's *leyenda negra*, or "dark legend" of sadistic cruelty and intolerance. According to that legend, the Spain united by

Isabella and Ferdinand was a primitive country of torture chambers, religious dogmatism, and bloody bullfights, peopled by a swarthy, suspicious people cut off from the mainstream of European culture—a distortion of the exotic mores and manners of the Hispanic culture.

After Isabella's death in 1504 the Spanish Inquisition, with its banned books and censorship of the arts and intellectual thought, would spread to Rome, France, and the German states. Later, in the sixteenth century, as Germany embraced Lutheranism and France and Italy remained Catholic, the Iberian Counter-Reformation under Isabella's great-grandson Philip II blocked Spain from fully participating in the intellectual life of post-Reformation Europe.

To this day Isabella's legacy has led to historical revisionism and debate. Some scholars have pictured her as a saint, and at this writing there are still efforts underway in Spain to have Isabella canonized.

After Isabella's death the Italian nuncio Baldesar Castiglione noted that "unless all the people of Spain, men and women, rich and poor, have combined to tell lies in her praise, there has not been in our time in the whole world a brighter example of true goodness, greatness of spirit, wisdom, religion, honor, courtesy, liberality, and every virtue, in short, than this Queen Isabella."[7] Exactly a century after Isabella's death those same lofty ideals of her reign were immortalized in Miguel de Cervantes's *Don Quixote*.

Others, however—including a contemporary traveler, Niccolaus von Poppelau, who visited Isabella and Ferdinand in Sevilla in 1484—noted that there was a terrifying side to Isabella's sense of justice: "everyone trembled at the name of the queen."[8]

The forced conversions and expulsions of the Jews and Moors from Spain drew oblique criticism from Isabella's contemporaries. In 1499 the *converso,* or converted Jew, Fernando de Rojas published *La Celestina,* the foremost literary epic of Isabella and Ferdinand's reign in which a virtuous girl, ruined by a mocking society, commits suicide. Despite its satirical tone, *La Celestina*'s final message was that Isabella's policies had destroyed Spain's old social order of Christians, Gentiles, and Jews and, with it, all human values for the sake of a superficial national unity.

In the early twentieth century, the Oxford scholar Martin Hume branded Isabella a sinner whose "saintly devotion to her Faith blinded her eyes to human things, and whose anxiety to please the God of Mercy made her merciless to those she thought his enemies."[9]

In truth, Isabella was neither saint nor sinner. Ultimately her monumental accomplishments were simply rooted in human fallibility. It is with Isabella's humanity, with her flesh-and-blood appetites and aspirations, rather than her exalted or debased representations, that her story begins.

CHAPTER TWO

Isabella's Castile, A Kingdom Divided

As Isabella was being crowned, Castile was straining under the heavy armor of medievalism that was fast giving way in other European nations to monarchial supremacy and a new sense of national pride. But Castile, unable to burst the iron seams of aristocratic control, floundered hopelessly under weak and disinterested kings. By the late fifteenth century, rivaling political factions, each struggling for domination, each wasting itself on territorial disputes, had splintered Castile into a dozen divisions that brought only bloodshed and a devastated countryside.

The most dramatic symbol of these divisions was a profusion of castle fortresses that pockmarked the kingdom's landscape and enabled the *grandees* to maintain private armies and live on their land in grandeur that often equaled or even surpassed that of Isabella's brother Enrique IV and her father, Juan II.

The terrain had fostered its political divisions. Isabella's Castile was the largest and most prominent kingdom of the Iberian peninsula, extending from Galicia in the north to Sevilla at the mouth of the Guadalquivir River in the south. Surrounding it were four smaller kingdoms whose history was inextricably intertwined with that of Castile—Aragón, Navarre, Portugal, and Granada. Like those kingdoms Castile had high-rimmed mountain ranges, lush forests, dense thickets, clear-running streams, and grassy plains where stag, wolf, bear, and boar roamed freely.

At the center of the Castilian kingdom was the *Meseta,* known as Old Castile. On this high tableland of fertile plains two to three thousand feet above sea level lived most of Castile's four to six million citizens. Here in the heartland of Castile's burgeoning sheep industry, the climate was as dramatic as the geography. In winter harsh winds, driving rains, and snow swept relentlessly over the plains, chilling nobles in their drafty castles as well as peasants bent over burning faggots in one-room huts. In summer the hot dry air of the plains raised temperatures to 100 degrees F—or more. These extremes have inspired sardonic native descriptions of Old Castile as *nueve meses de invierno y tres de infierno*—"nine months of winter with three of hell."[1]

North of Old Castile and the Cantabrian Mountains was the province of Vizcaya, today's Basque region, whose coastal ports on the Cantabrian Sea and rich iron ore deposits enabled merchants to develop a trade with northern European countries. In Spain's northwest corner was Galicia, bordered by the Bay of Biscay and the Atlantic, from whose busy harbors merchant ships and caravels sailed to England, France, Flanders, and Germany. Three hundred years before Isabella's birth Galicia was already internationally known to penitents and prelates, many of whom walked barefoot along its inland pilgrimage route past merchants hawking cockleshell badges, leather bags, and herbal remedies to the cathedral shrine of Santiago de Compostela where the remains of Spain's patron saint, St. James, were allegedly buried.

Directly south of Galicia lay the rugged and forested kingdom of León, incorporated into the Crown of Castile in the thirteenth century. South of the *Meseta,* stretching toward the North African coast, was Andalusia, Spain's coveted garden district, whose rich soil and mild climate produced lush harvests of oranges, figs, grapes, wheat, and olives on steep hills and shady groves cooled by the mountain air and sea breezes. There in the summer months shepherds migrated from Old Castile with thousands of the nation's nearly 4 million sheep to feed upon the pasturelands.

Life moved slowly in Isabella's Castile for in 1474 the kingdom was still primarily agrarian, connected by a few dusty highways and dotted with walled towns of straw-thatched wooden homes or whitewashed stuccoed dwellings roofed with red clay tiles. Nearly every Castilian town had its own small Romanesque or Gothic church, a central square, and at least one well. Beyond the city gates were pastures and great tracts of farmlands owned by the *grandees,* the church, and communities of monastic warriors where peasants cultivated Castile's main crops—wheat, barley, oats, and olives.

Madrid was still a small town whose old Moorish alcázar stood on a hill above the small Manzanares River near the site of the modern National Palace. Although fifteenth-century Castile monarchs frequently used that alcázar as a residence, Madrid was only one of several homes for the royal court, favored primarily for its central location. The sovereigns actually preferred other cities north of Madrid, such as Segovia, Toledo, and Valladolid, which were then thriving communities with spacious palaces and castles. But in Isabella's time no particular city was sacred to the Castilian crown, for the court was still peripatetic, wandering from town to town, as need, appetite, or political necessity demanded.

In 1474 change thus came to Castile gradually. News arrived from the outside world through royal courtiers or wandering peddlers whose mules were laden with brightly dyed bolts of cloth, herbs, spices, medicines, and ribbons. As early as the thirteenth century, a few enterprising Castilians had looked beyond their villages to trade wool, oil, leather, and iron with England, Flanders, and France for manufactured cloth and implements. By the fifteenth century, trading centers had envolved in a handful of Castilian cities—including Burgos, Segovia, Sevilla, Toledo, Cádiz, Valladolid, and Medina del Campo. The bi-annual wool fair held in Medina del Campo attracted merchants from lands as distant as Italy and Flanders.

While Castilian trade was slowly developing at this time, its sister kingdom of Aragón, located at its northern and eastern borders, participated in lively Mediterranean mercantilism. Although blocked by the Pyrenees on its north, Aragón was linked to the sea on the east through its territories of Catalonia and Valencia and their ports, Barcelona and Valencia. For centuries those majestic Mediterranean harbors had been a major conduit for the spices, perfumes, gold, and cultural ideas of the East. The resultant cultural interchange had given rise to an independent Aragonese middle class that became increasingly vocal about their political rights. Despite their geographical proximity, similar languages, and common enmity toward the Moors, Castile and Aragón remained independent countries with different customs and laws even after Isabella of Castile's marriage to Ferdinand of Aragón.

Directly to Castile's northeast was the Navarre, a tiny but fertile duchy strategically located on the edge of the Pyrenees spur with an independent rule and blood ties to Castile, Aragón, and France.

Portugal, flanking Castile on the west and bordering the Atlantic the full length of the Iberian peninsula, was a nation of fishermen, sailors and explorers. Until the twelfth century Portugal had been ruled by Castilian kings. Like Castile, its land was made up of mountains, plateaus, and plains. At the time of Isabella's birth, the Portuguese kings shared common blood with Castilian royalty, but the small country jealously protected its sovereignty.

At the base of the Iberian peninsula lay the kingdom of Granada, the last stronghold of the Moors, or North African Moslems, whose territory lay curled beneath the kingdom of Castile like an unsheathed scimitar. Centuries earlier, in A.D. 711, intrigued by the fertile Andalusian terrain across the Strait of Gibraltar, those fiery-eyed North Africans had swept over the Iberian peninsula under the leadership of Tarik the One-Eyed, governor of North Africa, and in the battle of Guadalete shattered the two-hundred-year-old Visigothic empire to its northern extremities.

With flashing swords and shields the Moors galloped north on African stallions through the Pyrenees and into France until Charles Martel repulsed them in A.D. 732. Afterward the Moors settled permanently on the Iberian peninsula, where other groups of invaders—Arabs, Syrians, and Berbers—were organized by Abd ar-Rahman I into a unified Islamic Spain. Along with their religion, Islam, their impressive body of knowledge—the martial arts, horticulture, astronomy, medicine, science—culled from the ancients made the Moors a sophisticated and formidable foe.

But the Christian Spaniards were determined to win back their territory. Led by Visigoth chieftain Pelayo in A.D. 718, they launched an offensive and regained the deep-gorged, lush mountain kingdom of Asturias in Castile's north. For the first three hundred years the *Reconquista,* or "reconquest," by the Christians was painfully slow, often involving hand-to-hand combat and surprise guerrilla tactics. Only gradually, valley by valley and town by town, did the Christians reconquer much of the territory once held by their Visigoth forebears. In the process the peninsula's various nation-states—Portugal, Castile, Navarre, and Aragón—were thus formed.

To ensure the permanence of those new conquests, the kings of Castile granted privileges and free land to any citizen, male or female, who would settle in the reconquered towns. But the Moors were as intransigent as they were militant, and in 1086, a year after losing Toledo to King Alfonso VI, they elicited help from their fanatic Moslem brethren, the Almoravids of Morocco. Eight years later Alfonso VI's legendary general El Cid, or Rodrigo Diáz de Vivar, repulsed the Almoravids' advance by conquering Valencia.

By 1212, after Alfonso VIII defeated the Moors at the battle of Las Navas de Tolosa, the Christians had gained the upper hand. In 1236 Ferdinand III, "The Saint King" of Castile, captured the key Moslem city of Córdoba, the intellectual and cultural center for Islam in the West and seat of its largest mosque outside Mecca. Twelve years later Ferdinand III took Sevilla. By the time of his death in 1252, the Moors had been permanently beaten back to the whitecapped Sierra Nevadas.

For the next two hundred years they were contained in the kingdom of Granada whose hillside capital city housed the famous Alhambra Palace built by the caliphs of the Nasrid dynasty.

The *Reconquista* drained the lifeblood of Spain's Christian kings and their vassals for nearly eight centuries. During that time the Moors became permanent settlers on the Iberian peninsula and by the mid-fourteenth century lived in *conviviencia,* or peaceful co-existence with the Hispanic Christians. Cultural cross-fertilization between Moors and Christians was inevitable, and eventually intermarriage between descendants of the old Visigoth empire and the Moors bred new populations and life-styles.

By the fifteenth century there were dark-skinned Christians, light-haired Moors, hybrids of every shape and complexion in Castile. Some Moslems adopted Christian manners of dress, speech, food, and even religion. Others who continued to practice Muhammadism but lived under Christian rule became known as the Mudéjars. Another group, the Mozarabs, were native Christians who learned to speak Arabic and adopted Moorish customs. Some Moslems shunned the Christian way of life altogether, keeping their women cloistered, avoiding pork, wine, and iconography; praying to Allah five times daily; and living in shuttered Islamic towns. But even in the strictest communities Moslem merchants and farmers traded livestock, produce, and fabrics with the Christians in exchange for iron plows, armor, chess sets, spectacles, and other new "gadgetry" of Western Europe.

Conversely, Moorish knowledge, habits, and life-style left an indelible mark on Christian Spain, inspiring the natives to imitate the more advanced Moslem techniques in horticulture, irrigation, medicine, and architecture. With the introduction of Moorish irrigation systems, fields of wheat, pepper, and saffron bloomed on formerly arid lands. Coconut and date palms, and orange, mulberry, and cypress trees transplanted from North Africa took root and began to spread throughout Andalusia. Christian physicians, trained by Moorish doctors, administered herbal poultices and purges, set broken bones, and cleaned wounds more efficiently for their patients than before. Astronomers and mathematicians, peering through Arabic texts or instructed by Moslem scholars, began to examine the universe scientifically and soon applied that knowledge to the development of such inventions as the magnetic needle and the compass.

By the time of Isabella's birth, high-born men and women had long since adopted Moorish fashions. The queen's own wardrobe included caftans, turbanlike hats, long veils, and embroidered chemise necklines. Frequently, Isabella and the members of her court dressed in the fine silks and brocades traditionally worn by Moslem women. This silk was grown and spun in the silk factories of Granada and North Africa.

The Christians also openly admired Moorish architecture, with its horseshoe arches, tiled walls and floors, polished marble arcades, fountains, and lushly landscaped gardens with cypress and orange trees. The finest example of Moorish architecture was the Alhambra, the royal palace of the Moslem kingdom, set high upon a hill overlooking Granada. Renowned for its delicately carved arches, twisted pillars, geometric arabesques, and brilliantly tinted stone lacework, the Alhambra inspired imitations that can still be seen in Castilian churches and palaces.

Eventually the Mudéjar style, as these filigreed Christian adaptations came to be called, began to appear in ordinary Castilian buildings, chapels, and even on city gates. The airy courtyards, fountains, and interior gardens that we think of as typical "Spanish" architecture were thus inspired by Moorish invaders.

Yet the fifteenth century papacy did not share Castile's traditional toleration of Islam. The church leaders became increasingly alarmed with what they perceived as a new wave of Islamic aggression against Christianity. Shortly after Isabella's birth, in 1453, the Turks invaded Constantinople, then the center of the Byzantine Christian empire and the heart of the Far East spice trade. In reaction, the church, still shaken by the Great Schism of 1378 to 1415 and the papacy's resultant removal to Avignon, spent the rest of the fifteenth century urging the kings of Western Europe to mount new crusades against Islam.

Although the Castilians tolerated the Moors, they were hostile toward the Jews. In the late Middle Ages the Castilian kings valued the Jews as an industrious and skilled minority. Many were doctors and artisans, but the Jews were prized primarily for their financial services to the crown as tax assessors, collectors, and moneylenders in this era before the development of a sophisticated banking system.

The Jews had been segregated into those professions by necessity. The tenets of the medieval Catholic church prohibited Christians from lending money or practicing "usury" in any form. Simultaneously medieval Jews were forbidden to engage in the "Christian" trades of carpentry, blacksmithery, or masonry and were excluded from those trade guilds. As a result, the jobs of moneylender, tax collector, and financier fell to the Jews. In those capacities, the Jews gained access to the throne. Their influence and wealth engendered hostility from both Christian courtiers and commoners.

Paradoxically, the Jews were among the oldest permanent settlers of Hispania, or ancient Spain. According to legend, they appeared on the Spanish peninsula in the pre-Christian era after being exiled by Titus or Nebuchadnezzar. Later, during the first centuries after Christ, other Jews emigrated to the peninsula from the Levant via North Africa. Some historians believe the Jews first encouraged the Moors to invade Spain, but such stories are difficult to document. Better historical evidence suggests that new populations of Jews emigrated to Spain after they were expelled from England in 1290 and from France in 1396. At the time of Isabella's birth, the Jewish population of the Iberian peninsula was between 50,000 and 200,000, the largest Jewish population in Western Europe.

The Jews were tolerated in Spain until the middle of the fourteenth century. Although the Christians occasionally vented their wrath against the Jews with mob violence and persecutions, in general they were allowed to live in peaceful, if segregated, *aljamas,* or ghettos, within the Castilian towns.

Besides their financial utility, there were other social and economic reasons for such tolerance. The Jews were familiar with the Semitic culture of the Moslems and since many of them spoke Arabic, they often served as translators and middlemen for the Christians. The most illustrious example of such cooperation was the foundation of the "Translators of Toledo," the renowed twelfth- and thirteenth-century schools where Moorish and Jewish scholars translated many of the ancient Greek and Roman manuscripts from Arabic and Hebrew into Spanish and Latin. These writings, which preserved the philosophical, mathematical, scientific, astronomical, and medical knowledge of the ancient world, were eventually carried to Italy where they inspired the birth of the classical Renaissance in Western Europe.

What changed Christian tolerance was the Black Death of 1348–51. The lethal new strain of *Yersinia pestis* bacteria, ratborne and transmitted to human beings by fleas, led to the deaths of millions of Western Europeans. Those lucky enough to survive the plague were battered by starvation and inflation brought about by the death of so many people and the subsequent abandonment of fields and industries. Anti-Semitism, which lurked just beneath the surface of Christian communities of the Middle Ages, burst forth with a vengeance. At the peak of the Black Death, Jews were accused of a variety of unnatural acts—of stealing Christian property and money, of poisoning the wells, of evoking the devil, and of causing the plague to spread—despite the fact that they too were dying.

In 1354, feelings reached such a pitch in Sevilla that superstitious mobs of Christians massacred many Jews. Nevertheless, famine, plague, and inflation continued to bedevil the Castilians through the rest of the century. In 1391 new generations of discontented citizens took to the streets again, this time in massive outbursts during which they slaughtered thousands of Jews in Sevilla, Toledo, Madrid, Barcelona, and Valencia. Afterward thousands of Jews converted, intermarried with Christians, and raised their children as Christians who would hence be known as *conversos,* or the converted. Some wealthy Jews even managed to marry into Castile's aristocratic, but impoverished, families where they were welcomed by calculating parents eager to obtain wealth for their offspring. Eventually their descendants became members of Castile's most powerful aristocratic families and even leaders in the church.

Yet, to the "old" Christians and their families, their descendants were still *conversos,* to be despised for their Jewish blood and suspected of still secretly practicing Judaism. Undoubtedly some did, while others simply maintained their contacts with old friends and family members who had remained Jewish.

Even those who led scrupulously "Christian" lives were suspiciously regarded by old Christians for signs that they had secretly "relapsed" into Judaism. In the end, the conversions of 1391 compounded, rather than resolved, the animosity between Spanish Christians and Jews. As Isaac Abravenal, Spain's last Jewish statesman, observed, "the native peoples will always call them Jews . . . consider them as Jews and falsely accuse them of Judaizing in secret."[2]

The plight of the ordinary Jew who refused conversion was no better. By Isabella's era, in many Castilian towns Jewish merchants and artisans were forced to conduct their business and live exclusively in *aljamas*. To distinguish them from Christians, they wore special yellow badges in some communities and were forbidden to own land or hold public office. Yet they remained important financial servants of the crown.

Ironically, the biggest political challenge facing Isabella at the time of her ascension to the Castilian throne came neither from the Moors nor the Jews but from within the nobility itself. Despite the division of Castilian citizens into the "three estates"—"those who fought, those who prayed, and those who labored"— feudalism, in the form of indentured servants and a centuries-old aristocratic class subservient to a king, had never really existed in Castile.

The *Reconquista* was partially responsible. Not only had Christian victories fostered a relatively autonomous population of commoners who were encouraged to settle new lands and establish towns along the Moorish border, but they gave rise to a formidable class of warrior knights who stood ready to defend Castile against the Moors at a moment's notice. Although these *grandees* were technically vassals of the king, many maintained their own militias. Because their combined forces were often stronger than the king's standing army, the nobles posed a significant threat to the authority of the Castilian crown.

In the fourteenth century tensions between the nobles and the crown grew so brittle that King Alfonso XI violently subdued the aristocrats. A generation later his son, Pedro I, or Pedro the Cruel, stripped them of seignorial rights altogether. But after murdering King Pedro, Enrique II of Trastámara, Pedro's illegitimate half brother, founder of the Trastámara line, and Isabella's great-great-grandfather, realized he needed a cadre of rich and powerful vassals and created a new noble class.

Eventually, this new set of *grandees* intermarried and established a hegemony strong enough by the fifteenth century to challenge the power of the crown. As late as 1500 the aristocrats still owned 52 percent of the land in Castile, and their "second sons," who often became prelates, owned another 45 percent. To placate them, Isabella's father, Juan II, later doled out so many land grants and inheritances in the first part of the fifteenth century that the revenues of the Castilian crown were depleted. Then, in a last-ditch effort to keep the royal treasury solvent, he levied higher taxes on the commoners. These, combined with the incessant territorial disputes among the aristocrats, contributed to a national mood of grumbling discontent.

In the next generation Isabella's half brother Enrique, "eternally enamoured of peace," repeated the same mistakes. During the first decade of his reign, Enrique's grants to the *grandees* bought him political stability. But ultimately his largesse backfired. By the time Isabella was an adolescent, Enrique's practices had provoked a civil war between rivaling noble factions that nearly lost him the crown.

Ultimately, aristocratic greed, rather than mere personal popularity, also lighted Isabella's way to the throne. The princess understood the power of the aristocrats early in life, saw it up close as a youngster in Enrique's court. Her own reign, she vowed, would be different.

This, then, was the Castile Isabella was to rule—a country surrounded by ambivalent Christian neighbors; internally splintered by warring families that owned nearly as much property as the crown; its southern border populated by a menacing, if temporarily subdued, foreign culture; its towns wary of new taxes, its citizens unnerved by years of chaos, seething with hatred for the Jews; its economy broken by a half century of political turmoil. The task before Isabella was formidable, one that would require psychological and physical stamina and clear vision if it was ever to succeed. Its achievement would shape Isabella as much as it would mold a new Spain.

CHAPTER THREE

Isabella, *Infanta* of Castile

No one expected Isabella to become Queen of Castile. So little attention was given to her birth that historians are not absolutely sure when it occurred.

One of the few contemporary clues was a letter written by Isabella's father, King Juan II of Castile, on April 26, 1451, to the town of Madrid announcing that his "dear and beloved wife" Queen Isabel had given birth to a baby girl the preceding Thursday. That was all. Although we know Isabella was a healthy infant, there were no records of special festivities or celebrations to mark her arrival, not even the mention of a court banquet.

Years after Isabella became queen, her private physician, Dr. Fernán Álvarez de Toledo, recorded her birth date in the *Chrónicon de Valladolid* as April 22 between four and five in the afternoon in the town of Madrigal de la Altas Torres. There, in a small alcove of an airless second-floor bedroom in King Juan's half Gothic-half Mudéjar palace, Isabella first saw the light of day.

In 1524 that palace was converted into a convent, which is still in existence, called the Monasterio de los Angustinas. Within its walls researchers have discovered remnants of the original brick building and its flat walls and small, low-roofed rooms. At its center was a small square patio surrounded by a low-ceilinged arcade reminiscent of Moorish courtyards.

Isabella's baptism is shrouded in similar mystery. Most historians believe she was christened in Segovia, at the Church of Saint Nicolas, although at least one sixteenth-century scholar claimed the ceremony took place in Madrigal's Church of St. María of Castillo.

The scanty information about the first days of Isabella's life suggests that her birth was barely acknowledged by either the court or the larger kingdom of Castile. When one of King Juan's messengers announced Isabella's birth to the city of Burgos, the city fathers were so unimpressed that the courier was tipped a mere 500 maravedís. Two years later, when another envoy proclaimed the birth of Isabella's young brother Alfonso, he was tipped three times that amount. Thus it was that the queen who was to unite Castile and Aragón, rout the Moslems from Granada, encourage Columbus on his famous westward voyage, and usher in Spain's "Golden Age" of literature and culture was received coldly into the world.

There were practical as well as dynastic reasons for that coldness. Isabella was the product of the second marriage of King Juan II of Castile, this time to a young, dark-haired princess named Isabel of Portugal. Although there was genuine affection between Isabella's parents, their match, like all royal marriages of the fifteenth century, began as a matter of political convenience. By marrying Isabel of Portugal, King Juan assured himself of a Portuguese ally against domestic enemies.

Juan's reign had been troubled from the start, both because of the prickly political situation he inherited and the personal idiosyncrasies that made him an inept king. In 1406 Juan had been born to Enrique III of the Trastámara line and England's Catherine of Lancaster, but before he was two his father had died. Consequently, the young prince had grown up in the coregency of his mother Catherine and his uncle Fernando de Antequera. That uncle, a harsh-tempered man who resented being second-born and thus ineligible for the Castilian throne, finally became King of Aragón-Catalonia in 1412 and took the title of Fernando I.

Even that acquisition, however, did not sate Fernando's ambitions; for he still longed to seize the Castilian throne from his nephew, Juan. As a result, he became locked in a power struggle against his coregent, the intrepid Queen Widow Catherine, which grew so bitter that Juan's education was sadly neglected.

Although Juan was taught to read, write, cipher, and speak Latin, his education was limited to books, as if he were destined for the university rather than the throne. Thus Isabella's father never received instruction in court politics, Castile's domestic problems, or international events.

The consequences of that neglect became almost immediately apparent in 1419 when, following the deaths of his coregents, the fourteen-year-old Juan was declared king. At first, the frightened young monarch turned for advice to his "bosom favorite," his Gentleman of the Chamber, Álvaro de Luna. Physically, Luna was most unattractive—short, prematurely bald, and with bad teeth. Yet to Juan, Luna's personal qualities far outweighed his physical deficits, for he was decisive, sophisticated, and politically shrewd.

For most of his life Luna would remain Juan's favorite at court. Although he was alternately promoted, honored, and dismissed during Juan's thirty-four-year reign, Luna was always recalled, for the king was unable to manage the kingdom alone. Temperamentally, Juan had neither the talent nor inclination to do so: Government administration bored him. Consequently, Isabella's father shucked off his regal responsibilities to Luna whenever he could.

Yet the real world was bound to intrude. Juan's uncle Fernando had left him with a perilous legacy. Although he served as the Castilian regent, Fernando had carefully protected his own, quite considerable Castilian landholdings. After his death these properties—and the frustrated ambitions that went with them—were passed on to his adult sons: his heir, Alfonso V, and his three younger brothers, the *Infantes,* or younger princes, of Aragón.

Soon after Juan II's 1419 ascension to the Castilian throne, the Aragonese *Infantes* determined to crush their cousin's authority and live on equal, if not superior, terms with him. On July 14, 1420, one of the *Infantes* stormed the royal palace at Tordesillas at dawn and kidnapped Juan. After Luna rescued the young king, the *Infantes* manipulated Castile's *grandees* into a grumbling constituency, which, like the well-trained falcons that perched on their own gloved hands during the hunt, methodically plucked choice parcels of land, inheritances, and political favors from Juan in exchange for temporary obedience.

When King Juan occasionally refused their requests, the nobles and *Infantes* threatened civil war; when he granted them privileges, they clamored for more. As a result, Castile became a battleground. Pastures and farmlands were burned, citizens rallied to one side or another of the quarreling factions, and villages were overrun with feuding militias.

It went on that way for nearly three decades until finally, on May 19, 1445, the *Infantes'* dynastic war against Juan ended with the battle of Olmedo. Although the victory was settled in the king's favor, Castilian peace was not yet assured. New Aragonese factions—in the person of the second *Infante,* another Juan, this one King of Navarre, later to become Isabella's father-in-law—still threatened Castile.

The recently widowed, thirty-nine-year-old Castilian king now pondered other ways to strengthen his country. Finally in 1447, largely at Luna's insistence, he married the seventeen-year-old Princess of Portugal, Doña Isabel, grandaughter of Portugal's King João I, thus gaining Portugal as an ally and adding dowry gold to the depleted Castilian treasury.

Although Juan's new queen was beautiful, heir-making was not a priority; twenty-six years earlier King Juan's first wife, María of Navarre, had given birth to a male child named Enrique. That prince, tall, blond, and irresolute like his father, had long since been sworn as heir to Castile. Since he was married and likely to produce his own heirs, nobody seriously entertained the idea that the little *Infanta* Isabella would be anything other than an auxiliary princess, a minor player to be dispensed with through marriage in some as-yet unforeseen political treaty.

And even if Isabella had not been the child of King Juan's second marriage, her female status would have made her an improbable candidate for the crown. However, Castilian inheritance laws, founded on Roman canons set down by Alfonso the Wise in the thirteenth century, did not specifically forbid female inheritance of the throne. In earlier eras, medieval Castile had, in fact, been governed briefly by such queens as Berenguela and Urraca, but those were exceptional instances with queens usually acting as regents for minor sons.

Two and a half years later any lingering thoughts about Isabella's potential as a future monarch must have disappeared altogether when her mother gave birth to a son, Alfonso. If by any chance Prince Enrique should perish before producing an heir of his own, the scepter, by all the traditional customs of ancient Castile, would pass to Prince Alfonso.

*   *   *

The twisted skein of political intrigues that confounded King Juan's reign persisted after Isabella's birth. Her mother had survived an uncomfortable pregnancy, marked by waves of illness and *profunda tristeza*, a profound sadness or depression she could not seem to shake off. At times, the usually lively and charming queen would speak to no one at all, stare vacantly into space, and break her silence only when her husband addressed her. Some of the queen's personal attendants attributed her behavior to the stress of giving birth, but others, including her doctors, suspected poison.

The alleged culprit was Juan's favorite, Luna, who, by the time of Isabella's birth, had been appointed to two of the most powerful positions in the kingdom—the constable, or grand military officer, of Castile, and the grand master of Santiago. The Order of Santiago, an honorary position that began in the twelfth century when Castile's monastic knights waged war upon the Moorish infidels, also made Luna the richest man in the kingdom.

Santiago was the largest and most important of the three monastic military organizations, which also included the Orders of Calatrava and of Alcántara. Although some of its knights still dwelled in monastic communities, the rules had grown lax over the centuries and many lived as ordinary citizens. As grand master, Luna controlled sixty towns and castles, commanded over 100,000 vassals, had more money than all the nobles and prelates of Castile combined, and was even said to wield more influence than the king.

By 1451 Luna was at the peak of his power. He managed the affairs of the Castilian kingdom so unilaterally that it was whispered that King Juan "had no other task except to eat."[1] Simultaneously, Luna lost no time in elevating his own relatives to high places at court in lieu of more deserving men. He also excluded representatives of the commoners from the king's privy council and raised taxes without the legislative approval of the Cortes. To maintain his supremacy, Luna systematically disposed of those who stood in his way with imprisonment, confiscation of their property, and even executions. Predictably, the courtier was soon surrounded with enemies. Ugly rumors scuttled through the court like nocturnal vermin; suspicions that Luna had bewitched King Juan, that he practiced sorcery upon his rivals, even that he had a homosexual relationship with the monarch.

Another formidable foe was Isabella's mother, the young Queen Isabel, who loathed Luna because of his seemingly hypnotic hold on her husband. When the seventeen-year-old Isabel arrived at court in 1447, her beauty and innocence convinced Luna that the new queen would be as malleable as the king. This was perhaps his most serious miscalculation. Gradually, as Doña Isabel became more comfortable as a wife and queen, she became annoyed, then anguished, and eventually outraged by Luna's influence and resolved to destroy it.

But Luna was hardly a man to be intimidated by a young, foreign queen. When he learned of her opposition, he confronted her directly. "I made your marriage and I will break it,"[2] the courtier announced venomously. What Luna did not, or perhaps could not fathom was the depth of the queen's fury and her considerable feminine wiles. Although she was twenty-five years younger than King Juan, Isabel had a much stronger sense of her own destiny as a queen than Juan had of himself as a king. The pretty young queen thus used every means within her power to restore her marriage—and her man—to their deserved integrity. Ultimately, as Luna's acts grew increasingly brutal towards his political rivals, the queen succeeded in her suit. Gradually King Juan began to treat Luna with a new coolness.

By 1452 Luna had acquired so many enemies that his defeat was inevitable. His fall came soon after he hurtled Juan's *contador mayor,* or chief auditor, from a tower in Burgos on Good Friday, April 9, 1453. Five days later Juan broke the safe conduct, or royal immunity, he had bestowed upon Luna and had his old favorite arrested.

Like a common criminal, Luna was imprisoned in a wooden cage, shackled to a mule, and taken to Valladolid. On June 3, without benefit of a trial, Luna, dressed in the dark clothes of the condemned, was led in an open cart through the streets of Valladolid toward a scaffold to be beheaded. As the executioner's knife pierced Luna's throat the crowd cried with horror as if in one voice. With Luna's death, the famed writer the Marqués de Santillana could at last gloat that "of your splendor, O Luna, Fortune has deprived you."[3]

Isabella, of course, knew nothing about those events for she was still a toddler under the care of her mother, who was then four months pregnant with another child. To the queen and to most of Castile, Luna's death was a relief, an event widely heralded as the beginning of a bright new era in Castile in which King Juan could finally rule his own kingdom. Shortly thereafter, King Juan took possession of Luna's vast holdings and replenished the lean coffers of the Castilian treasury.

Still, the new tranquility that descended on Castile with Luna's death was destined to be short-lived. In the months following his old favorite's execution, King Juan sank into a depression, one that even the queen's delivery of Prince Alfonso on November 17, 1453, could not allay. The king, his courtiers whispered, deeply regretted Luna's execution and now secretly mourned him.

As Juan grew increasingly depressed, his health began to fail. On July 21, 1454, just thirteen months after Luna was beheaded, Juan II of Castile died. He was forty-eight years of age. In his last moments, the king told an attendant that he despised his life. Why was it, he murmured with anguish, "he had not been born the son of a mechanic, instead of the King of Castile."[4]

Thus Luna's curse upon Doña Isabel's marriage to King Juan seemed to have reached beyond the grave. At the age of twenty-four she became Castile's queen widow. By the provisions of King Juan II's will, she was to receive the "rents" or taxes from the towns of Arévalo, Madrigal, Soria, and the suburbs of Madrid to support her household.

For her maintenance, little Isabella was given the taxes from the town of Cuellar. On her twelfth birthday the princess was also to receive a million maravedís from Madrigal; after her mother's death that town would become part of her own inheritance.

Prince Alfonso fared considerably better than his sister; the king had willed him the mastership of Santiago and, on his fourteenth birthday, the title of Constable of Castile. The young prince was also to acquire rents and jurisdiction over Escalona, Maqueda, Portillo, and Sepúlveda. At his mother's death Alfonso was to receive the towns of Soria, Arévalo, and the suburbs of Madrid.

Castilian custom demanded that a queen widow and her children leave the court after a reigning monarch's death. Soon after Enrique's coronation, Doña Isabel, Princess Isabella, and Prince Alfonso moved to the quiet agricultural town of Arévalo in Old Castile. While Arévalo was dozens of miles from court life, the town was a traditional retirement place for Castilian queen widows because it was accessible to major roads and contained both *casas reales*, or a palace, and a small castle.

Thus, Isabella's first memories would be of Castile's rolling hills, grazing sheep, and fields of wheat, oats, and barley rather than of the elegant banquets, mimes, and jousts of a royal court.

CHAPTER FOUR

Enrique *El Generoso*

King Enrique IV began his reign with the best of intentions. Peaceable and gullably optimistic, the twenty-nine-year-old Enrique was coronated in Valladolid on July 23, 1454, in accordance with King Juan's will. At the moment of his ascension, as throughout his life, the tall, blond king believed the best way to rule was through dialogue rather than a show of arms. He had been appalled by the violence of his father's reign. Shortly after the coronation he thus decreed that 159 appointees from King Juan's court could remain in their old positions instead of, as was the custom, being dismissed. He also pardoned those who had offended King Juan, freed those who were imprisoned or exiled, and returned land to former rebels.

In a more enlightened age Isabella's older half brother might have been praised for his tolerance, but in the mercurial fifteenth century, enthralled as it was with the chivalric ideal of decisive action, Enrique's actions smacked of cowardice. Even before the coronation courtiers and warriors had scoffed at Enrique's timidity and his lack of personal mettle.

For years stories had circulated through Castile that Enrique was unmanly, that he was, in fact, impotent and unable to ensure the Trastámara line of succession. Although Enrique had been married, a year before King Juan's death Enrique had divorced his wife of thirteen years, Blanca of Navarre, whose "bewitchment" was said to have made him temporarily impotent. That, at least, had been the judgment of the Spanish prelates who pleaded Enrique's case for an annulment before the pope. To prove that the fault lay with Princess Blanca, Enrique's counselors brought two prostitutes from Segovia "with whom the Prince had had intimate relations" who swore to his virility in the ecclesiastical hearing.[1]

In other respects Enrique's history as a prince was unremarkable. He was born on either the fifth or sixth of January 1425 in Valladolid to Maria of Aragón and King Juan II of Castile and declared Prince of Asturias—the royal title for the Castilian heir—at the age of six. In contrast to his father's upbringing, Enrique had been groomed to the crown from childhood. In the gilded and frescoed rooms of the Segovian alcázar where Enrique spent much of his youth, his tutor, the Dominican friar Lope Barrientos, drilled him in religious doctrine, the classics, mathematics, philosophy, and the rudiments of government—the standard fare of the humanist scholars who were then spreading the Italian Renaissance through the courts of Western Europe.

Daily Enrique practiced horsemanship, hunting, fencing, and tilting with *cañas*, or pointed eighteen-foot reeds. The last, in particular, was a skill that every *caballero* was expected to perfect to use in battle as well as in jousts.

Physically, the blond, blue-eyed Enrique was a vigorous, well-proportioned man who stood about six feet tall, well above average for fifteenth-century citizens. Besides his height, Enrique's most distinctive feature was his broken nose, the result of a childhood accident. From profile the king's flat nose, according to the chronicler Alonso Fernández de Palencia, made Enrique look rather like a monkey. To another courtier, however, Enrique's defect gave him a fierce appearance, "almost like a lion, the view of which struck terror to those who saw him."[2]

Yet Enrique's personality was anything but leonine. From the first days of his reign, the shaggy-haired king encouraged his courtiers to address him familiarly. Within his private circle Enrique even dismissed traditional displays of ceremonial allegiance—the bows of obedience, the seignorial kiss on the hand—that symbolically set him above his subjects. Moreover, he socialized with a raffish group of uncourtly men—uncouth peasants, jugglers, entertainers, muleteers, sharp-eyed peddlers—in short, anyone he found amusing.

Even his personal appearance revealed his disinclination for kingship. In spite of his broken nose, Enrique was reasonably attractive, but he paid little attention to personal grooming. He hated to wash, shaved infrequently, and scoffed at the perfumes and scented oils his courtiers used.

Another unconventionality was Enrique's habit of occasionally holding court in the Moorish style, seated upon cushions and rugs instead of his throne, fully dressed in the Moorish manner with turbans, short Oriental jerkins, and the *burnoose,* or hooded cape.

Enrique's disdain for courtly ceremony was but one side of an insecure man whose search for self-esteem was to remain unfulfilled throughout his life. Fearing criticism as he did, Enrique hated his royal responsibilities even more than ceremonial pomp. Like his father, Enrique was a loner whose happiest moments seemed to be when he buried himself in song and music, took long walks, or hunted with his greyhounds and bassets for deer, bear, or wild boar in the forests of Madrid or the dense Segovian woods of El Bazaín.

Personally vulnerable, easily swayed by the opinions of those he admired, Enrique developed into an indecisive monarch who fled from one faction of his nobles to another with the same skittish movements of the deer he loved to hunt. In time, broken loyalties became the signature of his reign. His nicknames suggest the subsequent disillusionment of his subjects. At the dawn of his reign when he bestowed lavish favors upon his subjects, the king was called *Enrique El Generoso,* "the generous" or "the liberal." Later, however, when his reign became turbulent and his leadership faltered, he was dubbed *Enrique El Impotente,* "the ineffective" or "impotent."

Years earlier, when he was still a prince, Juan Pacheco, the grandnephew of the Archbishop of Toledo, had captured Enrique's attention at court. A sly, confident youth with a quivering voice, Pacheco was a protégé of Luna's. As his father had done with others, Enrique became dazzled with Pacheco's cleverness and often sought his advice. In return, the ambitious Pacheco quickly ingratiated himself as a confidant, advisor, and according to some rumors, even lover.

To show his gratitude, Prince Enrique had named Pacheco the Marquis of Villena, thus granting his advisor untoward wealth. He even named Pacheco's scurrilous brother Pedro Girón to be master of the Order of Calatrava, the second-most powerful military brotherhood in Castile. Once he became king, Enrique saw no reason to curtail his practice of raising low members of the nobility to prestigious positions at court. In 1455 he named Pedro Portocarrero Count of Medelín, Juan de Silva Count of Cifuentes, and López Sánchez de Moscoso Count of Altamira. Similarly, Enrique ennobled a humble boyhood friend, Miguel Lucas de Iranzo, first as *corregidor,* or royal officer, of Baeza and then, in 1458, as Count of Quesada and Constable of Castile. Most shocking of all was Enrique's elevation of a handsome *caballero* named Beltrán de la Cueva, son of a town councilman, to *grandee* status in 1456. Two years later Cueva became Enrique's *mayordomo mayor* or chief steward.

To Enrique, such largesse was a means to gain new loyalties. And loyalty, in his simplistic view, was the handmaiden of peace. Unfortunately, the new king had no concept of diminishing resources, either in terms of the *grandees'* patience or the stability of the golden *doblas,* or ducats of Castile's coffers. When the royal treasurer complained about Enrique's extravagance, he retorted, "Kings, instead of hoarding treasure like private persons, are bound to dispense it for the happiness of their subjects. We must give to our enemies to make them friends, and to our friends to keep them so."[3]

In the first deceptively tranquil year after Enrique's coronation he decided to marry again. Enrique's second bride was Portuguese, this time a high-spirited, comely sixteen-year-old brunette princess named Juana of Portugal. She arrived at the village of Posadas, twenty miles from Córdoba, in May 1455 with an entourage of twelve gaily dressed ladies-in-waiting.

Despite Juana's beauty, Enrique was nervous: His expression, wrote Palencia, was "not one of fiestas."[4] Indeed, the thirty-year-old king seems to have presented himself at his worst, with his *bonete,* or soft rimless hat, hiding his face, a black cape hiding his drab clothes, his manner tremulous and tentative. In contrast, the new queen and her attendants were merry, and provocatively dressed. They infused a giddy, frivolous atmosphere into the banquets, jousts, and mimes held in the royal couple's honor at Córdoba.

Despite the frank aura of sexuality that enveloped the new queen, the wedding night was probably unsuccessful. According to Castilian tradition, court officials hovered at the bedroom door until the bridegroom displayed the bloody sheets. But although Enrique and Juana were ensconced in a curtained double bed on their May 20 wedding night, nothing happened. The next morning the queen, according to one chronicler, "left the bedroom as she entered"—that is, as a virgin, which "pleased nobody."[5]

Many modern historians believe Enrique may have kept his wedding night private so that no one except his queen knew what transpired. Having once endured the humiliation of having his first nuptial night observed, Enrique may simply have refused to let witnesses watch a second time. Whatever the real facts were, the new queen did not produce a child for seven years—a fact that Enrique's enemies later tried to use as "proof" of his impotence.

Enrique's alleged difficulties in the bedroom were repeated on the battlefield. The same spring that Enrique married Juana, he initiated a crusade against the Moors of Granada. But unlike earlier campaigns, Enrique did not intend to conduct an ordinary siege war with battering rams and catapults meant to penetrate the thick stone walls of Moorish towns.

Instead, Enrique ordered his army of 10,000 mounted knights and 20,000 to 40,000 infantry men to the Moorish kingdom between Moclín and Alcalá la Real to wage guerrilla warfare. In these surprise raids, Castilian soldiers swooped down from mountains or across gulches into Moslem towns, which they conquered within a few hours. Between those raids, Enrique ordered his soldiers to starve out the Moors by the *tala,* another traditional Moslem tactic in which soldiers destroyed surrounding croplands. But even here Enrique hesitated: There would, he commanded, be no destruction of the region's coveted olive trees, for they were slow to grow and bloom. His soldiers were incredulous. A *tala* was tedious enough, but a halfhearted one was more than they could stand.

Moreover, Enrique prohibited casual border skirmishes with the Moors. In an age when prowess in war was the measure of a man's honor, and booty—in the form of embossed Moorish swords, armor, and ornaments—its tangible reward, Enrique's approach was decidedly cowardly.

By 1457 the *grandees* were openly dissatisfied with Enrique. The Castilian clergy, fretting over the future of Christianity ever since the 1453 Ottoman conquest of Constantinople, continued to press for a victory over the Moors. The commoners were also disgruntled for they had been subjected to new taxes, raised by Pacheco. After the Jews had collected those taxes, they were delivered to the region's *grandees*, who, in turn, were to send them on to the King. But some angry *grandees* refused to cede them to the crown in lieu of money and privileges promised but still undelivered. Nor had the old aristocrats forgotten Enrique's elevation of new favorites.

Among the most vocal of Enrique's critics was the burly warrior-prelate Alfonso Carrillo de Acuña, Archbishop of Toledo and Juan Pacheco's uncle. His vast church holdings made him one of the most powerful ecclesiastics in Castile. Intelligent, bellicose, and worldly despite his crimson robes, Carrillo had earthly ambitions of his own—to amass more money and land, to settle a rich estate upon his bastard son Troilo, and especially to win enough influence from Enrique to become Cardinal of Castile.

Although related, Carrillo and Pacheco were rivals. In fact, to secure his own position Pacheco had warned Enrique about the archbishop, noting that his faction was a potential threat to royal authority. To subdue it Pacheco suggested that Enrique create an alternate faction that would dominate the *Consejo Real,* or royal council.

In 1457 Enrique, ever-enthralled with Pacheco's cunning, ever anxious to maintain peace in his realms, appointed his favorite head of the *Consejo Real.* Ultimately that promotion would lead to exactly what Enrique hoped to avoid—the polarization of the aristocrats into two distinct camps that would split Castile asunder.

As early as 1456 or 1457 Enrique, knowing that there was talk against him, began to worry that his half siblings, Isabella and Alfonso, might become the political pawns of his enemies. By then Isabella was five or six years old and Alfonso three or four—hardly old enough to understand the events that had brought them to Arévalo or their potential role in the coming dynastic struggle.

At first the queen widow's family lived in the small, tawny-colored Gothic castle that still stands on a barren promontory near the Adaja River overlooking pastures and grain fields. There, in compliance with King Juan's will, the queen widow supervised the youngsters' education in counsel with the thirty-year-old Gonzalo Chacón, *comendador,* or "knight commander," of Montiel. Because of Arévalo's distance from the courts of Segovia and Madrid, it was probably the queen widow, rather than her peripatetic court counselors, who first taught the young children their letters.

In those first tranquil years at Arévalo, Doña Isabel was a devoted mother with high standards and expectations for her young children. As befit a royal widow, she maintained a staff of servants—among them six Portuguese women who tended her personally, and the governor of Arévalo Castle, Pedro de Bobadilla. Despite the abundance of servants, the queen widow seems to have cared for her children personally. As a queen, Isabel had been a devout Catholic and now, in her widowhood, she turned even more passionately to her prayers. The church, with its promise of a glorious afterlife, provided the queen widow with solace for the injustices of her earthly existence. Thus she infused her children Isabella and Alfonso with the same devotional piety.

But Doña Isabel found adjustment to the shock of her husband's death and the move to the countryside difficult. Legend has it that it was in Arévalo where the bereaved queen became so guilty over her role in Luna's death that she began to lose her sanity. From a twentieth-century perspective, it is intriguing to contemplate whether guilt or rather the emergence of a constitutionally based mental disorder, albeit one precipitated by stressful life events, caused the queen widow's breakdown.

In any case, the queen widow's first symptom of mental instability was her insistence that Arévalo Castle was haunted. She claimed that the Adaja River flowing below the fortress whispered Luna's name day and night. Years later, long after Isabella left Arévalo permanently for Enrique's court, the queen widow would lose her sense of reality completely and sink into a nearly catatonic state.

According to legend, Isabel's mysterious complaints appeared some days after

Enrique, despite her wishes to the contrary, suddenly summoned young Isabella and Alfonso to court.

Isabella and Alfonso likely first went to court in 1457, when Enrique first noticed his *grandees'* discontent. Initially Archbishop Carrillo and his faction protested their presence. The pugnacious archbishop may have worried that Isabella and Alfonso would grow up as Enrique's allies, or possibly he feared for their lives. His objection has been preserved in a 1460 complaint to the king that demanded certain reforms going back to 1457. Among them was a mandate asking Enrique to "return the Infantas Don Alfonso and Doña Isabella to the most revered Doña Isabel's side."[6]

Were Isabella and Alfonso returned to Arévalo after 1457 and summoned to court again in 1460? Or, as some historians suggest, were they called to court in 1457 and forced to remain there until 1460? If so, they spent three of the most formative years of their childhood in Enrique's court, far from their mother and everything they once knew and trusted.

CHAPTER FIVE

Enrique *El Impotente*

Strange surroundings make youngsters cling to habits that represent earlier securities. For Isabella religion, learned at the queen widow's knee and practiced in Arévalo's tiny castle chapel, became such an anchor in the dizzying new world of Enrique's court. Thus it was that the auburn-haired Isabella was observed to be a "sedate," rigorously devout child who tended to her prayers without prodding from those appointed to supervise her in Enrique's careless, unceremonious court.

Traumatized children also tend to search for a substitute parent, someone they can entrust with their deepest, most irrational fears. Two men appeared at Enrique's court to fulfill those roles for Isabella and Alfonso. The first was the courtly Gonzalo Chacón, who, as co-executor of King Juan's will and husband of an attendant in the queen widow's household, took a keen interest in the young *Infantes* and protected their rights as descendants of the royal house of Trastámara.

The second, and far more influential surrogate, was Alfonso de Carrillo de Acuña, the tall soldier-priest and Archbishop of Toledo whose jeweled ecclesiastical robes and personal insistence that the *Infantes* be allowed to return to their mother soon won Isabella's trust. Eventually, as the children grew old enough to understand the tangled intrigues at court, Carrillo would become their most loyal advocate, the one to whom they consistently turned for counsel.

Being a "man of great heart,"[1] Carrillo was genuinely sympathetic to the *Infantes,* for he was a self-appointed champion of the innocent. When roused, the archbishop would defend his principles by summoning 1,000 armed men and the resources of 19,000 vassals to his side. Years before, in 1445, he had fought valiantly to defend King Juan at Olmedo and had been awarded an archbishopric for it. Ultimately it would be Carrillo, the fiery priest of "cape and sword," who would introduce Isabella and Alfonso to other *grandees* who would promote their claim to the throne.

Carrillo's motives were not, however, purely altruistic. There was another side to the archbishop—that of the alchemist who dabbled with test tubes and metal alloys in a laboratory in his palace at Alcalá de Henares in search of a formula to turn common objects into gold. Similarly, Carrillo pondered ways to transform Prince Alfonso into a king who would replace Enrique. If the archbishop could accomplish that feat, he knew that his reward would be more substantive gold than that created in his laboratory; Alfonso would almost certainly appoint him to the coveted cardinalship of Castile.

To elevate Alfonso, however, would take years of planning and preparation. Thus Carrillo enveloped the vulnerable and impressionable children in an atmosphere of paternal love when they arrived at Enrique's court, an advocacy that simultaneously attracted the discontented *grandees* to the archbishop's side.

Initially, Carrillo's plan to raise Alfonso as King of Castile had little effect on Isabella. From her first days at court—as from her very birth—the princess was perceived as a minor figure. Isabella's life was destined for the distaff side—as spinner, weaver, wife, and childbearer. No one expected that one day she would rule.

Accordingly, the young princess was taught her letters and numbers and exposed to conventional "women's books" such as Louis de León's *The Perfect Wife,* Martín de Córdoba's *The Garden of Noble Women,* and Juan Ruiz's *The Book of Good Love,* allegorical tales that illustrated the dangers of libidinous love and offered examples of virtuous women. Like most high-born children, Isabella also read heroic tales of chivalry, among them the tales of King Arthur, the adventures of Bernardo del Carpio, and the epic *Poem of the Cid.*

Such stories, filled with tales of courageous rescues by chivalric knights, still inspired the *grandees,* the *ricos hombres,* and even the newly promoted *hidalgos,* or rank and file of the fifteenth-century Castilian nobility, to think of themselves in heroic terms despite improved communications, ocean exploration, and the rise of the Renaissance nation-state.

Although Isabella's brothers were thoroughly schooled in the classics, the princess was taught "cultivation of the womanly virtues"—reading and writing in the Castilian vernacular, prayers, the Bible, embroidery, needlepoint, and gilded painting. If Isabella spoke French at all it was probably quite poorly. Modern historians have noted that even her handwriting revealed a lack of humanistic, or Renaissance, influence. Her education, thus, seemed to be quite limited.

Despite Isabella's royal birth and obvious intelligence, such neglect was not unusual: Rather it was in keeping with late medieval thought about women as essential, but inferior, creatures. According to the most influential theologian of the late Middle Ages, St. Thomas Aquinas, women were to be man's nonintellectual partner, a "helper in the work of generation."[2] Thus woman was naturally subservient to man in whom the "discernment of reason predominates."

For centuries the teachings of the church fathers, based on Aristotelian thought, emphasized that woman was morally inferior to man as evidenced by her sin in the Garden of Eden. Consequently women had to be carefully instructed in church doctrine to keep them pure and free from temptation. To allow them to delve in the mysteries of Greek philosophy, astronomy, or Pythagorean geometry was thus a dangerous venture that would lead women beyond their proper sphere and weaken their intrinsically frail moral fiber.

Years later when Isabella was queen and received letters from foreign kings and prelates in Latin, she deeply regretted her lack of education. But as a princess in Enrique's court, she had no recourse. During the early years at Arévalo there were at least two convents where Isabella may have received religious instruction. The first, within the town gates, was the royal convent of San Francisco, which Isabella's father had maintained during his lifetime. A few miles beyond Arévalo was the Convent of the Incarnation. For some months, or perhaps years, Isabella also studied with the nuns at Ávila's Convent of Santa Ana. There, in addition to prayers and study of catechism, Isabella learned to embroider altar clothes with gold and silver thread and emblazon banners still displayed in the cathedrals of Ávila and Toledo today. Isabella also learned to sew shirts and other garments. Later, as queen, she proudly continued that childhood tradition and insisted upon making Ferdinand's shirts as a sign of wifely devotion.

The country years spent at Arévalo made Isabella into an athletic child, one accustomed to far more physical activity than would have been deemed appropriate had she grown up exclusively at court. As a young girl Isabella rode horses through the countryside with her brother Alfonso and became an accomplished equestrian.

In that era, Castilian girls on the brink of puberty were expected to ride mules. However, Isabella, already showing signs of a strong, unbendable will, refused to comply. She continued to ride horses throughout her life, even when dressed in formal clothes, often in a sidesaddle.

Pastoral life also made Isabella an intrepid hunter. Noblewomen often accompanied men on royal hunts in fifteenth century Castile, but they rarely hunted alone. Isabella was an exception: From childhood she had prowled the plains and woods with her brother and developed a fearless attitude toward the chase. The future queen enjoyed all aspects of the hunt—falconry, stags, even the stalking of ferocious bears and boars.

Despite her athletic prowess, Isabella was an intensely feminine woman with a keen appreciation for close personal relationships. As a child she developed a friendship with Beatriz de Bobadilla, the intelligent dark-haired daughter of Pedro de Bobadilla, governor of Arévalo's castle. Although Beatriz was considerably older than Isabella, the natural fondness that often comes from such early associations bloomed into something much deeper. The future queen repeatedly sought the advice of the "wise, virtuous and valiant" Beatriz. Like Isabella, Beatriz was once described as a *mujer varonile*, literally a "manly woman," that is, one who is brave and courageous.

The event that brought Isabella and Alfonso to court in Madrid in late 1461 or early 1462 was the birth of a child to Queen Juana and King Enrique. After seven years of marriage, the still-giddy, now-twenty-two-year-old queen had become pregnant. Her child was to be named heir to the throne of Castile. In anticipation of that event, a train of attendants accompanied the *Infantes* to Madrid on gilded horses belonging to Juan Pacheco, Marquis of Villena, and his brother Pedro Girón, Master of Calatrava.

Thereafter the *Infantes*, then nine and ten years old, remained permanently at court, ostensibly because Enrique wanted to "have them educated properly."[3] But beyond the king's vaunted concerns there were other motives—among them Enrique's desire to monitor his half brother and sister's behavior and ensure their loyalty. Consequently he entrusted Alfonso's education to Diego de Ribera, a "cavalier of pure blood and many virtues," who would provide the prince with a suitable role model.[4] To her dismay, Isabella was entrusted to Enrique's wife, Queen Juana.

That Isabella and Alfonso were forcibly wrenched from their mother at Arévalo who went mad from anguish is an intrinsic part of the Isabelline legend, one that historians can neither refute nor affirm. The only first-person account of the *Infantes'* final move to Enrique's court comes from Isabella herself nearly a decade after the event. In 1471, when the twenty-year-old Isabella was struggling for recognition as heir to the Castilian throne, she reported that she and Alfonso had been taken against their will to Enrique's court and placed under the scrutiny of Queen Juana. She wrote: "When my brother Alfonso and I were children we were forcibly and intentionally taken from the arms of our mother and raised under the authority of the Queen Doña Juana during her pregnancy. . . . It was a dangerous guardianship for us and . . . had infamous influences."[5]

In that letter, which was designed to circulate through the towns of Castile, Isabella portrayed herself as an orphan essentially held hostage by a stepmother whose wicked and sinful ways terrified her and Alfonso. The historian Palencia subsequently wrote that Prince Alfonso was so outraged by Queen Juana's lascivious court that he forbade her ladies-in-waiting to associate with his sister. It seems unlikely that a country boy of nine or ten, even one who was a prince, could have intimidated his elders with his piety. Rather, modern historians suspect that this story—as well as Isabella's negative comments about the queen—were political propaganda designed to blacken Enrique's name and rationalize her claim to the throne.

Isabella's horrified reaction to Enrique's careless court may have had some validity. From the beginning Queen Juana had been *muy allegre,* a high-spirited queen who engaged in flirtation, frivolity, and sexual innuendo. In contrast to her shrinking husband Enrique, Queen Juana reveled in court celebrations, pageants, mimes, and banquets where she appeared provocatively dressed in satins, silks, and velvets designed to reveal her fine figure.

Nor was it a secret that Enrique's favorite, the handsome, high-living Beltrán de la Cueva, had more than a respectful interest in the queen. The muscular, ostentatiously bejeweled youth was frequently seen in the company of Enrique and Juana, at jousts, bullfights, and banquets. Cueva delighted the queen with flamboyant theatrical spectacles, mimes, dances, and other festivities funded by his new wealth—festivities Juana often attended without Enrique.

One episode in particular implies that la Cueva was Queen Juana's lover. During a state visit from Burgundian ambassadors, the royal party rode through the woods of El Pardo. Suddenly la Cueva appeared in the road, dressed in a suit of silvery armor. Behind him stretched an enormous painted canvas depicting an imaginary castle at whose wooden gate stood Cueva's servants, dressed in leaves like savages. To cross the path into the woods, Cueva announced to his amused guests that each knight in the party had to participate in six jousts. Then he pointed to an archway filled with dangling golden initials. Each contestant was obliged to chose an initial as an emblem of his sweetheart. The jousts continued well into the afternoon. When Cueva's turn came to, he plucked a golden *J* from the archway. Eyebrows were raised and the courtiers began to whisper that Cueva was Queen Juana's lover.

Cueva's selection was, of course, hardly proof that he had cuckolded the king. Nevertheless, Queen Juana's alluring manner, Enrique's alleged impotence, his disregard for ceremonial decorum and abrupt disappearances to the woods for long hunts with his cronies fed the illusion, if not the reality, of a raging permissiveness in the Castilian court.

No doubt that image was intensified by Enrique's own careless attitude toward extramarital sex. Less than a year after his second marriage, Enrique had an affair with a young beauty in his wife's court, a Portuguese named Doña Guimor de Castro. In return for Guimor's attentions, the enamoured king bestowed lands, annuities, and jewels on her while Juana smoldered. Although the affair was typical of high-born men of the fifteenth century, chroniclers subsequently observed that it was probably a ruse, another of Enrique's hollow attempts at redeeming his virility in the eyes of the court—an act "intended but not achieved."[6]

Soon Enrique acquired still another mistress or pseudomistress. The outcome of this amour with Catalina de Sandoval was even more of an embarrassment for him, for Sandoval secretly kept another lover on the side.

Such indiscretions, while juicy material for the tongues of court wags and gossips, were hardly unusual in the medieval courts of Western Europe where marriages were arranged for political advantage and romantic love was a matter of private prerogative. Still, for a girl like Isabella, accustomed to the solemn chants of nuns in their cloisters, the labor-filled lives of Arévalo's peasants, and the quiet grief of her devout mother, Enrique's perfumed, gloved, and careless courtiers must have seemed like a nest of hell-bent voluptuaries.

Despite court speculation about Queen Juana's fidelity, Princess Juana's birth in late February 1462 was celebrated with the usual expressions of thanksgiving to the Almighty for a first royal birth. There was no talk that someone other than Enrique might have fathered the child.

Princess Juana's birth was part of an orderly royal succession, duly recognized by papal legates from Rome and by French and Portuguese ambassadors who traveled to Castile in anticipation of the event. In early March Enrique circulated letters to the kingdom's major cities announcing the birth of the "most high Princess Doña Juana, my very dear and most beloved daughter and heir."[7] To mark the infant's arrival there were banquets and street celebrations in Madrid, dances and bullfights in Burgos and Toledo, even a solemn procession of thanksgiving to Toledo's cathedral.

The baptism was conducted by Archbishop Carrillo and witnessed by scores of

Castilian *grandees* in the royal chapel of the alcázar in Madrid. Four individuals were named as Princess Juana's godparents—Pacheco and his wife, the Count of Armagnac, and Princess Isabella, then just a month short of her eleventh birthday.

On May 9 Enrique convened the *Cortes* in Madrid to swear their allegiance to Princess Juana as heir to the Castilian throne. As the *procuradores,* or parliamentary representatives, rose for the oath, Princess Isabella and Prince Alfonso stood beside them to swear their allegiance to Princess Juana as Enrique's legitimate heir. The tiny baby who squirmed in Queen Juana's arms that day was to be the next Queen of Castile. No one doubted it, least of all the infant's stepaunt Isabella and stepuncle Alfonso, still God-fearing children themselves, who believed in the divine right of kings.

CHAPTER SIX

A Castilian Chess Game

Ultimately it was Alfonso and Isabella who kept Princess Juana from the Castilian throne. The young *Infantes* did not set about it deliberately, but as the offspring of King Juan, they were pawns in the hands of disgruntled *grandees* who manipulated them against Enrique for their own advantage.

The ensuing human chess game evolved slowly and was unwittingly fed by Enrique's untoward affection for the handsome Beltrán de la Cueva. During the celebrations for Princess Juana's baptism, the king surprised the *grandees* by elevating la Cueva to aristocratic status. After saying mass, the king ordered his courtiers into the throne room where, with trumpets blaring and a display of Castile's red and gold banners, Enrique named Cueva Count of Ledesma. This latest plum, the vast new lands added to Cueva's wealth, and his rapid rise from obscurity to ennoblement were more than Pacheco and his unhappy faction of counts and dukes could tolerate.

By August 1462, neither could Carrillo, for that month Enrique startled the court anew by marrying Cueva to Mencia de Mendoza, the youngest daughter of the second Marquis of Santillana. To Carrillo, that marriage was the final blow. The bride's uncle was the Bishop of Calahorra, Pedro González de Mendoza, Carrillo's rival for the cardinalship. Clearly he was in the king's favor.

The domestic tensions of Enrique's reign had long attracted interest from foreign rivals, particularly from the last of the *Infantes* of Aragón, King Juan of Navarre. In 1440 Juan had married his daughter to Enrique. Because of her alleged "bewitchment" of Enrique, the marriage had been annulled and Blanca had returned home in disgrace. Some years hence King Juan's ambitions for his son Ferdinand would enable Isabella to gain the Castilian crown.

Although Juan became King of Aragón in 1458, the early years of his reign were riddled with problems. By 1462 the short, wizened, sixty-four-year-old king was rapidly losing his eyesight to cataracts and his kingdom to his eldest son, Carlos, Prince of Viana. The bad blood between father and son had grown out of the widowed king's second marriage to Juana Enríquez, the brilliant daughter of an aristocratic Castilian clan.

The new queen had captivated King Juan with her brains and beauty, and on March 10, 1452, she completed his delight with the birth of a sturdy son named Ferdinand. Juan was so enamoured of his new family that he eventually seized the territory of Catalonia, which, by rights, had been left to Prince Carlos by his deceased mother.

To defend his claim as *primogenit,* or firstborn son and heir of Catalonia, the thin, scholarly, and probably tubercular Carlos sought help from France, Naples, and even Castile. The resultant treaty of December 1460 was one of Enrique's worst mistakes. In it he promised to provide Carlos with men and arms in exchange for Carlos's promise to marry Isabella when she came of age.

Before long, however, Carrillo and Pacheco learned of the pact and revealed the information to King Juan. On December 2, 1460, the infuriated Aragonese king clapped Carlos into jail. In response, the Catalonian *Cortes* rose in rebellion in Barcelona, imprisoned Juan's governor, and ran the king out of the city. Before long the rebellion had spread southward to Valencia, to Mallorca, Sardinia, even to Sicily.

Carlos's imprisonment left Enrique in an awkward situation. By 1461 his gifts to favorites and his war against the Moors had so depleted the treasury that he was unable to fulfill his obligations to defend Carlos. In desperation, Enrique decided to bargain with his betrayers. If Pacheco and Carrillo would lend him their private armies, Enrique promised to favor their faction again at court.

The two men agreed eagerly. Ultimately they consented to lease their soldiers to Enrique on one other condition: The king had to swear to make Isabella's brother, Prince Alfonso, his heir.

Initially Enrique agreed. Thus, in January 1461 Castilian soldiers crossed the Castilian-Aragonese border and marched into the Navarre. By early summer Carlos was freed and the Catalonians had declared their independence from the Aragonese crown. Shaken, King Juan agreed to name Carlos his successor. On August 26, 1461, he signed a treaty to that effect at Villafranca del Penedés.

That same day Enrique honored part of his pledge to Carrillo and Pacheco by agreeing to give their faction a stronger voice in the Royal Council. But the Castilian king balked at naming Alfonso as heir to Castile, for he had just discovered that Queen Juana was pregnant.

The Catalonians' triumph was short-lived. On September 23, less than three weeks after the treaty was signed at Villafranca, Prince Carlos died suddenly at the age of thirty-nine. Poison was, of course, was immediately suspected, and the Aragonese king and queen were named as the likely culprits.

Nevertheless, the prince's death galvanized the Catalonians into a single voice that refused to recognize King Juan's second son, the nine-year-old Ferdinand, as their new leader. By February crowds of Barcelonians had taken to the streets again. Queen Juana Enríquez, fearing for her life and Ferdinand's, fled.

By summer 1462, soon after Princess Juana of Castile was born, the Catalonians offered Enrique their crown. Immensely flattered, Isabella's older brother assumed the title of "Count of Barcelona and lord of the principality of Catalonia" and sent ambassadors to confirm his sovereignty. He had become the most powerful monarch on the Iberian peninsula.

Simultaneously, Juan appealed to the new French monarch, Louis XI, for succor. In exchange for 700 French "lances"—some 8,400 mounted knights and their infantry—Juan agreed to pay Louis the huge sum of 200,000 gold écus. But since the Aragonese king was penniless, he guaranteed his loans by granting the French king temporary jurisdiction over two Catalonian counties that stood north of the Pyrenees, Roussillon and Cerdagne.

Louis, perceiving Juan's "loan" as a means of permanently annexing those territories to France, eagerly accepted the offer. But Catalonian nobles protested bitterly, accusing Juan of callously bartering their liberty to a French rule they vowed never to accept.

Meanwhile, Enrique was stymied. Should he fail to fulfill his promise to Catalonia, he would lose its crown. Yet if he defended that principality, he would become embroiled in a war against France and Aragón.

Suddenly Louis stepped forward as peacemaker. That ugly, long-nosed French king was so new to the throne that he had not yet revealed the cunning that would later lead King Juan to nickname him the "universal spider." Enrique eagerly accepted Louis's offer and then gullably "trusted to those who sold him" by appointing Pacheco and Carrillo to negotiate a treaty with the French ambassador.

Ultimately, Enrique agreed to withdraw his troops from the Aragonese kingdom and cede his claim to the Catalan crown. In recompense, Louis awarded him the paltry border town of Estrella and the dubious promise that King Juan would respect the Catalan constitution.

Only Pacheco truly profited from the truce. In return for manipulating Enrique to surrender, Louis awarded him a French county, and Louis's illegitimate daughter became the bride of Pacheco's son. When Enrique learned about Pacheco's deception, he retreated abruptly to Segovia to sulk for weeks.

Even the news that his soldiers had wrested Gibraltar and Archidona from the Moors did not lighten the king's spirits. In retaliation against France, the Castilian king began to look eastward for new allies. Accordingly, he signed a trade treaty with England and entertained the notion of marrying Isabella to his brother-in-law, Afonso V, King of Portugal. He ordered the princess to accompany him and Queen Juana in late 1462 or early 1463 to meet Afonso in the newly conquered port of Gibraltar. Although the thirty-two-year-old Portuguese king was widowed and had a son nearly Isabella's age, he eyed the lithe princess approvingly.

But eleven-year-old Isabella stunned Enrique and Queen Juana by declaring that she had no intention of marrying Afonso. "The *Infantas* of Castile," Isabella solemnly reminded her brother, "could not be disposed of in marriage without the consent of the nobles of the realm," as provided in her father's will.[1] Doubtless the princess had been schooled to such thoughts by Pacheco, Carrillo, perhaps even by her childhood administrator, Gonzalo Chacón. Nevertheless, this reminder typified the future queen's sensitivity to public sentiment and the ancient laws of Castile.

In contrast was Enrique's 1464 award to Cueva of the mastership of the Order of Santiago, the largest landed estates in the kingdom of Castile except for the crown. The court, indeed all of Castile, were appalled, for by rights the mastership belonged to Isabella's brother Alfonso, as stipulated in his father's will.

Even before the appointment became official, Pacheco had prepared a protest. A week earlier he, his brother Girón, and Carrillo formed a "league" at the archbishop's castle at Alcalá de Henares to free Alfonso and Isabella from Enrique's authority. Now Cueva's appointment gave them the perfect excuse to challenge the king to restore Isabella and Alfonso's inheritance rights. In May 1464 Pacheco, Carrillo, and Girón thus circulated a proclamation explaining that Alfonso's birthright had been illegally assigned to Cueva and the public trust violated. Simultaneously, they protested Enrique's plans to marry Isabella to the Portuguese king.

The proclamation attracted thousands of discontented Castilians to their side. It also inspired some of Castile's most powerful *grandees* to join the rebels— among them the *Almirante,* or "Admiral" of Castile, Fadrique Enríquez, and other powerful landholders including Rodrigo Pimentel, Iñigo Manrique, Álvaro de Stúñiga and Garcí Álvarez de Toledo. Quietly, in the marbled rooms of ducal palaces, in the tapestried chambers and drafty sitting rooms of granite castles, the battle lines were drawn. By early summer 1464 the civil war against King Enrique had begun in earnest.

There are many ways to depose a king. Knowing that, Pacheco and Carrillo used every ploy within their means, every grumbling soldier and greedy courtier, to speed Enrique's fall. Both men knew that the quickest way to topple a presumably corrupt monarch was to produce a blameless new candidate for the throne, one whose royal blood was as pure as his past. A maligned innocent was even better, one who would immediately capture the sympathies of the poor, the ailing, and the downtrodden. The blond, devout, nearly ten-year-old Prince Alfonso was thus an ideal candidate for the role.

Still, before the rebels could establish Prince Alfonso on the throne, it was necessary to discredit the rights of his niece, the two-year-old Princess Juana. Thus insinuations that the toddler was illegitimate, that she was fathered by someone other than King Enrique, began to spread through the Castilian kingdom. Such tales were already so familiar at court that Gonzalo de Guzmán once observed there were three issues he refused to debate—the "pompous drawl of Pacheco, the gravity of Archbishop Carrillo and the virility of Don Enrique."[2]

Once begun, once spread through a few choice channels, the rumors wound their way through the Castilian towns and countryside, carried by couriers and minstrels over mountain passes and down long dusty roads, snatched up as eagerly by bored farmers and peasants as the cloth, spices, and herbal cures carried in the leather pouches of peddlers.

Ricos hombres, grizzled village wags, and common wenches all made great capital out of accusations that Enrique was impotent in his second marriage, that his new daughter and heir, the Princess Juana, was, in fact, fathered by the king's favorite, Beltrán de la Cueva, the new master of the Order of Santiago. So strong was the appeal of these rumors, so maliciously prurient, that before long the little princess was given a nickname—*Juana La Beltraneja,* or Joan, daughter of Beltrán—a sobriquet that has stuck to her throughout history.

Over the centuries scholars have suspected that Princess Juana's illegitimacy was specious propaganda, a ploy designed to turn the kingdom against la Cueva and Enrique. To explain the irregularities of Enrique's sex life that inspired these rumors, some historians have speculated that the king was sporadically impotent or even a victim of acromegaly, or constitutional eunuchoidism. The theory that King Enrique had hormonal deficiencies preventing normal masculinity finally led to the 1946 disinterment of his remains from the monastery at Guadalupe. The subsequent examination by physician-historian Gregorio Marañon and archaeologist Manuel Gómez Moreno revealed that Enrique's skeleton was normally virile and equal to that of "any robust living man."[3]

Was Enrique a homosexual? Or a bisexual who had an intimate relationship with Pacheco in his youth that he later refuted? Or was the king simply a normal but shy man who was inhibited from the sexual act on two wedding nights by a crowd of leering witnesses?

While the truth will probably never be known, the insinuation that Enrique was impotent, that Queen Juana had been unfaithful, and that Princess Juana was illegitimate had a powerful appeal to Enrique's disgruntled subjects. In time, these rumors prompted Enrique to submit to a physical examination to "prove" his masculinity. Somewhere too, in the desperate scuffle of the civil war years, an unnamed court attendant deliberately broke the unfortunate Princess Juana's nose to make her more closely resemble Enrique. Even so, the ugly accusations clung like burrs.

Inevitably, the allegations of sexual impropriety that tainted Enrique's reputation left an indelible impression upon Princess Isabella. As a member of the court, the princess doubtless heard the rumors and saw the snickers that greeted King Enrique and Queen Juana. Later, when she was drawn into the maelstrom herself, Isabella would personally witness how effectively the suspicion that a queen was unchaste could obliterate a dynastic line.

It was a lesson Isabella never forgot. Henceforth, as a young wife and later as queen, Isabella bound herself to irreproachable chastity.

CHAPTER SEVEN

The *Infantes* Imperiled

E nrique was trapped. All spring Pacheco fumed over Cueva's appointment to the mastership of Santiago, and by the summer of 1464 he fashioned a plan to force Enrique to retract it. First, he dispatched the chronicler Palencia to Rome to protest Cueva's appointment to Pope Pius II. Then he invited Enrique to a meeting with the rebels.

As usual the king longed only for *paz y sosiego,* or "peace and quiet," and ultimately he agreed to an interview. It was to take place on September 16 in the grassy plains between the northern Castilian towns of San Pedro de la Dueñas and Villacastin. On the appointed day, as Enrique and a handful of advisors rode toward the caucus, scouts warned the king of a rebel ambush inspired by Pacheco. Then, in a spontaneous show of public support, hundreds of Castilian commoners, waving rakes and scythes, gathered to repulse the rebels and accompany Enrique safely back to Segovia.

In Villacastin, meanwhile, the barons realized that the only way to depose Enrique was to expose his faults in such a way that the average citizen would feel threatened. On September 25 Pacheco and Girón thus gathered their followers in Burgos and issued an *amonestación,* or warning letter, to the Castilian towns listing their grievances. Among them was the flat statement that "Doña Juana, the one called the Princess, is not your daughter," thus reviving the ugly rumor about the little princess's paternity.[1] They also explained that King Juan's will stipulated that if Enrique left no legitimate children, the crown was to pass to Alfonso as his next living male heir. Should Alfonso die before bearing children, Isabella was to succeed him as queen.

Another complaint was Cueva's "power" over Enrique. Supposedly he wanted to control the royal *Infantes,* "to the great injury of your royal dignity and the shame of the inhabitants of these kingdoms, for they fear lest certain persons under the influence . . . of the said Count procure the death of the . . . Infantes, so that the succession . . . may devolve upon the said Doña Juana."[2]

The *amonestación* listed still other complaints designed to elicit citizen rage, among them that Enrique had abused royal authority by employing Jews and Moslems at court who had "corrupted the air and destroyed human nature,"[3] raised taxes without consent from the *Cortes,* and wreaked havoc with the coinage.

In Segovia, the royal council urged the king to punish the rebels at once. But Enrique, who loathed confrontations, stubbornly opted to ignore the insult. Instead he arranged a second meeting with the rebels, this time on the plain between Cigales and Cabezón. At the meeting the intimidated king agreed not only to exile his beloved Cueva from court and return the mastership of Santiago to Prince Alfonso, but to name his younger brother heir to the Castilian throne.

Enrique rationalized that he had not altogether abandoned his daughter's rights for he had attached one condition to Alfonso's ascension: The prince could become King of Castile only if he married Princess Juana. Through that marriage, facilitated by a papal dispensation, Princess Juana would thereby be queen consort, if not an independent Queen of Castile.

In late November 1464 the two sides met once again at the Cigales-Cabezón border to ratify the pact. This time Enrique brought eleven-year-old Alfonso to the meeting. In a simple ceremony, the king stood before the prince and swore "that the legitimate succession to these realms belongs to my brother the Infante don Alfonso, and to no other person whatsoever."[4] Then Enrique delivered the small, light-haired boy to Pacheco, who was to serve as his guardian and tutor.

The pact did not mention Isabella's rights. Although the rebels had discussed the possibility of returning the thirteen-year-old princess to her mother in Arévalo or even allowing her to live in an independent household, the negotiators abandoned both ideas. Instead, Isabella was to continue living under Enrique's authority. Nor was she to regain the town of Cuellar promised in her father's will, for it was still held by Cueva. At this time Isabella was still perceived as a minor figure, whose rights could easily be sacrificed.

The most important of Enrique's concessions was the creation of a council designed to reform the Castilian kingdom. The proposed commission was to include five appointees—two representatives from each faction and a neutral party. But the churning intrigues of Enrique's court soured loyalties faster than day-old milk. By the beginning of 1465, every man on the commission had joined the rebel cause, and on January 16 they published a harsh document known as the "Sentence of Medina del Campo." This "Sentence" not only reiterated many of the terms discussed at the first rebel conference, but contained other clauses that drastically reduced Enrique's authority and left him with little more than the title of king. Specifically, it prohibited Enrique from imprisoning a noble without a committee's consent. Nor could his royal appointments be passed from father to son. Finally the king's standing army was to be reduced from 3,000 to 600 lancers—considerably smaller than the militias many *grandees* maintained themselves.

Clearly, the sentence was a bold effort to strip Enrique of traditional seignorial rights and grant them to the rebellious nobility. To submit to those demands would have made him a laughingstock, an emasculated figurehead, forced to appeal to the *grandee* junta to exercise even the most elemental rights of monarchial authority. Ultimately, Enrique realized he had no other alternative than to declare war.

Enraged, the king ordered Cueva to mobilize a royal army. In February 1465 he decreed the Sentence of Medina del Campo null and void and annulled Prince Alfonso's title as heir to the throne. By late winter Cueva had assembled 5,000 citizens armed with lances and pitchforks to defend the kingdom. On the Granada-Andalusian border Enrique's soldiers occupied fortresses where crossbows, or *espingardas,* and *lombardas,* or early cannons, had been stockpiled. As a final precautionary measure, the king moved the royal treasury into the Segovian alcázar and placed that city under the aegis of his trusted allies Juan Arías Dávila, bishop of Segovia, and his brother Pedro.

Simultaneously, Enrique ordered Isabella, Queen Doña Juana, and Princess Juana moved from Madrid to Segovia under heavy guard. Years later Isabella would claim that she was virtually held prisoner in Segovia, but in reality she lived there as a member of the royal family. Isabella was housed in the royal apartments with the queen and her attendants, at Segovia's *casas real,* or royal palace, which stands in the center of town not far from the alcázar. Then, as now, Segovia was a beautiful, hilly city that sat majestically above the high plains dotted with trees and cut through by the Clamores and Eresma rivers, a city whose oldest homes are still emblazoned with aristocratic *escudos,* or shields. But while the princess was allowed to move freely within the city, every effort to communicate with the outside world was carefully observed.

On February 20, 1466, after Isabella had been confined to Segovia for nearly a year, Enrique awarded her the city of Trujillo. Initially, the gift, with its rent of 34,000 maravedís a year, may have come as a pleasant surprise to Isabella, but before long she gleaned her brother's motive. Trujillo, a whitewashed town near the Portuguese border, was politically strategic. Having declared civil war, Enrique realized that he needed a foreign ally. His first choice was the Portuguese king, Afonso V, Queen Juana's brother. Ever since his first meeting with Isabella in 1464, Afonso had retained interest in the princess as his future bride. In subsequent communications with Enrique, he demanded Trujillo as part of her dowry. Thus, Enrique presented Isabella with the town in anticipation of her fifteenth birthday—a marriageable age. He also may have believed the gift would bind her to him.

There is, in fact, evidence of at least superficial warmth between brother and sister. In a letter Enrique wrote to Isabella before 1468 he stated: "My virtuous lady and sister . . . Rest be assured that because you are my sister I will try to do everything you have requested . . . I am at your complete service. Also, Señora, if you ask anything of me, there is no one who would rather serve you than I. . . . With the privilege of a kiss, Your brother. . . ."[5]

There is less proof of Isabella's genuine affection, but from the tone of Enrique's letter the princess seems to have been appropriately respectful, even obsequious to her brother. As a child at Arévalo she had learned to pray; as an adolescent at Enrique's court she learned to dissemble. Now, as a young woman in Segovia, Isabella practiced both simultaneously—cordiality to her elders in public, fervent prayers for her brother Alfonso in private. As the ward of a nervous king, the fifteen-year-old Isabella knew the tactic was her only possible defense, the best ploy against the circumstances of her life.

In early spring 1465 the rebels and loyalists played an anxious game, trailing each other's armies across Castile and attempting to win uncommitted towns to their respective sides. Before long the rebels had won a handful of wealthy towns— among them Plasencia, Ávila, Medina del Campo, and Valladolid. The king had taken those defections badly, almost as badly as the betrayal of two men he once believed loyal to his cause—his cousin, the *Almirante* Fadrique Enríquez, father of the Aragonese queen, and the Archbishop Carrillo. When Enrique sent a messenger to the archbishop, the prelate had turned on him haughtily. "Tell your King that I am tired of him and everything about him," he snarled. "Now we shall see who is the real sovereign of Castile."[6]

In Carrillo's mind the "real" sovereign was the eleven-year-old Prince Alfonso, who despite his youth, was inevitably swept into the civil war and became its brightest symbol. In April the boy traveled with Pacheco to the hillside town of Plasencia at the foot of the Sierra Gredos. On May 10 the rebels dispatched a second circular from there to the Castilian towns, asserting that "the scandals, robberies, deaths and harm were the responsibility of the King and his inept counselors and not from us."[7]

When, later that month, the rebels learned that Enrique planned to visit Zamora to seal his alliance with the Portuguese king, Carrillo urged a dramatic civil gesture that would publicly humiliate Enrique. Thus on the morning of June 5, 1465, the rebels raised a high platform in a square behind the cathedral of Ávila outside the city gates. There, before a curious crowd, the *grandees* placed a crowned mannequin of Enrique upon a thronelike chair, dressed in sable, with a sword at his side and a scepter in his hand. In a grotesque, almost magical ceremony that smacked of Carrillo's alchemic transformations, the rebel leaders read a long list of complaints against King Enrique.

With a ceremonial flourish, the archbishop then lifted the crown off the dummy and declared Enrique unfit to be king. Other nobles then removed the sword, the scepter, the rest of the royal insignias, and booted the statue to the ground to signify Enrique's deposition. Below the platform a stupefied crowd of citizens wept aloud "for fear about the unluckiness of the dethronement."[8]

To both commoners and high-born of the mid-fifteenth century, anything was possible. It was an age steeped in magic and superstition, populated with demons, goblins, even Satan himself. Just thirty-nine years earlier Joan of Arc had been burned at the stake for being a witch. What then was to stop a saintly boy like Prince Alfonso, blessed by Archbishop Carrillo, from magically becoming a sovereign?

Triumphantly, the rebels raised Prince Alfonso to the throne and crowned him as Alfonso XII of Castile. Then one by one they knelt before the boy, kissed his hand, and swore their fealty. As trumpets pierced the still June air, the crowd then cheered Alfonso as their new king.

News of Enrique's dethronement in Ávila spread like summer lightning across

Castile's vast plains, speeding word of the impending conflict, jolting sleepy towns and bustling cities into action and splintering them into two camps.

On one side the rebel league was supported by some of Castile's wealthiest families—the Enríquezes, the Fajardos, the Manriques, the Guzmáns, the Giróns, and the Stúñigas as well as the Archbishop of Sevilla and hundreds of wealthy knights from the military orders of Santiago, Calatrava, and Alcántara.

Yet Enrique still had many formidable allies—most of Castile's bishops and powerful *grandees* such as the Mendozas, the Albas, Alver Pérez Osorio, Miguel Lucas de Iranzo, and Juan de Valenzuela. Moreover, the kingdom's outlying provinces remained squarely in Enrique's camp. Shortly after the "farce at Ávila," as the loyalists dubbed the dethronement, Enrique divided his army. Half his men were to battle the rebels; the other half prepared to march to the Portuguese border as escorts for Queen Juana and Isabella to meet Afonso V.

To Enrique's followers, the dethronement at Ávila was a sacrilege bordering on witchcraft, an unnatural act that desecrated the divine contract between the king and his subjects as established in the thirteenth century by Alfonso X's *Siete Partidas*. To defy it was to defy the natural order of the Almighty and the rudiments of Christianity. Consequently, both devout and superstitious Castilians feared that the dethronement would destroy the Castilian kingdom, much as the Black Death had a century earlier.

In contrast, the rebels viewed the dethronement as a necessary act that would rid Castile of an incompetent king.

By early summer the rebels were contesting Princess Juana's legitimacy on other grounds. On July 4 Carrillo wrote an open letter to the Castilian towns claiming Princess Juana was a bastard because Enrique's marriage to Queen Juana was canonically invalid. Like many members of medieval nobility, the Castilian king and queen were related—first cousins. Because the church prohibited marriage within four degrees of consanguinity, Enrique and his future wife had been obliged to obtain a papal dispensation at the time of their 1455 marriage. The reigning pope, Nicholas V, had, however, failed to issue such a dispensation because of the unusual circumstances surrounding Enrique's divorce. Instead, he sent a bull allowing Enrique to remarry with the promise of a subsequent papal dispensation if he proved capable of normal sexual relations with his second wife.

To verify Enrique's virility, Nicholas then appointed three prelates—Alfonso Carrillo de Acuña, the Archbishop of Toledo; Alfonso Fonseca, the Bishop of Ávila; and Alfonso Sánchez de Valladolid, the Archbishop of Ciudad Rodrigo. But Juana did not conceive for seven years, the documents were never sent, and the dispensation was never issued. On that basis Carrillo now claimed that Enrique's marriage to Queen Juana was invalid. That accusation—issued at the peak of Enrique's unpopularity and unresolved because of Nicholas V's death— shook the confidence of the devout Castilian citizenry in Princess Juana's "divine" right to the throne. By comparison, Prince Alfonso's claim no longer seemed sacrilegious, and even devout Castilians began to think of it as his "legitimate" right.

Castile, meanwhile, reeled under the strain of having two kings. Bandits preyed regularly upon highway travelers, robberies became increasingly common, and victims rarely received the satisfaction of trial. Assault, rape, and murder went unchecked, and decent citizens lived in constant fear.

Nobles, ensconced in impregnable castles across the Castilian landscape, now marshalled their private armies, battling rivaling forces for the throne. Peasants and commoners often were drawn unwillingly into these battles, either in homage to their lord or in defense of their modest cottages and fields. Sheepherding and agriculture, Castile's major industries, were maintained with increasing difficulty in a countryside wracked by war.

Castilian cities and towns were even more fractured, their citizens divided, their public buildings, even churches, used as strongholds. Everywhere the daily rhythms of life were disrupted. Towns, divided against themselves, had difficulty maintaining trade, markets and fairs were deserted or disbanded as communities closed their gates to their former trading partners. Merchants and moneychangers argued bitterly over the integrity of the coins that circulated through the countryside from the 150 new mints that sprang up around Enrique's decaying fiscal administration. The tenuous tranquility that Castile had enjoyed under Enrique's reign between 1455 and 1465 was permanently shattered.

In such an atmosphere, the *grandees* clung stubbornly to their cause and their symbolic leader, the boy-king Alfonso XII. By the spring of 1466 there was talk of dividing Castile into two zones—one loyalist and the other supporting the rebel cause.

Meanwhile the rebels had not entirely forgotten about Isabella, still at Segovia. The fifteen-year-old princess was a trump card Enrique intended to play in exchange for foreign protection. Although the 1465 talks at Zamora had not ended in Isabella's betrothal to Afonso V, the rebels feared that eventuality.

Thus in April 1466 they agreed to meet with the loyalists at Coca. Isabella's guardianship was the subject of an impassioned debate. Finally, after days of wrangling, the rival factions compromised. They decided to marry Isabella to Pacheco's brother, Pedro Girón, Master of Calatrava, thereby neutralizing her political utility. In exchange for Isabella as his bride, Girón and Pacheco promised to return the rebels to Enrique's obedience. The king, by then ready to sacrifice almost anything for peace, agreed to the plan.

Everyone was pleased with the marriage—everyone, that is, except Isabella, who was repulsed by the idea of marrying the forty-three-year-old Master of Calatrava. Girón, crude, jowled, foul-mouthed, corrupt, and notoriously lecherous, stood for everything Isabella personally despised.

But no matter how vile the man, how despicable his political and personal habits, there seemed no way Isabella could escape. Her only other option, to marry Afonso V, was just as distasteful. Essentially, Isabella was trapped. Even if she were to appeal to the Castilian *Cortes,* there was little chance the marriage would be denied because of its popularity with both factions. Nor could Isabella's mentor Carrillo offer her much consolation; despite his hopes for an Aragonese match for Isabella, he had conceded to political expedience.

In preparation for the wedding, Isabella had been ordered to move from Segovia to Madrid. Now there was nothing to do but sob, pray, and fast in her room at the Madrid alcázar for a day and a night, prostrating herself and begging God to let her die before the wedding.

According to legend, Isabella's friend Beatriz de Bobadilla shared Isabella's antipathy to the idea of marrying Girón. "God will not permit it and neither will I!"[9] Beatriz exclaimed when she first heard about Isabella's imminent wedding. Somehow the fiery young woman obtained a dagger, which she hid in her bosom and vowed to sink into Girón when he approached Isabella.

A few days before the wedding, Girón set out from the seat of the Calatrava knighthood in Almagro with an army of 3,000 lancers and presents for his bride. As he traveled north toward Madrid, he stopped at Barrueco Castle in Jaén. Above him a thick flock of storks circled and darkened the sky. Like most people of his era Girón was superstitious, and finally he polled his attendants about its meaning. His followers replied that they had never seen anything like it, but they noted the storks' path was the same one the bridegroom was following toward Madrid.

To at least one contemporary chronicler, the storks were an indisputable omen of impending doom. On the second night of the journey, Girón fell ill with an acute "throat abscess." On April 20, 1466, after several days of suffering, he died with "blasphemous words" on his lips, "cursing God for the cruelty of not allowing him to live forty more days to enjoy this last display of power"—that is, his marriage to Isabella.[10]

Girón may have died from complications due to a streptococcal throat infection; scholars have never settled the case. They agree only that Girón's death left Isabella free to pursue her future destiny. In the last years of the queen's life, as writers began to glorify Isabella and Ferdinand's accomplishments, "miracles" like Girón's death were increasingly seen as proof of the monarchs' status as chosen missionaries of God.

Isabella's reaction has also been lost to the dust of time, although she must have felt both shock and relief. But whether Isabella believed Girón's death was a matter of divine or human intervention, the incident left her with a chilling impression: Those who abuse political power create a debt of hatred that almost certainly brings them to a bad end. As monarch, Isabella would struggle to avoid such temptations.

CHAPTER EIGHT

Infanta No Longer

After Girón's death, Isabella returned to the cloistered environment of Segovia under Enrique's authority. But by 1467 the princess would become the subject of another marriage proposal, this time from King Juan, the troubled Aragonese monarch, on behalf of his fifteen-year-old son Prince Ferdinand.

Romance had nothing to do with it and political protection everything, for once again King Juan was desperate. Some months earlier the French king, Louis XI, his appetite whetted by his recent acquisitions of the Aragonese provinces of Cerdagne and Roussillon, dispatched troops to Catalonia, seized the strategic river city of Gerona, and established outposts in Barcelona. Although Juan mustered an Aragonese army to stem the French advance, he knew that in time Louis would invade Catalonia again.

Clearly, Juan needed additional military aid. Hoping to obtain it from his old allies Pacheco and Carrillo, in spring of 1467, he ordered a shrewd ambassador named Pierres de Peralta to Castile. As an additional incentive Juan secretly instructed Peralta to arrange a marriage between Ferdinand with either Princess Isabella or Pacheco's daughter Beatriz. Although King Juan preferred Isabella, he instructed Peralta to arrange a match with whoever had the larger dowry.

Girón's death led to strained relations between the rebels and the loyalists. For nearly a year the politic Alfonso de Fonseca, now Archbishop of Sevilla, tried to make peace between the two sides, but they never came to terms. In the resultant stalemate, the Castilian countryside was splintered into various political divisions, plundered by wandering groups of soldiers, who, lacking pay, swept vengefully over towns to steal household goods, pick the fields clean of crops, and create food shortages for Castilian citizens.

The rebels told Peralta they could not provide King Juan with soldiers despite his precarious political situation.

By August 1467, possibly through Peralta's machinations, rebels and loyalists finally met in a pitched battle on the desolate plains of the sleepy town of Olmedo—the same battlefield where, ironically, eighteen years earlier, Enrique had defeated King Juan.

While ultimately the battle was a draw, it so deeply disturbed Pope Paul II that he ordered the papal legate, Antonio Jacobo de Veneris, to Spain to make peace. Like Paul, Veneris favored King Enrique; thus he arrived with a bull of excommunication to threaten the rebels if they failed to come to terms.

To Veneris's surprise, both factions treated him shabbily. When the legate tried to persuade Enrique to pardon the rebels, the king angrily refused to cooperate. The rebels sneered at Veneris's threat of excommunication, insisting that the war was a domestic affair that did not require ecclesiastical intervention. "Those who advised the pope that he had a right to interfere in the temporal concerns of Castile deceived him," they told Veneris, for they had "a perfect right to depose their monarch on sufficient grounds, and should exercise it."[1]

But if papal intervention did little to resolve the dispute that paralyzed Castile, private opinion did. A month after the battle of Olmedo, Enrique's trusted *converso* guardians of Segovia, Juan Arías Dávila, Bishop of Segovia, and his brother, Pedro, betrayed the king by opening the city gates to the rebels. Suddenly Isabella was liberated from Enrique's control.

The king was dumbfounded. To him Segovia, with its towering alcázar, its rich treasury, its golden *Sala de los Reyes*, or Hall of the Kings, its lush woods and rich hunting fields, was the very symbol of the ancient Castilian kingdom. He had grown up there, spent much of his childhood wandering the alcázar's dank chambers and towers, had, as an adult, refurbished some of its crumbling Mudéjar rooms, even added defensive balconies and guard posts to the central keep, the *Torre del Homenaje*. As king he had stocked the woods of El Bazaín with deer, bears, and boars, built a wall around his hunting park, and spent long, happy hours there. To have the rebels take Segovia was the ultimate insult, a harbinger of aristocratic triumph over the divine rights of kings.

While Enrique's ward at Segovia, Isabella had maintained a neutral stance. But once she was freed in September or October of 1467, she immediately embraced Alfonso's cause. During the long years of her captivity, the future queen had blossomed into a comely young woman whose quiet manner, dignified reticence, and religious devotions belied a strong personality.

Upon obtaining her release, Isabella's first instinct was to return to Arévalo to tend to her mother who, despite moments of lucidity, was rapidly sinking into a permanent psychosis.

Shortly after her arrival, Alfonso joined her. On December 7, in the glow of their reunion, Alfonso awarded his sister the town of Medina del Campo in a document he signed as "King of Castile and León." Despite Isabella's acceptance of that gift, she was still considered a neutral party in the civil war. Nevertheless, she feared that if she attempted to travel outside of Arévalo she would be seized by loyalist soldiers. To clarify her status Isabella thus asked Enrique for a "guarantee" of her freedom.

The king, uncertain about Isabella's loyalties, readily granted his "dear and much loved sister" a safeguard on November 15. That decree assured the princess that she could "go to any town or place she chose and that there would be no objection to her movement, either from me or any *grandees*" as promised by "my faith and royal word."[2]

Despite Enrique's generosity, Isabella's sympathies remained with her younger brother. She had, after all, grown up with the little prince in Arévalo, and their subsequent years as newcomers to Enrique's court had bound them even closer.

After the rebels captured Segovia, the loyalists agreed to a six-month truce. As one of the conditions the royal treasury and jewels were to be moved to Madrid, where they would be returned to Enrique's safekeeping. In exchange, Queen Juana was ordered to live in Archbishop Fonseca's castle at Alaejos as a guarantee. Heartless as this arrangement sounds, such practices were common in the fifteenth century, the rationale being that if a cherished wife or child were kept in custody, promises about high matters of state would more likely be kept. Isabella had, in fact, been kept by Enrique when he released Alfonso to the rebels for similar reasons. Furthermore, by autumn 1467 relations between the king and queen were severely strained. Around that time a Bohemian visitor to the Castilian court who commented upon Enrique's Moorish dress and meals served upon rugs in the "heathen manner" could also not resist observing that the king and queen no longer slept together—that Enrique, in fact, "will have nothing to do with her."[3] Queen Juana, it was said, was thoroughly disenchanted with Enrique, who, because of his impotence, had encouraged her to take lovers.

Consequently, once the king "pawned" Queen Juana for the royal treasury, she gave up all pretense of fidelity. While living under Archbishop Fonseca's scrutiny, the embittered but still young and pretty queen fell in love with that prelate's nephew, Pedro de Castilla, and became pregnant with his son, Andrés. A year or two later Queen Juana gave birth to another son, allegedly by a second lover.

Meanwhile Pacheco, ever scheming, ever longing for more wealth, proposed a daring bargain. If Enrique would give him the Mastership of Santiago, Pacheco would ensure Segovia's return to the king. Admittedly the request was outrageous, especially coming from the man who had spearheaded a rebellion against Enrique three years earlier for awarding that same Mastership to Cueva. Yet Enrique agreed to the bargain.

Shortly after Pacheco received his new title, the rebels began to forsake Prince Alfonso's cause. Doubtless, Pacheco's assumption of Alfonso's inheritance contributed to those desertions for his appointment revealed the transparency of his loyalty. But once whetted, once fed, Pacheco's appetite for landed wealth was boundless. Before long he was quarreling with Carrillo, this time over the archbishop's efforts to marry Prince Alfonso to one of King Juan's daughters. Pacheco protested bitterly, claiming that any Aragonese match would threaten the rebels' authority. But beneath his impassioned condemnation, the new Master of Santiago had an ulterior motive—protection of his own Aragonese territories. Years before Pacheco had seized lands that belonged to King Juan; now he feared that if one of Juan's children married Alfonso or Isabella, the king would attempt to reclaim his lands.

Members of the rebel faction quickly became disgusted with such intrigues. Some knights were so weary of war that they openly longed for the stability of rule under one king—even one whose reign had proved less than brilliant. Many of them agreed with Enrique's favorite prelate, Bishop Mendoza, who, when learning of Enrique's dethronement at Ávila, condemned it because "without comparison, the destruction divided kingdoms endure is greater than what they suffer from an incapable king."[4]

By early 1468 many *grandees* had thus drifted back to Enrique. Among them were Miguel Lucas de Iranzo, the Constable of Castile; the Master of Alcántara; and Count Álvaro of Stúñiga, who returned the cities of Plasencia and Béjar to the king with the sheepish excuse that "most of the *grandees* wanted peace and agreed to surrender. . . ."[5] By spring the cities of Valladolid and Sevilla also supported Enrique; even the cathedral city of Toledo threatened to defect.

Despite his waning popularity young Alfonso continued to behave like an idealistic king. Repulsed by a wave of anti-Semitism then sweeping over Toledo and by the need to bribe subjects to his loyalty, Alfonso vowed to let the city slip from his grasp rather than have it held through bribery. "Much as I love power, I am not willing to purchase it at such a price," Alfonso declared indignantly.[6]

By late spring the prince's followers had dwindled so alarmingly that weeks often went by before he, Carrillo, and Pacheco learned about the movement of Enrique's troops. Nevertheless, on June 30 Alfonso left Arévalo with Isabella and a small coterie of followers. Their aim was to stop in Ávila to gather new soldiers in order to regain Toledo. They also sought to escape the plague.

By late June 1468 the Black Death, which had continued to rage sporadically on the Iberian peninsula throughout the fifteenth century, suddenly resurfaced in Arévalo. Citizens began to sicken and die. Frightened, Isabella, Alfonso, and their entourage set out rapidly for Ávila before Arévalo closed its gates in quarantine.

By twilight the prince's cortege arrived in the tiny town of Cardeñosa, about six or seven miles from Ávila. By royal tradition the prince and princess were housed in the community's most splendid home and fed its finest foods by the town's most prominent citizens. That night Alfonso was served one of his favorite dishes—a freshly caught trout.

The next day his attendants could not rouse him from his sleep. Isabella, closely trailed by Carrillo, Pacheco, and the Bishop of Coria, rushed to Alfonso's side. Although her brother seemed to have no fever, he lay in deep coma from which he could not be roused. A doctor was summoned to bleed the unconscious prince, but "there was no blood that flowed" from his veins and his "tongue was black."[7] Oddly enough, the critically ill youth did not display the conventional symptoms of the Black Death that covered its victims with pus-filled buboes and resulted in grotesque neurological and psychological symptoms. Still, it was clear that Alfonso was mortally ill.

News of Alfonso's critical condition quickly spread through the Castilian kingdom. From distant provinces concerned citizens offered public prayers for the prince's return to health. But there was no remedy, and on July 5, 1468, Prince Alfonso died. At the same hour and day, noted the chronicler Valera, many sick people died in Ávila and Segovia as well, "many of them children of whom it was said had gone to their glory and gave up their spirits to God in the company of King Alfonso."[8]

That night Alfonso's body was carried back to Arévalo where it was prepared for burial in the Monasterio de San Francisco. Isabella, tear-streaked and grieving, was not allowed to accompany her brother's corpse. Her elders had decided she should stay in the Monasterio de Santa Ana in Ávila for protection against the king.

The rebels were stunned. With the prince's death, their cause crumbled. As usual, the sudden demise of an important person provoked immediate suspicions of foul play. Had the trout Alfonso eaten been poisoned? If so, would not his official "taster" have been similarly affected? Had another lethal disease, not the plague, killed Alfonso? Or if it was the plague, as chroniclers Castillo and Pulgar insisted, why didn't Alfonso have the buboes that so obviously marked a stricken individual for the grave? Was that not circumstantial evidence that the prince had been poisoned?

Despite such theories, Isabella wrote letters unequivocally stating that "the king her brother died at three o'clock of the pestilence."[9] Alfonso had been, after all, living in Arévalo where there was a documented outbreak of the plague. Likely the prince—and the dozens of other youngsters who died on that same July 5—perished from that disease. The more lethal pneumonic variant of the plague strikes the respiratory system and renders its victims unconscious without disfiguring their skin; perhaps this had killed Alfonso.

With Alfonso's death, Isabella's role was transformed. Suddenly she was no longer an *Infanta* but next in line for the Castilian succession. As Alfonso lay dying Isabella had realized her situation and discussed it with Pacheco and Carrillo. On July 4, Isabella sent a letter to the distant town of Murcia near Castile's southeastern coast announcing that her brother "the lord king Alfonso" was gravely ill and that the doctors did not expect him to survive.[10] In that event, Isabella reminded them, "the succession of the reign and the dominions of Castile and León belonged to me as the legitimate heir and successor."[11] The letter was jointly signed by the princess, Carrillo, and Pacheco. Its message was unequivocal: Should Alfonso perish, Isabella intended to assume his duties and responsibilities as the legitimate heir of Castile and León.

On July 8 Isabella sent still another letter to the Murcia town fathers announcing her brother's death and reiterating the importance of guarding the city in her name as Alfonso's heir.

After reading the princess's second letter, Murcia's leaders assured her courier they would respond promptly. They never did. Other towns, once loyal to Alfonso's name, reacted with similar ambivalence.

Isabella had inherited Prince Alfonso's estate and with it his shadowy claim as heir to the throne of Castile and León. But by mid-July 1468, whatever political support Alfonso once commanded was already slipping away. All that remained were the strident voices of a few *grandees* and a seventeen-year-old girl, uninvited and ill prepared to be queen.

PART TWO

Heiress Apparent
1468–1474

CHAPTER NINE

Toros de Guisando

lfonso's death split the rebels into two groups, one militant, the other cautious. The first, a vocal minority led by Carrillo, immediately urged Isabella to be crowned Queen of Castile and León. But Pacheco's faction hesitated, partly because they were weary of war, partly because they lived "in great fear, dreading the indignation of the king, whom they had basely insulted with letters and words during the division."[1] Ironically, Alfonso's death also threw the king into a "chasm of melancholy" wrought from fears that it would ignite another round of civil war. To assess his popularity, Enrique quickly dispatched letters to the Castilian cities and towns asking for a pledge of support. Nearly all of them responded positively for the citizens were tired of war and had little faith in Isabella.

Putting a woman on the throne—even a rebel throne—was a bold but not totally unprecedented step in fifteenth-century Castile. Unlike Aragón, Castile did not follow the Salic law demanding male succession to the throne. Three royal daughters had already worn the Castilian crown: Doña Sancha in the eleventh century, Urraca in the twelfth, and Berenguela in the thirteenth, but all three were widows of Castilian kings and two had ruled as regents for male heirs. There was thus no real model for an unmarried female monarch to rule Castile, especially a seventeen-year-old princess who had never expected to reign nor been educated to the throne.

Moreover, by the summer of 1468 Isabella was a relatively obscure figure. Whatever attention she once commanded as King Juan's daughter had long since faded, and her three-year stay in Segovia had further dimmed that memory.

A week or so after Alfonso's death, Carrillo and his faction appeared at the iron gate of Ávila's Monasterio de Santa Ana. The abbess, startled by the fine dress of her visitors, immediately summoned Isabella from the central room above the cloisters where the princess spent most of her days. Isabella appeared at the entranceway in a long white woolen gown (then the prescribed color for mourning in the Castilian court) and greeted Carrillo from inside the cloister grille. The archbishop posed a solemn question: Would Isabella be willing to assume the rebel throne as Castile's new queen?

The tranquility of the convent and the opportunity it provided Isabella for personal reflection may have helped her prepare an answer. The princess replied that "while her brother Enrique lived, no other person had a right to the Crown: that the country had been divided long enough under the rule of two contending monarchs; and that the death of Alfonso might perhaps be interpreted as an indication from Heaven of its disapproval of their cause."[2]

Carrillo recoiled as if he had been struck. This was a new Isabella. Had the princess temporarily gone mad with grief? How else to explain a young woman whose lofty interpretation of moral law and religious justice deprecated the flesh-and-blood struggle Carrillo and his faction had waged against Enrique for the past four years.

But Isabella was unshakable. Nothing the archbishop said, including his plea for her to accept the crown in honor of Alfonso's beliefs, could move her. Even when, some days later, messengers arrived from Sevilla and other Andalusian cities expressing their support, the princess refused to change her mind. Isabella emphatically reiterated that to accept such an offer was to "bring the hardships of war between Enrique and me. . . . thus I am content with the title of Princess."[3] Her real aim was to inherit the throne legally from Enrique upon his death.

Isabella's reply was not merely rhetoric; for she had long been disturbed by the "destruction and tyranny that continued to increase in the kingdom."[4]

Moreover, Isabella believed that Alfonso's sudden death was divine judgment upon his attempted possession of the Castilian crown. It was not the first time Isabella had witnessed an offender's sudden death: Her prospective bridegroom Pedro Girón had also perished very quickly some fifteen months earlier. In Isabella's literal interpretation of the Holy Scriptures, such events signaled the presence of a divine moral force that demanded man's compliance to ethical behavior on pain of ruination or death.

The princess also felt guilty about Enrique. Although their relationship had always been tentative, Isabella nevertheless felt loyal to her older brother. Thus she balked at challenging his claim to the throne. Moreover, their father had clearly designated Enrique as his heir, and Isabella was not inclined to challenge his will.

A more formidable challenge to Enrique's throne came from an unexpected quarter. Immediately after Alfonso's death the rebels had notified their old ally King Juan of Aragón, who had responded by dispatching his envoy Peralta to Castile. This time Peralta brought an urgent message from Juan: If Isabella would marry Juan's sixteen-year-old son Ferdinand, Juan would support the rebel cause with Aragonese funds and forces.

Carrillo embraced the idea enthusiastically, but Pacheco made an impassioned speech to the rebels against the match. In his tinny, wavering voice the new master of Santiago argued that King Juan was a dangerously ambitious ally whose sole motive for allowing his son to marry Isabella was the acquisition of Castilian lands. Before long Pacheco had frightened the rebels with the prospect of losing their own lands to King Juan. Isabella, he observed, was unwilling to seize the crown. Most of the Castilian cities and the kingdom's powerful *grandees* had already defected to Enrique's cause. What harm then to reconcile with the king, provided that they received immunity from punishment for their rebellion?

The resultant peace talks were held at the northern Castilian town of Castronuño from August 17 to 22, 1468. In those five days Enrique agreed to name Isabella his legitimate successor to the Castilian throne in lieu of Princess Juana. In return, Isabella and the rebels agreed to relinquish all claims until Enrique's death.

But for Enrique it was *muy molesta cosa,* a tortured decision. Three days after that meeting, in fact, he solemnly promised a hysterical Queen Juana that his "very dear and beloved sister" Isabella "shall not be sworn heiress of these realms" and that "nothing will be done or accomplished that may be in any way detrimental for you or for the princess, my dear and beloved daughter."[5] He made the promise to placate Queen Juana so that she would join him in Madrid.

However, by now the queen was pregnant by her lover Castilla and thus refused to present herself before Enrique. Weeks earlier, or so Palencia reports, when Queen Juana still resided in Archbishop Fonseca's castle at Alaejos, she begged her dressmakers to invent a costume that would hide her bulging shape. Thus was Queen Juana credited with the invention of the hoop skirt—a style that, ironically, Isabella would later wear to advantage on important state events in her own reign.

The widespread realization that Queen Juana was an adulteress had appreciably weakened Enrique's bargaining position. According to one observer, the Castilians regarded Princess Juana so ambivalently that Enrique feared she would not be recognized as queen after his death. Another, perhaps more likely explanation for Enrique's naming Isabella his heir was that it was the most expedient way to achieve peace in the turbulent months immediately following Prince Alfonso's death. As subsequent events suggested, Enrique probably intended either to retract his oath to make Isabella heir to the throne once peace was fully established in Castile or to marry her to a foreign monarch who would remove her permanently from Castile.

Carrillo suspected as much. For days the archbishop had vehemently disapproved of the agreement reached at Castronuño and attempted to change Isabella's mind. By the end of August 1468 Carrillo consequently traveled to Cebreros, a small town near Ávila where the princess and the rebel faction then resided.

A few days earlier Pacheco had escorted Isabella from the convent to Castronuño. During that journey the courtier had applauded her decision to accept Enrique's offer to name her heir to the throne. Pacheco even insinuated that she would rule Castile during her brother's lifetime because Enrique was satisfied with the "mere title of King and intended to spend his life in the parks and forests among the animals," while Isabella, "married to some powerful prince, would be able to participate in the reform of the customs and laws" of Castile.[6]

Having assessed the princess's trusting personality, Pacheco then advised her to disregard advice from the archbishop, "who was stubborn by nature and recognized by everyone as only being interested in increasing his domain." Should she fail to do so, Pacheco warned Isabella "she should be prepared to participate in the universal ruin of Spain."[7]

When Carrillo met with Isabella at Cebreros, he attempted to dissuade her from accepting the peace treaty. Specifically, he reminded the princess that the treaty had been arranged by her "wicked brother and his Counts who were against God's law" and by Pacheco, who, since Alfonso's death, was "inclined toward Enrique" and who even earlier had proven untrustworthy.[8]

Carrillo also reminded the princess that the king had "torn her from her mother's lap when she was very young," that he "wanted to keep her in the company of the Queen so that being corrupted by her habits she [Isabella] would be unworthy of the throne." Finally, the archbishop warned Isabella not to underestimate her popularity among the Castilian citizenry "who had their minds set on her for the throne since Alfonso's death [for] they hated Don Enrique . . . and were . . . guided toward her with feelings of affection. . . ."[9]

On at least one point the archbishop's criticisms seemed justified. After escorting Isabella to Cebreros, Pacheco abruptly left the rebel camp and journeyed twelve miles to the king's temporary residence at the villa of Cadalso. Although Pacheco had told Isabella that he needed to complete details of the treaty, he was actually reconciling with Enrique.

Even so, Isabella was impervious to the archbishop's arguments, and the incensed Carrillo retreated to Ávila. Before Alfonso's death, the princess had been a respectful and sensitive young woman, willing to consider every aspect of a problem prior to making a decision. Now, within six weeks, she had twice refuted Carrillo. The archbishop believed Isabella was developing a stubbornness that was impeding her otherwise considerable intelligence.

Actually, beneath Isabella's seemingly inflexible stance, she was so anxious that she felt compelled to rationalize her decision in a public forum. Just before leaving Cebreros to sign the treaty with Enrique, she wrote to Carrillo explaining her refusal to take the crown because of the inevitable "hardships of war for me and my brother the Lord Don Enrique"[10] that act would create.

Even so, Carrillo continued to fret, for he was convinced Enrique would severely punish him for his rebellion. To placate the archbishop, Isabella wrote a second letter promising him immunity from Enrique's wrath. She even persuaded the papal envoy Veneris, who had been present at the conference at Castronuño, to write his own letter to Carrillo assuring him of immunity from Enrique's ire.

Ultimately, those letters convinced the archbishop to reconcile with Isabella. But the first cracks had appeared in the wall of trust that once encircled the two. In the summer of 1468 Isabella thus made her first independent political decision; in the ensuing years she would become increasingly determined to act on her own convictions. Still, the emotional price would be steep: the gradual erosion of the only father-daughter relationship Isabella had ever known.

On September 19, 1468, a few miles from the walled city of Ávila, just beyond a pine forest on a windswept plain named Toros de Guisando, Castile's rival factions met. The dramatic event that was about to occur was intensified by its symbolic location—an open field near a mysterious cluster of four prehistoric stone bull statues, the *toros,* or bulls of Guisando. There, at some unrecorded moment in the distant past, early inhabitants of the Iberian peninsula had once enacted primitive rituals. There too, the Romans had etched a record of one of Julius Caesar's conquests. Now, centuries later, on that clear September morning, still other ceremonies were to be performed with the same timeless hope: that they would produce a better life for the peninsula's inhabitants.

With a fanfare of trumpets and horns Enrique arrived at Toros de Guisando flanked by his closest associates, the newly reconciled Pacheco; Bishops Mendoza and Fonseca; the Archbishop of Sevilla; Andrés Cabrera, his *mayordomo;* and the Counts of Plasencia, Benavente, Miranda, and Osorno. These were quickly followed by the papal nuncio Veneris; Pedro de Padilla, the *adelantado,* or royal governor of Castile; and 1,300 armed horsemen on caparisoned horses.

Isabella's entourage was considerably more modest. The princess appeared on a richly harnessed mule whose reins were held by Carrillo. She was flanked on either side by the Bishops of Coria and Burgos behind whom rode 200 armed soldiers.

Isabella and Enrique had not seen each other in a year, and the first moment of encounter was tense. But as Isabella approached the king and bent to kiss his hand, Enrique waved away her gesture with an affectionate disregard for ceremony. Carrillo provided the only dissonant note. As he led Isabella's mule toward Enrique the archbishop refused to kiss the king's hand, despite the princess's pleas that he do so. He would, Carrillo replied, do so only after Enrique swore Isabella his heir.

The terms agreed upon at Castronuño in August and later signed into a treaty at Toros de Guisando demanded compromises on both sides. Although the original pact has been lost, three points sworn that day remain indisputable. The first was Isabella's promise to respect the monarchy and Enrique as her king, lord, and sovereign. The second was Enrique's promise to cancel his pledge for Princess Juana to inherit the throne and instead award the succession to Isabella, who henceforth would be known as "princess, legitimate heir and successor to the kingdoms of Castile and León." Third, Isabella was to receive properties and income commensurate with her new station—the principality of Asturias and seven towns in Castile's central tableland—Ávila, Huete, Ubeda, Alcaraz, Molina, Medina del Campo, and Escalona. She was also awarded Madrid, although that city was to be held by Enrique for another year to assure her compliance.

In addition, Enrique could initiate marriage proposals for Isabella. He could not, however, force her to marry against her will. Isabella and her three appointed guardians, Fonseca, Pacheco, and Álvaro de Stúñiga, could veto Enrique's suggestions. Nor, by the same token, was Isabella to marry without the king's approval.

Furthermore, Enrique was "informed"[11] that his marriage to Queen Juana was illegitimate and thus that he lacked a legal successor. According to Pulgar, Enrique promised to obtain a divorce from Queen Juana and send the disgraced queen and her daughter back to Portugal within a year.

Nevertheless, the closest Enrique ever came to admitting any irregularities in his marriage was a September 24, 1468, letter to the towns explaining that he had named Isabella his heir because "I married and procreated in such a manner in these kingdoms that I do not have legitimate successor to my lineage."[12] Enrique's comments may, of course, simply have referred to the missing papal dispensation that would have legitimized his marriage to Queen Juana.

On September 19, before hundreds of witnesses, Enrique read aloud the document that recognized Isabella as his legitimate heir. As Pope Paul's apostolic representative, Veneris then nullified any previous oaths Enrique made regarding the succession. Although the legate did not specifically name Princess Juana, the child's old claim was thus invalid.

After Isabella and the rebels pledged to recognize Enrique as their sovereign king, the monarch swore her as the Princess of Asturias and Castile's legitimate heir. Representatives of the kingdom's three estates—the clergy, the nobility, and the commoners—kissed the princess's hand in fealty and then swore their liege three times. At the end Veneris stepped forward and invoked an apostolic blessing upon the participants. Trumpets blared, the onlookers cheered, and Carrillo bent at last to kiss Enrique's hand. The king, either out of *noblesse oblige* or generosity, cheerfully excused the archbishop from doing so.

That same day Carrillo, escorted by the Bishops of Coria and Burgos, returned to the rebel camp at Castronuño in despair "for he could no longer control the Princess."[13] The next day he retreated to his book-filled estate at Yepes, a defeated man. In a sense he was: He had lost his innocent Isabella to the persuasions of two other men—the honey-tongued courtier Pacheco and an impulsive, fumbling king. Separately, each one posed a worrisome threat to the idealistic princess; together, Carrillo shuddered at the variety of ways in which they would attempt to bend Isabella's spirit.

Meanwhile, the newly reconciled Isabella and Enrique "no little excited and trad[ing] congratulations" traveled together to the king's camp at Cadalso to celebrate the end of the Castilian civil war.[14]

There, on Saturday, September 24, Enrique issued orders to have Isabella sworn heir by other Castilian officials who had not attended the ceremonies at Toros de Guisando. To ensure Isabella's kingdomwide acceptance as heir to the Castilian throne, Enrique promised to summon the *Cortes* to his court to swear their allegiance to the princess. With that pledge, whatever lingering doubts Isabella may have had about her future dissolved. In that moment of good faith, Isabella's destiny as the future Queen of Castile seemed sealed by all laws known to man and God.

CHAPTER TEN

Rapprochements and Regrets

In the first flush of her triumph at Toros de Guisando, Isabella had little reason to doubt Enrique's sincerity. The king, euphoric with the new peace, held talks with former rebels, collected *merindads,* or royal incomes, from previously unfriendly cities, and issued letters ordering the immediate release of the town of Medina del Campo.

The only disturbing note was Enrique's reinstatement of Pacheco as his *vasallo del rey,* or favorite counselor. From the moment Pacheco arrived at court he became the king's constant companion, a fitful shadow who hovered near Enrique as he moved from hunting lodge to throne room, always gesturing, always murmuring in his tremulous, persuasive voice to the credulous, adoring king.

Gradually Isabella began to withdraw from her old ally. Carrillo's recent warning and her own observations made her suspicious of his sincerity. Privately, she may have tried to assess Pacheco fairly, to equate his reconciliation with Enrique with her own, but ultimately she was repelled by his ruthless ambitions and his need to control those around her.

Nowhere was that more obvious than in Pacheco's suggestion that the court move south of Madrid across the Tagus River to Ocaña, the head city of the Mastership of Santiago. After Toros de Guisando, Enrique had promised to summon the *Cortes* to Ocaña so that Isabella could be sworn heir. For that reason the princess had not dared to object.

Pacheco's move to Ocaña was motivated at least in part by his desire to prevent Isabella's marriage to Ferdinand of Aragón. Although the peace had blunted the importance of that marriage, Pacheco knew that an avaricious and beleaguered ruler like King Juan of Aragón was not likely to abandon that proposal. Moreover, Pacheco's erstwhile ally and new foe, the Archbishop Carrillo, remained eager for the match. Nevertheless, Pacheco determined to prevent it and instead advance a match between Ferdinand and his own daughter, Beatriz.

But to block Carrillo's efforts meant Pacheco had to monitor Isabella's behavior, preferably from a town of his own, like Ocaña, where he could surround the princess with spies. Simultaneously, he planned to find Isabella a husband before an Aragonese marriage could take place.

Paradoxically, the young princess was now anticipating a new freedom, for as the newly declared Princess of Asturias and heir to the Castilian throne she was entitled to establish a small court of her own. Her only obstacle was an independent income, but in early October 1468 Isabella had every reason to believe she would soon receive *merindads* from the seven towns her brother had promised her.

In the interim, Isabella lived in the Ocaña mansion of young Gutierre de Cárdenas, nephew of her childhood administrator, Gonzalo Chacón, and *comendador* of León, or head knight of the largest province of the Order of Santiago. Like his uncle, Cárdenas was faithful to the rebel cause and remained so after Prince Alfonso's death. Officially, both men had reconciled with Enrique at Toros de Guisando. But their loyalty was largely ceremonial; beneath their smiling scrapes and bows to the king, Cárdenas and Chacón worried that Enrique would not keep his promises to the young Isabella.

Similar fears convinced the Archbishop Carrillo to settle in his fortress-palace at Yepes, seven miles south of Ocaña. He was so disturbed by the princess's move to a town owned by Pacheco that he had established secret communications with Chacón and Cárdenas through messengers. To ensure Isabella's safety, Carrillo doled out bribes to servants in the Cárdenas mansion. At Yepes he also ordered his soldiers on guard and solicited reinforcements from another old ally, Rodrigo Manrique, the Count of Paredes.

Ostensibly Castile was at peace, but underneath the old battle lines were drawn. Should events sour in Enrique's court, should the impulsive king change his mind about Isabella's status as heir, the archbishop was poised to rescue the princess at a moment's notice.

At least one other old acquaintance was scheming to displace Isabella from the throne, her old "guardian," Queen Juana. Two months earlier, when the queen learned about the events at Castronuño that threatened to disinherit her daughter, she made a nocturnal escape from Archbishop Fonseca's rural castle at Alaejos. To avoid Fonseca, the queen, then supposedly in her last trimester of pregnancy, was lowered by her servants by a rope-and-basket device. Even though the ropes broke before they reached the bottom, despite a few bumps and scratches, the queen and her unborn child were unharmed. Eventually the queen appeared at the Mendoza estate at Buitrago with a small entourage.

There Juana threw herself at the feet of Iñigo López de Mendoza, the first Count of Tendilla. Three years earlier Enrique had appointed him Princess Juana's guardian to guarantee his promise to favor the Mendozas at court. Now, when the queen reported that her daughter had been disinherited, the count became enraged.

Immediately he circulated a letter to the most powerful barons in Castile condemning the agreement as ludicrous, "as a great and enormous hurt, affront and injustice . . . null and no value . . ." and sternly reminded them that Princess Juana was the legitimate daughter of the said lord king, born of legitimate matrimony."[1] On October 24, 1468, after the treaty of Toros de Guisando was signed, the count and his brother, Pedro González de Mendoza, now the Bishop of Sigüenza, issued their own formal protest to Pope Paul II.

The Mendozas also took their case to the Castilian citizenry, nailing placards to the church doors at Colmenar near the court residence and at other villages decrying the treaty of Toros de Guisando as a political coup that "had been instigated by the *grandees* who oppressed the King."[2] A single placard was also posted on the door of the Cárdenas mansion. Isabella's reaction has not been recorded. But Enrique sank into a depression in which he "not only lost his love for the Princess [Isabella] but hated everything that happened."[3] In his black mood the helpless king delegated the crisis to Pacheco. Then he fled to the woods of El Pardo.

Pacheco used the opportunity to advance his plan to dispose of Isabella by marrying her to a foreign prince. By early November he was meeting with the Mendozas in the villa of Villarejo. For years Pacheco and the Mendozas had been rivals who jockeyed for Enrique's favor; for years they had slandered each other's reputation at court and even engaged in bitter property disputes.

Yet the Mendozas were no more eager to lose the king's favor than Pacheco had been, and after days of heated discussion, the two parties came to terms. Ultimately they agreed that Isabella was to marry Afonso V, the widowed Portuguese king who in 1464 had asked for her hand at Gibraltar. And when La Beltraneja came of age, she was to marry Afonso's son João. Should Isabella produce a male heir, he would inherit the Castilian crown. Should she, however, fail and La Beltraneja deliver a male, that child would become the next king of Castile.

By this compromise, Castile's dynastic line was thus hinged on biological chance. For Pacheco, it was a brilliant achievement, for in one stroke he had neatly undercut Isabella's prospective marriage to Ferdinand and disposed of her in a Portuguese match. In another, he had reconciled the Mendozas to the king and provided Princess Juana with a chance to compete dynastically for the crown.

Yet the compromise was never enacted. Soon after Pacheco presented it at court, Enrique asked Queen Juana to travel to Portugal to discuss the compromise with her brother, Afonso V. But the queen refused. She was no longer interested in pleasing Enrique, a man who, in her eyes at least, was cowardly to the core, who, instead of being her protector, had forced her to be confined for a year in Archbishop Fonseca's remote castle.

Now, having escaped and having, as some chroniclers attest, given birth to her lover's child, the queen resolved to thwart Enrique at every step.

Whatever Queen Juana's real reasons were—her rage over her daughter's disinheritance, her adulterous pregnancy, her vow to impede the treaty of Toros de Guisando, revenge against Pacheco, or some combination of them all—her refusal alienated everyone, her husband Enrique, Pacheco, and the Mendozas. After that the Mendozas lost all interest in championing the Queen. Although the clan continued to guard La Beltraneja, they promptly dropped their protest over the treaty to Pope Paul II.

Even before Enrique publicly expressed regrets about Toros de Guisando, Isabella sensed his feelings. In October 1468 when her assistant, Louis Velasco, attempted to take possession of the towns promised the princess in the treaty, he was rudely rebuffed. Although Velasco showed official letters to the gatekeepers at Molina's twelfth-century walls, they denied him entrance to the town. At the castle of Fuentelsas another official snickered at Velasco's parchment document and claimed that Enrique had sent him letters revoking that permission. Although Isabella finally did receive a few towns—the rustic *pueblos* of the Asturias and the Andalusian town of Baeza—those gifts were immediately offset by perplexing refusals from the towns of Pena de Mesa and Villel. At Zafra, a gatekeeper grumbled that since he and his guards had not been paid for their service in three years, he would surrender the town to Velasco only if he were given back pay. When, on November 15, Enrique released the town of Medina del Campo to Isabella, mysterious delays made it impossible for her to take control for over a year.

The stalemate left Isabella nearly helpless. Without the *merindads* from the towns, the princess could not establish her own household, hire servants, or conduct her personal affairs freely. Like her dead brother Alfonso, Isabella had quietly became "the ghost of a sovereign," a sworn heir of Castile but one whose title had little practical weight.

Her options were to remain financially dependent on Enrique, to rely on the generosity of her former allies such as Carrillo, Chacón, and Cárdenas, or to engage in a deliberately rebellious act that would violate the terms of the treaty of Toros de Guisando. But Isabella was too prudent to do anything so impulsive. In the two months since the treaty, the still-trusting princess had been disappointed but not demoralized. And disappointment was not cause enough to jeopardize her status as the legally sworn heir to the crown of Castile.

Like Queen Juana, Isabella had rejected the Mendoza compromise by the winter of 1468–1469. She would not marry Afonso V of Portugal under any circumstances, even if Enrique commanded her to do so. Moreover, by the terms of Toros de Guisando, he could not force her to marry against her will.

Enrique was incensed. He was not accustomed to having his subjects—least of all the younger sister he had just sworn his legitimate heir—chastise him for exercising his authority. In retaliation, he sent Pope Paul II secret letters "in his own hand in which he wrote with great insistence not to confirm the succession of the kingdoms to his sister, but only to his daughter Doña Juana."[4]

Pacheco took even firmer measures. He immediately wrote Afonso V, advising him of Enrique's interest in the marriage and urging him to send ambassadors to Castile as soon as possible.

In the ensuing weeks relations between the king and Isabella remained superficially cordial, but underneath the brother and sister seethed. Enrique, filled with regrets about the treaty of Toros de Guisando, peevishly regarded Isabella's refusal to marry Afonso as a threat to his sovereign authority. Isabella herself felt deliberately deceived. She had compromised with Enrique in good faith by delaying her claim to the Castilian throne until after his death. Moreover, she had urged the rebels to surrender and reconcile with the king. Despite warnings to the contrary from Carrillo, she had even agreed to live with the court in Ocaña. But Enrique had reneged on his promises. She had received only one of the major towns he promised her, and now he and Pacheco were attempting to coerce her into a marriage with Afonso V.

Carrillo's predictions, which the headstrong Isabella had denied in September 1468, had been fulfilled. In that bitter hour of disillusionment, the princess repented her proud words and once again turned to her former mentor, the Archbishop Carrillo.

Carrillo was probably relieved but not surprised by Isabella's change of heart. The vows at Toros de Guisando had meant little to the wary archbishop: The Mendoza compromise, combined with Isabella's difficulties obtaining the promised towns, merely confirmed his opinion that Enrique was untrustworthy. The only way to protect the princess's inheritance of the Castilian crown, he believed, was to marry her promptly to Ferdinand of Aragón.

Similar thoughts had occurred to King Juan. Like the archbishop, the shrewd Aragonese king knew Enrique would disapprove of the match because of his old bitterness over Catalonia. Moreover, now that Isabella had been sworn the Castilian heir, Enrique would be even more reluctant to wed her to Ferdinand, for if he attempted to rescind Isabella's title as heir, Aragón would defend the princess's claim with men and arms.

But Juan II of Aragón was a stubborn man, one who had spent most of his life in dogged battle and triumphed over seemingly impossible odds. At seventy-two he still burned with the fiery appetite of a younger man, still lusted for his own ascendancy in Aragón and a sizable inheritance for his son Ferdinand. In 1468 domestic troubles circled Juan like hungry hawks. After years of suffering, his beloved second wife and helpmate Juana Enríquez had finally died of cancer; the "spider king," Louis XI, perched beyond the Pyrenees holding Cerdagne and Roussillon in his hand, was waiting for the right moment to wrap the rest of Catalonia in his silken threads; in addition, cataracts had caused King Juan to become blind in one eye and nearly so in the other.

Nevertheless, with Prince Alfonso's death in July 1468, the prospect of marrying his son Ferdinand to the heiress of the Castilian throne brightened the future. To make his son a more eligible candidate, in June 1468 the Aragonese king had granted Ferdinand the title of King of Sicily. That distant, fertile island duchy, the stone beyond the "toe" of Italy's boot, gave Ferdinand international stature and a certain dignity. But for all its glamour, for all the wheat that made Sicily the coveted "breadbasket" of Western Europe in the late Middle Ages, the duchy was still a relatively primitive country, plagued by urban rivalries, foreign merchants, and economic instabilities. And the Aragonese kingdom that Ferdinand would inherit upon his father's death was far smaller than that of Castile. Nevertheless, if Juan could realize his dream of uniting Castile and Aragón through Ferdinand's marriage to Isabella, the resultant new Spanish kingdom would pose a formidable challenge to the Catalans and Louis XI of France.

On October 12, 1468, just two weeks after the treaty of Toros de Guisando, without benefit of medication or anesthesia, King Juan submitted to a cataract operation. A Jewish physician from Lerida had been summoned to perform the procedure. Using the most sophisticated medical techniques of the era, the doctor depressed King Juan's eye lens with a needle and removed it. Although painful, the operation was a success, and two weeks later the procedure was repeated in the other eye. Even with his newly regained vision, one image glittered beyond the rest: the prospective marriage of his young son Ferdinand to Isabella.

On November 1, King Juan dispatched his ambassador Pierres de Peralta to Castile again, this time with a bold if admittedly unlikely mission: to ask Enrique for Isabella's hand in marriage to Ferdinand, Prince of Aragón and King of Sicily.

CHAPTER ELEVEN

Flores de Aragón

A s the days grew shorter in November 1468, secret messengers rode horseback circuits between Yepes, Ocaña, and the Aragonese city of Zaragoza. The couriers carried letters that were coded or worded cryptically, often delivered under the cover of night. Within them were instructions from five men who plotted to marry Isabella to Ferdinand—Carrillo, Cárdenas, Chacón, Peralta, and King Juan— seasoned schemers all, wary of Enrique's disapproval but nonetheless determined to ensure that the young couple would be wed.

When Peralta arrived in Castile in November, Enrique and Pacheco greeted him coldly. The Aragonese ambassador seemed undeterred for he knew that Enrique would never accept Ferdinand's marriage to Isabella. His visit was really a pretext for secret talks with Carrillo. Consequently, Peralta led a double life, posing by day as a hopeful ambassador in Enrique's court, traveling secretly at night to the archbishop's castle at Yepes.

But Isabella was more problematic. Although the princess was living in the Cárdenas mansion, she was surrounded by Pacheco's spies. Yet Peralta was determined to visit her, for he was convinced it was the best way—perhaps the only way—he could obtain her consent. One night the indomitable ambassador boarded a small boat and forded the dangerously swift currents of the Tagus River until he reached a predetermined place on shore where Cárdenas and Chacón waited. Stealthily, the two men then led the ambassador to the Cárdenas mansion, through the darkened main courtyard, and upstairs to the princess's chambers where, with candlelight and drawn curtains, Peralta "reported . . . the state of affairs"[1] to the seventeen-year-old Isabella.

By day Isabella behaved as if nothing untoward had occurred. Gradually, like vulnerable women in every era, Isabella was learning to play upon her femininity to camouflage passion for passivity, resentment for docility, outrage for indecision. When she appeared gowned and coiffed with delicate *redecillas,* or net cauls, at Enrique's court Isabella adopted a neutral posture, smiling at the newly arrived Bishop of Lisbon and the other Portuguese ambassadors, but sidestepping all discussions about marriage. So maddeningly neutral, in fact, was the princess that before long the frustrated Portuguese ambassadors began to complain.

Cárdenas, who was not only Isabella's host at Ocaña but her *maestresala,* or representative at court, stepped forward in the princess's defense. Isabella's behavior, he coolly informed the impatient Portuguese, was typical of young Castilian women, who traditionally deferred to their elders. If the princess seemed hesitant it was due to a certain "modesty which usually affects unmarried women and prevents them from discussing or deciding their own marriages."[2]

Cárdenas's gallantry was not motivated purely by altruism. Weeks earlier King Juan had dangled vast riches before Isabella's *maestresala,* a promise of two thousand gold florins, ownership of the town of Maqueda, and authority over the royal seal if he would help effect Ferdinand's marriage to Isabella. The Aragonese king had also bribed Cárdenas's uncle, Chacón. Juan was even prepared to buy the papal nuncio's loyalty. In exchange for Veneris's pledges of support for the Aragonese match, the king promised the prelate eight hundred ounces of gold, the *merindad* of the Aragonese city of Orihuela, and the bishopric of Tortosa. But these promises, the shrewd and still-penniless Juan stipulated, were contingent upon the successful realization of Ferdinand and Isabella's marriage.

Cárdenas's explanation of Isabella's "modesty" was more accurate than any courtier, foreign or domestic, could have guessed. By late 1468 Isabella was still undecided about her course—whether to continue to feign obedience to Enrique or to break with him completely and commit herself openly to Carrillo and Peralta.

But as the skies turned gray with winter rain, it became increasingly obvious that Enrique had no intention of releasing the rest of the promised towns to Isabella. Nor was there talk of Enrique's divorce from Queen Juana or of her exile with La Beltraneja to Portugal. Even so, Isabella did not want to further antagonize Enrique for officially, at least, the treaty of Toros de Guisando was still intact. Moreover, she fervently believed that when the *Cortes* met in early 1469 Enrique would order the *procuradores* to swear her as the Castilian heir.

Nevertheless, Isabella was leaning toward marriage with Ferdinand. Years later the future queen's marriage would be hailed as a romantic symbol of "one soul in two bodies," but in its inception, love was an irrelevant factor. At seventeen Isabella must have felt the normal stirrings of sexuality, but she had never met Ferdinand, nor even glimpsed a miniature portrait of him. Nor had she expected to, for in the fifteenth century royal marriages were arranged almost exclusively for dynastic purposes. It was simply that Ferdinand was the best choice. Unlike the middle-age Afonso V, the Aragonese prince was young and vibrant. Moreover, the Aragonese prince spoke Spanish and shared similar food and customs. The same immortal vows had been pledged by the Castilian and Aragonese kings for over seven hundred years—the *Reconquista,* a constant battle cry for the conquest of Granada and the defeat of the Moors to reunite the Iberian peninsula under Christianity.

Most important, Isabella and Ferdinand were blood relatives, second cousins who shared the same paternal great-grandfather, Juan I of Castile, son of the founder of the Trastámara line. Their marriage would thus reconnect the scattered lines of the dynasty formed five generations earlier. Such a marriage, as Isabella later explained to her subjects,

> will unite the crown of our ancient kingdoms and the wishes of
> King Ferdinand of Aragón, grandfather of the said prince of Sicily
> and brother of the very illustrious king of glorious memory, don
> Enrique, grandfather of your sovereign and mine, who later ex-
> pressed in his will, that there should always be new matrimonial
> concessions with the descendants of the direct line of the said king
> don Ferdinand his brother.[3]

Although it was necessary to obtain a papal dispensation, few individuals understood or even considered the genetic implications for the offspring of marriages between close relatives. Rather, a union between the Castilian princess and the Aragonese prince was considered an advantage, a fulfillment of a common ancestral heritage. Moreover, there were other obvious political advantages to Isabella and Ferdinand's union. Most of the Iberian peninsula would hence be united under one authority, the double crowns of Castile and Aragón. Ferdinand would eventually inherit Aragón and other territories from his father while Isabella would inherit Castile from Enrique.

Historically, the marriage was a brilliant union that destroyed medieval provincialism and gave birth to the modern Spanish state. In the late 1460s neither the princess nor her allies could appreciate those implications, nor the threat that nascent Spanish nationalism would eventually pose to other European nations, most of which were still struggling with warring duchies left over from weak, largely feudal kings. In 1469 Isabella and her advisors saw the marriage as a political expedience, a vehicle by which the princess could "guarantee" her claim to the Castilian throne.

But if romance had a negligible role in Isabella's decision to marry Ferdinand, its potential had great appeal to the Castilian commoners. Shortly after Enrique's court moved to Ocaña, groups of young boys gathered outside the palace gates singing satirical ditties about the advanced age of the Portuguese king and the extreme youth of the princess. To the pragmatic and superstitious commoners, Isabella's proposed marriage to Afonso was an "unlucky" event bound to bring the princess misfortune. Above all, they objected to the age difference between the king and princess, who, being a "tender rosebud," would "become in the flower of youth the stepmother of stepchildren who were older than she."[4]

Moreover, urban citizens saw little, if any, political advantage for Castile in the Portuguese marriage. Afonso V already had heirs from his first marriage and thus Isabella's children would not inherit the Portuguese throne. After Afonso's death, they worried that his heirs might seize Isabella's inheritance and "inhu-manely subject the kingdoms of Castile and León to cruel enemies . . . which would overpower the country's honor and freedom."[5]

Gradually, these anti-Portuguese ditties were adopted by youths who marched through Ocaña waving handmade banners with Aragonese insignias. Before long the songs spread to other towns and cities. When news of marriage proposals from Portugal and England filtered down from the courts to the commoners, adults began to join youngsters in the parades. By late 1468, the demonstrations had become ritualized patterns. Groups of commoners now walked through the streets singing the stanzas while mounted knights with *cañas,* or reed lances, roared back the refrain "Banners of Aragón/Banners of Aragon."[6] After the songs had been repeated five times, a priest read aloud a passage from the Bible.

To Enrique the demonstrations were a defiance of royal authority, ominous sparks from a rebellion he thought had been permanently quelled. At first, he ordered the local authorities to ban the street demonstrations. Finally he sent out his own armed soldiers "to stop those tunes and severely punish those who would dare to repeat them. . . ."[7]

It was an uncharacteristic act for the usually timorous and tolerant king. But the civil war had irreparably shaken Enrique's confidence in himself as a monarch. To steady his grip, to convince himself and his subjects of his authority, Enrique now deemed a show of force necessary.

By early January 1469 Isabella had made her decision: She would marry the Aragonese Prince Ferdinand "and no other" suitor. In anticipation of that event, the Aragonese royal secretaries had already drafted a marriage agreement based on Peralta's discussions with Carrillo. The resultant document, or "capitulations" as they were called, was signed by Ferdinand on January 7, 1469, in the Aragonese town of Cervera. Five days later King Juan ratified the terms and dispatched copies to Carrillo at Yepes.

Isabella spent the month of January in suspense, caught between her commitment to marry Ferdinand and the need to seem obedient to Enrique. Moreover, members of the *Cortes* who had been called to Ocaña months earlier now began to arrive. Despite long advance notice, the *procuradores* from only ten of the seventeen towns represented by the *Cortes* appeared.

The *Cortes*'s importance was largely fiscal. Originally, the parliament was composed exclusively of aristocrats and ecclesiastics who acted as advisors to the king. But the advance of the *Reconquista* and the growing number of settlements on the shrinking Moorish border had forced the Castilian kings to grant the commoners a larger voice in government than in most other Western European countries. As early as 1169 the king invited deputies from some of the towns to appear in the parliamentary sessions. Although it would take another two hundred years before the townsmen, merchants, and burghers of the "third estate," the *estado llano,* would have their votes counted, eventually they outnumbered the aristocracy.

By the fifteenth century, the first two "estates," the nobles and prelates, had almost disappeared from the *Cortes,* largely because only commoners were obliged to pay taxes to the king. At sessions convened at the king's pleasure, two *procuradores* from each town appeared to express their grievances and vote upon requests for taxes. By the time Isabella was born, the *Cortes* had become a powerful governing body that controlled the kingdom's purse strings and reflected popular opinion. Enrique's promise to have Isabella sworn by the *Cortes* as his legitimate heir thus signified the highest approval in the land. Without it, the oaths taken at Toros de Guisando were not fully recognized as law.

The *Cortes* that met in Ocaña in January 1469 did little to consolidate Isabella's position. The *procuradores* from the three provinces that had objected most strenuously to the treaty of Toros de Guisando—Murcia, Andalusia, and Extremadura—simply did not appear. When Enrique learned that only slightly more than half of the *Cortes* members had arrived, he decided to cancel the parliament. But the *procuradores,* who had not met for four years, complained until Enrique finally opened the meeting. Then he delegated the parliament to Pacheco and his assistant, Archbishop Fonseca, and left for the woods of El Pardo.

To prevent the *procuradores* from confirming Isabella as heir, Pacheco and Fonseca buried the deputies in piles of petty paperwork, so much that some left in disgust before the meeting officially closed in April 1469.

To this day, historians debate whether the *Cortes* ever swore Isabella heir to the Castilian throne. According to some reports the remaining *procuradores*—fewer than half the official body of representatives—did so. Some months later Isabella would bitterly remind Enrique that she had been sworn his heir by the *Cortes* in Ocaña "by the commandment of Your Lordship, many other prelates and procuradores of the cities and towns of your kingdom have sworn it . . . that your Lordship knows it well and it is well publicized."[8] Nevertheless, the oath was not recorded in the official papers of the *Cortes.*

Even if her claim to the Castilian throne was never officially verified by the *Cortes,* a strong constituency of aristocrats and commoners did approve Isabella's marriage to Ferdinand soon thereafter. Generations later historians would praise Isabella for her sensitivity to popular opinion, but in reality, she and Carrillo had no other choice but to seek consensus in the winter of 1469. By her decision to marry Ferdinand, Isabella was already defying Enrique. If she could not command support from the old rebel constituency, she would have left herself in a precarious position. Knowing that, knowing how swiftly the pendulum of public opinion could swing from one side to another, either catapulting Isabella to new heights of popularity or plunging her into an abyss of disfavor, Carrillo sought assurances. Thus before the archbishop agreed to sign any papers with King Juan, he insisted on polling the rebel barons of Castile.

Like everything else surrounding Isabella's marriage to Ferdinand, Carrillo's poll was conducted in utmost secrecy. By late January fleets of couriers were dispatched to the far corners of the kingdom, south over the snowy passes of the Alpujarras and the Sierra Nevadas, north beyond the Galician and Cantabrian mountains into the rustic villages of Asturias and beyond the Vizcaya to the Cantabrian coast.

After three suspenseful weeks the rebel constituency returned a consensus: Overwhelmingly they believed Isabella should marry Ferdinand to fortify her claim to the Castilian crown.

Thus reassured, on February 3, 1469, Carrillo and Peralta signed an agreement affirming that the prince and princess were "ready and agreed to certain notes and items" that would formalize their marriage.[9] With those signatures, the betrothal promise became official and the destiny of Isabella of Castile and Ferdinand of Aragón was inextricably intertwined.

CHAPTER TWELVE

Flight from Ocaña

I mmediately after the betrothal agreement was signed, Peralta and the Castilian courtier-poet Gómez Manrique carried the news to King Juan in Aragón. At the same time they brought a sealed parchment document from Isabella to Ferdinand—the first letter the princess ever wrote to her future husband. Fearing that the document would be intercepted by Pacheco's spies, Isabella worded her message enigmatically. "To the lord, my cousin, King of Sicily, cousin my lord: Since the high constable is traveling [to you], it is not necessary for me to write more, except to apologize for such a delayed answer. . . . And you will understand the reason from him because it is not fit to be written. From the hand which will do whatever you command. The Princess."[1]

Clearly, Isabella's letter was an attempt to impress Ferdinand with traditional feminine acquiescence. It was also a coy apology to the prince for Carrillo's delay in responding to the Aragonese "marriage capitulations" sent to Castile a month earlier. At eighteen Isabella may have dreamed of a cooperative and loving marriage with the Aragonese prince, but her Castilian elders were willing to grant Ferdinand few political powers.

In fact, the prince's "rights" as future king-consort of Castile had become the subject of heated debate after Carrillo had received the first draft of King Juan's capitulations at Yepes. Without certain changes, the archbishop warned Peralta before he left for Aragón, the marriage between Isabella and Ferdinand could never take place.

The amended capitulations finalizing the marriage were thus not signed until March 5 by Ferdinand in Cervera and on March 12 by King Juan in Zaragoza. Part of the agreement was typical of royal marriage pacts of the era; Ferdinand pledged to respect the laws of Castile and its subjects as "should be and is expected from a good king toward his subjects."[2] But much of it was clearly humiliating, especially for a prince who would one day rule his own kingdom and, as tradition suggested, would wield similar authority over his wife's inheritance.

But the fiery, iconoclastic Carrillo had little respect for historical conventions. Determined king-maker that he was, the archbishop was intensely covetous of Isabella's rights to the Castilian throne, perhaps even more so than the princess herself, who, he suspected, was vulnerable to romantic dreams of equity between a husband and a wife. Knowing Isabella had the advantage, that Castile was larger and wealthier than Aragón, and that King Juan's Catalonian kingdom was menaced by Louis XI's smartly trained French army, Carrillo and the rebels were willing to grant Ferdinand practically nothing beyond the honor of marrying the princess.

Consequently, the Aragonese prince was to pledge that he would live permanently in Castile and would ask Isabella's permission before leaving the kingdom or taking their children with him. He also was to agree to leave the crown's property intact, to wage no wars through conspiracies, and significantly, to make no attempt to reclaim any Castilian lands once owned by his father King Juan. While Ferdinand and Isabella could jointly publish royal ordinances, the prince would not be allowed to make municipal or civil appointments without Isabella's consent. Nor would he be permitted to make any ecclesiastic appointments. Those important prizes, usually awarded to the "second sons" of the aristocracy, were solely Isabella's jurisdiction.

The capitulations also stated that Ferdinand was to serve as Isabella's military defender. As commander of the army, the prince was thus expected to "wage war against the Moors who are enemies of the Catholic faith as have other Catholic sovereigns in the past."[3] As Isabella's husband, Ferdinand was to honor and obey Enrique as king of Castile "as long as he would respect the peace that had been given between him and his sister."[4] But if "the treaties of Castile were broke"—a reference to a possible new outbreak of civil war—Ferdinand was to provide 4,000 lancers in Isabella's defense.

As a final concession that was to anger his fellow Aragonese, the prince was to award Isabella an *arras,* or marriage gift far more generous than was usually given Aragonese queens for their dowries. It was to include a rich parcel of Aragonese and Sicilian towns and 100,000 gold florins to be paid four months after the marriage took place. Moreover, in recognition of the betrothal, Ferdinand was to send Isabella 20,000 gold florins and a magnificent ruby and pearl necklace once owned by his mother and valued at 40,000 ducats.

On this last point, however, King Juan managed to gain one concession: Aragón would send neither the money nor the jewels until the princess had escaped from Enrique's authority.

Despite the rebels' initial flutter of joy that followed ratification of the marriage contract, Carrillo managed to keep the news hidden from Pacheco and Enrique. Doubtless, the king and his favorite suspected secret communications between Carrillo and the Aragonese king, but they were too preoccupied with an incipient Andalusian rebellion to do more than maintain spies in Ocaña.

At the time of the treaty of Toros de Guisando, many southern Castilian cities still refused to recognize Enrique as king. More recently, the southern provinces of Murcia and Andalusia and the western province of Extremadura had failed to send representatives to the *Cortes*. Some Andalusian towns, had even continued to agitate openly for Isabella's coronation.

By early spring 1469 Enrique had decided to subdue the uncooperative territories himself. He had been urged to the campaign by Pacheco, who, as a former member of the rebel faction, was intimately acquainted with the depth of that resistance. To bring all the cities of Castile directly under royal authority, Pacheco thus urged Enrique to begin his campaign in Córdoba and proceed south to Sevilla.

But to order the royal army south and leave the still tenuously held lands of Old Castile without adequate surveillance would have been foolhardy. Obviously it was essential to leave powerful *grandees* who would ensure peace and safeguard Isabella from the Aragonese in Enrique's absence. The Mendoza clan was well suited to the task: Its members were wealthy, influential, and had recently reaffirmed their old allegiance to Enrique through their leader, Bishop Mendoza. To bind the clan to his side, Enrique now formally forgave them for their criticisms of the treaty of Toros de Guisando. In return, the bishop and his brothers agreed to protect Isabella in Enrique's absence and persuade her to marry Afonso.

But Enrique's last charge to the Mendozas was an acknowledged impossibility. Several courtiers had already vainly attempted to persuade the princess to marry the Portuguese king, among them a brash *grandee* named Pedro de Velasco. That courtier (no relation to Isabella's assistant Louis de Velasco) had tried to coerce the Princess by reminding her that at Toros de Guisando she had promised to wed in accord with Enrique's wishes.

Isabella curtly replied that "my marriage is not supposed to be arranged against my will."[5] Moreover, she coolly reminded Velasco, any decision about her marriage had to be approved by the *Cortes*, as had been decreed in her father's will.

Velasco, surprised by the usually docile princess's impassioned words, lost his temper, threatened to imprison her in the alcázar at Madrid, and spoke with "such excessive liberty" that she burst into tears. Isabella then fell to her knees and "sought help from the Almighty to liberate her from such shame and to reject such a cruel affront."[6] Unable to placate the princess, Velasco stomped out of the chamber, promising to report her impertinence to Enrique.

Isabella's reaction was not simply that of a young woman bullied by an older, powerful man. Secretly, she feared that she was being forced to commit a sin. She had already promised to marry Ferdinand and thus could not, in her own conscience or in the eyes of the church, agree to marry another man—even under threat of imprisonment.

Carrillo rallied immediately to Isabella's side. But instead of appearing with armed men, he dispatched two innocent-looking priests to Ocaña who ordered the city fathers to shut the gates against Velasco's soldiers.

Ultimately, Enrique forbade Velasco to carry out his threat. Although the king wanted a Portuguese match, he was about to launch his Andalusian campaign. This was, he sharply informed Velasco, hardly the time to stir up more angry feelings among the citizens by imprisoning Isabella or forcing her to marry Afonso.

By the winter of 1469, Enrique abandoned the idea of the Portuguese marriage altogether. Disgusted, he summoned Bishop Mendoza and instructed him to dismiss the Portuguese ambassadors who had been waiting for months at the nearby town of Ciempozuelos for an answer. Pacheco, however, immediately sought another suitor for Isabella. Through secret communication with his old ally, Louis XI of France, he now maneuvered for a marriage between Isabella and the king's younger brother Charles, Duke of Berry. Louis embraced the idea immediately. With such a match France and Castile would become allies and hence unite against King Juan of Aragón—"the wolf," as Louis called him.

On the eve of his May 1469 departure for Andalusia, Enrique made one final effort to keep Isabella yoked to his authority by asking her to promise that she would neither leave Ocaña nor make any marriage commitments until his return. To ensure the princess's obedience, he promised that after the campaign he would arrange a marriage that would please her.

Isabella agreed. She had pledged to marry Ferdinand in January; thus she would not be making any *new* commitments. Pacheco, however, remained deeply suspicious. Before departing, he enlisted new spies to watch Isabella, among them several servants in the Cárdenas household. Finally on May 7, 1469, Enrique, Pacheco, and their entourage passed through Ocaña's arched gates and headed south to war.

For weeks Isabella had been preoccupied with the idea of flight. She was tired of living in Ocaña with its spies and informers, tired of the bitter events that had revealed the transparency of Enrique's promises at Toros de Guisando. Now she longed to return to Arévalo, the simple country town of her childhood, and to her mother.

For weeks too, the Archbishop Carrillo had begged the princess to wait, even though he, like Isabella, believed that now would be the perfect opportunity for her escape. But before Isabella was to risk such a journey, Carrillo insisted she first obtain guarantees of King Juan's commitment to the marriage. Specifically, Carrillo was waiting for the arrival of the *arras*, the betrothal money and necklace King Juan had promised in February. Without them, Carrillo argued, Isabella's flight would be reckless: Were she to leave Ocaña during Enrique's absence without his approval and without tangible proof of Ferdinand's commitment to defend her, the King might send soldiers to seize Isabella. Moreover, once received, the promised money and jewels could be used in an emergency to hire soldiers, purchase munitions, and buy new loyalties.

Isabella had listened dutifully to Carrillo. But by the time Enrique departed, she had still not received the gifts. The delay was deliberate. In April 1469 the Aragonese political situation had grown tense when French soldiers again stormed Gerona. King Juan, already pressed for money to hire troops and fearing that Isabella would never escape Enrique's control, refused to send "one single florin" until the princess bolted.[7]

Clearly, it was imperative for Isabella to leave Ocaña as soon as possible. Any pretext would do, even a feeble one, as long as it enabled her to depart. Coincidentally, nearly a year had passed since Prince Alfonso's death. As his devoted sister, Isabella was obliged to return to his burial site at Arévalo's Convent of San Francisco for memorial funeral rites. Few people, including Enrique, could object to that visit, even though Isabella had promised to remain in Ocaña until his return.

Still, symbolically, by fleeing Ocaña, Isabella was not merely leaving a town: She was deliberately shattering a commitment, a pledge of obedience sworn to Enrique some eight months earlier. Even worse, she was rushing into the arms of a man whom Enrique flatly forbid as a marriage partner. Whatever excuses she might offer Enrique, Isabella knew that her *salto,* her flight or leap from Ocaña, would be construed as treason. Nevertheless, it would also be a release, a deliberate thrust simultaneously piercing Enrique's façade and freeing Isabella from the necessity of pretending that she still trusted him.

Isabella left Ocaña in the middle of May. Little is known about the *salto* except that the princess left on horseback at night, accompanied by the Bishop of Burgos and the Count of Cifuentes. As the princess and her entourage spurred their horses northwest toward Arévalo, they learned that one of the king's knights named Álvaro de Bracamonte had seized the town in the name of the Count of Plasencia and that in the ensuing turmoil, Isabella's deranged mother, the queen widow, had been bundled off to Madrigal with her attendants.

Alarmed, Isabella turned toward Madrigal, where she was reunited with her mother. After spending several days resting in the royal palace, the same galleried building where Isabella had been born eighteen years earlier, the princess, the queen widow, and their entourage crossed the Ambles Valley to the cathedral town of Ávila, where Prince Alfonso's memorial funeral rites were now to be held.

CHAPTER THIRTEEN

Surprise Visits

On the morning of June 18, 1469, a solitary *caballero* spurred his horse through groves of olive trees and vineyard-covered hills toward the Aragonese city of Zaragoza. Everything about the stranger suggested his journey was urgent: his dusty boots, his flagging horse, and the fact that he traveled alone. His name was Alonso de Palencia, the forty-six-year-old man of letters who would later chronicle Isabella and Ferdinand's reign and had just been dispatched by Carrillo to collect Isabella's betrothal gifts.

Just before Palencia reached Zaragoza, he heard disheartening news. French soldiers had just taken the Catalonian city of Gerona. That walled "city of a thousand sieges," at the junction of the Ter and Omar rivers and south of the Pyrenees, was strategically important to Catalonia's defense. Its fall bode ill for the security of the kingdom of Aragón. "The news profoundly saddened my soul," wrote Palencia, "for I knew that the disaster would disturb the anguished monarch in such a manner that it would be impossible for him to surrender the [promised] sum [of money] and the necklace."[1]

Nevertheless, Palencia managed to meet with King Juan in the elegant eleventh-century Mudéjar palace that still stands in Zaragoza today. There, beneath Moorish stone traceries and delicately painted wooden ceilings, Palencia described the urgency of Isabella's situation and the consequent importance of the betrothal gifts so vividly that Juan agreed to order their release from Valencia at once.

By August 7 Palencia had returned to Castile with the promised gifts and presented them to Carrillo.

The archbishop, Palencia could not help noting, "was very happy with our arrival and thanked God for overcoming at such low cost such great difficulties."[2]

In August 1469 when the tawny fields of wheat stood tall in the fields of Madrigal, Isabella wrestled with a new problem—the arrival of the French ambassador, Jean Jouffroy, Bishop of Arras. On August 8 his stiff entourage of liveried attendants and richly harnessed horses trotted through Madrigal's high stone gates and appeared at the royal palace where Isabel now lived with her mother.

The princess had not anticipated Jouffroy's visit. In fact, until his arrival she was not even certain that Enrique knew her location. But the French bishop's visit changed everything. As Isabella soon discovered, the tall broad-chested bishop had tracked the princess from Córdoba, where he just met with Enrique, and convinced him, on the basis of the "antique and ancient"[3] friendship between Castile and France, to forsake his treaty with the English. To seal the new French-Castilian pact, both men agreed to betroth Isabella to Louis's brother Charles, Duke of Berry. Thus it was that Enrique had urged the bishop to meet Isabella on his return trip north.

Jouffroy summoned his considerable powers of persuasion to make the princess accept the betrothal. She was, the bishop shrewdly reminded her, the daughter of King Juan II of Castile, who had been a lifelong friend of France. Her father would never have approved her marriage to the widowed Portuguese King Afonso with his grown heirs; nor would he have agreed to a marriage with Ferdinand, son of his old enemy.

Initially Isabella smiled and "paid great honor to the Cardinal [Jouffroy, later a cardinal] and the knights who accompanied him."[4] As a show of respect the princess even had her mother dressed, coiffed, and seated with her in her interview with the bishop. Then Isabella explained that she could make no decisions about Jouffroy's proposal "without first seeking the counsel of the *grandees* and *caballeros* of the realm."[5] When a verdict was returned, she would notify the bishop.

Doubtless Jouffroy was surprised. He had not expected Isabella to respond so coolly or to place the ultimate responsibility for the betrothal on the Castilian *Cortes*. Still, the princess had not refused to marry the Duke of Berry; in fact, the bishop left Madrigal believing Isabella had given her tacit consent to the match. Thus when news of Isabella's marriage to Ferdinand reached the French court in November 1469, Louis XI was astonished. Until that moment he had fully expected Isabella to marry his younger brother.

Isabella's polite response to Jouffroy did nothing to mollify Enrique's suspicions, however. She had, after all, disobeyed him by leaving Ocaña without his permission. He was certain the princess was scheming with Carrillo to obtain a better grip on the Castilian throne.

Events had not gone well in Andalusia. Rather than showing obedience, the citizens had demonstrated their resistance to his authority. And much of their resentment, Enrique could not fail to notice, grew out of their loathing for Pacheco. At Córdoba the city officials had allowed the king to enter the gates, but once he was inside, they protested violently. At Jaén, Enrique's old favorite

Miguel Lucas de Iranzo, Constable of Castile, had welcomed the king warmly but refused to allow Pacheco to enter the town. At Écija, the citizens greeted Enrique begrudgingly, and at the whitewashed town of Antequera the town gates were firmly closed against him. As Enrique's cortege approached Sevilla, the rebellious young Duke of Medina Sidonia menaced the king in the Guadalquivir valley with a private army.

Something had to be done to quell the rebellious Andalusians who still clung to dreams of civil war. Once Enrique's spies confirmed that Isabella had settled in Madrigal, the king decided to punish her for her flagrant disobedience. By mid-August Enrique thus dispatched letters to Madrigal's officials, threatening the town's citizens with "harsh penalties" if they supported Isabella in any marriage to Prince Ferdinand.[6]

But Enrique had misjudged popular sentiment. The Madrigalians sympathized with the princess and showed her the king's letters. Still, no one wanted to anger Enrique. Even Isabella's faithful attendants, Beatriz de Bobadilla and Mencia de la Torre, who had followed her to Madrigal, were hesitant. Perhaps, they suggested, she should reconsider her marriage to Ferdinand.

Isabella had not made her decision lightly. She told her timorous companions that she had no intention of changing her mind and had written Carrillo for help. Nevertheless, fearing that her friends would be punished on her account, she hurried them out of Madrigal to Coca, a few miles north.

Suddenly Isabella was alone, surrounded by the anxious faces of the Madrigalians, some of whom genuinely sympathized, others of whom were almost certainly Pacheco's spies. Four silent days crept by. Help finally came from the south, from Carrillo and from Ferdinand's uncle, Alonso Enríquez, who combined their armies into a five-hundred-man force at the tiny hamlet of Pozaldes near Madrigal. Beneath the archbishop's scarlet cape, he carried even more formidable ammunition than a sheathed sword: two leather pouches containing the *arras* from Aragón. As the prelate advanced toward Madrigal, he dispatched a messenger to Isabella with the necklace and 8,000 golden florins. He retained the other 12,000 florins for future use.

Isabella's situation was thus immediately transformed. Henceforth she would wear the jewels proudly, as a defiant statement to Pacheco's spies that she intended to marry Ferdinand. In later years Queen Isabella wore other gems that dazzled visitors to the Castilian court. Jewels, in fact, would become Isabella's one vanity. In her will she left hundreds of diamonds, rubies, sapphires, and pearls behind that she had collected during her lifetime. But never was Isabella more proud of jewels than those she wore in Madrigal that August day in 1469, for they signaled her imminent freedom from Enrique.

The money was even more useful; Isabella immediately used it to recompense her nervous allies for their support. In her exuberance, Isabella doled out the money generously, almost extravagantly—2,000 florins to Chacón, "many others to Gutierre de Cárdenas"[7] and 1,000 to Clara, one of her cousins.

Some of Pacheco's spies now began to reveal themselves—servants, artisans, even some of her personal attendants. Some even threw themselves at the princess's feet, "begging and praising her for saving their lives and not allowing them to be thrown in prison or suffering some [other] misfortune."[8] Taking pity on those who had confessed, Isabella dispatched them to Coca, where they could escape Enrique's wrath, at least temporarily. But not all the spies had been exposed.

Madrigal was obviously no longer a safe place for Isabella. The next day, surrounded by a cavalcade of piked men, she moved into a convent a few miles beyond her birthplace. Fearing the princess's flight, the Bishop of Burgos, who had secretly spied on Isabella since her *salto* from Ocaña, visited her and urged her return to Madrigal. When Isabella refused, the bishop, ". . . dejected by his inability to retain her," returned to the town alone.[9]

As he left, Carrillo and his forces appeared at the convent and surrounded Isabella again. Then the princess mounted a mule and "with great joy and the sound of many trumpets and drums" the cortege marched toward the village of Fontiveros.[10]

No sooner had Isabella left the convent than Alfonso de Fonseca, the Archbishop of Sevilla, arrived in Madrigal with four hundred horsemen intending to seize the village and capture the princess in the king's name.

At Fontiveros, meanwhile, Isabella and her followers were nearly ensnared in another trap. Originally Carrillo had planned to hide the princess there under the custody of the Duke of Alba, but after a clash with Alba's treacherous guards, Carrillo's party fled south with Isabella toward Ávila.

Death seemed to stalk the princess. As the entourage approached Ávila's majestically turreted walls, anxious messengers waved them off. The pestilence had made its dread appearance and the city streets were already choked with corpses. Carrillo now turned his party to Valladolid, forty miles to the north. Weeks earlier, he had selected that city as a backup in the unlikely event that the other shelters had failed. On July 20, 1469, he had written the town officials asking their permission to bring Isabella to the house of his niece, Doña María, wife of Juan de Vivero. The city fathers had agreed; Valladolid had long been sympathetic to the rebel cause.

Thus, on August 30, 1469, after a dusty ride that lasted for a full night and a day, Isabella and her cortege arrived at the Vivero palace. There "half an hour after the sunset" a crowd of *grandees* and commoners clustered around the weary princess with "solemn cheers of jubilation."[11]

CHAPTER FOURTEEN

A Wedding in Valladolid

W ith her first breath of freedom in Valladolid, Isabella no longer had to feign obedience to Enrique; no longer would she have to simper at his courtiers or struggle with her conscience about her disobedience. Heady with her recent escape, poised to marry Ferdinand, Isabella now confronted the king boldly, defending her deeds as necessary reactions to his tyranny.

Consequently, Isabella wrote Enrique on September 8, 1469, informing him of her intentions. The letter began with the princess's reminder of her former acquiescence to her brother's wishes.

> Very high prince and most powerful King and Lord. It is very well known that after the very illustrious King Don Alfonso brother of your Lord left this life some *grandees,* prelates and *caballeros* . . . asked that I assume the title that belonged to the said King Don Alfonso my brother . . . but because of the great and genuine love I always had for you and dedication to your royal person and [desiring] peace and tranquility . . . I agreed to submit to your wishes . . . in which it was agreed that the true succession of these said your kingdoms would belong to me as your legitimate heir and successor.[1]

Isabella then reminded the king that she had received marriage proposals from Afonso V, the "brother of the King of England," the Duke of Berry, and Ferdinand of Aragón. Enrique's attempts to force her to marry Afonso V were, she observed, reinforced by "certain persons who wanted to coerce me to such an agreement."[2]

Nevertheless, in a secret poll the *grandees* and prelates of Castile had supported her marriage to the Aragonese prince, King of Sicily, in "consideration of the age and unity of our old lineage."[3]

The next part of Isabella's letter was even more confrontational. Within it she accused Enrique of attempting to prevent her marriage to Ferdinand by "employing certain women as my attendants and servants . . . to oppress and endanger my freedom."[4] Moreover, he had sent letters to the officials of Madrigal commanding them "to detain and apprehend me."[5] To defend herself, Isabella was finally forced to call upon Archbishop Carrillo and the Almirante Enríquez.

Now, having arrived in the "noble city of Valladolid," Isabella begged Enrique "for the glory of his crown and the health and well-being of his kingdoms that Your Highness would agree . . . that the above mentioned reasons made it obvious and favorable that he consent to the marriage with the . . . Prince of Aragón, King of Sicily. . . ."[6]

Enrique never wrote back. Instead, he quickly completed his affairs in Andalusia and ordered his troops to march north toward Valladolid. Along the route he commanded the royal army to stop and attack the Extremaduran town of Trujillo. Only after weeks of a frustrating and ultimately unsuccessful siege would the king finally reach central Castile.

Personally as well as politically, Isabella had good reasons for choosing Ferdinand. Yet while she had consented to marry him, as the months passed she became increasingly uneasy about her choice. To defy Enrique was difficult enough, but to do so and reject the French Duke of Berry for a weak or dull-witted suitor who lacked military prowess would have been a tragic mistake. To assure herself of Ferdinand's vitality, Isabella dispatched her chaplain, Alfonso de Coca, to France and Aragón shortly before she left Ocaña. To her relief, Coca returned to Valladolid in September with grave doubts about Berry and glowing reports about Ferdinand.

The French duke was only five years older than Isabella, but, Coca reported, he seemed like an old man in frail health. Berry, in fact, was "made ugly by extremely misshapen thin legs and watery eyes that were sometimes so bad as to be nearly blind so that rather than weapons and a horse what he needed was a skillful guide."[7] In contrast, the Aragonese prince, who was a year younger than Isabella, was "a young man with a gallant presence who could not be compared to the duke."[8]

Subsequent descriptions of Ferdinand verify that the prince was a vigorous and charming young man, who, if not exactly handsome by twentieth-century standards, was nevertheless quite attractive. An anonymous court historian later noted that Ferdinand had "marvelously beautiful, large slightly slanted eyes, thin eyebrows, a sharp nose that fit the shape and size of his face," a slightly full, sensual mouth and lips that were "often laughing." Although Ferdinand seems to have had a slight cast in his left eye, he had an attractive face framed by a high forehead. His well-shaped legs and an average height body were "most appropriate to elegant suits and the finest clothes." Ferdinand was also an athlete, "a great rider of the bridle and the jennet, and a great lance thrower and other activities which he performed with a great skill and a grace."[9]

The future king, Pulgar later observed, was also an excellent horseman who "jousted with ease and with so much skill that no one in his kingdom did it better . . . an avid sportsman and a man of good effort and much activity in war."[10]

Ferdinand, like Isabella, was a compassionate individual who "felt sympathy for miserable people in unfortunate situations." Naturally affable and gregarious, he had a "singular grace, to wit, that all who spoke with him at once loved him and wished to serve him." Yet, despite his charm, Ferdinand was seemingly unflappable, a man in whom "neither anger nor pleasure could alter . . . very much." His personal habits were similarly conservative and he exercised "moderation in food and drink."[11]

Yet Ferdinand was already showing tendencies that must have at least fleetingly disturbed the young princess. The year before his marriage, Ferdinand had lived in a military camp on the banks of the Segre River where he acquired several *barraganas,* or mistresses. By September 1469 the Aragonese prince had already fathered two illegitimate children, one, a son born that same year, known as Alfonso of Aragón, upon whom he would later dote.

Almost nothing is known about Isabella's reaction to Ferdinand's premarital affairs. In all likelihood the princess dismissed them as a male prerogative common to high-born men of the era. In an age of arranged marriages, royal *barraganas* were often stoically, if unhappily, accepted by the wives of Spanish kings and treated with respect by their courtiers.

Yet the young Isabella, like brides since time immemorial, must have hoped that, once wed, Ferdinand would remain faithful to her. In any case, nothing would change Isabella's own ideas about the sanctity of the marriage sacrament. She would wed Ferdinand and prove herself a chaste wife regardless of her husband's former or future sexual behavior.

Enrique's failure to respond to Isabella's letter worried Carrillo, especially after his spies reported that the king's army was marching north from Andalusia. Meanwhile, Fonseca's forces lingered near Madrigal, waiting for orders. Former allies of Isabella mysteriously changed sides, and some enlisted as spies for Enrique's cause. In that atmosphere of shifting loyalties, the archbishop dispatched Palencia and Cárdenas to Aragón to bring Ferdinand to Castile. The two men left Valladolid on a moonlit night "with great secrecy in the small hours of the morning when the moon was full" and rushed past the nearby castle of Castroverde.[12] Two days later they arrived at the town of Burgo de Osma near the Aragonese border where they expected to receive aid from Osma's bishop, Pedro de Montoya, and the powerful Count of Medinaceli, Luis de la Cerda.

Because of the secrecy of their mission, neither Palencia nor Cárdenas initially revealed the purpose of his trip. To their astonishment, they discovered that the bishop had defected from Isabella's camp and had assembled unfriendly soldiers to "capture Prince Ferdinand."[13] Moreover, the prelate revealed that Bishop Mendoza had alerted his clan to patrol the hilly Aragonese border to apprehend Ferdinand if he attempted to cross into Castile.

Palencia maintained his composure and ultimately obtained a safe conduct so that he and Cárdenas could travel unimpeded to Aragón. By September 25 or 26 the chronicler and Cárdenas arrived in Zaragoza only to learn that the kingdom of Aragón was straining under new misfortunes. King Juan was on a battlefield in Gerona attempting to maintain an army that threatened to desert because they had not been paid. Ferdinand, meanwhile, was preparing to mount a new offensive against the French.

Clearly, this was an inopportune time for the prince to leave Aragón. The French had occupied the southern Aragonese town of Segorbe. King Juan's old Catalonian allies, the Margarits, had defected. The French were advancing south daily. Then more than at any previous time in the war, Juan regarded Ferdinand as his one hope, his most trusted military commander.

The king had prepared Ferdinand for that position almost from birth. It was, in fact, because of Juan's preference for him over his firstborn son Carlos that the Catalonian rebellion had begun. By the age of eight or nine, Ferdinand had been forced to flee with his mother from Barcelona's murderous crowds. Later he lived on Catalonian battlefields with King Juan and, as an adolescent, led attacks against the French. War had been Ferdinand's cradle, much of his childhood, and ultimately his legacy from his fond father Juan. Although Ferdinand could read and write, he later described his childhood education as one in which he "had seen much but read little."[14] Little wonder then that by September 1469 King Juan looked to the vibrant seventeen-year-old prince as his fondest hope to direct a counteroffensive against France.

But Isabella, Palencia argued, needed Ferdinand even more urgently in Castile. Should the prince fail to marry her promptly, Enrique's soldiers might seize her and make the marriage impossible. In that event Aragón, lacking a Castilian alliance, would be even less likely to defend itself against France.

After a hurried consultation with his illegitimate half brother, the Archbishop of Aragón, Ferdinand agreed to leave immediately for Castile. Although the Aragonese treasury was bankrupt, the prince schemed to circumvent his poverty and hide his identity from his Castilian enemies by disguising himself as a humble muleteer and leaving Aragón with only a few companions.

On the night of October 5, 1469, Ferdinand, disguised in ragged clothes, set out with five friends and a guide for Castile. Except for the strange sight of the tattered prince whipping the mules to speed their way, the journey was unremarkable. The only mishap was Ferdinand's loss of a purse of gold left behind at an inn.

Ironically, the poverty of the Aragonese kingdom was the vehicle of Ferdinand's salvation. Not even the Mendozas' border spies paid attention to the shabby muleteer and his young traveling companions. The group's most dangerous moment came when they were within Castilian borders. On the night of October 7, the chilled, exhausted prince and his companions arrived at the Count of Trevino's castle near Burgo de Osma and knocked at the gate. Palencia was asleep inside. Because he did not expect Ferdinand until the next day, he had failed to notify the guard of the second watch of the prince's arrival. Consequently, the sentinel raised the alarm and hurled a large stone from the castle ramparts that narrowly missed Ferdinand's head. Palencia, awakening from the din, scolded the guard. As soon as Ferdinand heard Palencia's voice, he begged entry to the castle.

Palencia immediately awoke the Count of Trevino, who descended to the castle courtyard with his knights and large wax torches to welcome the Aragonese prince.

After the inhabitants of the castle prostrated themselves before Ferdinand, Trevino's trumpeters played so loudly that they "astonished those in the [nearby] villas and terrified the guards of the next castle."[15] Then, flanked by Trevino's two-hundred-man escort, Ferdinand entered the town of Burgo de Osma and proceeded on to the fortress at Curiel, where Carrillo and Juan de Vivero waited.

By October 9 the prince, accompanied by Carrillo and Vivero, had arrived in the mountainside town of Dueñas, just twenty miles north of Valladolid, where cheering citizens greeted him.

Isabella was, of course, immediately notified about Ferdinand's arrival. The only remaining record of that moment was a second letter she addressed to Enrique on October 12, once again asking for his approval of her marriage. Isabella noted that while Enrique had failed to reply to her first letter and "had given orders to block the entrance of the above said King and Prince," Ferdinand had arrived in Castile. Therefore, Isabella wrote, "I beg of your Highness, my very high and illustrious Prince, Lord and King, to approve of his arrival and of my purpose [my marriage]."[16]

Once again Enrique remained silent. Nothing could have been more frustrating to the princess who desperately wanted to establish a relationship with her brother on terms agreeable to both of them, such as had been implied at Toros de Guisando. But it was not to be.

On that same October 12, 1469, Isabella and Ferdinand signed a document with Carrillo formalizing their friendship. The date has perplexed Spanish scholars for centuries for there is no other historical evidence that Isabella and Ferdinand met before October 14. Nevertheless the pact, which is still preserved on parchment in the General Archives of the Kingdom at Simancas, suggests the prince and princess had already met, or at least communicated their mutual consent, to honor the archbishop. Within it the *novios*, or betrothed couple, solemnly pledged to protect the archbishop's property, honor his vassals, and govern in accordance with his counsel. To the eighteen-year-old Isabella, the pact was a sign of appreciation, a logical extension of her former dependence on Carrillo. To Ferdinand, it was a dutiful son's compliance with his father's demand that he obey the archbishop.

The pact stated that in view of the "good and true friendship" Isabella and Ferdinand enjoyed with the archbishop, "all three of us have agreed and . . . are determined to act as if we had one body and soul to appoint offices, give privileges and thanks following your counsel. . . ." The archbishop also promised to "guard your [Isabella and Ferdinand's] lives and royal persons and houses and estates and to use by faithful power to honor with esteem, royal dignity so that the three estates will be conserved and grow. . . ."[17]

The first meeting between Isabella and Ferdinand occurred on either October 12 or 14, 1469. Palencia, the only chronicler who recorded it in detail, reported it took place on the fourteenth.

It is certain that Isabella and Ferdinand first met at night. To avoid attention, Ferdinand arrived by horseback at the back entrance to the Vivero mansion around midnight. Behind him lay a large tract of fields and the rutted path he had followed with several attendants from Dueñas. In front of him stood the beaming Archbishop Carrillo, who bent to kiss the prince's hand. But Ferdinand would not hear of such deference from the man who was to make him King of Castile. He told Carrillo that he regarded him "like a father," one whom he, in fact, revered for he had endured "much suffering and danger in pursuit of the Aragonese house."[18]

After that warm greeting, the archbishop led Ferdinand and his attendants through a courtyard to an inner chamber where Isabella waited. Days earlier Isabella and the archbishop had quarreled about the meeting. Carrillo and other advisors had insisted that the prince kiss her hand in deference to Isabella's superior status as heir to the Castilian crown. But Isabella had rejected that notion. She and Ferdinand would recognize each other as equals, she insisted, just as they would live together as man and wife. Moreover, Isabella argued, Ferdinand was now the King of Sicily and thus "participated in a dignity that she did not receive as well as superior rents and incomes." It was, she added, widely agreed that "the quality of man put him over the woman by right and reason as was the natural law in all communities."[19] Ferdinand would not be required to kiss Isabella's hand when they met.

The couple's first assessment of one other was unequivocally favorable. According to one account, they gazed at each other approvingly and Isabella received her future husband "happily with the respect with which a fiance was due."[20] Palencia even insists that Isabella and Ferdinand fell passionately in love. "In that meeting," he writes, "the presence of the Archbishop restrained the amorous impulses of the lovers, whose strong hearts filled with the joy and delight of matrimony."[21]

That night the prince and princess were formally betrothed. Then Ferdinand and his attendants returned to Dueñas at two or three in the morning. It was, of course, one of the most memorable nights in Isabella's life. After months of anticipation the princess had finally met the young prince who would be her husband and had found him attractive. Even for a princess taught to marry for political expedience, it must have been a pleasant surprise to learn that love, or at least sexual attraction, would be part of her marriage.

The wedding festivities began on St. Luke's Day, Wednesday, October 18, at the Vivero palace. It is said that the prince and princess were so impoverished that they were forced to rely on friends to defray the cost of their clothing and the expenses of the celebration. Even so, Ferdinand's arrival in Valladolid on that day, accompanied by a thirty-man escort, was sufficiently impressive to attract large crowds of Valladolidians to the entranceway of the palace for the first civil ceremonies.

There, toward dusk, in a "rich room" in the presence of the Archbishop Carrillo, the papal nuncio Antonio Veneris, members of Isabella's court, the *Almirante* Fadríque Enríquez, the Manriques, and other *grandees,* Ferdinand and Isabella exchanged vows and signed documents that bound them together as man and wife. During the ceremonies Carrillo presented a papal bull from Pope Pius II dated March 24, 1464, sent by King Juan that allowed Isabella and Ferdinand to marry within the forbidden degrees of consanguinity. The religious ceremonies, however, would not be held until the next day. Consequently Ferdinand slept alone that night in the archbishop's house.

The next morning the prince returned to the Vivero palace. There Carrillo, the *Almirante,* Veneris, and 2,000 observers watched as Isabella and Ferdinand participated in a high nuptial mass and exchanged wedding vows. Some witnesses, filled with "sadness and anger of those loyal to the Master of Santiago [Pacheco]," stood by in sullen silence.[22] Most, however, were genuinely thrilled by the marriage. During the ceremony Carrillo read aloud the papal dispensation for a second time. Then, in keeping with royal tradition, Ferdinand promised to honor the customs, laws, and privileges of Castile. Once again he reiterated the marriage capitulations signed at Cervera ten months earlier.

After the ceremony the day was spent in feasting, dancing, and festive jousts until finally, at nightfall, Isabella and Ferdinand retired to the royal bedchamber.

Even in that most intimate of moments, the prince and princess had no hope of privacy. Below them, in other rooms of the palace, wellwishers celebrated loudly with songs, dances, and raucous comments about the event that was about to take place. At the door to the bridal bedchamber, witnesses waited until Ferdinand drew back the velvet curtains of the bed, walked to the door, and handed the officials the bloodstained sheet that proved he had consummated his marriage with Isabella. In response, the witnesses then "commanded that trumpets and drums and other instruments be played as they showed it [the sheet] to all of those who were waiting. . . ."[23]

The wedding was thus declared a success. In marked contrast to Enrique's two dubious nuptial nights, Isabella's marriage had been consummated and the proof of her virginity confirmed. Whatever emotions Isabella felt, pride was certainly one of them and perhaps also pleasure. Ferdinand, having already fathered several children by two different women, must have been a lover of considerable experience. Moreover, fifteenth-century women were permitted to enjoy the sexual act. Although the church condoned marital sex for procreation rather than pleasure, St. Paul's advice "Let the husband render to his wife what is due to her and likewise the wife to her husband" was often interpreted to mean that both sexes should experience sexual satisfaction.

Moreover, at the time of Isabella's birth there was widespread acceptance of the theories of the second-century Greek physician Galen suggesting that when a woman climaxed she ejaculated sperm that enabled conception. As a result, husbands were encouraged to enable their wives to experience orgasm.

The day after the wedding Ferdinand dutifully reported his union with Isabella to the *grandees* of Valencia. In Latin, the prince wrote that "there was a high nuptial mass. And last night, in service to God, we consummated our marriage."[24]

By vow and deed, Isabella and Ferdinand had become man and wife. Privately, they also fell in love. In time, the passion that glowed between them from the first days of their marriage was to melt the brittle terms of the marriage contract. Gradually too, their love kindled mutual respect that enabled the prince and princess to govern equitably, each according to his individual strengths and talents for the common good of Castile.

Sparked by political expedience, forged in youthful passion, Isabella and Ferdinand's union was to last nearly thirty-five years in one of the most remarkable monarchial partnerships ever known to Western Europe.

CHAPTER FIFTEEN

I Must Take Counsel with My Advisors

T he rapture of Isabella and Ferdinand's marriage was woefully short-lived. The nuptial celebrations lasted for six days, during which the young bride and groom were feted with banquets, fiestas, and processions. A spirit of thanksgiving overflowed into the streets of Valladolid where almost everyone, "whether *grandees* or not," rejoiced in Isabella's marriage. Nobles and commoners began to talk of Ferdinand as "the peaceful king" of Castile to distinguish him from Enrique.[1]

But outside the city the wedding was received with ambivalence. While citizens celebrated the event with religious processions in Valencia, Zaragoza, and the Sicilian capital of Palermo, there were bitter protests in Catalonia. Towns in Castile received the news coolly, fearing the match would precipitate a new civil war. And Enrique remained silent.

Nevertheless, Isabella and Ferdinand determined to extract a response from the king. On October 22, 1469, they dispatched three envoys to Segovia to present their letter directly to Enrique. Within it the prince and princess formally announced their marriage, describing themselves as "truthful younger siblings and obedient children" who wanted to bring "harmony and peace" to Castile.[2]

To emphasize their sincerity, the couple even enclosed details of Ferdinand's marriage capitulations. In addition, Isabella and Ferdinand conceded they "should have waited until seeing your Highness's consent and the vows and counsels of all the prelates and great men of all these kingdoms . . ." before becoming man and wife. But, they explained, "were it necessary to wait for everyone's agreement and consent this would be very difficult to obtain or else so much time would have passed that in these realms great danger would arise because of the absence of children to continue the succession."[3]

Although the letter closed with reassurances that Isabella and Ferdinand intended "to obey him as they ought . . . to avoid irreparable harm" to the kingdom,[4] it was clear that they wanted Enrique to recognize them as potentially obedient subjects, but nevertheless independent future rulers.

As usual, the king became skittish when confronted. Days earlier when he first learned about the wedding, he and Pacheco became "no little distressed" at the news. In disgust they abandoned the siege of Trujillo and marched north to Segovia. Along the way Pacheco, still smarting from Isabella's triumph, had fallen ill and was left in Ocaña where he would spend the next ten months recovering.

In Segovia, Enrique dismissed Isabella and Ferdinand's messengers without a response. "The matter was of such great importance," Enrique solemnly told them, that he "would have to take counsel with his advisors"[5] before he could decide anything.

The ensuing silence unnerved Isabella. She knew that Enrique's failure to respond was a bad sign, an indication that the king was either deliberately avoiding a painful decision or intended to delegate it to Pacheco. On October 30 Isabella wrote her old friend, Doña Leonor de Pimentel, Countess of Plasencia, to ask for help. The Countess was married to one of Enrique's favorite grandees, Álvaro de Stúñiga, Count of Plasencia, who had once been allied to Isabella's faction. But Enrique refused to be appeased. On November 2 he awarded the town of Arévalo to Doña Leonor's husband. As that town had belonged to Isabella's mother, the queen widow, according to King Juan's will, Enrique's award was clearly a spiteful act meant to punish the princess for her marriage.

Even that did not sate the king's anger. A few weeks later Enrique publicly denounced Isabella and Ferdinand's marriage as invalid by claiming that the papal dispensation presented at their wedding was false. For once this was not simply Pacheco-inspired rhetoric. The bull of May 28, 1464, that Carrillo read aloud at the wedding had indeed been forged by him and King Juan of Aragón. It was, as a deeply distressed Isabella would later understand, the desperate act of men determined to see the prince and princess married at a particular time.

Of course, neither King Juan nor Carrillo had originally intended to have the marriage performed under false pretenses. As early as 1467 King Juan had asked Pope Paul II for a dispensation that would have allowed Ferdinand to marry any one of several women who fell within the forbidden degrees of consanguinity. But Paul, who favored Castile over Aragón, had refused the request, stating that a bull had to be written with a specific party in mind. Some months later Juan requested a second bull, but again the pope had refused it.

Juan, however, persevered. Through letters and ambassadors he continued to beseech the pope for a dispensation until just a few weeks before Ferdinand's departure for Castile. Ultimately the pope agreed to issue a dispensation—but only, or so Juan claimed, after the wedding was performed. Consequently, when faced with the imminence of Ferdinand and Isabella's marriage, King Juan and Carrillo falsified the bull, backdated it to 1464, and forged it with the name of the deceased Pope Pius II.

The king and archbishop had relied on the papal legate Antonio Veneris to complete the hoax. At the time of the wedding the *nuncio* was claimed to have a "secret dispensation" from the pope, which he later failed to produce. More likely Veneris fabricated the story to facilitate the marriage and collect King Juan's bribe. On October 18 and 19 Veneris thus blindly accepted the falsified bull and gave the wedding the image, if not the reality, of canonical sanction.

To Isabella, as to any devout Catholic in fifteenth-century Europe, an uncanonical marriage was equivalent to a spiritual condemnation. Hence, she and Ferdinand were candidates for the eternal flames of hellfire.

Now, ironically, Enrique's faction could accuse the princess of the same sin her faction once flung at the king—namely that her marriage was invalid and that she lived in a graceless, "unclean" state.

An ominous silence now surrounded the newlyweds in Valladolid. Enrique sent no further communications from Segovia, and the *grandees* who had balked at news of Isabella's wedding joined the king in a new series of alliances. Uneasy, Ferdinand appealed to his father to send a thousand lancers to protect him and his new wife. The Aragonese king also dispatched another envoy to the pope requesting the dispensation.

Despite those tensions, the newlyweds settled happily into married life. It is said that after the wedding festivities Isabella and Ferdinand spent a few quiet days of *la luna de miel,* or honeymoon, at the nearby castle of Fuensalida. From their first days together, the young couple discovered many compatibilities. In spite of the false bull that marred their marriage, the prince, like Isabella, was a devout Catholic who attended daily mass. Both were moderate in food and drink. Isabella, in fact, drank no alcohol at all. Both were skilled equestrians, and enjoyed the hunt and the quieter amusements of chess and cards.

After her marriage Isabella continued to read and pursued the "womanly" occupations she had been taught by the convent nuns of her childhood—spinning, weaving, embroidery, and sewing. As a sign of wifely devotion, she soon added a new task, the sewing of Ferdinand's chemises.

Early on, in the tradition of courtly love and marriage, the prince and princess chose objects that were symbols for the first letter of each other's first name. Isabella thus chose *flechas,* or arrows, for the *F* of Ferdinand. The prince adopted the *yugo,* or yoke for the *Y* or *I* of Isabella. These symbols, when combined with the royal arms of Castile and Aragón and bordered with a chain, the Gordian knot, and a sphere, would become their new *escudo,* or shield at Isabella's coronation five years later. As emblems of the permanent union, the new *escudo* would appear on everything the sovereigns touched—in churches, cloister archways, on fortresses, books, furniture, even on their clothes.

No doubt, Isabella and Ferdinand's determination to become the next monarchs of Castile was an important common bond. But to achieve the crown meant they would confront enormous obstacles. Temperamentally they were well suited to the task, for Ferdinand, like Isabella, was an ordered, self-disciplined individual. Years later, courtiers observed that both were inveterate list-makers who kept tiny notebooks of individuals and events that would be potentially useful to them.

Their most immediate problem was poverty. To stretch their meager resources, Isabella and Ferdinand often dressed in borrowed clothes and ate at the charity of friends. Still, the goodwill of allies could not protect the prince and princess from the fear that Enrique's troops might seize them. In order to maintain the thousand lancers and their horses Juan sent from Aragón, the newlyweds were compelled to raise 40,000 florins—something they failed to do. "Now," Ferdinand wrote his father, "I am in a worse situation than I was a short time ago because my followers have lost hope and I cannot give them money to support themselves and their retinue. . . ."[6]

In a similar effort to raise cash, Isabella dispatched another envoy to Aragón to claim the towns promised in the marriage capitulations. But the towns were not forthcoming, partly because of the Catalonian war, partly because of Aragonese resentment of Isabella's large dowry. As a result, the couple was forced to remain financially dependent on Carrillo and King Juan.

Soon after the wedding, the newlyweds' dependence on the archbishop became problematic. On October 22, when the newlyweds held their first council meeting, Ferdinand and Carrillo quarreled. The archbishop, apparently interpreting his new pact with the prince and princess to mean that he would share their authority, had so dominated the meeting that Ferdinand began to bristle. Finally, when the prince complained that Carrillo was treating him with little respect, the archbishop, whose authority had been virtually unchallenged for a year, flew into a rage.

Clearly, Carrillo had mixed motivations. His paternalistic instincts to guide Isabella to the throne were combined with his own desire to dominate her and enjoy power for himself. The seventeen-year-old prince, married just a few days to Isabella, was both a source of pride and a threat to his own relationship with the princess. The archbishop most probably envied the emotional bond the newlyweds had forged through their sexual union. That October day the two men parted unhappily, Ferdinand to grumble about the overbearing archbishop, Carrillo to slip into one of his dark moods.

Isabella witnessed at least part of the dissension. But the princess was a seasoned veteran of Carrillo's acidic temperament and accustomed to his moods when crossed. Eventually she and Ferdinand came to believe that the contract they signed before their wedding naming Carrillo their most trusted counselor was a mistake. Advice, Ferdinand would later observe, did not constitute ultimate authority. He would not be ruled by any counselor.

If little else, the quarrel enabled Isabella to discover a new side to her husband, a willful streak Ferdinand would subsequently hide from the world under a veneer of congeniality. But at seventeen Ferdinand was still a brash and unformed youth, who "wore the joy of his heart on his face."[7] Although the prince had been "educated in the school of dissimulation" by his father Juan, he had not yet acquired the self-control that would subsequently enable him to "sacrifice his passions, and sometimes, indeed his principles, to his interests."[8] Only gradually would Ferdinand develop the diplomatic skills that Machiavelli later used as a model for his depiction of the shrewdly opportunistic Renaissance prince.

Some weeks after that argument, the two men quarreled again. This time, Ferdinand told the fuming prelate "that he would not be put in leading-strings like so many of the sovereigns of Castile," for that practice had contributed to the kingdom's current problems.[9]

Years later, when Isabella and Ferdinand ruled Castile, they invited talented individuals to join their court and often solicited their advice. But ultimately they ruled alone to assure that the authority of the crown remained in their control. As Pulgar later observed, "The King's favorite was the Queen and the Queen's favorite was the King."[10]

Nevertheless, in 1469 Carrillo had little patience for Ferdinand's notions. To him, the prince was simply an arrogant and privileged youth with no experience in Castilian politics who was attempting to undercut his authority. Simultaneously, Isabella's sexual passion for the prince was drawing her more and more under Ferdinand's control and away from the archbishop's influence.

Carrillo was not the only one alarmed at Ferdinand's manner. Other courtiers who witnessed the hostility between the two men found the prince unnecessarily provocative.

In Aragón King Juan was so distressed by these reports that he sent his secretary, Juan de Coloma, to Castile. The ambassador lectured Ferdinand sternly: Without Carrillo, Ferdinand and Isabella would not have been married; without the archbishop's support, he and Isabella would have little chance to obtain the throne; without Carrillo, it was still possible for Enrique to disinherit Isabella. Thus the archbishop was to be respected. "Surely the day will come," Coloma dourly predicted, "when you will be more secure and more thoughtful about the possibility of being forced to leave Castile."[11]

Ultimately, Coloma's lectures were only partially successful. Although Ferdinand and the archbishop subsequently established a superficially cordial relationship, the rift between them never completely healed.

Other dark forces pressed around the newlyweds. With Enrique's return to Old Castile, it was rumored that his soldiers were preparing to seize Isabella in Valladolid. The townspeople, fearing an invasion, gradually became less enthusiastic about the marriage. Some citizens, in fact, even became hostile to Isabella and Ferdinand. In other small towns and *pueblos* of Old Castile the meager support the princess once commanded withered. To the south of Valladolid in the Duero River valley, the towns of Tordesillas, Sepúlveda, and Olmedo still privately supported Isabella but were too fearful of Enrique's wrath to proclaim their allegiance openly. "Few *grandees*," the Aragonese ambassador Coloma wrote King Juan, "wanted it to be known that they supported the 'young sovereigns.'"[12]

In February 1470 Isabella became pregnant. In Aragón, King Juan received the news with delight; in Castile, Enrique trembled. Because Isabella and Ferdinand were heirs to the Castilian and Aragonese thrones, their child, especially if it was male, would inherit the twin crowns. Hoping that Isabella's pregnancy would persuade Enrique to recognize her marriage, the prince and princess wrote the king once again.

Their letter of March 8, 1470, was even more forceful than earlier communications. "It has been four months since Your Lordship has failed to respond to us," Isabella and Ferdinand began. During that time they had observed peaceful and faithful behavior toward Enrique as their "King and Lord and true father." But Enrique had employed individuals who had "committed certain actions against them" despite the fact that Isabella was still his acknowledged heir. In the interests of maintaining peace in the kingdom, Isabella and Ferdinand now begged Enrique to accept them as his "obedient subjects."

Should he refuse again, Isabella and Ferdinand suggested that Enrique delegate the problem to a council consisting of the four Castilian ecclesiastical orders—the Dominicans, the Franciscans, the Cartujans, and the Hieronymites—an offer they intended to publicize "both within and outside Castile." If their petitions were not respected, the couple threatened, they would do "whatever is allowed by all divine and human laws in defense of their rights [for which] they could not be held responsible by God and men."[13] This time Enrique replied enigmatically, reiterating his need to consult with his advisors.

While awaiting a response, Isabella and Ferdinand's host, Juan de Vivero, became embroiled in a bitter fight between the old Christians and the *conversos* of Valladolid. In the subsequent street riots, the security of Vivero's home was threatened. Now, more than ever before, the prince and princess needed a safe haven, a place removed from the "mutabilities of a large city" so that Isabella could wait out her pregnancy in peace. On March 8, 1470, the same day Isabella and Ferdinand sent their letter to Enrique, the newlyweds thus moved eighteen miles north to Dueñas, the same town where Ferdinand stayed before his wedding. Doubtless Carrillo had suggested the move. The couple would live in a small mansion owned by Carrillo's brother Pedro de Acuña, who was *alcaide,* or military governor, of Dueñas.

In Segovia, meanwhile, Enrique began to strip Isabella of the privileges he agreed to at Toros de Guisando. On April 30, 1470, he awarded Pacheco the town of Escalona, one of the seven towns he had promised the princess. Four days later Enrique transferred the *merindads* of Medina del Campo to the Count of Urena.

Slowly, but surely, in deed, if not in word, Isabella was being disinherited. On June 18, the infuriated princess and her husband wrote Enrique again. This time their letter was to the point. As before Isabella and Ferdinand assured the king that if he accepted them "with love," peace would settle over Castile. On the other hand, if he preferred to work against the prince and princess, "it would not be strange that this would release the powerful elements of war. . . ."[14] In the end the Almighty, Isabella and Ferdinand predicted, would make a judgment on those events. Once again Enrique's response was silence.

In addition to the escalating hostility between Isabella and Enrique, Castile was beset with other problems. The year 1470 had begun badly, with severe winter snows and heavy spring rains that devastated most of the country.

When the rain finally stopped and the plains of the *Meseta* turned green, a withering heat descended upon the kingdom, dessicating wheat, oats, and barley seedlings. From Andalusia to Galicia the crops began to fail. Animals died from thirst, and there were bread, meat, and wine shortages. Even worse, Enrique had recently devalued the coinage, and the resultant monetary confusion drove food prices even higher. People sickened, and so many died from hunger that the mood of angry discontent that descended on Castile was reminiscent of the civil war years.

In that bleak atmosphere Isabella and Ferdinand passed the summer of 1470, surrounded by poverty and popular disfavor in the "prison of Dueñas." After their move to the Castilian countryside, Enrique seized the opportunity to reinstate La Beltraneja to the Castilian crown. Realizing that to disinherit the princess and elevate his daughter Juana was a politically dangerous act, likely to incite Aragonese hostility, Enrique sought the aid of a foreign ally. The most obvious candidate was Louis XI of France, who, having been disappointed in his plan to marry his brother to Isabella, had his own reasons for revenge. Shortly after Isabella's marriage had been announced, Enrique thus convinced the French king to have his brother marry La Beltraneja instead.

CHAPTER SIXTEEN

Val de Lozoya

On October 2, 1470, Isabella gave birth to a daughter. Few details have been preserved except that the labor began during the night of October 1. Thereafter "the *caballeros* and Ferdinand spent many anxious hours worrying about Isabella's dangerous condition" until finally somewhere "between nine and twelve"[1] on the morning of October 2, Isabella *de a luz,* that is, "gave to the light," a baby girl. The child, who was blond and well formed, was christened by Carrillo and named Isabel for the three generations of women on her maternal side who bore that name before her.

It is said that Isabella delivered the child with the assistance of one, or possibly two, midwives, for in fifteenth-century Castile physicians rarely attended births, even of royalty. In accordance with Castilian tradition, five other witnesses attended the royal birth, as had been the practice for a century ever since Pedro the Cruel's wife had attempted to pass off a Jewish male infant as her own. Almost certainly, Isabella delivered her daughter while sitting upright or reclining slightly upon a birthing chair or stool. In the late Middle Ages such devices were made of wood with an opening at the bottom to facilitate the mother's expulsion of the baby with minimum pain and the aid of gravity.

Women of the time universally anticipated the pain of natural childbirth. While midwives occasionally administered alcoholic beverages to retard labor in difficult births (as, for example, in breech deliveries), no other anesthesia was available. Death from the delivery itself, from infections, or from subsequent complications was a real possibility. Mortality studies of the era suggest that one-quarter to one-third of female deaths were related to childbirth. As a result, most marriages seldom lasted more than a decade.

Thus any pregnant woman had reason to be anxious. Doubtless, during her pregnancy the devout Isabella had contemplated the possibility of her own death as well as the spiritual implications of her afterlife. But as a princess and future Queen of Castile, Isabella was also concerned about her dignity on earth during the birth process itself. Her one request during labor was that a silken veil be placed over her face so that her attendants would not see her grimace.

Later that same day, Isabella sat up in bed and dictated a letter to the governor of Valencia announcing that "Our Lord has given us a princess."[2] Subsequently, Isabella and Ferdinand notified the towns of Castile and Aragón of their daughter's birth and introduced her as "the Infanta of Castile and Aragón."

While Isabella would retain a special affection for this first daughter throughout her life, the baby's gender elicited sharply negative responses outside the nursery. The Aragonese, and particularly King Juan, were openly dismayed. His kingdom still adhered to the Salic or Germanic inheritance law that specified that the crown could be inherited only by a male child. Consequently, the tiny infant, already swaddled and fed by a royal wet nurse in the Acuña mansion, could not legally inherit the kingdom of Aragón. Thus was Isabella's dream of uniting Castile and Aragón through her child temporarily shattered.

It is likely that Isabella raged privately against the Aragonese prejudices toward the female sex. Although the princess had long accepted the biblical notion that the "man was natural lord over the woman" and even argued for that subservience before her first meeting with Ferdinand, her personal experiences in Enrique's court made her exquisitely sensitive to the vicissitudes of birth. Moreover, as the future heir to the Castilian crown, the princess could have few objections to the idea that a woman could rule as well as a man.

The issue would gnaw at Isabella throughout her life. Four years later, shortly after her coronation, Isabella would argue the question with Ferdinand. To exclude half the healthy children born to a royal couple from the possibility of ruling a kingdom because of their female gender, Isabella would observe, was to place that nation in dynastic jeopardy. Twenty-five years later as queen, she would debate the same question again before the Aragonese *Cortes*. But in October 1470 Isabella could not speak her mind. She was merely the younger sister of a hostile king and had just given birth to that most undesirable of all creatures, a female child.

When Enrique learned of the birth, he must have been as relieved as the Aragonese king was disappointed. Although the kingdom of Castile recognized female succession, Isabella's claim as heir would have been immensely bolstered had she delivered a boy because the child would have been the first living male descendant of King Juan after Enrique. But as a female, the infant was a political nonentity, as meaningless to the Castilian succession as she was to Aragón.

With that news, Enrique proceeded to divest Isabella of the rest of her royal privileges. First he seized the rich trade town of Medina del Campo in his name. Then on October 12, 1470, Enrique announced Princess Juana's engagement to Charles, Duke of Berry.

By the time of Enrique's announcement, Berry was no longer Louis XI's heir. That past August, just as Louis's ambassador Jean Jouffroy, the new Cardinal of

Albi, traveled over the Pyrenees to Castile, the French queen gave birth to a baby boy, the future Charles VIII. Suddenly, Berry was reduced to secondary importance in France, and so was Jouffroy's mission. The ambassador was nevertheless obliged to carry out Louis's orders and thus continued his march through the searing August heat with 250 armed men to Medina del Campo.

Enrique was still so eager for the French alliance that, "contrary to his habit," he arrived first in Medina del Campo and participated in the welcoming ceremonies. But Jouffroy, vexed both over the French prince's birth and Isabella's duplicity from the previous year, now angrily attacked the Castilian court. Although he directed most of his criticism at Isabella, who he claimed had "married illegally," and upon Ferdinand, who he believed wed "so that he would have new resources to fight the French," the cardinal's attacks upon the "infidelity of the Castilian people" created bitter resentments at court.[3]

Jouffroy also delivered an ultimatum: There could be no betrothal unless La Beltraneja was made heir to the Castilian throne. Enrique conceded. To prove his sincerity, the king even signed letters echoing the cardinal's accusations that Isabella had married without either his approval or that of the *Cortes* and that she was living in an incestuous marriage that lacked proper papal dispensation.

Enrique lost no time honoring his promises to Jouffroy. By mid-October Enrique planned a double ceremony that would simultaneously create the ten-year-old La Beltraneja his heir and betroth her to the Duke of Berry. The ceremony, which was to be held in an open field of the *Val de Lozoya,* or Valley of Lozoya, near the town of Buitrago close to the northern Aragonese border, bore striking similarity to the bucolic setting of Isabella's oath at Toros de Guisando two years earlier.

October 26, 1470, was a sunny day. Few clouds were visible in the skies above the fields of the *Val de Lozoya.* Near the shores of the small Angostura River, the flutter of royal banners around an assembly of *grandees* mounted upon caparisoned horses attested to the importance of the occasion. Enrique stood in the center of the finely dressed, gloved, and bejewled men with Queen Juana, La Beltraneja, Pacheco, and Fonseca. Jouffroy and his French associates stood at Enrique's side. As the sun danced brightly over the king's shaggy blond hair and set the jewels in his crown gleaming, he read aloud a letter than canceled his previous oath at Toros de Guisando.

His sister Isabella, Enrique observed, "had not paid attention to what she had promised by marrying without his permission and . . . against his will and disregarding the respect she should have paid . . . [Enrique] as a father and older brother and marrying the King of Sicily, Prince of Aragón as if there were no prohibitions against him." Therefore, Enrique could no longer consider Isabella his legitimate heir and successor to the throne. "With this letter," he announced, Isabella was "disinherited" and he would "give no value to any letter or title as Princess and successor" of his crown.[4]

Turning then to his audience, Enrique ordered the *grandees,* knights, and prelates of his reign to "neither consider the princess the legitimate heir nor to obey her as such."[5] To lend further legitimacy to his denunciation, Enrique then produced a dispensation from Pope Paul II that nullified all oaths made to Isabella at Toros de Guisando.

Jouffroy then asked Queen Juana to swear that La Beltraneja "was the true daughter of the King her husband."[6] Raising her right hand, the still-pretty thirty-one-year-old queen responded affirmatively. Finally the cardinal asked Enrique if he thought Princess Juana was his child. The king responded that he "believed she was and that he had considered her so from the time she was born."[7] Afterward the *grandees* and prelates, "bribed with rents and privileges,"[8] swore their fealty to Princess Juana and kissed her hand as Enrique's legitimate heir. Jouffroy then joined the small hands of La Beltraneja with the larger ones of the Duke of Berry's proxy and the ceremonies ended in a fanfare of trumpets and drums.

Three days later in the ancient cathedral of Segovia, the king and queen participated in a ceremony designed to quell any lingering doubts Jouffroy had about La Beltraneja's legitimacy. Before an assembly of knights, *grandees,* and prelates, Queen Juana received the host and heard mass. Then she mounted a high altar and before the mitered Jouffroy swore once again that the princess was Enrique's daughter. Afterward La Beltraneja's engagement to Berry was solemnized in a religious service officiated by the cardinal. On November 3, 1470, Enrique issued letters to the Castilian towns announcing that "I have publicly betrothed the Duke of Guyenne [Berry] with the said Princess my daughter, and the prelates and *grandees* of my kingdom joined with me and the *procuradores* of the cities and villages and ratified and sworn to make the Princess my daughter the heir and successor to these kingdoms."[9]

With those words Isabella was no longer the legitimate heir to the Castilian throne. Once again she was simply *Infanta* of Castile.

CHAPTER SEVENTEEN

Bad Blood

Isabella and Ferdinand were stunned when they heard about the disinheritance. The blow fell at a particularly difficult time for the couple, just as Isabella was recovering from the birth of her daughter and soon after Ferdinand suffered a serious injury. In early November 1470, as messengers sped toward Dueñas with Enrique's announcement, Ferdinand was running a high fever subsequent to a fall from his horse. On November 7 the prince's physician, Llorenc Badoc, wrote King Juan that Ferdinand had "damaged his blood" from the fall and might even have permanently injured his health.[1] Nevertheless, by November 12 Ferdinand recovered sufficiently to write his father that he had attended mass.

Disturbed as Isabella and Ferdinand were over Enrique's retraction, they were still young, filled with optimism, and determined to rule Castile. To their constituents, the prince and princess's marriage was a mystical union whose magnetic force either attracted talented individuals to their side or repulsed them. That force—youthful love, limitless ambition, the juxtaposition of high birth and personal integrity—was so strong that even Carrillo, perpetual alchemist in search of the secret of eternal life, could never dominate it. Left outside the bond of their love, the archbishop decided to abandon the prince and princess.

He would do so, however, only gradually. By the time Isabella and Ferdinand had moved to Dueñas, their relationship with Carrillo was already faltering, and once Enrique repossessed Medina del Campo, the archbishop became even more distant. No longer would he spend hours talking with Isabella about plans to help her secure the crown. At council meetings he sought to dominate every discussion. In the same November 12 letter to his father Ferdinand complained bitterly about the archbishop. "Believe me, your Lordship, it seems that nothing can be done or determined without his counsel and there is nothing that can satisfy him."[2]

By late autumn the young couple were clearly vulnerable. In Aragón King Juan fretted to his counselors about "the great danger that existed to the persons of the said princess, his children, and his granddaughter, the Infanta."[3] At any moment he fully expected that Enrique, joined by French soldiers provided by the Duke of Berry, would attempt to seize Isabella and Ferdinand in Dueñas. And indeed, on December 8, Enrique wrote Berry urging him to dispatch his "most powerful" soldiers to Castile to apprehend the prince and princess.

A week later Isabella and Ferdinand moved to the busy market town of Medina del Rioseco, home of Ferdinand's uncle Alonso Enríquez and his family. The town, about thirty miles northwest of Valladolid, was a logical refuge for it was surrounded by estates owned by the Enríquez clan.

Although Carrillo escorted the prince and princess there, he complained bitterly about the move, asserting that their host would inevitably "govern everything" regarding the couple.[4] The archbishop's behavior was at least partially to blame. But like most neurotics, he failed to understand that his domineering personality had actually caused the alienation between him and Isabella and Ferdinand that he had tried so desperately to avoid.

The news about Enrique's disinheritance had rocked Castile. As soon as La Beltraneja's reinstatement as heir was announced, an uproar sounded from one end of the kingdom to the other "accusing the magnates of injustice and evil and disloyalty and brazenness for having so many times approved and condemned the same cause."[5] In the north, the provinces of Vizcaya and Guipúzcoa revolted against the king. In Andalusia, the cities of Jerez, Baeza, and Ubeda refused to swear obedience to La Beltraneja. And in Sevilla, the powerful Duke of Medina Sidonia sent letters reaffirming his support for Isabella and Ferdinand against Enrique.

Even in sunny Jaén, posed at the bottom of the Castilian kingdom near Granada, Enrique's childhood friend, Miguel Lucas de Iranzo, Constable of Castile, protested. When Enrique ignored his friend's arguments, the constable privately sent a squire to the Duke of Berry informing him "that Princess Juana was the daughter of the adulterous Queen Doña Juana." Then, to impress the duke with the fact that by birthright Isabella was "the true successor to the kingdom," he even described "the impotence of King Don Enrique and the wickedness that the Queen committed at her husband's command."[6]

Ultimately Berry decided against sending Enrique soldiers. The duke, who was already embroiled in a bitter feud with his brother Louis, became convinced he was being pawned off in a bad marriage for his brother's expedience. In retribution, Berry began secret talks with Louis's enemy, Charles the Bold, Duke of Burgundy, whose independent duchy bordered France, stretching from Provence in the south to the Low Countries of Belgium, Flanders, and Holland in the north.

Temperamentally, Isabella was hardly content to let others take the initiative in her defense. From the moment of her *salto* at Ocaña the princess had become an activist, and now, after the events at *Val de Lozoya,* she longed to confront her brother directly and reassert her claim to the Castilian crown. Lacking men and munitions, the princess struck back with the only tools at her disposal—pen and parchment. The resultant letter, dated March 7, 1471, was an indignant justification of her acts and a reaffirmation of her position as heir to the throne.

Insisting that she had been slandered by Jouffroy, Isabella argued that she had never "deliberately offended, either in thought or word, her brother the King." Moreover, she was the indisputable heir of Castile by the oath Enrique signed at Toros de Guisando which affirmed that "the Queen had used her body uncleanly" and in which Enrique was "informed he was not legitimately married to her."[7] The king had even sworn to the papal legate Veneris that the queen's daughter was not his own.

Despite these pledges, Enrique had failed to deliver what he promised—to divorce Queen Juana, to return her and her daughter to Portugal, and to give Isabella certain cities.

> And in the case that you, by passion and ill advice, were to deny
> this, I ask and demand of you in the name of God and by the loy-
> alty you owe to these kingdoms to clearly see what you are
> obliged to by the law and right . . . by your conscience and
> loyalties . . . it will be a great disgrace and insult in the future
> times for the old nobility and the honest Castilian community . . .
> will give you copper instead of gold, . . . and an alien heiress
> instead of a legitimate successor . . . And if . . . there are
> fires . . . robberies . . . deaths God will . . . make you . . .
> the consenters responsible for such a great evil, while my Lord,
> the Prince, and I and the ones who follow . . . will be free of
> all blame.[8]

It was an admittedly brazen letter for a woman one month short of her twentieth birthday, but the legal issues the princess had raised were valid. According to Castilian law, the oath at Toros de Guisando and the pledge of the *Cortes* at Ocaña could not be reversed "by a single oath against it," such as the one sworn at *Val de Lozoya*.

Essentially, Enrique was obliged to call the *Cortes* to session again so that the *procuradores* could vote upon which princess held the right of succession. On February 1, 1471, just a month or so before Isabella sent her new letter, Enrique had, in fact, called the *Cortes* to Segovia to discuss the kingdom's finances. At that time it was said that Enrique asked the *procuradores* to swear allegiance to La Beltraneja's claim to the throne, but reports about the oath were vague and not published until four years later.

In 1471 the *Cortes* had even more pressing matters to consider than the Castilian succession—the monetary confusion that threatened to shatter civil and international security of the kingdom. For years Enrique had so carelessly supervised the Castilian coinage that by 1471, 150 mints, many unlicensed by the crown, were churning out coins. As a result, ordinary citizens often confused legal tender with counterfeit money and each coin became the subject of sharp debate. "All the money, especially gold," wrote a contemporary, "was so false that nothing was worth its right price and because of the situation [worth] half its true value."[9] "A bolt of cloth that used to cost two hundred maravedís," observed another, "now costs six hundred and a standard of silver valued at fifteen hundred now costs 6,000."[10] In desperation, many citizens reverted to the more primitive system of barter, "exchanging bread for wine," a scythe for a flail, an iron plowshare for a prize lamb.

The bad weather and crop shortfalls of 1470–71 worsened the unstable economic situation. Food prices soared beyond the reach of many ordinary citizens. Children and adults sickened and died from malnutrition and other diseases. Subsistence living and a constant struggle against the specter of death became a horrifying reality for the masses.

Yet it would be from the decaying soil of Enrique's reign that the seeds of Isabella's Castile would finally take root. The low morale and pervasive discontent that characterized Castile in the early 1470s soon embittered the very same *grandees* who had pledged themselves to La Beltraneja at *Val de Lozoya*. Feuds between dissenting nobles shattered what little peace still remained in the chaotic kingdom.

Robberies and homicides became as common as they had been during the civil war. Even the *Hermandades,* Castile's network of civilian police forces, were paralyzed. A general mood of malaise, hopelessness, and despair swept over the weary Castilian citizens.

Ordinary citizens, embittered and starving, refused to become involved in the aristocratic feuds. Individually and collectively the officials of the Castilian cities, "knowing of the King's weakness and inability to conserve the Crown," likewise hedged, scrupulously avoiding allegiances to the aristocrats who almost inevitably plunged the towns into dissent.[11] In the wake of *Val de Lozoya,* a few towns took Isabella's side; others equivocated, denying their allegiance to either the king or the princess.

By early 1471 things began to change. Suddenly a Mendoza relative, Luis de la Cerda, Duke of Medinaceli, abandoned Enrique's cause and threw the weight of his vast estates and subjects on the side of the prince and princess. The duke had recently married King Juan of Aragón's granddaughter Ana de Navarra, and either connubial bliss or material gain had swayed him to his new opinion. The ever-conniving Aragonese king, realizing how important the Mendozas could be as allies, had dangled the match in front of Medinaceli, knowing full well that once he wed and became kin, the duke would be obliged to help Isabella and Ferdinand.

In late February or early March 1471 the duke had journeyed to Medina del Rioseco to meet with Isabella, Ferdinand, Carrillo, and Alonso Enríquez. There, before an audience of her allies, Isabella read her condemnatory letter of March 7 aloud before it was sent to the king. The princess then distributed copies of the letter to her allies, who had them nailed to church gates and public buildings throughout Castile.

Isabella's condemnation was only the first step. Above all the princess and her faction needed money to support their campaign; to find it, the princess launched an aggressive campaign to collect her dowry from Aragón. In May she sent an envoy to Sicily to take possession of the lands promised her in Ferdinand's marriage capitulations. In July she dispatched another envoy to Aragón to claim Elche and Crevillente. When those towns resisted, Isabella protested sharply. If nothing else, Enrique's disinheritance had taught the princess the folly of passivity in the face of broken promises.

The young princess consequently penned a letter of complaint to King Juan reminding him that "you willfully accepted the responsibility and offered to carry it out." In a second letter, she chastised Juan for his failure to keep his solemn promise "to order the conclusion of these affairs . . . without changing a single point." The king should not, Isabella observed, "act without my knowing and should let me do what I consider appropriate because the truth is that I will only do what is just."[12]

Impressed by the young woman's determination and moral indignation, the Aragonese sovereign soon conceded and urged his subjects to do the same. "It is best that you fulfill your promise as Your Ladyship has reminded me," the Aragonese king wrote his subjects. "For not to do so would be unjust."[13]

King Juan's respectful, almost reverential tone would characterize his attitude toward Isabella for the rest of his life. Although he was half a century older and served as an advisor to Isabella and Ferdinand, the Aragonese Wolf knew that he had met his match in his stalwart daughter-in-law.

Meanwhile, by late spring 1471 Enrique had still not received soldiers from the Duke of Berry. The frail duke, disquieted by Iranzo's reports, now longed to break free from both the French and Castilian kings. In the summer he thus sent an envoy to Pope Paul II asking for a release from two promises—the first his pledge of loyalty to Louis, the second his betrothal to La Beltraneja. By August, Enrique realized his link to France was in jeopardy. Several months later his suspicions were confirmed when the duke made a formal appeal for marriage to the Duke of Burgundy's daughter, Mary.

By then something even more dramatic had happened to snap the frayed harnesses of Enrique's restive kingdom. On July 25, the Castilian king's most loyal and powerful ally, Pope Paul II, suddenly died. The new pope, Francesco della Rovere, crowned on August 22 as Sixtus IV, had an entirely different attitude toward Isabella and Ferdinand. Instead of viewing the young couple as obstacles to Castilian peace, Sixtus IV regarded them as a solution to the chaos that would threaten Castile after Enrique's death. On December 1, Sixtus IV granted Isabella and Ferdinand the long-sought bull that sanctioned their marriage.

In the eyes of the church, the prince and princess were now legally wed. The old accusations hurled at them by Enrique and Jouffroy were no longer valid. Neither, by then, was the French threat of Berry's marriage to La Beltraneja. In Sixtus IV, Isabella and Ferdinand had found a new ally who would help them transform Castile, the church, and ultimately the course of Western European history.

CHAPTER EIGHTEEN

An Anguished Princess

I n the plains surrounding Simancas, in the foothills of the steep Guadarrama mountains north of Madrid, humble land tenants and simple townspeople quietly embraced Isabella's claim to the Castilian throne. Aware of those sympathies, Ferdinand and his newly reunited faction bolstered Isabella's cause by moving from town to town, drilling their soldiers, gathering arms, and preparing for battle against Enrique.

They did not have to wait long. On January 16, 1472, when Enrique announced he was awarding his "dearly loved Master" Pacheco the town of Sepúlveda in the Guadarrama foothills, the citizens protested. The independent-spirited Sepulvedians did not want to be governed by the tyrannical royal favorite. In defiance, they hung banners throughout the town in support of Isabella and Ferdinand.

Enrique, determined to subdue the hilly town, ordered his supporters to be armed with "shields, lances and crossbows and barricaded the streets."[1] But the very next night, in the wee hours of the morning, the city fathers helped Ferdinand and his soldiers enter Sepúlveda. By daybreak the Aragonese prince had claimed the town in Isabella's name.

After that victory, other towns began to defect to Isabella—among them Ágreda and Moya in the north and Aranda in the Duero River valley. Slowly Isabella and Ferdinand's prospects were brightening, and eventually would light their way to the Castilian throne. But first the prince and princess would have to endure dark years of *grandee* intrigues and the desperate fumblings of a troubled king in the dusk of his reign.

In Aragón, meanwhile, King Juan was achieving his own military victories. The political tide had shifted in his favor in late 1470 when Jean of Lorraine, chief military leader of the Catalonian rebellion, died. With his death, French support for the revolt crumbled and Catalonian aristocracy renewed its allegiance to Juan. For the first time in over a decade, Juan now saw the possibility of reclaiming a victory in Catalonia. In August 1471 he recaptured the city of Gerona. Although the truce would not be completed until November, Juan carved out a pact with Charles the Bold, Duke of Burgundy, and his own nephew Ferrante, King of Naples, against Louis XI. Now, with his Burgundian-Neapolitan-Aragonese "triple alliance," Juan planned to isolate the Spider King and eliminate his influence over Catalonia.

By late autumn only the proud city of Barcelona held out against Juan. The Aragonese king ordered his armadas and armies to initiate a blockade, and little by little the wealthy city on the Mediterranean was starved out of food and munitions. Meanwhile, in the north, Juan's troops successfully invaded the Ampurdán, today's modern province of Gerona.

But even with those triumphs, King Juan summoned Ferdinand to his side. Simultaneously, Louis XI promised Rêné of Anjou, leader of the Barcelonian rebellion, an army of 300 lancers, thousands of infantrymen, and 3,000 *ballesteros,* or primitive guns, capable of thrusting stones or arrows at great distances.

The French aid never materialized. On May 25, 1472, Charles, Duke of Berry, died in Bayonne at the age of twenty-six. Charles the Bold and Francis, Duke of Brittany, immediately accused King Louis of poisoning his brother.

Shortly before his death, Berry became violently ill. His hair, beard, and eyebrows were said to have fallen off and his nails "parted from his flesh with great pain."[2] Those symptoms, according to the era's chroniclers, strongly suggested that he had ingested poisonous herbs or arsenic.

But perhaps not. A full two years earlier Isabella's chaplain Coca had reported that the duke's health was alarmingly fragile. Berry may well have suffered from a chronic illness that had simply progressed. From descriptions of Berry's symptoms modern scholars now speculate that the duke died from syphilis, possibly complicated by tuberculosis.

Whatever its cause, Berry's death unleashed Charles the Bold's fury upon France. Convinced that Louis had poisoned his brother, the Burgundian duke dispatched soldiers to attack the northern French province of Vermandois. That invasion so distracted Louis that he never sent reinforcements to defend Rêné of Anjou at Barcelona.

Berry's death shocked Castile as well. Enrique, with no more hope of allying the ten-year-old La Beltraneja with France, sent his ambassadors scurrying off to Naples to find her a new prospective husband. Shortly before Berry's death, Enrique had already met with King Afonso V of Portugal in the vain hope of arranging a marriage between him and the girl.

Now Enrique made overtures to the son of the Neapolitan king Ferrante, who himself was the bastard of the long-deceased Alfonso V of Aragón, a former *Infante* of Aragón. By virtue of that old relationship, Enrique's new son-in-law would have become Prince of Castile and thus would pose a challenge to his cousin Prince Ferdinand. As Ferrante was bound in a diplomatic pact with his uncle, King Juan of Aragón, he soon turned down Enrique's proposal.

Like Louis XI, Enrique was beginning to find himself alone and friendless, grasping at shadowy allies in a world that was bound by treaties whose unifying link seemed to be the King of Aragón.

King Juan continued to triumph. In May and June the perseverant Aragonese monarch wore down the Catalonian towns of Montserrat, Sarria, Badalona, Vic, and Manresa. The once-proud and well-governed port city of Barcelona with its beautiful plazas and parks now languished in a state of siege. There was every reason to believe that its hungry citizens would soon be brought to their knees. Already songs were circulating among the Barcelonians reproaching them for their political "infidelity" to Aragón—to their betrayals with France, with Portugal, even with Castile—and admonishing them to return faithfully to Juan or, if not, at least to his son Ferdinand.

King Juan had summoned Ferdinand to Aragón at the end of the winter in 1472. In March the prince traveled to the Aragonese capital Zaragoza on the Ebro, where, acting as *lugartemiente general,* or lieutenant general, of the crown of Aragón, he remained for three months. Then, in July Ferdinand traveled to the royal palace in Pedralbes near Barcelona where he was finally reunited with his father. Three years had passed since they had met. During that time Ferdinand had married, fathered a child, and won battles of his own on Isabella's behalf. Now, at the age of twenty, the prince was an adult in all respects, a fitting heir to the Aragonese throne. As such, King Juan thus wanted his son by his side, both to complete negotiations to end the Catalonian war and to cement an alliance with Charles the Bold.

Juan had another motive for summoning his son to Aragón that spring—to meet Rodrigo Borgia, Sixtus IV's papal *nuncio,* whose arrival from Rome was imminent. Borgia was bringing with him the long-sought papal dispensation legitimizing Isabella and Ferdinand's marriage and something else equally precious—an open mind and a sybaritic appetite for worldly goods that the Aragonese king was prepared to sate. Shrewd politician that he was, Juan knew the value of a face-to-face meeting. Once Borgia had the opportunity to meet Ferdinand, Juan was convinced that the legate would champion Isabella's cause.

Little is known about Isabella's life during Ferdinand's absence, but there is enough evidence to suggest that these must have been among the most unsettled days of her life. At the beginning of March 1472, Isabella, the prince, their infant daughter, and their small court had traveled with Carrillo back to Alcalá de Henares and from there Ferdinand had left for Aragón. For the first time in Isabella's marriage, she was to be separated from Ferdinand for more than a few days. And to make his departure even more wrenching, she was now left to live under the jurisdiction of the temperamental archbishop.

The separation undoubtedly unnerved Isabella. With every departure for war or battle, husbands and wives wondered if they would see each other again. On the eve of Ferdinand's departure, Isabella sent her father-in-law a note that expressed the depth of her grief. "Lord, my excellence, I was greatly distressed to learn about the entrance of the French against Your Royal Lordship and the other things that happened as a result, and it gives me great anguish not to accompany the Prince with help to Your Majesty."[3]

In addition to her fears about Ferdinand's safety, Isabella was plagued with other worries. Her husband was traveling back to Aragón, to the kingdom not only of his birth but where other women had welcomed him into their beds. It was entirely likely that when he arrived in Aragón, Ferdinand would embrace the two *barraganas* he had made mothers, and perhaps others as well.

But if the princess suffered normal pangs of jealousy over Ferdinand's paramours, she was also a sensitive judge of her man. Isabella, as the chroniclers had already begun to observe, knew how to treat Ferdinand *con blandura,* with tact. More than likely on the eve of his departure she treated him with soft words and tenderness. She knew that when he returned, Ferdinand would bring the papal dispensation that would at last validate their marriage. No woman, no matter how beautiful or alluring, could compete with the laws of the church and the crown of Castile.

To comfort herself and proclaim her unity with Ferdinand to the world, Isabella did what sweethearts have done since time immemorial when faced with a long separation—she wore his emblem. Thus in July 1472 when ambassadors from the Burgundian court of Charles the Bold arrived in Alcalá to seal an alliance with Isabella and Carrillo, they were honored with jousts, bullfights, and banquets. Isabella and her ladies-in-waiting appeared at those festivities in such splendor that even the ambassadors from the opulent Burgundian court were impressed. The coppery-blond princess arrived on a horse covered with gilded silver armor that glittered in the sunlight. Isabella was crowned with a jeweled coronet and wore a *brial,* or rich dress of crimson velvet trimmed with green hoops topped by a fringed satin coat. The magnificence of her costume was completed by thick golden strands that prominently displayed "a necklace of arrows"—the *flechas* that Isabella had taken at the time of her marriage to symbolize her love for Ferdinand.

CHAPTER NINETEEN

Rodrigo Borgia

Rodrigo Borgia, Cardinal–Vice-chancellor of the Catholic church, arrived in the coastal port of Valencia on June 18, 1472. Tall, dark, and strikingly handsome, the forty-year-old cardinal had returned to his episcopal see of Valencia after an absence of many years. Officially, the new pope, Sixtus IV, had dispatched Borgia to Valencia to ensure peace in Aragón and Castile. But before he finished, the pleasure-loving cardinal would forge alliances that not only advanced his own Aragonese properties but secured Isabella's claim to the Castilian crown.

Borgia was a native Valencian, born to an aristocratic family in the nearby village of Játivia in the southern Valencian *huerta,* or fertile valley. In 1455, when his uncle Alonso Borgia became Pope Calixtus III, he heaped titles on Rodrigo, who became a cardinal at the age of twenty-five. Rodrigo, who would himself someday become Pope Alexander VI, was urbane, politic, and charming. He also had an eye for the ladies. Early in his career his tutor, Gaspare da Verone, noted that Borgia "excites the weaker sex in a strange manner more powerfully than iron is drawn to magnet . . . Yet he skillfully hides his conquests. . . ."[1] Still, Borgia's intelligence and energy quickly made him a favorite of the next two popes, Pius II and Paul II, and through their influence he gradually amassed power within the church and a huge personal fortune.

Finally, on August 22, 1471, when Borgia crowned Sixtus IV as pope, he was awarded even greater honors—the rich Benedictine abbey church of Subiaco, and the title of Cardinal Bishop of Albano and the treasurer of the Sacred College of Cardinals. Despite his high rank and oaths of chastity and celibacy, Borgia maintained a liaison with a beautiful and wealthy woman named Vannozza Cattanei.

Nevertheless, two days after his June arrival in Valencia, the urbane, bejeweled cardinal made a triumphal march through the city under a glittering canopy. As Borgia passed through the Serrano gate, which was bedecked in satin for his arrival, Valencian dignitaries stepped forward to greet him. Trumpets blared, bulls were "run" through the streets, and knights jousted in nearby tilting fields to honor the papal *nuncio*. That night Borgia hosted the city fathers in a banquet with food so rare and opulent that the city historian refused to describe it "in order not to shame St. Peter."[2]

Borgia had arrived in Valencia with the papal dispensation that legitimized Isabella and Ferdinand's marriage. In addition, he brought several other papal bulls, granting favors to the Valencian clergy. But those were only gilded trifles meant to dazzle and obscure Borgia's true mission. The new pope had resolved to renew his predecessor's plan of routing the Ottoman Turks from Europe. In one year he already spent 144,000 gold ducats to build a fleet of twenty-four galleys and amassed a 4,000-man force. Now, to continue the crusade, Sixtus needed to solicit support from the Christian kings of Western Europe: Thus he had appointed five other legates including Borgia, to raise funds from his Christian subjects. But to do so in Spain, to ask Aragón and Castile to pool their resources, meant each kingdom must first be at peace.

Thus Borgia met with Ferdinand on August 13–14, 1472, in the coastal city of Tarragona to discuss the Castilian succession. The cardinal was immediately impressed with the Aragonese prince. Several days later, in a meeting with King Juan, he affirmed his commitment to Isabella and Ferdinand as the next monarchs of Castile. In exchange for Juan's pledge to support Sixtus's crusade, Borgia even promised to advance Isabella's claim to the Castilian crown.

Borgia was to be well recompensed for those efforts for he had hinted, if not directly stated, his preference for a fiefdom near his native Játivia, which would provide a princely inheritance for his eldest bastard son, Pedro Luis. There was only one obstacle: The cardinal had promised Sixtus that he would refrain from interfering in the quarrel about the Castilian succession. Thus Borgia's promise to King Juan and Ferdinand had to remain a matter of strictest secrecy.

Enrique had similar plans for currying favor with Borgia. Eager to win the *nuncio* to his side in supporting La Beltraneja, the king had dispatched his most respected prelate, Bishop Mendoza, to Valencia. The bishop had gone willingly for he too sought a favor—a cardinalship. In a carefully staged show of power, Mendoza swept into Valencia on October 20 in his own dramatic procession. Once again the native Valencians rushed into the streets to witness his arrival, announced by two blacks beating enormous drums and a brightly dressed band playing trumpets and smaller drums. Like the papal *nuncio,* Mendoza was celebrated with fiestas, bullfights, and jousts that were so elaborate the citizens gleefully dubbed the two prelates "rivals of ostentation."[3]

There were, however, deeper currents of *simpatico* between the prelates. Both men were not only *bon vivantes* but intelligent, political creatures whose acumen had enabled their rise in the church. Accordingly, Mendoza presented himself most amiably to the cardinal and, gleaning Borgia's loyalty to Ferdinand, espoused his own secret preference for the prince and princess. Before long the shrewd Aragonese king stepped in to seal the pact. To ensure Mendoza's pledge to Isabella and Ferdinand, Juan promised to surrender certain Castilian properties to Mendoza and his clan.

This new agreement also had to be kept strictly secret—this time because neither prelate was in a position to alienate Enrique. Borgia was still obliged to talk the Castilian king into supporting the Turkish crusade, and Mendoza hoped to win more land and favors from him. Thus, as the two strategists left Valencia on November 2 and traveled north toward Madrid, few people suspected that their meetings had involved anything more than spiritual matters.

For weeks Enrique had anticipated Borgia's visit as a prelude to the same warm, favored relationship he had enjoyed with Pope Paul II. Thus, when on November 15, 1472, Borgia was escorted by Mendoza through the gates of Madrid, a massive conclave of knights, *caballeros, grandees,* and ecclesiastics "dressed in very rich clothes and capes" dutifully assembled. In tribute to the friendship with the Holy See, *regidores,* or urban counsellors, and knights held a brocade canopy above Borgia upon which were painted the arms of the pope and the king. Slowly, with all the dignity of his papal rank, Borgia, flanked on the left by Enrique who walked "a few steps ahead," proceeded to the Church of Santiago for a high mass.[4]

By late December, Borgia had so thoroughly charmed the king and assured him of Sixtus's favor that Enrique stated that "as a Catholic King and son of obedience he was ready to agree with the bull that the Holy Father had sent him."[5]

Ironically, Isabella's older brother had little inkling that the greatest threat to his kingdom lay not with the infidel but with Christians who lived considerably closer to home.

By December 22 Ferdinand had returned to Castile and hurried to Isabella's side in the town of Torrelaguna. Just why the princess had moved with her daughter and her court to that small town south of the Tagus River is not known. Possibly she wanted to distance herself from Carrillo, or perhaps she had moved there to garner more political support from the neighboring citizens.

Isabella received Ferdinand there before Christmas, joyous with his safe return, grateful for the bull that sanctioned their marriage. To add to her happiness, Ferdinand reported that Borgia had promised to legitimize their blond, blue-eyed daughter, who was by then already over a year old. In fact, the *nuncio* had even agreed to serve as the child's godfather. Moreover, in the last weeks of Ferdinand's visit to Aragón the city of Barcelona had finally surrendered to King Juan, making Ferdinand the heir to the Aragonese kingdom and all its principalities.

If Borgia had any doubts about the wisdom of supporting Isabella and Ferdinand over La Beltraneja, they were quickly resolved at Alcalá de Henares, Carrillo's castle palace. The *nuncio* already knew Ferdinand, but had not yet met the princess. While the details of their first meeting have not been preserved, Borgia's subsequent behavior suggests he found Isabella intelligent, sensitive, and worthy of assuming the Castilian throne.

Carrillo, meanwhile, went nearly bankrupt in his efforts to flatter Borgia and win his favor. So intent was the archbishop upon winning the miter that when the *nuncio* arrived at his castle, Carrillo virtually overwhelmed him with ceremonial pomp. In Borgia's honor, the archbishop staged grandiose receptions followed by a dizzying series of processions, banquets, and entertainments.

To feed the hundreds of guests whom he summoned for the festivities, Carrillo's servants collected, as Palencia wryly observed, "so many chickens from the surrounding villages that all the cocks were left looking frightfully lonely. . . ."[6] Mountains of barley were transported to the fields near the archbishop's palace as fodder for his guests' horses and mules. In addition, Carrillo's servants gathered "herds of sheep and calves, turkeys, capons," grain, and countless gallons of wine.

But while Borgia was cordial and polite, he was obviously not impressed. Despite Carrillo's efforts to pander to the *nuncio*'s creature comforts, the archbishop had "not captured the spirit of the cardinal."[7] Three weeks after his arrival, Borgia left Alcalá de Henares and moved twenty-four miles north to Mendoza's palace in Guadalahara. Before leaving, he proposed that the young prince and princess join him there for a more lengthy visit.

Carrillo was crushed. To prevent Isabella and Ferdinand from accepting the *nuncio*'s offer, he frightened them with predictions of imminent ruin. If they were foolish enough to move to Mendoza's estates, they would "be conceding the oath [to the throne] to the daughter of the Queen." And once in the possession of the Mendoza clan, he believed they would risk "losing their privilege of freedom."[8]

In Aragón, meanwhile, King Juan, knowing Mendoza's secret commitment to Isabella and Ferdinand, encouraged them to accept his offer. But ultimately Isabella and Ferdinand refused. Perhaps they felt guilt about defying the archbishop. And they were also genuinely worried about Pacheco. On March 17, 1473, Ferdinand wrote his father that he and Isabella had decided against the trip because they feared "the Master of Santiago [Pacheco] was going to mediate in the agreement."[9] A week later Ferdinand wrote Juan that Borgia's invitation to Guadalahara was not important because "all the work that had been done to assure the succession of the most serene Princess, my Ladyship wife, and everything that surrounds it has been completed."[10]

Indeed, Borgia had faithfully fulfilled his part of the bargain. Before leaving Alcalá de Henares, the *nuncio* had declined an invitation to visit Queen Juana and La Beltraneja. Furthermore, as Ferdinand wrote in that same March 24 letter, Borgia refused to grant a dispensation for another of Enrique's marriage schemes for La Beltraneja ". . . and other things that would damage and do a disservice to our Ladyship [Isabella] and yours."[11]

Meanwhile, on March 7, with the high pomp of an important religious ceremony, Borgia had entered Guadalahara in his scarlet surplice to confer the cardinal's miter on Pedro González de Mendoza, Bishop of Sigüenza and the youngest brother of the Mendoza clan. After the ceremonies Borgia and the Mendozas had returned to Madrid where they were received by Enrique, Pacheco, and the rest of the court. With the acquisition of the purple beretta, Mendoza, now Archbishop of Sevilla and Cardinal of Santa Maria in Dominica by order of Pope Sixtus IV, was suddenly the most powerful prelate in Castile.

Carrillo was devastated by the news. He had been Archbishop of Toledo for twenty-five years, and that, it appeared, would be the highest position he was to attain in the church. Despite his valiant efforts, the fiery archbishop had not transmuted anything into gold—especially his own life of sixty years which he now began to regard as little better than mortal dross.

CHAPTER TWENTY

Concessions

During Borgia's visit to Castile, a foppish young *caballero* and his mother traveled from Aragón to the Castilian village of Requena. By Enrique's orders, attendants escorted the youth and his entourage to the castle of Garcí Muñoz near Madrid, which had been lavishly outfitted for his arrival.

Enrique Fortuna, as the pompous young man was called, was Enrique's latest candidate as bridegroom for La Beltraneja, chosen to challenge Isabella's husband Ferdinand as a parallel cousin in the Trastámara line. Fortuna, like Ferdinand, was one of Fernando I's grandsons and, thus, King Juan's nephew.

During the Catalonian civil war Juan had protected Fortuna's lands from the French. Yet when, in late 1472 or early 1473, Enrique dispatched an envoy offering the youth La Beltraneja as his bride, Fortuna promptly forgot his uncle's generosity and instead boasted about his willingness to pit himself against his cousin for the Castilian crown.

Pacheco was at least partially responsible for the youth's bravado, for he had filled Fortuna with images of becoming the most powerful king of the Iberian peninsula. That courtier had conceived the match months earlier and eventually persuaded Fortuna's Castilian uncle, Rodrigo Pimentel, Count of Benavente, to suggest it to Enrique. As usual, Pacheco's motives were money and power.

But Fortuna was a pauper as well as a blowhard. To the initial amusement and eventual contempt of the Castilian court, he became a habitual guest at the tables of his fellow *grandees,* repeatedly borrowing money, clothes, and other essentials "to satisfy the necessities" of life.[1] Moreover, after Cardinal Borgia deliberately failed to provide Fortuna with a papal dispensation, the youth's status as a suitable marriage prospect for La Beltraneja dimmed. Nevertheless, by the spring of 1473

Pacheco had succeeded in negotiating the match. For his efforts he demanded a reward of 15 million maravedís.

Enrique initially agreed to Pacheco's request. However, the king's *mayordomo mayor,* or chief steward Andrés de Cabrera, who administered the Segovian alcázar and royal treasury, was appalled at Pacheco's request and balked. The *mayordomo*'s reluctance, Fortuna's poverty, and his failure to obtain a papal dispensation made him an even less attractive candidate than before. Gradually Enrique lost his enthusiasm for the marriage and began to think of Fortuna only as a bridegroom of last resort. Finally, in 1474, when it became blatantly obvious that Enrique had lost all interest in Fortuna, the youth and his mother returned to the kingdom of Aragón.

Cabrera's reluctance to pay Pacheco was a carefully calculated act. The *mayordomo,* a forty-three-year-old *converso,* was bright, judicious, and admired by his contemporaries for "his generous qualities, his singular prudence in government and his solicitude for his vassals." It was, in fact, precisely because of those qualities that Enrique had gradually elevated Cabrera to the position of *mayordomo.* By 1466 Cabrera was so highly esteemed that he had even married Isabella's childhood friend, Beatriz de Bobadilla.

Pacheco, however, envied Cabrera's rise. By 1472 he was so alarmed by Cabrera's position that he pitted himself against the *converso* for control over the royal alcázar of Madrid. Finally in September, after a bitter struggle, Cabrera agreed to cede the Madrid palace to Pacheco on the condition that the match between Fortuna and La Beltraneja was arranged. Cabrera insisted, however, upon maintaining control over Castile's "second capital," Enrique's beloved Segovia.

When in the spring of 1473 Cabrera refused to release the 15 million maravedís to Pacheco, the embittered favorite vowed to wrest Segovia from the *mayordomo* in revenge. To do so, Pacheco set about fomenting dissension between the old Christians of Segovia and the *conversos.* He blamed their complaints on the city's highest official, Cabrera.

Anti-Semitism smoldered just beneath the surface of everyday life in fifteenth-century Castile. In the years immediately before Isabella's birth, relations among the old Christians, the *conversos,* and the Jews had gradually worsened. In 1449, for instance, the old Christians of Toledo had protested the new taxes that Álvaro de Luna had imposed on them and stormed the houses of the *converso* tax collectors and the city's Jewish section in revenge.

Sixteen years later the *conversos* of Sevilla defeated the old Christians in a street battle. In 1467 the old Christians of Toledo beat the *conversos* into submission and hanged their leader from a church belfry. The following year Enrique's allies capitalized on that animosity to win the city to his side and abandon the cause of Isabella's brother, Prince Alfonso.

By 1473, four years after Toros de Guisando, the old Christians and *conversos* still maintained little more than an uneasy peace. In spring of that year their ill feelings, aggravated by food shortages, inflation, and Enrique's devaluation of the coinage, finally exploded.

In Andalusia, as in most of Castile, tensions over money and power were at the root of the turmoil. After 1391 many *conversos* had intermarried with members of the old Castilian aristocracy, and in Córdoba their descendants had become influential citizens. By 1473 a chronicler noted that "there was great enmity and jealousy because the new Christians of that city were very rich and continued to buy offices [high positions] in such numbers that the old Christians were not able to bear it."[2]

One March day a *converso* girl in Córdoba dumped a chamber pot out of a second-story window. The contents splashed onto a statue of the Virgin Mary being carried through the streets by members of a religious fraternity that excluded *conversos*. The procession came to an immediate halt. The silence was broken by a blacksmith who angrily observed that the fluid dripping over the statue was urine. Before long, other members of the fraternity denounced the act as a symbol of *converso* desecration, a "deliberate defiance" of the "holy Christian faith."[3]

Within hours, throngs of infuriated Córdobans were howling in the streets for retribution against the *conversos*. "We are going to avenge ourselves for this great injury and everyone will die who are traitors and heretics!" they vowed.[4] In a murderous rage, the crowds stampeded through the city, leaving plundered homes and bloody corpses of the *conversos* in their wake. So frenzied were the vigilantes that when Córdoba's *alcalde,* the justice of the peace, Alonso de Aguilar, appeared, hoping "that his presence would restore peace to the people," he was brutally battered and robbed.[5]

By then the whole city was at war: the old Christians against the *conversos,* the townspeople against the aristocrats, the rich against the poor, the privileged against the commoners. On the third morning, a few miles beyond the charred beams and burning embers of the blood-soaked city, rampaging crowds appeared in Córdoba's suburbs. To the west, the *converso* Constable of Castile, Miguel Lucas de Iranzo, was bludgeoned to death at the altar of the Church of Santa Maria. Thereafter the riots spread to other Andalusian towns, including Écija, Jerez, Carmona, and Andujar.

The timing of these pogroms was not surprising. Easter was traditionally a season when anti-Semitic sentiments were whipped to a froth by fanatic preachers with stories of *converso* or Jewish desecration of the host and ritualistic murders of Christian children. Over the years superstition and hearsay had jumbled together in the minds of the ordinary citizens, to be exploited by the priests as a means of recalling their wayward flocks to worship. During Isabella's lifetime the most famous of those preachers was Fra Alonso de Espina, confessor to Enrique IV, whose slanderous tract *Fortalitium Fideli,* or "Fortress of the Faith," methodically condemned *conversos* and Jews for corrupting the Christian faith.

In the wake of the 1473 Córdoban riots, it was thus relatively easy for Pacheco to stir up similar anti-Semitic sentiment in Segovia. His specific target was Cabrera, both because of his Jewish blood and his sympathy for the Segovian *conversos*. Playing on the recent events in Andalusia, Pacheco spread stories that the *conversos* had commandeered the most influential positions in the city. With his usual eloquence Pacheco also persuaded the old Christians of Segovia that the *conversos* were defiling the church with secret Jewish rites. Before long there were protests in the streets.

Some of Segovia's old Christians nevertheless regarded Pacheco as a master schemer who was "the friend of the Christian religion only to extend his tyranny."[6] Suddenly, new groups of protestors gathered to avenge their wrath upon

Pacheco himself. Within a few days they had driven Enrique's favorite out of Segovia and forced him to seek refuge in a nearby monastery.

Subsequently, Cabrera and the *conversos* made peace with the old Christians. Pacheco was never to see Segovia again—henceforth he was forbidden to enter the city.

Pacheco's final act of aggression convinced Cabrera to pledge Segovia to Isabella's cause. For years he had secretly sympathized with the princess's claim to the Castilian throne, but even after his marriage to Isabella's closest friend, he had not defected from Enrique. Instead, the prudent *mayordomo* adopted a posture similar to that assumed by Cardinal Mendoza, one of public obedience to Enrique but private support for Isabella.

Pacheco's machinations at Segovia finally forced Cabrera to confront an unpleasant truth: Enrique would never agree to make Isabella his heir as long as he remained under Pacheco's influence. Thus Cabrera decided to effect a reconciliation between the king and Isabella.

At first Isabella hesitated. To assure the princess of her safety, Cabrera penned an agreement dated June 15, 1473, in which the "Monarchs of Sicily"—Isabella and Ferdinand—agreed to "honor the Lord King" by traveling to Segovia with Carrillo to meet the King.[7] In turn, Cabrera assured Isabella of his support by guaranteeing that if Enrique failed to reconcile or if civil war erupted again, he would place Segovia, its alcázar, and the royal treasury at her command.

When Isabella signed Cabrera's document on June 15, 1473, she was alone. Ferdinand had gone to his father's aid in Catalonia. By late spring 1473, King Juan was trapped in Perpignan, the capital city of Roussillon, surrounded by 30,000 French soldiers and heavy artillery.

His earlier victory over the French was the cause of his predicament. After the October 1472 surrender of Barcelona, the citizens of French-held Roussillon and Cerdagne began to agitate for freedom. Juan, lured by the chance to reclaim his old lands, went to their rescue. At first, victory seemed assured. Louis XI was involved in a war against Burgundy and had already evacuated his men to northern France. The Aragonese army crossed the Pyrenees to Cerdagne and Roussillon, and by late winter had reconquered all their old territories except a few towns. But on April 10 Louis moved 30,000 soldiers back south.

On April 30, just before Ferdinand left for Aragón, Isabella wrote King Juan to express her sympathies for the French counteroffensive: "I was so sad about the attack of the French against your royal domain that if things here allowed it, I would not restrain myself from going with my lord the Prince to succor your Majesty, because the trip would be less painful than his lordship's departure . . ."[8]

But Isabella had her own problems within the Castilian court. Unlike Ferdinand, who could wage a war for repossession of his Catalonian inheritance, Isabella's only hope of reclaiming the Castilian crown depended on her passivity, and her ability to trust the goodwill of her friends, Beatriz de Bobadilla and Andrés de Cabrera.

Little by little the political pendulum was swinging in Isabella's favor. By August several new towns in the Castilian *Meseta* pledged their allegiance to the princess—Moya, Aranda de Duero, Agreda, and the Vizcayan town of Bilbao. For years the Andalusian Duke of Medina Sidonia had publicly declared his loyalty to Isabella, and in the summer of 1473 other nobles began to join him—among them Carrillo's old ally, Rodrigo Manrique, the Count of Paredes; Alonso de Cárdenas, the *commendador mayor,* or knight commander of León; and Gabriel Manrique, the Count of Osorno.

Even Pacheco, never comfortable with a losing cause, switched sides in Isabella's favor. Characteristically, he did so for a price: In return for a pledge of loyalty to Isabella and Ferdinand, Pacheco secured a promise from King Juan to arrange a marriage between his daughter and the Aragonese king's illegitimate son, the Archbishop of Zaragoza.

Enrique, too, now began to think about Isabella in a new light. He had still not secured a marriage between La Beltraneja and Afonso. Moreover, most of Andalusia and many towns in northern Castile now supported Isabella's claim to the crown. In addition, so did many trusted counselors.

With the approach of the Christmas holidays, Enrique traveled to Segovia, hoping, as usual, to spend his days hunting in the woods of El Bazaín. But this time he had to travel without Pacheco. As a result, Enrique was alone and more vulnerable than he had been in years.

No one was more aware of the king's mood than Cabrera and his wife. Soon after Enrique's arrival, Beatriz met privately with him. Enrique had always been fond of the dark-haired young woman, and now he listened to her respectfully as she pleaded forgiveness for Isabella. Now, Beatriz reasoned, if Enrique would reconcile with the prince and princess, the kingdom of Castile would be returned to peace, "like a tree whose dried branches turned green again" and "would never again weep."[9]

Enrique was deeply moved by Beatriz's speech. Clearly, he was as anxious about the future as he was chagrined about the past. Thus he finally agreed to meet with his half sister.

> . . . Not because I believe this to be the remedy to the problems
> of my royal position but to try this path and see whether it is freer
> of obstacles than the others . . . If my evil doings and thoughts
> have brought this on me, it is natural that I . . . should be pun-
> ished now and so I am pleased to see the Prince and Princess.
> And as I don't see any solution . . . they, more innocent than I
> am, maybe will be able to find one . . . In these matters I can-
> not lose anything that I have not already lost. I am like a man
> numbed in his limbs and mind by many wounds, and who is
> healed back from death . . .[10]

On December 27, 1473, an old peasant woman knocked at Isabella's palace in Aranda de Duero near Valladolid. After inviting the woman in, the princess discovered her visitor was Beatriz de Bobadilla, elaborately disguised. Beatriz's message was simple and direct: Enrique had agreed to meet with Isabella in Segovia. But the princess had best come at once in utter secrecy before the king had a chance to change his mind again.

CHAPTER TWENTY-ONE

A Visit to Segovia

The end of December 1473 must have been one of the happiest times of Isabella's young life. A few days before Beatriz's visit Ferdinand had returned from Aragón where he had become a national hero. In June Ferdinand and his Aragonese *grandees* had led 1,300 lancers and 7,000 infantrymen into battle against the French in Perpignan and, in a driving rain, achieved a "wondrous triumph."[1]

When the French surrendered, the small, aged King Juan "marched out, with colors flying and music playing at the head of his little band."[2] Then, in a touching moment observed by both armies, Juan embraced his son and in a voice filled with emotion declared, "Lucky me who can call myself the father of my liberty and the liberator of my country!"[3]

Finally, on July 14, Louis and Juan signed a truce in which they agreed that the Aragonese king would pay 250,000 écus within a year to ensure the return of Cerdagne and Roussillon. If he failed to do so, the two provinces would be permanently annexed to France. Despite their official agreement, neither Juan nor Louis XI trusted each other. In the tenuous peace that followed, Ferdinand was thus compelled to remain in Aragón for another five months to help re-establish the civil order.

Ferdinand's victory elevated him to nearly saintly dimensions. "The French had to make peace with our prince, whose name is exalted on this day. Thus begins his rule of the Spains," wrote an Aragonese canon, in what would be the first of many such accolades.[4] Once Ferdinand returned to Castile and was greeted by Isabella with reports about a meeting with Enrique, the Aragonese prelate's pronouncements must have seemed prophetic.

On December 25 Isabella, Ferdinand, and their three-year-old daughter spent

Christmas together in Arando del Duero. In the fifteenth century, Christmas was celebrated simply, even among members of the royalty. Minstrels sang carols in anticipation of the holiday and town markets were piled high with goods—plump fowl and handsome bolts of cloth. On Christmas Eve the citizens lighted tiny oil lamps in their homes, and at midnight they attended a Christmas mass. Although Christmas dinner was traditional, the festivities—the exchange of gifts, the parade of city officials dressed as Oriental kings who tossed sweets and coins to the bystanders—all were saved for Epiphany, or January 6.

Despite her pleasure at Beatriz's announcement, Isabella had a new cause for anxiety: Both Enrique and Cabrera requested that she bring her child to Segovia to be placed in the *mayordomo*'s guardianship. The little girl was to serve as a "guarantee" of Isabella's good faith in exchange for Cabrera's own promises. Although Ferdinand and Carrillo agreed to the request, Isabella flatly refused. She was passionately attached to her young daughter and too familiar with Enrique's vacillations to risk her child. Instead, as she coolly told the archbishop, she intended to reward Cabrera by awarding him the town of Moya when she became queen.

As if in one voice Ferdinand and Carrillo observed that it made no sense for Isabella to jeopardize the meeting by refusing to accommodate Cabrera. But the princess was adamant: The child, she reiterated, would remain in Aranda del Duero when she visited Enrique in Segovia.

This was one of the first times Ferdinand found himself locked in a struggle with his wife. The other side of Isabella's stalwart personality, he was gradually learning, was obstinacy. In a pique of temper that would be repeated later in his marriage, Ferdinand accused Isabella of "stubbornness."[5]

There was, however, little time for argument. According to Beatriz, Enrique had left the Segovian alcázar on December 26 and departed immediately for his hunting lodge in El Bazaín. On December 28 the princess and Carrillo traveled to Segovia where they were greeted by Beatriz, Cabrera, and the Count of Benavente. Simultaneously, a messenger was dispatched into the woods to notify Enrique of his sister's arrival.

Late that afternoon Isabella and Enrique were finally reunited in the courtyard of the Segovian alcázar. Brother and sister embraced, and then Enrique led Isabella into an interior chamber of the castle "where they spent a long time talking."[6] The years had changed them both. At forty-nine Enrique was aging, his white skin even paler now from a recent illness. At twenty-two Isabella was less a girl than a woman in her prime childbearing years, the slender lines of her figure already beginning to fill in with maturity.

After dining together, Enrique and Isabella sequestered themselves again. Isabella told him:

> Lord, I have arrived for two reasons. "The first to see your High-
> ness as a father and lord and older brother as blood relations de-
> mand. In the second, to beg you to erase any grudge you may
> have against me, and, as I begged in my letters, to maintain and
> observe what you promised and ordered, when you wanted me

sworn as crown princess and legitimate successor to your position, because in this way the will of God will be fulfilled and otherwise to do the contrary would be certain to bring great evils upon these realms.[7]

Enrique may have been surprised by Isabella's bold words, but he merely answered that he was delighted with her visit.

The next day a magnificent feast was held in the alcázar. As was the custom in great households of fifteenth-century Europe, the floors were strewn with sweet-smelling rushes and spices and white linen tableclothes were spread upon the long trestles that served as dining tables. Servants rushed between the great hall and kitchen with large covered tureens and plates of wild boar, venison, salmon, and other delicacies, perhaps even the swans and peacocks that were frequent fare at royal banquets. At the end of the meal, musicians strummed on lutes and other *rodallas,* or string instruments.

A day or so later, in a gentle, snowy mist, Enrique walked through the city streets holding the reins of Isabella's white horse. Above him, the russet-haired young woman rode silently, with modest dignity at the honor. The moment was so poignant, so moving that it has been recorded in several contemporary accounts. To the Segovian citizens this public display of affiliation meant the king and the princess had reconciled.

To Isabella and Enrique, the *paseo,* or walk, after the largest meal of the day was less a promise than the first tentative steps toward a renewal of old filial affections that had been nearly extinguished during the princess's winter in Ocaña. Nevertheless, Enrique still scrupulously avoided all talk about the succession of the Castilian throne.

Ferdinand waited in the nearby town of Sepúlveda, and on New Year's Day 1474, at Isabella's invitation, appeared in Segovia to meet Enrique. The king treated Ferdinand warmly—so affectionately, in fact, that the prince wrote enthusiastically to Barcelona's city fathers about the *confederacio e concordia,* the "fellowship and harmony" they enjoyed together.[8] Inevitably, Enrique warmed to Ferdinand. "Everybody was delighted," an observer reported. "The Prince danced in the King's presence and it would take too long to tell how much the latter rejoiced in this. The King could not have been more satisfied with the Prince."[9]

In the first days of 1474 Enrique, Isabella, and Ferdinand were constant companions, dining, riding their horses together through the streets of Segovia, obviously "abiding with much love."[10] But although the delicate subject of the succession had been broached, it had not yet been resolved.

On Sunday, January 9, Cabrera invited the king, the prince, and princess to a banquet at the home of Segovia's bishop, Juan Arías Dávilla. The house, the *casa episcopales,* adjoined the city's cathedral, which then stood across the square from the alcázar. Isabella and Ferdinand had been living there during their stay in Segovia.

In fifteenth-century Castile, as now, it was customary to serve the major meal of the day in early afternoon. Thus after Enrique, Isabella and Ferdinand made a morning tour of Segovia by horseback, they arrived at Arías's handsome stone palace and seated themselves around a white-linen table that was laden with food.

During the meal the king sat at the head of the table. Next to him sat Isabella and Ferdinand.

At the meal's conclusion, Enrique, Isabella, Ferdinand, and the other guests retired to an adjacent room where musicians entertained with instruments and singers and where they nibbled leisurely at a "sumptuous collection" of desserts—fresh cheeses, puff pastries, fried dough cakes, and *almojevanes,* or cheese tarts. By then it was late afternoon. Attendants lighted wax candles and torches that must have contributed to the feelings of warmth and good humor from the banquet.

Suddenly the brightness of that afternoon banquet flickered and was extinguished forever. The king doubled over in his chair in pain, clutching one side of his abdomen. Isabella and Ferdinand rose from their chairs, as did others in the room. Then Enrique's attendants helped the king to another room where he could rest. Moments later they carried him across the square to the alcázar and into the royal bedchamber where doctors rushed to his side.

Whispers that the king had been poisoned filtered past the musicians who still sat mute in Bishop Arías's home, past the servants and guests who attended the banquet, and out into the icy, rutted streets of Segovia. In the alcázar, Isabella and Ferdinand kept an anxious vigil outside the royal bedchamber throughout the night.

CHAPTER TWENTY-TWO

Ninguna Cosa Respondio

ith news of the king's illness, Segovia became hushed with prayers. Priests marched through the narrow, hilly streets in solemn processions for the king's recovery. Special masses were held in the cathedral and churches. Chanting monks and nuns knelt in the monasteries and convents that ringed the city. Isabella and Ferdinand visited the king and prayed daily for his recovery, fearing that the momentum for their reconciliation had been shattered.

Their fears were soon realized. At first Enrique was too ill for the young couple to speak with him about the succession, and after he was better he avoided the subject altogether. Pacheco was at least partially responsible for the king's new diffidence, for from his watchpost in the northern village of Cuellar he sent messages insinuating that Enrique's illness was the result of foul play. Had it not occurred to the king, he wrote, that he had been poisoned by Isabella and Ferdinand, with Cabrera as an accomplice?

Enrique never completely recovered. For months after he was well enough to dress and resume his normal activities, he suffered bouts of diarrhea and bloody urine. Gradually his vigorous frame began to waste away.

His symptoms could well have been the result of poisoning, by arsenic or mercury. Another possibility was bacterial food poisoning, although no one else who attended Cabrera's banquet fell ill at that time. The king might also have been affected with diverticulosis, a condition common to middle-age people involving a small weakening, or herniation, in the intestinal wall, which, if left untreated, often results in hemorrhages. Or he might have been suffering from one of several other diseases, including ulcers, diverticulitis, gall bladder problems, appendicitis, or cancer.

Enrique recovered neither his health nor his initial enthusiasm for Isabella and Ferdinand. Whether he had been poisoned or not, the very possibility that the prince and princess could have been responsible for the attack made Enrique rethink his willingness for reconciliation. Thus he avoided all discussions about the succession to the Castilian throne.

Even so, Pacheco was not satisfied. His next impulse was to imprison Isabella, Ferdinand, and Cabrera.

Cardinal Mendoza scolded Enrique for allowing Pacheco to advance such a scheme. Enrique, had he reminded the king, had sworn Isabella as his legitimate heir. To imprison her or harm her in any other way would be to "do a great disservice"[1] to Castile. Without disclosing his secret loyalties to Isabella, the cardinal alluded to Enrique's precarious hold on the throne and his sister's growing popularity, which, if challenged, might very well open the floodgates of a new civil war. Chastened, Enrique ordered Pacheco and his spies to abandon their plans to incarcerate Isabella and Ferdinand or to harm them in any way.

Thereafter the charades between Isabella and Enrique began anew. Repeatedly the princess and her husband tried to reconcile with the king, but he brushed them aside. Isabella, meanwhile, was so worried about the safety of her daughter, who had been left with caretakers in Aranda de Duero, that Ferdinand fetched Isabel and brought her to Segovia.

The Segovians who had followed the events at court with keen interest wondered at Ferdinand's sudden departure and began to speculate about its cause. Before long the community was buzzing with rumors that the king and Ferdinand had quarreled, that the prince was being blamed for Enrique's illness, and that the king no longer trusted either Isabella or Ferdinand. To put an end to the gossip, Enrique and Isabella walked through Segovia to show that "none of their deeds were broken."[2] This time their *paseo* was calculated rather than spontaneous.

Soon afterward Ferdinand returned to Segovia with Isabel. But for all Mendoza's assurances that Isabella and Ferdinand were safe in Segovia, the city still held too many risks to keep their daughter with them. A few days later the youngster was bundled anew in heavy wraps and taken to the safer town of Ávila. Even though it meant separation from her daughter, Isabella was determined to stay in Segovia for she still clung to the dream of being reconciled with Enrique.

But it was not to be. One March night the impulsive king slipped out of Segovia. Possibly it was another of Pacheco's sleight-of-hand schemes. Or perhaps the king left on one of his own whims. Whatever his motives, Enrique's abrupt departure released him from the necessity of receiving a formal farewell visit from Isabella and confronting the succession issue again.

Nevertheless, Enrique was to pay a heavy price for his departure, for by so doing he symbolically ceded Segovia to Isabella. Isabella had waited Enrique out of the city through the sheer force of her will; her forbearance overcame his restlessness, her determination bested his indecision. The city of Segovia, its alcázar and royal treasury, now remained under Cabrera's control and thus implicitly belonged to Isabella.

Yet the princess may have only dimly understood her advantage. Enrique returned to Segovia several times during 1474, if only for short visits. Carrillo had become nearly as untrustworthy as Enrique for he had received private reassurances of royal support, and these, combined with his jealousy of the prince and princess's friendship with Cardinal Mendoza, had unraveled his loyalties. The only stability in Isabella's life was Ferdinand, and thus it was in him alone that the princess ultimately placed her trust.

Still, Pacheco refused to be defeated, to have his own lands repossessed by Aragón if Isabella and Ferdinand should become the next rulers of Castile. In the face of the couple's rising popularity, the guileful courtier renewed his efforts for a new marriage agreement for La Beltraneja.

Now Afonso V of Portugal was more amenable to the match than in 1473, but he demanded new terms, among them assurances that Juana would be named heir to Castile and that as her future husband, he would become king. Afonso also expected to receive specific funds and lands as part of La Beltraneja's dowry—including the town of Trujillo near the Portuguese border.

In Segovia, meanwhile, Ferdinand waited for the next opportunity to advance Isabella's cause. On June 20, 1474, the prince gathered three hundred lancers and marched north; two days later the prince, the Count of Alba, and their men scaled the walls of Tordesillas above the Duero River. The next day Ferdinand and his men captured that town's fortress and, to the undisguised joy of its citizens, claimed the town in Isabella's name.

Enrique, who had returned to Madrid, "declared his bitterness about the notice."[3] Even more upsetting, Ferdinand's victory had come just after another attack of the mysterious disease that was wasting his body. A day earlier Enrique had gone hunting in El Pardo when he suddenly doubled over in pain. This time, the *mal de sus gomitos*, the waves of nausea and vomiting, were so debilitating that Enrique failed to make his way back to the alcázar and was forced to seek refuge in the monastery of Santa María del Paso. After dark the monarch finally returned to the royal palace, so weakened that his servants had to carry him into his bedchamber.

But Pacheco would not let Enrique rest long. Bent on meeting Afonso's terms for marriage to La Beltraneja, Pacheco now sought to secure possession of Trujillo. Previous efforts to wrest that town from the new Duke of Arévalo, Álvaro de Stúñiga, had failed. Even when Pacheco had offered to exchange Trujillo with the duke for other privileges, Stúñiga had consistently declined. To Pacheco's irritation, even the noble's *alcalde* did not respond to the royal letters. The best solution, Pacheco thus reasoned, was for him and the king to appear personally in Trujillo.

Initially Enrique protested for he was afraid of becoming ill again far from home. Moreover, Trujillo was located in Extremadura, south of the Duero River, where the summer heat roared over the high plains like a furnace. It was bound to be an unpleasant trip, one that would test anybody's stamina, let alone the ailing king's. But Pacheco wheedled and coaxed relentlessly. Without Trujillo, he reminded Enrique in his urgent, tremulous voice, Afonso would not marry La Beltraneja.

Ultimately the king conceded, and in late July the two men and their entourage traveled the steaming, dust-filled roads to Trujillo. As they rode southwest from Madrid, Enrique and Pacheco learned that Extremadura was *mal sana*, stricken with the pestilence. When the king and Pacheco finally arrived in the granite-ledged town of Trujillo in the foothills of the Guadalupe Mountains, the Duke of Arévalo rebuffed them. Moreover, Trujillo's *alcalde,* Gracian de Sese, informed Enrique's messenger that he would not allow the king access to the town's square-towered fortress.

For several weeks Enrique and Pacheco stayed in the nearby village of Santa Cruz to plot their next strategy. But the king grew impatient and anxious in the relentless heat and, finally, observing that considerable "delays . . . would be involved in the negotiations," left for Madrid.[4] Pacheco, iron-willed to the last, resolved to stay.

The courtier's truculence did him in. By late September he finally arranged an exchange with the Duke of Arévalo by trading the fortress of Trujillo with the town of Sahelices de los Gallegos. Just as the final terms for the agreement were drawn up, Pacheco developed a throat abscess. Soon he was wracked with high fevers and began vomiting blood. The doctors lanced the abscess four times, but finally when it "grew hard like a stone" they were unable to relieve the courtier's suffering.[5]

Death now stared Pacheco directly in the face. But Pacheco, determined to obtain Trujillo, stared back just as boldly and continued with the final negotiations. Demanding that his servants tie him in a chair and make the bedroom *escura,* or dark, so that "the *alcalde* would not see how weak he was," Pacheco met for the final time with the official and obtained the keys to Trujillo.[6]

Pacheco had little time to savor his triumph. The next day he slipped into a coma and died. His servants promptly stripped him of his money and jewels and then, to avoid being caught, hid his corpse in a giant wine vat. Days later Pacheco's body was found and buried in the monastery of Santa María de Guadalupe.

In Madrid Enrique received the news "very heavily," as if it were a confirmation of his own death sentence.[7] So frequently had Pacheco provided the spark for Enrique's decisions that without him the king felt powerless. In his grief Enrique issued only one decree. He conferred Pacheco's highest title, the Master of Santiago, on his son, Diego López Pacheco. Enrique was exceedingly fond of Diego. He had, wrote Palencia, hinting at Enrique's homosexuality, an inordinate love for the youth.

In contrast, the Castilian citizens publicly rejoiced when they learned about Pacheco's death. With equal passion they protested the king's nomination of Pacheco's son as the new Master of Santiago. But Enrique was too sunk in grief and too ill to care any longer about popular opinion. The impolitic king had lost the one ally who had steered him through the shoals of aristocratic ambitions. In Enrique's loveless world, he was now dangerously adrift.

On October 24, 1474, Ferdinand received an urgent letter from Isabella's *maestresala,* Gutierre de Cárdenas. "My highest and most powerful Prince and King My Lord," the letter began, "I am writing to tell you that the Master of Santiago has died."[8]

Already, Enrique's appointment of Pacheco's son to the mastership had stirred up dissension, already other *grandees* were vying for the title. With King Juan's blessings, Ferdinand left Barcelona, abandoning the chance to help his father save Perpignan from a second French invasion. Unfortunately, the French truce of June 1473 had only lasted a few months.

The arrival of Cárdenas's letter presented Ferdinand with a new dilemma. By leaving Aragón, Ferdinand would abandon his father once more on behalf of his wife's claim to the Castilian Crown; yet if he stayed, Isabella's interests might well be trampled under the stampede of Castilian *grandees* vying for the Mastership of Santiago. In the end, Ferdinand compromised by traveling to Zaragoza from where he could cross the deeply gorged Ebro Valley and arrive in Castile in a few days.

At Zaragoza, Ferdinand tried to wrest a promise of war funds from the *Cortes,* but the *procuradores* dawdled. As the days passed the prince became increasingly worried, for Isabella's most recent letter suggested he should return to Castile at once. Less than a month after Pacheco's death, the Count of Osorno, a rival for the Mastership of Santiago, had imprisoned Pacheco's son. At least five other Castilian *grandees* were also competing for the title, and Isabella had refused to take sides. Instead she sent secret messengers to Pope Sixtus IV asking him to appoint Ferdinand the new Master of Santiago.

Meanwhile Ferdinand presided unhappily over the *Cortes,* growing more edgy every day, torn between loyalties to his Aragonese father and his Castilian wife. These two competing allegiances would perplex Ferdinand for most of his marriage, long after his father's death.

But on December 17, Ferdinand received news so shocking that he was forced to abandon the Catalonian cause altogether. A letter arrived notifying the Aragonese prince that Enrique IV, King of Castile and León, had died suddenly in Madrid.

Enrique's last days were as turbulent as the rest of his reign. In late October when he learned that the Count of Osorno had imprisoned Diego Pacheco, the king became so anguished that he "behaved like a madman," broke down in tears, and "would take no council" from his advisors.[9] He became so obsessed with the idea of freeing the young Diego himself that, despite doctors' protests, the agitated king, "whose affection [for Diego] overruled his reason" set out angrily for the Extremaduran town of Villarejo.[10] Among his escorts were Cardinal Mendoza, Carrillo, and the Count of Haro.

After three weeks Osorno agreed to free Pacheco's son and grant him the village of Maderuela. Still, the Mastership of Santiago remained unresolved.

Slowly Enrique retraced his steps to Madrid and sank into a langorous state. The king began to "live by caprice," eating excessively and refusing to take the medicines prescribed by his physicians.[11] Emotionally, his life was nearly as wasted as his body. Everything the monarch had once treasured or held dear seemed to be falling away from him. His oldest, best-loved advisor Pacheco was dead, and Enrique could not even reward his son Diego with assured possession of the Mastership of Santiago; Enrique was alienated from his wife, Queen Juana, who lived in Segovia's Convent of San Francisco; his daughter, La Beltraneja, was an unpopular choice for the Castilian throne; and his sister, Isabella, protected by

Cabrera and the royal treasury, maintained her little court in his beloved city of Segovia.

By December Enrique was too ill to travel to Segovia for the Christmas holidays. To soothe his spirits the king frequented the woods of El Pardo. But on Friday, December 9, he began to bleed profusely from his bowels. His appearance, says a chronicler, "was so disfigured . . . that it was awesome to see him."[12] For two days Enrique lay moaning and half conscious on his bed while his doctors stood by helplessly.

On Sunday, December 11, Enrique rose abruptly, pushed back the bed drapes, and dressed in his hunting clothes. Disregarding his physicians, the king insisted that being in the fresh air and seeing the wild animals of El Pardo would "strengthen" him. Enrique thus set out for the woods from the Madrid alcázar with a small escort, but before he got very far, he clutched his stomach and began to lose his grip on his horse. Attendants caught the king and carried him back to the palace where they lay him on his bed. For hours Enrique lay there dazed and bleeding, "half dressed . . . covered with a shabby tunic," and still in his Moorish hunting boots, which he refused to have removed.[13] Physicians and courtiers clustered around him. "Knowing he was near his end" and had failed to name a successor, they called a confessor and a handful of his closest advisors, among them the Cardinal Mendoza and the Count of Benavente.[14]

But Enrique refused "to receive the sacraments as a Catholic."[15] Then the courtiers at his side began to press him for answers. Was La Beltraneja really his daughter? Which princess, Isabella or La Beltraneja, was to be successor to the throne? Enrique, still conscious but writhing in pain and weakening by the minute, would give no answer.

At this point contemporary reports about Enrique's last moments become contradictory. Palencia, who was still in Aragón at the time of Enrique's death, wrote that the king told his confessor, Juan de Mazuelos, "I declare my daughter to be the heir to the kingdom."[16] On the other hand, Valera reports that when Enrique was asked which princess—Isabella or La Beltraneja—should inherit the crown, the king referred the question to his chaplain, Alonso González de Turegano. When Turegano, in turn, asked Enrique for an answer, the king would not reply. "*Ninguna cosa respondio*,"—"He will not say anything"[17]—that chronicler wrote with frustration.

Both Pulgar and the king's official chronicler, Castillo, however, reported that Enrique named certain counselors "who knew his conscience" about the succession. Supposedly, he listed six men—the Cardinal Mendoza, the Marquis of Santillana, the Count of Benavente, the Duke of Arévalo, the Constable of Castile, and Diego López Pacheco—as the ones who should make the decision. Since four of the six men were clearly in favor of Isabella, wrote Pulgar, Enrique's choice was obvious. Still other historians claim that Enrique left a will naming La Beltraneja as his heir. Although a priest was said to have taken it to Portugal, the alleged will—obviously favorable to Afonso V's interests in Castile—was never found.

As Enrique's condition worsened the attendants pressed him for an answer, but in his final agony he was permanently mute. Then he became delirious. Sometime around the first minutes of December 12, 1474, the fifty-year-old Enrique died.

Like deserting rats, the king's attendants and servants scattered, taking with them gold dishes, jewelry, and other treasures. Hired servants, *gentes alquiladas*, had to be called in to lay the king out in state. He was buried at the monastery of Santa María de Guadalupe at Cardinal Mendoza's expense "without the pomp usually accorded to the deaths of great Princes."[18]

That same night, somewhere on the highway from Madrid, Rodrigo de Ulloa thrust his spurs hard into the sides of the horse speeding him toward Segovia to awaken the twenty-three-year-old Isabella with the news that her brother, Enrique IV, was King of Castile no more.

PART THREE

Queen of Castile and León

1474–1482

CHAPTER TWENTY-THREE

Tanto Monta, Monta Tanto

Three days after Enrique's death, Ferdinand received an urgent letter from Carrillo. Falling to his knees, the messenger kissed Ferdinand's hand, which he said "had to be kissed once and a hundred times because it belongs to my King and Lord."

"Did the king die?" asked Ferdinand. "The letters will tell about it, most illustrious monarch," the messenger replied.

The Archbishop's letter did indeed announce Enrique's death. With tears in his eyes, the prince told Palencia, who was then living with him in Zaragoza, that Enrique's sudden death and his "corrupt habits" had impressed upon him the importance of living a life of "worth and honor."[1]

As the shock of Enrique's death sank in, Ferdinand began to wonder why he had not heard from Isabella.

On Friday, December 16, another messenger finally brought the prince a "very brief notice" from Isabella confirming Enrique's death and requesting his immediate appearance in Castile. There was no mention of the coronation held in Segovia three days earlier, on Tuesday, December 13, 1474, that made Isabella and Ferdinand the new sovereigns of Castile and León.

Despite the obvious urgency of Ferdinand's return to Castile, he was obliged to remain in Zaragoza until the *Cortes* disbanded on December 19. Finally, on December 21, just as the Aragonese prince reached the town of Calatayud, a messenger intercepted him with a letter from Gutierre de Cárdenas announcing Isabella's coronation and describing the ceremony.

Ferdinand was stunned. He had not expected that Isabella would be crowned without him or that the unsheathed sword, that ancient symbol of the highest sovereign authority, would be raised aloft in that ceremony for a female monarch.

"I never heard of a Queen who usurped this male privilege," he complained to Palencia after he read the letter.[2] Moreover, the ceremony had been held for Isabella alone. Although Ferdinand had been named "King of Castile and León" at the coronation, the proceedings suggested that he was to be little more than a king-consort rather than a full-fledged monarch in his own right.

The marriage capitulations Ferdinand had signed in 1469 before his wedding to Isabella had unequivocally restricted his rights to those of a consort in the event that she succeeded to the throne. But a reigning queen was an anomaly in fifteenth-century Castile unless she was linked to a king with authority of his own. Besides, Ferdinand grumbled to Palencia, it was he who had enabled Isabella to rise to new power and popularity.

Privately, Palencia could not resist noting that although Isabella was a queen, she was "after all, a woman" who, despite her "arrogance and haughtiness" would ultimately have to depend on male military prowess for her protection.[3] And ancient Castilian law decreed "that in the marriage of a crown heiress, even though the husband be of inferior lineage, he must enjoy the scepter and the title of him together with her as well as all the other priorities accorded to males all over the world."[4]

Despite Ferdinand's bruised feelings, he set out briskly for Castile with Palencia and a *converso* legalist named Alfonso de la Caballeria. The *converso* had been dispatched specifically at King Juan's request to keep peace between his son and his strong-willed daughter-in-law.

In Castile, meanwhile, Isabella justified her actions as not only appropriate but essential. She was, after all, the acknowledged successor in Castile by virtue of the oath Enrique had sworn to her at Toros de Guisando. Her marriage contract with Ferdinand unequivocally affirmed the supremacy of her rights over his in Castile. And Isabella's allies had pressed for her immediate coronation in order to deter La Beltraneja's faction from a similar claim.

On December 16 Isabella wrote to the towns of Castile announcing her coronation and inviting them to display banners for her "recognizing me as your natural Queen and for the very illustrious and most powerful Prince Don Ferdinand, my lord, as my legitimate husband."[5] Shortly thereafter several communities responded, including Ávila, Tordesillas, and Valladolid, which festooned their streets with pennants. On December 24 Cardinal Mendoza, the Constable of Castile, the *Almirante* Enríquez, and even the Count of Benavente pledged their fealty to the new queen. Other knights soon followed, among them Beltrán de la Cueva, the handsome *grandee* who was said to have sired Queen Juana's daughter, but who now attached himself to her rival Isabella with the fervor of an intimidated vassal.

Despite those successes, however, Isabella remained apprehensive. Instinctively she knew that Ferdinand would be angry with her coronation. In an effort to soothe his hurt feelings, she instructed the *grandees* to treat her husband most solicitously. Thus when Ferdinand arrived in Turegano on December 31, he was greeted warmly by a large assembly of *grandees* and prelates, among them the Segovian Bishop Juan Arías; the new *Almirante* of Castile, Alonso Enríquez; and the Count of Trevino, Pedro Manrique.

In the last days of 1474 Isabella prepared an elaborate reception for her husband's entrance to Segovia—so elaborate, in fact, that she sent messages to Turegano asking him to delay his arrival for three days. This reunion would be a dramatic contrast to Ferdinand's earlier arrivals into his wife's arms and would set the precedent for all greetings between the new king and queen for the next thirty years as public celebrations heralded with trumpets, and drums, with rich clothes, and festivals.

In contrast to Enrique's disdain for ceremony, both Isabella and Ferdinand embraced courtly ritual, indeed, exploited it to its fullest measure, if for no other reason than to assert symbolically their sovereignty over a torn kingdom. From her first days as queen, Isabella also recognized the importance of costume. Already her gowns had been admired by ambassadors from the courts of Burgundy for they were made from satin, velvet, gold cloth, or fine spun silk, often embellished with handsome brocades sewn with silver and gold thread. Gradually, as the wealth of her kingdom increased, Isabella would adorn herself with jewels, both on her person and sewn into her clothes.

King Ferdinand cut an equally impressive figure in *ropas,* or long robes, and *sayos,* or knee-length jerkins, of finely woven silk, satin, gold cloth, and velvet, and often trimmed with golden embroidery or in rare furs, including ermine and sable. Upon his neck Ferdinand wore stiff velvet collars from which were hung thick gold necklaces and pendants of state; on his feet finely cured leather buskins, or half boots; upon his hands perfumed gloves. The cumulative effect unequivocally marked him as the king.

When Ferdinand approached Segovia at sunset on January 2, 1475, he was greeted by Cardinal Mendoza, the Archbishop Carrillo, and other *grandees* under a brocade canopy of state. As the new king drew close to the city, its suburbs were hung with banners. Music floated through the air, and the village streets were filled with singers, jugglers, and fiestas. Just before the new king approached the hills of Segovia, he was helped out of his dark mourning clothes into a rich *ropa* woven with gold threads and trimmed with *martas,* or sables.

At twilight the new king passed through Segovia's Gate of San Martin, as dignitaries carrying lighted torches stepped forward and knelt in homage. Ferdinand, in turn, swore his allegiance to the city and promised to honor the laws of Castile as its new king. Afterward the large body of assembled *grandees* and prelates entered the cathedral for a thanksgiving mass.

In the alcázar Isabella waited with "deep affection" for her husband.[6] When she saw the torchlit procession approaching the plaza, she descended to the first floor of the castle. Finally the new king walked through the entranceway and was reunited with Isabella.

Despite the public warmth of their reunion, it was soon obvious that Ferdinand and Isabella were quarreling. The new king bitterly resented the role he had been assigned as king-consort while Isabella, as queen, held the reins. For her part, Isabella maintained that she had simply acted in accordance with the marriage capitulations that assigned her the larger sovereign authority for the Castilian crown. Moreover, that agreement and Castilian custom dictated that upon Isabella's death, the throne would be inherited by her oldest son or, barring any, by her oldest daughter, Princess Isabel. Because Ferdinand was not directly but only laterally descended from the reigning Trastámaras of Castile, he could never become King of Castile in his own right, no matter what military aid he rendered to the country, whatever lands or justice he administered. After Isabella's death the throne would pass only to her children.

Those judgments profoundly rankled Ferdinand. It was absurd, he contended, that if Isabella should die an untimely death the crown would fall to their four-year-old daughter, while he was still capable and in good health. Was it not more sensible to have a kingdom managed by a man than a child?

Ferdinand finally became so agitated that he threatened to return to Aragón despite Isabella's efforts to win him over "with sweet words." She had not meant, the queen explained, "to cause any problem to her very beloved consort for whose joy and honor she was ready to sacrifice with dignity and by duty not only the crown but her own health." But the decision was not hers alone. The debate had been created "by the *grandees* and jurists in charge of defending the laws regulating inheritances, who were asking her not to allow them to be changed with permanent harm for the throne's succession."[7]

Still, Ferdinand would not be placated. As a last resort, the young monarchs agreed to plead their differences before a formal council of legal experts. That meeting proved to be one of the most extraordinary examinations of female inheritance rights in prefeminist Europe, one whose highly emotional tone would finally be resolved by Isabella's cool logic. The council convened in Segovia on January 15, before a large audience of aristocrats. Among the listeners were Aragonese advisors to Ferdinand such as Caballeria, and allies for Isabella, among them her new confessor, a Hieronymite monk named Fernando de Talavera. As agreed, Cardinal Mendoza was to plead for Isabella's rights and Archbishop Carrillo, for Ferdinand.

In the midst of the negotiations, Isabella addressed Ferdinand on the delicate question of the succession rights. Before the gathered assembly she told her husband:

> This subject, Lord, need never to have been discussed because
> where there is such union as by the grace of God exists between
> you and me, there can be no difference. Already, as my husband,
> you are King of Castile, and your orders have to be obeyed here;
> and these realms, please God, will remain after our days for your
> sons and mine. But since it has pleased these knights to open this
> discussion, perhaps it is just as well that any doubt they have be
> clarified, as the law of our kingdoms provide.[8]

Isabella further reminded Ferdinand that it "has not pleased God thus far to give us an heir" except their daughter Princess Isabel. If Ferdinand were to insist on male inheritance, it was entirely possible that a distant male relation, someone from a collateral Trastámara line, might claim the throne as well. "Hence we can well see," Isabella responded, "what great embarrassment would follow for our descendants."[9]

The queen also observed that in all likelihood their daughter would marry a foreign prince to whom, under Ferdinand's proposed scheme of male supremacy,

Castile would then belong and "who may desire to place in command of the forts and royal patrimony other people of his nation." As a result, Castile "may pass into the hands of a foreign race," a situation that would be a "great burden on our consciences and a disservice to God and a great loss to our successors and subjects."[10]

Ferdinand listened to Isabella's arguments and "knowing [them] to be true, was much pleased." In the end he accepted the Castilian concept of female inheritance and ordered that "nothing more be discussed on the subject."[11] Years later, in fact, when Ferdinand was faced with the painful subject of his own succession, he would present those same arguments to the Aragonese *Cortes* who still stubbornly clung to the Salic law of male inheritance.

Nevertheless, in 1475 Ferdinand continued to be frustrated by the Castilian insistence upon maintenance of the exact terms of his capitulations. The queen was to have ultimate authority over tax collections for the crown. She also retained sole authority over the appointment of military governors and the summons of soldiers to war. And it remained her sole duty to appoint and promote ecclesiastics to positions of power.

There were a few concessions to Ferdinand. The king's name was to precede Isabella's on all documents and ceremonial addresses. Ferdinand was also to take full responsibility for waging war. Although the queen would determine the salaries of the soldiers, Ferdinand's martial expertise entitled him to serve as supreme commander of the army. Independently he could punish criminals, order expeditions, and render military justice. That, however, was the extent of Ferdinand's privileges. His "masculine rights" were only superficially honored. As king, he was given little independent authority. Should Ferdinand and Isabella write separate opinions on matters of mutual concern, the queen's opinion "would be valued over all."[12]

Despite these dissatisfactions, the conference averted a serious rift between Isabella and Ferdinand. In time, love would take care of the rest. Within the next three months Isabella would privately assign Ferdinand privileges so that he could cogovern Castile in deed as well as in name.

To emphasize their mutual authority, the king and queen created a new coat of arms. Within it they blended the royal symbols of Castile and León—castles and lions–with the gold and red bars of Aragón and the eagles of Sicily. Beneath the new heraldic emblem, the couple placed their personal insignias of devotion to each other—the *yugo*, or yoke, for Isabella, the *flechas*, or arrows, for Ferdinand. Both symbols were intertwined with a Gordian knot, signifying the perpetuity of their union.

The new sovereigns also took a motto, *Tanto Monta, Monta Tanto, Fernando como Isabel, Isabel como Fernando*, or "One is equal to the other, Ferdinand as much as Isabella, Isabella as much as Ferdinand." The slogan *Tanto Monta* appeared everywhere—on coins, documents, stone friezes, churches, cloisters— and became the most famous epithet for their reign. But *Tanto Monta* was more than a public proclamation of mutual rights: It was a private creed of mutual respect. During the first five years of their marriage, Isabella and Ferdinand had already endured injury, war, disinheritance, and disloyalties and thus discovered the wisdom of their interdependence. In spirit, if not law, their marriage was already one of equals.

CHAPTER TWENTY-FOUR

I Am Like an Anvil

I sabella and Ferdinand's reign began with disappointments. The first bad news came from King Juan in Aragón, announcing that Perpignan was surrounded by the French. The new queen, acutely aware of Ferdinand's sacrifice for the Castilian crown and indebted to Juan for his previous aid, resolved to help her father-in-law. In the young monarchs' first council meeting on January 18, 1475, they thus ordered 2,000 lancers to Aragón.

Isabella then dispatched Pulgar to Paris to propose a peace treaty with Louis XI. The Spider King, anticipating the fall of Perpignan, returned a polite, noncommittal answer.

In addition, the Castilian treasury was nearly depleted. To raise new monies and have themselves sworn King and Queen of Castile, the monarchs summoned the *Cortes* on February 7 to Medina del Campo. This time most of the *procuradores* appeared and swore their allegiance. Nevertheless, they refused to vote the monarchs funds. Many Castilian towns were still undecided about supporting Isabella and Ferdinand, and a few from the provinces of Andalusia, Galicia, Guipúzcoa, and Extremadura had failed to send representatives.

Without an infusion of funds, Isabella and Ferdinand could hardly rule Castile, let alone help King Juan. On March 6 an embarrassed Ferdinand was thus forced to write to the counselors at Barcelona that Castile was *desberatas,* "ruined," because its income, the "royal rents," had *dissipades,* or "evaporated."[1]

Soon trouble came from a closer quarter. In February Carrillo quarreled bitterly with Ferdinand about the award of certain Aragonese *oficios* and *privilegios,* "titles" and "privileges" promised to the archbishop when Ferdinand became king. Because the Catalonian war made it impossible for Ferdinand to deliver those properties, he had offered the archbishop other gifts and privileges.

But Carrillo refused to accept anything but "his [original] intention." For months he had been brooding over Isabella and Ferdinand's friendship with the Mendozas, and now, having failed to be properly rewarded, he vowed to break with the young couple permanently. On February 20 Carrillo thus ordered his servants to pack his belongings, "turned his face away from the monarchs who had rewarded him so poorly for his large service," and left Segovia.[2]

That spring Carrillo sulked in his palace at Alcalá de Henares. Isabella and Ferdinand sent him conciliatory letters. From Aragón King Juan tried to persuade the archbishop to reconcile with his son and daughter-in-law. But every effort to placate the fuming prelate met with failure. Carrillo was a man of extremes, a man who either loved or hated passionately. In the spring of 1475 he thus switched allegiances and pledged himself to Afonso V of Portugal, who, as La Beltraneja's uncle and potential husband, had his own ambitions for Castile.

The archbishop was not alone in his defection. Shortly after Enrique's death, Pacheco's son Diego had promised obedience to Isabella, but he remained loyal to La Beltraneja. The youth had retained his allegiance in accordance with his dead father's wishes: Along with Diego's title as the Marquis of Villena and its vast agencies was Pacheco's old enmity toward King Juan. Moreover, Pacheco had named his son La Beltraneja's guardian. Now, to fulfill his father's wishes, to pose a challenge to Isabella and Ferdinand's Castilian crown, the young Villena plotted to marry La Beltraneja to Afonso V.

After Enrique's death another young *grandee,* the red-haired Marquis of Cádiz, Rodrigo Ponce de León, had offered to support Afonso V from Andalusia. Before long other wealthy nobles joined the rebel party, among them the Duke of Arévalo, who owned large tracts of land in Extremadura, and the Master of Alcántara, leader of Castile's second largest military order.

The forty-six-year-old Portuguese king had welcomed those alliances and considered them a necessary prerequisite to any action against Isabella and Ferdinand. By 1475 Afonso was already a wealthy monarch in his own right. In 1471 he had successfully invaded Berber Morocco, captured four ports including Tangiers, and earned the title of *El Africano,* or The African. That same year seafaring explorers under the Portuguese flag had sailed south of Sierra Leone on the African Guinea coast to Cape Three Points and founded a rich gold trade at St. George La Mina.

To add Castile to the Portuguese crown would be the best prize of all. Officially, Afonso intended to present his invasion of Castile as a heroic effort to protect the rights of his niece, La Beltraneja, to the Castilian crown. Then, to ensure Castile's absorption into Portugal, Afonso planned to marry the thirteen-year-old girl himself. Through that ruse—a "wooden horse," as one Castilian chronicler called it—the Portuguese king ultimately planned to leave Castile to his son and heir, Prince João.

To do so, however, would require foreign aid. Thus the "prudent" Portuguese king turned northward to Louis XI of France. It was probably his worst mistake. Before agreeing to any alliance, the Spider King forced Afonso to break his treaty with England: Only then would he promise to invade the Basque provinces of Vizcaya and Guipúzcoa on Castile's Cantabrian coast.

Shortly afterward Afonso sent Isabella and Ferdinand a letter demanding that they resign the Castilian throne to La Beltraneja. "It is well known," the Portuguese king announced, "that my niece is the daughter of the King Enrique and as legitimate heir she has the right to the title of Queen of Castile."[3]

The queen and king replied sharply through their secretary Pulgar.

> I see those who call you to carry out this design are the Arch-
> bishop of Toledo . . . the Duke of Arévalo . . . and the Grand
> Master of the Order of Calatrava. . . . they are the ones who
> asserted all over Spain . . . that this lady did not have right to
> succeed King Enrique and that she could not be his daughter due
> to his proven impotency . . . we would like to know how it is
> that they found this lady not to be the rightful heir then . . . and
> how they find her now to be. . . .[4]

Afonso ignored the letter. Instead he sent gold crosses, silver cups, and other tokens to Castilian knights still loyal to Isabella and Ferdinand. He even issued gold coins with his image and labeled them the "King of Castile." Finally in mid-spring 1475 Afonso and his son, Prince João, summoned an army of 5,600 cavalry and 14,000 footsoldiers and began moving toward the Castilian border.

Despite Afonso's letter, neither Isabella nor Ferdinand believed that the Portuguese king was ready to declare war. Consequently they spent their days attempting to win the loyalties of Castile's most important *grandees.*

On April 3, 1475, Isabella and Ferdinand attended a joust hosted by the Count of Alba. The *grandees,* accompanied by their wives, relatives, and servants, arrived at Valladolid by horse and mule in an ostentatious display of wealth designed to impress each other and the new king and queen. Even their horses and mules, it was said, were caparisoned with gold embroidery and sable fur.

Most impressive of all, however, were the contestants themselves, who arrived at the grassy arena dressed in glittering suits of armor, decorated with silver and gold, topped with steel helmets in "the latest fashion."

"Who," an anonymous chronicler observed, "would be able to describe the wealth . . . the beautiful new fashions and the ceremony with which each of those richly dressed knights surrounded by servants and relatives came out to the field?"

The pageantry was so extraordinary, the parrying between the armored men so thrilling, the spectacle of knights dismounted with "broken lances and helmets" so impressive that the audience was swept away with "the impression that more than a usual tournament this was an encounter of the knights of the Round Table."[5]

Inevitably, the young monarchs were the center of attention. Isabella's arrival on April 3 was preceded by fourteen female attendants, who were crowned and attired in green brocade and crimson velvet. The queen then appeared at the tilting yard in a blaze of light. Her dress was a brocade *brial,* her crown glittered with gems, and Isabella was mounted upon a horse harnessed in silver and decorated in golden flowers.

That same day Ferdinand appeared on the field in a sparkling suit of Toledo armor inlaid with gold and silver and a helmet bearing the insignia of an anvil. The king had always been a skilled combatant, and during the joust he defeated so many knights that the significance of his symbol soon became clear. "I am like an anvil," read his motto. "I suffer without making sound/for as long as I am bound."[6]

In the midst of the celebrations, a message arrived from Afonso V that cast a permanent pall over the jousts. The document announced the Portuguese king intended to marry La Beltraneja in order to "defend" her claim to the Castilian crown. It was, in effect, a declaration of war.

The rest of April was spent in feverish activity. Isabella continued to press Louis XI for a treaty. Simultaneously she and Ferdinand gathered an army from both the aristocracy and ordinary citizens. Fearing internal revolt, the young monarchs even resurrected the *Hermandad*, or citizen police force, in such towns as Toledo, Talavera de la Reina, and Ciudad Real. Before long it was obvious that Ferdinand needed independent authority to summon soldiers, collect munitions, and protect fortresses against the Portuguese. Although the king had been denied that right at Segovia in January, Isabella now disregarded those judgments and granted him total authority.

Then, at the beginning of May, Isabella left Valladolid and traveled south to Alcalá de Henares. Over the protests of her counselors, Isabella intended to ask Carrillo for a reconciliation on the basis of their old relationship and his former allegiance to her cause.

Along the way the queen made what may well have been a tactical error by visiting the Mendoza clan at Guadalahara. Then, on May 10, as she approached the city of Alcalá de Henares, she sent ahead one of the Mendozas, the Count of Haro, to notify her former mentor of her arrival.

But Carrillo had no interest in talking with Isabella. He may have known she had just visited the Mendozas. Or perhaps he was already so committed to Afonso V that he saw no point in discussion. Months earlier he had sworn he would not be cowed again by sovereign authority, especially from the young princess he had made queen. Now he was determined to bring her down. "If the Queen comes in one gate of Alcalá, I will go out the other," he vowed.[7]

The archbishop's words fell on Isabella like a thunderbolt. Grasping her head with anguish, she fell to her knees and prayed. "My Lord Jesus Christ," she said tremulously, "I leave everything in your hands and I expect to be defended by your favor and help."[8] For one brief moment, Isabella's prayers seemed to be answered. Soon after Carrillo's rejection she traveled to Toledo, the seat of her former mentor's archbishopric. There, on May 20, its citizens received Isabella joyously as the Queen of Castile.

A week earlier, on May 12, Afonso's troops had invaded Castile. At the heart of the Extremadura plateau, high above the Jerte River, the town of Plasencia had opened its gates to the Portuguese king. The Duke of Arévalo and the young Marquis of Villena then joined Afonso V, who on May 25, was betrothed to La Beltraneja in Plasencia's ancient cathedral. Afterward the young girl and the middle-age king proclaimed themselves the new sovereigns of Castile. The actual marriage, however, was delayed because Afonso was La Beltraneja's uncle and the requisite papal dispensation had not yet been granted.

A few days after the betrothal festivities, Afonso and his army of about 15,000 men marched north to Arévalo to wait for Castilian reinforcements. The news came as a terrible jolt to Isabella and Ferdinand. Now they responded with feverish activity—Ferdinand summoning and training soldiers, Isabella raising money and scouting the countryside to enlist more men for the imminent battle.

In desperation, Isabella issued a general pardon to all the Castilian cities that had been disloyal to her as a princess in hopes that they would join her cause as queen. She worked through the night, writing letters, issuing orders, and raising funds. With total disregard for the usual customs of her sex, Isabella mounted a fast horse and rode from town to town with a few attendants, hoping that her personal pleas would win the undecided Castilian towns to her cause.

Despite their relative inexperience, the young monarchs mounted a formidable counteroffensive. On May 19 Ferdinand wrote to the *adelantado*, or royal governor, of Murcia, ordering him to attack the soldiers of the four aristocratic traitors, the "foes to the Castilian throne"—Villena, the Master of Calatrava, the Count of Urena, and the Duke of Arévalo. Five days later Isabella signed a *cedula*, or document, condemning the rebellion of those same four barons. On the twenty-seventh of that month Ferdinand announced that Castile was officially at war "by sea and by land against the King of Portugal and his subjects" and ordered similar notices circulated throughout Castile.[9]

Afonso and his future bride retaliated with war propaganda of their own. On May 30 La Beltraneja issued a manifesto accusing Isabella and Ferdinand of ruining the economy of Castile, poisoning King Enrique, and illegally seizing the throne. To protect herself, La Beltraneja thus asserted she sought marriage with Afonso V, who had invaded Castile in her defense.

The frenzied nature of Isabella and Ferdinand's preparations for war and defense of the lands west of the Duero River meant they could not always communicate or know each other's location. Nevertheless, they were bound by love and mutual faith. On May 23, on the eve of the Portuguese war, Ferdinand composed his first will. Within it, the young king ordered that if he died, his body was to be buried in the Madrid monastery of Santa María del Prado or any other place "the above-mentioned Queen, my dear and well-loved wife" should choose for her own burial so that "as we were [together] by marriage and singular love in life that we not be separated by death."[10] In addition, Ferdinand entrusted Isabella with the legal and financial care of his illegitimate children and their mothers. Clearly the king considered his sexual transgressions far less important than his love for the queen.

Moreover, in the four months since their quarrel at Segovia over the rights of female succession, Ferdinand had completely reversed his position.

> I appoint universal heir . . . our very dear and beloved daughter, princess Isabel. Especially I institute her heir of my kingdoms of Aragón and Sicily, in spite of any laws . . . and customs of the said kingdoms, which may forbid a female to succeed in them. And this is not because of ambition, greed or the inordinate affec-

tion I may have for the said princess . . . but I . . . order it in
this way due to the great benefit resulting for these kingdoms of
their union with Castile and León. . . .[11]

Still, the enforced days of separation, the uncertainty of Isabella and Ferdinand's imperiled crown, and the constant movements of the queen through the Castilian countryside unnerved the king. Almost certainly he had not approved of Isabella's decision to attempt a reconciliation with Carrillo, for she had not communicated with him after her encounter with the archbishop on May 10. By May 16 Ferdinand had grown so edgy that he wrote to Isabella from Tordesillas:

My Ladyship, now at last it is clear which of us two loves
best . . . I can see that you can be happy while I lose my sleep,
because messenger comes after messenger and brings me no letters from you. The reason why you do not write is not because
there is no paper to be had, or that you do not know how to
write, but because you do not love me and because you are
proud . . . Well! One day you will return to your old affection.
If you do not, I shall die and the guilt will be yours. . . . Write
to me and let me know how you are. . . . For God's sake remember her [Princess Isabel] as well as her father, who kisses
your hands and is your servant. The King."[12]

Two weeks later the strain of the impending war took its toll upon Isabella. On May 31, a day or so after she left Ávila and galloped south to the village of Cebreros, she began to suffer excruciating abdominal pains. A few hours later the young queen miscarried a male fetus—the son she and Ferdinand had so desperately longed for. Both the queen and the king reacted to the loss with "great emotion," all the more because it was a boy.[13]

CHAPTER TWENTY-FIVE

Not a Single Tower

O n July 9, 1475, Ferdinand and Isabella were reunited in Tordesillas. Despite their long separation their reconciliation was consumed in feverish preparations to repulse Afonso's advance. By then Afonso was publicly proclaiming himself and La Beltraneja "the King and Queen of Castile" and had taken the town of Toro in Extremadura.

Within a few weeks, Isabella and Ferdinand amassed an army of 42,000 men to check the Portuguese advance. The monarchs' army was an eclectic militia, composed of men from different regions, social strata, and goals. Within it were squadrons of thickset, muddy booted *peóns,* or peasant footsoldiers too poor to own a horse. There were the most affluent and better disciplined *escuderos,* or shield carriers, who arrived outfitted with swords, breastplates, and steel helmets. Most conspicuous of all were the aristocratic *lanceros,* or lance-bearers, knights dressed in custom-made armor, booted with spurs of gold and helmeted in steel. As a point of ancestral pride, these elite units were accompanied by standard-bearers carrying heraldic symbols.

In addition, raw units of private citizens had appeared in response to Isabella's personal call for help, some like the battalions of archers from Vizcaya, with wooden *ballesteros* and crossbows; others with no weapons at all. Money was needed to support these men and their munitions. As the funds could not be raised through the *Cortes,* Isabella was forced to ask Cabrera for a loan from the royal treasury. To guarantee it Isabella now awarded Cabrera and Beatriz de Bobadilla custody of her daughter, Isabel, as she no longer had to fear Enrique. As a token of appreciation, the queen then elevated her friends to aristocratic status as the Marqués and Marquesa of Moya.

Despite the respectable size of Ferdinand and Isabella's army—some 30,000 footsoldiers, 8,000 cavalry, and 4,000 lancers—the forces were an undisciplined militia whose individual units harbored internecine grudges. On July 16, Ferdinand and a cadre of his most trusted advisors nevertheless led the army west along the Duero toward Toro. But no sooner had they begun traveling through the scorching heat than they learned Afonso had taken the city of Zamora, twenty-two miles west of Toro, the very community Ferdinand had planned to use as a base of operations. By July 19 Ferdinand's army arrived exhausted, sweaty, and "covered with dust" below Toro's towering walls and arranged themselves for a pitched battle.

For two days they waited, wilting in the relentless sun. To Ferdinand's consternation, his army was incapable of attacking Toro for he lacked certain *ingenios,* or inventions, such as battering rams, catapults, and movable assault towers indispensable to invade walled cities. To end the stalemate, Ferdinand dispatched a messenger to Afonso, challenging him and his army to hand-to-hand combat. As an alternative, Ferdinand offered to duel against Afonso himself. The Portuguese king agreed but shrewdly failed to specify the time, place, or conditions for the contest, and ultimately the plan was abandoned.

Meanwhile, the heat had become unbearable and food supplies began to run low. Finally, "seeing there was no way for them to break into the fortress," Ferdinand ordered a retreat.[1] But the oppressive temperatures, the enforced inactivity of the men and their internal resentments took its toll. With the announcement of the retreat the common soldiers revolted, blaming the decision on aristocratic cowardice and storming a church where Ferdinand met with his counselors. Ultimately the king made peace between the factions.

On July 22 the army retreated in sullen chaos. Without glory, without plunder the men freed from Ferdinand's command wreaked their frustration on innocent Castilian communities, leaving terrible devastation in their wake. They pillaged villages, robbed citizens, raped their daughters and wives, picked farms clean of crops.

Isabella, waiting upriver on the Duero in Tordesillas, grieved deeply when she heard about the defeat. But when messengers brought the queen reports about the retreating army's wanton destruction, her grief turned into rage. Isabella was, in fact, so angry that as the first soldiers began to reappear in Tordesillas, she ordered the entrance to the town closed against them. The next day when Ferdinand approached, Isabella rode from her temporary quarters in the Convent of Santa Clara to meet her husband and his army at the edge of town.

It was hardly a loving welcome. Isabella seemed "more sorry to see the army return without glory than glad to see them safe" and with "words more like those of a forceful man than a timid woman" accused Ferdinand and his army of cowardice.[2]

"With such good knights, such horses and gear and such infantry, what fight would be dangerous enough to rob them [the army] of the daring and action that normally grows in manly hearts?" she demanded of the king. "If you had forced the forts open, and I don't doubt that you would if you had my will, Portugal and its sovereignty would have been lost in memory."[3]

In her fury Isabella was inconsolable. "You may say now that women should not speak of dangers because they are not the ones who suffer them and . . .

it's always the ones who don't risk . . . who speak louder," she observed, "but I would tell you that nobody was risking more than I because I was wagering my Lord, the King, whom I love more than anything in this world and betting so many . . . good knights, people and money that losing them I would also lose these realms."[4]

In a final outburst that revealed the depth of Isabella's frustration at her position, she then confessed that she had spent the last few days waiting "with an angry heart, gritting my teeth and clenching my fists." It was, she added, "as if revenge itself was fighting with me. . . . I wonder about my rage, being a woman and about your patience, you being men."[5]

Ferdinand, barely able to contain his anger, attempted to explain the arduous conditions at Toro and the wisdom of his retreat from a situation in which his men were outnumbered "ten to one." But even if the conditions had been more favorable, he observed vitriolically, Isabella's reaction was unconscionable. He said:

> I thought that coming back defeated I would find words of conso-
> lation and encouragement from your mouth but you complain be-
> cause we have returned whole and with no glory lost? Well, we
> will certainly have a heavy task to satisfy you from here on! But
> women are always difficult to satisfy, even though their men be
> ready and diligent to act and do it with joy, especially you, my
> lady, who can never be satisfied by any mortal man.[6]

"Especially you, my lady." The words must have cut through Isabella like a knife. Would the women Ferdinand lusted after in Aragón have been as critical? Did, as her husband had so cruelly implied, Isabella routinely demand too much of him? Without giving Isabella a chance to respond, Ferdinand reminded her that men faced battle and death primarily out of a sense of "their own honor and not to satisfy women or to gain advancement in the world." Having vented his own anger, the king, in considerably more chastened tones, then urged Isabella to remember the Almighty.

"Let us be humble in front of the One for whom the most powerful are weak and . . . have faith and hope that He will always relieve our grief, even though by our sins we may not deserve to reign peacefully."[7]

Isabella never forgot Ferdinand's words. After all other battles in their reign, the queen greeted Ferdinand and his soldiers with warmth and solicitude regardless of their arrival in triumph or defeat.

The bitterness of Isabella and Ferdinand's defeat at Toro was compounded by Carrillo's sudden defection to the Portuguese king. Interpreting Afonso's triumph as a sign of divine favor, the archbishop appeared in Arévalo with five hundred lancers whom he placed at the Portuguese king's disposal with the boast that "he had raised Isabella from the distaff and would soon send her back to it again."[8]

Meanwhile, in retaliation for the defeat at Toro, forces of light cavalry from Andalusia and Extremadura faithful to the king and queen tore across the Portuguese border, attacking villages and leaving behind charred fields of wheat, oats, and barley. From Andalusia, other loyalists seized the Portuguese cities of Elvas, Ongella, and Nodar. From Extremadura, still other allies took the Portuguese towns of Alegrete and Noroeste.

Neighboring kingdoms joined the cause as well. From Valencia, King Juan ordered soldiers to cross their western border and attack Villena's estates in southeastern Castile. Aragonese boats sailed into the Strait of Gibraltar, entered the mouth of the Guadalquivir, and seized rebel-held territories in Andalusia. And on July 25, 1475, the King of Granada, Ali Abu-l-Hasan, signed a pact with Isabella and Ferdinand. Although he refused to pay them the traditional tribute money, the Moorish king promised to protect Isabella and Ferdinand against a Portuguese invasion.

Simultaneously, Isabella tried to choke off Portugal's rich trade routes. In August she urged Castilian mariners to sail as far south as the Portuguese-dominated Canary Islands and claim those lands and their wealth for Castile. Other Spanish fleets were ordered to disrupt Portuguese trade routes in Africa and northern Europe.

Meanwhile, Afonso's army remained in Toro. After Ferdinand's retreat, the Portuguese king, growing edgy with reports of invasions in his own kingdom, returned thousands of soldiers to defend Portugal. With only a fragment of his army left and a fraction of the promised reinforcements from Villena and the Duke of Arévalo, Afonso began to reconsider the wisdom of his declaration of war. Finally he proposed a settlement. He would cede his claim to the Castilian crown in exchange for Castile's province of Galicia, the cities of Toro and Zamora, and a large sum of money.

Initially Ferdinand considered the idea, but Isabella was violently opposed. "Not one tower," she vowed, not one piece of Castilian property formerly held by her father King Juan would be surrendered to Afonso.[9]

To accept Afonso's offer would have been an easy way to end the war. But Isabella was intransigent. Her refusal to compromise, her "stubbornness," as Ferdinand once called it, was already making her a formidable monarch. In time, Isabella's faith in her own convictions would become the whetstone of her greatness, enabling her and Ferdinand to carve out a world empire for Spain.

Now more than ever, Isabella and Ferdinand needed an influx of money to defeat the Portuguese king. With new funds they would be able to summon and train new soldiers, buy provisions, and import cannons from Italy and Germany. Otherwise Afonso might remain in Castile indefinitely, free to batter and wheedle his way to the Castilian throne. But *dinero,* money, was in short supply. The barons faithful to Isabella's cause had contributed all they could, and the *Cortes* of February 1476 had failed to vote any new funds.

To solve the predicament, King Juan suggested that his daughter-in-law and son raise new subsidies by granting the *grandees* new titles and lands. Isabella rejected this idea outright. As a girl in Enrique's court she had witnessed the disastrous results of that practice; it enabled nobles to manipulate the king, impoverish the crown, and make Enrique little more than "king of the highways." Isabella was determined to avoid such a struggle in her own reign. From childhood she had believed that the Castilian crown was sacrosanct, its authority supreme.

Thus the king and queen must stand above the aristocrats, not work in partnership with them. To strengthen her own tentative grasp on the Castilian throne, Isabella thus established the concept of an absolutist king and queen that would later typify the monarchies of other courts in Western Europe at the peak of the northern Renaissance.

In 1475 the only remaining repository of wealth in Castile was the church. Initially Isabella shrank from using ecclesiastical funds—the idea was unprecedented, perhaps even uncanonical. But Cardinal Mendoza and other prelates supported the idea, even cited scriptural arguments in its defense. Ultimately Isabella conceded, and by autumn 1476 the Castilian church lent the young monarchs half their "gold and silver plate," a contribution amounting to some 30 million maravedís that was to be repaid in three years.

More help came from Aragón. After the humiliating defeat at Toro, King Juan dispatched one of his illegitimate sons, the talented general Alonso de Aragón, to Castile, "a master of the arts of war." Alonso arrived in Castile on November 22, fresh from the Catalonian battlefields with fifty armed men and one hundred light cavalry, *a la jinete*. Best of all he brought along artillery and equipment that enabled Isabella and Ferdinand to build *inventios,* or war machinery of their own. For several days thereafter Isabella, Ferdinand, and Alonso plotted new strategies to foil the Portuguese king.

Then Ferdinand and his half brother launched a new offensive against the castle of Burgos by creating a blockade. Scores of Castilian soldiers dug tunnels and built barriers around the castle to prevent the enemy from delivering supplies, and by December 2 the hungry Portuguese surrendered. Ironically, Ferdinand was not present, for five days earlier Isabella had urged him to travel to Extremadura. Secretly the queen had learned from the *alcalde* of Portuguese-held Zamora that his city was ready to overthrow the Portuguese king if Ferdinand and his soldiers appeared to help them.

The task of formalizing the surrender at Burgos thus fell to Isabella. On January 10, 1476, the queen wrapped herself in wool gowns and fur-lined cloaks, left Valladolid, and proceeded through knee-deep snowdrifts and high winds to arrive in Burgos in a blinding blizzard. By January 28 the queen had obtained an oath of allegiance from the city fathers and a promise of support for her cause.

Despite the pressing duties of war, Isabella was still haunted by the miscarriage she had suffered eight months earlier in Cebreros. She longed to give birth to a male child who would become heir to the twin crowns of Castile and Aragón. For months she had prayed to conceive again, and now she took even more definitive steps. One bitter January day she rode north of Burgos to an outlying hamlet where a chapel had been erected to the memory of an eleventh-century saint, San Juan de La Ortega. That Romanesque church, which housed the saint's tomb, contained an odd bas relief of a woman in childbirth who, according to tradition, San Juan protected. It was to that saint that Isabella now prayed. As a sign of her devotion, the queen donated alms and gave funds for the construction of a larger church to be annexed to the chapel.

Then Isabella headed south again, stopping briefly in Valladolid before riding to Tordesillas. From that town high over the Duero, Isabella was close enough to Ferdinand to receive daily reports about his siege upon Zamora.

But prayers for victory over the Portuguese king and for her husband's safe return failed to satisfy Isabella's passionate disposition. Though female, as the frustrated Isabella had unhappily reminded Ferdinand six months earlier, revenge against the Portuguese burned within every fiber of her being. To expel it, she assumed the role as quartermaster of the Castilian army. Thus in February 1476 it was Isabella who dispatched squadrons of light cavalry to patrol the Duero valley and block Afonso's supply lines. Like her husband Ferdinand, Isabella had vowed to be monarch of Castile in deed as well as in name.

CHAPTER TWENTY-SIX

A Battle at Toro

Even before Isabella's return to Tordesillas, her allies at the Portuguese border had blocked the enemy. In late 1475 Afonso had dispatched urgent letters to his twenty-year-old son João in Portugal asking for reinforcements. The prince had responded by raising an army of 2,000 lancers and 8,000 infantrymen, but when he marched to the Castilian border he was violently repulsed. João and his men were forced to follow a circuitous northern route through Galicia before turning south again toward the Duero River valley.

Meanwhile, on December 5 Ferdinand and 5,500 armed men arrived across the river from Zamora. In the distance above them loomed the city's church towers from where, in clear weather, it was possible to see into Portugal. Below them swirled the treacherous currents of the Duero spanned by a single fortified bridge. Just before Ferdinand's arrival, Afonso had ordered new reinforcements for the bridge and other gates leading into the city.

Nevertheless, Zamora's *alcalde* managed to smuggle the keys of the city to Ferdinand. As the Castilian army crossed the bridge the Portuguese sounded an alarm and Afonso's soldiers rose to defend the city. Simultaneously, the loyalists barricaded themselves in one of the ramparts and with *bombardas,* or primitive cannons, dropped white-hot stones on Afonso's army. Then three battalions of Castilian *escalanados,* or wall-scalers, climbed Zamora's towers and entered the city. Shortly before dawn Ferdinand and his army entered the city as well.

Faced with the citizens' treachery, Afonso first retreated to the castle, which lay north of the city walls. Then, leaving some of his men behind, he rode east to Toro to meet João. Afonso was so heartened by his son's approach with the promised reinforcements that he wrote Pope Sixtus IV, Louis XI, and his

Portuguese subjects that he intended either to capture Ferdinand or to "driv[e] him from the country."[1]

At dawn on a mid-February morning in 1476 Ferdinand awakened to the sound of cascading retorts from arquebuses and *bombardas* across the Duero. In the dead of night a large Portuguese army had arrived on the other side of the river and taken possession of Zamora's one bridge. The Castilians' position was clearly perilous, bound as they were by the bridge to the south and the Portuguese-held castle on the north. Moreover, so much snow-melted water flowed in the Duero that no one could safely ford it. Ferdinand and his army were thus trapped, and their food and munitions soon began to dwindle.

Ironically, Afonso's situation was not much better. His army, living in canvas tents, was poorly protected from the winter cold. From Tordesillas, Isabella dispatched units of light cavalry that menaced the Portuguese camp and cut off their supplies. In addition, Ferdinand's half brother sent fresh Castilian troops from Burgos who lurked in the countryside, literally at Afonso's back.

On March 1 or 2 Afonso abruptly retreated from Zamora. In the process his men deliberately destroyed the bridge. Ferdinand's army had to repair it before they could follow. Three hours later, the Castilians finally crossed the Duero and chased the Portuguese over the narrow mountain passes of the Sierra de la Culebras. There, on the north side of the Duero, they entered a wide plain near the village of Peleagonzalo and the city of Toro. Above the plain on the opposite hill the Portuguese army had arranged themselves in formation for a pitched battle. It was nearly four o'clock, and in the fading light of that winter afternoon Afonso's thick form, gleaming in his armor and mounted upon a tall warhorse, was visible. To his right was Carrillo, flanked by his men; to his left rode the auburn-haired Prince João at the head of a battalion of armored knights.

The Castilians quickly prepared for battle on the opposite hill. Ferdinand was stationed at the center of his troops. His left wing was commanded by his uncle Enrique Enríquez, the Duke of Alba, and Cardinal Mendoza. To Ferdinand's right, six other battalions stood at attention. With the rising beat of war drums, the blare of *clarines,* and spirited shouts of "St. James and St. Lazarus," Ferdinand's right wing charged the Portuguese, who promptly discharged their cannons and arquebuses.

In the crackle of exploding gunpowder and the subsequent rain of fiery lead balls, stones, and long-shafted arrows, Ferdinand's right wing splintered. Its men were injured, their armor blown apart or ripped open, their horses bleeding and fallen. But as the Portuguese advanced on the wounded and dying Castilians, Ferdinand's left wing rallied. Within minutes, squadrons of mounted knights thrust lances at the enemy and engaged in hand-to-hand combat with swords, each side responding to respective shouts of "Afonso!" and "Ferdinand!" Carrillo, unmistakable in his scarlet mantle, raised his sword against his former Castilian allies while Mendoza led his men against the Portuguese in another part of the battlefield.

An icy rain began to fall. In the deepening twilight the outcome of the battle remained undecided. The Portuguese flag was ripped apart as its courageous bearer, losing one arm and then the other, clenched the banner in his teeth until finally he was cut down. Hundreds of wounded Portuguese fell or leapt into the

Duero and were washed downstream. In the darkness a spirited and bloodied Ferdinand continued to shout, "Charge forward, my Castilian knights, I am your king!"[2]

In three hours of battle, more than twelve hundred Portuguese soldiers perished. Afonso had disappeared, but Ferdinand remained on the battlefield until midnight, convinced "that night that Our Lord had given him all of Castile." In the tradition of the victorious, the Castilian soldiers "took prisoners, gold, silver, clothes and many other things" from the dead Portuguese and their horses.[3]

Both sides subsequently claimed victory, but the battle of Toro permanently damaged Afonso's credibility as a contender for the Castilian crown. Within weeks Prince João returned to Portugal to disband the remnants of his army. On March 19 the fortress of Zamora surrendered to Ferdinand.

"To describe Isabella's joy when she heard about the victory at Toro would be impossible," wrote Palencia.[4] As a sign of her gratitude, the queen walked barefoot to the monastery of San Pablo despite the winter cold. Solemn religious processions filed through the streets of Tordesillas in honor of the event. Isabella sent jubilant letters to the major cities of Castile describing how "with the help of God our lord and his blessed mother the King conquered and destroyed the said enemy and his people."[5] She also vowed to found a monastery and church in Toledo in honor of Ferdinand's victory. On March 5, Isabella joined Ferdinand in Zamora for peace negotiations with the city's *alcalde*. Three weeks later the young king and queen marched through with their soldiers and dignitaries to take formal possession of the city.

After the battle of Toro, Afonso retreated to a defensive position and refortified the towns still faithful to his cause—among them Cantalapiedra, Castronuño, Portillo, and Mayorga. But the Portuguese king was clearly a defeated man, forced to send his betrothed niece, La Beltraneja, to Portugal for her protection. Finally, on June 13, realizing he had "little money and few followers" and concluding that "his stay in Castile was unsafe," Afonso left the kingdom and returned to Portugal where he and João "were received with great sadness and many tears by their people."[6]

By then, many Castilian rebels had already reconciled with Isabella and Ferdinand. In April the Duke of Arévalo, Álvaro de Stúñiga, was among the first to beg the king and queen for pardon. The monarchs had responded by excusing the duke and even allowing him to retain the lands he had received from Enrique. They did demand, however, that the duke return the town of Arévalo to Isabella's mother, the queen widow. Heartened by Isabella and Ferdinand's clemency, other aristocratic rebels sought forgiveness and were duly pardoned.

Only Carrillo and Villena remained at war. Well into the spring of 1476 they continued to battle royal troops in the greening Castilian countryside. Finally, after suffering an additional series of humiliating defeats, even those two rebels sought reconciliation.

To forgive the two men who had encouraged Afonso to invade Castile was a decidedly difficult task, and the negotiations lasted all summer. Villena's pardon was easier for Isabella and Ferdinand to effect, for his behavior was a direct result of the feuds of his dead father, Pacheco. By early September the king and queen had thus restored the youth as the Marquis of Villena. Several towns formerly in Villena's possession, however, now reverted to the Castilian crown.

From Aragón, King Juan had prevailed upon the young monarchs to forgive Carrillo as well. It would be better, the old king wrote, for Isabella and Ferdinand to think of the archbishop "with the memory of all his deeds on their behalf at the time it was important and forget the short time that he was alienated from them."[7]

Carrillo, who had pleaded for a pardon through a relative, now waited uneasily in Alcalá de Henares. He was unable to bring himself to appear personally before Isabella and Ferdinand. Finally, begrudgingly, Isabella issued him a pardon. Then she and Ferdinand restored nearly all of the archbishop's property, except for three fortresses, which royal officials were to hold for twenty months.

The archbishop reluctantly signed a pledge on September 20 promising new obedience to Isabella and Ferdinand. In a second sign of repentance, Carrillo wrote to the pope confessing that he had erred gravely by swearing obedience to the King of Portugal and attesting to his reconciliation.

By the harsh standards of fifteenth-century justice, Isabella and Ferdinand's restoration of rights to the rebel aristocrats was remarkably merciful. But there was an underlying rationale for their decision. It was clear that whatever support La Beltraneja once elicited from Afonso had crumbled with the battle of Toro. In the wake of that defeat, the young monarchs now had two choices: to wreak their vengeance upon the perpetrators of the rebellion or to build new bonds between those dissidents and the crown. Isabella and Ferdinand chose the second course and, by so doing, gained a reputation for being merciful Christian monarchs.

Underneath, the young king and queen were more than that. Although still in their mid-twenties, Isabella and Ferdinand were already practitioners of an astute political psychology. They knew nothing was more disarming to a defeated enemy than a show of cautious generosity. Ultimately their decision would enhance their victory by transforming the still-powerful but penitent barons from adversaries to allies.

CHAPTER TWENTY-SEVEN

Scales of Justice

The war released terrifying forces of greed and destruction upon Castile. For months soldiers faithful to Isabella and Ferdinand galloped over the Portuguese border seizing towns, burning croplands, and returning home with plunder. Others shadowed the Portuguese army as they tramped through the Castilian countryside, intercepting messengers and blocking supplies. Armed groups of men thus became an ordinary sight in the kingdom, and some, more criminal than patriotic, began to plunder the villages of Castile for selfish gain.

Burglaries, rape, and murder became commonplace, committed by anonymous, brutal groups of men who passed through Castilian villages in unpredictable waves. Fortresses, which could have been used as defenses against the Portuguese, were converted into outlaw hideouts. Churches and monasteries were stripped, their sacristies invaded for their jeweled and gilded treasures. To maintain peace within their walls, affluent towns, including Ávila, Salamanca, and Segovia, were forced to pay robber barons blackmail money.

The Castilian economy was in an equally bad state. At Burgos, the center of Castile's wool-exporting industry, trade with Flanders was disrupted by the Portuguese invasion. Consequently, the usual flow of foreign funds into the Castilian economy slowed dramatically. Moreover, merchants and moneylenders quibbled over the validity of every coin. The kingdom's already wobbly financial system, weakened still further by the war, thus veered toward bankruptcy.

In that worrisome atmosphere, Isabella and Ferdinand called the *Cortes* to Madrigal in April 1476. Eight months earlier Carrillo had boasted that he had raised Isabella from the distaff to the scepter and would bring her back to the distaff side again. Now, in the *Cortes* of 1476, the queen would prove him wrong.

Isabella's particular genius, in fact, was to blend the skills of the distaff with those of the scepter, to apply a meticulous, housewifely order upon the corruption-infested Castilian government. The resultant harmony, coordinated by a strong monarchy, would later epitomize Renaissance, rather than medieval, forms of government in other fledgling European nation-states.

Out of sheer necessity Isabella laid the groundwork for that evolution by reorganizing the kingdom's money system. First, the king and queen urged the *procuradores* to pass acts standardizing values for denominations of the Castilian coin. Then they abolished nearly all of the 150 mints of Enrique's reign, leaving only five to stamp coins for the crown of Castile.

More ominously, the *procuradores* restricted the fiscal activities of non-Christian Castilians. Jews and Mudéjars were forbidden to wear expensive silks and pearls, to adorn their clothes with silver and gold, or to similarly decorate the harnesses of their horses. Limits were established on the amount of interest Jewish moneylenders could collect. By the end of the *Cortes* session, Isabella and Ferdinand had thus established regulations for virtually every important fiscal transaction within the Castilian kingdom.

Financial reform was only the first step in their reorganization. To ensure compliance with their laws, Isabella and Ferdinand appointed ten men as *corregidores,* or crown officers, to live in the Castilian cities. Although some members of the *Cortes,* convinced their presence would curtail local autonomy, protested, Isabella was adamant: There was, she believed, no other way to enforce obedience to crown authority.

With similar energy Isabella and Ferdinand virtually overhauled the Castilian judicial system. Judges were appointed by the queen, but permitted to act independently. Once a week they or their assistants were obliged to inspect the prisons and hear the pleas of the accused. Prisoners were not to languish in prison indefinitely but to be brought to a speedy trial. Poverty was no excuse for delay. Special attorneys were hired at the crown's expense to serve as "advocates for the poor."

But efficient courts, while admirable in themselves, were of lesser importance to Isabella and Ferdinand than the task of apprehending criminals. The *procuradores* grumbled incessantly about the widespread crime that afflicted their communities. With Isabella and Ferdinand's approval the royal auditor, Alonso de Quintanilla, and Juan de Ortega, head priest of the bishopric of Villafrance de Montes de Oca, proposed a solution—a kingdom-wide *Hermandad,* or civilian police force.

In Castile, the *Hermandad* dated back to the twelfth and thirteenth centuries. The original *Santa Hermandad,* or Holy Brotherhood, as it was first called, was a loose collection of citizen police units designed to maintain civilian peace. It was formed primarily to suppress violent crimes, particularly those on the highways, in the open countryside, or by fugitives who had eluded town authorities.

More recently, Enrique had resurrected the *Hermandad* to keep peace in his tottering kingdom. In 1464 he ordered the local chapters from Madrid, Segovia, Cuenca, and Huete to coordinate their activities, and in the last faltering years of his reign, he ordered "constitutions" for the creation of a larger *Hermandad.*

Although Enrique died before those "constitutions" were established, Isabella and Ferdinand now framed a similar plan. To coordinate local units of the new *Hermandad,* the king and queen approved the establishment of a central *junta* in Toledo. By that authority every 100 *vecinos,* or Castilian householders, were to pay 1,800 maravedís to employ one policeman. This *cuadrillero,* or trooper, was expected to arrest any individual guilty of violent crimes in his region and bring him to trial in a two-man court. Anyone who committed robbery, murder, rape, housebreaking, or rebellion was to be apprehended. Since "rebellion" included those who supported the Portuguese cause, Isabella and Ferdinand could thus use the *Hermandad* as army adjuncts.

The capture of criminals was practically assured. If local *cuadrilleros* failed to apprehend a miscreant, they signaled neighboring members of the *Hermandad* by ringing church bells. If the fugitive eluded the *cuadrilleros* for more than five leagues—about fifteen miles—the obligation fell to the *Hermandades* of adjacent towns. Through such regional tracking techniques, criminals were almost always caught within a few hours or days.

Punishments were severe, their harshness underscored by the fact that they were written in blood. At the very least, petty thiefs were beaten with whips. Those convicted of stealing property worth 500 to 5,000 maravedís routinely lost an arm or a leg. The most serious offenders were tied to a post, where, as it was stipulated, "his body shall be taken for a target" with arrows.[1]

Three years after its creation, the *Hermandades* had succeeded in restoring peace to Castile so dramatically that the cities voted its continuation until 1498. To its credit, the *Hermandades* cleansed Castile of the swarms of robbers, murderers, and rapists who infested the land during the Portuguese war; to its detriment was the legacy of cruel, even sadistic punishments it perpetuated into the sixteenth century.

Gradually a new optimism began to flower in the fragile Castilian kingdom. Order, perhaps even prosperity could be restored to Castile with Isabella and Ferdinand as its monarchs. The reforms of the *Cortes* of 1476 had been the first step toward restoration of that peace. The vigilant militia of the *Hermandad* was a second effort. Its dedicated men, its terrifying punishments were already crushing the spores of anarchy that had spread so widely across Castile in the wake of Enrique's death. Once tamed, once disciplined and prosperous, the Castilians of Isabella's reign would be ready to drive invaders from their kingdom and make new conquests on their own.

Neither Isabella nor Ferdinand believed that force was the only way to subdue the conflicting interests of Castile's various factions. The queen, in particular, was a firm believer in the power of personal appearances. Vanity had less to do with it than piety. Isabella was convinced that the righteousness of her ideas would inevitably win over her subjects because the Almighty was on her side. The phrase "with the help of Our Lord" frequently appeared in her letters and conversations.

At the beginning of her reign, an observer reported that "Many men believed that Isabel was created miraculously for the Redemption of lost kingdoms."[2] The queen was also referred to in contemporary chronicles as a "second Virgin Mary." Similarly, the prelate Fray Iñigo de Mendoza perceived Isabella and Ferdinand's union as an embodiment of a national Christian identity that would soon encompass all of Spain.

By the end of the 1470s, the idea that Isabella and Ferdinand were messianic beings inspired their subjects to rally behind them in a Holy War against the Moors. But in 1476 those beliefs were not yet firmly established. The queen's fearless attitude and insistence upon her authority as an agent of justice would contribute to that legend. In the summer of 1476 that attitude was put to a public test.

At dawn on August 1 Isabella was awakened in Tordesillas by a messenger from her *converso* governor, Andrés de Cabrera. Segovia was in an uproar and the life of the queen's daughter Isabel was threatened. For months the five-year-old princess had been living peacefully in the Segovian alcázar under Cabrera's guardianship. But during the Portuguese invasion the Segovians became resentful of Cabrera's strict discipline over the town. A city officer named Alfonso Maldonado stirred their discontent.

When Cabrera left Segovia for a few days, Maldonado smuggled armed men into the town who killed the guards of the alcázar and imprisoned Cabrera's father-in-law, Pedro de Bobadilla. They then took possession of the rest of the castle, including the tower where the queen's daughter lived. From the turrets, the princess's attendants called for help. Ultimately royal soldiers drove Maldonado's men from the tower. Meanwhile Segovia's *converso* bishop, Juan Arías Dávila, incited the population to seize the city gates of San Martin and Santiago.

Isabella, fearing for her daughter's life, reacted "with much spirit" and determined to leave for Segovia at once. Coincidentally, the princess's coguardian, Beatriz de Bobadilla, was visiting Isabella at the time. The queen promised her that she would punish Maldonado for his treachery. Without waiting for the royal army, Isabella set out for Segovia accompanied only by Cardinal Mendoza, the Count of Benavente, and Beatriz. Tordesillas was sixty miles northwest of Segovia, a long arduous ride over mountainous terrain, but Isabella and her entourage rode continuously, arriving at dawn after a twenty-four-hour journey.

Outside the city gates Isabella learned that nearly the entire population, including Bishop Arías, was calling for Cabrera's dismissal. The prelate, who had known Isabella from her Segovian years, now advised her against passing through the gate of San Juan because it was barricaded by hostile Segovians. Moreover, he warned her against entering the city accompanied by Beatriz and Benavente, for to do so would almost certainly incite the crowd to new violence.

Incensed by Arías's disrespectful tone, Isabella replied: "Tell those *caballeros* and citizens of Segovia that I am Queen of Castile and this city is mine for my father left it to me and I do not need any laws or conditions set for me to enter what is mine. I shall enter by the gate I want and the Count of Benavente shall enter with me and all others I think appropriate to my service."[3] With that, Isabella and her entourage proceeded through the San Juan gate and into the angry crowds. Despite their hostility the Segovians did not injure the riders as they passed through the city's winding streets to the open square of the alcázar.

Isabella and her friends then crossed the drawbridge and entered the central courtyard beneath the tower where Isabel was imprisoned. Above the din of the crowd, Cardinal Mendoza and the Count of Benavente begged Isabella to close the gates to the courtyard behind them. But the queen refused. Instead she announced in a loud voice that anyone who wanted to enter the alcázar should. As a crowd squeezed into the courtyard, Isabella faced them and said, "My vassals and my servants, tell me what you desire for if it is for the good of my city and kingdom, I want it too."[4]

A murmur rippled through the crowd. The townspeople had expected a reprimand and were certainly not prepared for the queen's willingness to entertain their complaints. Finally a citizen spoke out, listing grievances against Cabrera and requesting his removal as *alcalde* of Segovia. Isabella interrupted him, announcing that she would act as governor herself and would subsequently appoint someone else who would be acceptable to the Segovians.

"What you want I want," said Isabella. "Therefore climb now those towers and those walls and push off all the steward's men and all the others who have this castle occupied because I want to deliver it to the custody of one of my servants, one who keeps my allegiance and who keeps the honor of you all."[5]

"*Vive la Reina!*" "Long live the Queen!" the crowd shouted. Later, having restored the alcázar to her command, having folded her five-year-old daughter in her arms, Isabella rode through the streets to the royal palace, followed by cheering crowds. There she assured the Segovians that they "would no longer be troubled by the *mayordomo* [Cabrera] and his officials" for she intended to investigate the matter thoroughly.[6] To begin with, she asked the citizens to send several representatives to discuss their grievances.

Soon afterward a citizens' committee presented their case against Cabrera. Isabella inquired into their accusations "with great diligence" but ultimately determined Cabrera's innocence. Whatever abuses the Segovians had suffered under his leadership were "mostly committed by his officials." But as a *converso,* hated for his wealth and influence, Cabrera became a scapegoat for those who lusted after his position. Isabella, "knowing that this scandal had been incited by some nobles and rich citizens,"[7] thus commanded that Cabrera be fully restored in his authority as *alcalde* of Segovia and its alcázar. This time the Segovians did not protest.

In mid-November 1476 Isabella was presented with another dilemma, the sudden death of the newly appointed Master of Santiago, Rodrigo Manrique. Immediately the nobles began to quarrel among themselves for the position. Carrillo, still uneasily reconciled to the king and queen, sought the mastership for one of his relatives. Villena also eyed it longingly. Nevertheless, electorates soon determined that Alonso de Cárdenas, *encomienda mayor* of León, or head of the largest province of the Santiago order, was the candidate of choice. He was a proven military leader who had successfully led raids against the Portuguese in Extremadura and who repeatedly inspired members of the order in battle. According to ancient tradition, the master was to be elected by thirteen counselors. In early December Cárdenas thus traveled forty-four miles southeast of Madrid to the convent of Uclés where the election was to take place.

Isabella, fearing Carrillo would foment a new rebellion among the nobles over the mastership, left Valladolid on December 9, determined to neutralize the struggle by claiming the position for the crown. After riding for three days and a night, Isabella arrived at Uclés and entered the monastic hall where the electorates, the *treces* and *comendadores* of the order, were meeting.

To her astonished audience Isabella explained that the Mastership of Santiago "is one of the great honors of this realm" and, because of its many fortresses bordering the Moorish frontier, the "Kings my ancestors always controlled it, giving it to their second sons or some other royal person. While the *comendador mayor* of León was loyal to the King my lord and me, I have decided that his Majesty ought to have the administration of the Mastership."[8] For that reason, Isabella added, she had already requested a bull of investiture from Pope Sixtus IV. Intimidated by Isabella's forceful words, the knights conceded.

In Rome, meanwhile, Isabella's request that the order be awarded to her husband shocked members of the Holy See. Confidentially, Isabella's ambassador wrote, "The Pope and Cardinals held it to be a most monstrous thing and contrary to all precedent that a woman should have any rights over the administration of orders."[9] Eventually, however, the ambassador convinced Sixtus to grant Isabella her request.

For nearly a year Ferdinand administered the order. But eventually the young monarchs, who were becoming increasingly sensitive to the needs of their constituency, began to worry about the long-range implications of seizing the mastership from Cárdenas. If Isabella and Ferdinand had learned anything from the Portuguese war, it was that old allies who felt their loyalties insufficiently rewarded were apt to turn traitorous.

A delicate equilibrium thus had to be established between the authority of the crown and the rights of its subjects—a balance as honest and clear as the one the monarchs demanded in their reforms of Castile's money system.

Eleven months after accepting the Santiago mastership, Ferdinand voluntarily relinquished it to Cárdenas. In return, the new master agreed to pay the crown 3 million maravedís each year, to be drawn from the order's income and used to maintain fortresses at the Moorish border. The king would have to wait twenty-two years until Cárdenas's death before he could again claim the Order of Santiago for himself. But by then the political scales had tipped decidedly in favor of the Castilian crown.

CHAPTER TWENTY-EIGHT

Certainly No Good Monarch
Would Do Less

B ehind Isabella and Ferdinand's efforts to secure the monarchy were fears about a second Portuguese invasion. In September 1476 Afonso V, still obsessed with the dream of wearing two crowns, assembled two hundred men and a fleet of ships and sailed east through the Strait of Gibraltar to Marseilles. Through a face-to-face meeting with Louis XI, Afonso hoped to bind the French king to his cause and use his well-trained army to invade Castile.

The devout, middle-age monarchs first met in Tours in an atmosphere of ceremonial warmth and hyperbole. Louis, still awed by Afonso's conquests in Berber Africa, embraced the Portuguese king obsequiously. He was, he told Afonso, "the very happiest ruler in the world because he saw the most noble and virtuous King of all Christendom."[1]

The two kings traveled north together to Paris, where Louis, although notoriously parsimonious, feted Afonso with celebrations. Banquets were held in his honor. Prisoners were freed from the dungeons. Afonso was presented with the keys to the city. The Portuguese king thus had every reason to believe Louis would support him, even though six months earlier the Castilians had defeated Louis's soldiers in an invasion of the Vizcaya.

Louis had not accepted this defeat easily. Nor had he earned the sobriquet Spider King on a whim. By the time Afonso arrived in France, Louis was engaged in a double intrigue. Just before Afonso's arrival, the French king had, in fact, been negotiating with Ferdinand's ambassadors. During those discussions he had even referred to Ferdinand as the "King of León and Castile."

Now, during his visit with Afonso, Louis took full measure of the plump, idealistic Portuguese king and determined to manipulate him for his own gain.

Ostensibly he promised to provide Afonso with aid against Isabella and Ferdinand, but he set forth two conditions: first, that he conclude his war against Burgundy; second, that the pope grant Afonso a dispensation for his marriage with La Beltraneja. The pope's approval, Louis observed with his usual iron-clad logic, had to be obtained "before everything else," for without the marriage, Afonso had no justifiable claim to the Castilian crown.[2] Louis did, however, agree to urge his own ambassadors at the Holy See to persuade the pope to grant the dispensation.

Simultaneously, the French king emphasized the importance of concluding his war with Burgundy. For years Louis had feuded with his powerful and intelligent cousin Charles the Bold, the Duke of Burgundy, the "oldest lord without a crown," and by late 1476 the struggle was drawing to a climax. In preparation for that decisive battle, Louis was feverishly stockpiling men and arms. To buy more time, Louis capitalized on Afonso's gullibility by dispatching him to Charles's camp in Nancy with the absurd mission of achieving a reconciliation.

Nevertheless, the elegant, still-handsome forty-eight-year-old Charles the Bold received Afonso respectfully. After listening to the Portuguese king's impassioned pleas for peace, Charles explained that Louis was untrustworthy and hence any hopes for a reconciliation were futile. Afonso refused to believe him. On January 21, 1477, he returned to Paris and wrote confidently to the Castilian Count of Ciudad Real that "I have the promises of the King of France who will help me with all his strength to conquer Castile."[3]

A few days later Afonso learned that during his return trip to Paris, Louis's soldiers and his Swiss mercenaries had crushed the Burgundian troops and killed Charles the Bold. Louis now seized the vast Burgundian territory for the crown of France.

Still, Louis's treachery made little impression on Afonso. In fact, he continued to trust Louis implicitly. When, on February 3, Pope Sixtus IV granted Afonso a dispensation to marry a close blood relation, the Portuguese king's faith in Louis was affirmed. Now that both conditions for French aid had been fulfilled, Afonso expected Louis to honor his promise. Louis, however, continued to procrastinate, for he was engaged in final negotiations with Aragón and Castile. The resultant pact, which would not become official for a year, stipulated that the provinces of Roussillon and Cerdagne were to be turned over to France; in exchange, Louis agreed to avoid aiding Portugal against Castile.

Before long Afonso became agitated, then disillusioned, and finally depressed. By summer he had retired to a remote monastery in Normandy and written his son João that "as all earthly vanities were dead within his bosom" he planned to renounce his kingship by "performing a pilgrimage to the Holy Land . . . devoting himself to the service of God."[4] Since he was abdicating the throne, Afonso ordered João to have himself crowned as Portugal's new monarch.

Alarmed by the Portuguese King's behavior, Louis insisted that Afonso be removed from France at once. Tactfully and diplomatically, he arranged for the departure by providing Afonso with a fleet of ships that returned him to Portugal in early autumn 1477.

A few weeks after Charles the Bold's death, the Castilian monarchs met in Toledo to fulfill Isabella's promise to found a church in commemoration of the victory at

Toro. That "imperial city," poised above the deeply etched ravines of the encircling Tagus River, was a leading center of scholasticism and culture in fifteenth-century Castile, as it had been through most of the Middle Ages. Four hundred years earlier El Cid had entered Toledo in triumph after defeating the Moors. It was in the "schools" of twelfth- and thirteenth-century Toledo that Jews, Moors, and Castilians had translated the ancient Greek and Roman manuscripts into Latin, an act that, in turn, had sparked the fourteenth-century Italian Renaissance.

Over the long centuries of the Spanish *Reconquista,* a majestic Gothic cathedral had slowly risen on Toledo's highest hill. It was the first cathedral to be built in Castile. As such, it made Toledo the primate or most venerable seat of Catholicism in the land. Therefore, Isabella and Ferdinand had chosen Toledo as the site for the Franciscan monastery "which they had promised for the victory God had been pleased to give them" at Toro a year earlier.[5]

On January 28, 1477, the king and queen arrived at Toledo's Moorish gate, the *Puerta de Visagra,* on the north side of the city where they were greeted by large crowds.

The next morning Isabella and Ferdinand presented their war trophies to the cathedral. To emphasize the importance of the event, the queen wore a white brocade dress embroidered with the insignias of Castile and León—golden lions and castles—and a long flowing cape of ermine. As they entered the cathedral and approached its Chapel of the New Kings, the monarchs offered spoils from the battle of Toro to their common ancestor, their great-grandfather Juan I, and hung the torn Portuguese standard over his tomb.

Later, in another ceremony on the crest of a hill overlooking the Tagus, they laid the foundation stone for the monastery and church of San Juan de los Reyes. The resultant building, a central-nave church with four symmetrical vaults, was designed by Juan Guas in what is now known as the Isabelline style of architecture. Among its most characteristic features were intricate stone carvings, fanciful pinnacles, and a stone ballustrade crowning the top of the church that blended features of Mudéjar and flamboyant Gothic architecture. Surrounding the inner cloister were arches and marble pillars carved with elaborate lacework, Isabella and Ferdinand's monogrammed crest, and their personal emblems—the *yugo* and the *flechas*—all of which can still be seen today.

The king and queen stayed in Toledo only a month, for at the end of February 1477 they rushed to Madrid to avert a *crisis triguera,* a wheat crisis. The devastation caused by the Portuguese war and the severe weather of 1476 had contributed to a crop shortfall. Then Castilian merchants, especially those from Andalusia, where cereal crops grew in abundance, had raised their prices and precipitated a panic.

The wheat shortage had far-reaching consequences for every level of society. Although bread flour could be made from a variety of grains, including barley, oats, and even beans, the best bread was from wheat. In an age when commoners often lacked tableware, bread was used as a crude kind of spoon, as a means to sop up juices, gravies, and wines. Stale bread was also used as a trencher, or dinner plate upon which food was placed in lieu of an earthenware dish.

To the church, wheat was also an important grain. In the thirteenth century the theologian Thomas Aquinas had decreed that the wafers of the Holy Eucharist should be made from wheat. Although other grains could be mixed into the dough, the church demanded that the main ingredient must be wheat.

In the ensuing crisis, Isabella and Ferdinand saw an opportunity to ingratiate themselves with the pope. By sending wheat to Italy, they hoped to win Sixtus IV's favor so that he would annul Afonso's betrothal to La Beltraneja and support their claim to the Castilian crown instead. Consequently, over the objections of Andalusian merchants, the king and queen decreed that there would be no wheat sales abroad except to the Holy See. To enforce those prohibitions, Isabella and Ferdinand appointed royal officers to supervise wheat transactions in some of Andalusia's most important ports—Sevilla, Jerez, Cádiz, Sanlucár de Barrameda and Puerto de Santa María. To defy the decree was to incur the monarchs' wrath and face penalties, imprisonment, and a loss of property. For the first time in its history, the kingdom of Castile had an organized, albeit primitive, trade policy.

In spite of Afonso's long absence from the Iberian peninsula, a stubborn nucleus of the Portuguese army continued to defend La Beltraneja's cause in Castile. Near the border, cities including Castronuño, Cubillas, Cantalapiedra, and Sieteiglesias still resisted Isabella and Ferdinand. Moreover, traitorous factions within largely loyalist cities often split those communities in two. In Extremadura, Trujillo was rent by a feud between the Monroys and the Stúñigas. In Castile's northwest corridor, pockets of Portuguese sympathizers had infiltrated Galicia. In the south, the Andalusian provinces were splintered by feuds between the Duke of Medina Sidonia and the Marquis of Cádiz.

To rally support in the face of such farflung resistance would require the energies of both monarchs. But to do so, to win the kingdom piece by piece, to bind the fragmented loyalties of Castile to Isabella and Ferdinand's cause, meant that the king and queen had to separate.

Their parting on April 21, 1477, was a painful wrench. Since the first year of marriage Isabella and Ferdinand had been continually separated by wars in Aragón, Catalonia, and Castile. Their only child was six years old, and they longed for a male heir. In the last twelve months the two had spent more time apart than together. A year earlier in late spring 1476, Ferdinand had been called to the Navarre by King Juan to protect that duchy from the French. Now the prospect of still another separation, another series of battles and more lost chances to conceive a male child, pressed heavily on the queen's mind. Isabella parted from Ferdinand most unhappily. Ferdinand, too, was deeply anguished.

First the king traveled north to Medina del Campo where, from the formidable brick and battlemented castle of La Mota, he formulated an attack on the rebels who clung to Castronuño and its three neighboring Extremaduran towns. On April 25, in a stunning blaze of artillery, cannon, and *ingenios,* the Castilians simultaneously besieged the castles of Sieteiglesias, Cantalapiedra, Cubillas, and Castronuño. Only Castronuño held out; it did not concede to the Castilians until October 1.

In southern Extremadura Isabella worked with similar tenacity. At first, when she had proposed that journey, Ferdinand, Cardinal Mendoza, Gutierre de

Cárdenas, and other members of the royal council had protested because of Extremadura's proximity to Portugal. But Isabella had insisted; she considered the conquest of southern Extremadura an obligation.

The queen told her counselors:

> I have always heard it said that blood goes to the part of the body that is wounded in order to heal it . . . then it would not be [for me] to act as a good monarch if I were to hear constantly about the war that the Portuguese . . . tyrannically wage against the Castilians in those parts and . . . bear it with a good face. The kings who want to reign must work for it. My opinion is that my Lord, the King should go to those areas beyond the mountain pass and I should go to the other areas in Extremadura and so we would take care of both.[6]

When Isabella spoke with such pious conviction, Ferdinand knew there was no point refuting her. After seven years of marriage, it was clear that "his wife had great spirit . . . and once her mind was made up it was difficult to change it."[7] Besides, Isabella was beginning to think of herself and Ferdinand as instruments of God, chosen to elevate Castile to its highest potential through their bravery and commitment. Ferdinand, too, had embraced that theory, although perhaps not with as much intensity as the queen. And as their marriage evolved, he had come to respect his wife's judgment as much as his own. Over the years Ferdinand would, in fact, concede ever more frequently to Isabella for, as Pulgar observed, she had "great ability and a good natural intelligence."

In April 1477 Isabella had thus proceeded west to Extremadura, stopping first to pray at the Hieronymite monastery at Guadalupe and then, on May 15, the troubled city of Trujillo. Twice she sent her secretary Fernán Álvarez de Toledo to demand entrance to the enormous Moorish castle that loomed over the city, and twice the *alcaide,* Pedro de Baeza, had refused. The official did so, he told Isabella's secretary, because of orders from the Marquis of Villena. In reality, the marquis had no authority over the castle for he had ceded it to the crown when he reconciled with Isabella and Ferdinand in 1476. Baeza nevertheless steadfastly denied the queen entrance and announced that if she insisted, he would use artillery.

Isabella was enraged. "I tell you that I will enter my city understanding that it is mine through God's service," she retorted coolly, "for I will not be stopped by the inconveniences that my arrival has caused this *alcaide.* Certainly no good monarch would do less and neither will I."[8]

Then Isabella summoned a large army of Andalusian soldiers stationed in Guadalupe to march to Trujillo. At the same time, she ordered Villena to her side. The marquis appeared most reluctantly, still insisting that by rights he owned the castle. But Isabella was so enraged that Villena, "seeing the determined will of the Queen," commanded his *alcaide* to cede.[9] Trujillo surrendered, Baeza apologized for his mistake, and Villena was ordered to relinquish some of his lands. Gradually Isabella was learning that the mercy she and Ferdinand had initially showed old enemies was a calculated risk. While some had blossomed into loyal allies, others were like weeds, pulled from a freshly tilled field, who reappeared in nefarious form with frustrating persistence.

The queen next turned her energies to establishing new branches of the *Hermandad* in Extremadura. As Isabella's counselors had reported, the province was overrun with robbers, outlaws, and Portuguese sympathizers. Through spies she soon identified the fortresses the brigands used as hideouts and then ordered the *Hermandad* to raze them. From the fortresses of Madrigalejo, Figueruela, Castronuevo, Palacios, and Orellana scores of outlaws fled, some apprehended by the *Hermandad,* others killed by Isabella's soldiers, others escaping across the Portuguese border.

Isabella had one more task to accomplish in Extremadura. On July 1 she rode to the ocher-walled city of Cáceres. Like Trujillo, Cáceres had been riddled with feuds. A year earlier the queen had dispatched a *corregidor* there to reestablish peace. Now, as she passed through its city gates flanked by three hundred knights, the entire population had appeared in the streets displaying banners, crosses, and insignias of their trade.

Isabella immediately assembled one hundred of Cáceres's most important *grandees* and, in an impassioned speech, chastised them for civil disobedience. Despite her orders, the nobles had still not destroyed their defensive fortresses. Moreover, they had continued to interfere in the election of city officials. Henceforth, Isabella pronounced, all those who had been appointed as officials would retain those positions for life. After their death, Isabella "and the sovereigns who followed her would appoint new ones."[10] Thus the privilege of free election was removed from Cáceres and subsumed under the authority of the crown.

The citizens greeted Isabella's announcement with relief. To them she was a new type of monarch. Even those who had lived under Juan II or Enrique IV had little experience with strong sovereigns and certainly not with one who was female. On July 9, with peace restored and her popularity reaffirmed, Isabella left for Andalusia.

Extremadura had been Isabella's first solo campaign as queen, and she had left impressive accomplishments in her wake. In a sense that western province had served as a training ground for the task that still lay ahead in Andalusia. But to Isabella, as to her subjects, it had illustrated a basic fact: Efficient government had less to do with gender than with character and skill. At the age of twenty-six Isabella was already proving a more successful sovereign than her father Juan II or her brother Enrique IV.

CHAPTER TWENTY-NINE

Triumphs at Sevilla

Isabella was received in Sevilla with flowers, cheering crowds, fiestas, and banquets. She had approached the city from the lime-washed village of Rinconada at the shores of the Guadalquivir River. On July 25, 1477, the queen sailed into the "city of reflections" on a luxurious barge hung with tapestries and gold ornaments owned by the Duke of Medina Sidonia. She disembarked at the Bridge of the Macarena where Sevillian officials and the duke presented her with the keys to the alcázar.

Often, in the first weeks after Isabella's arrival in Sevilla, the forty-three-year-old duke Juan Enrique de Guzmán visited her at the alcázar in an effort to retain her favor. The duke, who had inherited vast estates in the fertile valleys of western Andalusia, had been one of Isabella's most steadfast advocates during the Portuguese war. In the wake of those skirmishes, however, he had seized properties that belonged to the crown and the city of Sevilla—among them the castles of Alcalá de Fuadayra and Utrera and the city and fortress of Tarifa.

By mid-1476 groups of armed men overran the valley of the Guadalquivir like locusts, making the province notoriously ungovernable. The duke "worked to prejudice the Queen in whatever manner he could"[1] by placing the blame for that anarchy on his rival, the redhaired Marquis of Cádiz, Rodrigo Ponce de León. Cádiz was heir to equally vast domains in southern Andalusia and, as Juan Pacheco's son-in-law, had sided with the Portuguese.

Nevertheless, Isabella took no action against Cádiz. She knew that for generations the Medina Sidonia family, the Guzmáns, and Cádiz's clan, the Leóns, had been embroiled in feuds. Instead, Isabella informed Medina Sidonia that while she intended to honor him for his past loyalty, she had come to Sevilla to render justice and "rid it of all crimes and tyrannies and . . . work to do so with the help of God to make everything secure."[2]

In the ensuing weeks, although Medina Sidonia continued to pay Isabella homage, he retained the fortresses he had taken and made no efforts to return them. Isabella could have simply demanded that the duke relinquish his castles; she could also have summoned Cádiz to her court and ordered him to do the same. But force, as the queen had learned in Segovia a year earlier, had to be exercised cautiously, and only as a last resort. She preferred to have both Medina Sidonia and Cádiz come to her side voluntarily and cede their illegal possessions of their own free will.

By the late fifteenth century, Sevilla was already Castile's largest city, with 40,000 inhabitants and another 133,000 in its environs. The lifeblood of the region was the four-hundred-mile Guadalquivir River, rising in the east in the Cazorla Sierras, flowing past Sevilla on two sides and through a gently undulating valley into the Atlantic Ocean on Castile's southwest coast. The rich soil of the river valley was ideal for farming, and the plains surrounding Sevilla burgeoned with plantations of olive, fig, and orange trees, grape vineyards, cereals, beans, and peppers. Palm and banana trees, brought from North Africa by the Moors generations earlier, dotted the terrain; bees buzzed through the wildflowers producing thick combs of honey; Arabian horses, cows, and merino sheep grazed at the shores of the river, whose lush vegetation inspired the Andalusian proverb that "the water of the Guadalquivir fattens horses better than the barley of other countries."

From its earliest discovery by the Romans, Sevilla had been an important inland port connecting the Andalusian interior with trade routes to Western Europe, Africa, and the Mediterranean. But despite its obvious geographical advantages, fifteenth-century Sevilla lacked a strong central government. The anarchy that dominated the Andalusian countryside was matched, or even surpassed by the crimes committed within the city itself. As a result, ordinary law enforcement became impossible. Property owners squabbled constantly. Urban officials, bribed or intimidated by hired criminals, rarely intervened. Taxes remained uncollected. Courts were backed up for years on end and trials were often a mockery of justice. Dung heaps obstructed the streets. Disease-carrying rats slithered through alleyways, around patio corners, and beneath bridges. Petty crimes were ubiquitous, violence ordinary. For the common man, everyday existence had become a hazardous venture.

Undaunted, Isabella established a tribunal in a "great room" of the alcázar, which was later known as the *Sala de Justicia,* or Hall of Justice. Although not formally trained in Castilian law, the queen established herself there as chief magistrate. To fill the gaps in her knowledge, Isabella appointed *letrados,* or university-trained legal experts, to serve as specialists in the tribunal's most difficult cases. Contrary to Castilian tradition, some of those *letrados* were not aristocrats, but rather middle-class men, sons of burghers who had been sent to the university to become legal clerks. In this way Isabella was already laying the groundwork for a new kind of monarchy, one supported by men of talent and intelligence as well as those of high birth.

The queen's tribunal followed an orderly pattern. Every Friday morning

Isabella presided over the assembled body from an elevated chair covered with a gold cloth and placed on a long raised platform. Earlier each week the *letrados* and members of Isabella's royal council had considered each case and retained those that were most difficult for the Friday morning sessions.

Many suits involved property disputes and murders, but the most pathetic were crimes committed against orphans and widows. Isabella listened to these petitions with great "diligence." Those she believed too technical were referred to the *letrados*.

Within two months of the new *audiencia,* or criminal court, Isabella settled so many cases and rendered justice so harshly that the Sevillians grew fearful. In her zeal the queen became excessive, following, as Pulgar observed, "more the path of sternness than of compassion."[3] Some Sevillians guilty of crimes but not yet apprehended grew so anxious that they left the city, fleeing west to Portugal or south to Moorish Granada. In fact, so many Sevillian homes were abandoned that the alarmed city fathers sent their spiritual leader, the Bishop of Cádiz, to talk with the queen.

"My highest and most Excellent Queen and Ladyship," the bishop began, "since your arrival the great rigor of your ministers have demonstrated the execution of justice and changed everything that was once sad into a place of great fear." The bishop reminded the queen that men were generally "inclined to evil" and while this was particularly true in Spain where they had languished under the rule of "inferior lords . . . it should not close the door to clemency."[4]

Isabella, surprised by the bishop's criticism and "moved by his tears," agreed to show more mercy.[5] Her initial harshness, it seemed, had sufficiently impressed the Sevillians with the fact that criminal acts would not be tolerated during her reign. Ultimately, the queen issued a general pardon to all who had committed crimes with the proviso that they made fair restitution of property to their victims. Only one crime was inexcusable: heresy.

Shortly after Isabella's arrival in Sevilla, she heard the passionate sermons of a Dominican priest named Alonso de Hojeda, who accused the *conversos* of Sevilla of secretly practicing Judaism. Although the idea that the church had been corrupted by some Christians who secretly embraced another faith was not new, Hojeda's fiery delivery and his visions of a deliberately falsified Christianity terrified his listeners. No one was more affected than the queen, who, as a devout Catholic monarch, envisioned her domain as a law-abiding country dominated by a pure church. To verify Hojeda's accusations, Isabella launched her own investigation through several ecclesiastics, among them Cardinal Mendoza and an austere Dominican friar from Segovia named Tomás de Torquemada whom Isabella had known from adolescence. Some months later those prelates returned a report that at least partially verified Hojeda's accusations: *Conversos* were practicing Jewish rites not only in Sevilla but throughout the Castilian kingdom.

The only solution, Hojeda, Torquemada, and others insisted, was an ecclesiastical inquisition similar to the one that had existed in Aragón since the thirteenth century. Such a tribunal, Torquemada argued, would ensure punishment for "blasphemers, deniers of God and the Saints . . . magicians and diviners."[6] As the Queen of Castile, Isabella was obliged to dispel religious anarchy from the Castilian church just as she had checked criminal disorder in its towns.

Ultimately, Isabella conceded to her religious counselors. In early 1478 she and Ferdinand applied to the Holy See to establish an inquisition. On November 1, 1478, Pope Sixtus IV thus issued a bull, *Exigit sincerae devotionis,* granting the monarchs permission to appoint several priests to investigate those alleged to have perpetrated crimes against the Castilian church.

But still Isabella hesitated. To use the bull, to burrow beneath the peaceful surface of the practice of Christianity, the queen sensed, would be to raise questions Castile was not yet stable enough to absorb.

In August 1477 the Marquis of Cádiz appeared unannounced at the Sevillian alcázar. The thirty-three-year-old *grandee* arrived under unusual circumstances—late at night at a back door of the palace; presumably to avoid attracting the attention of his rival, the Duke of Medina Sidonia. Isabella had already retired, but when she heard about Cádiz's arrival, she summoned her counselors to her side and welcomed her guest.

The red-haired and bearded marquis was not only handsome but charming. "If it pleases your Royal Majesty, I will show my innocence and do whatever your Royal Majesty wishes," the marquis began on bended knee. "I did not come here with any assurances that Your Royal Majesty gave me but . . . with the innocence I have . . . Ladyship, please send [officials] to receive your fortresses of Jerez and Alcalá."[7] In the next breath, Cádiz begged the queen to forgive him and his followers for the crimes he had committed in support of Afonso V, which, he explained, was his duty as Juan Pacheco's son-in-law.

Clearly, Isabella was pleased with Cádiz's words. She replied:

> I have heard many good things about you, but the trust that
> pushed you to come to me is a clear sign of your innocence, and
> even though you deserve a punishment, the fact of delivering
> yourself into my hands would force me to be merciful. Deliver
> those fortresses you hold in Jerez and Alcalá and I will mediate in
> the differences between you and the Duke of Medina and decide
> what is just. . . .[8]

When Medina Sidonia learned about Cádiz's offer, he resolved not to be outdone by his rival. Three days after Isabella took possession of Cádiz's castle of Jerez, Medina Sidonia signed his own pact with the queen, authorizing her to take possession of his five illegally held towns. For the first time in years, the bloody skirmishes that raged between followers of the duke and the marquis ceased. By September 13, 1477, when Ferdinand arrived in Sevilla, all of Andalusia was at peace.

Nevertheless, Ferdinand's return was marked with tensions. Like Isabella, he traveled down the Guadalquivir by barge and arrived at the same Bridge of Macarena where he was greeted by the city fathers. But in contrast to the queen's arrival six weeks earlier, few crowds had appeared. This was not necessarily alarming, as Palencia observed, for Ferdinand had arrived during siesta time "when the heat . . . obliged people to retire into their homes."[9]

For months Ferdinand had been preoccupied with the failing Aragonese war against France. No sooner was he reunited with Isabella in Sevilla than the citizens began to protest the wheat shortage. The peninsula-wide crop shortfalls of 1476–77 had affected Catalonia more severely than other regions because of the war's devastation. Knowing that, Ferdinand's Castilian relatives, the Enríquezes, had ordered the Sevillian merchants to export Andalusian grain to the kingdom of Aragón.

Isabella was deeply torn. On one hand, she was "inclined to look out for the good of her subjects" and to quell any additional protests by the Sevillians;[10] on the other, she understood the importance of sending grain to Catalonia, the "buffer" province between France and Spain. Furthermore, because Isabella did not want to undermine Ferdinand's already tenuous leadership in Catalonia by restricting the exports, she wrote the king "with urgency" to travel south to Sevilla and judge the situation for himself.

Initially, Ferdinand's arrival did little to calm the Sevillians' fears. With each passing day the resentments between the privileged, who could afford to buy wheat at inflated prices, and the commoners intensified. Before long, the two groups were exchanging "taunts and insults" and again threatening the newly established Sevillian peace.

In the interim Cádiz had still not signed a pact with the king and queen. To ensure that the *grandee* would fulfill his promises, Isabella and Ferdinand left Sevilla on October 4 and traveled down the Guadalquivir toward Jerez on Castile's southeastern coast. By October 7 the royal party arrived at the port city of Sanlúcar de Barrameda where three tributaries of the Guadalquivir converge and open like a broad window onto the Atlantic.

Isabella had seen the sea only once before, as a child when she traveled with Enrique to Gibraltar. The azure stretch of water pounding against the rocky shore fascinated her. On the trip down the Guadalquivir the queen had talked of sailing on the high sea, but at the last minute she had given up the idea "because she suspected she was pregnant."[11]

A year earlier, a twenty-five-year-old Genoese navigator named Christopher Columbus had been washed ashore in a shipwreck in Lagos, Portugal, only a few miles from the Castilian border. Yet another decade would pass before that intrepid navigator would appear before the queen to share his excitement about the Ocean Sea, as the Atlantic was then called.

But in Sanlúcar de Barrameda in October 1477 there was little time for idle speculation about the sea. The Duke of Medina Sidonia, threatened by Isabella and Ferdinand's visit to the Marquis of Cádiz, entertained them in his hilltop palace with "costly celebrations" and "excessive" banquets. Thereafter, the monarchs proceeded south, arriving in the rolling hills and freshly harvested vineyards of Jerez, which were already famous for their sherries, where they were entertained by Cádiz.

By the time the monarchs left Jerez they had accomplished their goal: Cádiz had signed a pact granting the towns of Alcalá de Guadiar and Constantina to the crown. Although Cádiz feared that if he ceded his fortresses to the crown, he would be vulnerable to new attacks from Medina Sidonia, both nobles ultimately surrendered their properties. Nevertheless, the difficulty of the armistice had impressed Isabella and Ferdinand with the enmity of the rivals, which, at the slightest provocation, could easily spark new violence in Andalusia. Doubtless, Isabella's newly established Andalusian *Hermandad* would go a long way to reinforcing civilian peace. As an additional precaution the monarchs permanently banned both the Marquis of Cádiz and the Duke of Medina Sidonia from Sevilla.

Within weeks of the monarchs' return to Sevilla, there were ominous new rumblings from the Portuguese border. Afonso V had returned home on November 14, 1477, to reclaim the crown less than a week after his son was coronated, and by winter 1478 was preparing for a second invasion of Castile. Villena, never fully reconciled to the king and queen, secretly gathered and trained new soldiers in Castile. Carrillo also invited Afonso to enter the town of Talavera de la Reina near his own Toledo so that he would be strategically headquartered in central Castile.

When Ferdinand learned about these activities, he abruptly left Sevilla, arriving in Madrid on February 27, 1478. By then most of the Castilian *grandees,* clergy, and commoners supported Isabella and Ferdinand as their lawful queen and king. Increasingly, the citizenry had come to regard the couple as saviors, as beings who had been touched by divine grace and thus had restored civil order to the war-torn kingdom.

Yet Ferdinand had journeyed north with trepidation for, as he confided to a companion, he would have preferred returning to Aragón to conclude the Catalonian war. But once again the affairs of Castile were to take precedence. By late winter 1478 Ferdinand had a second compelling reason to remain in Castile—the anticipated birth of his second child. As he wrote to his father King Juan on March 11:

> The main obstacle [for traveling to Aragón] is Her Majesty's
> pregnancy . . . this is now the most serious and important matter
> in Spain and . . . there is nothing else that could be more neces-
> sary or desired. If Our Lord, using his mercy and compassion in
> the benefit of Spain grants us what we need and desire [a male
> heir] Your Majesty will . . . understand how necessary it is for
> King Ferdinand to stay here. . . .[12]

In this second confrontation against the Portuguese, Ferdinand displayed a new confidence. The vision of "El Africano" ruthlessly cutting down the Moslems of Morocco no longer intimidated him as it had earlier in the war. Moreover, the king could now rely upon the *Hermandad* to provide him with reinforcements. Thus, with Ferdinand's call to arms in March 1478, 3,000 lancers and 11,000 footsoldiers appeared in Madrid and marched south to Toledo. The formidable presence of the *Hermandad* soon frightened Afonso and sent him and his soldiers scurrying off to Portugal again. With peace thus assured, Ferdinand returned to Sevilla.

Carrillo's bitter prediction of 1475 had not come true. The queen had not returned to the distaff side nor did it seem likely that she ever would. With Afonso's second failed offensive Isabella now wielded the scepter with uncontested authority. And before long the life that now stirred within her womb would permanently silence La Beltraneja's claim to the Castilian crown.

On June 30, 1478, between ten and eleven in the morning, Isabella gave birth to a baby boy. Sevilla went wild with celebrations. So did the rest of Castile and all of Aragón. In Barcelona there were festivals and religious processions. The city of Lonja was lighted with torches and bonfires for a public dance.

The little prince was named Juan for both his grandfathers and for John the Baptist. Among the devout the prince was regarded with messianic fervor. Politically, in fact, the baby was a savior, for as a male he would inherit the twin crowns of Castile and Aragón. And as the only living male descendant of King Juan II of Castile, the prince dealt a final blow to La Beltraneja's claim to the Castilian throne.

The baby, wrote Ferdinand to the counselors of Barcelona, had "united all the kingdoms and estates." With the birth of the prince, Pulgar instructed a contemporary to ". . . raise your hands to the sky. Now it is given that . . . our eyes behold the salvation of this kingdom."[13]

On Thursday, July 9, in honor of Prince Juan's baptism, *regidores,* or urban officials, dressed in long black velvet gowns led an enormous procession through the streets of Sevilla to the Church of Santa María. It was said that every cross in the city and its monasteries was displayed in that procession and the air was filled with music from trumpets, horns, and drums. The citizens had never seen such pageantry. The infant prince, swaddled in rich clothes, was carried in the arms of his aristocratic nurse, Doña Maria de Guzmán, beneath a brocaded canopy of state. An elegantly dressed young page carried the heavy silver baptismal basin on his head. Close behind him was Pedro de Stúñiga, the *justica mayor,* or lord chief magistrate, of Sevilla, who brought the baptismal candlesticks and the offering, a gold *excelente,* made from fifty gold pieces.

At the high altar of the church, Cardinal Mendoza presided over the baptismal ceremony. Beside him stood the prince's ecclesiastical godfather, Nicolás Franco, Pope Sixtus IV's *nuncio.* Ferdinand and Isabella were not present, for, according to custom, parents did not attend their child's baptism.

The magnificence of Prince Juan's baptism was followed by the appearance of a celestial event that had been predicted by astronomers at the University of Salamanca for months. Twenty days after the ceremony, on St. Martha's feast day, there was an eclipse of the sun, an occurrence said to be "more frightening than anyone could remember," turning the sky so black "that the stars appeared in the sky as if it was night." The commoners, convinced it was the Day of Judgment, fled to the churches to pray for the return of the light. The sun did, of course, reappear, although one chronicler, fearing the eclipse was a harbinger of bad luck or impending doom for Prince Juan, insisted it "never returned to shine as brightly as it had before."[14]

But such rumors did not stop Isabella or Ferdinand from formally presenting the prince to the people of Sevilla. The queen, who "abhorred sorcerers and soothsayers," had probably been warned about the eclipse by university astronomers. In any case, the event did not appear to have caused her any special concern. A fanfare of trumpets, horns, and other instruments soon announced Prince Juan's presentation to the citizens of Sevilla. Then Ferdinand appeared mounted "very jovially upon a silver-gray horse," harnessed with black velvet. For the occasion the king was dressed in a brocade gown "braided and fringed in gold and a hat . . . fringed with gold thread."[15]

Although it was not quite six weeks since Isabella had given birth, she appeared before the Sevillians in full vitality "capering on a white palfrey in a very richly gilt saddle and a harness of gold and silver." She was dressed in a very rich *brial* of brocade bedecked "with pearls of many kinds." Beside her rode her sister-in-law, the Duchess of Villahermosa, wife of Alfonso of Aragón. On Isabella's right, holding the bridle of her horse, was the Count of Haro; to her left walked Prince Juan's godfather, the Count of Benavente. The infant prince was carried by a nurse who rode on a mule "saddled in velvet and pillowed in a colorful brocade."[16] To the delight of the admiring crowd, the nurse held Prince Juan up so that he could be seen by all. The procession ended at the Cathedral of Sevilla where a "very festive" mass was said at the high altar for Prince Juan's birth. Then the queen offered the gold *excelentes,* one for the fund to complete the cathedral, the other to her chaplains.

The ceremony must have been one of the most joyous moments of Isabella's life. After eight years of marriage she had produced a male child who united the main and lateral branches of the Trastámaras and would someday rule over Castile and Aragón. In the ensuing years the queen would expend singular energy on the preservation of Prince Juan's health and happiness.

CHAPTER THIRTY

Surrender

By the summer of 1478 Castile was still not wholly at peace. In Córdoba a feud raged between the Aguilars and Fernández de Córdoba. In Extremadura, where Villena hoped to recover the properties he had lost, there were ominous new border skirmishes. And in Old Castile, despite Carrillo's recent defeat at Talavera de la Reina, he continued to act as "more a pope than a prelate" by excommunicating Ferdinand's military officers.

Less than a week after Prince Juan's birth, Isabella and Ferdinand publicly chastised the archbishop by circulating a notice accusing him of disloyalty to the crown. Carrillo, they proclaimed, had persistently attempted to start "new wars in great disservice to God and to them" despite the fact that a year earlier they had pardoned him for his treachery.[1] Yet now he had waged war "as he did before and created new scandals in our kingdoms."[2] As punishment, the king and queen intended to embargo the archbishop's rents and seize his fortresses and towns. They also dispatched their secretary Alfonso Colón to Pope Sixtus IV to explain their occupation of Carrillo's fortresses and to appeal his excommunications.

Simultaneously, the monarchs ordered a final offensive against all remaining Portuguese sympathizers. On August 1, 1478, the Master of Santiago, Alonso de Cárdenas, led thousands of lancers across the Duero to crush all lingering signs of Portuguese support in Extremadura. South of Cáceres, the *clavero,* or municipal key-keeper, of Alcántara attacked the rebellious village of Merida. Soldiers commanded by the Bishop of Evora stormed Medellín. On the high seas, Ferdinand alerted an Aragonese armada in Sicily to step up its watch over Portuguese boats in the Mediterranean. In the Atlantic, the Castilian navy seized thirty-five Portuguese ships laden with gold from St. George La Mina.

These, however, were only vicarious victories. Ferdinand and Isabella were hands-on monarchs who enjoyed resolving conflicts in person. To do so, they planned a tour to Andalusia's most unstable cities to personally bring "the lands under their obedience."[3] On October 2, 1478, the royal court journeyed northwest from Sevilla toward Écija and then on to Córdoba. In that ancient city on the Guadalquivir, once the intellectual center of the Moorish kingdom, Isabella and Ferdinand ended the feud between the Aguilars and the Fernández de Córdobas through a series of negotiations similar to those in Sevilla. And again they conducted a weekly tribunal with themselves as magistrates. Outside the city limits the *Hermandad* enforced the peace.

By November 22 Isabella and Ferdinand had restored eight new towns to their obedience. To consolidate their achievements, Isabella remained in Córdoba until Christmas while Ferdinand rode north with a battalion of armed men to Trujillo. That Extremaduran city, having been reconciled to Isabella in 1477, was to serve as military headquarters for the last stages of the Portuguese war.

From the moment of his birth, Isabella kept Prince Juan by her side. She did not, however, nurse the infant prince. In fifteenth-century Castile high-born children were routinely suckled by wet nurses carefully chosen for their health and character. A healthy woman with a placid disposition was thought ideal, for it was believed that the child imbibed her character in her breast milk. Thus the Mendoza noblewoman Maria de Guzmán became the prince's wet nurse.

The queen was already a devoted mother, and her maternal instincts were doubtless intensified by the fact that Juan was heir to twin crowns. Consequently, Isabella watched the infant warily, ever vigilant about his health, ever fretful over any cold or stomach upset, which, in that preantibiotic era, could easily escalate into a serious illness.

The queen was not the only one who fretted over the newborn's life. From Aragón, his paternal grandfather, King Juan, sent congratulatory letters about Prince Juan's birth as well as instructions about the child's education. Above all, he warned Ferdinand to avoid raising the Prince under the tutelage of any one particular *grandee*. To do so, the Aragonese king wrote, was a dangerous practice for it provided the guardian with inappropriate influence over the heir. "In any case," he wrote, "the child should not be educated in Castile, but should be brought with care to the kingdom of Aragón."[4]

Isabella probably rejected the idea outright. King Juan was hardly qualified as a guardian: He was eighty years old, in fragile health, and his kingdom was still at war. Nor was Isabella the type of mother to relinquish her children easily. Years before, on the eve of her meeting with Enrique in Segovia, she had quarreled with Carrillo and Ferdinand, refusing to entrust Princess Isabel to Cabrera as a guarantee for Enrique. Only after his death had she done so, and then only temporarily. With Prince Juan she was even more protective. From the moment of his birth, the little prince had sparked a fervent maternal nature in Isabella that grew even stronger as the boy matured. Judging from the surviving records of his childhood court, it developed into an intense, even neurotic attachment.

Those feelings may well have been exacerbated by Isabella's gradual realization that the prince, who was unusually prone to cold and digestive upsets, had a sickly constitution. In an effort to improve their son's health, the king and queen offered special prayers to the Sevillian cathedral's Virgin of Antiquity. When the child grew more sturdy, they requisitioned a silver statue of the Christ Child for the Lady's Chapel there. Through prayer, the donation of alms, and meticulous surveillance of Prince Juan's health, Isabella and Ferdinand thus attempted to ensure their son's development into a healthy adult.

By late 1478 other issues clouded King Juan's relationship with Isabella and Ferdinand. For two years their Castilian ambassadors had been negotiating a peace treaty with Louis XI of France over Portugal. It was finally resolved in June 1478. By August Louis proposed a revised treaty that provided different terms for peace in Castile and in Aragón. The resultant pact was signed by French and Castilian ambassadors on October 9 at St. Jean-de-Luz.

The treaty was divided into several parts. The first section reestablished the ancient peace between Castile and France and demanded that Louis cease all aid to Portugal. The second delineated the terms of peace between Ferdinand and other participants in the French-Catalonian struggle, among them Ferdinand's half sister Leonor of Navarre, Ferrante of Naples, Rêné of Anjou, and Louis XI. In the third and most thorny part of the treaty, worded with deliberate ambiguity, Louis agreed to peace with King Juan of Aragón "if he felt inclined to it."[5] In that eventuality, four counselors from Cerdagne and Roussillon were to meet to determine Louis's claims to those counties.

Months earlier King Juan had vehemently objected to Louis's effort to hold Roussillon and Cerdagne in perpetual trust until he was able to redeem them for 300,000 escuderos. So intent was the Aragonese king upon regaining the provinces that when Cardinal Mendoza suggested he cede them temporarily to Louis, Juan accused his old friend of being a francophile. Juan's paranoia even spilled over onto his son. To encourage Ferdinand to continue the Catalonia war in 1478, he had peevishly written:

> Is my son waiting for a more favorable time to avenge this offense
> to our honor and recover this land? Because now his foe, the King
> of Portugal has nothing to eat, the *grandees* of Castile are more
> united than ever before, if he wants to destroy the archbishop of
> Toledo [Carrillo], in five days there will be no memory left of
> him, and the King of France, his natural foe, is in dire straits be-
> cause of his endeavor [in Burgundy]. He [Ferdinand] will not be
> able to find a more favorable time than the one he has now.[6]

Juan had so exacerbated Ferdinand's guilt over his repeated abandonment of the Catalonian war that in the October 9, 1478, treaty with Louis, Ferdinand sidestepped terms of an Aragonese peace altogether, leaving them contingent upon Juan's willingness to negotiate with France himself. To discuss that strategy, Ferdinand and his father planned to meet after the New Year in the hillside town of Daroca, fifty miles south of Zaragoza.

In January 1479 ambassadors from the court of Louis XI arrived in Guadalupe to meet Isabella and Ferdinand and ratify the peace treaty. Meanwhile, King Juan traveled to the pine-forested town of Daroca to await Ferdinand. Although Juan had recently been ill, he felt sufficiently recovered to make the trip.

On January 18, still ailing, contemplating the French treaty, perhaps sensing the end of his life was near, Juan wrote again to Ferdinand. This time the old Aragonese king confessed that "under these circumstances, kingdoms, subjects and human powers, great as they may be, cannot help me. Only our Creator . . . in whose hands I am, can help me. Right now, in this difficult moment, I would prefer to have been one of the lowliest men of my kingdom."[7]

King Juan then cautioned his son to "not be fooled by the world . . . keep always in front of your eyes the fear of God . . . Make justice, above all things, the mirror of your heart." Above all, warned the once-bellicose Juan, "keep your realms and your subjects in peace and justice, with no offense to the neighbor and, as much as you can, the world free of war and strife."[8]

King Juan of Aragón died the next day, January 19. With his death Ferdinand and Isabella became King and Queen of Aragón. Henceforth they were proclaimed "King and Queen of Castile, of León, of Aragón, of Sicily, of Toledo, Valencia, Galicia, Mallorcas, Sevilla, Córdoba, Corsica, Jaén, Algarve, Algeciras and Gilbraltar, Count and Countess of Barcelona, Lords of Vizcaya and Molina, Duke and Duchess of Athens, Count and Countess of Roussillon and Cerdagne, Marqueses of Oristan and Gociano . . ."[9]: rulers of essentially the entire Iberian peninsula, except for Portugal and Moorish Granada.

Meanwhile, the Portuguese war was winding down. In Lisbon, Prince João and King's Afonso's powerful sister-in-law, the *Infanta* Beatriz, Duchess of Viseu, refused to support Afonso's plan for a second invasion of Castile. There Afonso retained only a handful of supporters—Villena, his sister the Countess of Medellín, and his cousin, the Master of Calatrava—and even they were steadily losing enthusiasm for La Beltraneja's cause. By late 1478 Isabella and Ferdinand had succeeded in winning Sixtus IV's sympathy: In December the pope retracted his prior dispensation for Afonso's marriage to La Beltraneja "because of all the evils and wars" that dispensation had created.[10]

Even the acrimonious Carrillo was finally subdued. In late 1478 royal soldiers had impounded the archbishop's rents and seized his fortresses. Thereupon the archbishop sold sacred objects from the Toledo archbishopric—ceremonial silver cups, glassware from the cathedral sacristy, gold ornaments, and jewels— everything, it was said, that would provide him with "the means to hire supporters."[11] Simultaneously, he imprisoned Isabella's sympathizers and exiled others from the archbishopric in order to confiscate their wealth and property.

But the archbishop's efforts were futile. In the end, his soldiers were defeated by royal troops, and on January 16, 1479, the king and queen permanently stripped Carrillo of his fortress. Although they agreed to pardon their old mentor, the archbishop refused to appear before them and sent a proxy instead. The sixty-nine-year old archbishop then retired to the Convent of San Francisco in Alcalá de Henares "where he lived peacefully without causing any more scandals to the Queen of Castile."[12]

* * *

Despite the confluence of events that mitigated against Portuguese victory, Afonso launched a last attack on Extremadura in early 1479. At his instigation, Portuguese sympathizers infiltrated a half-dozen Extremaduran border towns but were quickly subdued by knights from the Order of Santiago. By February 22 the ragged and bloodied remnants of Afonso's army surrendered to the order's master, Cárdenas, at Albuera.

By that act the Portuguese king was obliged to make peace with Castile. He did not, however, negotiate the treaty himself, but instead assigned the negotiations to his sister-in-law Beatriz.

On March 4, with two counselors and an armed escort, Isabella thus traveled northwest from Cáceres. She arrived the next day in the Castilian border town of Alcántara, headquarters for the military order by that same name.

But the Portuguese duchess did not appear for nearly two weeks. Finally, on Thursday, March 18, Beatriz arrived borne by servants on a litter chair at the twelfth-century castle of the Knights of Alcántara. Although Beatriz was sister to Isabella's mother and wife of Afonso's brother Fernando, it was the first time they had met. Isabella received her aunt with "great veneration" and "much love" and despite their opposing political interests, a friendship soon developed.[13]

By Sunday, March 21, the two women began their talks in earnest. At their request, they were held in private. Initially Beatriz proposed two marriages—the first, a match between Prince Juan and La Beltraneja, the second between the Princess Isabel and the Portuguese king's young grandson. She also proposed that Castile absorb the costs for the war and that Isabella issue a general pardon to those who had sided with the Portuguese.

But the queen objected to nearly all her aunt's proposals. In particular, she disputed the idea of marrying La Beltraneja to Prince Juan, because that would have required a thirteen- or fourteen-year wait for her son to grow to young manhood. To leave La Beltraneja unwed for that period of time, she argued, would be to invite some other European king or prince to betroth her and "open the way for an invasion here."[14] Instead, Isabella "insisted that [La Beltraneja] become a nun in Castile" and immediately relinquish her title as "Queen of Castile."[15] Nor would Isabella grant permission for a marriage between her daughter Isabel and Afonso's grandson because the girl was already promised to the son of the Neapolitan king. The other issues—the costs of the war, the general pardon for the Castilian nobility—would have to be considered individually.

The duchess listened respectfully, but in the end she insisted on one point: La Beltraneja should have the option of marriage or the convent. The talks ended on Monday, March 22, with Beatriz's promise that she would send a reply to Isabella as soon as she had spoken with Afonso.

Convinced that her aunt was sincere, Isabella waited dutifully in Alcántara for a reply. But no answer came from Lisbon. After a month the queen returned to Cáceres, reuniting with Ferdinand on April 24. Two days later Beatriz wrote Isabella apologizing for her delay in answering because "certain persons" had not yet examined the proposed terms for peace.

Isabella then waited several more weeks. When she could no longer stand the suspense, she dispatched a letter to Afonso observing that although her aunt "had worked with good intentions" it was essential to formalize the treaty to clarify if the two kingdoms were in a state of "peace or war."[16]

Isabella's document elicited an immediate response from the Portuguese court. In a return letter, King Afonso and Prince João agreed to peace but disputed several of Isabella's suggestions—among them the release of La Beltraneja to Castile and the insistence that she become a nun.

A stalemate ensued and there were new skirmishes in Extremadura. Finally, in late summer, Afonso agreed to set a time and place for the peace treaty. On September 4 ambassadors thus signed a treaty in Alcaçovas, Portugal, renewing a 1432 armistice between Castile and Portugal and establishing "perpetual peace" between the two nations. By its terms Isabella, Ferdinand, and Afonso renounced their claims to each other's crown and refuted their claims to territories taken during the war. As a result, the African countries of Guinea and Fez and the islands of Madeira, Cape Verde, and the Azores reverted to Portugal while the Castilians regained possession of the newly conquered Canary Islands. Isabella and Ferdinand ceded their exploration rights to the southern end of West Africa and agreed to limit their own maritime expeditions to the latitudes of the Canaries—a concession that some years later, in the golden age of sea exploration, they would sorely regret. But in 1479 those rights seemed less important to Isabella and Ferdinand than international recognition of their claims to the Castilian throne.

To ensure fulfillment of the terms, their ten-year-old daughter, Princess Isabel, and the Portuguese heir were to be held *en terceria,* by a mediator, for a year. The princess was to live in the Duchess of Viseu's palace in Moura near the Castilian border.

The second part of the treaty outlined the disposition of La Beltraneja. The eighteen-year-old girl was offered two options: She could wait fourteen years to marry Prince Juan of Castile, at which time the Castilian monarchs would pay Portugal a dowry of 100,000 doblas, or she could enter one of the five Portuguese convents of the Sisters of Santa Clara. In either case La Beltraneja was no longer to refer to herself as a "Princess of Castile." *La Excelente Señora,* or "the most excellent lady," as the Portuguese had begun to call her, was given six months to make a decision.

The treaty of Alcaçovas was signed by Afonso V in Portugal and ratified by Isabella on September 27, 1479. Three weeks later, when Ferdinand arrived from Aragón, he too signed the document that would keep Castile and Portugal at peace for 101 years.

Had Isabella had her way, La Beltraneja would have been immediately confined to a Castilian convent. In her heart the queen believed that La Beltraneja was illegitimate and thus had no right to the throne. Nor did Isabella seem to have any guilt over her proposed disposition of *la mochacha,* or "the girl," as she now referred to her. Nevertheless, for strategic reasons, the queen had conceded to the Portuguese demand that La Beltraneja be given an opportunity to marry her son. Despite the awkward discrepancy in their ages, such a marriage would have eliminated all potentially antagonistic Portuguese claims to the Castilian crown.

For La Beltraneja, however, whose life had been a series of broken engagements, the option of marrying Prince Juan was not appealing. During the requisite fourteen-year-waiting period, she would be supervised by the Duchess of Viseu in her castle at Moura. The prospect of such scrutiny, even by the "discreet" and worldly duchess, could not have been very attractive to the already disheartened young woman. And after such a long wait—by which time La Beltraneja would be thirty-two years old—the possibility remained that Prince Juan would refuse the proposed marriage.

Isabella had pondered these prospects carefully. By giving La Beltraneja a choice, the image-conscious Isabella and Ferdinand must have realized that they would appear more merciful toward the pretender than they really were.

La Beltraneja did not wait even six months to make her decision. On October 6, 1479, she entered the Portuguese convent of Santa Clara de Santarém. Less than a year later she left, claiming that the plague had appeared in the nunnery. At Isabella and Ferdinand's insistence, she then entered the convent of Santa Clara de Coimbra. On November 15, 1480, in the presence of Isabella's confessor Fray Fernando de Talavera and one of her other counselors, Dr. Juan Díaz de Madrigal, a white-veiled La Beltraneja took her vows. With her disappearance into the cloister, Isabella and Ferdinand became the uncontested monarchs of Castile and León.

Only a few documents reveal La Beltraneja's reactions to the events that led her to become a *monja,* or nun. Pulgar, with his usual pro-Isabelline bias, reported that on the eve of La Beltraneja's vows Talavera reassured the young woman of the wisdom of her decision. She had, the monk told the young woman, "chosen the better part in the Evangelists" for as a "spouse of the church, her chastity would be prolific of all spiritual delights."[17]

Similarly, La Beltraneja assured Isabella's confessor that she was entering the convent willingly, for she was disillusioned with the secular world and believed that becoming a "bride of Christ" would give her a better life. Allegedly she told Talavera she had chosen religion over marriage "because God had shown her many times that the royal status and other worldly rewards were temporary."[18]

La Beltraneja's subsequent behavior, however, belied her words. Beneath her meek, submissive exterior was an enraged young woman who remained convinced that she was the rightful heir of Castile and had been robbed of her birthright by Isabella.

During her long life La Beltraneja was to leave the convent repeatedly and live in ducal homes and palaces under the protection of Portuguese kings. Each time she made a lengthy excursion into the Portuguese court, Isabella and Ferdinand protested and enlisted the help of the pope to force her back into the convent. Neither monastic walls nor stark chapels would, however, change La Beltraneja's conviction. To the last days of her life in 1530 La Beltraneja continued to sign her letters *Yo la Reina,* or "I the Queen."

The bitter struggle over La Beltraneja's claim to the Castilian throne broke Afonso V's spirit. After that defeat it was said that the Portuguese king was "never again merry, and always went withdrawn, musing and pensive, like a man that abhorred the things of the world rather than a king who prized them."[19]

A month before La Beltraneja entered the convent at Santa Clara de Coimbra,

Afonso, "melancholy and shame-faced,"[20] announced his intention to renounce the throne a second time. Then, perhaps following La Beltraneja's example, he withdrew into the monastery of Varatogo to become a Franciscan monk. That monastery, set upon a cliff high above the pounding Atlantic north of Cintra, would be Afonso's last home. On August 26, 1481, the fifty-two-year-old Portuguese monarch died, a shadow of the proud Christian king who, a decade earlier, had conquered the Berber Moroccans and had been widely revered as "El Africano."

CHAPTER THIRTY-ONE

The Great Cortes of 1480

A week after Isabella signed the treaty of Alcaçovas, she moved her court to Toledo. She arrived in that imperial city on October 14, 1479, after what must have been an uncomfortable journey, for she was in the last month of another pregnancy. Even so, Isabella had braved the desolate plains and bumpy mountain roads in anticipation of a still more luminous event—the *Cortes'* oath of allegiance to the infant Prince Juan as the future King of Castile. Although that parliament would not meet until January, Isabella wanted to reach Toledo before the winter rains and the birth of her third child. Like Ferdinand, she prayed for another son, the proverbial "heir and a spare," who would serve as insurance for the throne in the event that Prince Juan died.

Ferdinand had not seen his wife for four months, for in June 1479, when the peace treaty with Portugal seemed assured, he had returned to Aragón to assume his dead father's throne.

Two weeks after Ferdinand's arrival in Toledo, on Saturday, November 9, between six and seven in the morning, Isabella gave birth to a robust female child. The baby, named Juana, was somewhat darker in complexion than her siblings and bore such a striking physical resemblance to her namesake, Ferdinand's mother Juana Enríquez, that Isabella nicknamed her *suegra,* or mother-in-law. But as she grew to maturity Juana appeared to have strong temperamental similarities to her other grandmother, Isabella's mother, the queen widow. By late adolescence, the comely auburn-haired Juana had already begun to display those same terrifying symptoms of emotional instability that had gripped Isabella's mother and would eventually earn the young princess the sobriquet of *Juana La Loca,* or Joanna the Mad.

* * *

In January 1480 an enthusiastic *Cortes* of thirty-four *procuradores* from the seventeen cities of Castile convened in Toledo at the Church of San Pedro de Matir. The full representation of this body was a result of the recent peace with Portugal and Isabella and Ferdinand's now internationally recognized right to the Castilian throne. The king and queen arrived at the *Cortes* with similar optimism, determined to impress their authority upon Castile as its supreme rulers. The absolute power they sought and would eventually achieve was new to Castile, wracked as it had been by warring barons and weak kings in the waning years of the Middle Ages.

A cooperative atmosphere permeated the opening sessions, and Isabella and Ferdinand quickly capitalized on that mood to manipulate the "third estate" as a counterfoil to the nobility. Consequently, they listened sensitively to the grievances and petitions of the *procuradores*.

They also conceded to the *procuradores'* petitions to segregate the Jewish population strictly. By 1480 a new wave of anti-Semitism had swept over Christian Castile, exacerbated by the recent economic havoc and the Portuguese war. With their jobs as moneylenders and merchants, their fine clothes, and their pride as "the chosen people," the Jews were increasingly perceived as a godless, but powerful population who controlled the kingdom's financial system.

In reality, the Jews (whose population was estimated at no more than 200,000, probably less than 2 percent of the Christian population) were a disenfranchised people who were often forbidden to own land, join trade guilds, or hold high public office. Most of them held urban jobs in lower levels of trade and finance—as tax collectors or tax middlemen for the crown—or as merchants, peddlers, artisans, and physicians. "None," as the anti-Semitic chronicler and curate of Los Palacios, Andrés de Bernáldez, wrote, "broke the earth or became a farmer, carpenter or builder, but all sought . . . comfortable posts and ways of making profits without much labor."[1]

Nevertheless, Isabella and Ferdinand had elevated several Jews to key positions in their courts. Among them were Abraham Seneor, who served as treasurer of the *Hermandad* and chief treasurer of Castile, and Isaac Abravanel, who supervised collection of the kingdom's sheep tax.

When, in the first years of her reign, Isabella longed for a male heir, she had enlisted the services of a Jewish doctor, Llorenc Badoc. And as early as 1468 the Catalan Jew, David Abenasaya, had been one of Ferdinand's most trusted physicians.

During the anti-Semitic protests of the late 1470's, the king and queen had taken measures to protect the Jews. In March 1475 they revoked discriminatory laws that forbade the Jews of the northern village of Medina de Pomar from "purchasing bread, silk and linens" in the nearby city of Bilbao. In 1477 Isabella and Ferdinand interceded in Sevilla and ordered reluctant Christians to allow the Jews to continue buying cattle in the marketplace. That same year the queen affirmed an old law in Burgos prohibiting a tax on the export of Torahs. When, in 1479, the townspeople attacked the Jews of Cáceres, Isabella donated money to help them rebuild their community. And she had already stated in Trujillo that "all the Jews in my realms are mine and under my care and protection . . . to defend and aid them and keep justice."[2]

Traditionally, the Jews were not governed as ordinary members of the Christian Castilian community, but rather as unique *vasallos y subditos,* as vassals and subjects of the king and queen, who were obliged to pay special taxes and were subject to special protections. Yet, in the *Cortes* of 1480, anti-Semitic sentiment had grown too strong for either Isabella or Ferdinand to oppose. Ultimately, they conceded to the *procuradores'* demands that Jews be identified by special yellow badges and restricted to *aljamas,* or ghettos, as they had been in earlier eras so as to minimize their contact with Christians and *conversos.*

Despite these concessions, Isabella and Ferdinand initiated a series of reforms at the *Cortes* that established them as the highest authority in the land. Of utmost importance was the collection of the *hacienda,* or national income, which in the wake of Enrique's careless reign had fallen to a mere 30,000 ducats a year. It was obvious that the third estate, already heavily taxed for the *Hermandad* and the Portuguese war, could not contribute much more. Thus the *procuradores* agreed to permit the monarchs to sign into law a series of new taxes that would provide perennial income for the crown—among them an *alcabala,* or sales tax, duties on imports and exports, and "passage" taxes, such as those issued for the annual sheep migrations from northern Castile to Andalusia.

But even those would not sufficiently restore the kingdom's coffers. During his twenty-year reign, Enrique had doled out territories and estates traditionally held by the crown to his favorite *grandees* and prelates. The attendant loss of revenues from those properties and the power they afforded the nobles had profoundly disquieted Isabella. "No monarch," she observed, "should consent to alienate his domains since the loss of revenue necessarily deprives him of the best means of rewarding the attachment of his friends and of making himself feared by his enemies."[3]

To regain those estates was an admittedly tricky challenge that would require help from the *Cortes.* If the revenue from those properties remained uncollected, Isabella and Ferdinand explained, the crown would have to raise the missing funds from the *Cortes* itself. As the monarchs anticipated, the *procuradores* responded by drafting measures demanding that the *grandees* contribute their fair share to the crown by returning all estates, towns, and funds improperly held since 1464.

Predictably, some of the nobles protested, but with the consensus of the *Cortes* behind them, Isabella and Ferdinand stood firm. Ultimately the nobles and prelates conceded, and the resultant Act of Resumption signed by the *Cortes* into law allowed the crown to retrieve some 30 million maravedís.

Isabella and Ferdinand, ever sensitive to aristocratic opinion, moved slowly. To fulfill the unsavory job of removing property from the *grandees* they chose their most fair-minded associate, Fray Talavera, Isabella's personal confessor. Their choice was brilliant. In his former capacity as prior of Valladolid's convent of Santa María, the soft-spoken Talavera had become an astute observer of humanity. Ascetic in his food, garb, and tastes, the Hieronymite monk was so removed from worldly temptations that he was widely acknowledged as incorruptible.

It was Talavera's legendary rigor, in fact, that had inspired the queen to choose him as her confessor above all others. In 1474, shortly after her coronation, Cardinal Mendoza had introduced the monk to Isabella in Segovia. After a brief meeting, Isabella knelt to be confessed but Talavera remained seated. When the queen observed that it was "usual for both parties to kneel," the monk replied, "This is God's tribunal; I act here as his minister, and it is fitting that I should keep my seat, while your Highness kneels before me." So impressed was Isabella with Talavera's uncompromising standards and refusal to be intimidated by her station that she told Beatriz de Bobadilla, "I have found my confessor."[4] Once appointed, the monk proved himself a strict guardian who set standards for the young queen's life-style. Although Talavera was a member of the court, he disapproved of frivolity and such trappings of state as rich foods, dancing, ostentatious clothes, and the display of jewels. On more than one occasion he had criticized Isabella for allowing such luxuries or indulging in them herself. He continued to do so throughout her reign.

Thus Talavera was the perfect agent for the delicate task ahead. Rather than ordering a uniform return of all crown properties, he heard and judged each case individually. In a series of hearings that bore an eerie resemblance to church confessionals, Talavera asked each *grandee* to explain the circumstances under which he held crown property. Ultimately no one, not even Ferdinand's maternal family, escaped.

Gradually the royal coffers began to fill. By 1482 the returned properties and new taxes swelled Castile's domestic income sixfold. Not all the funds were used for the greater glory of the crown. At the earliest possible opportunity Isabella distributed some of the new revenue to the orphans and widows whose fathers and husbands had been killed in the Portuguese war.

The 1480 Act of Resumption restricted other aristocratic abuses as well. To underscore their monarchial authority, Isabella and Ferdinand stripped the *grandees* of all symbols that intimated they held power equal to that of the crown. Thus nobles were forbidden to display insignias of royalty, such as crowns, above their shields or upon their banners. Nor were they allowed to display their titles at the beginning of letters or employ mace-bearers and bodyguards. Moreover, the *grandees* were not permitted to construct new castles, and many of their old ones were razed. Duels between *grandees* were also forbidden, for Isabella and Ferdinand believed such practices not only encouraged new rivalries but also created unnecessary discord in the kingdom.

At first, some *grandees* refused to take the new laws seriously. A year after the 1480 *Cortes* two young barons, Ramiro Núñez de Guzmán, the Lord of Toral, and Don Fadrique Enríquez, Ferdinand's cousin and son of the *Almirante* Enríquez, quarreled bitterly in Valladolid. To ensure that there would be no bloodshed, Isabella granted Toral, who was younger and weaker than Fadrique, a safe conduct. Nevertheless, Fadrique, behaving "as if he was above the laws of the Queen," vowed to take vengeance in his own hands.[5] Several days later, when Toral rode a mule through Valladolid's main square, three men beat the youth brutally. By nightfall messengers brought Isabella the news. Although a violent storm raged outside, the queen was so infuriated that her orders had been ignored that she threw on a cloak and called for her horse. She then galloped seven miles south through the muddy roads that led to the castle of Simancas owned by Don Fadrique's father.

The queen banged on the castle gate, which the elder Enríquez soon opened. "*Almirante,* take me to the place where your son, Don Fadrique, is because he defied my safeguard," Isabella said.[6]

"Ladyship, I cannot do so nor do I know where he is," Enríquez replied.[7]

"Then if you don't know where he is, allow me to enter this fortress of Simancas and the fortress of Rioseco," the queen ordered.[8] Although the *Almirante* complied, Don Fadrique was not to be found. Nor did he turn up in a subsequent search at the castle of Rioseco. To ensure that Don Fadrique would not return to either fortress, Isabella placed both under surveillance.

The next morning, back at Valladolid, the queen awoke feverish and in pain, too ill to leave her bed. When her doctor asked about her symptoms, Isabella replied, "My body is lame with the blows given by Don Fadrique in contempt of my safe-conduct."[9]

A few days later the youth's uncle, the Count of Haro, brought Don Fadrique before the queen, pleading that because the youth was not yet twenty he "is not capable of knowing the authority and obedience which you have commanded in these kingdoms. Please," the count begged, "consider this, Your Highness, in the justice which you render or the punishment you make."[10]

But once deliberately crossed, Isabella was not to be mollified. The youth had defied royal authority twice, first by quarreling with Toral, second, by ignoring her safe conduct. To impress others with the preeminence of royal law, she decided to make an example of Don Fadrique, despite his status as Ferdinand's cousin. Subsequently, an *alcalde* marched the guilty youth through Valladolid's main plaza and dispatched him to the castle at Arévalo, where he was placed under heavy guard. Months later, out of deference to his kinship to Ferdinand, Isabella exiled Don Fadrique to Sicily.

During the 1480 *Cortes* Isabella debated the wisdom of stripping too many powers from the nobility at once. To reduce resentment, the queen allowed the barons to retain certain privileges. The nobles were still to be allowed the unique privilege of "being covered"—that is, of wearing hats when in the presence of the monarchs. They also remained exempt from imprisonment, torture, and the payment of taxes. Simultaneously, Isabella granted new titles to lower members of the nobility. By the end of her reign the number of Castilian dukes had risen from seven to fifteen.

At the same time, the queen reduced aristocratic access to the inner sanctums of power. The *consejo real,* or royal council, the monarchs' main advisory body, was cut to one prelate, three *grandees,* and eight or nine *letrados.* By such measures, *grandee* influence was diminished and that of the university-trained legalists elevated. As before, Cardinal Mendoza presided over this *consejo real;* now the cardinal was so close to Isabella and Ferdinand that he was dubbed "the third king" of Castile.

Beyond its advisory duties, the *consejo real* functioned as Castile's supreme court. Like the prototype Isabella had established three years earlier at Sevilla, this *consejo de justicia,* or council of justice, as the royal council was also known, met with Isabella and Ferdinand on Friday mornings to decide cases that had stymied the lower courts. By 1485 though, as the monarchs' duties increased, the judicial function of the royal council was moved to Valladolid where the new supreme court—the *audiencia* or *chancelleria*—would be permanently located.

Isabella wrought changes in the composition of her new *consejo real* tactfully, with the same diplomacy later Renaissance monarchs would adopt as fitting strategies for an increasingly complex world. Already, by 1480, the queen was fond of saying that "the man who has good taste bears a letter of recommendation."[11] Exquisitely fearful that the changes she was making in the *consejo real* were too abrupt, Isabella maintained a show of respect for baronial privilege. Any aristocrat with hereditary "rights" to sit on the council was thus allowed to appear, but only in an honorary capacity—he could no longer vote in council matters or otherwise participate in the transaction of royal business.

The strong monarchy Isabella and Ferdinand envisioned meant their advisors had to be not only well informed but readily available. Consequently, members of the *consejo real* were obliged to live near the king and queen, preferably, as the *Cortes* recommended, within the royal residence itself.

This, however, was not an easy task for in fifteenth century Castile, the court was still itinerant, traveling from town to town as political necessity, bad weather, the appearance of the plague, or an area's dwindling food supply required. In anticipation of a move, servants in Isabella and Ferdinand's court often traveled several days ahead of the king and queen to prepare the new royal residence. They rode by mule and horse, guarding the *fardage,* or baggage train, loaded on beasts or in wooden carts, which contained dishes, bedding, tapestries, and other possessions of the royal household. Despite these preparations, the palaces and mansions where the king and queen were quartered were not always large enough to accommodate the entire court. As a result, the *consejo real* was sometimes obliged to live nearby.

Hard workers themselves, Isabella and Ferdinand demanded similar efforts from those in their service. The *consejo real* met every morning of the week except Sundays and religious holidays, convening from 6:00 to 10:00 A.M. during spring and summer and from 9:00 A.M. to noon in fall and winter. With such hours, the late-night carousing enjoyed by members of Enrique's court was obviously impossible to sustain. Within Isabella's court there were, of course, the usual amusements—hunting, hawking, chess, board games, and cards. But gambling was strictly forbidden in the royal residences. And so were drunkenness, wanton flirtations, and dishabille costumes.

Instead, Ferdinand and Isabella now introduced a new elite, young daughters and sons of the nobility who were to be educated in the humanities, the classics, music, literature, and poetry. By the turn of the sixteenth century, those young people would make the Castilian court one of the most erudite in Western Europe. To encourage that interest, Isabella allowed books to be imported tax-free. She endowed Toledo's Church of San Juan de los Reyes with a library. And by 1482, regretting her own lack of a formal classical education, the queen herself began to study Latin. An atmosphere of culture, intellect, and dignity thus began to permeate the Castilian court.

Licentiousness was poorly regarded. Even Ferdinand's sexual escapades were handled with discretion. Although he would father two illegitimate children during his marriage besides those sired before his wedding, the king's mistresses never appeared at court. But Ferdinand's illegitimate children were treated kindly. As they grew to maturity, they lived at court and were often seen with the queen. Ferdinand's illegitimate son Alfonso of Aragón was named Archbishop of Zaragoza while still a child. One of his daughters, Doña Juana, married the Constable of Castile, and the other two—both called María—became prioresses at convents in Madrigal.

That is not to say that Isabella tolerated Ferdinand's flirtations gracefully. She had difficulty accepting adultery despite its prevalence among high-born men of the era. To her male historians, Isabella's failure to accept Ferdinand's indiscretions was one of her few faults. Even her admiring secretary Pulgar noted that the queen was "jealous beyond all bounds" of Ferdinand's amours.[12]

"She loved after such a fashion, so solicitous and vigilant in jealousy, that if she felt he looked on any lady of the court with a betrayal of desire, she would very discreetly procure ways and means to dismiss that person from her household . . ." wrote the contemporary humanist and courtier Lucio Marineo Siculo.[13]

Although the details of the king's affairs remain shrouded in secrecy, at least one instance of Isabella's vengeance upon his paramours has been preserved. In 1480 the queen noted that a beautiful green-eyed brunette attendant in her employ named Beatriz de Bobadilla—not her close friend, but a cousin with the same name—had attracted Ferdinand's roving eye. That same year Fernán Peraza, governor of Gomera, the most remote of the Canary Islands, arrived at court to answer accusations that he caused a rival's death. In punishment, Ferdinand had ordered Peraza to subsidize eighty men out of his own pocket and subdue the rest of the Canaries. Isabella, seeing an opportunity in it for herself as well, had this Beatriz de Bobadilla married to Peraza. By so doing, the flirtatious lady was exiled eight hundred miles south to the most distant corner of Castile's foreign properties off the coast of West Africa.

That Isabella was an ordered woman was undeniable. Over time, her belief that an efficient state could best be maintained by a disciplined and disciplining monarch would make her the most powerful ruler in Western Europe. It was said that she delighted in seeing four things—"men-at-arms in the field, a bishop in his robes, a lady in a drawing room, and a thief on the gallows."[14]

Still, to run an efficient government in which every man and woman understood his place required well-formulated laws. At the time of the 1480 Cortes, the Castilian laws were chaotic. Consequently, Isabella asked the Cortes to order the converso legalist Dr. Alfonso Díaz de Montalvo to revise the laws of Castile. Montalvo's resultant work, the eight-volume Ordenanzas Reales de Castilla, or Royal Laws of Castile, would take five years to complete and was written in the Castilian vernacular. By 1485 it was also printed, thus becoming one of the earliest books published in Castile.

At the monarchs' urging, the Cortes of 1480 created several other governmental councils to ensure civil order. Like the consejo real, these new councils were closely supervised by the monarchs and traveled with the court. By that year the council of the *Hermandad* was already established; it was soon followed by the *Contadores Mayor,* a financial body composed of "officials who kept the accounts of the royal treasury and the crown domain."[15] There was also a primitive Council of State within which the king and queen briefed the *grandees* "to advise ambassadors from other kingdoms."[16]

Finally, to assuage Ferdinand's lingering guilt—and perhaps Isabella's own—over his distant rule over Aragón, the *Cortes* approved a separate council to administer the king's non-Castilian domains—Aragón, Catalonia, Barcelona, Valencia, and Sicily. Despite the Aragonese presence at the Castilian court, their council continued to function independently. Thus, in spite of the much-vaunted "union of two crowns" implicit in Isabella and Ferdinand's marriage, the kingdoms of Castile and Aragón remained separate entities, proudly maintaining their own customs and laws. During Isabella and Ferdinand's subsequent reign, the twin crowns would be increasingly identified as "Spain" by them and by foreign rulers. Still, the governments of Castile and Aragón would not truly be blended until the sixteenth century, long after the deaths of the king and queen.

Even the establishment of new councils would not necessarily guarantee the smooth operation of a strong monarchy. To ensure that every town had a bureaucracy answerable to the crown and a place to house its records, Isabella and Ferdinand ordered all cities still lacking a town hall to construct one from public funds.

Simultaneously, they summoned royal officials, *corregidores,* to "all the cities and villages of all their kingdoms where there were none before."[17] This time the king and queen met with little resistance for they had developed a new strategy: the addition of *pesquisidores,* or ombudsmen whose job was to monitor the *corregidores'* activities and report any abuses to the crown. Thus assured, the *Cortes* approved a kingdom-wide system of court representatives that made every city and town answerable to royal scrutiny.

The *Cortes* of 1480 was to be the most productive parliament of Isabella and Ferdinand's reign. It was, as a contemporary observed, "so well weighed and executed that it seemed a divine work for the correction and resolution of past disorders."[18] Yet this *Cortes* was only a first, human step toward the great glory that Isabella and Ferdinand envisioned for Castile. Their greatest challenge still lay ahead—the social and spiritual homogenization of their subjects under one authority and one church.

CHAPTER THIRTY-TWO

Edicts of Faith and Grace

I n February 1481 three prominent Sevillians were burned at the stake for heresy. One of them was a wealthy *converso* named Diego de Susan, "said to be worth ten millions of maravedís," who had conspired against officers of the Sevillian Inquisition. Weeks earlier Susan had gathered other prominent *conversos* from nearby towns to meet in the Church of San Salvador. "How can they come against us?" he asked. "We are the principal members of the city and well liked by the people. Let us assemble our men. If they come to take us, we will set the city in turmoil with our followers and our friends."[1]

In anticipation of attack, the *converso* patriarchs stockpiled weapons and alerted their friends. Ultimately they were betrayed by Susan's lovely daughter, Suzanna. *La Hermosa Hembra*, the beautiful woman, as Susan's daughter was called, had fallen in love with a Christian and, fearing for his safety, had revealed her father's plot.

The *converso* and his friends were tried for heresy in a formal ecclesiastical ceremony known as an *auto-da-fe*. After their conviction, municipal authorities prepared a field outside the city gates for their execution. Susan was dignified to the end. As he walked to the *quemadero*, or burning place, the halter placed around his neck to tie him to the stake dragged heavily behind in the mud. "Be so good as to lift up the end of this Tunisian scarf of mine," he asked an observer.[2]

Afterward, the sight of Susan's burning flesh and his death cries haunted his daughter. Seeking solace in religion, the guilt-ridden young woman retired to a convent. Later, *La Hermosa Hembra* took to the streets where, sick and impoverished, she died a premature death. Her last request was that her skull be nailed to the door of her old home in Sevilla to warn others about her mistake.

The circumstances that preceded the 1481 Sevillian *auto-da-fe* illustrated the depth of *converso* resistance to the Spanish Inquisition. Intuitively, Isabella had sensed that resistance and thus delayed implementing Pope Sixtus's 1478 bull to allow an Inquisition for two years. Meanwhile the queen, convinced that *converso* failure to truly embrace Christianity was the result of poor childhood training, ordered a public campaign of religious education.

To head the effort, Isabella commanded Cardinal Mendoza and Talavera to Sevilla to instruct *conversos* in the rudiments of Christianity. For two years, a virtual army of prelates lectured on Christianity, convinced that if they could show "how much perpetual damnation [would be inflicted] on their souls and . . . bodies if they practiced Jewish rites" the *conversos* would voluntarily embrace Christianity.[3] Yet there were few gains. The *conversos,* the Sevillian priests soon began to complain, seemed impervious to conversion.

Not all *conversos,* however, were unfaithful Christians. Many who held prominent positions in Castilian society led perfectly regular Christian lives. Three of Isabella and Ferdinand's secretaries—Alfonso de Ávila, Fernando Álvarez de Toledo, and Fernando del Pulgar—had *converso* blood. Even Tomás de Torquemada, the devout Dominican priest who had agitated for the inquisitional bull of 1478, was of *converso* descent. Ferdinand relied heavily on his *converso* financial advisors, among them Luís de Santángel, Alfonso de la Caballeria, and Gabriel Sánchez. "We have always had *conversos* in our service, like any other people, without distinction of persons and they have served us well," the king once observed.[4]

Nevertheless, stereotypes about the *conversos,* rather than exemplary individual cases, were what impressed most Castilians. *Converso* power, wealth, and influence combined with the suspicion that they still secretly practiced Judaism engendered perpetual hatred from the old Christians of Castile. Even now, three generations after the massive conversions of 1391, the *conversos* and Jews were still lumped together as a privileged, seditious lot. By 1480 circumstances were ripe for another round of persecutions.

Certainly some *conversos* had maintained close ties to Judaism. Many "new" Christians still had Jewish relatives and friends. Others had difficulty relinquishing foods, customs, and language their parents had taught them in childhood. Still others refused to abandon Judaism but practiced it alongside their newfound Christianity.

Those who stubbornly retained their religion, the so-called *marranos*—a derisive old Christian name for *conversos* meaning "pigs"—secretly practiced Judaism behind closed doors or under the cover of night, often without the knowledge of their Christian spouses. Many second- and third-generation descendants taught their youngsters Judaism at the same time they sent them to church.

Other *conversos* refused to have their children baptised, or washed away the holy water after the ceremony. Covertly, they attempted to retain Jewish customs in their homes. Some cooked their meat with oil rather than lard or fat from pigs. Others eschewed pork "unless forced by necessity." The most determined observed the Jewish holidays and the Sabbath, "sent oil to the synagogues," and "discussed their affairs . . . with the rabbis." Still others, it was said, profaned Christian custom by eating meat during Lent and on fast days. In church they "made excuses for avoiding the sacrament" and, when they attended confession, they "never confessed the truth."[5]

Another group of *conversos* were simply halfhearted practitioners of two faiths. Sometimes, as the *converso* court secretary Pulgar himself observed, "they kept neither one law nor the other. They did not circumcise themselves as the Old Testament admonishes, and although they kept the Saturdays and fasted during some of the fasts of the Jews . . . they did not . . . observe all of the fasts . . . if they observed one rite, they ignored another with the result that they were false to both laws."[6]

Records from the first decade of the Inquisition were, in fact, filled with case histories revealing the *conversos'* conflicted status. In Sevilla a *converso* silk weaver was apprenticed to a Jewish silversmith around 1460 who taught him Jewish prayers and laws. In 1486 a *conversa* from Valdeiglesias recalled that when she was a child, a Jew visited her father's home and urged him to buy Jewish books and observe Jewish holidays. A *converso* priest from Talavera had been educated as a Jew and fasted on Yom Kippur as atonement for his sins.

Other *conversos* even managed to "judaize"—as the secret worship of Judaism was called—in the very face of the church. In 1450 a *converso* youth named Diego de Marchena became a Hieronymite priest and lived at the famous monastery of Guadalupe until 1485 when inquisitors condemned him for giving other *conversos* unorthodox spiritual advice.

In Toledo's Hieronymite monastery of La Sisla, another monk was accused of encouraging *conversos* to bless their children as Jews. That same monk, who was eventually sentenced to death by the Inquisition, debunked the statutes of Jesus and the saints as "a jest and a derision."[7]

Like the inquisitors, the rabbis debated the true status of the *conversos*. Most maintained that they were not Jewish by faith or deed and should thus be considered Christians. A minority, however, unwittingly echoing their anti-Semitic persecutors, insisted the *conversos* were Jewish because they fulfilled the tenets of the faith under arduous circumstances.

The *conversos* were thus both a troubled and troublesome population in late fifteenth-century Castile. By 1480 Isabella and Ferdinand reluctantly conceded that all their efforts to "persuade" or educate the *converso* population to Christianity had failed. A steady stream of complaints about *conversos* followed the monarchs north from Sevilla, and as they accumulated the king and queen began to fear for that city's fragile peace.

Isabella was also deeply disturbed about the integrity of the church. As queen, she held herself responsible for the spiritual well-being of her subjects and thus believed it her duty to ensure purity within the church. In 1479 she had asked the pope to grant Castilian bishops permission to reform the monasteries. She also requested authority to appoint native prelates to the Castilian bishoprics herself. In 1480 Isabella and Ferdinand tried to eliminate concubinage from the church by banishing the nonmonastic clergy's *barraganas*.

But heresy remained the most thorny problem of all. To allow it to continue, to deliberately avert her eyes from the crime, was, to Isabella's scrupulous conscience, spiritually irresponsible, tantamount to committing heresy herself.

That message had been drummed into Isabella's head years earlier when she was a princess in Segovia. There, during a confession to the fanatic Dominican priest Tomás de Torquemada, it was said that Isabella promised that if she ever became queen, "she would devote herself to the extirpation of heresy, for the glory of God and the exaltation of the Catholic faith."[8]

In later years, even after Isabella had chosen Talavera as her new confessor, Torquemada retained his grip on the queen. After all, it had been his pleas for a papal inquisition in 1478 that finally persuaded the queen to write Sixtus for authorization of the bull. Yet by 1480 Isabella had still not fulfilled her vow. The promise hung heavily over her, a silent indictment of her inability—or unwillingness—to fulfill what she had promised.

Clearly, stronger measures than proselytization were needed. The Mendoza-Talavera campaign had failed. Even more alarming were reports from those prelates that the "ugly disease" of *converso* duplicity was not unique to Sevilla but pervaded all of Castile. The infidel, it seemed, had become a permanent resident in Isabella's Christian kingdom.

The threat of a defiled Christian church was exacerbated by foreign enemies who now seemed to endanger Christianity on all sides. On December 4, 1479, the Ottoman Turks sailed from the Albanian coast and set siege to the Greek island of Rhodes. Then, on August 11, 1480, an Ottoman naval expedition under the command of the Grand Admiral Gedik Ahmed Pasha cut through the Balkan Sea and captured the Italian port city of Otranto.

Within the Iberian peninsula itself, the Islamic Crescent was poised for war. Since 1476 the Moorish king, Ali Abu-l-Hasan, had refused to donate the *paria,* or gold tribute, traditionally paid the Castilian monarchs. By 1480 groups of turbaned Moors were raiding the Andalusian border towns so often that Isabella and Ferdinand talked of mounting their own Holy War against their ancient enemy. But it would be difficult to mobilize a divided Castile for another war. There seemed only one way to "cleanse" the land of heretics. Thus on September 27, 1480, Isabella and Ferdinand activated the 1478 inquisitional bull by issuing their own royal order:

> Therefore We, the said King Ferdinand and Queen Isabella, with
> the great desire we have to elevate, honor and preserve our Catho-
> lic Faith and that our subjects and people born in our realms live
> in it and save their souls, and in order to avoid the great evils and
> harms that would occur if the aforementioned behavior went un-
> punished and uncorrected, and because, as monarchs and sover-
> eign lords of these realms . . . we must provide the remedy for
> this and because we want that such bad Christians be punished
> and the faithful and good Christians be free of all stain and
> infamy, . . . we accept the said commission and faculty to us
> granted by our most Holy Father.[9]

In that same document Isabella and Ferdinand named two priests from Burgos to serve as the first inquisitors in Sevilla: the Dominicans Fray Miguel de Morillo and Fray Juan de San Martín. It was traditional to assign Dominicans to such posts, for the mendicant Order of Preachers, as the Dominicans were known, had been founded in the thirteenth century by St. Dominic to combat heresy and teach doctrine. When, in that same century, the first papal inquisition began, the Dominicans were thus called upon to serve as official examiners for the church.

Those first tribunals had appeared in the kingdom of Aragón, in southern France, and in northern Italy, largely in reaction to the rise of heretical sects such as Waldensianism and Catharism. The rationale for those tribunals was based on the writings of theologians including Master Gratian of Bologna, Pope Gregory IX, and St. Thomas Aquinas to identify nonbelievers and win them back to true faith. Inquisitional examiners were, according to Gregory IX, to "seek out diligently those who are heretics or are infamed of heresy" so that through inquiry and accusation they could be corrected or "reconciled" to the orthodox church through mercy.[10] If, after a thorough investigation and proof of heresy, a "sinner" refused to repent, he was condemned as a heretic. That crime, according to the canons of Roman law adapted by the church, was analogous to treason and hence punishable by death.

The Castilian Inquisition of Isabella and Ferdinand's reign was based on this earlier papal model. Like its medieval predecessor, the Spanish Inquisition—or Holy Office as it was later called—used torture and the confiscation of property to punish the accused. But while Sixtus IV had granted permission for the Castilian Inquisition, the new tribunal was administered and financed by the crown under Isabella and Ferdinand's direction. The inquisitors and their staffs were salaried by the monarchs, and proceeds from the confiscated property of the condemned reverted to the Castilian treasury.

Soon after Isabella and Ferdinand signed the September 27 order, the Sevillians panicked. Many *conversos,* either out of guilt or terror, abandoned the city. Some 4,000 men, women, and children, it was said, fled to seek refuge in distant parts of Castile, in Portugal, and even in the city of Granada. As influential and prominent citizens who held key positions in Sevillian finances and mercantilism, the *conversos'* flight devastated the economy. Shops run for decades by fathers and sons were boarded up and abandoned. Trade barges disappeared from the port. Cloth and silk markets vanished. The flow of commodities from foreign countries dwindled.

In Medina del Campo, Isabella received news of the exodus calmly. Once having made the decision, she had steeled herself to its unpleasant consequences. Economic ruin, even the prospect of torturing and burning heretics, horrible though it was to a usually compassionate woman like Isabella, was a relatively minor price to pay for the glory of purifying the church.

Resistance, as the unfortunate *converso* Susan and his friends had learned, was impossible, for the Inquisition was founded upon an anonymous spy system. Within two weeks, members of the old Christian nobility had turned over many of the fleeing *conversos,* having been ordered to do so by their priests on pain of excommunication. Such threats foreshadowed the coercive techniques and mutual denunciations that would characterize the sixteenth-century Inquisition as it spread from Spain into other Western European nations.

For weeks before the inquisitors arrived in a town, the local clergy prepared their parishioners for the tribunal with sermons designed to impress them with a "horror of heresy." To encourage the laity to act as informers, the priests described thirty-seven ways Christians could discover judaizing *conversos*. Among them were telltale behaviors such as *conversos* who wore better clothes on Saturdays than during the week, who refused to eat on Jewish holidays, or who avoided pork. The Inquisition formally began with the appearance of the court-appointed examiners. In church the inquisitors would read aloud the *Edicto de Gracia*, or Edict of Grace, to the parishioners, notifying them of the Inquisition and giving them a certain period of time—usually one to three months—to step forward and confess their sins.

Good Christians were expected to identify those they suspected of heresy. To fail to do so, whether one was a queen or a commoner, was to disqualify oneself from salvation in the afterlife for it implied that the observer himself had "relapsed" into heresy. Should any Christian be found guilty of failing to name a suspect, he would be "relaxed"—a sardonic inquisitional term meaning apprehended by the state authorities—and condemned to death.

The inquisitional process—the naming of suspects, the denunciations, the trials—thus spun out of a web of fear. To avoid being named by others, many *conversos* confessed themselves. Added to this paranoia was the fact that inquisitional denunciations were always made in secret, so that the condemned never knew who had accused them.

Those accused of heresy suffered agonizing ordeals that often lasted for months, even years. After a preliminary investigation, the accused was imprisoned and his property held in custody: As a result, his family was often left without a means of support.

At first Sevillian Inquisition suspects were imprisoned in the Monasterio de San Pablo, but as their numbers grew they were moved to the Castle of Triana in the city's outskirts. Later, as the Inquisition spread northward through Castile, its prisoners were housed in monasteries and castles whose conditions, it was said, were often better than those of ordinary prisoners in municipal jails.

Inquisitional prisoners were fed at their own expense from funds taken from their confiscated properties. Their diet consisted primarily of meat, bread, and wine; no worse, and probably somewhat better than the fare in local prisons. But unlike ordinary prisoners, who were mandated to speedy trials by the monarchs' 1476 ruling, inquisitional suspects often languished behind bars for months. To ensure secrecy about their accusers, those prisoners were isolated from the rest of the world. Those who refused to cooperate within the prisons were "controlled" through two devices—the *mordaza,* or gag, to prevent them from blaspheming, and the *pie de amigo,* an iron fork designed to keep a captive's hands raised.

The accused were considered guilty unless proven innocent. Although ignorant of the charges against them, prisoners were given several chances to confess before trial. Should they do so, they were expected to repent and seek "reconciliation" with the church.

Yet the inquisitional concept of "reconciliation" was rarely kind. Sometimes prisoners were still burned at the stake but shown "mercy" by being strangled first. "Reconciled" heretics might also be imprisoned indefinitely, severely flogged, forced to serve in a galley boat, ordered to make a pilgrimage or to serve penitentially in religious service.

Their sins were never to be forgotten. If confessed heretics were allowed to live, they were ordered to wear a *coroza,* or tall conical hat, and a *san benito,* or yellow woolen knee-length gown, often painted with their name and decorated with devils and the flames of hellfire. Even after death reconciled heretics' transgressions lived on, for their *san benito* was publicly displayed in the family's parish church.

In the fifteenth century torture was a normal part of prison life. Thus it was a normal inquisitional device used to extract a confession or clarify a statement. Such confessions, however, were not considered valid unless reaffirmed the next day. As prisoners were often still suffering from those tortures, they rarely recanted.

Punishment took many forms, and none were unique to prisoners of the Inquisition. Once accused, no one was spared—females as well as males, old women as well as young pregnant women, boys as young as thirteen or fourteen, men into their eighties and nineties. In preparation, victims were stripped to a loincloth and tortured by a member of their sex. One of the most common tortures was the *toca,* or forced imbibement of large amounts of water. Another was the *garrucha,* or pulley that hoisted the prisoner to the ceiling and then dislocated his or her limbs. Still another was the *potro,* or rack upon which the victim was placed and bound with cords that the torturer tightened until they cut deep into the flesh. And there were dozens of others just as grisly—flogging, disfigurement, dismemberment, partial burning of flesh.

If prisoners still failed to confess, they were compelled to appear in court to hear the rest of the evidence for trial. Then inquisitors, theologians, and a bishop's deputy consulted on a verdict. The sentences were issued in a large public ceremony known as the *auto-da-fe,* literally an "act of faith." The ritual began with a grand ecclesiastical procession that ended in a public presentation in which a prelate preached a sermon of faith to the accused. The inquisitors then pronounced the sentences. Those who failed to be "reconciled" to the church were declared heretics and "relaxed" to the crown. Theoretically, the inquisitors could not condemn anyone to death because scriptural law and the church forbid it. Nevertheless, the secular punishment for heresy in Castile was death, usually by burning alive at the stake.

Historians have long debated the number of people executed in the first years of the Spanish Inquisition. Estimates run from Bernáldez's report of 700 between 1481 and 1488 to some 8,800 between 1480 and 1498. Whether Isabella ever attended an *auto-da-fe* is not clear. Almost certainly she never witnessed the death of a condemned heretic at the stake for she abhorred bloodshed, even when she believed it was deserved. Paradoxically, the queen's personal fear of hellfire and her fervent desire to cleanse the church of heresy thus led her to initiate one of the most cruel and enduring religious persecutions known in the history of Western Europe.

PART FOUR

A Holy War
1482–1492

CHAPTER THIRTY-THREE

Ay de mi, Alhama!

By late 1481 the Moorish king Ali Abu-1-Hasan could no longer contain his animosity as a tribute state of Castile. For the last six years he had refused to pay Isabella and Ferdinand the traditional tribute money. Now, on December 27 a battalion of Moors scaled the walls of Christian Zahara, killed the guards, and entered the sleeping city. After slaughtering Zahara's *alcalde* and some of its citizens, the turbaned soldiers claimed the city in the name of the Granadan king. By daybreak, the Moors had chained together 150 of Zahara's men, women, and children and marched them to Ronda where they were to be enslaved.

Isabella and Ferdinand were stunned by the news. At the time of the attack the monarchs were in Valencia, completing a tour of the Aragonese cities where Prince Juan had been sworn as royal heir. Although Isabella and Ferdinand knew the border clashes between the Moors and Christians were intensifying, they did not expect an invasion because their treaty with Hasan was still in effect. Moreover, Zahara, perched at the edge of the Andalusian border and built atop a mountain, was considered an impregnable fortress, perhaps the safest in Castile—so famous, in fact, that the Castilians colloquially called a virtuous woman a *Zaharena*.

To Isabella, the invasion was intolerable, for once having attained the Castilian crown, she was determined to maintain the borders of her kingdom and keep them safe for Christianity. Ferdinand was equally distressed. Decades earlier it had been his grandfather, Fernando I, who had wrested Zahara from the Moors, and now he could not allow it to slip back to Islam. But with the Moors' *rebato,* or guerrilla attack, the monarchs' dynastic inheritances were suddenly challenged. Overnight, the *Reconquista* that Isabella and Ferdinand considered an ancestral obligation had become a political necessity—a Holy War against Granada fully as compelling as Pope Sixtus's campaign against the Turks of the Albanian peninsula.

By the time the Moors took Zahara, Isabella and Ferdinand shared equal responsibilities in Castile and Aragón. The previous April they had traveled to Calatayud where the Aragonese *Cortes* conferred Isabella with royal authority equal to that of King Ferdinand. From there the monarchs had journeyed to Barcelona and then to Valencia, where Isabella's monarchial rights were again confirmed and Prince Juan sworn as heir.

In January 1482, as Isabella and Ferdinand rode toward Castile, they issued notices affirming their declaration of a Holy War against Granada. To that effect, the monarchs ordered all the Andalusian border towns to strengthen their fortresses. They then instructed the Castilian navy to block the Strait of Gibraltar so that Hasan could not summon troops from Morocco or other Moslem nations. They also ordered Alfonso de Cárdenas, Master of Santiago, to Écija and Rodrigo Tellez Girón, Master of Calatrava, to Jaén.

Meanwhile, the Marquis of Cádiz collected his own army of 5,000 men. As his commanders he appointed Ferdinand's uncle, Pedro Enríquez, *adelantado* of Andalusia, Diego de Merlo, *alcalde* of Sevilla, and two other officials.

Cádiz's fiery disposition may very well have ignited the Moorish war. By 1480 he was already fuming over Moorish attacks on his estates and had retaliated by storming the Moorish fortress of Villalonga. Ali Abu-l-Hasan, in turn, sought revenge by invading Zahara. But his actions had a negative effect. In the capital city of Granada, Hasan's subjects were terrified and convinced the invasion had destroyed the tenuous equilibrium between their kingdom and Castile.

Meanwhile, Cádiz sought another Moorish town in revenge. Before long a young Catalan named Juan de Ortega, captain of the *escaladores,* or wall-scalers, learned that the Moorish town of Alhama was poorly guarded and could be taken with little effort. The idea was admittedly daring: Alhama was situated in the heart of the Moorish kingdom, less than forty miles from Granada and prized by the royal court for its baths. Moreover, it was located in the middle of a fertile plain and poised upon a high cliff. Although Alhama's battlemented walls were well guarded, its castle, which seemed to rise out of the sheer granite wall of the mountain below, was poorly patrolled.

This was exactly the kind of challenge that appealed to Cádiz. By February 27, 1482, the marquis, with 2,400 light cavalry and 3,000 infantrymen, had assembled in a valley less than two miles from Alhama. Then he called for volunteers. Just before dawn thirty *escaladores* slithered up the walls of Alhama Castle, killed the guards, and stormed onto the streets between the castle and the walled city. Simultaneously the Castilian army waiting below blew trumpets to distract the citizens. In the resultant tumult, an *escalador* opened the back door to the castle, enabling the Castilians to enter. By then it was dawn, and the Moors barricaded themselves within the city walls. From the ramparts turbaned soldiers aimed poisoned arrows, and shot stones and lead balls from primitive artillery, while their wives and children threw boiling water and pitch from the rooftops.

Finally, Cádiz's battering rams tore through a city wall from the castle side. With a blare of trumpets, they stormed Alhama. By day's end the Castilians had slaughtered 800 Moors and taken 3,000 captive. The streets were littered with corpses. To prevent the stench of death, Cádiz ordered the bodies thrown over Alhama's walls. Within hours many of their skeletons were picked clean by vultures and wild dogs.

"Ay de mi, Alhama!"—"Woe is me, Alhama!"—are the words Ali Abu-l-Hasan supposedly cried when he heard about the town's fall. But the Moorish king did not weep for long. The following Tuesday, March 5, he arrived outside the walls of Alhama with 3,000 cavalry and 5,000 infantrymen. Surrounded, Cádiz dispatched messengers for help—to Isabella and Ferdinand, to the Andalusian nobles, even to his wife.

The Moorish army, meanwhile, enraged by the sight of the skeletons and half-eaten corpses ringing Alhama, threw themselves on the city walls and like human inchworms wriggled toward the top. As Hasan's men reached the battlements, they were cut down with swords, spears, and arrows and fell to their death. Within hours the Moorish king realized that in his haste to rescue Alhama he had failed to bring along battering equipment. But there was one other way to rout those living in a state of siege—cut their supplies.

Alhama "the Dry" had only one water source—a small river that gushed out of the mountains near the city gates. To reach it Cádiz's soldiers were forced to make daily forays outside. Consequently, Hasan ordered his men to divert the river, reducing it to a mere trickle. Cádiz's parched soldiers were thus compelled to scurry beneath the swift Moorish arrows to collect water for their comrades. The trip was so hazardous that it was said "every drop of water was purchased with a drop of blood."[1] Within three weeks the situation had become so grim that Cádiz's prisoners were dying of thirst and his men weakening. Once again the marquis dispatched urgent requests to the monarchs and his friends for aid.

By March 14 Isabella and Ferdinand received Cádiz's first letters from Alhama announcing his initial victory. Although the marquis and his men were now trapped, neither his messenger nor the monarchs knew of his predicament. The king and queen received the news with "more anxiety than joy," falling to their knees in chapel and offering prayers of thanksgiving to the Almighty.[2] That day an observer noted that Isabella and Ferdinand ate their main meal in near silence. Then they went to the Church of Santiago to hear *Te Deum Laudamus* sung and to offer prayers for success in the forthcoming Holy War. By late afternoon the monarchs made their decision: They would travel to Andalusia and supervise the war personally.

At twilight, the king and a group of barons that included Beltrán de la Cueva, the Count of Tendilla, and the Count of Trevino left for Andalusia. Isabella, then in the fifth month of pregnancy, planned to follow them in a few weeks.

In Andalusia, meanwhile, the Marquesa of Cádiz, having learned of her husband's plight, searched for reinforcements. She knew, of course, that the most powerful of the Andalusian barons was her husband's arch rival, the Duke of Medina Sidonia. Valuing Cádiz's life more than his pride, she appealed to the duke, who agreed not only to send men but volunteered to lead the expedition himself. Before long he had summoned 5,000 men and set out with them toward Alhama. Moslem spies, meanwhile, tracking Medina Sidonia's large army, relayed the news to Hasan, who became so unnerved by their approach that on March 29 he retreated.

That same day Cádiz's guards saw the bright glint of Castilian banners and weapons. At the head of the advancing forces was Medina Sidonia, dressed in full battle regalia. Cádiz stepped forward to meet the duke and express his gratitude. As their armies watched, the two rivals embraced. Afterward, the two leaders evacuated their men from Alhama and left the town under a small patrol.

The queen, traveling slowly because of her pregnancy, journeyed over the well-worn roads from Old Castile toward Andalusia and arrived in Córdoba on April 23. Isabella had spent her last weeks in Medina del Campo summoning recruits for a new Castilian army and ordering munitions—hemp, lead, *bombardas*, catapults, battering rams, and other *ingenios*. At the same time she ordered sacks of cereals and wheat, *botas* or sheepskins of wine, thousands of dried fish, and 150 freshly slaughtered cattle.

Meanwhile from Alcalá de Henares came reports that must have saddened Isabella. The seventy-year-old Archbishop Carrillo lay dying in the Convent of San Francisco. Isabella's former mentor would linger for nearly three months, but there was no time for the queen to visit him. Nor was there a point in such a visit. Carrillo had never personally reconciled with Isabella, never embraced her warmly again, never even seen her since those first terrifying weeks of the Portuguese war.

Isabella did, however, pay indirect homage to her old mentor. After leaving Medina del Campo at the end of March, she stopped in Toledo for three days. It was Easter. She attended high mass in Castile's oldest cathedral, which was still technically under Carrillo's authority, and offered prayers for Castile, for the Holy War against the Moors, and for her loved ones—Ferdinand, her children, and the new life stirring in her womb.

But once she arrived in Andalusia, once she breathed the sweetened air of jasmine, lavender, and roses, once she rode through the land where spring had already blossomed, Isabella became wholly preoccupied with the Moorish campaign. Shortly after her arrival in Córdoba, Isabella and Ferdinand learned that the Granada king had returned to Alhama with siege equipment. Ferdinand's counselors advised the monarchs to abandon that town immediately, arguing that its craggy site deep within enemy territory made it difficult to supply and costly to retain.

Isabella would not consider the idea. "It was well known that all wars extracted high costs and required labor," she said. "That had been carefully considered before the King and I entered upon the idea of the conquest against the King of Granada; this city [Alhama] is the first we have won and it was thus impossible to contemplate giving it back."[3]

The queen's spirited words ended the argument, and Ferdinand thus marched toward Alhama with a new army. Hasan, learning of the Castilians' approach, again retreated. On May 19, 1482, Ferdinand took formal possession of the city. But this bloodless victory was not enough to satisfy Isabella and Ferdinand: There had to be tangible signs that the conquest was permanent.

Months earlier, in Medina del Campo, Isabella had prepared for that moment by providing the Castilian army with bells, crosses, altar clothes, and the sacramental utensils of the Catholic church. Consequently, by late May the prelates who traveled with Ferdinand embellished the freshly built altars of the city's new churches with the traditional symbols of Christianity. And above the city, from the highest tower of Alhama's largest mosque, hung a large silver cross given to the monarchs by Sixtus IV to proclaim the Castilian triumph.

The next object of Ferdinand's campaign against the Moors was Loja. Only about fifteen miles from Alhama, its conquest seemed the logical next step. But the Marquis of Cádiz and other Andalusian *grandees* acquainted with the region's geography advised Ferdinand against it. Like many Moorish towns in Granada, Loja was surrounded by inhospitable mountains and could be approached only by climbing over rocky ravines. Such a siege, they warned Ferdinand, was premature. If attempted, it would demand a better knowledge of the terrain and a cadre of carefully trained men. Instead, they suggested the royal army attack Málaga, a wealthy port city on the peninsula's southern coast whose victory would cripple Granada's maritime trade and thwart Moslem reinforcements from North Africa.

Nevertheless, Diego de Merlo, a deeply respected *alcalde* and former judge in Sevilla, persuaded Ferdinand to take Loja first.

Isabella, who considered military strategies Ferdinand's domain, consequently issued a new call for men, munitions, and *repartimiento,* or provisions, throughout the kingdom. Rural communities picked their fields clean. Grains were harvested as soon as they were barely ripe and quickly ground into flour. Cows, chickens, and sheep were herded onto carts and sent south. The Sevillian area alone was responsible for 4,000 *fanegas* (a measure equal to 5.5 liters of grain, or the produce of 1.59 acres) of wheat, 8,000 *fanegas* of barley, 12,000 fish, 150 cows, and 15,000 *arrobas* (barrels) of wine.

Before long, cavalry and infantrymen had gathered in Castile. As was the custom, the *grandees* were expected to provide the king and queen with most of the men and equipment. Nearly all of those nobles chose to direct their own troops in battle as a symbol of seignorial rank and privilege rather than to turn them over to the king. Isabella and Ferdinand, in turn, were expected to reward the *grandees* with some of the conquered territory.

The Castilian cities provided other military units known as the *concejos.* The crown itself sent a royal army from the *guardas reales,* its standing militia of 500 cavalry and 500 men-at-arms. Another 1,500 horsemen and crossbowmen from the *Hermandad* were supported by special funds from local towns. Finally, there were battalions of "lesser nobles," vassals of the king and queen, who joined the royal army for pay. Despite her well-advanced pregnancy, the "attentive" queen worked feverishly to coordinate these units just as she had during the Portuguese war. By May, Isabella was very large with child and it was suspected she was carrying twins. Despite her physical awkwardness, the queen's efforts as quartermaster succeeded. By the end of June, the army, artillery, provisions, and the mule train needed to transport them, had assembled in Córdoba.

On June 29, just as the army made final preparations for its departure, Isabella went into labor and delivered another daughter. The blond child was named María in honor of the Virgin. However, the labor pangs continued. Thirty-five hours later Isabella's midwife and a court physician finally delivered the exhausted queen of another child—a stillborn daughter. Ferdinand stood by anxiously, relieved to hear that his wife had survived the ordeal.

Nevertheless, Isabella's difficult birthing "did not delay the enterprise" any longer.[4] On July 1 Ferdinand and an army of 5,000 cavalry and 8,000 infantrymen departed for Loja. After crossing the Jenil River and reaching Écija, the king left most of his army behind to be used later as reinforcements.

By July 9 Ferdinand and the rest of his militia had arrived at Loja's outskirts. As Cádiz had predicted, the ravine-gnashed terrain made capturing the city difficult. The landscape, broken up by small mesas, olive tree groves, and steep hills, prevented Ferdinand from settling his camp around his own pavilion. As a result, his army was forced to pitch their tents on several plateaus. Moreover, the Castilian cavalry was useless in the rocky terrain, and Isabella's siege equipment and heavy artillery could not be moved close enough to penetrate the city's walls.

On Saturday, July 13, Loja's seventy-year-old governor, Ali Atar, attacked the Castilians below their encampment. The Castilians rushed forward to chase their assailants as other Moors, hidden in the bushes above, gained control of the strategic hill of Albohacen. The Castilians, reversing direction, fought their way slowly up that hill, losing hundreds of soldiers, among them the handsome, twenty-four-year-old Master of Calatrava.

Utterly demoralized, Ferdinand ordered a retreat to nearby Río Frío where fresh reinforcements would meet his army. Just as the last tents were packed away, the Moors swarmed out of Loja's gates with bloodthirsty cries for revenge. With only a handful of men the king slashed blindly at the Moors with his spear, wounding some, killing others, toppling still others into the Jenil River below. Cádiz, realizing the king was outnumbered, fought his way to Ferdinand's side. By then Ferdinand was in a perilous position. After lancing a Moor, he was unable to remove his spear from the victim or even reach for his sword. Above him, a tall Moor poised his scimitar. At the last moment Cádiz threw a spear under the Moor's arm, thereby deflecting the blow.

In the end the Castilians retreated, leaving some of their artillery behind. Pounding behind the broken army that dragged its gory lances, swords, and crossbows to the Río Frío were 300 Moorish jennets spurred by the jeering Moors of Loja.

By mid-July Ferdinand had returned to Córdoba. The Marquis of Cádiz did not remind the king of his former advice, nor did any of the other commanders. But Ferdinand's mistake was obvious. If the Castilian monarchs were ever to conquer Granadan territories, they would require bigger and better guns, soldiers trained in guerrilla warfare, and familiarity with the terrain.

At the Córdoba alcázar, a still-pale and weak Isabella greeted her husband sympathetically. But while she "suffered keenly," wrote Pulgar, "no one could tell from her words or her actions the grief which she felt."[5] The words Ferdinand spoke to her six years earlier at Tordesillas after his defeat at Toro had been seared into the queen's memory. Like the men under her command, Isabella had vowed to remain courageous in war, to learn from disappointments, and, with dignity befitting a queen, to present a calm face to the world.

CHAPTER THIRTY-FOUR

Indulgences

The pope was angry. Despite the careful establishment of the Inquisition at Sevilla, the first tribunal had failed to publish the requisite Edict of Grace that allowed individuals to confess their sins before the arrests began. Soon after the deaths of Susan and his friends, Pope Sixtus received complaints from Castilian bishops that the Inquisition had been unduly harsh and failed to follow the due process of papal law.

Privately, some members of Isabella and Ferdinand's court disapproved of the Inquisition. One of them was the queen's secretary, Pulgar, who complained to Cardinal Mendoza about the injustice of punishing innocent children brought up in *converso* homes who had never "learned any other doctrine but that which they had seen their parents practice at home."[1]

Others, like the *converso* humanist and former ambassador to Rome Juan de Lucena, questioned the validity of *converso* Christianity, performed two or three generations earlier under duress and then transmitted to their children. Believing that Jews "baptized through fear did not receive the sacrament properly," he maintained that *conversos* should not be treated as heretics "but rather as infidels."[2]

Even the queen's confessor Talavera was troubled by the use of the Inquisition to win *conversos* to Christianity. Although he agreed that condemned heretics should be burned at the stake, he urged a more moderate approach for all *conversos* before they were tried. "Heresies," he maintained, "need to be corrected not only with punishment and lashes but even more with Catholic reasoning"—that is, through teaching and inspiration.[3]

Nevertheless, Isabella and Ferdinand had approved the Inquisition. In 1481 the king and queen were, in fact, so convinced of its worth that when they traveled to Aragón, Ferdinand reestablished the tribunal there. But before the end of 1481, Sixtus received still another batch of complaints, this time from *converso* bishops in Aragón.

On January 29, 1482, just after Isabella and Ferdinand returned to Castile, Sixtus suspended the papal bull of 1478 that had established the Sevillian Inquisition. The Castilian tribunal, wrote the pope, had proceeded with "no regard to law, have imprisoned many unjustly, have subjected them to dire torments and have unjustly declared heretics and despoiled them, once dead, of their goods."[4] The contention that the Castilian crown would grow wealthy from confiscation of the property of their victims is still a matter of debate today. With that in mind, Sixtus reestablished the Inquisition under his own authority on February 11 and appointed seven new Dominican inquisitors to Sevilla.

On April 18 the pope similarly condemned the Aragonese Inquisition. "In that kingdom," Sixtus wrote, "the Inquisition has for some time been moved not by zeal for the faith and the salvation of souls, but by lust and wealth. . . ."[5]

Then Sixtus ordered a series of reforms. Among them were the demand that the accused should know the names of their accusers, that bishops should preside with inquisitors, that the papacy should hear appeals, and that heretics could be absolved after making secret confessions to inquisitional officers. That document, said to be "the most extraordinary bull in the history of the Inquisition,"[6] established heresy as a crime, which, like any other, was entitled to a fair trial in the ecclesiastical courts.

Despite their involvement in the Moorish war, Isabella and Ferdinand protested Sixtus's actions as an infringement of their royal autonomy. From Andalusia, Ferdinand wrote Sixtus in May that he refused to obey papal orders because without royal authority over the Inquisition, heresy would never be eliminated in Castile and Aragón.

"Things have been told me, Holy Father, which, if true, would seem to merit the greatest astonishment," Ferdinand wrote. "It is said that Your Holiness has granted the *conversos* a general pardon for all the errors and crimes they have committed." Yet neither he nor Isabella believed those rumors because they were "things which would in no way have been conceded by your Holiness, who has a duty to the Inquisition." Moreover, Ferdinand warned, "if by chance concessions have been made through the persistent and cunning persuasion of the said *conversos,* I intend never to let them take effect. Take care therefore not to let the matter go further and to revoke any concessions and entrust us with the care of this question."[7]

The king's confrontational tone reflected not only the monarchs' commitment to the eradication of heresy but another, equally important goal—their determination to control the Spanish church independent of the pope. The struggle had been building for years. Twice since 1479 Sixtus had overruled requests from Isabella and Ferdinand to have native prelates named the new bishops of Cuenca and Tarragona. In spite of that conflict, the king and queen had complied with Sixtus's call for a crusade against the Turks by sending an armada in 1481 to drive the infidels from the Italian port of Otranto. But when, in the winter of 1482, the papal envoy Domingo Centurion arrived in Medina del Campo from Rome,

Isabella and Ferdinand refused to meet with him. "The Pope," the monarchs were said to have grumbled, "had dealt with them more unjustly than with any Catholic prince."[8]

Sixtus retaliated almost immediately. Shortly after he received Ferdinand's May 1482 letter, he arrested the Castilian ambassador. Ferdinand, in turn, apprehended Sixtus's papal *nuncio* and recalled the Spanish representatives from the Holy See. Isabella and Ferdinand even threatened to call a general council of all the princes of Christendom to reform the church.

The pope relented. Exactly why is not fully understood. Cardinal Borgia, still faithful to Isabella and Ferdinand, may have convinced the pope about the folly of such a break. Besides, the victory at Otranto was just a year old, and Sixtus knew that in all likelihood he would have to appeal to Spain again for military aid against the infidel.

While Sixtus considered his options, Cardinal Mendoza took steps toward a reconciliation. In letters to the Holy See, the cardinal outlined Castile's peculiar political situation, which, he explained, was imperiled both by Moors and *conversos*. In that seditious atmosphere it was imperative for Isabella and Ferdinand to control all appointments to the bishoprics. In addition, they must retain authority over the Inquisition.

Gradually the pope softened. On July 3 he agreed to remove his nephew, Rafael Sansoni, as Bishop of Cuenca and replace him with Isabella's chaplain, Alfonso of Burgos. The following October Sixtus rescinded the April bull that had demanded papal control over the Spanish Inquisition. Two months later the pope published a new bull approving the appointment of Cardinal Mendoza to the cardinalship of Toledo, whose see had become vacant with Archbishop Carrillo's death.

On August 10 Sixtus also issued Isabella and Ferdinand a Bull of Crusade for the Holy War against the Moors. By that bull the king and queen received new "indulgences," or papal letters, meant to encourage soldiers to fight against the infidel. Those indulgences, which were distributed in churches throughout Castile, could be purchased by parishioners as a guarantee of spiritual salvation after death. Soldiers could buy them from their priests to receive earthly dispensations for sins and were told they would automatically acquire martyr status if they died in battle. The indulgences were also offered to those who did not, or could not, fight in the Granada war but were willing to donate money.

In September Isabella wrote the pope assuring him of her gratitude and filial devotion. She had not, however, forgotten his criticisms about the Castilian Inquisition and, during their estrangement, had pondered how to prevent future abuses. In those letters (which have not been preserved and whose content can only be gleaned from the pope's subsequent response), the queen now suggested that the inquisitional court of appeals Sixtus had proposed for Rome be located instead in Castile.

Vice-Chancellor Cardinal Borgia read Isabella's letter aloud to the pope. Shortly thereafter, Sixtus fell ill and consequently delayed answering the queen until February 25, 1483. His response letter was a resounding affirmation of the reestablishment of the Spanish Inquisition along the lines suggested by Isabella and Ferdinand. He wrote:

Your letter is full of your piety and singular devotion to God. We rejoice exceedingly, daughter, very dear to our heart that so much care and diligence are employed by Your Highness in those matters [the inquisition] so eagerly desired by us. We have always striven to apply suitable remedies for the wretched folly of those people [the heretics] as for a pernicious disease.[9]

In answer to the bishops' accusations that Isabella had initiated the Castilian Inquisition "more by ambition and by greed for temporal goods than by zeal for the faith and for Catholic truth," Sixtus assured Isabella "that we have no such suspicion."[10]

He also assured Isabella that he was still seriously considering her proposal to establish an Inquisitional Court of Appeals in Castile. He was, in fact, in the process of consulting with his cardinals and "so far as we may be able before God, we shall endeavor to grant your will. . . ."[11]

The pope then reemphasized his confidence in Isabella and Ferdinand's ability to administer the Inquisition by the highest standards of the Christian church. Nevertheless, Sixtus remained genuinely troubled about the Inquisition and its potential abuses under the twin crowns of Castile and Aragón. In particular, he worried about Isabella and Ferdinand's deputies, the inquisitors:

Since we behold, not without wonder, that which proceeds, not from your intention or that of our previously mentioned beloved son [Ferdinand], but from your officials, who, having put aside the fear of God, do not shrink . . . from breaking our provisions and the apostolic mandates . . . we urge and require that you carefully avoid censures of this kind. . . .[12]

How to avoid those "censures" or abuses perplexed Isabella and Ferdinand for the rest of their lives and left a permanent stain upon their reputations after their deaths. While it was impossible for the monarchs to monitor the details of every tribunal conducted in Castile and Aragón, the fact that they had requested that responsibility from the Church made them culpable for all Inquisitional excesses of the era. Moreover, Isabella and Ferdinand had demanded that responsibility at a time when the pope and his church were politically vulnerable.

As the tone of Sixtus's letter implied, Ferdinand too had reconciled with him. The Castilian king had regained Sixtus's favor through what was rapidly becoming his personal forte—diplomatic and military assistance to the troubled Holy See.

For years, Sixtus had been caught between the warring city-states of Italy whose rivalries had at least partially encouraged the 1480 Turkish invasion of Otranto. By 1482 the papal states of Venice, Florence, and Naples were entangled in new imbroglios and their energies spent on internecine bloodshed rather than, as Sixtus urged, on a unified Christian defense of the Italian peninsula. As King of Sicily and cousin to the Neapolitan monarch, Ferdinand ordered his ambassadors to negotiate a settlement between those papal states. Finally, through their efforts, peace was declared on the Italian peninsula on December 12.

On January 2, 1483, Sixtus consequently addressed a letter to Ferdinand thanking "Your Royal Majesty for enabling the cause of peace to his everlasting glory."[13] Then he rewarded Isabella and Ferdinand by granting them permission to collect 100,000 ducats, a tax of one-tenth called *la decima,* out of the church revenues of Castile and Aragón. With that influx of funds, Isabella and Ferdinand suddenly could mount a formidable campaign against the Moors.

The monarchs learned about that award while in Madrid, for every winter of the Moorish campaign they traveled north from Andalusia. Every spring they reversed the process, arriving in the south with new men and arms. Despite the seeming perversity of traveling north in winter, the migrations fulfilled several purposes. First, they enabled the Andalusian countryside to recover from the strain of supporting a large army year-round. Moreover, they enabled Isabella and Ferdinand to tour other parts of their kingdom, gathering new soldiers, supplies, and munitions. Now, with Sixtus's *decima,* Isabella and Ferdinand ordered dozens of *lombardas,* primitive cannons, to be cast at the Aragonese city of Huesca. In the Andalusian town of Sierra de Constantina, they commissioned thousands of stone balls as ammunition. From distant corners of Castile they stockpiled gunpowder, catapults, and other *ingenios de guerra* for Ferdinand's 1483 campaign.

On January 1 the Castilian monarchs also issued a startling religious *cedula.* All Jews living in Sevilla and Córdoba were to be expelled in one month. By then Isabella and Ferdinand believed the Jews were at least partially responsible for the *converso* controversy, a decision doubtless abetted by Sixtus's October 1482 retraction of his criticism. And as the Moorish war progressed, the monarchs had become increasingly fearful about all non-Christians.

Nevertheless, the expulsion came as a shock to the Jewish community, for in 1480 Isabella had assured the Jews of Sevilla that the Inquisition would not threaten the security of their *aljamas.* But the growing number of confessed heretics, the Sevillian tribunal's indictment of more than three hundred *conversos,* and the fear that thousands of others remained at large had poisoned the atmosphere between man and man, between Christian and *converso,* and finally, between monarch and subject.

By February 1483 the largest Jewish population in Castile had been uprooted. Forced to sell their homes, vineyards, and livestock in what the Christians quickly recognized as a buyer's market, the Jews became a dispossessed population overnight. Some moved north to Old Castile, to Extremadura, to Portugal, and even to Granada. By mid-1484 not a single Jew was left in all of Andalusia.

Ironically, that exodus did little to stem the tide of *conversos* convicted of heresy by the new Inquisition. Instead, it foreshadowed a solution Isabella and Ferdinand would reconsider nine years later: the permanent expulsion of all Jews living in the kingdoms of Castile and Aragón on pain of death or forced baptism.

True to his promise, Sixtus IV established an Inquisitional Court of Appeals in Castile in May 1483 and appointed a native, Iñigo Manrique, Bishop of Sevilla, as its head. Yet by early summer the flow of complaints to the Holy See about inquisitional injustices had not abated. And a growing number of *converso* fugitives from Castile and Aragón began to arrive regularly in Rome seeking the pope's protection.

On August 2 Sixtus abruptly refuted the Castilian Court of Appeals in a ten-page bull, *Ad Futuram rei memoriam*. Within it he criticized the long delays prisoners endured before Manrique heard appeals and complained that the inquisitors' decrees "exceeded the moderation of law."[14] Many of the accused were not given a chance to appeal; others, despite papal letters of pardon, refused to present them because their names had already been burned in effigy. To those who had automatically been condemned, Castile's Inquisitional Court of Appeals was thus useless.

So widespread were those abuses that Sixtus now decreed that all appeals accepted in Rome were to be honored in Spain. Those who repented were also to be privately absolved by the inquisitors and, once freed, were never again to be tried. Additionally, Isabella and Ferdinand were to ensure that all confiscated property was returned to the absolved penitents.

Had it gone into effect, that remarkable bull would almost certainly have destroyed the underpinnings of the Spanish Inquisition. A mere eleven days later, however, it was followed by a brief from Sixtus, who, conceding to objections from some of his cardinals, canceled the August 2 bull.

Nevertheless, the critical tone of Sixtus's August 2 brief suggested that Isabella and Ferdinand were headed for still another papal confrontation. An anxious Isabella thus proposed that the Spanish Inquisition be reorganized along more merciful lines with a uniform set of procedures. To enforce that standardization, she thought it necessary to appoint an overseer, one with impeccable standards. In October Sixtus thus named the sixty-three-year-old Tomás de Torquemada as Inquisitor General in Castile and on the seventeenth of that month named him to a similar position in Aragón, Catalonia, and Valencia. Under the auspices of a man like Torquemada—stern, ascetic, uncompromising—the Spanish Inquisition would, or so the pope and the Castilian monarchs believed, surely be administered with a minimum of corruption.

Torquemada was well suited to the position, for in his twenty-year service as prior of the Dominican monastery of Santa Cruz in Segovia, the aquiline-nosed monk had led an exemplary life of study, prayer, and penitence. Some of those years had coincided with Isabella's adolescence in Segovia, and it was there that Torquemada had served as her confessor. In 1477 Isabella had ordered Torquemada to investigate Hojeda's accusations about the "judaizing" *conversos* of Sevilla. Five years later Sixtus had named him as one of the seven inquisitors for the tribunal then under his authority. As a Dominican priest his personal asceticism was legendary. At night, Torquemada slept on a board; he abstained from meat, fasted endlessly, wore a hair shirt next to his skin, and endured all sorts of other penitences in hopes of achieving spiritual grace.

Religious rigor burned through every inch of Torquemada's gaunt frame. In addition, his hatred of Jews and *conversos* had long ago reached obsessive proportions. His sermons against the *conversos* were vehement, filled with allusions to the devil and eternal hellfire, so vivid that they inevitably frightened his listeners to new acts of devotion. So masterful was Torquemada at intimidation that he is usually credited with having persuaded Isabella to ask Sixtus for the original 1478 bull of Inquisition.

With the blessings of the pope and the Castilian monarchs, Torquemada assumed the role of Inquisitor General of the Spanish Inquisition in late 1483. To administer the new tribunal, Isabella and Ferdinand established a new royal council, the *Consejo de la Suprema y General Inquisición,* the Supreme Council of the General Inquisition. Under Torquemada's aegis this council—the sixth one of Isabella and Ferdinand's court—had jurisdiction over both Castile and Aragón. It was, in fact, to be the only institution shared by both kingdoms during the monarchs' reign.

Each new tribunal was to have two judges, an assessor, or legal advisor, a guard, a prosecuting attorney, and notaries, all of whom were considered employees of the crowns of Castile and Aragón. As before, the appearance of the Inquisition in a new community commenced with the publication of an Edict of Grace that allowed a thirty- or forty-day grace period before the arrests began. Only those who confessed before the trial could be "reconciled" to the church. The new inquisitors, like the old ones, were expected to determine guilt, impose fines and confiscations, and "relax" those condemned as heretics to the "secular arm" of the state. Whatever differences existed between the earlier Castilian Inquisition and its 1483 version were, in the end, quite minimal.

Gradually the Inquisition spread north through Castile, and by November 1483 it reached Ciudad Real, a small town on the road between Andalusia and Old Castile known for its prominent *converso* population. By the end of February 6, 1484, thirty-four people and the effigies of forty fugitives had been burned at the stake.

From there the new Inquisition moved on to Guadalupe, Toledo, and Valladolid. Invariably, the announcement of the tribunal terrified every citizen— even those who were old Christians—for with its approach, many *conversos* fled, taking money, possessions, and trade with them. As a result, towns often became impoverished overnight. In addition, the inquisitional mandate that good Christians were obliged to accuse others they suspected of heresy spread fear and suspicion through every community. Every citizen was vulnerable, if only because anyone could be a victim of a spiteful accusation from an enemy.

By the time Torquemada was appointed to his new post, citizen protests were common. As the Inquisition moved north, they evolved into public demonstrations. When Ferdinand reestablished the Inquisition in Aragón in 1484, the city of Teruel bolted its gates against the inquisitors for a year. In 1485 eight *conversos* finally murdered the inquisitor Pedro Arbués in the Zaragoza cathedral.

Yet even in the face of such open public protest, Ferdinand and Isabella persisted, for they were convinced that the Inquisition was the only way to save Christianity, to protect souls for the church, and to keep Christian Castile safe from the infidel.

CHAPTER THIRTY-FIVE

Boabdil *El Chico*

I n March 1483 war broke over Andalusia again. All winter Castilian soldiers stationed at the Moorish border had longed for a new victory, and by spring their commander, Alfonso de Cárdenas, envisioned an easy triumph in the Ajarquía. That mountainous region, just north of Málaga, surrounded by deep valleys famed for its mulberry trees, had given rise to a rich silk industry. In fifteenth-century Europe, silk was nearly as valuable as gold, and thus Cárdenas's capture of the Ajarquía would have been an important economic victory.

By mid-March hundreds of soldiers joined Cárdenas and his men at Antequera. With them came commanders such as the *adelantado* of Andalusia, Pedro Enríquez; the Count of Cifuentes, Juan de Silva; Alonso de Aguilar; and the Marquis of Cádiz. Spirits ran high among the warriors, all except for Cádiz. Repeatedly the marquis's Moorish guides, or *adalides*—deserters from the Granadan kingdom, now employed as scouts—had discouraged the invasion because of the Ajarquía's deeply ravined valleys, high mountains, and fiercely patriotic peasants. But Cádiz's warnings were shouted down by younger men bursting with enthusiasm for battle and booty.

On March 19 a Castilian army of 3,000 cavalry and innumerable infantry left Antequera. Behind them scurried a motley group of fortunehunters, who had joined the campaign after learning of the proposed invasion and its rich booty. Most were merchants and peddlers who carried large sums of money in leather pouches, intending to buy silk, gold, and slaves in the spoils of the *caballeros'* invasion. Others wielded daggers and swords "with the intention of robbing and profiteering rather than serving God by destroying the infidel."[1]

As the Castilians penetrated the lush Ajarquía valley, Moslem peasants fled to its heights taking most of their valuables with them. When the Moorish king's brother, El Zagal, or The Valiant, learned about the invasion, he summoned an army and dispatched half to the mountains to attack the Castilians from the rear. El Zagal then rushed north with the other half to meet the enemy head on.

Meanwhile, the Castilians, proceeding with little resistance through the valley, grew discontent with the lack of rich plunder. Some of the malcontents broke out of the army's main column and rode off in search of booty as far south as Málaga. Suddenly El Zagal and his cavaliers appeared over a rock-filled gorge and swooped down. Amid shouts, flying arrows, the thud of stones against shields, and the cries of the wounded and dying, Cárdenas's soldiers held their ground bravely. But the mountain pass was too narrow for the Castilian battalions to maneuver, and they were forced to retreat. The safest path back through the Ajarquía was a shortcut known to the Castilians' guides. Even that effort was ill-fated, for the Castilians were so loaded down with bolts of silken cloth, gold and silver ornaments, Moorish shields and helmets that they had difficulty following a circuitous retreat.

Toward dusk on the night of March 20, "through either the treachery or ignorance of the guides" the Castilians entered a wooded gulch ringed by impassable mountains. In the fading light, the soldiers abandoned their loot. As they retraced their steps to a safer valley, the hills above them blazed with fires—"ten thousand torches glancing along the mountains," says one chronicler, revealing the enemy.[2] When the exhausted and by then thoroughly disoriented army refreshed themselves at a stream, a shower of arrows and stones fell from the heights, killing many men. The attack was so frightening and the Castilians so defenseless that "sons abandoned their fathers to their fate, brothers did not help brothers, and officers did not care about their troops."[3]

"Let us die, walking forward with our hearts if we cannot advance with our weapons and let us not perish here of this wretched death," Cárdenas bellowed. "Let us climb this range as men and let us not stay in this ditch waiting to die and watching our people die and being unable to help them." As the men climbed higher the earth fell away from their feet and "with shrieks and shouts their bodies fell to the ground."[4] Meanwhile the Moors continued to pelt the Castilians with arrows and stones from *La Cuesta de la Matanza,* or the Hill of the Massacre, as it is still known today.

At daybreak the scene was even more grim. In place of proud columns of advancing Castilians were haggard, blood-streaked men, their clothes ripped, their armor dulled and dented, their horses wounded and spiritless, their spirits so broken that "no one listened to the sound of the trumpet or the wave of a banner."[5] In their desperation, some soldiers abandoned their weapons in order to retreat faster. Others, it was said, dropped dead in their tracks without the sign of a wound. Still others staggered back to Málaga and gave themselves up as prisoners. A few lived on nuts and berries and, after walking for days, finally found their way to Alhama. Many, including most of the leaders of the campaign, eventually returned to Antequera. Cifuentes had been taken prisoner by the Moors. Cádiz, who had fled into another valley, saw his three brothers and nephews killed before his eyes, and barely escaped.

The Castilian casualties were embarrassingly high. According to one account only seventy Moorish knights had "defeated two thousand knights, the best in Spain."[6]

All of Andalusia mourned. Bernáldez, the moralistic curate of Los Palacios, wrote that the disaster was God's judgment upon the evil motives that had inspired the campaign. "The truth is that the majority of the troops had come more with the intention of looting and trading than to serve God . . . and win over the enemy to favor the Holy Catholic faith. There were very few with this intention. Most . . . were dominated by the greed of looting objects and jewels . . ."[7]

The king and queen "suffered deeply" when they learned about the disaster, their second defeat in less than a year.[8] But before Isabella and Ferdinand had a chance to retaliate, the Moorish king's son, Abu Abdallah, or Boabdil, as he is usually known, invaded the mountain town of Lucena. Boabdil's motives for the attack were not solely patriotic: He planned to besiege that Andalusian town to prove to his fellow Granadians that he was a better leader than his father, King Hasan.

For several years the Moorish kingdom had been divided between father and son. In keeping with the customs of Moslem emirs, Hasan maintained several wives and fathered many children. For twenty years his favorite concubine had been a beautiful blue-eyed, blond Christian slave named Isabela de Solis. The Moslems knew her as Zoroya, Star of the Morning, named for her radiant appearance. In time the lovely sultana bore Hasan a small, blond son, Boabdil, "El Chico," or the Younger.

From birth, the young prince had been recognized as heir to the Granada kingdom, but King Hasan never held his son in high regard. Legend has it that at his birth the Moslem astrologers had been called to read the prince's fortune. "*Alla Achbar!* God is great," these prophets had pronounced. "He alone controls the fate of empires: It is written in the heavens that this prince shall sit upon the throne of Granada, but that the downfall of the kingdom shall be accomplished during his reign."[9] As a result, King Hasan was most reluctant to have Boabdil rule.

Indeed, Boabdil had inherited physical characteristics from both parents—his mother's diminutive height, blond hair, and limpid eyes, his father's hollow cheeks and long face—but none of their spirit. By the time he had grown to manhood, his detractors snidely observed that he preferred lovemaking by the fountains and baths of the Alhambra to battling the Christians.

Meanwhile, months before the Moors' 1481 attack on Zahara, the aging Hasan became infatuated with a new paramour—a Greek slave, Ayesha, whom he soon married. Sultana Zoroya, by then approaching middle age, worried that Hasan would disinherit Boabdil in favor of Ayesha's future children. The sultana appealed to members of the Zegrie clan, who promptly took up arms against Ayesha and her allies, the Abencerrages.

By spring 1482 the two factions had clashed and spilled blood in the streets of Granada. In retaliation, King Hasan locked the sultana and Boabdil in the Alhambra Tower of Comares just before he left for Alhama. By the time Hasan returned in defeat from that city, Boabdil had not only escaped from the tower but been declared the King of Granada. Yet even as late as the spring of 1483, Boabdil's popularity extended no further than Granada's high walls; the rest of the

Moorish kingdom still preferred King Hasan and even his brother, the warrior El Zagal, to the blond prince.

In mid-April 1483, less than a month after the battle of the Ajarquía, Boabdil rallied 7,000 cavalry and 9,000 horsemen and marched toward the Castilian border. Although he was only nineteen, the prince was confident. The recent defeat in the Ajarquía left the Castilians with only the shards of an army. Moreover, Boabdil was accompanied by his octogenarian father-in-law Ali Atar, who had defeated Ferdinand at Loja in 1482.

By April 21 Boabdil had arrived at the town of Lucena in the Sierra Morenas, about ten or eleven miles northeast of Sevilla. Diego Fernández de Córdoba, the *alcayde de los donzeles,* or captain of the royal pages, immediately warned his uncle, the Count of Cabra, in nearby Baena of the Moors' approach. With such short notice, Cabra was forced to dispatch the few forces then at his disposal—250 knights and 1,200 infantrymen. Nevertheless, Cabra's soldiers climbed over the Sierra Morenas and lighted watchfires on the evergreen-covered hills above Lucena. A fog set in and, as at Ajarquia, hid the small size of Cabra's army from the Moors. On a signal from Cabra, the Castilians then swept over the hills and descended into the valley. Simultaneously, the count's young nephew and his own soldiers burst out of Lucena and charged the Moors. From both sides of Lucena Castilian soldiers played trumpets to confuse the enemy.

Soon the Moorish infantry, thinking only of booty, abandoned the field to the knights. Meanwhile Boabdil, conspicuously mounted on a white, richly caparisoned horse and dressed in a red velvet tunic, attempted to rally his soldiers. Suddenly Ali Atar, "the best lance in all of Morisma [the Moorish kingdom]" fell to the ground, his skull cleaved in two by a Castilian war ax.

News of the great warrior's death spread quickly through the Moorish camp. Without Ali Atar's leadership, the Moslem knights lost their nerve and retreated to the banks of the Jenil River. As the defeated Moors attempted to ford the river, Boabdil remained on its shores, resting his horse. Three Castilian footsoldiers then surprised the prince, who, explaining that he was of high rank and hence a valuable political prisoner, begged for mercy. Finally Boabdil was presented to the Count of Cabra, where his true identity was revealed.

Cabra's first thought was to ensure Boabdil's safety so he could be safely turned over to Isabella and Ferdinand. Therefore he treated the prince with every courtesy. Not only did he ensure that Boabdil was well fed and clothed, but he personally attempted to console him. Eventually Cabra transferred the young Moorish prince to his own castle at Baena, where he lived in luxury.

By then Isabella and Ferdinand had journeyed to northern Castile. Preoccupied with difficulties in the Navarre and Galicia, the monarchs hardly expected such good fortune to be dropped into their laps from Andalusia. Finally they agreed that Isabella would remain at the Castilian border near the Navarre while Ferdinand traveled south to determine Boabdil's fate.

A day or two after the battle at Lucena, a bedraggled Moorish cavalier named Cidi Caleb rode into the city of Loja with news of the defeat. A great lamentation echoed through the streets of Loja and Granada, reaching its height as the humiliated survivors of Boabdil's army reappeared. Women beat their breasts and sobbed behind closed doors. Men, their clothes rent with grief or smote with dust, went numbly about their business. "The hostile star of Islam now scattered its malignant influence over Spain and the downfall of the Mussulman empire was decreed," wrote one Arabic historian.[10]

But Sultana Zoroya, unable to accept this fate for her son, ordered messengers to Córdoba to offer an extravagant ransom. With it was the tantalizing promise that she would release hundreds of Christian prisoners held by the Moors.

The offer immediately prompted a heated debate. Some advisors urged Ferdinand to release Boabdil for the enormous sums that the sultana dangled before them. Others argued that Boabdil was too important a prize to be released for such sanguine purposes. Shrewdly, Cádiz and Cardinal Mendoza suggested that Ferdinand not only release Boabdil but offer to support him against his father and uncle.

Ultimately, the royal council could not agree and the decision was left to Isabella. The queen, who had already dispatched sympathetic messages to Boabdil from the north when she heard of his capture, now ordered his release. He was to become a vassal of the Castilian monarchs who, in exchange for freedom, would be obliged to assist them in conquering the Granada kingdom. Neither Boabdil nor the sultana cared about this betrayal. Son and mother, blinded by hatred and the need for vengeance, had only two goals—to free Boabdil and destroy King Hasan and his brother El Zagal.

Isabella's proposal fit those goals perfectly. In the resultant treaty, Boabdil was freed on condition that his realms observed a two-year truce with Castile. In that first year Boabdil was to release four hundred Christian captives without ransom, then seventy Christian prisoners for the next five years. He was also obliged to pay an annual tribute of 12,000 doblas of gold.

Far more extraordinary, however, was Boabdil's concession to permit Castilian troops to pass through his domains and to supply them with provisions so they could "wage war in the places where the King his father dwelt."[11] To guarantee the treaty, Boabdil and his nobles were to entrust their young sons to the Castilian monarchs.

Once the terms of the treaty were established, Ferdinand agreed to receive Boabdil in Córdoba. Boabdil was allowed to march there from Baena flanked by his own knights and members of the Córdoban aristocracy. Ferdinand deliberately had granted that dignity to the captive prince, partly to ameliorate his humiliation, partly to create an atmosphere of trust. When Boabdil rode into Ferdinand's presence, dismounted and bent to kiss his hand "as his lord," Ferdinand ordered the youth to rise and greeted him as a fellow monarch.

As they talked an Arab interprete lavished praise upon Ferdinand for freeing Boabdil until finally the Castilian king waved him away. "Such tributes are unnecessary," said the king, "because I believe that he [Boabdil] will keep his faith as becomes a true knight and King."[12] Those words epitomized Ferdinand's tactful management of his captive and eventually made him a consummate politician.

But words, Ferdinand also knew, lost their validity unless supported by action. Once the treaty was signed, Ferdinand thus showered Boabdil with rich presents:

prize horses, embossed armor, royal ornaments, and purses stuffed with gold to pay for the Moorish king's return to Granada.

Finally, with a flutter of royal banners and a flourish of drums and horns, Boabdil, mounted upon a mule and flanked by members of the Castilian cavalry, was escorted to the frontier. In that ludicrously festive moment, the young Moorish prince was honored as if he had just achieved a diplomatic triumph rather than participating in an ignominious deed—the wholesale pawning of the kingdom of Granada for his personal freedom.

Enrique IV, artist unknown (courtesy Foto Oronoz)

Juan II of Aragón, by Juan de Borgona (courtesy Arxiu Mas)

Etching of Louis XI of France, "The Spider King" (courtesy of the Print Collection, Miriam & Ira D. Wallach Division of Arts, Prints and Photographs, The New York Public Library, Astor, Lenox and Tilden Foundations)

Inset: *The Catholic Sovereigns*, artist unknown. This portrait is believed to have been painted around the time of Isabella and Ferdinand's marriage. Isabella is shown wearing the famed ruby and pearl necklace. (courtesy Convento Agustinas, Madrigal)

Western view of the alcázar at Sevilla. The Eresma and Clamores rivers cross in the valley below the castle. The city of Segovia lies to the southeast. (photo by Harry Lentz/courtesy Art Resource)

Alfonso Carrillo, by Juan de Borgona (courtesy Foto Oronoz)

Pedro González de Mendoza, by Juan de Borgona (courtesy Arxiu Mas)

Ferdinand of Aragón, artist unknown (courtesy Windsor Castle/copyright reserved to Her Majesty Queen Elizabeth II)

Isabella of Castile, artist unknown (courtesy Windsor Castle/copyright reserved to Her Majesty Queen Elizabeth II)

Two details from the fresco *Batalla de la Higueruela* in the Library of El Escorial. The fresco illustrates a fifteenth-century battle between the Spaniards and the Moors, including the use of cavalry, lances, and cross-bows. (courtesy Patrimonio Nacional)

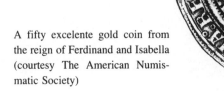

A fifty excelente gold coin from the reign of Ferdinand and Isabella (courtesy The American Numismatic Society)

Fray Fernando de Talavera, artist unknown (courtesy Patrimonio Nacional)

Marble relief of Jiménez de Cisneros (courtesy Foto Oronoz)

Auto de Fe Presided Over by Saint Dominick of Guzmán, by Pedro Berruguete. Center, top: inquisitional tribunal presided over by St. Dominick and six ecclesiastical judges. Left: another tribunal with penitents wearing *san benito* and *coroza*. Bottom, center: guards conduct "reconciled" heretics to witness the burning of two condemned heretics at the stake (far right). (courtesy the Prado Museum)

La Virgen de los Reyes Católicos, artist unknown. To the left of the Virgin and the Christ child is St. Thomas. Kneeling beneath him is King Ferdinand. To his left is Tomás de Torquemada, the Inquisitor General. At bottom left kneels Prince Juan. On the right is St. Dominick. Kneeling beneath him is Queen Isabella. To her right is allegedly Pietro Martire d'Anghierra, the Italian humanist. At bottom right kneels Princess Isabel. (courtesy the Prado Museum)

Pope Alexander VI, by Pinturicchio (courtesy Art Resource)

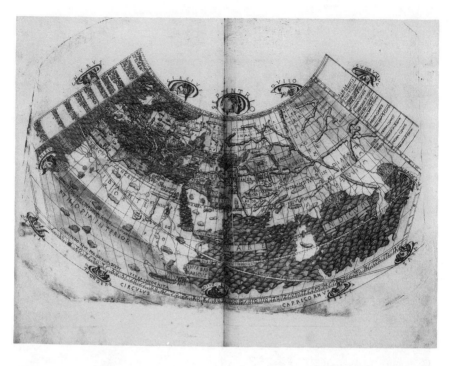

A 1477 map from Ptolemy's *Geographia* illustrating the known landmasses at the time: Europe, part of northern Africa, and Asia. (courtesy The John Carter Brown Library, Brown University)

Christopher Columbus, artist unknown (courtesy Art Resource)

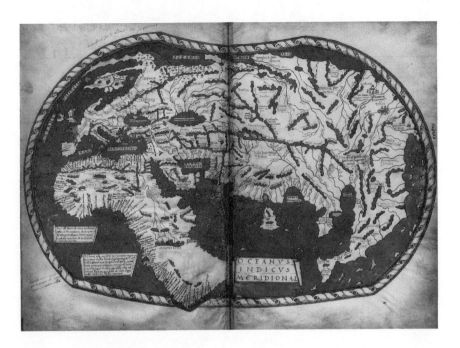

Henrius Martellus Germanus's 1492 Map of the World, drawn during the same year as Columbus's first expedition and reflecting the recently discovered southern tip of Africa. (courtesy The British Library)

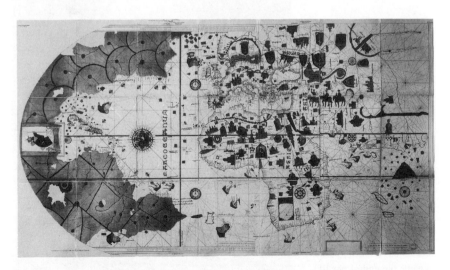

Map of the World drawn at the end of the fifteenth century by Juan de la Cosa, a crew member on Columbus's second voyage. (courtesy of the Map Division, The New York Public Library, Astor, Lenox and Tilden Foundations)

The Seal of "Isabel la Católica" (courtesy Archivo Historico Nacional)

Isabella the Catholic, painted towards the end of her life, by Juan de Flandes (courtesy Patrimonio Nacional)

Los comentarios de Gayo Julio Cefar.

The royal shield of Isabella and Ferdinand. The shield incorporates the royal insignias of Castile and León (the castles and lions) and the bars and eagles of Aragón. At the base of the shield are the words "Tanto Monta," meaning "One Is Equal to the Other." At the bottom, center, is a pomegranate, the symbol for Isabella and Ferdinand's conquest of Granada. Beneath the shield to the right is Isabella's personal symbol for her marriage to Ferdinand, *flechas* (arrows) to symbolize *F*. Beneath the shield to the left is Ferdinand's personal symbol for Isabella, the *yugo* (yoke) to symbolize *Y* (*I*). The final element is the Gordian knot, to symbolize indissoluble union. (courtesy The Hispanic Society of New York)

Emperor Maximilian I, by Albrecht Dürer (courtesy Art Resource)

Philip the Handsome, artist unknown (courtesy of the Print Collection, Miriam & Ira D. Wallach Division of Arts, Prints and Photographs, The New York Public Library, Astor, Lenox and Tilden Foundations)

Juana la Loca, by M. Michel (courtesy Foto Oronoz)

Catherine of Aragón, artist unknown (courtesy National Portrait Gallery, London)

Detail from the tomb of Isabella of Castile (photo courtesy Art Resource)

CHAPTER THIRTY-SIX

Reconciliations

Isabella arrived in the northern city of Bilbao on September 6, 1483. Its citizens were spellbound; the queen, still handsome at thirty-two, immediately conveyed the impression of an authoritative monarch. Before long the Bilbaons would know Isabella's personal mettle at close hand, for she had journeyed to the Vizcaya to accomplish a specific task.

At the time bands of brigands still roamed the Vizcaya, today's Basque region, plundering its quiet fishing hamlets on the Cantabrian coast and ravishing its snug agricultural villages in the mountainous interior. Local justice was poorly administered and criminals were seldom apprehended. As queen, Isabella would not tolerate such anarchy, especially in the northern reaches of her kingdom that were situated so close to France. That spring, similar disorders had brought Ferdinand to Galicia on Castile's northwesternmost coast to subdue feuding *grandees.*

Now Isabella intended to restore the Vizcaya to similar order. As in Sevilla and other Castilian cities, the queen established a weekly tribunal to frighten the "marauders of the land" and convince the regional population "not to think of committing the crimes they had committed before."[1] First she appointed new judges. Then she ordered an examination of the Vizcayan *fueros,* or common laws, and had them refined to conform with existing Castilian law. Finally she gathered new armies and munitions for the Granada war.

On September 28 Isabella rode south from the lush green hills of the Cantabrian coast to the walled city of Vitoria, capital of the largest of the Vizcayan provinces, where she was "happily reunited with her beloved consort."[2] Isabella and Ferdinand had not seen each other for five months, the longest separation in their marriage.

Conditions within Castile had changed dramatically during their separation: Galicia had been subdued, the Vizcaya restored to law and order, and Boabdil made an ally against his father, King Hasan. A month before Isabella and Ferdinand were reunited there was still another surprise: On August 30, in his shaded bedroom in the castle at Plessis, King Louis XI of France had died. In Louis's last moments, his confessor, Saint Francis de Paula, made him promise to return Roussillon and Cerdagne to Ferdinand.

That autumn, as peasants swung scythes through golden fields of wheat surrounding Vitoria, French ambassadors arrived at Isabella and Ferdinand's court. Their avowed purpose was to announce King Louis's XI's death, name his thirteen-year-old son, Charles VIII, as the new heir, and confirm the peace between France, Castile, and Aragón. Although Isabella entertained the French ambassadors courteously, Ferdinand, mindful of the reports about Louis's death-bed promise, met with them only briefly. Pointedly he delegated most of his communications to his assistants, implying that renewal of warm relations with France was contingent upon return of the disputed provinces.

In mid-October other, more welcome visitors arrived in Vitoria—the Count of Cabra and his young nephew, Don Diego—who were to be honored for their capture of Boabdil. Within the audience hall the Count of Cabra and Don Diego knelt before the smiling king and queen and kissed their hands. Then the monarchs honored the warriors by inviting them to sit upon cushions at their feet as they held court.

Three days later Isabella and Ferdinand awarded Cabra and his nephew the right to display an insignia of the Moorish king's face and his banners on their coat of arms. Then, in what was considered the highest personal honor of all, the two warriors were invited to share the same banquet table with Isabella, Ferdinand, and Princess Isabel.

Despite the momentary distraction of those festivities, Ferdinand was growing increasingly frustrated. His father had been dead for nearly four years, yet the provinces of Roussillon and Cerdagne were still in limbo, belonging neither to France nor to Castile but claimed by both. Initially, Louis's "well-publicized" deathbed promise suggested that the struggle had finally been decided in Ferdinand's favor. But the French ambassadors' silence on the subject had suggested otherwise.

Because Louis's son, the future Charles VIII, was only thirteen, France was to be ruled under the regency of his elder sister, Anne de Beaujeu. The new regent, who was once praised by Louis as the "least silly" of all women, had immediately understood why Ferdinand had treated her ambassadors frostily. Her suspicions were soon confirmed when the Castilian ambassadors, Juan Arías Dávila, Bishop of Segovia, and Juan de Ribera, Lord of Montemayor, arrived at the French court to demand restitution of Roussillon and Cerdagne. Anne was too shrewd to refuse Ferdinand's ambassadors outright. She simply told them that Charles VIII was "too young to execute his father's will."[3] Any settlement of the disputed provinces, she coolly announced, would have to wait until the young king came of age.

That Anne de Beaujeu had purposely deferred the decision was more than

Ferdinand could bear. For too long he had postponed securing those two counties in lieu of Castile's interests. He would, he now grimly announced to Isabella, declare war upon France.

From his perspective, there was no reason why the Holy War against Granada could not be postponed until he retrieved Roussillon and Cerdagne. By late 1483 the Castilians had a decided advantage over Granada. He and Isabella had just honored the two men who had defeated the Moors at Lucena and captured Boabdil. Ferdinand had personally liberated that Moorish king and made him a vassal of the Castilian crown. Since Ferdinand's arrival in Vitoria, the Marquis of Cádiz and Luis de Portocarrero had defeated the Moors at Lopera. And most recently, on October 29, Cádiz had recaptured Zahara. Given those victories, Ferdinand reasoned, there could be no harm in postponing the Granada war for a year or two and concentrating their efforts on resolving the French question. Isabella was stunned. To lose the momentum they had finally attained against Granada seemed ludicrous, contrary to everything she and Ferdinand had sworn, everything they held sacred. The Granada war, she reminded Ferdinand, was a Holy War, a Crusade against the infidel. As such, it was imperative for that war to take precedence over everything else.

But Ferdinand was as adamant as Isabella. For once he would not sacrifice Aragón for Castile. The longer he waited to claim those counties, the less likely were his chances. So much time had passed since those provinces had been ruled by Aragón that Ferdinand feared the citizens "would resign themselves to be subjects of the King of France. . . ."[4]

Isabella was not moved by those arguments. While she agreed that there were "good reasons to fight against France and leave Granada for later," they were already deeply embroiled in the Moorish war in which they had "suffered great labors" and incurred enormous expenses. Under those circumstances it was impractical to abandon the campaign and "start another war."[5] However, if Ferdinand insisted and could raise the requisite money from the Aragonese *Cortes,* he had her permission to pursue Roussillon and Cerdagne. To help him in this effort the queen agreed to leave some Castilian troops in Aragón. But she would not allow herself to be deterred from the war against the Moors. In fact, Isabella now intended to return to Andalusia and supervise the Holy War herself.

The clash of wills between two strong personalities like Isabella and Ferdinand was inevitable. Nevertheless, neither had forgotten the principles of *Tanto Monta, Monta Tanto,* which had guided every aspect of their married lives. Despite their differences, Ferdinand and Isabella thus dispatched notices as King and Queen of Castile to Valladolid and other cities advising their leaders to prepare for a spring campaign against the Moors.

On December 24, 1483, in hopes of obtaining men and money for his French campaign, Ferdinand called for a general *Cortes* at Tarazona. As Queen of Aragón, it was incumbent upon Isabella to attend the first sessions of that *Cortes,* which consisted of the combined parliaments of Aragón, Valencia, and Barcelona. Thus, shortly after New Year's 1484, the Castilian court traveled south across the Ebro River to Tarazona. There, on February 12, the *Cortes* opened the sessions with a petition to renew the war against France. But the Barcelonians, claiming the meeting violated their constitution, forbade their representatives to attend.

Consequently the daily sessions of the *Cortes* passed in argument and little was accomplished.

By mid-March, Isabella had become so impatient with the dissension that she left Tarazona and returned to Castile. Despite her disgust, she more than likely departed from Ferdinand tactfully, letting the intransigence of the *Cortes* speak for itself. Nevertheless, the king could not have helped feeling abandoned because most of the Castilian court left Aragón with Isabella. The queen, however, had carefully honored Ferdinand's decision to pursue the French war and, as promised, left behind several battalions of Castilian soldiers who stood ready to "execute anything the King wanted."[6]

Isabella and her court then began the four-hundred-mile trek south toward Córdoba, cutting west to spend Easter in Toledo, then stopping in Ubeda, Baeza, Andújar, and Jaén to recruit soldiers for the Granada campaign. From those posts the queen sent letters to Andalusia ordering food, wine, and artillery for the new army.

Isabella now also assumed a new responsibility—the requisitioning of medicines, slings, bandages, army tents, and physicians. During the long years of the Portuguese war the queen had pondered the sufferings of the wounded and the attendant loss of life from lack of immediate medical care. Why not, she mused, attach a medical unit to the army as it rode into battle and improve her men's chances for survival? As queen and now military commander of the Castilian army, Isabella thus established *El Hospital de la Reina*, the Queen's Hospital, to travel with the militia. Within it were special tents designated for ill and wounded soldiers, medical supplies, medicines, doctors, and other medical attendants. This was the first military hospital to appear on the battlefields of Western Europe, created with the express purpose of reducing war casualties. By the sixteenth century the Castilian medical units were so widely admired by foreign generals that they became a standard feature of European army life.

When Isabella and her court reached Córdoba in early May, the army had already convened. Each year more men had rallied to the Holy War. This time the force included 12,000 cavalry and 6,000 infantrymen. In addition, there were scores of heavy guns and cannons from France and Germany, mule trains loaded with sacks of flour, dried fish, cured meat, wineskins, and "a great number of carts and timbers and iron and stones."[7]

As a female Isabella could not, of course, lead the troops into battle herself. Thus she had appointed Cardinal Mendoza her proxy general. Alonso de Aguilar was to command the first battalion of the queen's army; the second was to be led by the Marquis of Cádiz and the Master of Santiago. Other brave and familiar *grandees* had arrived as well, among them the Duke of Medina Sidonia, the Count of Cabra, and the Duke of Medinaceli.

Already part of Isabella's army was conducting the spring *tala*, cutting a wide path of destruction through the fertile Granada *vega*. But the charred farmlands, granaries, and orchards of the *tala* were only a prelude to the formal war that would commence under Cardinal Mendoza's leadership in June. Despite Ferdinand's absence, the Granada campaign of 1484 had begun in earnest.

Isabella's departure disturbed Ferdinand profoundly. All spring members of the Aragonese *Cortes* bickered among themselves and had refused to grant Ferdinand funds for the French campaign. Meanwhile, he had received reports from the queen about her arrival in Andalusia and her preparations for war. From the town of La Membrilla in the southern province of Ciudad Real Isabella wrote on May 2 that "It is widely known that the King my lord and I have ordered the protection from the city of Alhama for the *tala* of Granada for the many footsoldiers and horsemen and our guards and the *Hermandades* and other *grandees* of our reign."[8]

By then Ferdinand, still unable to win support from the Aragonese *Cortes,* realized that he had no other option but to abandon the French war. Thus on May 1 the frustrated king ordered the dismissal of the Valencian *Cortes.* On the same day Isabella wrote from La Membrilla, Ferdinand wrote to Cardinal Borgia in Rome. In a thinly veiled effort to hide his argument with Isabella and her early departure from Aragón, he wrote:

> We have such a desire to continue the war against the Moors of
> Granada [that] in order not to allow them to recover their strength,
> which we have, by grace of God, considerably weakened, we
> have decided to go to Andalusia. Her Majesty the Queen has al-
> ready departed . . . we hope that, with God's help, we will be
> able to injure those infidels considerably this summer . . . obtain
> a final victory . . . and organize that kingdom in the service of
> our Lord.[9]

On May 13, after the remaining members of the *Cortes* refused to vote Ferdinand money, he dissolved the entire Aragonese assembly, leaving its closing ceremonies to his illegitimate son, the sixteen-year-old Alfonso of Aragón, Archbishop of Zaragoza. By May 29 Ferdinand had arrived in Córdoba where Isabella, it was said, met him with "great happiness" in what was doubtless a tender, if initially awkward, reconciliation.[10] Although the *grandees* had gossiped about the monarchs' argument for months, Ferdinand was greeted warmly by his subjects and "with all the due given a great general."[11] In early June the king and the army departed for Sevilla, and by the eighth Isabella had assumed her old role as provisioner, dispatching orders for wheat, wine, and barley to be sent to the army camp "where the King my Lord is."[12]

On June 10, 1484, an army of some 30,000 cavalry, an indeterminate number of footsoldiers, and a caravan of heavy guns and twelve-foot *lombardas* mounted on crude wooden carts thundered out of Sevilla and turned southwest toward Alora. That town was about twenty-five miles northwest of Málaga and, like most fortified settlements of the Moorish kingdom, sat upon a cliff over a river—the Guadalhorce—making conquest difficult.

Now, however, the Castilians had a winning combination; Ferdinand, anxious to reaffirm himself as general of the Holy War, and the new cannons and artillery that had arrived at the queen's request from France and Germany. Shortly after Ferdinand's army arrived in Alora, the Moors rained poisoned arrows and darts upon them. But this time the wounded were immediately taken to the six medical tents of *El Hospital de la Reina.*

Simultaneously, Ferdinand ordered the new artillery fired at Alora's thick stone walls. Before long the *lombardas,* twelve-foot Italian cast-iron tubes, were discharging iron or marble balls, propelled by exploding gunpowder. Although they weighed about 165 pounds and were difficult to fire, the *lombardas* shook the very foundations of Alora's fortress and shattered its stone ramparts. On June 20 Alora fell and Ferdinand claimed it for Castile.

Strategically, Alora was one of the least important battles of the Moorish war. Psychologically, however, Alora symbolized Ferdinand's renewed commitment to the Holy War. As such, the battle marked a turning point in Ferdinand's marriage, an end to his old arguments and a breaking away from paternal loyalties in favor of those of his wife.

Perhaps privately, in the months of Ferdinand's unhappy separation from the queen, as he witnessed the weaknesses of his kingdom up close, Ferdinand realized the bleak future that would have been his had he married a less powerful woman and ruled Aragón alone. In the years to come Ferdinand would return to Aragón and again press for Roussillon and Cerdagne's return, but he would more stoically accept the Castilian wars as his first priority.

Isabella must have sensed Ferdinand's transformation but, being sensitive to her husband's pride, probably did not gloat over her triumph. To the faithful and devout queen, the most important fact was that Ferdinand had returned home to her and the Holy War. The *Reconquista,* Isabella believed, was too strong for any true Christian monarch to resist, for the challenge was divinely inspired and would guide her and Ferdinand to certain victory.

CHAPTER THIRTY-SEVEN

Granada's Right Eye

From Sevilla in the winter of 1485, Isabella and Ferdinand mounted their greatest military effort yet against the Moors. That winter they gathered a new armamentarium of gunpowder artillery that would soon make the lance, sword, and battering ram of medieval warfare obsolete.

In Écija, blacksmiths, smelters, and engineers created molds for the manufacture of the new weapons. Nearby, carpenters built forges, kilns, and workshops to assemble primitive guns and cannons. Iron, mined near Huelva on Castile's southeast coast, was fashioned into *robadoquines*, projectiles used for small artillery. From Sicily, Flanders, and Portugal Isabella imported gunpowder, which was stored in deep vaults and placed in strategic locations along the Andalusian border. And to coordinate the weaponry for the new campaign, the queen named a brilliant military engineer, Francisco Ramírez de Madrid, nicknamed *El Artillero*.

Simultaneously, Isabella and Ferdinand gathered a new army. To supplement the men drawn from the *Guardes Reales*, the *Hermandad*, and the *grandees*, they summoned soldiers from the Vizcaya, Galicia, and Asturias. They even allowed Castilian fugitives to join the army in exchange for restitution of their rights.

Then, backed by church funds, the king and queen hired the Swiss Guard. By the late fifteenth century those mercenaries from across the Alps had already gained a formidable reputation among the crowned heads of Europe. Some of them already guarded the pope at the Holy See, and in 1477 Louis XI of France had hired them to help defeat Charles the Bold at Nancy.

Legend had it that the Swiss Guard never turned their back on an enemy and thus wore armor only on the front of their bodies. Although they were mercenaries, they disdained booty. Unlike the *condottiere* of the Italian papal states, the Swiss Guard chose their battles carefully, in strict accord with their ethical beliefs. As thoroughly Christian soldiers who would espouse "only a just quarrel," their appearance on any European battlefield immediately intimidated the enemy.[1]

Yet even with the combined might of the new Castilian army and its state-of-the-art artillery, Isabella and Ferdinand knew victory was not assured. The fearless Moslem soldiers had defied Christian conquest for seven hundred years and might well do so for another seven hundred. Moreover, the treacherous mountain passes of the Granada kingdom, its rock-filled valleys and badlands, posed special problems for the mules and ox carts that transported the *lombardas* and other heavy artillery to the site of a siege. Consequently, Isabella hired 2,000 sappers, or military miners, who could dig roads through mountains and build new bridges on demand.

With similar thoroughness, the queen provisioned the army. To inspire the soldiers in battle Isabella also ordered new war drums. For the hospital there were bandages, bedclothes, medicines, and surgeons. To convert captured mosques into churches, there were crosses, sacramental dishes, candlesticks, incense holders, and altar cloths. Finally she ordered great quantities of bells—not just those to be hung from new church towers, but small ones for soldiers to ring in battle because they were known to frighten the Moors.

For the campaign of 1485 not a detail was overlooked by the queen, not a possibility left unexplored, not even in her private thoughts. Several times a day the devout queen prayed in the chapel of the Sevillian alcázar for victory over the infidel.

As a mother, Isabella applied the same meticulous standards to the establishment of her personal household. By 1485 her eldest daughter, Isabel, was fourteen years old—educated in the classics, imbued with religious piety, skilled in the womanly arts of embroidery, weaving, and sewing—in short, an accomplished Renaissance princess on the threshold of young womanhood. Between 1481 and 1483 the pretty, blond princess had lived under the guardianship of Isabella's aunt, Beatriz, Duchess of Viseu, at her castle in Moura, Portugal, to comply with the peace treaty. Now the princess was treated as a young adult, permitted to eat with Isabella and Ferdinand, to attend official court functions, even to dance with honored guests like the Count of Cabra at his banquet.

By 1485 the focus of Isabella's maternal attention fell more heavily upon her other children—two-year-old María, four-year-old Juana, and especially six-year-old Prince Juan. From birth the prince, like his sisters, was surrounded by personal attendants. In time the prince became so fond of his second nurse, Juana de Ávila, that he even wrote her a childish letter demanding that "you must have me for your husband more than anyone else."[2]

That noble men and women acted as servants for Prince Juan was only an extension of Isabella's practice in her larger court. From her first days as queen, Isabella, recalling Enrique's rebellious *grandees,* had established the practice of using aristocrats as personal attendants for herself and Ferdinand—as dressers, chamberlains, stewards. Symbolically, the practice set the king and queen a rank above the *grandees;* it was natural that the queen continued that practice for her children.

From childhood the prince's day began with an orderly, highly ritualized routine that was meant to emphasize his future sovereignty. Upon waking, Juan was greeted by a royal chamberlain, Juan de la Calatayud, and two assistants who brought him freshly laundered and pressed clothes. At first the chamberlain entered the royal bedchamber alone with the boy's shirt wrapped in a towel. After assisting Juan with his hose and jerkin, two other attendants appeared to help the prince dress. Then they poured water over Juan's hands from a silver bucket and, after kissing a towel, presented it to the child. Finally a cobbler and barber arrived to inspect the prince and help him complete his toilet. At night that same process was reversed.

After morning prayers in the royal chapel and a light breakfast, the prince appeared before his tutor, the Dominican Fray Diego Deza. Although the theologian was an erudite Latin scholar from the University of Salamanca, he was not a Renaissance humanist, and thus placed the greatest emphasis on the prince's religious education. Deza was, in fact, a Catholic of such intense religious conviction that he would later be appointed Grand Inquisitor of Spain. Consequently, as a contemporary would later note, Prince Juan was "very well learned in all that which was proper to his royal person; especially was he a very Catholic and great Christian."[3] Eventually, the young boy's education would be broadened by the Italian humanist Pietro Martire d'Anghiera, who arrived in Castile in the late 1480s.

Despite Prince Juan's Catholic training, the queen worried about her son's character. Fearing that the prince would grow up pampered and willful because he lacked peers, as reputedly had happened with Louis XI's son, the queen invited the sons of aristocrats to live at court. She also populated the court with a slightly older group of aristocratic youth who were to serve as models for the impressionable prince. Among them were men who would become famous in their own right: Nicolás de Ovando, future governor of the Indies, and Gonzalo Fernández de Oviedo y Valdés, future historian of the Indies.

As part of his education the prince and his young companions learned to ride and joust, to hawk and hunt, to play chess and cards, to sing and recite poetry. In addition, Juan was a naturally gifted musician and played the clavichord, violin, and flute with ease and even joined an orchestra with his peers. Moreover, he developed a fine tenor voice and often sang with his siblings and companions in choral recitals.

Isabella gave the young prince autonomy over his possessions and encouraged him to reward his servants for their loyalty. But initially Juan was not inclined to generosity. When the prince was about eight years old the queen once asked him whether he had given away a certain suit of clothes. The boy replied that he never donated his possessions to anybody nor did he want to. Isabella, worried that the prince was "stingy," instructed his chamberlain that all his possessions—his doublets, capes, jerkins, gowns, and even the harnesses that belonged to his horse, mule, and pony—be laid out before her on his birthday. Then, with a list in her hand, Isabella called her son to her side. "Son, my angel," the queen said, using her customary address for Juan, "princes should not be old-clothes men or keep their *arcas* [trunks] full. Henceforth, each year on this day, I wish you to distribute before me all things among your servants and those whom you like to favor."[4]

Isabella's technique eventually transformed the prince. As he matured, Juan developed into a charitable young man, one whose mercifulness toward those less fortunate than himself suggested he would become a compassionate king.

Despite the exquisite care Isabella lavished on her family within the Sevillian alcázar, she was not able to control the hazardous and unsanitary health conditions of the city beyond its gates. By early winter 1485 Sevilla's large rat population, gorged on city garbage, nesting in alleyways and the reedy banks of the Guadalquivir, began to die in heaps. Few people realized the rodent corpses were harbingers of epidemic even when, in February, hundreds of Sevillians fell ill with a new wave of bubonic plague. On March 4, after several servants within the royal court died, the frightened monarchs moved their household to Córdoba.

Soon after their arrival Ferdinand completed preparations for the spring campaign. On April 5 he left Córdoba at the head of an enormous army. In addition to the military forces there were groups of carpenters, "blacksmiths with their forges, master gunners and engineers [and] all the artillery experts needed for essential tasks." By 1485 the royal army had, in fact, become a moving city that included great herds of steers, cartloads of bread, wine, and flour, medical equipment, and a "large number of beasts and carriages to transport them."[5]

The new army was financed in part by church revenues. Non-Christians were expected to contribute as well. In late 1484 Isabella and Ferdinand had ordered Abraham Seneor to collect 16,000 *castellanos* from the Jewish *aljamas* of Castile; similar instructions were given to those living in Mudéjar ghettoes.

The aristocrats had dutifully supplemented those funds with their own personal contributions of men and arms. By late March or early April 1485, dozens of barons from Castile's aristocratic families had thus assembled in Córdoba, among them the Count of Haro with 500 pikemen, the Count of Benavente with 250, Pedro Hurtado de Mendoza with another 250, and Beltrán de la Cueva with 80 armed men and 100 light cavalry.

Despite their willingness to risk their lives in the Holy War, the aristocrats had not forgotten their rivalries. Forbidden to fight openly among themselves, the *grandees* now tried a new tack—a lavish show of wealth designed to put their fellow warriors to shame. Many of them thus arrived in Córdoba for the spring campaign outfitted opulently in silk and satin clothes, embossed armor, and fanciful silver helmets and with elegant silken tents, trimmed with gold thread and emblazoned with their escutcheons. Personal servants, dressed in the livery of their masters' houses, accompanied their commanders and waited on them as if they still lived in their palaces.

Isabella and Ferdinand, shocked by their ostentation, lectured the barons about the folly of such vanity. It was, they told the aristocrats, "without purpose . . . especially in the time of war for the [poor] example it set" for the less wealthy men in the army and for its distraction from their holy mission.[6]

Ferdinand and his commanders knew that if they were ever to achieve a permanent victory over the Moors, it was first necessary to conquer Málaga. That wealthy port city lay at the base of the Iberian peninsula on the Mediterranean and was a major conduit for soldiers and munitions from Africa's north coast. Yet before besieging that city, the Castilians had to subdue Moorish settlements in the adjacent valleys of Santa María and Cartama, a region known as Granada's "right eye."

By April 20 the Castilians had crossed the Yeguas River south of Córdoba and stormed the village of Benamaquez with their new *lombardas*. A year earlier that community had surrendered to the Castilians, but later its citizens had rebelled. Now Ferdinand vowed to avenge himself. "I shall make their punishment a terror to others . . . they shall be loyal through force, if not through faith."[7]

Within hours, the constant thrust of stone and iron projectiles from the Castilian *lombardas* had reduced the turrets and towers of Benamaquez into dust. Afterward Ferdinand and his army occupied the village and executed 180 men who had fomented the rebellion. By the end of April Ferdinand had conquered the villages of Coin and Cartama as well.

Isabella, meanwhile, waited anxiously in Córdoba for news. As soon as she heard about Ferdinand's triumph, she ordered new supplies sent to the Castilian army. To ensure their prompt arrival she instructed her accountant to release funds from the treasury. She also wrote "kind letters" to the *grandees* who participated in the war, congratulated others on their bravery, answered complaints, and tended to all the other details "so that the work of war would get accomplished."[8]

By 1485 Isabella's duties were clearly expanding. Not only was she a provisioner and quartermaster, but she had become a behind-the-scenes administrator and morale booster. Years earlier Isabella's tact, efficiency, and competence had won enough political respect to achieve the Castilian crown. Now she was fast becoming an indispensable military partner in the Holy War, an accomplished strategist who stood just beyond the battlefield with her prayers and provisions, an inspirational symbol of Christian forbearance.

News of the Castilian victories quickly spread through the valleys of Málaga and terrified the Moors. In reaction, King Hasan's brother, El Zagal, fortified himself and his soldiers in Málaga and ordered reinforcements from nearby cities and towns. Then his warriors launched a bitter *rebato* attack in which so many Castilians were killed that Ferdinand and his leaders reconsidered their plan to besiege the city.

The quick-witted Marquis of Cádiz soon devised a new strategy. Since thousands of Moorish soldiers were then gathering in Málaga, the surrounding towns were only minimally protected. One such town was Ronda, a whitewashed town about twenty-five miles north of Málaga, which, along with Coin, Cartama, and Setenil, comprised Granada's "right eye." Why not, the marquis suggested, poke out that eye while the Moors were looking the other way—especially since many of the Christian prisoners taken at the battle of Ajarquía two years earlier were still held at Ronda?

Moreover, Cádiz did not think Ronda would be difficult to win, despite its location over a 300-foot gorge and protection by three sets of walls. Believing Ronda's formidable site and a few guards would ensure its protection, its military leader, El Zegri, was then attacking the Andalusia *campinas,* or pasturelands where sheep grazed in summer.

When on May 18, El Zegri returned to Ronda and heard sharp retorts of the Castilian *lombardas,* he quickly realized his mistake. To his horror, Ronda was ringed with the white tents of the Castilian army. For four days Ferdinand's artillery had battered its *arrabales,* or suburbs, and now the Castilian *lombardas* were shattering the walls of Ronda itself.

El Zegri promptly ordered his men to climb the mountains above the Christian camp. That night his soldiers attacked the Castilians but were brutally rebuffed. To summon help, El Zegri then ordered watch-fires to be lighted in the hills. Simultaneously he dispatched soldiers to Málaga for reinforcements. But each time El Zegri ordered an attack on the Christians, his men were roundly beaten. In the end he ordered a permanent retreat.

Cádiz, meanwhile, pondered how to gain access to Ronda. Through his native guides, the marquis learned that the town's main water source was a tributary of the Rio Verde that flowed outside a deep tunnel cut through the town's tall rock foundation. To keep Ronda supplied with water, the Moors had forced the Christian prisoners to work as fetchers, carrying jugs of water up a stone staircase from the tributary below.

The marquis ordered his men to block the tunnel that led from the city. Hundreds of feet above him, on the opposite side of the gorge, Ferdinand's *lombardas* simultaneously battered Ronda's thick walls and shattered its defensive towers. The Castilian soldiers now cast flaming hemp missiles upon Ronda's buildings so that at night "the city looked like a fiery furnace."[9] In the ensuing thunder from the *lombardas,* the city was filled with women and children "howling with grief over the deaths of their husbands and sons."[10]

The army, divided into sections that were commanded respectively by the king, Cádiz, Medina Sidonia, the Count of Benavente, and the Master of Alcántara, now readied itself to invade. Finally, on or around Easter Sunday, the citizens of Ronda surrendered.

The first thing Cádiz did was rush into the dungeons of Ronda to free the Christian prisoners, many of whom were indeed survivors from the Ajarquía. Some of them, the young sons of nobles, were now aged beyond their years. Others, their faces haggard with illness and exhaustion, had long been thought killed in battle. Among them were also forty emaciated women and children, many barely able to walk.

Once the prisoners had been fed and revived, they were given mules and escorted to Córdoba to meet the queen. There, in a moving ceremony Isabella, newly pregnant, appeared with the Princess Isabel to greet the prisoners. After a mass of thanksgiving, the queen ordered food for the prisoners and presented each with eight *reales,* or silver pieces, to cover his expenses home. Then Isabella ordered the prisoners' manacles hung on the outer walls of Toledo's Church of San Juan de los Reyes. Today visitors to that famous church will still see rusty handcuffs displayed on its walls in tribute to the iron-willed prisoners of Ronda.

CHAPTER THIRTY-EIGHT

A New Road Through the Mountains

The loss of Ronda sent shock waves through the Granada kingdom. That summer ninety-four Moorish castles fell to the Castilians. With its "right eye" taken and the rest of its face ruled by two kings, the Moorish emirate was crippled. In Granada the citizens grumbled in the streets, placing the blame first upon the aged King Hasan, then upon his son Boabdil.

The Moorish *alfaquis,* or counselors, of Granada denounced the behavior of both kings. Boabdil, they reminded the agitated citizens, had divided the kingdom into two factions through his "vileness and cowardice or bad fortune."[1] His father, the old King Hasan, had fallen ill and was equally powerless to defend the Moors. The future, the *alfaquis* preached, lay with the fearless warrior El Zagal, King Hasan's brother, whose high birth and military prowess made him eminently qualified to be king.

Before long the entire city of Granada was clamoring for El Zagal to be coronated. Consequently he was summoned from Málaga. To travel from that port city to Granada meant El Zagal had to traverse the Sierra Nevadas near the Castilian-held city of Alhama. Knowing that the surrounding area was patrolled by Castilian soldiers, El Zagal sent scouts ahead. One of them had observed a group of knights from the Order of Calatrava resting with their horses by a riverbank. Those men, El Zagal decided, would be perfect "trophies" for him and his soldiers to display on their arrival in Granada.

Soundlessly the Moors edged close to the Castilians and descended upon them in a *rebato* attack, slaughtering ninety-seven and taking eleven as prisoners. As was traditional in Moorish victories, the soldiers decapitated their victims and attached their heads to their saddle bows. Several days later the eleven captive knights of Calatrava appeared at Granada's Gate of Elivra followed by ninety horses of their slain peers still displaying their shields and armor. Finally, a triumphant El Zagal swept through the gates with seventy Moorish soldiers and their grisly Christian trophies bobbing at their side. The city went wild with celebrations and proclaimed El Zagal Granada's new monarch, a man blessed with both "good fortune" and "bravery."[2]

Meanwhile, by August 1485 the Count of Cabra discovered that the town of Moclín, the so-called shield of Granada, was poorly defended. As the city was less than twenty miles north of Granada, its capture would have been an important coup for the Castilians, one Cabra hoped to achieve before summer's end. But Ferdinand's military advisors opposed the idea, arguing that its proximity to Granada made it a hazardous venture. Ferdinand, however, was still so dazzled by Cabra's capture of Boabdil the year before that he decided to proceed with the siege. The king planned to conquer Moclín by enforcing a blockade. To that end he ordered the count and Don Martin Alonzo to surround the town with soldiers. At a predetermined hour they were to be joined by 10,000 troops commanded by the Master of Calatrava, the Count of Buendia, and the Bishop of Jaén.

On September 1 Cabra thus welcomed Isabella to his castle at Baena and established her court in a rich suite of rooms; then he and his soldiers left for Moclín. To escape Moorish detection the count's militia marched until dawn. Just as the army planned to sleep, Cabra's scouts reported that El Zagal himself had arrived in Moclín with 20,000 soldiers and 1,200 *jinetarios,* or jennet riders.

Cabra was not a man to be deterred from his dream of taking the shield of Granada. Perhaps overly impressed with his military prowess, perhaps lured by the idea of capturing another Moorish king, the count now resolved to push on to Moclín alone, without waiting, as he had promised, for the rest of the Castilian army. Consequently he urged his tired men through the valley of the Velillas River on September 2 and well into the following night. As they marched, the moon came up full and the count's militia found themselves in a scrubby ravine surrounded by towering cliffs.

Suddenly, a torrent of poisoned arrows and stones fell upon Cabra's men, thrown by Moors hidden in the hills above them. The moonlight, glittering against the Castilians' armor, made them a perfect target and dozens of them, including Cabra's brother, were killed. The count, who had been wounded and lost his horse, finally ordered a retreat. But as the Castilians backed out of the valley, the Moors rushed down from the hills with frightening war cries and slaughtered Cabra's men. Over 1,000 were killed and nearly all the survivors were taken prisoner.

A day or two later messengers rode into Baena with news of the defeat. For once, the usually dignified queen, who was then in her fifth month of pregnancy, lost her composure. In her despair, Isabella began to worry that the defeat at Moclín would give the Moors so much confidence they might attempt to rebel in Alhama and in every other reconquered town of the realm.

At Baena, the graying, fifty-seven-year-old Cardinal Mendoza, "understanding the Queen's anguish," tried to comfort her. Every war, he reminded Isabella, had defeats as well as victories. "You should thank God . . . that you have conquered more cities in three years than . . . any of the former kings acquired in two hundred."[3]

To allay the queen's fears, the cardinal volunteered to send 3,000 of his own cavaliers at his own expense to Alhama as reinforcements. Ultimately Mendoza's words comforted Isabella so that she was able to present a brave face to Cabra's critics. To those who began to refer to the count as "the King-Catcher," Isabella sharply reminded them that a victory had been just as likely as a defeat. "The enterprise was rash," she conceded, "but not more rash than that of Lucena, which was crowned with success and which we have all applauded as the height of heroism. Had the Count of Cabra succeeded in capturing the uncle as he had the nephew, who is there that would not have praised him to the skies?"[4]

Ferdinand, meanwhile, had arrived within fifteen miles of Moclín before learning of Cabra's defeat. In the wake of that news his original strategy had to be discarded. But the next step was not at all clear. Some of Ferdinand's military advisors argued that since the Castilian soldiers were already assembled, the time was right "to avenge the Moors for their triumph."

Still others argued that "the defeat of one *caballero*'s battalion was not sufficent reason for the King to cancel his campaign" and that to do so would be to demonstrate "great weakness" to the Moors.[5] Another contingent argued that Moclín's location was so treacherous that the project should be scuttled in favor of a more vulnerable town.

In the interim Don García Osorio, the Bishop of Jaén, visited Isabella at Baena to make a special appeal. For years the sheep and cattle herders of his wealthy bishopric on the Granadan border had been harassed by the Moors. So frequently did turbaned Moslems ride into the Castilian pasturelands killing shepherds and scattering livestock that Jaén's citizens were afraid to walk outside the city walls.

The headquarters for the raids were two turreted fortresses called Cambil and Alhabar located about fifteen miles from Jaén in a deep river valley. Those castles, reputed to be the "largest and most secure in all of Spain," stood on two tall rocks connected by a bridge that spanned the Río Frío, which passed over the gorge. As Ferdinand's army was already at the Moorish border, the bishop proposed that he attack those castles instead of Moclín, thus ridding Jaén of the Moors at last.

Although too old to join the fight himself, Cardinal Mendoza convinced Isabella, and eventually Ferdinand, of the argument's validity. Soon afterward the Marquis of Cádiz and 2,000 *caballeros* rode toward Cambil and Alhabar to blockade the valley. On September 16, they were joined by Ferdinand and his army.

The journey had been difficult for the mountainous terrain above the Río Frío was steep and deeply gorged. Even when the Castilians finally picked their way through the broken terrain and descended into the river valley, the soldiers were forced to pitch their tents on three sites, much as they had at the battle of Loja three years earlier.

The treacherous terrain also posed immediate problems for the artillery. The heavy *lombardas* and other siege equipment transported by mule and oxen in carts lagged ten or twelve miles behind the rest of the army. Gradually, as his army had climbed the rocky heights ringing the river valley, Ferdinand realized the futility of attempting to bring the heavy cannons there.

Then, through what was later hailed as "divine intervention," a shepherd appeared and showed Ferdinand where a path could be hacked through the mountain passes to move the artillery. By "order and concern" of the queen, 6,000 sappers thus ascended the mountain and with shovel and pickax carved a new road through the steepest part of the slope, which was reputedly "so high that a bird could hold on there only with difficulty."[6] Thick-rooted cork trees were uprooted and tossed into a nearby valley, rocks splintered, and an entire hill leveled for the road.

After twelve days of labor, the Castilian sappers carved out a nine-mile path through which oxen promptly dragged the heavy guns. On a Wednesday morning, the Moors gawked from the ramparts of Cambil and Alhabar as the Castilian artillery inched its way up the mountain like fat giant snakes. The valley was filled with the sounds of cheering Castilian soldiers as the *lombardas* arrived for "more than anything else [they] showed the great determination the King and Queen had to make this conquest."[7]

Without further delay Francisco Ramírez, *El Artillero,* ordered the *lombardas* pointed at the twin castles and ordered his men to fire. By day's end the *lombardas* had discharged 140 volleys against Alhabar, destroying two towers and a wall. Two days later, on September 23, the Moors, "seeing their defense could bear no other fruit than to die," surrendered the twin castles.[8] By Ferdinand's terms, the Moslem leader, Mahomet, and his soldiers were allowed to retreat to Granada.

Isabella and Ferdinand were reunited in Jaén on September 27 in a triumphant procession through the city. The Castilian army recognized that the queen's brilliant military preparations had been a key element in their latest conquests. Without Isabella's artillery, ox carts, and sappers, the Moors would have remained ascendant and the chances for Castilian victory would have been as remote as they had been for the last 750 years.

By early October Isabella, now nearly eight months pregnant, Ferdinand, and the court moved to Cardinal Mendoza's permanent home in Alcalá de Henares. There, on December 16, 1485, in a bedchamber of that magnificently appointed palace with its tapestried and frescoed walls, its glittering silver ornaments and velvet hangings, Isabella birthed her fifth and last child, Catherine, named after the queen's paternal grandmother, Catherine of Lancaster.

Very little is known about the details of this birth except that it was received "with great delight" even though the child was a female. Like the royal couple's other three daughters, Catherine was considered an important political asset, one who would be wed to a foreign prince to increase Castilian influence abroad.

In honor of Catherine's birth, Mendoza hosted a lavish banquet for the king, queen, and all the knights and ladies of the court. The object of these festivities, the pink-and-white-skinned, reddish-haired infant, would eventually demonstrate a keen intelligence and a hardy disposition. Of all Isabella's daughters, it was said that Catherine most closely resembled her mother. Yet the princess's fate would be considerably different. In obedience to her parents' subsequent marriage arrangements, Catherine of Aragón would spend her adult life on English soil as the anguished wife of King Henry VIII.

CHAPTER THIRTY-NINE

Buscar El Levante por El Poniente

uring that same winter of 1485–86 a liveried messenger arrived in Alcalá de Henares with a letter addressed to Isabella and Ferdinand. The parchment document was sealed with the crest of the Duke of Medinaceli, one of the most powerful *grandees* in Castile. The count had written to the king and queen for advice about a foreign navigator's proposal to sail to the Orient. In late 1485 a tall, aquiline-nosed sailor had arrived at Medinaceli's castle from Portugal with a scheme—*buscar el levante por el poniente,* to reach the East by sailing West. By doing so, the foreigner claimed, he would circumvent the Ottoman blockade of the rich Asian spice trade that European maritime merchants had enjoyed before the 1453 fall of Constantinople.

The blue-eyed navigator, a Genoese named Cristobal Colón, known alternately as Christofo Colombo or Colomo or Christopher Columbus, had already proposed his venture to Medinaceli's Andalusian neighbor, Medina Sidonia. But when that noble had rejected Columbus's scheme, the mariner appeared at Medinaceli's riverside castle.

Columbus's perseverance paid off. Although Medina Sidonia was the wealthiest *grandee* in Andalusia, Medinaceli was even more influential. His domains were immense, stretching from the provinces of Soria and Guadalahara in northern Castile to ports in Andalusia. His military might was considerable, and because of his royal blood he had influence with the king and queen. Moreover, Medinaceli maintained oceangoing caravels in El Puerto de Santa María.

At first Medinaceli listened to Columbus dispassionately, but as the seaman talked, the count grew impressed. Columbus intimated that he intended to present his *La Empresa de las Indias,* or expedition to the Indies, next to the King of

France. Moreover, the future explorer came with solid recommendations, among them one from Fray Antonio de Marchena, a cosmographer-humanist known to Isabella's court and a member of the La Rabida monastery in the nearby town of Palos. It was, in fact, to the Franciscan monks at La Rabida on Castile's southwestern coast that Columbus had entrusted his five-year-old son Diego that past summer. Columbus's second recommendation came from Father Juan Pérez, prior of the monastery.

Now, as Columbus talked, his navigational knowledge, his convictions about the spherical shape of the earth, and his voyage's potential for discoveries and riches convinced Medinaceli that the project was a worthwhile investment. Finally the count agreed to furnish Columbus with a handful of ships and a small sum of money to support the voyage.

But before releasing the boats and funds, Medinaceli hesitated, recalling that after the 1480 Portuguese peace treaty at Alcaçovas, Isabella and Ferdinand had decreed that no international explorations were to be conducted by private individuals without royal permission. Medinaceli, powerful as he was, had no intention of angering the king and queen and consequently wrote them a tactful letter. In it he described Columbus as a man "who came here from Portugal and wished to go to the King of France to . . . find the Indies under that King's protection. . . . I myself offered to send him from El Puerto with three or four caravels, since he asked for no more than this."[1] Because the navigator's plan seemed plausible, Medinaceli intended to lay out the 4,000 ducats himself to build the caravels and provision them for a year at sea. However, as the count wanted the credit for the expedition to go to Isabella rather than the King of France, he had written the queen for advice.

From Alcalá de Henares Isabella wrote back a surprising answer. "She replied," Medinaceli recalled many years later, "by telling me to send this man to her."[2] Isabella may have felt that she had no other option but to listen personally to the foreign navigator's suit. Although the treaty of Alcaçovas had restricted Castilian exploration to no farther south than the Canary Islands, there were no prohibitions about sailing west into the watery void known as the "Atlantic abyss." Despite the anticipated difficulties of such a journey, Isabella was not willing to let any exploratory opportunities escape, especially not into the hands of the French king. Nor, for reasons of obtaining complete control, did Isabella allow Medinaceli to finance such a voyage. On the slim possibility that a western passage to the East could be discovered, she resolved that the Castilian crown must have all the credit.

Columbus appeared "with all haste" at the royal court in Córdoba on January 20, 1486, only to learn that Isabella and Ferdinand were still in Alcalá de Henares. In their absence the disappointed explorer was presented to their *contador mayor,* the royal auditor, Alonso de Quintanilla. As with nearly everyone he met, Columbus charmed Quintanilla with his eloquence. Although he was not of high birth, the ambitious thirty-five-year-old mariner had long since adopted the mannerisms, language, and appearance of an aristocrat.

Bartolomé de Las Casas, an early historian of Columbus's voyages and author of *Historia de las Indias,* observed that he was "affable and cheerful in

speaking . . . eloquent and boastful in negotiations . . . serious in moderation, affable with strangers and with members of his household gentle and
pleasant, with modest gravity and discreet conversation."[3]

Quintanilla's initially favorable impression of Columbus was underscored by
the mariner's presentation of two letters. The first was the recommendation that he
had shown to Medinaceli from Fray Pérez of the La Rabida monastery. Pérez had
been in Quintanilla's service as a *contador* years before. The second was Isabella's
letter to Medinaceli, instructing that noble to send "the man" to her at Córdoba.
It would, however, be four months before the queen and her court would return to
Andalusia. For Columbus, who lacked money to sustain himself for that length of
time, it seemed an interminable wait. In the service of the queen, Quintanilla
granted the future explorer a small allowance until she arrived.

By 1486 Columbus had already led a full and colorful life. For centuries
historians have argued about the events that preceded the future explorer's arrival
in Castile, the details of which are sketchy at best. As a result, a thicket of
contradictory theories have been proposed to explain Columbus's religious and
national origins. Various historians have claimed Columbus as a *converso* Jew
from Majorca or Aragón, a Catalan, a Frenchman, an Armenian, and a Greek, just
to mention a few of the prevalent theories.

Yet contemporary Castilian chroniclers and Columbus himself maintained that
he was born in the northern Italian city-state of Genoa. The future explorer was
almost exactly Isabella's age, for he was born in 1451, sometime between August
25 and October, the son of a master-weaver Domenico Colombo and Susanna
Fontanarossa. Like most Italians of that era, Columbus did not celebrate the exact
date of his birth but rather his patron saint's feast day, St. Christopher, which fell
on June 25. Before long he would be followed by four other siblings—
Bartholomew, Giacomo later known as Diego, Giovanni Pellegrino, and a sister,
Bianchinetta.

In those early years Columbus's parents lived in Genoa's Porta dell'Olivella
quarter where Domenico, a master weaver, was an active member of his trade
guild. Like most artisans of that era, Domenico probably depended on the services
of his young children to card the raw wool that his wife Susanna spun and dyed.

Because of his humble background, Columbus's formal education was limited,
although he did learn to read and write the Genoese dialect. Susanna and
Domenico were probably devout Catholics, who raised their children in keeping
with the traditional practices of the church. In 1470 Columbus's parents moved
twenty-three miles west to the port city of Savona, where, in addition to their
wool-trade business, Domenico sold wine.

By then Columbus was nineteen years old and had spent most of his youth as
a wool carder or weaver. Genoa, in particular, and, to a lesser degree, Savona
were bustling northern Italian ports whose lifeblood was trade and mercantilism.
By the mid-fifteenth century Genoa's expansive harbors, backed by the purple-
hued Apennine Mountains, were filled with carracks, caravels, and xebecs topped
with forests of masts and ropes.

Years before the Ottoman invasion of Constantinople, fleets of light Mediterranean cargo ships arrived regularly in Genoa with precious spice stores from the
East—Malabar pepper, cinnamon, cloves, nutmeg, ginger, and sugar. They

carried other coveted goods as well, rare fabric dyes, ivory, and gold from the North African coast. But after the 1453 fall of Constantinople, Genoese trade in the Red and Black seas was blocked. As a result, capital-rich Genoa looked westward to Spain and Portugal, transferring its trade to Barcelona, Valencia, Sevilla, Lisbon, and points beyond on the Atlantic. Genoese merchants and captains then financed journeys down the African coast in search of gold. In time, they also traveled north past Lisbon to ports in western France, Flanders, and England, even into the North Sea toward Iceland.

The exotic aura that pervaded the Genoese ports inevitably stimulated the young Columbus to consider a seafaring life, although exactly when the future explorer first sailed remains conjectural. Columbus may have gone to sea even before adolescence, as a ten- or eleven-year-old ship's assistant or cabin boy. By young manhood Columbus probably had traveled along the Italian coast to ports like Nervi, Portofino, Rapallo, or Corsica as a merchant sailor entrusted with the delivery of cargo for his father and others.

By 1473 Columbus had ventured as far east as Chios, an Aegean island off the west coast of Turkey. Through a special arrangement with the Ottoman Grand Turk, Chios was one of the few islands still permitted to trade with Genoa and other Italian city-states in the Turkish-dominated Aegean. Onboard a three-master called the *Roxana,* the helmsman did something Columbus had never before witnessed: He abandoned the traditional short voyages from port to port and ventured into the open seas. Once surrounded by an endless azure horizon, the helmsman steered by dead reckoning, that is, by mathematically computing a ship's position from one point to another without visual aids. This navigational feat left a deep impression on Columbus, who, nearly twenty years later, would use it to plot his course to the unknown half of the globe. Still, by the mid-1470s Columbus was either an ordinary sailor or a merchandise transporter, an obscure Genoese, one among hundreds of others who boarded ships to ensure the safe delivery of goods to distant ports.

But in 1476 Columbus's life was transformed. In May he joined a Genoese merchant marine fleet bound for Lisbon, England, and Flanders with a cargo of Chian mastic, a yellow resinlike powder from Mediterranean trees used for varnish and adhesives. Once again the twenty-five-year-old Columbus must have served as a merchandise transporter or a common seaman, for his name was not listed either as an officer or passenger.

The Genoese fleet sailed on May 31 and progressed uneventfully through the Strait of Gibraltar. On August 13 as the boats drew near Lagos and Portugal's southwesternmost point, Cape St. Vincent, they were attacked by thirteen Franco-Portuguese warships. Politically, the Genoese flotilla was neutral, but its flagship, the *Bechalla,* sailing under the red and black Burgundian flag, had provoked the assault.

The Genoese sailors threw flaming pots upon the warships, hoping to set those wooden hulks ablaze. However, the warships were so close that fire spread from the enemy vessels to three of the five Genoese boats. In the ensuing panic, hundreds of sailors from both sides jumped into the sea and drowned. Columbus, who was a prodigious swimmer from youth, propped himself on a floating oar and stayed afloat for six miles until "by miracle" he was washed ashore in Lagos.

Later the young sailor journeyed to Lisbon, then the premier European center of navigation, mapmaking, and sea exploration. The city, bordered by the Tagus estuary that drains into the Atlantic, stirred Columbus profoundly. All of Lisbon buzzed with the idea of global exploration. Sea captains, sailors, and adventurers from many nations gathered in the shops, taverns, and docks of the sprawling harbor town to discuss those theories between voyages at sea. Discovery was a favorite topic of speculation, second only to news that a new fleet of masted ships had arrived in Lisbon that needed sailors to sail south of the Canaries and the Azores to fetch gold from West African Guinea or to seek a sea route to the Indies around the southern coast of Africa.

Before Columbus could participate in these discussions, he had to learn Portuguese. Eventually, he would learn also Spanish and Latin, the latter of which enabled him to read the works of classical antiquity and correspond with princes and scholars.

It was probably in the shops of Lisbon's cartographers that Columbus first heard the geographical theories of Ptolemy, then newly discovered through a Latin publication of his *Geography*. In that work the second-century Hellenized Egyptian astronomer had proposed that the world was round and composed of three clustered land masses—Europe, Asia, and Africa. Those continents, in turn, could be divided into mathematical coordinates of longitude and latitude, comprising 180 degrees of the earth's surface, the rest being bordered by a boundless sea. In the thirteen hundred years since Ptolemy's death, no one had crossed that sea because of its vast distances and the fear that monsters lay within its depths. Moreover, fifteenth-century sailors and astronomers pondered how explorers would "hold on" if they reached the other side of the world. When Columbus arrived in Lisbon in 1476, no European sailor had yet successfully ventured past "Cape Nun" or "Cape No," the westernmost point on the Moroccan coast near the Tropic of Cancer in the Atlantic abyss.

Yet by the time Columbus was born nearly all educated men believed the world was round. So did most Portuguese sailors, if only from their practical observation of the curved horizon while at sea. To the educated, rather than the common, seaman, the theoretical basis for that assumption came from renewed interest not only in Ptolemy but also in other classical thinkers whose work was disseminated in the humanistic revival of the Italian Renaissance. It was well known, for instance, that Aristotle believed it possible to circumnavigate the globe from Spain to the Indies in a few days. The writings of Strabo, a first-century Greek geographer, suggested that the feat had once been attempted. In the late fourteenth century at a scholarly conference in Paris, a French bishop named Nicole Oreseme again proposed that the earth was circular. By then, observations by late medieval astronomers of the curved shadows of the earth's surface during lunar eclipses reconfirmed the ancients' suspicions that the planet was spherical.

Thus by the mid-fifteenth century, most European princes not only accepted the notion that the earth was round but had spherical globes in their palace libraries.

Although no man had yet circumnavigated the globe, the idea had stirred

Columbus. "I have made it my business to read all that has been written on geography, history, philosophy and other sciences," the explorer would explain years later to the Castilian monarchs.[4] Specifically, he had read books like Zacuto's *Perpetual Almanac, The Book of Marco Polo,* Piccolomini's *Historia Rerum Ubique Gestarum,* and *Imago Mundi* by Cardinal Pierre d'Ailly, an early fifteenth-century geographer. The last of these, a copy of which Columbus bought around 1483 and is still preserved in Sevilla's Archives of the Indies, was a digest of Greek and Latin thought on the world's geography encapsulating the theories of Plato, Aristotle, Cicero, Seneca, and other philosophers. This volume exaggerated Asia's proximity to Western Europe, and in its margins Columbus eventually penned his own theories: "all seas all navigable," "all seas are peopled by lands," "the Ocean Sea is no emptier than any other," and "every country has its east and west."[5]

The future explorer would develop these concepts gradually, and then only as his comprehension of theoretical geography matured. But during his first years in Lisbon Columbus inevitably associated with sailors and captains who had ventured south past the equator down the coast of Africa, past St. George La Mina in search of a sea route to the East. In those same years Columbus was reunited with his brother Bartholomew, who either lived in Lisbon already or arrived shortly after Columbus to establish his own cartography shop.

By January 1477 Columbus was on the high seas again, this time on a merchant marine to Iceland, crossing the *Mare Tenebroso,* or "dark sea" of the northern Atlantic. On his return, the fleet stopped in Galway where Columbus saw flat-faced people adrift in a boat. The sight of those strange beings convinced him that Cathay was attainable. Subsequently, he would scribble in his copy of *Historia Rerum,* "Men of Cathay which is toward the Orient have come hither. We have seen many remarkable things, especially in Galway of Ireland, a man and a woman of extraordinary appearance in two boats adrift."[6]

In all likelihood, the "extraordinary people" were Eskimos, Finns, or Lapps, but Columbus was obsessed with their Oriental origins. Somewhat later, a Portuguese helmsman named Vicente found an unusual piece of driftwood beyond the Azores "ingeniously wrought but not with iron" unlike anything grown in Africa or Asia.[7] And in Flores, the westernmost island of the Azores, there were reports that the bodies of two broad-faced Orientals had been washed ashore.

A century before Columbus, Marco Polo had written of faraway Cathay and of *Cipangu,* or Japan, a golden-roofed island kingdom he calculated to be 1,500 miles off the Asian mainland. Few fifteenth-century scholars trusted Polo's observations, for they contradicted Ptolemy's theories that suggested the Asian mainland and its adjacent lands were considerably smaller in size. Yet Columbus pondered these conflicting theories and concluded that Polo's estimates were correct, that the eastern part of Asia was closer to Portugal than was generally believed.

Similar thoughts had already occurred to other men. In Lisbon, a canon of the cathedral named Fernão Martins had befriended a Florentine physician and humanist, Paolo dal Pozzo Toscanelli. Like many physicians of the era, Toscanelli was well versed in mathematics and astronomy, and through them he had developed an interest in geography.

Mathematicians and astronomers had long believed the earth's circumference could be discovered by multiplying the length of a degree by 360. The length of the degree, however, had remained a source of heated debate among the ancients, despite the fact that around 200 B.C. the Greek mathematician Eratosthenes had placed it at a nearly correct 59.5 nautical miles. Now, in the late fifteenth century, Toscanelli developed a new formula for the degree and concluded that the Asian mainland lay 30 degrees closer in longitude to Portugal than was previously believed. Eventually, he explained his new calculations to Martins who, in the early 1470s, relayed the idea to the Portuguese King Afonso V.

That monarch, fresh from his triumphs in Africa against the Barbary Moors and intrigued by the idea of discovering a shorter route to the East, asked Toscanelli to send a letter of explanation. On June 25, 1471, the Florentine responded with a chart to show "a route shorter than the one which you are pursuing by way of Guinea."[8] But within a year, war against Isabella and Ferdinand in Castile forced Afonso to ignore Toscanelli's proposal.

By the late 1470s Columbus had learned about the physician's theories and wrote him. Toscanelli responded:

> Paolo the Physician, to Cristobal Colombus, Greetings: I perceive your noble and grand desire to go to the places where the spices grow; and in reply to your letter I send you a copy of another letter which some time since I sent to a friend of mine, a gentleman of the household of the most serene King of Portugal, before the wars of Castile, in reply to another which by command of His Highness he wrote to me on this subject; and I send you another sea-chart like the one which I sent to him, that your demands may be satisfied.[9]

The letter was the same one as that in which Toscanelli, in exquisite detail, had explained his calculations to Afonso V. But Columbus, dissatisfied with the information, wrote the Florentine physician again. Toscanelli, believing Columbus was Portuguese, replied somewhat impatiently, repeating much of the information of the first letter. "I do not wonder," he concluded, "that you, who are of great courage and the whole Portuguese nation, which has always distinguished itself in all great enterprises, are now inflamed with desire to undertake this voyage."[10]

Columbus did not agree completely with Toscanelli's proposition. In fact, he did not trust Ptolemy's, Eratosthenes', or Toscanelli's estimates about the size of the degree. By his estimates, the degree was only 45 nautical miles, a figure that made the globe 25 percent smaller than Eratosthenes' estimate and 10 percent smaller than Ptolemy's figures. In reality, Columbus foreshortened the ocean between Europe and Asia to 5,000 miles, or 68 percent of its true size, making Japan appear considerably closer to the Azores than it really was.

Columbus did not, however, spend his eight years in Portugal spinning abstract theories. By 1478 he had assumed his old position as merchandise transporter for a Genoese named Paolo di Negro, an associate of the same man who had hired him for the Chios voyage. This time Columbus's task was to arrange for the transportation of 60,000 pounds of sugar from Madeira to Genoa—a position of considerable responsibility, given the size of the shipment and high price of that commodity.

That same year he married Doña Felipa Perestrello e Moñiz, daughter of an aristocratic Portuguese family. Columbus had met his future wife at the chapel of the Convento dos Santos, which served both as a public church and a boarding school for aristocratic young women. Felipa's father, Gil Ayres Moñiz, had died in 1457 and since then her mother, Isabel, had struggled to maintain Felipa and herself on her slender widow's income. By 1479 Felipa's mother was thus eager to marry her twenty-five-year-old daughter to the ambitious and courtly Columbus.

Coincidentally, the bride's father had been one of the early colonizers of the island of Porto Santo, thirty miles northeast of Madeira. Felipa's mother, knowing Columbus's interests in exploration, gave her new son-in-law her husband's sea charts and writings "by which the Admiral was the more excited, and he informed himself of the other voyages and navigations that the Portuguese were making."[11] Shortly after their marriage, the young couple had journeyed to Porto Santo, then governed by Felipa's brother. It was there in 1480 that their son Diego Colón was born.

By the time Columbus left Portugal in 1485, Felipa had died. Little is known about the circumstances of her death or even when it occurred. Her only trace was a grave in Lisbon's Church of Carmo and the small boy Columbus brought with him to Castile in 1485.

It is widely believed that Columbus first proposed *La Empresa de las Indias,* or his "Enterprise of the Indies," before King João in late 1484. After João assumed the Portuguese throne in 1481, he had attempted to subdue the nobles to his obedience and crushed a plot, led by the Duke of Braganza and his wife's brother, the Duke of Viseu. In 1483 João ordered Braganza's execution, and in 1484 he finally murdered Viseu himself.

With Portugal restored to order and Isabella and Ferdinand embroiled in the Granada war, João then turned his attention to exploration. To supervise the navigational efforts already underway on behalf of the Portuguese crown, he created a *Junta dos Mathematicos,* or Maritime Advisory Committee. That council was composed of three men, two Jewish physicians and an ecclesiastic, whose job was to provide explorers with standardized navigational charts and instruments.

It was during that period that Columbus proposed his Enterprise of the Indies. The future explorer had chosen that moment, according to the Portuguese historian João de Barros, because he knew of the king's keen interest in finding another sea route to the Indies from the south.

But King João, Barros wrote, "observed this *Christovao Colom* to be a big talker and boastful in setting forth his accomplishments and full of fancy and imagination with his Isle Cypango than certain whereof he spoke."[12] Nevertheless, on the outside chance that Columbus's project was indeed worthy of merit, João relegated the matter to his *Junta dos Mathematicos.* In the end, that committee rejected Columbus's theories for they "considered the words of Christovao Colom as vain, simply founded on imagination or things like that Isle Cypango of Marco Polo."[13]

Still, João and Columbus parted so amiably that the navigator would be able to propose other projects in the future.

Soon afterward Columbus traveled to Castile. The details of this journey, like most of the mariner's early life, are shrouded in mystery and have thus become an endless source of speculation. What is certain, however, is that Columbus arrived in the seaport town of Palos in mid-1485, that he walked along the shore road to the monastery of La Rabida where he left his son Diego, that he stayed at the palaces of Medina Sidonia and Medinaceli, and ultimately that he appeared in Córdoba in January 1486.

Besides Quintanilla, Columbus would eventually befriend other key members of Isabella and Ferdinand's court, among them the Queen's *comendador mayor,* Gutierre de Cárdenas, Prince Juan's tutor Diego de Deza, the Cardinal Mendoza, Ferdinand's steward Juan Cabrero, and his *converso* Aragonese treasurer Luís Santángel.

During his four months' wait for Isabella and Ferdinand in Córdoba, Columbus fell in love with a young woman named Beatriz Enríquez de Harana, cousin to a *hidalgo* whom he had befriended. This Beatriz was orphaned, but born to what may have been a prosperous family that owned vineyards in Santa María de Transierra. She may even have been an aristocrat because she knew how to read and write, but almost everything else about her—her appearance, age, and marital status—is sketchy. In any event, Beatriz soon became mistress to the thirty-four-year-old navigator, and in 1488 she bore Columbus a second son, Fernando.

Although Beatriz never did become Columbus's wife, the memory of their liaison would haunt him for the rest of his life. In a 1506 codicil to his will, Columbus left instructions with his son Diego to ensure that "Beatriz Enríquez, mother of Don Fernando my son, is put in a way to live honorably, as a person to whom I am in great debt, and thus for discharge of my conscience, because it weighteth on my mind."[14] By 1492 the couple seems to have permanently separated.

On April 28, 1486, the monarchs finally appeared in Córdoba and passed through the gates of the old Moorish alcázar in a stately procession. A week or so later Columbus was ushered through those same gates and presented to them.

Years later Columbus would describe his feverish mood as he prepared for that meeting. "Our Lord revealed to me that it was feasible to sail from here to the Indies and placed in me a burning desire to carry out his plan. Filled with this fire I came to Your Highnesses" even though "all who knew of my enterprise rejected it with laughter and mockery."[15] Columbus then delivered an imposing explanation of his "Enterprise of the Indies" and his theories about sailing west to arrive at the East. To support his hypothesis, Columbus showed Isabella and Ferdinand his own hand-sketched map of the world with its greatly shrunken distances between the European coastline and Cypango.

By May 1486 Columbus was nearly thirty-five, and if his previous experiences with high-born men and women had taught him anything, it was to address a prospective sponsor's personal interests. Knowing Isabella's two passions were purification of the church and conversion of the infidel, Columbus raised the possibility of discovering new lands and people who could be converted to Christianity as well as the wealth that would accrue to the crown from a new route to the Orient.

The queen listened to Columbus's suit with considerably more interest than Ferdinand, who, according to Las Casas, "heard the request very superficially, being so occupied with the war."[16] Subsequently, Columbus heaped praise upon both the king and queen for their support of his expedition to the New World, but he reserved special accolades for Isabella and her unshakable faith in his proposal.

Because of Columbus's passionate adulation of Isabella, some historians have conjectured that a love affair blossomed between them. If so, that union must have been a spiritual one for Isabella was still an intensely chaste queen, as covetous of her reputation for marital fidelity as Queen Juana had been careless. Both Isabella and Columbus were reflective, highly motivated, driven individuals, visionaries who dreamed of a perfectable world and those aspirations may well have inspired a certain *simpatico*. Besides their obvious physical similarities—above-average height, reddish hair, blue eyes, fair skin, and birth dates only a few months apart—Isabella and Columbus shared the belief that they were divinely inspired and destined to change the world.

But in 1486 Isabella was not prepared to make a commitment to Columbus. With a new Moorish campaign, a rebellion simmering in faraway Galicia, and a depleted treasury, Columbus's proposal could not have come at a worse time. Still, his theories might be correct, a possibility Isabella, painfully aware of her own educational gaps, was in no position to judge. Instead of sending the mariner away, the queen thus entrusted him to Quintanilla, who once again hosted him in his home. Simultaneously, the queen ordered a committee of scholars and theologians to study Columbus's proposed enterprise and placed her trusted confessor Talavera at its head.

Therein would begin six long years of uncertainty and torment for Columbus. This was one of the bleakest periods of his life, even darker than the moonless nights on the Atlantic when a grumbling crew would curse their captain and fear they would never see land again.

CHAPTER FORTY

The Work of a Month

There were other reasons why Isabella and Ferdinand would not immediately embrace Columbus's proposed Atlantic expedition. By the spring of 1486 the Islamic Crescent was again poised menacingly over Christian Western Europe. After Pope Sixtus IV's death in 1484 and the ascension of Pope Innocent VIII, the Ottoman Turks had invaded Moldavia, a Balkan province now part of modern-day Romania. A second wave of Turks swept over the northwestern end of the Black Sea and seized the Danube River fortresses of Kilia and Akkerman. At the same time, a fleet of Turkish ships ominously prowled the Mediterranean near Italy.

To make matters even more alarming, the usually contentious leaders of the Moslem Empire, having learned about Isabella and Ferdinand's conquests in Granada, united in a new pact. In Egypt the *Gran Soldan,* Sultan Kait-Bey, gathered an army intended to reinforce the Granadan Moors. Simultaneously, Bayezid II, head of the Ottoman Turks, launched an armada to menace Ferdinand's island kingdom of Sicily.

The new pope, Innocent VIII, a fifty-two-year-old man with weak eyes, poor health, and a disposition "guided rather by the advice of others than by his own lights," promptly warned Ferdinand about the threatened invasion.[1] Yet the Holy See and confederation of Italian kingdoms known as the Papal States were unable to help, for they were crippled by a bitter domestic struggle of their own. In June 1485, at Isabella and Ferdinand's insistence, Innocent did, however, grant the Castilian monarchs a new Bull of Crusade that granted them a *tercero,* or third part of all funds from Castilian tithes.

That same summer the pope became enmeshed in a conflict against Ferrante, King of Naples, whose soldiers stormed the Italian countryside to the very gates of the Eternal City. The alarmed pope appealed to his Italian subjects for help. Finally on December 28—less than two weeks after Isabella gave birth to Catherine in Alcalá de Henares—Venetian reinforcements repulsed Ferrante's soldiers and rescued the Holy Father.

In the heat of that crisis Innocent had also appealed to all the crowned heads of Christian Europe. Once again Ferdinand served as a mediator. To make peace between the pope and the Neapolitan king, Ferdinand appointed the forty-three-year-old Count of Tendilla, Iñigo López de Mendoza, his papal ambassador and promptly dispatched him to Rome.

Meanwhile, Ferrante was wrestling with internal domestic problems of his own—rebellious barons who so loathed him that they vowed to topple him from the throne. In desperation, they even threatened to enlist the help of the Ottoman Turks. When Innocent learned about that scheme, he seriously considered a previous offer from the French king, Charles VIII, to invade Naples. Ferdinand, fearing the French presence in the Trastámara-held kingdoms of Naples and Sicily, immediately protested to the pope through Tendilla and Cardinal Borgia. By August 1486 those two shrewd diplomats had succeeded in convincing the timorous and by then thoroughly intimidated pope to sign a peace treaty with Ferrante.

But the Neapolitan king proved as deceptive as he was ruthless. Before the end of the year Ferrante had murdered his rebellious barons, doled out benefices without the pope's permission, and once again refused to pay Innocent tribute money.

In May 1486 Ferdinand and Isabella, menaced by the triple threats of the Turkish and Granada Moslems and France, launched their most aggressive campaign yet against the Moors. To the monarchs the infidel was rapidly assuming satanic dimensions, perennially fomenting dissension between the Christian leaders of Western Europe and at their own borders in Castile.

In that retributive mood, Isabella and Ferdinand collected their largest army yet—some 52,000 men who assembled in the valley of the Guadalquivir near Córdoba under Sixtus IV's large silver cross. Repeatedly, that cross had been carried into battle as a symbol of the Holy War whose religious aura grew more intense each year. Now new soldiers arrived in Córdoba with Christian emblems of their own—the traditional red cross of the ancient Crusades worn upon jerkins over their armor. Increasingly too, prelates like the Bishop of Jaén and the Archbishop of Sevilla appeared to fight alongside their secular peers. Even the fifty-eight-year-old Cardinal Mendoza, although too old to fight, regularly accompanied the king on excursions to conquered cities.

The idea of spiritual redemption and an imminent Christian apocalypse pervaded everything, especially after Innocent issued his 1485 Bull of Crusade. Since then Isabella and Ferdinand reported each victory to the pope from the battlefield as a Christian triumph. Innocent, in turn, acknowledged those triumphs with special masses and celebrations held in the Eternal City.

In spring 1486 the monarchs decided to again attempt a conquest of the whitewashed city of Loja, one of the last Moorish-held communities in Granada's western province, about forty miles from the capital and the scene of the 1482

Castilian defeat. But now, Isabella and Ferdinand's victories over the Granada Moors were rapidly assuming legendary proportions in ducal palaces and manor houses across Western Europe. Thus a new crop of foreign soldiers arrived to join the army at Córdoba. Among them were a French chevalier named Gaston de Lyon, an Irishman named Ubertus Stantum, and the English Sir Edward Woodville, or Conde de Escalas as he was known to the Castilians.

A year earlier Escalas, a "cavalier young, wealthy and high-born . . . allied to the blood royal of England," had commanded a company of sharpshooting archers at the battle of Bosworth Field that had raised his Tudor brother-in-law, King Henry VII, to the English throne. It was thus with considerable excitement that Escalas, "attended by a beautiful train, armed after the fashion of their land with long-bow and battle-axe," was welcomed to Ferdinand's camp.[2]

Nevertheless, the attack upon Loja was bound to be difficult. Although the old Moorish king Ali Abu-l-Hasan died in 1485, his son Boabdil had broken his pact with Isabella and Ferdinand in early 1486 by uniting with his uncle, El Zagal. Believing Ferdinand ignorant of his defection, Boabdil boldly notified the Castilian monarchs that he held Loja as a vassal of Castile. Ferdinand, however, immediately retorted that since Boabdil had broken his promise, he could no longer be considered an ally.

On May 13 Ferdinand and his army left Córdoba to invade Loja. Initially Cádiz and his men stormed the town but Boabdil and El Zagal's men countered them on three sides. Just as Cádiz and his men were beaten back into the deeply ravined hills, Ferdinand arrived with the rest of the army.

A ferocious hand-to-hand battle ensued. In its midst Escalas and three hundred of his men dismounted. Then "with a battle-axe in his hand and with a band of men in a wedge behind him, all armed like him with axes," the count rushed toward the Moors "with stout and valiant heart giving blows right and left, killing and knocking them flat." Despite the brutality of the Moorish counterdefense, "neither courage nor might failed" the Englishmen.[3]

The Castilians, especially those under the command of the young Duke of Infantado, Iñigo Hurtado de Mendoza, were astonished at the ferociousness of their English allies. Although the duke and his men had been mocked for their frivolity and dandified ways, their ferocity now so inspired the Castilians that "without waiting for a moment . . . [they] did such execution among the Moors that they turned their backs in flight."[4]

Escalas and his battalion then attacked one of Loja's suburbs. As the English lord and his men mounted a ladder placed against a town wall, a Moor hurled an enormous rock upon them. Three Englishmen were killed and Escalas, whose front teeth were knocked out by the blow, fell unconscious.

Ferdinand, meanwhile, ordered the *lombardas* and the lesser guns discharged "at certain parts of the wall where they would not harm those involved in battle."[5] The siege raged for a day and two nights until at last, on May 28, Loja was forced to surrender.

Once again Boabdil was taken prisoner. As before, the young Moor approached Ferdinand humbly. The king, although filled with contempt, treated him with courtesy. Privately Isabella and Ferdinand still believed that Boabdil's fecklessness would make trouble for the Moors so they could be manipulated to the Castilians' advantage. Consequently, Ferdinand freed Boabdil again. This time, however, the young Moorish king was not only to pay tribute as a Castilian vassal but his freedom was restricted to Guadix and seven other towns north of Granada. Boabdil also agreed that if he ever broke the truce and the Castilians seized the towns of Almeria, Baeza, and Guadix, he would surrender the city of Granada.

On May 29, in a ceremony repeated for virtually every city conquered in the Moorish war, Ferdinand entered Loja surrounded by his barons and prelates.

In Córdoba, meanwhile, a relieved Isabella, keenly recalling Ferdinand's former defeat at Loja, rejoiced in her husband's triumph. In gratitude, she walked to the cathedral barefoot to attend mass and to offer prayers of thanksgiving for the victory.

After the victory Isabella's role in the Holy War would become increasingly visible. No longer was she content to sit on the sidelines of the Granada campaign. Eleven years earlier, during an argument with Ferdinand at Tordesillas, Isabella had admitted her restlessness: Had she been born a man she would have led her subjects into battle herself.

That the queen's work as a military provisioner, quartermaster, and strategist was highly valued was obvious. Nevertheless, Isabella still felt removed from the war and deeply frustrated that she was forced to wait at a distance from the battlefield for news of triumphs and defeats.

Just how Isabella effected the change in her role has never been made clear. Her contemporaries disagreed as to whether it was Isabella or Ferdinand who first proposed that the queen visit the army at Loja, but in any case, both monarchs ultimately embraced the idea. All thoughts of danger were brusquely pushed aside.

The queen's visit was meant to inspire the rank and file of the Castilian army—most of whom had never seen Isabella personally—to new heights of bravery. After nearly seventeen years of marriage, Ferdinand understood that the men symbolically fought for Isabella, a direct descendant of the Trastámara line and Castile's premier monarch, rather than for him. Despite *Tanto Monta,* despite the king's revered role as army general, despite even his proven courage on the battlefield, the queen still elicited higher respect. Accepting that, Ferdinand enthusiastically welcomed Isabella to the army camp. Her presence, the rhetoric that flowed around her as a second Virgin Mary, the public perception that she was an instrument of God through which the infidel would be routed from Castile would inevitably rouse his men for the next battle. And selfishly, as Ferdinand wrote Isabella, she would no longer have to endure the long separations enforced by war, but instead would always be available to "provide the King with council."[6]

By the time Isabella received Ferdinand's letter requesting her presence, he had already pressed on to Íllora, a small town in the Parapanda Mountains, about twenty-four miles northwest of Granada. After a four-day siege, the Castilian *lombardas* smashed Íllora's walls, and on Friday, June 9, the town surrendered to Ferdinand.

That same Friday Cádiz, the Count of Miranda, and a thousand armed guards left Ferdinand's camp and traveled to the *Fuente de Archidona,* the Archdeacon's

Fountain at the Yeguas River to meet the queen. From Córdoba, meanwhile, Isabella rode south to the Yeguas with her closest companions—the Princess Isabel, Gutierre de Cárdenas, Gonzalo Chacón, and Diego Hurtado de Mendoza, the Archbishop of Sevilla. In Isabella's honor, Cádiz ordered his men to pitch handsome silk tents and furnished them with tables, chairs, couches, and other comforts. Isabella was surprised by such luxury in a rustic setting. "Marquis, it seems that your fields are filled with joyfulness," she began. "You deserve to receive much honor for this and the King my lord and I will grant you great privileges."[7]

Cádiz then feted the queen with a magnificent meal of white bread, poultry and other meats, fruit, pastries made of sugar and honey, fine wines and sweet-smelling water, all of which were served on golden, bejeweled plates. Afterward the royal party was escorted to a local landmark called the Rock of the Lovers just four or five miles from Moclín, where Isabella was greeted by Infantado and other nobles.

There, on a broad plain, the Castilian army stood at attention in full military regalia, their individual battalions distinguished by colorful heraldic standards. As Isabella approached, she had reason to feel pride at the sea of faces turned toward her that had gathered to fight the Holy War on behalf of Castile. The soldiers, in turn, gazed with admiration upon the thirty-five-year-old queen, who, although heavier now than in her youth, was still a handsome woman.

Everything about Isabella attested to her majesty. On that day she appeared on a chestnut mare caparisoned in crimson cloth embroidered in gold. The queen herself was dressed in Andalusian style with a rich crimson velvet skirt covered with layers of brocade. A matching red mantle decorated with Moorish embroidery fell from her shoulders, and her head was protected from the strong sun by a brimmed, gold-trimmed black hat. Beside her rode the Princess Isabel from whom she was "never separated" and who, at fifteen, was budding into a beautiful young woman.

The queen and her daughter remained mounted as thousands of helmeted and armored men, holding their lances and swords, filed past them "with great joy." The soldiers' obvious delight in Isabella's arrival "pleased her Highness very much."[8] As the leaders of each battalion approached Isabella, they lowered their standards in a sign of respect.

"You should be happy," the queen told the men, "because as knights you have defended the Faith from the dangers that threaten the land and that have caused us so much hardship in this life. God knows our cause and will not forget our difficulties and will remember them in the other [world]."[9]

Ferdinand, surrounded by a cortege of Castilian nobles, then made his own dramatic entrance. Like the queen, the king was garbed *à la Andaluz,* with a scarlet doublet and yellow silk *quezote,* or breeches. His shoulders were covered with a mantle of richly embroidered brocade and at his side hung a Moorish scimitar. Like Isabella, the king wore a sombrero that covered a thin cap.

At Ferdinand's approach, Isabella made three reverences and the king bowed in a similarly gallant fashion. To the delight of the curious men, Isabella then removed her hat, revealing her auburn hair, which flamed in the sun beneath a silken net, and her fine, pale cheeks. The king, smiling as he approached, embraced Isabella and kissed her on the cheek. Then he hugged the princess, made a sign of the cross, and kissed her as well.

At the end of the entourage, Escalas appeared on a white horse. The Englishman was dressed in a full suit of armor over which he wore a coat of dark brocade and a white plumed hat. As Escalas smiled, the queen noticed his front teeth were missing and expressed her sympathy for his disfigurement. Escalas grinned again. "It is a small thing to lose a few teeth in the service of Him who gave them to me," he said. "Our Blessed Lord, who built all this house, has merely opened a window in it, that he may more easily see what passeth within."[10]

Even in her first moments reviewing the army, Isabella was thus sharply reminded of the sufferings of her soldiers. In the first of many subsequent tokens of appreciation, Isabella presented Escalas with rich gifts—twelve Andalusian horses, two beds with rich coverlets of gold, fine linens, and luxurious tents. These, she knew, could never compensate the Englishman for the loss of his men or his own injuries. That the war was a holy one, that it was being conducted in the hope of arresting the infidel and winning new souls to Christianity, was her only solace.

The queen's presence had just the kind of inspirational effect Ferdinand hoped for. The following day he and the Castilian army stormed Moclín with 2,000 *lombardas* and other heavy artillery. For two harrowing nights and a day the Castilians battered the city with their fiery projectiles until, finally, the walls began to crumble. On June 17, after *El Artillero,* Francisco Ramirez, aimed a *pelota encendida,* or heated iron ball, into a Moorish magazine, the Moslems surrendered.

Throughout the war, but especially after Isabella's appearance at Loja, the army viewed every battle as a judgment from the Almighty. Accordingly, the stunning brevity of the siege at Moclín was perceived as having been accomplished by the "hand of God."[11]

Now too, instead of waiting anxiously for days, Isabella learned about the victory in minutes. She promptly rode from her nearby encampment to congratulate Ferdinand and the army. Then, in a solemn procession, the prelates raised Sixtus's silver cross, and Isabella, Ferdinand and the army entered Moclín to consecrate its mosques as churches.

Shortly thereafter, Ferdinand and his men swept through the Málaga plains to conduct the *tala.* In their fury, the army subdued the towns of Montefrio and Colomera, cutting a wide path of destruction through orchards and croplands to within six miles of the city of Granada.

Isabella stayed behind. Moclín had been her first excursion to an actual battlefield, probably her first glimpse of the corpses of the enemy and the feeble state of the recently released Christian prisoners. Every day she visited the army hospital to cheer the sick and offer her prayers.

During that same period she also fretted about the Christian soldiers who had been buried near Moclín in unconsecrated graves a year earlier. Believing it incumbent upon her to rectify the situation, she ordered their remains disinterred and reburied in newly consecrated churches.

By July 1486 the Castilian monarchs' martial objectives for the year had been fulfilled. Loja, Íllora, and Moclín had been conquered in "the work of a month."[12]

Ferdinand's *tala* had destroyed all food supplies within six miles of the Moorish capital. Slowly but surely the Castilians were tightening the noose around Granada's neck. In Rome Innocent VIII celebrated the Castilian victories with a high mass in the Church of St. John the Divine and took up a special collection for the Moorish Crusade.

On July 10 Ferdinand, dressed in gold, rode through Córdoba's gates with a richly dressed cortege of warriors to be greeted by his eight-year-old son, Prince Juan, the Master of Calatrava, and the city's knights. Then, under a golden canopy, the king proceeded to the cathedral, *La Mezquita,* an enormous tenth-century converted mosque, to attend a thanksgiving mass. Afterward Ferdinand and his party arrived at the alcázar where Isabella, the Princess Isabel, and their attendants waited "dressed in rich adornments" to receive them "with great rejoicing."[13]

Still, there was little time for rest. The drive for conquest burned as relentlessly within Isabella and Ferdinand as the hot Andalusian sun. From Córdoba they issued orders for the next year's campaign—new shipments of iron, cattle, flour, wine, and munitions.

The Moslem kingdom had been temporarily beaten into submission. But the port city of Málaga, opening on the Mediterranean and still held by the Moors, remained a major threat, a potential conduit for the sultan's Egyptian army. And from foreign reports Isabella and Ferdinand learned that white-sailed Moslem ships skirted the Italian peninsula restlessly, hungering for prey along Sicilian shores.

CHAPTER FORTY-ONE

The Siege of Málaga

In an apocalyptic era, natural events are likely to be misinterpreted as omens of divine will. So it was on Sunday morning, April 7, 1487, when the city of Córdoba began to tremble. Buildings rattled, towers teetered, loose stones toppled from city ramparts, and potted plants fell from balconies into narrow streets. To those who witnessed it, the earthquake seemed particularly severe around the Moorish alcázar.

As soon as the quake ceased the terrified citizens poured from their homes into the streets searching for an explanation. Some "considered it a sign of future events that would befall the population." Others believed it an "omen of good luck," portending that the very foundations of Granada were about to be destroyed.[1]

Coincidentally, the quake had occurred on the eve of the 1487 Granada campaign, but since neither Isabella nor Ferdinand were superstitious they attached little meaning to it. The next morning, as scheduled, Ferdinand's army, now enlarged to 50,000 infantry and 20,000 cavalry, left Córdoba. Their first destination was Vélez Málaga, the lush port city on the Mediterranean that lay between Castilian-occupied Marbella and Moorish Málaga.

By May 3 that city had fallen and its inhabitants released 120 Christian prisoners. Before long a string of adjacent Moorish strongholds surrendered as well—among them Benamix, Comares, the towns of the Ajarquía, and forty other communities in the Alpujarras Mountains.

By early summer most of the Granada coast belonged to Castile. Only Málaga resisted. That proud port of the Granada kingdom stood essentially alone, glittering like a solitary jewel along the Iberian coastline, only a few miles from the Strait of Gibraltar and the tip of North Africa through which men and munitions continued to flow, despite a Castilian naval blockade.

To pluck Málaga from the diadem of Granada's crown would be no easy enterprise. From the foothills of the Sierra Blancas Ferdinand and his army gazed down upon that city, which even at a distance was studded with palm trees, stately cypress, and shady gardens. As Granada's premier port, Málaga curled around a point of land, protected on one side by cliffs, on the other by 112 defensive towers and two looming fortresses.

Opening to the Mediterranean, Málaga was a bustling city whose docks welcomed ships from the African coast. Although most of its population of 11,000 to 14,000 were native-born Moslems, there were also North African Berbers and a renegade Castilian population—criminals as well as "relapsed" Moors who, fearing the Inquisition, had fled Castile. Several hundred Jews also lived there, having sought sanctuary after their 1482 exile from Andalusia.

The taller of Málaga's two castles, Gibralfaro, was located on a height overlooking the sea. It was there that the military defender of Ronda, El Zegri, and his band of North African warriors, the Gomeres, now lived. That proud warrior, still remembering the humiliation of his defeat at Ronda and still "panting for vengeance against the Christians,"[2] now fiercely protected the city. Below Gibralfaro stood another citadel, the Alcazaba, Málaga's lower castle, which protected the city and its ramparts.

Cádiz, as usual, asked Ferdinand for the most dangerous post, the plains closest to Málaga's ramparts and Gibralfaro. Soon his 2,500 mounted knights and 14,000 infantrymen had created a bunker that stretched from the foothills toward the sea, thus cutting the city off from the interior. Then armed Aragonese ships commanded by the Catalan admiral Mosen Requesens surrounded the port.

With the North African coastline thus severed, Castilian ships arrived with some of the *lombardas* that could not be transported earlier. Sailors then unloaded seven cannons, dubbed *las siete hermanas Ximonas,* or the "seven sisters of Jiménez" for a notoriously stern Franciscan friar, Francisco Jiménez de Cisneros, later important to Isabella's reign. Simultaneously they delivered a "lucky" load of one-hundred-year-old marble bullets taken from the fields surrounding the port city of Algeciras, site of a Christian victory a century earlier.

Without further delay *El Artillero* arranged the *lombardas* on ox carts at key points along the walls of Málaga and ordered the gunners to commence. In the ensuing thunder, holes began to appear in the city's thick walls. But since the *lombardas* were difficult to pivot and awkward to load, the Moors stationed upon the ramparts soon learned to anticipate each blow. As soon as a *lombarda* blasted a hole in the city walls, Moslem soldiers hastily patched it up. Consequently the siege dragged on for days.

By late June, the heat brought swarms of insects and with them an outbreak of pestilence in Málaga's suburbs. Several Castilians died and some soldiers, frustrated by the stalemate, began to grumble. A few were so unhappy that they deserted to the enemy, spreading exaggerated stories about an epidemic in the Castilian camp and a shortage of gunpowder. In their efforts to discredit the Castilians, they even boasted that Isabella had advised Ferdinand to abandon the siege.

The queen, of course, had not done so, but to dispel those rumors, Ferdinand asked her to visit. There was no question that the queen's arrival would quickly restore goodwill. Ever since Moclín the superstitious soldiers had come to regard Isabella as a saintly creature, a lucky portent, bound to bring them victory. Her reputation had also spread to the Moors who, consequently, dreaded her arrival as a harbinger of certain defeat.

Isabella's attitude toward this adulation was characteristically muted. As a devout Catholic she had, after all, been taught to avoid pride. On the other hand, she must have appreciated the fact that the warriors' adulation reinforced her supremacy as a monarch. There was, moreover, a grain of truth to her reputation: Isabella's appearance inevitably did inspire the Castilian soldiers to new acts of bravery. Like Joan of Arc a half century earlier, Isabella "made men forget their past labors and encouraged them to persevere."[3]

By early June the queen, escorted by Cádiz and his men, thus rode into the Castilian camp. To honor her arrival Ferdinand had ordered the Castilian artillery to be silenced. He then offered the Málagans generous terms for a surrender. If they refused, he vowed "with the blessing of God to make them all slaves."[4]

The Moslems, however, believing the Castilians' artillery had fallen silent from a lack of gunpowder and celebrating their presumed advantage, stoutly refused Ferdinand's offer. When the king heard the Moorish rumors, he resolved to correct them at once. Before long the *lombardas* had resumed their incessant thunder.

Although Isabella and Ferdinand were living on a battlefield, they felt personally secure. A few weeks after Isabella's arrival, a Tunisian *alfaqui* named Ibrahim Algerbi, accompanied by four hundred Moslems, stole into the foothills above Ferdinand's camp and swooped down in a *rebato* attack. After a bitter struggle the Castilians repulsed Algerbi's warriors and took him captive. The Tunisian was brought before Cádiz. Claiming he was a "saint" with holy knowledge, he begged the marquis for an audience with the monarchs. Despite Cádiz's skepticism, Isabella agreed to grant him the interview.

However, because Ferdinand was napping, Isabella "moved by some divine inspiration" ordered the man held in a neighboring tent until the king awoke.[5] Algerbi was thus taken to the next pavilion where Beatriz de Bobadilla and a Portuguese nobleman were playing chess. The Moor did not understand Castilian and, mistaking the richly dressed pair for the king and queen, feigned thirst and asked the guard for water. The moment the guard's back was turned, Algerbi pulled a scimitar from his Moorish cape and stabbed the baron. He then attempted to attack Beatriz. In the ensuing struggle, Algerbi's scimitar became tangled in the drapery of the tent and his blow was averted by the gold ornaments of Beatriz's headdress. Her sharp cries, meanwhile, attracted the attention of two courtiers and the royal guards.

The Castilians were so horrified by Algerbi's attempted assassination that they murdered him on the spot and threw his mangled corpse over the walls of Málaga.

The incident marked the end of an innocent era. Thereafter, the Castilians would maintain tight security over the royal pavilion and the other tents of the court. Henceforth two hundred men would guard the king and queen. Never again were unfamiliar armed warriors or Moors permitted to enter the royal quarters.

Inevitably, Isabella's arrival had a civilizing influence upon the Castilian camp. Although on one occasion she visited Cádiz's dangerous post at the border of the Málaga blockade, peace and the medicinal arts were more suited to Isabella's temperament than were war machines. Thus the queen spent most of her time in the army hospital tents with the wounded. Encouraged by the queen, priests and friars said mass daily at various locations throughout the camp.

Some aspects of Christian devotion were also exploited to intentionally rattle the Moors. Sixtus's silver cross was prominently displayed over the Castilian camp. Its fiery reflection in the strong Andalusian sun could not help but attract the attention of Málaga's rampart guards. Isabella had provided the army with forty silver bells to be used in the newly consecrated churches of conquered cities, but now they were hung in the camp to ring the hours of the military watch. Night and day they sounded in various pitches and tones, giving "very bad comfort" to the Moors who feared them as portents of certain doom.[6]

In reality, the Moslems had abandoned the city of Málaga. Whatever help the Moors could have gained from the interior was now eroded by new rivalries between the two Granadan kings. After El Zagal's defeat at Vélez Málaga, he had been jeered from the gates of Granada and retreated to Guadix to rule over the eastern half of the Moorish kingdom. Although Granada's fickle citizens now embraced Boabdil as their new king, El Zagal was determined to become Granada's sole monarch. Within a few weeks he dispatched a new battalion of cavalry toward Málaga. In response, Boabdil ordered his own shock troops to fight against his uncle's soldiers. Realizing that he was no military match for the Christians, Boabdil then dispatched a messenger to Málaga laden with gifts— perfumes and silks for Isabella, a dozen Andalusian horses for Ferdinand.

Subsequently the monarchs fashioned a new truce with Boabdil in which the Moor agreed to a momentous concession: He would permanently surrender the city of Granada to them "when he was able"—that is, when he was secure enough politically to do so.[7] In exchange, the Castilian monarchs would allow Boabdil to live in peace as king over a small portion of the old Granada kingdom—Guadix, Baeza, and several other cities.

In contrast to the divided Moorish kingdom of Granada, the Castilians continued to attract support from all corners of the Spanish peninsula and points beyond. One day two ships arrived from Flanders with *lombardas* and other artillery, a gift from Maximilian, heir to the Holy Roman Empire. Another day a ship arrived from Portugal with a gift of gunpowder from King João. A fleet of one hundred Castilian ships arrived from the Duke of Medina Sidonia with new supplies. Then the duke himself appeared with reinforcements and a loan of 20,000 gold doblas.

Yet Isabella was deeply disturbed by the lives lost at the siege of Málaga. To prevent more bloodshed, she urged Ferdinand to offer El Zegri new terms for surrender. At her insistence, Ferdinand thus tendered a new peace treaty, this time offering to let the Málagans go free and retain their personal property in exchange for a prompt surrender. But should they refuse and force Ferdinand to shed more Castilian blood, the king promised stern vengeance.

By then Málaga's food supplies were running low and its citizens were clamoring for peace. Nevertheless, El Zegri entrusted his decision to a fanatic *alfaqui* who assured him of victory if he held out longer. To placate the hungry Moors, that prophet promised they would soon eat the grain that was piled high in the Castilian camp. So persuasively did the *alfaqui* present his case that, in the end, the citizens relented and refused Ferdinand's offer.

But as the days became weeks the citizens ran out of food and were forced to eat palm leaves and finally their horses, dogs, and cats. The Málagans were by then so infuriated with the *alfaqui* that they threatened murder, and he retreated into the castle of Gibralfaro.

Meanwhile, in the Christian camp Ferdinand was growing equally impatient. Finally he ordered the *lombardas* to be fired anew. At the same time Castilian soldiers rolled out *El Artillero*'s battering rams and movable wooden towers whose drawbridges and galleries enabled access to walled cities. Despite the Moors' weakened condition, they rallied for a last fight. Stones, poisoned darts, and arrows fell from the city ramparts upon the Castilian soldiers below. Teams of Moslems hacked *El Artillero*'s wooden towers to pieces with war axes. In the ocean a small armada of Moorish boats sparred with the Castilian fleet. And in tunnels beneath the cliffs of Málaga, the Moslems feverishly repulsed the Christians. The battle raged for four days.

Finally, *El Artillero* mined one of Málaga's towers. After it exploded, the Christians gained access to an important bridge and stormed the city.

Subdued, the terrified Málagans begged El Zegri to surrender. But that warrior and his African band, caring less about the plight of the citizens than about their vow to destroy the Castilians, bid the Málagans to make their own arrangements with Ferdinand. Then they retreated into the fast granite walls of Gibralfaro.

A committee of Málagans led by a rich merchant named Ali Dordux then begged the Castilian king for a surrender. But Ferdinand was still seething over the senseless sacrifice of his men in the last battle. "Send them to the devil," he told his envoy Gutierre de Cárdenas. "I will not see them."[8]

Once again the committee approached Ferdinand. This time the Málagans agreed to surrender everything to him—their personal property as well as the city—if he would grant them personal freedom. If Ferdinand refused, they threatened to hang every Christian captive from Málaga's ramparts and place their women, children, and old men in the fortress at Gibralfaro. Then they vowed to burn the city and fight to the death.

Ferdinand was not moved by these threats. Instead he countered that if the Moors hurt one single Christian prisoner, "not a single Moor would live in the city of Málaga because he would put them all to the sword."[9]

A third time Ali Dordux tried to placate the Castilian monarchs, this time sending them bolts of cloth and brocade, gold, precious jewels, spices, and perfumes. Now he pleaded only for his own liberation and forty families of his friends. Dordux also offered up twenty of the city's most prominent citizens to be held as hostages until the Castilians occupied the city. And finally he presented a letter of surrender from the citizens of Málaga.

With that document in hand Ferdinand reluctantly agreed to the surrender. Had the Málagans conceded to his earlier offers, they would have been free to live in other parts of Spain or abroad. "But since I have had to wait so long I have no other choice but to tell you that I cannot guarantee you any mercy."[10]

On August 18, 1487, after a siege that had lasted three months and eleven days, Málaga formally surrendered. That morning Gutierre de Cárdenas and his soldiers took possession of the Alcazaba. Suddenly, the banners of Christian Spain were unfurled. Afterward twelve Christian traitors were tied to stakes and then executed Moorish style—Castilian soldiers rode by shooting them with *canas*, or reed darts, to ensure a slow death. That same day relapsed Christian and Moslem heretics were burned at the stake.

The rest of Málaga's population received food distributed at the orders of the king and queen. Ironically, the Moorish *alfaqui*'s prediction had come true: The Málagans had eaten the Castilian grain, but not as free men.

The most poignant moment of all was the release of six hundred Christian prisoners from the city dungeons. Blinking in the unaccustomed sunlight, the men and women were "so thin and yellow with the great hunger that they all desired to die" and threw themselves with tears at the feet of the protesting king and queen.[11]

To symbolize the Christian occupation, the city's mosques were purified and the forty silver bells that had rung in the Christian camp were hung from the new church towers. The king, queen, prelates, courtiers, and warriors then marched through Málaga to attend a high mass in that city's largest mosque, now renamed Santa María de la Encarnación.

The next day El Zegri surrendered the fortress of Gibralfaro and was put in chains. Simultaneously, the Moorish citizens' fate was announced. Earlier that morning the frightened Málagans had walked through the streets clenching their hands, raising their eyes to the heavens and crying aloud: "Oh, Málaga, famous and very beautiful city, your citizens are deserting you! How could your land nurture them in life and not shelter them in death? Where is the strength of your castles? Where is the beauty of your towers? The thickness of your walls could not defend your dwellers because their Creator is angry with them. What will your old and your women do?"[12]

Isabella and Ferdinand's announcement confirmed their worst fears: The entire population was to be sold into slavery. This was to be the monarchs' most merciless treatment of the conquered in the entire Granada war. One-third of the Moors were sent to Africa in exchange for Christian prisoners held there. Another third were given to the aristocrats and others who had helped finance the war. Of the remaining third, one hundred were sent to the pope to be made part of his guard and converted to Christianity. Isabella gave fifty of the most beautiful girls as a token of friendship to the Neapolitan queen. Thirty others were presented to King João's wife, Leonor. Still others went to women in Isabella's court.

The only remaining hope left to the Málagans was the monarchs' offer that if the captives could pay thirty doblas a head within nine months, the entire population would be freed. To finalize their liberation Moslem men, women, and children voluntarily delivered their jewels and money to the Castilian monarchs. But the sum, generous as it was, never totaled to the requisite amount.

On only one point did Isabella and Ferdinand concede. A committee of Castilian Jewish leaders, headed by Abraham Seneor, asked to ransom back the 450 Jews, most of whom were women, who were to be enslaved. Seneor, head rabbi of Castile, a treasurer in Isabella and Ferdinand's court, and one of the chief financiers of the Granada war, wielded such influence with the monarchs that he was not refused. By the appointed date the Jewish leaders had scraped together the required 20,000 doblas so their brethren could live as free men and women.

CHAPTER FORTY-TWO

St. Augustine Doubts

After Isabella and Ferdinand's victory at Málaga, Columbus rushed to the monarchs' side, hoping that triumph would free them to focus upon his Atlantic expedition. But although the king and queen had willingly paid his expenses, they still refused to commit themselves to financing his voyage. While Málaga had been a key battle and a final victory over the Granada kingdom seemed more likely now than ever before, it was by no means assured. Thus Columbus was told he would have to wait longer, perhaps until the conclusion of the Holy War. Moreover, Talavera's committee had still not rendered a final decision on the merits of Columbus's proposal, even though it had been meeting for over a year.

That past November 1486, the committee had moved with the Castilian court to the revered university city of Salamanca and established a meeting place in the Dominican monastery of St. Stephen's College. The monastery was located between the university buildings and the "old," or first, cathedral of the city. Its prior was Fray Diego Deza, professor of theology at Salamanca and Prince Juan's tutor.

To this day historians have never determined whether Deza served on Talavera's committee or was merely a consultant to answer theological questions. In either case, Deza's university position and intimacy with Isabella's court gave him considerable influence over the committee. Moreover, Deza had supported Columbus's project from the start, either because he was impressed with the navigator's theories or because he applauded the foreigner's conviction that to discover the "Indies" would be to win new souls to Christianity.

But Deza's enthusiasm was counterbalanced by the frank disapproval of other committee members. Among those who opposed Columbus's theories was Dr.

Rodrigo Maldonado, a distinguished *letrado* of Isabella's court. Some years after Columbus's death, Maldonado recalled the skepticism with which he and other members of the committee initially listened to the mariner's *empresa* and "agreed that what the Admiral said could not possibly be true."[1]

The committee was, in fact, topheavy with theologians and *letrados* rather than astronomers and cosmographers, a fact that worked to Columbus's disadvantage. Although the names of most of those who served on the committee have not been preserved, they were—or so Columbus's son Fernando later claimed in his biography of his father—largely ignorant about navigation.

Like most educated men, Maldonado believed that the world was round. In fact, mathematicians and astronomers at the nearby University of Salamanca were still working out that theory. Foremost among them was the Jewish astronomer Abraham Ben Samuel Zacuto, who, eight years earlier, had completed the *Perpetual Almanac* containing mathematical tables that enabled navigators to calculate their latitude without depending on the sun's meridian.

The committee's arguments were thus not about the shape of the earth, but about Columbus's estimates of the size of the Atlantic Ocean. Talavera's examiners doubted the mariner's theory about a 5,000-mile ocean separating Europe and the fabled "Indies." According to their own calculations, it would take Columbus three years to sail to the Orient.

Columbus vainly insisted that the length of a latitudinal degree was only forty-five nautical miles. He alluded to Toscanelli's calculations, to Marco Polo's *Travels,* perhaps even to his own observations of "Orientals" who had appeared in boats off Galway. Yet, in order to protect himself, Columbus did not explain all of his supporting data. As Fernando Columbus later put it, his father did not "wish to reveal all the details of his plan, fearing lest it be stolen from him in Castile as it had been in Portugal."[2] After Columbus's departure from Portugal, or so wrote his son Fernando, King João used some of the navigator's information to support his own expedition to the Atlantic. By March 1487 King João had, in fact, sponsored a journey to the legendary Atlantic island of Antillia with the explorers Fernão Dulmo of Terceira and João Estreito of Funchal. Although the expedition failed, its attempt evidently made Columbus wary about fully disclosing his plans to anyone, including Talavera's committee. Not surprisingly, several committee members thus concluded that Columbus's proposed *empresa* was an impossibility.

Most of the men on Talavera's committee seem to have been steeped in that curious blend of naturalistic-theological theory embodied in the writings of St. Augustine. According to that fourth-century father of the Christian church, the only habitable zones on earth were Europe, Asia, and Africa. The ocean's equatorial zones, its "antipodes," were thought to be so hot that they consumed ships and men. Even Columbus's retort that the Portuguese had successfully explored the African coast south of the equator failed to convince the committee members. The vast Atlantic abyss, they contended, was one of God's mysteries, and thus unknowable. Some were "absolutely certain that one who left the hemisphere known to Ptolemy would be going downhill and so could not return; for that would be like sailing a ship to the top of a mountain: a thing that ships could not do even with the aid of the strongest wind." Finally "they all repeated the Spanish saying that is commonly used of any doubtful statement, 'St. Augustine doubts' . . ."[3]

While the committee members considered his case, Columbus, untrained in the collegial tradition of dialectic debate, "always remained silent on the most important matters."[4] Curiously though, he seemed arrogant, even contemptuous of his erudite examiners.

Such haughtiness did little to win Columbus favor with the committee. The navigator did not mean to seem self-important, but like the Caribbean blowfish he would later discover, Columbus would puff himself up with pride when he was rattled or threatened. Unfortunately, this posture served only to rankle Talavera, whose rigorous Christianity inevitably disapproved of the pride he saw in others.

Yet, after spending years in Portugal tinkering with his *empresa,* after being subjected to humiliation by King João's committee, after pitching his theory to Medina Sidonia and Medinaceli, and finally having achieved an audience with Isabella and Ferdinand, Columbus was convinced he had been "called" by the Almighty to a divine purpose. No amount of doubt or scorn from theological experts could shake him. Columbus burned with an "intuitive" hunch that is often called genius.

Despite many hours spent arguing in the halls of St. Stephen's, by the end of 1486 nothing was resolved. Neither Talavera's committee nor Columbus had been able to convince each other of the validity of their respective theories. Isabella was left in an awkward position; if the most learned and respected counselors in her kingdom could not assess the plausibility of Columbus's proposed expedition, how then, could the poorly educated queen?

Perhaps through Deza's encouragement, her own intuitive gleam, or the kindred spark she glimpsed in Columbus's eyes, Isabella did not give up on him. Instead, she urged the committee to study the matter further and placed Columbus on retainer. In May 1487 she ordered the royal treasury to release 3,000 maravedís to him. In August, October, and June of 1488 the queen saw to it that the same payments were awarded him again. The sum was not extravagant, merely commensurate with the wages paid to a capable seaman. Still, it was enough to keep body and soul together and to provide Columbus with a tantalizing incentive to remain under the Castilian flag a few months longer.

By the beginning of 1488, however, Columbus was clearly discouraged—so disheartened, in fact, that he wrote to King João of Portugal asking him to reconsider the *empresa.* But since the navigator had left Portugal with unpaid debts, he could return to the service of the Portuguese flag only if the king granted him a safe conduct from his creditors. On March 20, João wrote to "our particular friend," urging Columbus to return immediately to Portugal where his "industry and good talent" would be welcome. João further assured the mariner that ". . . during your coming, stay and return, you shall not be arrested, held up, accused, remanded or made to answer for any thing, whether civil or criminal, of any kind."[5]

João had good reasons for welcoming Columbus back to Portugal then. The summer after Dulmo and Estreito's unsuccessful 1487 voyage, the king had supported a second naval exploration headed by Bartholomew Dias to reach the southern tip of the African continent. More than six months had passed without a word from Dias. João had become discouraged and longed to launch other explorations to hitherto unknown waters.

Despite João's warm invitation, Columbus hesitated. Historians have developed many theories to account for the navigator's sudden change of heart. Perhaps it was because Columbus's mistress, Beatriz Enríquez de Harana, was pregnant; indeed, five months later, on August 15, 1488, she gave birth to the son, Fernando, who subsequently wrote his father's biography. Perhaps too the navigator felt obliged to wait until Talavera's committee rendered a final decision. During his stay in Castile Columbus had earned the friendship of many influential members of the Spanish court—not only Castilians, such as Quintanilla, Deza, Mendoza, Cabrera, and Beatriz de Bobadilla—but powerful Aragonese, such as Juan Cabrero, *camerero* (chamberlain) to Ferdinand, the *converso* general treasurer Gabriel Sánchez, and the *escribano de ración* (finance minister) Luís de Santángel. Those men and women, intrigued by Columbus's theories and knowing the monarchs' nascent interest in exploration, may well have persuaded him to stay on a few months longer.

Thus it was not until late 1488 when Columbus traveled to Lisbon, just in time, ironically, to witness Dias's triumphant arrival from the Cape of Good Hope. Columbus scribbled in his copy of *Imago Mundi*:

> Note that in this year '88 in the month of December arrived in Lisbon Bartholomaeus Didacus, captain of three caravels which the most serene king of Portugal had sent to try out the land in Guinea . . . He says that in this place he discovered by the astrolabe that he was 45' below the equator . . . and plotted it league by league on a marine chart in order to place it under the eyes of the said king. . . . I was present in all of this.[6]

With Dias's discovery of an African route to the East, King João no longer needed Columbus. Timing, as the navigator was learning through trial and error, was an essential ingredient of success, and timing was not yet on his side.

In early 1489 Columbus left Portugal and returned to Castile to await Talavera's verdict. In the navigator's absence Isabella and Ferdinand had not reissued grants for his support. Where he lived and how he survived are unknown, although most historians believe that he divided his time between at least two places—in Córdoba with his mistress Beatriz and their infant son and in the La Rabida monastery in Palos with his older son Diego. He may also have sold books and charts in Sevilla or depended on the generosity of his old sponsor, the Duke of Medinaceli, for support.

CHAPTER FORTY-THREE

International Alliances

T
he conquest of Málaga dealt a harsh blow to the faltering Granada
kingdom. With its major port destroyed and most of its coastline
taken, the Moorish kingdom was trapped within, cut off from African
reinforcements of food, men, and munitions. Internally, Granada was
even more fragile because of the conflict between its two kings. From
the throne room of the Alhambra, poised high above the city of
Granada, Boabdil sent obsequious congratulations to Isabella and Ferdinand for
their triumph at Málaga. Meanwhile, north of Granada, El Zagal gathered men and
stockpiled weapons to repulse future Castilian attacks.

Those contradictory responses so worried Isabella and Ferdinand that after
their triumphant entrance to Córdoba on September 21, 1487, they immediately
set about preparing for a new campaign. Since 1482 the monarchs had collected
money from every source under their authority—from the *Hermandad*, the royal
treasury, church tithes, and Jewish and Mudéjar citizens. Only one source of
income had yet to be tapped for the Holy War, the kingdom of Aragón.

Nearly three years had passed since Ferdinand had visited Aragón, having left
there in disgust in spring 1485 when the *Cortes* refused to vote money for a war
against France. The kingdom had languished under the king's absentee rule.
Brigands and criminals had overrun the land, and its divisive political factions had
failed to restore law and order. Aragonese citizens still lived unhappily under
French control in the occupied provinces of Cerdagne and Roussillon. Moreover,
Prince Juan was now ten; and it was appropriate for him to be sworn again by the
Cortes as the new heir of Aragón. For those reasons, the king and queen planned
to travel to Aragón in late 1487 with their children and the court.

The monarchs' stay in Zaragoza was brief and productive. By the end of 1487

Ferdinand had reestablished law and order in the Aragonese city in much the same way Isabella once did in Sevilla. Upon his arrival, the king had removed corrupt judges from the courts, appointed new ones, and reorganized the kingdom's judicial system. At his insistence the newly established Aragonese *Hermandad* was approved for another five years. The Zaragozan city council was reorganized and governed by a triumvirate of capable men. To help effect these reforms, the king relied heavily on two men—his eighteen-year-old illegitimate son, Alfonso, Archbishop of Zaragoza, who served as his lieutenant general, or deputy, and the *converso* Alfonso de la Cabelleria, vice chancellor of Aragón.

On January 4, 1488, the Aragonese *Cortes* had dutifully appeared at Zaragoza's *Casa de Deputación,* the meeting house for Aragón's Council of Estates. This time, in contrast to the stormy Aragonese *Cortes* of 1485, the representatives greeted Isabella and Ferdinand enthusiastically. In a solemn ceremony they raised their right hands and pledged homage to the frail blond prince who would someday become King of Aragón. Then, in tribute to Isabella and Ferdinand's victories against the Moors, the representatives voted the king and queen 125,000 libras, 5,000 of which was to be paid annually to support the Holy War.

Isabella, Ferdinand, and their court then traveled to Valencia, where, on March 20, that *Cortes* duly swore homage to Prince Juan. Whatever tranquility the monarchs initially enjoyed in that sunny Mediterranean city was soon shattered by the arrival of a Gascony aristocrat named Alain d'Albret, Lord of Labrit, who proposed a tantalizing offer to help Ferdinand regain Cerdagne and Roussillon. Labrit professed that while he had faithfully served the late French king Louis XI, he could no longer support his successor. Labrit's son Jean had married Catalina, the young Queen of the Navarre, and had become involved in a land dispute with the French. By 1488 those young Navarrese monarchs were so embittered that they joined forces with the Duke of Brittany for a rebellion against the French crown, then still held for Charles VIII by his sister Anne de Beaujeu as regent. Labrit now proposed that if Ferdinand would support the Duke of Brittany's rebellion with men and arms, the Navarrese queen and king would later help Ferdinand regain Cerdagne and Roussillon.

Although Ferdinand embraced the offer, Isabella was wary. She still believed, as she had in 1485, that all Castilian and Aragonese manpower should be reserved for the Granada war. The queen had not forgotten the bitterness of her struggle with Ferdinand over the French question three years earlier. Since then he had committed himself wholeheartedly to the Granada war, often at peril to his life. As King of Castile, he had ignored Aragón in favor of the Holy War and even relegated the government of his kingdom to deputies. If ever it was appropriate to sacrifice men and munitions to Ferdinand's claims for Cerdagne and Roussillon, this was the right time.

Out of love, gratitude, and probably guilt, Isabella thus conceded. Consequently, by early spring 1488 several thousand Spanish soldiers sailed north from ports in the Cantabrian Sea at a time when, ordinarily, they would have marched south from the Vizcaya and Guipúzcoa to Córdoba.

That same spring the Ottoman Turks were quietly preparing for the long-feared attack on Italy. On March 16 Bayezid II ordered an army of 100,000 men to march through Russia to the Hellespont where a fleet of galley ships waited to take them to Sicily. To the fiery Turkish sultan, the Sicilian peninsula, the "toe" of Italy's boot, was an ideal springboard from which to launch a series of invasions upon Italy, upon the rest of Western Europe, and even upon his erstwhile ally, Sultan Kait-Bey of Egypt.

To effect such plans, Bayezid had to proceed slowly, first by occupying the lesser islands of the Mediterranean as a base of operations. Thus, on May 16, a Turkish armada of fifty-five galleys set sail for the Aragonese-owned island of Malta, which lay only fifty-five miles south of Sicily. Ferdinand consequently sent fifty warships to Sicily and commanded that "the greatest attention" be paid to fortifying its coast.[1] Maritime security was promptly tightened around the islands of Goza and Malta. Ferdinand, who had already resumed friendly relations with the Egyptian sultan, now began sending him Sicilian wheat. Finally, he distracted the Ottoman Turks by dispatching part of his fleet to attack Moslem cities on the coast of Tripoli.

In the end the Turkish invasion miscarried. Pope Innocent was elated and the Italian states once again escaped.

During the spring of 1488, El Zagal determined to redeem himself as a hero to the citizens of Granada. That March he burst from Guadix and overran Castilian towns to the border near Jaén, killing Christian inhabitants, burning villages, and carrying off rich booty in a gleeful reversal of the Christian *tala*.

In retaliation, Ferdinand gathered a new army. But so many soldiers had been sent to the Mediterranean and France that he could amass only 14,000 infantry and 5,000 cavalry. With that militia Ferdinand marched south into the eastern Granada kingdom and in a series of bloodless victories took sixty small towns—among them Vera, Vélez el Rubio, and Vélez el Blanco. But when Ferdinand reached Almeria, the last important Moorish port on Spain's southeastern coast, Moslem forces overwhelmed the Castilians.

After an initial skirmish, it became clear that Ferdinand's army was too small for victory. Afraid to disclose his weakness, Ferdinand hastily retreated to the shores of the Guadalentin River and dismissed his army. With only a handful of attendants the Castilian king then marched west to the city of Caravaca de la Cruz at whose shrine he repented his earthly sins and prayed for victory over the Moors.

Isabella, meanwhile, had traveled to nearby Jaén with the children and her court. Politically as well as spiritually, the queen had no objections to Ferdinand's defensive actions against the Ottoman Turks. But privately she was still ambivalent to his struggle against the French. On July 28, 1488, her intuitions that the conflict should have been postponed until the end of the Granada war were confirmed. That day the Duke of Brittany's rebels were roundly defeated at St. Aubin du Cormier and 1,000 Castilian and Aragonese soldiers were captured or killed.

Other leaders in Western Europe sought alliances with Castile and Aragón against France. The most powerful of these was Prince Maximilian, heir to the German Hapsburg states and elected leader of the Holy Roman Empire, whose domains bordered France from the Danube River in Austria to the Low Countries.

In late December Maximilian dispatched ambassadors to Isabella and Ferdinand who, in an effort to avoid overland travel through France, had braved the Atlantic and landed at Spain's northwesternmost port of La Coruña. Upon their arrival Isabella promptly dispatched one of her treasurers to Burgos with animals, clothes, and other essentials to enable their safe arrival at the Castilian court's residence in Valladolid.

In 1477 Maximilian had married Mary, Duchess of Burgundy and daughter of Charles the Bold. But in 1482 the young woman had been killed in a horseback-riding accident, and since then Maximilian intended to recover her Burgundian domains from France. In preparation for that invasion, the Hapsburg widower had already allied himself with England. Now he hoped to strengthen that alliance by binding himself to Castile. To entice Isabella and Ferdinand, Maximilian's ambassadors promised to help them regain Cerdagne and Roussillon with the combined military might of Flanders, the Holy Roman Empire, and England. As an added incentive, the envoys proposed a marriage between the Princess Isabel and Maximilian's young son, Philip, the Archduke of Flanders.

For forty days the ambassadors remained at Valladolid where they were lavishly entertained with "jousts, tournaments and many celebrations" while Isabella and Ferdinand debated Maximilian's proposal.[2] The Castilian monarchs finally agreed with one proviso: They would offer no military aid until the conclusion of the Granada war. To seal the treaty they also agreed to a Spanish-Hapsburg marriage—not with the Princess Isabel, who by the treaty of Alcaçovas was to marry the Portuguese prince—but with their second daughter, Princess Juana.

Years later Isabella and Ferdinand would deeply regret this match. But in 1488 the king and queen, beset by conflicts to the north and south, could not foresee the troubles that lay ahead. At that time, promising a daughter to the Hapsburg heir seemed a small price to pay for assurances of a strong offensive against France.

The gossamer threads of chance that had hitherto connected Castile to England were fast being spun into a permanent knot that would last for thirty-five years. Although the two nations were rivals for Western Europe's maritime hauling business, they already conducted a lively trade, exchanging Castilian wine, wool, iron, and oil for English cloth. England, still smarting from the Hundred Years' War, retained an antipathy toward France. In 1488 Henry VII, blond, attractive, and insecure in his position as England's first Tudor king, feared that the duchy of Brittany would be subsumed by the French crown.

Early that year Henry thus proposed a pact with the Castilian monarchs. By its terms England and Castile would agree to protect each other from France and conduct a joint campaign to reclaim properties still held by that nation—namely Normandy and Aquitaine for England, Cerdagne and Roussillon for Spain. To seal the agreement Henry proposed that Isabella and Ferdinand's fifth child, the three-year-old Catherine, marry his two-year-old son Arthur when the youngsters came of age. Henry had other reasons to seek the match beyond the merely formulaic custom of sealing peace treaties, for the young Tudor king was still threatened by pretenders to the crown.

Knowing that, Isabella and Ferdinand demanded a high price for the betrothal.

In March 1488 they dispatched their ambassador Dr. Rodrigo González de Puebla to England to negotiate a treaty whose terms were so onerous that the betrothal was never formalized. But Henry remained intent upon the match and in early 1489 dispatched his own ambassadors to Castile.

Thus, on February 16, 1489, just as Isabella and Ferdinand were completing talks with Maximilian's ambassadors, Henry's emissaries, Dr. Thomas Savage and Dr. Richard Nafan, arrived in Laredo on the Basque coast. Nearly a month later the Englishmen appeared in Medina del Campo where Isabella and Ferdinand staged a reception calculated to display the full splendor and glory of their estate.

On the evening of March 14, Savage and Nafan were led by torchlight over the drawbridge of the castle of La Mota and into its interior where Isabella and Ferdinand received them under a golden canopy emblazoned with the arms of Castile and Aragón. The king was dressed in a gold cloth gown trimmed with sable and Isabella, in a gold cloth gown, literally glittered with jewels. The neckline of the queen's dress was wreathed with a black velvet collar slashed through with gold cloth and finger-length golden ornaments studded with precious gems—"a thing so rich no man ever has seen the equal."[3] Ribbons, set with large diamonds and other gemstones, also hung from her neckline. To complete her splendor Isabella wore a golden necklace of enameled roses in whose center gleamed a large jewel. A red satin cloak lined with ermine hung from her left shoulder and on her head she wore a simple, gold net, a *coifa de pleisance*.

During the ensuing jousts and bullfights held to honor the ambassadors, the wealth of the Castilian court was again displayed. At one memorable event Ferdinand appeared in a golden gown lined in ermine and a large collar "in the German mode." That day Isabella wore a velvet cape over another spun-gold dress decorated with large pearls and gems. Her hair was decorated with a large jeweled setting—two huge pink rubies bordered by an enormous pearl at either side.

A few days later the ambassadors finally had an opportunity to meet the little red-haired Catherine who was to be England's next queen. The three-year-old child, who would wed Prince Arthur and later become the first wife of Henry VIII, appeared at a *cañas* tournament in a tiny dress of brocade and jewels with her young sisters, Juana and María. As was traditional in reed-spear tournaments, Ferdinand arrived in a black cloth gown with open sleeves, but his clothes had a special flair—a left sleeve was bordered with jewels and pearls. Isabella wore one of her favorite color combinations that day—a green satin dress edged in gems and set off by crimson velvet sleeves, decorated with golden letters spelling *Tanto Monta*.

For all of Isabella's piety, chastity, and temperance, she clearly enjoyed splendid clothes and jewels. On a subsequent occasion, her confessor Talavera would chastise Isabella on the cost of her outfits and the personal vanity it implied, which, he fervently maintained, was sure "to offend God."[4] An irate Isabella retorted that she only dressed in such splendor for state occasions and not for ordinary days. Her magnificent clothes, Isabella maintained, and those of the royal family were designed for political rather than personal purposes: to convey the impression that Castile was strong and wealthy, foremost among the nations of Western Europe and hence, not easily intimidated.

This message was not lost on Henry VII's ambassadors. Two weeks after their arrival, the Englishmen agreed to the terms for the Castilian marriage. By their consent Catherine's dowry was to be less than Henry had originally hoped for, now 200,000 scudos or nearly 40,000 pounds. The ambassadors further agreed that if the prince died after Arthur and Catherine were wed, Catherine would inherit one-third of all the revenues from Chester, Cornwall, and Wales—an amount that would become appreciably higher if she were widowed after becoming queen.

Four days later Savage and Nafan left for England, still mesmerized by the splendor they had seen at Isabella and Ferdinand's court. To those Englishmen from the still-poor island kingdom across the Channel, the magnificence they witnessed at Medina del Campo defied description, despite their best efforts to share it with the delighted King Henry VII.

CHAPTER FORTY-FOUR

Brokered Jewels of Baeza

T he successful negotiations at Medina del Campo were a brief ceremonial interlude in an otherwise embattled year. After meeting with the English ambassadors, Isabella and Ferdinand headed south toward Córdoba to open the 1489 campaign. High winds and heavy rains buffeted the itinerant court with its unwieldy *fardage* as it crossed the Sierra Morenas, making their entrance to Andalusia unusually difficult.

Bad weather had, in fact, plagued Castile since the first weeks of 1489. That spring Andalusia was shrouded in relentless showers that flooded the Guadalquivir and caused Sevillians to abandon their homes for higher ground. The foul weather dashed caravels upon the rocks, destroying men and cargo. Newly sown fields of wheat, oats, and barley were transformed into muddy quagmires. Exacerbating these troubles were new outbreaks of the pestilence in towns across Castile, among them Sevilla, Toledo, and Córdoba.

Undaunted, Isabella and Ferdinand proceeded with their plans. Initially they reconnoitered in Córdoba where they collected an army of 40,000 infantry and 13,000 cavalry, but fearing the plague, they prepared to leave for Jaén. Before doing so they met with Columbus, who, having just returned from Portugal, was eager to try his suit with the Castilian monarchs again. Once again the navigator's request was ill-timed: With Isabella and Ferdinand on the eve of a new campaign, his Atlantic expedition was hardly a priority. Nevertheless, the monarchs did what they could to show Columbus their goodwill. On May 12 they provided him with an open letter informing all Castilian innkeepers and town officials to provide Columbus with free room and board.

A week later the king and queen traveled sixty-two miles south to Jaén, arriving in that castle-crowned city in the foothills of the Sierra de Jabalcuz Mountains on May 20. Jaén, or *Geen,* as it is called in Arabic, means "caravan route," and was named for its location between the plains of La Mancha and Andalusia near a mountainous region still held by El Zagal.

That region would be Ferdinand's next object of attack. Specifically, he planned to lay siege to Baeza, a key city in the eastern half of the Moorish kingdom held by El Zagal. Wresting the city from the Moors would be a formidable task for the citizens of Baeza were reputed to be "the most ferocious and warlike of all the Granadians."[1]

Isabella, her children, and the royal court were soon settled in the Mudéjar palace of El Condestable at Jaén. The city was a good place to settle with the *Infantes,* rich with Moorish remnants from the past, stately mansions, and *Reconquista* cloisters.

That spring Isabella had turned thirty-eight, an age when she increasingly measured the passage of time by the growth of her children. When she was pregnant with her fourth child in 1482, Pulgar had written the queen that "If you have two or three more daughters, within [the next] twenty years your children and oldest grandchildren will rule all of Christendom."[2] The queen had not forgotten her secretary's prediction.

But to raise competent daughters meant they had to be educated wisely—not merely to read and write but to be versed in Latin, the international language of court diplomacy, which Isabella was still struggling to master. Although poorly educated herself, the queen had a keen appreciation for higher learning. After the 1475 introduction of the first printing press in Valencia, Isabella had encouraged a domestic publishing industry. By the end of the fifteenth century at least twenty-five Castilian towns would have printing presses of their own.

Through the constant flow of ambassadors to the Castilian and Aragonese courts from Italy, Flanders, and the German states, the queen had become at least superficially apprised of the new humanism then sweeping over Western Europe. She may well have heard of the remarkable paintings of Sandro Botticelli, whose *Primavera* had been painted for the Medicis of Castello in 1478, of Hans Memling's triptych the *Adoration of the Magi* created the following year for the Hospital of Saint John in Bruges, of the 1481 discovery of an ancient Roman statue of Apollo found in Cardinal Giuliano della Rovere's vineyard at Grottof-errata and subsequently displayed as the Apollo Belvedere. Papal envoys may also have mentioned Pope Sixtus IV's 1481 assemblage of Italy's best painters—Botticelli, Ghirlandaio, Cosimo, and Rosselli—who decorated the Sistine Chapel. That a new spirit existed, one celebrating the uniqueness of mankind and of the human individual, was undeniable. Its influence had permeated the arts, letters, and culture, finding expression as far south as Italy where, in 1483, Leonardo da Vinci painted the *Virgin of the Rocks,* and Matteo Maria Boiardo published the first two volumes of his epic chivalric poem *Orlando Innamorato,* to the northern reaches of England with William Caxton's 1485 publication of Sir Thomas Malory's *Morte d'Arthur.*

In such an atmosphere Isabella resolved that her daughters too would become as well educated as any prince in Western Europe. To that end she had engaged a Latin master, Fray Pedro de Ampudia, for Princess Isabel in 1484; that same year she hired another Latin expert named Fray Andrés de Miranda, who became tutor for Princess Juana in 1486. During that same period the queen also hired two Italian humanists, Antonio and Alessandro Geraldino, to teach the *Infantas* the classics.

In time Isabella's daughters, especially Juana and Catherine, would become so fluent in Latin that they astonished foreign ambassadors. Years later Catherine would impress Luis Vives and the Dutch scholar-philosopher Desiderius Erasmus with her intellectual accomplishments, then practically unknown to women outside of Spain.

Gradually, too, Isabella's attention to her youngsters' education would draw a new breed of scholars and humanists to the court and beyond it into the universities of Castile. Already, under the patronage of the erudite Mendoza, Count of Tendilla, the Italian humanist Pietro Martire d'Anghiera had arrived to participate in the Granada campaign of 1489. In time he would become Prince Juan's tutor. Other learned men appeared as well, scholars such as the Sicilian humanist Lucio Marineo Siculo, a professor of oratory and poetry at the University of Salamanca, and Antonio de Nebriga, who returned to Castile from Bologna to teach Latin at the universities of Salamanca and Alcalá. At Salamanca in 1489 the Portuguese classical scholar Arías Barbosa taught Greek and rhetoric—long before similar chairs in the "new learning" were established at Oxford or Paris.

Learned women appeared at Isabella's court as well, savants such as Juana de Contreras and the Latin scholar Doña Lucia de Medrano, who lectured on the classics at Salamanca. During this same fertile period in Castile new colleges were founded whose curriculum included civil law as well as theology, among them Cardinal Mendoza's Colegio de Santa Cruz established in Valladolid in 1484. New universities appeared as well—in Ávila in 1482, Barcelona in 1491, Valencia in 1500, and Santiago in 1504. These institutions, while somewhat muted in their emphasis on humanism compared to the full-blown expressions of the Italian Renaissance, would, in time, give rise to a flowering of Spanish arts, letters, and the humanities.

In the pull of learned men and women to Isabella's court, and the new learning that the queen sought for herself and her children, an erudite new society was gradually emerging. In such an atmosphere, it seemed logical that innovative thinkers such as Columbus would be regarded favorably. In 1489 the new humanism slowly pushing through Castilian soil was still a delicate seedling, quietly nursed in palace drawing rooms by royal tutors and the university dons attached to Isabella's court.

But imperialistic conquests still took first precedence. In the last half of 1489 the queen's interest in her children's education was subsumed by the crushing duties of the Holy War.

From Jaén, Ferdinand and his army had proceeded north, first storming the nearby village of Cujar, then proceeding into the mountainous tableland of Baeza's *hoya*, or broad, fertile valley. On one side the town was protected by jagged mountainous cliffs and a castle and on the other by battlemented walls. There two tributaries of the Guadalquivir river nourished lush fields of vegetables and fruits, culminating in a luxuriant, but deceptively ravined woods that shielded the town. Behind

Baeza's garden district, or *huerta*, were wealthy suburbs, which, like the town itself, were fortified against invasion.

By the time Ferdinand arrived on June 1, 10,000 Moorish soldiers had already been garrisoned in Baeza by El Zagal to defend the town from both his enemies—his nephew Boabdil and the Castilians. That Moorish king, however, had remained in Guadix and entrusted Baeza to his brother-in-law, Prince Cidi Yahye Almazar Aben Zelim, *alcayde* of Almeria, who arrived with thousands of his own reinforcements. In anticipation of a summer siege, Baeza's citizens had stockpiled enough food and provisions to last fifteen months. When they heard about Ferdinand's advance, they promptly stripped Baeza's fields of its half-ripe spring crops.

It soon became obvious that Baeza's *huerta* had to be conquered before Ferdinand could take the city. Consequently, he ordered his soldiers to advance, but the thickets of underbrush and ravines made the task onerous. Meanwhile, Cidi Yahye's men, poised for battle on the far side of the *huerta,* attacked Ferdinand's knights, who had been forced to dismount. For twelve hours the Castilian *caballeros* and Moorish knights fought in a hand-to-hand battle. Unnerved, the king's advisors advocated giving up the siege altogether. First, they feared that the Castilian encampment would be attacked by El Zagal's soldiers from Guadix, twenty miles south. They also worried that the army would be subjected to the flash floods that came with the autumn rains.

However, Ferdinand, who had known nothing more than small victories and retreats for a year, was ambivalent. On one hand, he wanted to conquer Baeza for its strategic significance as one of the few Moorish cities still under El Zagal's control. On the other, he was loath to shed Castilian blood unnecessarily. Finally, he wrote Isabella. The queen wrote back promptly but did not comment directly on the wisdom of continuing the siege.

Instead, she appealed to Ferdinand's highest instincts. Although she believed that God was on the Castilians' side, victory would only be assured if Ferdinand's men rallied to the cause. As queen, Isabella was prepared to assist the army by providing it with provisions and artillery. At that moment she was already dispatching 14,000 mules and ox carts daily from Jaén with bread, meat, and wine at a monthly expense of 19 million maravedís, and she had every intention of fulfilling that obligation as long as Ferdinand required it.

The queen's words filled Ferdinand with new conviction. But to win Baeza it was first necessary to remove its troublesome *huerta*. Consequently, he divided the army and placed the men on both sides of Baeza. Then he ordered Isabella's 4,000 sappers to destroy the *huerta* that lay between them.

For seven weeks the sappers chopped trees, cleared underbrush, and razed vegetation. They then dug a deep trench between the two camps and filled it with mountain water to blockade Baeza on the south. To defend the new Castilian lines, they built mud or clay towers on the far side of the trench. Afterward they dug another trench and connected it to two stone walls on Baeza's north side, essentially surrounding the city.

El Zagal made one halfhearted attack on the Christians, but after being repulsed he never attacked again, fearing that in his absence Boabdil's soldiers would seize Guadix.

In Granada, the situation was equally static. During the summer of 1489, Boabdil languished in the Alhambra while the Granadian citizens grumbled about his cowardice. Gradually, their complaints changed into demands for his abdication. But the young Moor was determined to retain his grip on Granada. With uncharacteristic resolve Boabdil ordered his soldiers to suppress the rebellion and execute its instigators. To emphasize his authority, Boabdil then had the heads of the rebellion's leaders displayed on the ramparts of the Alhambra. While the civilian population was subdued for a time, the Granadians waited sullenly for another opportunity to rise against their cowardly master.

On a hot day in July 1489 two brown-robed Franciscan monks rode mules into Ferdinand's camp. The first, Antonio Millan, was the portly prior of the Church of the Holy Sepulcher in Jerusalem; the second was an unnamed Castilian who had emigrated to Palestine many years ago. The monks had been sent by the Sultan of Egypt, Kait-Bey, with a letter for Isabella and Ferdinand. As in a similar communication to the pope, the sultan chastised the Castilian king and queen for persecuting the Moors and contrasted their behavior to his own respectful treatment of the Christians in Palestine. If, the sultan now threatened, Isabella and Ferdinand did not desist from waging war on the Moors, he would "be forced to treat the Christians in his domains like the King and Queen of Castile treated the Moors."[3]

The infuriated monarchs soon drafted a reply. When they first assumed the throne, they wrote, they had allowed the Moors to practice their religion peacefully. But by 1482 they had grown impatient with the Moors who refused to acknowledge them as sovereigns and constantly invaded their borders. In earlier eras when the Moors treated the Christians peacefully, the Castilian kings had responded generously allowing them to remain with "their persons in liberty . . . free to possess their property and . . . allowed to live within their own law without outside pressures."[4] In the future, after the Moors were conquered and lived as vassals of the Castilian crown, they would, Isabella and Ferdinand assured the sultan, be allowed to practice Mohammedanism freely.

Despite their stern letter, Isabella and Ferdinand were too worried about the sultan's threats against the Christians of Jerusalem to let his messengers return to Egypt empty-handed. The pious queen "in all modesty and lowliness of spirit" thus awarded the Franciscans an annual stipend of a thousand ducats to maintain their monastery.[5] She also gave them a finely embroidered veil to place in the church of the Holy Sepulcher. To foil any repercussions from the Granadian court, the queen dispatched the diplomatic and erudite humanist Pietro Martire to inform Boabdil of their response to the sultan.

Summer turned brutally hot in the Baeza valley, but the Moors continued to live quietly within their walls. The Castilians grew more anxious every day, exhausted from the relentless heat and the unchanging quality of the siege. The only break from the monotony was occasional skirmishes between Castilians and Moors, which drew blood, wasted ammunition, and decided nothing.

Inside Baeza, *alfaquis* comforted the citizens with the promise of autumn rains that filled the riverbeds with fast-running torrents and created flash floods. That dramatic transformation, Baeza's leaders predicted, would uproot the Castilian army and force them to a new site. Moreover, the anticipated deluge would destroy the road between Jaén and Baeza and hence cut off Christian supplies.

In preparation for the bad weather, Ferdinand ordered his men to build permanent huts in place of their canvas tents. Within four days a city of thatched and tiled-roofed clay huts had arisen in the Christian camp.

No amount of foresight could, however, prevent the return of the region's dreaded autumn weather. Toward the end of September two "horrible hurricanes" whiplashed Baeza, provoking the enemy into "great cheer for they were sure it would destroy everything."[6] Before long floodwaters cascaded over the mountains and into the valley that surrounded the Castilian camp, devastating the newly built huts. The rains continued, creating mudslides, dislodging boulders, and destroying the roads between Jaén and Baeza. As the *alfaquis* had predicted, Isabella's 14,000 supply-laden mules were unable to pass into Baeza.

The queen, however, had "worked ceaselessly" to hire auxiliary sappers. As soon as the skies cleared, she dispatched 6,000 more to the mountains between Jaén and Baeza to build new bridges, clear the boulders, and hack out two new mule paths. Upon their completion, Isabella sent Ferdinand fresh supplies and new soldiers. But those efforts had cost more than the funds available in the Castilian treasury. Aragón's contribution had already been spent, as had the donations from the church for the original 1489 campaign. In desperation, Isabella thus asked the *grandees* and *ricos hombres* of Castile for extra contributions. She also petitioned the Jews who, eager to retain their dwindling favor, made generous contributions and loans. Still, the net value of these funds fell short of the enormous debts incurred by Isabella's posthurricane rescue of the Castilian army.

There was only one other solution: Isabella would have to pawn her jewels, not only the personal gems she wore so proudly at Medina del Campo in February 1489 but also the *collar de balajes y una rica corona,* the crown jewels and ruby necklace that Ferdinand had given her at the time of their marriage.

Her one vanity had to be sacrificed to the greater glory of the Holy War.

With a fresh influx of Isabella's supplies, conditions improved dramatically at Baeza. Spiritually, however, the soldiers were at their lowest ebb since the siege began: weary of war, racked with illnesses, and discouraged by what they perceived as an impossible task. No amount of food, warm clothes, or fresh munitions, the *grandees* and *caballeros* insisted, would improve the soldiers' emotional state as much as Isabella's appearance in the camp. Finally the queen, "moved by the requests of the King as well as the petitions . . . of the *grandees* and *caballeros,*" entrusted Prince Juan and his younger sisters to attendants at nearby Ubeda, and began the thirty-mile trek to Baeza.[7]

Moorish spies immediately relayed news of the queen's arrival to the citizens of Baeza, who "were astounded by her approach in winter."[8] The morning of November 7, the Moors climbed atop their red-clay roofs and hung over the city's battlemented walls to gaze at the royal entourage threading its way along the newly reconstructed mountain road.

To some observers, Isabella's arrival seemed like the approach of the Virgin Mary herself. "She came surrounded by a choir of nymphs," Martire wrote, "as if to celebrate the nuptials of her child; and her presence seemed at once to gladden and reanimate our spirits, exhausted by our lengthy duties, the difficult watches, the heat and cold and hunger."[9]

The Moors regarded Isabella with similar awe. Ever since her arrival in Moclín two years earlier, the queen's reputation had grown. To the Moslems, steeped in superstition and demoralized by eight years of Christian invasions, the queen was a harbinger of certain defeat. Now, after watching Isabella's 4,000 sappers cut new roads through the mountains, they regarded the queen with even more trepidation. Three days after Isabella's arrival, Baeza's *caudillo,* or leader, agreed to a surrender. The queen's presence had so thoroughly intimidated the Moslems that they saw no other option.

In Guadix, El Zagal accepted Baeza's surrender calmly. Although he praised Cidi Yahye's valiant efforts to defend the city for five months, the Moslem king conceded there was little he could do to aid Baeza. Instead, he urged his royal relative to obtain the best terms of surrender possible.

This time, Ferdinand's terms were considerably more lenient than they had been in Málaga. He permitted the Moorish mercenaries to leave the city freely. Then he allowed the citizens a choice: either leave Baeza with their worldly goods and live elsewhere in Castile or remain in its suburbs as vassals of the crown. Should the Moors choose the latter, their religious habits, customs, and life-style would be respected.

The king and queen's merciful treatment of the Baezans has intrigued historians for centuries. Although the siege lasted longer than the struggle at Málaga, it was not nearly as bitter; nor was the surrender as difficult. Isabella and Ferdinand also may have been intimidated by the Egyptian sultan's threats. In addition, their long-term goals for the Granadian kingdom had almost certainly influenced their decision, for by 1489 they already envisioned themselves leaders of a Moslem nation. In anticipation of that conquest, they recognized the impossibility of instantly converting the Moors to Christianity; such an effort would almost certainly provoke a rebellion. To mollify the conquered, it was thus better to allow the Moors to retain their customs—at least temporarily.

On December 4 the surrender of Baeza became official. That day the king, queen, and members of their court entered the city, bells were rung from the newly consecrated churches and Sixtus's cross was displayed upon its highest tower. Meanwhile, Isabella and Ferdinand had treated El Zagal's deputy, Cidi Yahye, so kindly and regaled him with so many presents—robes, horses, gold—that he agreed to become their vassal.

In that capacity Yahye now visited El Zagal at Guadix to persuade him to an unconditional surrender of all his Moorish holdings. There was, he explained, little point in prolonging the war, for the Castilians had won virtually every major city in the Moorish kingdom. Moreover, at his birth Boabdil's horoscope had predicted the inevitable fall of Granada.

El Zagal listened quietly and sat for a time in silence. "What Allah wills, he brings to pass in his own way. Had he not decreed the fall of Granada, this good sword might have saved it; but his will be done!" he finally concluded.[10] With those words, the unhappy monarch thus surrendered the towns of Almeria, Guadix, and the rest of Granada's eastern kingdom.

With characteristic efficiency, Isabella and Ferdinand hastened to formalize El Zagal's surrender. Thus on December 17, Ferdinand ordered his army to march through the snow-covered passes of the María mountains toward Almeria. Stinging winds, subzero temperatures, and snowstorms swirled over the mountains, causing many soldiers to suffer frostbite and others to lose their way. Finally, on December 22, the exhausted army staggered onto the warmer coastal plains of the Mediterranean at the port of Almeria where Isabella and Ferdinand were to meet with El Zagal.

The next day Ferdinand and a small entourage rode to a designated place on the plain of Tabernas to meet the elder Moorish king. After years of bitter enmity the dignified, aging El Zagal, dressed in a regal "peace" outfit consisting of a black silken mantle and camelskin jerkin, came face to face with Ferdinand. "I almost felt sorry for him," Martire would subsequently write. "It is true that he was an infidel and a barbarian but a king, nevertheless, and foremost in military virtues."[11]

At Ferdinand's approach, El Zagal dismounted and attempted to kiss the Castilian king's hand. But Ferdinand leapt from his saddle to embrace the Moorish king and insisted he mount his horse again and ride by his side as befit the sovereign's station. Nevertheless, El Zagal was determined to show humility. "O victorious King!" he exclaimed. "Though I have committed unforgivable acts against you, your kindness has given me a hope of salvation which I had not anticipated. I wanted to defend the land of the Moors from your great power . . . But, as it has been the will of God to deliver you with prosperity from the dangers of the siege at Baeza . . . I have decided to become your vassal."[12]

Ferdinand, deeply moved by El Zagal's supplications, assured the Moor that his life was secure and his freedom preserved. Then he made El Zagal a vassal of the Castilian crown and pronounced him "king" of the city of Andaraz, the valley of Alhaurin, and the salt pits of Maleha.

With the surrender of *Almeria dorado,* or golden Almeria, as the early-twentieth-century Spanish poet Antonio Machado once called it, the eastern kingdom of Granada had fallen. Every "jewel" in the Moorish diadem had been plucked but one—Granada, the proud city of the Alhambra, the traditional seat of the Moorish kings. For Baeza Isabella had pawned her own gems. Now Granada, the most precious diamond of the pagan kingdom, glittered just out of reach, held in the soft hands of Boabdil.

CHAPTER FORTY-FIVE

A Bittersweet Year

With El Zagal's surrender, the Castilian monarchs expected Boabdil to release Granada. By the terms of his 1487 pledge the Moor had promised to cede the city once El Zagal had been conquered: In exchange Isabella and Ferdinand had agreed to give him Baeza, Guadix, and several other towns. But when the Count of Tendilla arrived in Granada to effect the surrender, Boabdil balked, claiming he could not yet cede the city because of citizen resistance. Granada was filled, he said, with "such a division in votes and . . . goals that it was not possible to urge them [the citizens] to consent to what had been promised."[1]

Boabdil's words contained at least one grain of truth. By late 1489 the population of the city had swollen to 200,000—three or four times its original size. Most of the newcomers were Moors whom Ferdinand had allowed to migrate from conquered towns such as Alhama, Loja, and Vélez Málaga. Now, having settled in Granada and having lived through the humiliation of defeat once at Ferdinand's hand, those Moslems were determined to defend the city with their lives.

In the two years since his pledge, Boabdil had resolved to maintain his grip on the city, and the citizens' new resistance now gave him a perfect excuse. But to maintain the monarchs' goodwill he wrote Isabella and Ferdinand on January 22, 1490, assuring them of Granada's eventual surrender and requesting that they "have faith in everything we have said regarding our position."[2] Shortly thereafter, the Granadian Moors burst forth from the city gates and seized the nearby Christian fortress of Padul. By winter's end, Boabdil's soldiers took Alhendin and several other towns. In addition, they fomented a rebellion against the Castilians in Guadix.

Incensed by Boabdil's repeated treachery, Isabella and Ferdinand vowed to seek revenge. Two years had passed since Ferdinand had conducted a *tala* near Granada—two years in which he had allowed the Moorish countryside to regenerate in keeping with his truce with Boabdil. But in May 1490, with that treaty broken, the king and 5,000 soldiers swept through the fertile *vega,* burning crops and destroying orchards in a blackened path that led to the very gates of Granada.

A broad band of charred acreage surrounded the city as far as the eye could see. The ruined land would take months, even years to produce food again. Moreover, with the old ports of the Granada kingdom blocked, the Moors were deprived of all hopes of obtaining food and supplies from Africa. Ferdinand and Isabella anticipated that it would be only a matter of time before the Granadians would be forced to surrender.

That same spring Prince Juan accompanied his father on the battlefield for the first time. On June 30 the prince would be twelve, an age when many aristocratic boys were knighted. In anticipation of that event, Juan and several of his companions thus accompanied Ferdinand and the Castilian army on the Granadian *tala.*

Afterward the prince prepared for the knighthood ceremony. In accordance with tradition, Juan fasted the day before the ceremony and offered prayers over his armor for knightly courage. The next morning, on a plain within sight of the walls of Granada, the Castilian nobility assembled in full battle regalia as the armored prince, flanked by his sponsors, the Duke of Medina Sidonia and the Marquis of Cádiz, walked solemnly toward his father. The youth knelt and raised his right hand to swear allegiance to God and the King of Castile and Aragón. Then Ferdinand touched his sword on the shoulders of his kneeling son and dubbed Juan a knight.

With the completion of that *rite de passage,* the prince was recognized as a fledgling warrior, old enough to engage in military conflicts in defense of the kingdoms of Castile and Aragón. With time and more experience in war, Ferdinand would mold the prince into a brave commander, much as his father King Juan had once trained him. There was, however, one major difference: Juan was already heir to vast domains—Castile, León, Aragón, Sicily. If events went as Ferdinand and Isabella anticipated, he would also inherit the entire Granadian kingdom.

But if, that spring, Ferdinand was to gain a fellow warrior, Isabella was preparing to lose a daughter to marriage. The terms of the 1480 treaty of Alcaçovas had provided that at maturity Princess Isabel would marry Afonso, João's son and the Portuguese heir.

For years this marriage had been uncertain, largely because relations between Castile and Portugal had remained tense. First, there were recurrent rumors that the Castilians had supported an aristocratic conspiracy against King João. Secondly, there were lingering problems with La Beltraneja. In June 1487, after she made several excursions from the monastery at Coimbra to the Portuguese court, Isabella and Ferdinand persuaded Pope Innocent VIII to issue a bull ordering her to permanent confinement within the cloister. No one dared disobey the bull, least of all King João and his prelates, because failure to comply carried the threat of excommunication. By late 1487 relations between Portugal and Spain had improved dramatically and even blossomed into a friendship.

Thus it was that in April 1490, just before he left for the *tala,* Ferdinand and Isabella greeted the Portuguese ambassadors warmly in Sevilla. On Easter Sunday, April 18, Cardinal Mendoza then presided over a betrothal ceremony in the Sevillian cathedral with Princess Isabel and the Portuguese prince's proxy, Fernão de Silveira. In honor of the bride's new status, she was now known as the Princess of Portugal.

This was the first of Isabella and Ferdinand's children to be wed and the first Castilian alliance to be sealed by a marriage since their own wedding twenty-one years earlier. To celebrate the union that was to "bring peace and other good fortune" to Castile and Portugal, Sevilla was festooned with flowers and silken banners.[3] Jousts and tournaments were held on the listing field by the Guadalquivir and silken canopies, embroidered with emblems of Castilian heraldry, were draped over the arena to block the hot Andalusian sun. Before long the "flower"of Castilian chivalry appeared in their finery, eager to pit themselves against their fellow cavaliers and to demonstrate the military skills that had enabled them to subdue the Moors. The ensuing display of wealth defied description.

From the far corners of Castile, Aragón, Valencia, Sicily, even from islands owned by the king and queen, dozens of cavaliers arrived to join the lists. Among the more familiar contenders were the Dukes of Medina Sidonia and Cádiz, Villena, Beltrán de la Cueva and the king, the last of whom "broke many lances," to the roaring approval of the crowds. Inevitably, though, the center of attraction was the beautiful bride-to-be Princess Isabel, dressed in brocades and glittering with jewels, who sat quietly at the sidelines surrounded by seventy ladies-in-waiting and one hundred pages.

The celebrations lasted for fifteen days and nights. At dark, eight or nine torchbearers led the richly dressed women of the royal court on mules through Sevilla's twisting streets to the dances, concerts, and banquets held in honor of the royal betrothal.

It was said that Isabella was very "pleased" by her daughter's marriage because of its political implications. But the queen had always been very close to her oldest child. The Portuguese courts at Evora and Lisbon were at least five or six days' ride from Castile, which meant the queen and princess would be separated for months, perhaps years at a time. Marriage, as Isabella knew from her own experience, was not always easy and might well be more difficult for a bride living among strangers in a foreign land. Nevertheless, the queen had long anticipated this marriage and thus dedicated herself to preparations for the wedding.

There was much to be done—hundreds of dresses, headdresses, mantles, and hats to be ordered for the princess and the nine female attendants who would escort her to Portugal. No expense was spared. Despite the incessant drain of funds for the Holy War, Isabella and Ferdinand wanted to wed their daughter with magnificence so as to "show the generosity of their souls and the wealth of their kingdoms" to the Portuguese court.[4]

Consequently, the princess was outfitted with an extensive trousseau. In addition to dozens of silk, velvet, and brocade gowns, Isabella ordered gold and silk threaded tapestries, fifty linen chemises, twenty brocade coats, and six other silk robes "edged with pearls and encrusted with gold."[5] Perfumers, glovers, and shoemakers were busy for months. Carpenters built beds and other household items for the members of the princess's court. The cost of the entire trousseau amounted to 5.3 million maravedís.

Even that sum paled when compared to the princess's dowry: Beyond the "customary sum" given in gold coins for an *Infanta*, the Portuguese were to receive 500 gold marks, 1,000 silver marks, and "four gold collars with many pearls and precious stones and other chains and gems of great cost the value of which was estimated at 100,000 florins."[6]

By November all was in readiness. From Portugal, King João and his son Prince Alfonso signaled the Castilian court that the royal palace at Evora had been prepared for the nuptials. On November 11 the blond bride kissed her mother farewell. Then, in a grand procession heralded by trumpets, horns, and sackbuts, festooned with flowers and swathed in purple and white banners, the future Portuguese queen left Córdoba. She was escorted by the Cardinal Mendoza, the Count of Benavente, and dozens of other *grandees* and female attendants, all of whom were to witness the wedding. Behind the royal cortege trailed 1,500 mules and oxen hitched to carts that carried the princess's possessions to her new home across the border.

As was then the custom of kings and queens when a royal daughter wed, Ferdinand and Isabella stayed behind. Whether monarch or commoner, they suffered that same bittersweet emotion that parents have always felt when their children come of age—a surge of joy at the miracle, a prayer for their well-being, and a sudden emptiness at their unaccustomed absence.

The vacuum left by Princess Isabella's departure was quickly filled by a series of new concerns. During the fall of 1489 Talavera's committee seems to have rendered a decision about Columbus. After nearly four years of deliberation they "condemned the enterprise as vain and impossible."[7] The navigator's proposed Atlantic expedition, the committee reported, "did not conform with the dignity of such great princes to support a project resting on such weak foundations."[8]

Among their reasons, the committee cited the length of the journey, the difficulty, if not impossibility, of navigating the "Western Oceans," and the assumption that even if Columbus could sail west to arrive in the East, he could probably not sail back the other way. Furthermore, the committee still believed that human beings could only survive on three-fifths of the world's "zones" and that if they were able to exist elsewhere they would already have discovered those lands.

Yet Isabella and Ferdinand still did not reject Columbus outright. Instead, they remained "undecided" because of their preoccupation with the Granada war. They thus informed the navigator that he could apply to them again when the surrender was complete.

For the next six months Columbus, "finding their Highnesses still undecided, resolved to bring his project to the attention of the Duke of Medina Sidonia."[9] But by the summer of 1491, the future navigator was so discouraged and so weary of waiting for the end of the Granada war that he wrote to the French king. Then, in anticipation of traveling to France, Columbus returned to the monastery of La Rabida in Palos to fetch his son Diego.

Columbus was determined to find a king or noble to sponsor the journey. If the French king should prove unreceptive, he intended to "set out immediately for England" to find his brother who had journeyed there to petition Henry VII on his behalf.[10]

CHAPTER FORTY-SIX

El Niño de la Guardia

Under Torquemada's ubiquitous gaze, new waves of the Inquisition were sweeping over the Castilian towns in the late 1480s with a virulence that was rapidly bringing anti-Semitism to a head. In 1488 two booklets appeared that were designed to intensify anti-Jewish and anti-*converso* sentiment. Both were dedicated to Torquemada and contained an introduction written by a Segovian inquisitor named Fray Fernando de Santo Domingo. The first was an instructional guide for inquisitors urging them to prosecute without mercy *conversos* who had "relapsed" into Judaism; the second pamphlet described the *alborayco,* or Jew forcibly converted to Christianity, as an individual who had dedicated his life to robbing "true Christians" of their money and property.

In the ensuing paranoia, few Jews dared to protest. To complain publicly was a dangerous act, one that could be cited as proof of Jewish hostility and used to feed the flames of a fulminating anti-Semitism. Should a Jew dare to complain he would thus be doubly condemned.

Yet occasionally, against the better judgment of their peers, some Jews retaliated. One particularly notorious instance occurred on Holy Thursday 1488 when several Jews picnicked in an orchard near the village of Casar de Palomero, south of Salamanca. In that community, as in many others in Castile, Christian law specifically forbade Jews to congregate in public places on Holy Thursday. Thus, when their gathering was discovered, a group of angry young Christians beat the Jews and drove them back to their homes.

The next morning while the Christian community attended Good Friday church services, the same Jews reconvened in a field called Puerto del Gamo where a large wooden cross stood. In revenge, the Jews toppled the cross and shattered it, supposedly "doing and saying all that their rage dictated against the Nazarene." Secretly an old Christian, Fernán Bravo, witnessed that event and promptly reported it to the Christian community. This time, the Christians left the church en masse and fell upon the Jews. In the ensuing fray, three Jews were stoned to death and two, including a youth of thirteen, lost their right hands.

By the fall of 1490 a string of new insinuations made their way from the town of La Guardia near Toledo into the Castilian court—rumors that a Christian child had been crucified in a ritualistic murder by *conversos* and Jews. Allegedly a three- or four-year-old boy had been kidnapped at a doorway of the La Guardia cathedral and, after being hidden in a cave, had been nailed to a cross. Afterward the boy's heart was said to have been cut out and used in a magical ceremony with a sacramental wafer to protect the offenders from the Inquisition and infect all Christians with rabies.

The odd thing about this ugly story was that, unlike the description of the shattered cross at Puerto del Gamo, there was no documentation about the child's existence. Reports about the child's identity varied, and even his town of origin was hotly debated. The remains of his body had "disappeared" from the grave where he was allegedly buried. All that remained were tales that the child's death had produced miracles, among them the restoration of sight to his blind mother.

The only historical "proof" of the story of *El Niño de la Guardia,* or the child of La Guardia, comes from two sources—an eighteenth-century rendition of the tale by an inquisitor named Mártinez Marino and a nineteenth-century discovery of the inquisitional proceedings against the accused.

Today historians are divided about the veracity of the accusations. Many cite the La Guardia story as a glaring example of the anti-Semitic propaganda then circulating in Castile about ritualistic murders and crucifixions of Christian children. Such tales, they contend, were simply expansions of medieval legends that appeared in the 1460 circulars of the anti-Jewish preacher Alonso de Espina. Others maintain that in a superstitious age there may well have been *converso* or Jewish attempts to stop the Inquisition or destroy Christianity through the use of magic incantations. The subsequent trial has been cited as a notorious example of abusive inquisitional techniques such as intimidation and the use of "leading questions." The *Niño de la Guardia* trial is usually regarded as a turning point in the extension of the Inquisition from *conversos* to Jews, and as such, the final incident that sparked their expulsion from Spain.

The case came to light in an unusual way—not through reports of a missing child by his parents (for none, apparently, existed)—but rather, from confessions extracted under torture. In June 1489 a sixty-year-old *converso* woolgatherer named Beníto García stayed at an inn in the northern Castilian village of Astorga. As he sat in the common room of the hostel, several drunken guests emptied the contents of his backpack for amusement. To their surprise they found herbs and a sacramental wafer.

"Sacrilege!" the travelers exclaimed with sardonic glee. Then, tossing a rope around García's neck, they dragged the woolgatherer to an Astorgan ecclesiastic named Dr. Pedro de Villada. That prelate, who would soon be appointed an inquisitor for the province of Ávila, tortured García in hopes of learning the truth.

In his subsequent confession, García admitted that he secretly practiced

Judaism, having reembraced the faith five years earlier. Initially, when Dr. Villada offered García mercy if he would name those who had corrupted him, the prisoner refused. Later, however, he confessed that he had been reconverted by a *converso* named Juan de Ocaña and often ate on Fridays and Saturdays in the home of a young Jewish cobbler named Yuce Franco who lived with his eighty-year-old father in the nearby village of Tembleque.

By July Juan de Ocaña, Yuce Franco, and his aged father had been arrested by the Holy Office and brought to an inquisitional jail in Segovia. Since the tribunal did not allow its suspects to know why they were accused or the names of their accusors, the three men did not know they had been charged with "corrupting" García.

Yuce fell desperately ill in prison. Believing he was dying, he begged to have a rabbi sent to him. Hoping to extract a confession, the inquisitors sent a Dominican priest, Alonso Enríquez, disguised as a rabbi. Through that pretense, Fray Enríquez wheedled a confession out of the ailing cobbler who thought he had been arrested because of his involvement in "the murder of a boy who had been killed after the manner of that man [Christ]."[1]

A few days later when Fray Enríquez returned to visit Yuce, the youth had recovered and refused to say any more. The affair was brought to Torquemada's attention and interested him so much that he decided to judge the case himself. Coincidentally, Isabella and Ferdinand had just summoned Torquemada to Córdoba, but the Grand Inquisitor stalled, citing urgent business in Old Castile.

By August 27 Torquemada moved Yuce Franco to Ávila where the case was entrusted to his deputies, Dr. Villada and Fernando de Santo Domingo—the same man who had written the introduction to the 1488 anti-Semitic booklets. In a formal document on that same day Torquemada informed the inquisitors that he was now "occupied with other and arduous matters and therefore may not personally acquaint ourselves with the said cases."[2] Consequently, he instructed the Ávila inquisitors to "seize and examine any witness and inquire, learn, proceed, imprison, sentence and abandon to the secular arm such as you may find guilty."[3]

During the subsequent trial, Yuce admitted that he had traveled to the town of La Guardia three years earlier to buy wheat for *matzos,* the unleavened bread used in the Jewish Passover *seder*. He had purchased that wheat from four *converso* brothers who, coincidentally, were also named Franco, but were not related to Yuce. One of them, Alfonso, knowing Yuce to be a Jew, confided that he wished he knew more about his Jewish heritage. Moreover, he told Yuce that he and his brothers had crucified a Christian boy from La Guardia "in the manner that the Jews had crucified Christ."[4]

That admission, combined with Yuce's earlier sickbed confession to the "rabbi" that he had participated in the ritualistic murder of a Christian boy, convinced the inquisitors that Yuce Franco was guilty of a heinous crime. On December 17 they accused him of crucifying a Christian boy on Good Friday "almost in the manner and with that hatred and cruelty with which the Jews, his ancestors, crucified our Redeemer Jesus Christ. . . ."[5]

Yuce was also accused of obtaining a "consecrated Host to be outraged and mocked in vituperation and contempt of our Holy Catholic Faith, and because among other Jews—accomplices in the said crime—there were certain sorcerers, who, on the day of their Passover of unleavened bread were to commit enchantments with the said Host and the heart of a Christian boy."[6]

Once in possession of that heart, Yuce allegedly used *comulgar*, or a magic enchantment, which was intended to destroy Christianity. Through this sacrilege Yuce was attempting to ensure that "all Christians . . . [should] enrage and die" for his intention was "that the law of Moses should be more widely kept and honored in rites and precepts and ceremonies . . . that the Christian religion should perish."[7]

Yuce Franco declared the charges to be the "greatest falsehood in the world."[8] Five days later his attorney, Martínez Vazquez, argued that the trial was illegal for it fell under the jurisdiction of Toledo, where, by all rights, it should have been judged. Second, the charges were vague, making no reference to specific time, date, place, or persons where the "crimes" had been committed. Third, the accused denied participation in the crucifixion of a Christian boy and in any knowledge of sorcery. Fourth, and most important, Yuce Franco was a Jew, and because he lacked a baptized soul, he was technically ineligible for denunciation as a heretic.

Nevertheless, the trial dragged on for another year. During that period the inquisitors arrested still more suspects, tortured the accused repeatedly, and played them off against each other, promising each mercy if he would "confess" the truth. Finally, in October 1491, the "confessions" were brought to a dramatic climax when, in an unprecedented act, the inquisitors ordered the suspects to appear simultaneously before them. The men had not seen each other in over a year. Now, having mutually incriminated each other, they were mortal enemies, eager to blame each other for the alleged crime. In the subsequent hearing, the suspects thus repeated their accusations in hopes of saving themselves.

Finally, on November 16, Yuce, his father, and another Jewish suspect were accused of having "induced and persuaded the Christians their accomplices" into defiling the Christian religion.[9] Those men, as well as Beníto García, Juan de Ocaña, and the four Franco brothers, were condemned in an *auto-da-fe* as heretics to be "relaxed" to the secular arm of Avilian justice.

In their last moments García and the other *conversos* embraced Christianity for the privilege of being strangled before being burned at the stake. Yuce and his octogenarian father, however, refused to convert. In retribution for their stubbornness, the executioners tore their flesh with white-hot instruments before burning them to death.

By then anti-Semitic sentiment ran so high in Ávila that no Jew dared appear outside his home. The next day rumors began to circulate that the burial place of the *niño* had been discovered and that their "Highnesses and the Lord Cardinal [Mendoza]"[10] planned to visit the site. Anti-Jewish riots broke out in Ávila and in several other Castilian towns.

Weeks later the citizens of Ávila were still so aroused that the Jews finally appealed to Isabella and Ferdinand to ensure protection for their *aljamas*. From Córdoba, on December 9, the monarchs accordingly issued the Jews a letter of safe conduct prohibiting citizens from destroying Jewish property or individuals under threat of heavy financial penalties or death. The recent trial of the child of

La Guardia, Isabella and Ferdinand observed, had subjected Jewish men, women, and children to "much abuse and mistreatment." As a result, the monarchs wrote, "we beg that they be treated mercifully and with justice . . . as our privileges to them require."[11]

Ávila, however, was only a microcosm of the anti-Semitism that had infected the Castilian kingdom, and the La Guardia trial was merely its most blatant symbol. In earlier inquisitional trials Jews had occasionally been implicated as contributors to the judaizing tendencies of *conversos,* but this was the first time a Jew had been accused as a central figure. Through the trial of the *Niño de la Guardia* old suspicions about the Jews thus seemed affirmed.

Nor was the trial likely to be forgotten, for the old Christians of Castile resolved to keep its memory alive. By 1501, a shrine had been established in the basement of the razed home of one of the Franco brothers; later it was transformed into a church. Two other shrines were built—one in the cave where the child was allegedly crucified, another near the village of Santa María de Pera, where the child's grave was allegedly located. And in La Guardia the villagers elected the child their patron saint and still celebrate his feast day on September 25.

Isabella and Ferdinand's personal reaction to these events has not been preserved. But the length of the case and the Christian reaction to it undoubtedly left them with a vivid impression. The anti-Semitism that surrounded the trial of the *Niño de la Guardia* proved beyond a doubt that royal efforts to protect the Jews of Castile were dangerous—a powder keg that might explode into civil disorders as destructive as those common to the dark days of King Enrique IV's reign.

In early autumn 1490 Torquemada had hurried to Andalusia to join the king and queen at court. No doubt it was during this period that the inquisitor began to insist that the *converso* "problem" would never be resolved until the Jews were expelled from Spain.

CHAPTER FORTY-SEVEN

The Last Sigh of the Moor

I n the last weeks of April 1491 Ferdinand and an army of 50,000 men pitched their tents four miles from Granada. To the Moors, the presence of the white-pavilioned city and the Castilians' silver cross was an omen, as foreboding as a flock of vultures encircling the verdant fields of the *vega*. And indeed, that was precisely the effect Ferdinand intended. Granada, the sole jewel left in the Moorish crown, was doomed.

The Castilian king had every reason for optimism. As spring returned to Andalusia, a bright new army of cavaliers and infantry had arrived in Córdoba for the "honor" of participating in the last siege of the Moorish war. Among them were fresh faces from England, Germany, Switzerland, France, and Burgundy as well as Moorish renegades and warriors who, disenchanted with Boabdil, had defected to the Christian side.

In 1490 the kingdom's war chest, administered by Talavera and Luís de Santángel, was replenished from new taxes levied upon the Jews, by church donations, and by loans from Castilian nobles. With fresh funds at her disposal, Isabella ordered enormous shipments of food and weapons from distant parts of Castile and supplemented them with imports, including, ironically enough, wheat from North Africa.

As in previous campaigns, Castile's bravest nobles formed the vanguard of Ferdinand's army—Cádiz, Villena, Medina Sidonia, Gutierre de Cárdenas, the Counts of Tendilla, Cabra and Urena, and Alonso de Aguilar. These barons had aged in the decade-long Holy War. The sixty-four-year-old Cardinal Mendoza had long since stopped leading men into battle. Cádiz's once bright red hair had turned white, and although his body was still sinewy, the knight spent the winter ill with fever. The gallant Medina Sidonia was nearing sixty, Tendilla was just fifty, and even Villena was approaching middle age. Still, the anticipated end to the Holy War that had been the dream of Christian kings for nearly eight centuries had stirred those veterans so profoundly that once again they arrived in Córdoba with vigorous new battalions.

Like his peers, Ferdinand longed to subdue Granada without pitched battles or the thunder of *lombardas*. The girth and length of Granada's walls, the legendary beauty of the Alhambra, and especially the knowledge that the city was unable to receive provisions convinced him and Isabella that the best strategy was simply to starve the Moors out. Despite the tedium of a blockade, it was preferable to the spilling of more Christian blood. "Hunger alone," Isabella told a French ambassador who visited the monarchs at the Granada encampment, "will win the city for us."[1]

Before Ferdinand settled his camp in the Granada *vega*, he made every effort to tighten security around the city. From Córdoba, Ferdinand had dispatched Villena and his men to the nearby Alpujarras Mountains to raze twenty-four Moorish towns. Later the Castilian army pitched its tents along the shores of the Jenil River. Above them hovered Granada, sheltered on the east by the perennially snowcapped Sierra Nevadas. On its south were massive walls and dizzying towers that looked out upon the *vega* and the Christian army. Within Granada, 20,000 Moslem soldiers peered from its ramparts, longing to throw open the city gates and storm the foes who squatted so brazenly at their doorstep.

King Boabdil hesitated, afraid to attack the Christians en masse for fear they would retaliate by storming the beautiful city and the Alhambra. But the explosive spirits of the Moors could not be contained indefinitely, and before long they were engaging in skirmishes at the edge of the Christian camp.

Nevertheless, Ferdinand asked Isabella to join him in the Christian encampment. On June 18 the queen and her eleven-year-old daughter Juana left their quarters at Alcalá de Real and arrived in the Granadian *vega* where they were greeted with music and cheers from the Castilian soldiers.

After Princess Isabel's marriage, the queen's second daughter Juana had become her special companion at formal events. But Isabella's relationship with Juana was fraught with tensions. Although Juana, like her older sister, was beautiful and had already acquired a reputation as a gifted student, she was moody and had an uncontrollable temper.

Upon her arrival at the Castilian camp, Isabella donned a full suit of armor, mounted a warhorse, and reviewed the army. And as in the past, she spoke with some of the soldiers and spent many days at *El Hospital de la Reina* tending to the sick.

Wherever she went, Isabella was surrounded by a cadre of barons, each vying for her approval, each offering her courtesies and favors. Cádiz even offered his tent as her temporary residence. The marquis's pavilion was the most beautiful in the camp, even more elegant than Ferdinand's. With his penchant for splendor, Cádiz had outfitted the tent with every comfort: Its silken walls were hung with tapestries, its floors lined with rugs, its tables graced with pretty lamps. During earlier sieges it had been customary for Isabella and Ferdinand to sleep in separate tents because of the parade of soldiers that appeared in the king's doorway. Thus there was nothing untoward or improper in Cádiz's offer, only his respectful wish to see Isabella living in comfort. Thus the queen graciously accepted her courtier's offer.

The Moors had taken careful note of Isabella's arrival. Like their defeated compatriots, they regarded her with a mixture of fear, admiration, and contempt. But unlike the soldiers at Baeza, the Granadian Moors were less easily intimidated. "We have nothing left to fight for but the ground we stand on," the Moorish commander Muzar had reminded them. "When this is lost, we cease to have a country and a name."[2]

With that steely attitude, a gigantic Moslem soldier named Yarfe galloped close to the Castilian encampment and hurled a spear toward the royal pavilion. An insulting note was attached addressed "for the Queen of Castile." News of the rude message spread quickly through the Castilian camp. To degrade the queen was to degrade everything the Christians held sacred. Retribution, the soldiers grumbled among themselves, had to be exacted for the insult.

A soldier named Fernando Pérez del Pulgar—not related to the chronicler with a similar name—swore immediate revenge. That night he and fifteen companions stole across the *vega,* through a poorly guarded Granadian gate, and into the Moors' central mosque. There, in whispered voices, he and his companions dedicated the mosque to the Holy Virgin and left a dagger stuck in the door with a placard that read "Ave Maria."

From her first moments in the Christian encampment, Isabella longed for a closer look at Granada. To accommodate the queen, Ferdinand ordered Castilian scouts to scour the *vega* and clear it of Moorish renegades on Saturday morning, June 18. That same morning Cádiz and 2,000 men marched to a part of the *vega* that lay between the hilly town of Zubia and Granada. Although they were to serve as a buffer between the Christian and Moorish camps, Ferdinand gave Cádiz's men strict instructions to avoid provoking the Moors. Isabella, the king reminded Cádiz, abhorred bloodshed and insisted no lives be sacrificed to her curiosity.

Shortly thereafter the queen, king, and their children, all of whom had since arrived at the royal camp, were escorted to a house in Zubia that had a spectacular view of Granada. From a window, Isabella and Ferdinand gazed over Granada's walls and into the wealthiest part of the city. They also glimpsed the rambling walls of the Alhambra embellished with stately gardens and arching fountains, the inner sanctum of the Moorish empire that had sustained Islam on the Iberian penninsula for nearly eight hundred years. It was this Alhambra, symbol of the Moorish presence in Castile, famed for its intricately mosaicked rooms and tiled floors, whose chambers opened endlessly from one sunlit courtyard to another, for which thousands of Christian soldiers had died, many within the monarchs' lifetime. Soon, Isabella and Ferdinand prayed, the kingdom would be in their possession and the long centuries of bloodshed would cease.

But their wish was not to be immediately granted. As the king and queen peered at Granada, its citizens, agitated by the sudden presence of Cádiz's troops in the nearby *vega,* sounded an alarm. Suddenly a city gate burst open and howling bands of turbaned Moors, scimitars flashing, galloped out. Behind them tramped the Moorish infantry, a motley band of soldiers and untrained commoners, dragging cannons and *espinagardas,* bullet- or arrow-shooting artillery.

Cádiz, ever mindful of Ferdinand's orders, commanded his men to stand by silently and resist all efforts at battle. Puzzled by what they perceived as Castilian cowardice, the Moslems charged. One of their most prominent warriors was Yarfe. His huge body was encased in armor and he was mounted on a black horse upon whose tail was pinned Pulgar's "Ave Maria" placard. The insult was more than the Castilians could stand. They cursed, muttered angry imprecations, even picked up their weapons, but Cádiz refused to let them attack.

Finally a young *caballero* named Garcilasso de la Vega rode to Zubia and begged Ferdinand to allow the army to avenge themselves upon the Moors. Reluctantly the king agreed, and before long Vega himself had locked lances with Yarfe. Soldiers from both sides watched as Yarfe, who was by far the taller and more powerful of the pair, wrestled the Castilian from his saddle and pinned him to the ground with his knee.

The Moor then drew a dagger out of his belt and raised his arm toward Vega's throat. Suddenly the Moor's body began to shudder, and with an ungodly howl, he fell back in a death agony. While Vega was on the ground he had somehow managed to unsheath his sword; when Yarfe released his grip to stab Vega, the Castilian quickly plunged the sword into the Moor's side. Afterward Vega leapt to his feet and retrieved the "Ave Maria" placard from the dead man's horse. Then, to the ecstatic shouts of his fellow Castilians, he stuck the sign on the tip of his raised sword and galloped away in triumph.

By then Cádiz had given orders for his men to charge the Moorish army. "St. James! St. James! Castile! Castile!" he bellowed as his men had rushed forward. In the din and smoke of the ensuing battle, the Moorish cavalry, confounded by their infantry's undisciplined movements, had been forced to break formation. Scattered, no longer able to move as a coordinated group, the Moors were forced to fight the Castilians hand to hand.

The ensuing casualties—600 Moors by some accounts, 2,000 including prisoners by others—left the Moslems badly broken and beaten back to the gates of Granada. Out of Isabella's peaceful intentions had come war and ultimately, a Castilian victory, the last of the Granada war.

Whatever guilt Isabella may have felt for provoking the battle at Zubia was ameliorated by gratitude for the victory. In the thick of battle the horrified king, queen, and their children had fallen to their knees to pray to St. Francis. Hours later the monarchs had descended into the *vega* where the exhausted but jubilant Cádiz and his men still stood.

"Señora, this victory comes from God and from the good fortune of Your Highness," Cádiz said with a courtly flourish.

"Duke," Isabella responded, "we have been indebted to your service before and it is you who have brought [this victory] about."[3]

The Moors were so humiliated that they stopped their raids. For the first time in weeks, peace settled over the Castilian camp. In commemoration of the battle and the prayers Isabella had offered to St. Francis, she founded a monastery at Zubia. In its garden she planted the saint's symbol, a laurel tree.

* * *

The new peace was destined to be short-lived. On Thursday night, July 14, the queen was awakened by the pungent odor of smoke and a curtain of flames that steadily consumed a section of Cádiz's tent. While Isabella slept, the flames from a small lamp had ignited a silken drape in the pavilion. A light breeze had carried the flames to adjacent tents, endangering the whole Castilian encampment within minutes.

Isabella escaped from the tent unharmed and burst into the adjacent tents to warn Ferdinand, Prince Juan, and Princess Juana. Ferdinand, convinced that the fire had been set by the Moors, immediately fastened on his sword and buckler and escaped with his wife and children. A general warning sounded and before long half-dressed courtiers, drowsy barons, and common soldiers evacuated the camp. Although no one had been injured, the suddenness of the conflagration convinced Ferdinand that the flames were the first stage in a Moorish attack.

By then the flames had become a white-hot furnace enveloping the tents as well as the knights' clothes, jewels, silver dishes and ornaments. The glare of the fire was so bright that it even illuminated the walls of Granada where curious Moors stood on the battlements to watch the spectacle.

In the fire, Isabella's entire wardrobe had been destroyed. To help the queen, the valiant warrior Gonzalo Fernández de Córdoba offered her his wife's clothes. Within a day or two, the promised gowns, skirts and mantles had arrived, and Isabella was so pleased with their beauty that she later honored de Córdoba and his wife for their kindness. She was, in fact, so delighted with the clothes that she told de Córdoba "your household has lost more in this disaster than mine."[4]

Soon after the fire, a somber-faced messenger from the Portuguese court arrived at the Castilian encampment. Instead of the usually happy reports Isabella received from her daughter Isabel, there was heartbreaking news. In July, while the newlyweds were visiting the city of Santarem, Prince Afonso had gone hunting with his father along the Tagus River. During the chase he had been thrown from his horse, suffered a blow to his head, and died a day or two later.

With his death the twenty-year-old Princess Isabel had become a widow. In her sorrow, the young woman had cut off her glorious blond hair, and donned *jerga,* or sackcloth, and a heavy veil. The princess was so despondent that she refused all food except soup and would not undress. Now she was traveling back to Andalusia in grief. Shocked, Isabella immediately removed Countess de Córdoba's beautiful gowns and, as befit a Castilian queen of that era, donned dark mourning clothes. Before long she was followed by the entire Castilian court, who, in keeping with medieval tradition, wore white mourning clothes. Isabella and Ferdinand then set out for Íllora to meet their daughter.

In spite of the "Queen's victory," as the battle near Zubia was called, the fire in the Castilian encampment had left Isabella and Ferdinand with new worries. To prevent a repetition of the disaster and to prepare for the approach of winter, the monarchs ordered the army to erect permanent housing on the Granada *vega.* Representatives from nine Castilian cities were selected to coordinate the project, foundations were dug deep into the earth, and quarried rocks were hauled from nearby gulches. Overnight, entire battalions were transformed into laborers who wielded hammers and nails instead of swords and lances.

By October a new city had been erected near Granada. The oblong settlement was divided by two perpendicular streets that formed a cross and was bordered on four sides by gates. On one end stood a massive stable large enough to hold a thousand horses. Towers and battlements ringed the settlement, and from the tallest height the Castilian army's silver cross glittered in the sunlight.

The Castilians wanted to name the city Isabella after their queen, but she would not hear of it. This was, Isabella reminded her soldiers, the last siege of the Holy War and it was through faith that the battle would be won. The city could thus be named *Santa Fe,* or Holy Faith, to reflect the solemnity of the Holy War. Santa Fe, a Castilian would later observe, was "the only city in Spain that has never been contaminated by the Moslem heresy."

Before long merchants and peddlers were streaming into the new city with their wares—rich bolts of cloth, leather goods, ornaments, silver vessels, perfumes and oils. Fresh supplies of food, wine, and wheat arrived daily from the far corners of Castile. Clearly, Santa Fe had become a permanent part of the *vega,* and, the Moors feared, so had the Christians who were determined to make Granada their own.

Granada was soon filled with grumbling factions, some urging immediate surrender, others agitating for still another battle, still others murmuring that Boabdil should be expelled for the curse he had brought upon them. Exacerbating the citizens' sense of hopelessness was a worsening food shortage. Although it was October there were few crops to be harvested, for the Castilians had burned the fertile fringe of the Granada *vega.* Moreover, Ferdinand's army had cut off all access to the lush valleys of the Alpujarras. There was not even the possibility of help from North Africa or the Egyptian Grand Sultan because the Moors no longer held ports along the Mediterranean.

In the Alhambra, Granada's leaders searched vainly for a solution. Finally, on a dark October night, Boabdil dispatched his minister Abul Cazim Abdelmalic to arrange for a surrender. To represent the Castilians, Isabella and Ferdinand appointed two men—one of their secretaries, Fernando de Zafra, and Gonzalo Fernández de Córdoba, who, in addition to his military prowess, was fluent in Arabic.

Meanwhile, Granada's streets were filled with turmoil. Children wailed with hunger. Soldiers, still dreaming of rescue from North African allies, urged patience. Veiled women remained behind shuttered windows, whispering fearfully to their sisters. Rabble-rousing *alfaquis* stirred the commoners to seek Boabdil's downfall. Old men beat their breasts in anticipation of Granada's imminent destruction. Because of the widespread civilian unrest, the peace talks were conducted in utmost secrecy. Sometimes they were held within the city of Granada, at other times in the nearby village of Churriana. By November 25 the terms of the surrender were complete.

As at Baeza, Isabella and Ferdinand offered the Granadian citizens a generous treaty that was to become effective at the end of sixty days. Their largesse had been inspired by several factors—among them their confidence that they could easily maintain civilian peace and their belief that the oppression of large conquered populations was a dangerous policy that could incite future rebellion. Consequently, the Castilian monarchs decided to leave the everyday lives of the Granadian Moors much as they had been under the Moslem kings.

The terms of the resultant pact allowed the Moors to practice their religion freely. Crimes and civil lawsuits were still to be judged by Moslem law under the Moors' own officials, who were now accountable to the Castilian king and queen. In addition, the citizenry retained the right to maintain their traditional dress, language, and customs.

The conquered population was free to migrate to other parts of Castile. Should they choose to emigrate to North Africa within three years, Isabella and Ferdinand agreed to provide ships for the journey. As vassals of the Castilian throne, the citizens of Granada would pay taxes to Isabella and Ferdinand at the same or, by some reports, even lower rates than they once paid the Moorish king. Finally, Boabdil was to be given a small territory in the Alpujarras as a vassal of the Castilian king and queen.

But before the sixty days had elapsed, news of the surrender had leaked to the citizens of Granada. Angry crowds began to gather in the streets. A riot ensued and there was fear of a full-scale rebellion. Boabdil, fearing for his life, dispatched messengers to Ferdinand and Isabella requesting an earlier surrender. January 2, 1492, was chosen as the new date on which the Castilian monarchs would occupy Granada and the nearly eight-hundred-year-old *Reconquista* would come to an end. On that day the Cross would, at last, achieve ascendancy over the Crescent.

At daybreak on January 2 the Count of Tendilla, a retinue of barons, and a company of soldiers prepared to pass through the gates of Granada. With them was Talavera, who was charged with the duty of hoisting the Castilian banners from the tallest towers of the Alhambra. Immediately after the occupation, these two men would assume key roles in Granada: Tendilla was to become *alcaide* of the Alhambra as well as captain general of the kingdom of Granada, and Talavera was to become Archbishop of Granada.

But on this date the two men moved gingerly toward the city for the situation within was tense. By previous arrangement, Ferdinand and Isabella remained in the *vega* below, waiting for signs that Tendilla had successfully entered the city. To commemorate the event, the monarchs and their court had exchanged their mourning clothes for festive brocades and silks, ironically in the Moorish style.

At first, Tendilla and his escorts ascended an outer road of the city by the Puerta de los Molinos, or "Gate of the Mills," and proceeded toward the Hill of Martyrs. There they met Boabdil who was just leaving Granada with fifty Moorish knights and was to meet Ferdinand farther down the path. At Boabdil's approach, the Castilian king nudged his horse forward until the two kings were nearly face to face. The Moor dismounted and threw himself at Ferdinand's feet. Ferdinand, protesting, embraced Boabdil respectfully.

Then, with trembling hands, Boabdil presented Ferdinand with the keys to Granada. "These keys are the last relics of the Arabian empire in Spain," he said sorrowfully. "Thine, O King, are our trophies, our kingdom and our person! Such is the will of God!"[5]

"Doubt not our promises," Ferdinand replied. "Or that you shall regain from our friendship the prosperity of which the fortune of war has deprived you."[6]

Afterward Isabella greeted Boabdil kindly. The queen then surrendered Boabdil's son Ahmed, the boy who had been repeatedly held as a guarantee for Boabdil's truces. But even the sight of his son, grown tall now with the passage of years, could not cheer Boabdil. Anxious to avoid witnessing the Castilian occupation of Granada, his face blurred by tears, the defeated Moor rode off with Ahmed to a secluded spot where his family, laden with household possessions, waited to accompany him to the Alpujarras.

By then Tendilla, Talavera, and the Castilian army had arrived at the Alhambra. Although bright sunlight now flooded Granada's streets, the city was unnaturally quiet. Not a Moor was in sight. In anticipation of the occupation, they had sequestered themselves in their homes.

Moments later Ferdinand's silver cross was attached to the top of Alhambra's tallest tower, the Torre de la Vela. Then, with a flourish of trumpets and drums, the standards of Castile and the banners of Isabella and Ferdinand were unfurled to flutter in the breeze. To witness that historic moment Isabella, Ferdinand, the *Infantes,* and courtiers had proceeded to the village of Armilla, about two miles to the south. Below them, on the shores of Jenil, came a roar from the Castilian army: "Granada! Granada for the monarchs Don Ferdinand and Doña Isabella!"[7] Canons and *lombardas* thundered in salute. Isabella, Ferdinand, and their court fell to their knees and in one voice sang *Te Deum Laudamus.*

Isabella and Ferdinand would never forget the moment, nor would the rest of the spectators. That day the assembled Castilians had come to "worship the Cross with the greatest tears and devotions in the world."[8] They had fulfilled their ancestors' fondest hopes and dreams, succeeded even where such legendary leaders as Alfonso X and El Cid had failed. Afterward, the story of Isabella and Ferdinand's exploits would be repeated in song and story and their reign glorified beyond that of any other in Spanish history.

Miles away, on a certain hilltop at the edge of the Alpujarras, Boabdil stopped and turned for a last look at Granada. As he gazed at a vista of the city and the red-towered Alhambra shimmering in the morning sun, tears streamed down his face. "You do well to weep like a woman for what you could not defend like a man," said his mother, Sultana Zoroya.[9]

Then the grief-stricken Moor and his cortege disappeared around the corner of the hill that led to the Alpujarras. To this day Boabdil's sorrows have been preserved in the name given to that vista, *El Ultimo Sospiro del Moro*, "The Last Sigh of the Moor."

Four days later, on Epiphany, January 6, Isabella and Ferdinand entered Granada for the first time, accompanied by members of their court and the most powerful prelates in Castile. The procession, emblazoned with heraldry and glittering with all the finery the court could muster, moved solemnly through the city streets. At Granada's largest mosque, newly consecrated as a church, the procession attended a high mass of thanksgiving.

Then the royal cortege ascended a slight hill and rode through the Gates of Justice into the fourteenth-century palace of the Alhambra, the famed inner sanctum of the Nasrid dynasty. With wonder, Isabella and Ferdinand gazed upon its richly decorated walls, the stone lacework that surrounded its azure- and emerald-tinted stalactite ceilings, the intricately carved traceries of vines, leaves, and Arabic poetry that decorated a seemingly endless series of courtyards and fountains, until finally they arrived at the Hall of the Ambassadors, the throne room of the Moorish Caliphs.

At that moment, the world of the Christians and the Arabians interlocked. Beneath the domed cedarwood ceiling of the hall and around walls filigreed with Arabian words from the Koran were gathered the most cherished courtiers and prelates of Castile and Aragón—Cardinal Mendoza; Talavera; the Dukes of Cádiz and Medina Sidonia; Gonsalvo Fernández de Córdoba; the Master of Santiago; Alonso de Aguilar; Garcilasso de Vega; Luís de Santángel, Gutierre de Cárdenas; and many others. Then, for the first time in Western European history, Christian monarchs assumed the ivory thrones of the ancient caliphs. The Moslem people had brought an extraordinarily rich mixture of knowledge, beauty, and bloodshed to the Iberian peninsula; in the process Spain had been permanently transformed. For one more moment in Spanish history—a brief ten years—the two cultures would live in harmony.

The implications of Isabella and Ferdinand's conquest of Granada transcended their ancestors' vows to rout the infidel from the Iberian peninsula. Internationally, the victory was hailed as a monumental advance for Christianity, retaliation for the 1453 Turkish occupation of Constantinople. As such, it symbolized the end of the Western European Crusades.

In the Alhambra, the king and queen were nearly as awed by their victory as their subjects. Soon after they were ensconced in the Moorish palace, they notified city officials throughout Castile and Aragón that "this city of Granada is greater in population than one can imagine, the royal palace greater and richer than that of Seville."[10]

To the Sevillians they noted it has:

> pleased Our Lord after many great efforts, costs and exhaustion of
> kingdoms, deaths and bloodshed of many of our subjects . . .
> we have the good fortune to end the war with the king and Moors
> of the kingdom and city of Granada this second day of January in
> '92 in the power of our lordship. I have entered the Alhambra and
> the city and other places and won all the other castles and for-
> tresses and towns that belong to this kingdom. Thus I am writing
> to inform you that we owe thanks to Our Lord of glorious victory
> who has given us this victory and our holy Catholic Faith, and
> brought honor and rewards to our kingdoms and lordships which
> so much faith and loyalty in this holy conquest that we have
> served.[11]

With similar jubilation, Ferdinand announced to Pope Innocent VIII that "this kingdom of Granada, which for over 780 years was occupied by infidels, the fruit that past pontiffs, your predecessors so much labored to obtain, in your days and with your aid has been secured."[12] On February 1, Innocent ordered church bells to be rung throughout Rome. Despite stormy weather, an enormous procession wended its way to the Church of San Giacomo degli Spagnoli to celebrate a thanksgiving mass, and that night Rome was illuminated to celebrate the Castilian triumph. In honor of Granada, Cardinal Borgia hosted five bullfights in the Eternal City and a fellow cardinal presented a dramatization of the victory at Granada. From Florence, Venice, and other Italian cities came letters of congratulations.

When England's Henry VII heard the news, he summoned London's lord mayor and aldermen to march to St. Paul's Cathedral for a high mass. In a laudatory speech to the assembled dignitaries Henry's most trusted advisor, the Lord Chancellor John Morton, praised Isabella and Ferdinand's conquest as a "new song unto God." He said:

> [In] these many years, the Christians have not gained new ground or territory upon the infidels, nor enlarged and set farther the bounds of the Christian world. But this is now done by the prowess and devotion of Ferdinando and Isabella, kings of Spain; who have, to their immortal honor, recovered the great and rich kingdom of Granada, and the populous and mighty city of the same name from the Moors . . . for which this assembly and all the Christians are to render laud and thanks to God, and to celebrate this noble act of the King of Spain, who in this is not only victorious but apostolical in the gaining of new provinces to the Christian faith.[13]

Morton's words were more prophetic than he knew. Joining in the procession that witnessed Isabella and Ferdinand's occupation of Granada was Christopher Columbus, who had traveled north to plead his cause once again to the king and queen.

PART FIVE

Dynastic Dreams
1492–1504

CHAPTER FORTY-EIGHT

1492: Columbus

Columbus had not expected to appear before the monarchs again. Six months earlier, in the summer of 1491 Columbus had returned to the La Rabida monastery. Embittered by the six years he had "wasted" in Castile, the forty-year-old navigator now intended to take his son Diego to France to try his suit with King Charles VIII. But Fray Juan Pérez, head of La Rabida, "much distressed at the admiral's decision and the loss that Spain would suffer thereby," hotly protested Columbus's departure.[1]

Having listened a second time to the navigator's theories, Pérez now consulted with a local physician and cosmographer, Dr. García Fernández, and perhaps also with the Palos shipowner Martín Alonso Pinzón. Then Pérez wrote the queen "in the hope that as he was her confessor, she would credit what he might tell her about the affair."[2] Isabella must have been impressed with the fervency of Pérez's suit for she urged him to visit her at Santa Fe and instructed Columbus to expect an invitation of his own. And, indeed, in late summer Isabella summoned Columbus to Santa Fe and enclosed 20,000 maravedís for him to buy a mule and clothes for court.

That summer or in early fall Columbus appeared before the monarchs. Again the navigator framed his *empresa* in terms designed to appeal to Isabella and Ferdinand's ambitions, insisting that his discovery of a western route to the Orient would not only bring Castile new riches but acquaint him with the Orient's pagan natives. Through that acquaintance, Columbus maintained, he would discover "measures which could be taken for conversion to our Holy Faith."[3]

Once again Isabella relegated the navigator and his theory to a committee of *astrologos* (astronomers), *filosofos* (doctors of philosophy), mariners, and pilots.

Columbus, determined to win this committee to his side, seems to have shown them one or perhaps several maps illustrating his concept of a shorter ocean passage between Europe and the Orient. The new committee approved Columbus's *empresa* and soon forwarded it to the royal council, which only considered schemes important to the crown.

Yet in the royal council Columbus's venture became bogged down—not, historians believe, because of its credibility, but because of the future explorer's excessive demands. Exactly what he requested in 1491 is not known, but judging from the contract Columbus later signed with Isabella and Ferdinand, he must have pressed for privileges rarely extended to commoners or foreigners. Among them may have been the demand that he and his descendants receive the titles of *almirante*, or admiral, and viceroy over any lands he discovered and retain a portion of all profits of those discoveries.

Such privileges were unprecedented. *Almirante* was, after all, a hereditary title, reserved for those related by blood to the king and queen. Certainly such an honor could never be shared with a foreigner like Columbus, even if he did discover new lands for Castile.

Yet Columbus's deep-rooted conviction that he was destined for greatness justified his requests, he believed. For years he had been the butt of crude jokes and had suffered poverty and a string of rejections in the courts of Portugal and Castile. Gradually, as Columbus approached middle age, he had nursed these wounds into an enormous hurt, a debt that he expected mankind—in the person of some powerful monarch like Isabella, Ferdinand, or Charles VIII—to repay with lavish honors.

Moreover, during Columbus's wait in Castile he had become convinced that his theories were valid. He had continued to read extensively, not only from ancient and medieval geographers but also from a 1489 Italian translation of Pliny's *Natural History,* and a 1485 version of Marco Polo. Moreover, Columbus seems to have repeatedly reread d'Ailly's *Imago Mundi,* and Piccolomini's *Historia Rerum.* These books, still preserved in Sevilla and containing the navigator's inspired marginal notes, reveal Columbus's deepening conviction about a narrow ocean.

By late 1491, when Columbus's *empresa* was brought to the attention of the royal council, he was thus even less conciliatory than he had been in 1485. Having been subjected to what he felt was unnecessary humiliation by Talavera's committee and by an interminably long wait for the end of the Granada war, Columbus had already psychologically broken with Castile. Thus, he was fully prepared to appeal to Charles VIII of France, where, he fancied, he would be treated more generously.

Several weeks after Isabella and Ferdinand occupied Granada, they had a final meeting with Columbus in Sante Fe. While they believed his *empresa* worthwhile, the sovereigns informed the navigator that they could not grant his extravagant demands.

Disheartened, Columbus made preparations to leave Isabella and Ferdinand's court and shared his disappointment with his friends—among them Beatriz de Bobadilla, Alonso de Quintanilla, and Luís de Santángel. The same January 1492 day that Columbus left Santa Fe with Fray Pérez, those courtiers begged the king and queen to reconsider their rejection. The most influential of them, the *converso escribano de ración,* or keeper of the privy purse, Luís de Santángel, made an impassioned and eloquent appeal to Isabella. Just why is unclear. Cynical historians contend that Columbus had so stirred Santángel's cupidity with the promise of private profits from the Orient that the financier volunteered to be his agent at court. Others claim that Columbus, like Santángel, was a *converso,* and thus the two men had naturally collaborated. Still others believe that Columbus was an exceptionally charming and imaginative man who had simply captivated Santángel with his radical ideas.

In any case, Santángel pleaded with Isabella to support Columbus's *empresa* with all the fervor of a shrewd and cunning tactician who knows his audience's appetites. Columbus's expedition, he observed, offered the prospect of considerable gain for the crown at a relatively low cost. Santángel professed to be "surprised that her Highness, who had always shown a resolute spirit in matters of great weight and consequence, should lack it now for an enterprise that offered so little risk yet could prove of so great service to God and the exaltation of His Church, not to speak of the very great increase and glory of her realms and kingdoms."[4]

Moreover, Santángel warned, should Isabella let this opportunity escape, another monarch might very well support Columbus's expedition, an eventuality that would "clearly be a great injury to her estate and a cause of just reproach by her friends and of censure by her enemies." Even if the expedition should fail, the sovereigns would nevertheless be regarded as "generous and high-minded princes for having tried to penetrate the secrets of the universe, as other princes . . . had been praised for doing."[5]

Although the cost of the proposed expedition was relatively modest—around 2 million maravedís—the crown was still impoverished from the Granada war. Nevertheless, Santángel proposed a way to finance the expedition with little strain. As co-treasurer of the *Santa Hermandad,* Santángel and his associate Francisco Pinelo had access to public funds. He proposed to draw part of them as a loan to the crown.

Isabella, moved by Santángel's arguments and his plan, thus agreed to support Columbus's expedition. The Inquisition was gradually "cleansing" Castile and Aragón of heretics. With the recent triumph in Granada, the Moslems had been subdued and many had already migrated to North Africa. If Columbus's theories proved correct, Isabella and Ferdinand might also convert the pagan Indies. The gamble, as Santángel had so eloquently argued, seemed worth the potential risk to the Castilian crown.

In that luminous vision of herself and Ferdinand as champions of Christianity at home and abroad, Isabella even offered to lend her jewels as collateral against Santángel's loan—an offer the *converso* financier deemed unnecessary, but one that later gave rise to the legend that the queen had, in fact, "pawned her jewels for Columbus's expedition." In the next breath the queen did, however, send an *alguazil* (court bailiff) "posthaste" after Columbus and Pérez, who by that time had traveled four miles south.

To Columbus and Pérez, the approach of Isabella's *alguazil* must have seemed a hallucination, a mirage sailors are prone to after staring at the horizon for too many hours while at sea. But the messenger was real and so was his startling order for Columbus to return immediately to the Castilian court as "Her Highness is ready to conclude the affair."[6]

This time the king and queen greeted Columbus warmly and granted approval for his *empresa*. It would be nearly three months before the documents relating to Columbus's *empresa* were completed in the small gray-and-white palace that still stands in the plaza of Santa Fe. Altogether there were seven sets of agreements: the "Capitulations" or "Articles of Agreement" of April 17, 1492; the *Titulo,* or Title of April 30; a "Letter of Credence," or introduction to foreign kings; a "passport," and three royal orders about preparations for Columbus's fleet.

The most important were the Capitulations, so called because they granted certain privileges to the explorer should he discover new lands and a western route to the Orient. Columbus's earlier extravagant demands—to be ennobled, to be made *almirante* and viceroy of any discovered lands, to receive a portion of its profits and to have those privileges conferred on his descendants—were all ultimately granted.

The Capitulations thus already addressed Columbus as "Don Cristobal de Colón" in recognition of his new noble status. They provided that he would be entitled viceroy and *almirante* of all lands "that shall be discovered by his effort and diligence in the said Ocean Sea." He was also promised the title of viceroy and governor-general "in all islands and mainland that, as has been stated, he may discover and acquire in the said Seas." Moreover, the explorer was to retain one-tenth of all the profits, "whether pearls, gems, gold, silver, spices or goods of any kind" acquired on his journey, the rest of which would revert to the crown.[7]

The last two clauses of the Capitulations provided for any long-term conflicts from the anticipated profits of Columbus's discoveries. Should any dispute arise over the mercantile interests of individuals, only the *almirante* or his deputy could act as judge. Finally if Columbus chose, he could pay for an eighth of any ship's expense and collect an eighth of its profit.

The *Titulo* of April 30, or official deed, reaffirmed the terms of the Capitulations. The monarchs wrote:

> We declare Our will and pleasure that when you have discovered
> and acquired the said islands and mainland in the said Ocean Sea,
> you Christopher Columbus shall be Our Admiral of the said
> islands . . . and shall be Our Viceroy and Governor therein, and
> shall be entitled to style yourself Don Christobal Colón. Your sons
> and daughters in the said office and duty shall likewise be entitled
> to call themselves Don and Admiral, Viceroy and Governor
> thereof.[8]

For the journey itself, Isabella and Ferdinand provided Columbus with two documents attesting to their support. The first was a Latin passport, the second a "Letter of Credence" addressed to the Great Khan of China and all the rulers of India and "of any other region that he might find" introducing "our noble captain

Christopherus Colón to you, with letters, from which you may learn of our good health and prosperity."[9]

In the end, the Castilian crown did not provide all the financial backing for the expedition. Santángel advanced Isabella and Ferdinand 1.2 million maravedís from the *Santa Hermandad* treasury. The rest of the funds came from a variety of sources. Columbus may have contributed about 250,000 maravedís himself, which was probably borrowed from his friends at court or wealthy sponsors, including Medinaceli.

Nevertheless, in a decree read on May 23, 1492, Isabella and Ferdinand ordered the city fathers of Palos to provide Columbus with two *caravelas,* caravels or light seagoing ships, within ten days in repayment for an old war debt. The third ship, as well as the rest of the journey's expenses, were probably funded by Santángel, either privately or through some manipulations of the Aragonese treasury. Despite Santángel's fiscal ties to Aragón, the expedition was to sail under the Castilian flag. Consequently, any new lands or riches realized from Columbus's voyage would be claimed in the name of Isabella and Ferdinand of Castile.

Although there was a flourishing shipbuilding industry at Palos, an inland port on the Rio Tinto near Castile's southwestern coast, the city fathers could hardly have been pleased with the royal order demanding that their community outfit two ships at public expense. To begin with, the ten-day requirement was unreasonable. To provide a caravel, or light sailing vessel, with a year's supply of food was already a major task, not to mention the chore of ensuring the seaworthiness of the vessels. It would be ten weeks rather than ten days before Palos could honor its obligation and provide Columbus with two high-hulled caravels: the *Niña,* a swift seventy-foot three-masted vessel with lateen, or triangular, sails and a storage capacity of sixty to seventy tons, and the slightly larger *Pinta,* a sturdy *caravela redonda,* or square-rigged vessel, owned by a local citizen.

In addition, Columbus was obliged to charter a third craft—the *Gallega,* a Galician cargo ship owned by a shipbuilder/sailor named Juan de la Cosa. Rechristened the *Santa María,* this boat was the flagship of Columbus's tiny fleet. Although it was considerably larger and heavier than a caravel and better suited than the other ships for the rough waves of the Atlantic, Columbus never liked it. He found the *Santa María* "very cumbersome and not suited to the work of discovery."[10]

The explorer's next task was to hire a crew. Once again, this proved difficult. The mysterious nature of Columbus's expedition to the Ocean Sea had already stirred fears among superstitious sailors of sea monsters that lay beyond the waters of the Atlantic, of a giant waterfall that would drop them off the end of the earth, or of sailing so far west they would be unable to return. In addition, Isabella and Ferdinand's May 23 directive in Palos had contributed to that mystique, for the monarchs had offered any citizen involved in civil or criminal lawsuits an automatic pardon if he signed up with Columbus.

But such provisions were unnecessary. Nearly all of the ninety men who signed on for Columbus's first voyage were listed on the royal payroll as law-abiding sailors.

By the beginning of August all was in readiness. For weeks carpenters and chandlers had swarmed over the three ships, checking the rigging and planking, caulking the seams against leaks, ensuring the bilge pumps were in good working order. Each ship had been outfitted with extra sails, hemp ropes, and heavy anchors and supplied with hardtack, salted meat, cheese, rice, almonds, and casks of fresh water and wine. In view of the daring and presumably holy purpose of Columbus's expedition, the sails of the three vessels had been painted with large red crosses, and probably also heraldic emblems.

Finally, in the wee hours of the morning on Friday, August 3, Columbus and his crew received communion at Palos's Church of St. George. As dawn broke over the city, the air was unnaturally still and hot. It was the day of the halycon, a day so airless that seagulls build nests of algae at sea. To Columbus the unnaturally still air meant little, for he planned to use the Tinto River's ebb to carry his small fleet to the mouth of the Atlantic. Thus it was that at 5:15 A.M. the navigator ordered the crew "in the name of Jesus" to weigh anchor and sail south into the River Saltes, known today as the Rio Odiel. Then, propelled by dreams of the blue expanse that stretched south from the Iberian peninsula, serenaded by the spirited songs of his crew, Columbus and his three-ship fleet floated downstream past the skeptical stares of the few mariners who stood on the docks of Palos watching. By sunrise, the tiny flotilla was drifting past La Rabida from whose whitewashed walls the friars' morning hymns emanated in a final prayer. Upon hearing them, Columbus removed his hat, as did many of his men who knelt for the last stanza of the ancient hymn:

> Glory be to God the Father,
> and to his only Son
> with the Holy Spirit
> who resides Now and Forever.

By 8:00 A.M. the *Niña*, the *Pinta* and the *Santa María* crossed the sandbar of the River Saltes. Suddenly the sails swelled with a freshening sea breeze as the ships entered the frothy waves of the Atlantic that would first take them south to the Canary Islands and then across the Ocean Sea. For Castile and Aragón, for Europe—indeed for all of humanity—a new era had been unfurled.

CHAPTER FORTY-NINE

1492: The Expulsion

L uís de Santángel's eloquence and financial acumen on behalf of Columbus could not rescue his brethren from the anti-Semitic fury again enveloping Castile and Aragón. By the last months of 1491 the embers of inquisitional fervor had flared into a violent conflagration as the trial of the *niño de la Guardia* drew to its searing conclusion.

Torquemada, who had traveled to the court at Santa Fe in late 1491 to witness the surrender of Granada, capitalized on the horror of that trial by repeatedly denouncing the "corrupting" influence of the Jews upon the *conversos*. He reminded Isabella and Ferdinand of the Jewish cross-shattering at Casa de Palomero; of anti-inquisitional conspiracies in Sevilla, Toledo, and Zaragoza; of the scores, perhaps hundreds, of *converso* priests and prelates who had been condemned by the Inquisition as heretics. Castile and Aragón, the Dominican grimly predicted, would never be safe from heresy until its Jewish population was expelled.

Despite their own efforts to protect the Jews, Isabella and Ferdinand knew that Torquemada's views reflected public opinion. By late 1491 a new rash of stories were circulating through Castile and Aragón about other alleged Jewish crimes— about a Valencian crucifixion, about a Jewish doctor who poisoned Christian patients with his fingernail, even about an international conspiracy among Jews to promote heresy in the twin kingdoms.

Despite the wave of anti-Jewish riots following the trial of La Guardia, the king and queen continued to resist Torquemada's suggestion. To the monarchs, the Jews were valuable citizens who, for generations, had faithfully served the crown in financial and other areas. By 1492 the Jews were an important link in the primitive banking system of fifteenth-century Castile and Aragón. Jewish pawnbrokers had held Isabella's jewels in trust, paying the crown millions of maravedís to finance the final years of the Moorish war. Moreover, Talavera and Abraham Seneor had collected some 58 million maravedís from the Jews in special taxes to help end the Holy War.

To expel the Jews now, Isabella believed, seemed both cruel and foolish, a dramatic break with the long-held tradition of *conviviencia*, or toleration, that had existed between Christians and Jews for centuries. Despite the Queen's devotion to the True Faith, she thus balked at the idea of exiling an entire population, especially one as skilled and industrious as the Jews.

For weeks the king and queen pondered Torquemada's entreaties that Castile and Aragón had to be "cleansed from the great pestilence [the Jews]."[1] Their growing acceptance of the idea was reflected in Castilian domestic policies. In 1491 Isabella and Ferdinand renewed their four-year contracts with Jewish tax collectors as usual, but that December, just before the formal surrender of Granada, the sovereigns redesigned Castile's tax system, reserving the rights of supervision for themselves and allowing them to cancel all previous contracts contradicting the new laws.

Undoubtedly, those changes made the Jews nervous for they seemed to verify rumors that Torquemada had urged the monarchs to expel them. Soon after the surrender at Granada, Jewish leaders sent Abraham Seneor and Isaac Abravanel to Isabella and Ferdinand to defend their brethren. In an account of those meetings, Abravanel, collector of the crown's sheep tax, reported that he begged Ferdinand to reconsider the expulsion on three different occasions.

"Please, O King. What is it that you want from your subjects? Ask us anything: presents of gold and silver and whatever you want from the house of Israel that we can give to your native land."[2] But Ferdinand refused to commit himself.

Abravanel then begged his friends at court—among them Cardinal Mendoza, the Marquis of Cádiz and Talavera—to intercede on his behalf. Finally, he appealed to the queen. In words strikingly similar to the pronouncements of King Solomon, Isabella was said to have replied, "The King's heart is in the hand of the Lord as the rivers of water God turneth it whithersoever He will."

Then, scrutinizing Abravanel, she asked, "Do you believe that this comes upon you from us? The Lord hath put this thing into the heart of the King."[3] There was, in other words, no way to change Ferdinand's mind for his thoughts had been determined by God.

In another version of that story, Jewish leaders held several audiences with Isabella and Ferdinand to remind them of the Jews' considerable service to the crown and their potential value in the future. To strengthen their case, Abravanel and Castile's chief treasurer, the eighty-year-old Rabbi Abraham Seneor, offered to contribute 30,000 ducats to help defray old war debts.

The sum, though generous, proved to be an unfortunate figure. Legend has it that, in the midst of the negotiations, Torquemada burst into the palace chamber where Isabella and Ferdinand sat with the Jewish leaders and pulled a crucifix from his robe. Scowling at the frightened king and queen, Torquemada then held the crucifix on high. "Judas Iscariot sold his master for thirty pieces of silver," he said with a snarl. "Your Highness would sell him anew for thirty thousand; here he is, take him and barter him away."[4] With those words, the fanatic priest threw the crucifix on the table and stormed out of the room.

Allegedly, Isabella and Ferdinand were so overcome by Torquemada's words that they broke off negotiations with the Jewish leaders. To those intimately acquainted with the monarchs, their reaction was not surprising. Three months after that famous meeting, the Italian humanist Martire wrote the Count of Tendilla about the queen's extraordinary fear of God and of Torquemada's powerful grip on her and "the secrets of her heart."[5]

Shortly after the priest's outburst Isabella, probably contemplating threats of eternal hellfire and mindful of her old oath to rout heresy from Castile, acquiesced to his demands. On March 31, 1492, Isabella and Ferdinand signed an edict demanding that all Jews who refused baptism must leave Castile and Aragón within three months.

> It is well known that in our kingdom there are some bad Christians who have judaized and abandoned our holy Catholic faith because of much communication between the Jews and Christians. The 1480 *Cortes* ordered to separate the Jews from the cities, towns and villages of our kingdoms and territories, and keep them in separate ghettos . . . in the hopes that this separation would resolve the problem. We have also ordered the Inquisition in our kingdoms for twelve years, and in which we have seen many cases of their guilt. We have been informed by the inquisitors and many other religious individuals . . . that it seems that great damage to the Christians from their participation, conversation and communication with the Jews, of whom it has often been proven that they have been able to betray our Catholic faith . . .
> . . . Thus, we, in consultation with the prelates, *grandees* and *caballeros* and other knowledgeable persons in our reign, after much deliberation . . . have agreed to order the Jews of our kingdoms to leave and never to return.[6]

The Edict of Expulsion was to take effect on July 1, at which time all Jews and their children, servants, and associates "in whatever condition of life" were to leave. The document further stipulated that all personal property owned by the Jews in Castile and Aragón—homes, farms, furniture, and animals—be sold by the time of exile. Although the Jews could take portable property with them, they were forbidden to remove any gold, silver, and "other monies" from the country. While designed to protect Castile and Aragón from losing their gold reserves, this measure exacerbated the hardships the exiled Jews suffered.

With characteristic efficiency, Isabella and Ferdinand mandated the departure to be conducted in an orderly fashion. By the time the edict was released in late April or early May, the crown had already ordered local authorities to pay their debts to the Jews and enable them to dispose of their properties equitably.

The Jews were stunned by the edict. Just how many individuals were affected is unclear. Expulsion estimates range from 75,000 to 200,000 people. Within three months the entire Jewish population was to leave the country where many of their ancestors had lived for at least a millennium, stripped of everything they knew, disenfranchised from homes, businesses, and communities and forced to seek a new home in a strange land. Henceforth, the Castilian crown itself paid the Jews a debt of 1.5 million maravedís. To underscore Isabella and Ferdinand's efforts to expel the Jews "fairly," their possessions were converted into letters of exchange by Genoese bankers, to be redeemed abroad. And to prevent abuses by the Christians, the monarchs issued a series of royal letters "protecting" the Jews from assault.

Nevertheless, human cupidity, the free-market system, and the haste with which the Jews were compelled to leave, wreaked havoc upon those plans. After the edict was published, many Jews rushed to liquidate their property. In the ensuing stampede, the market value of Jewish homes, farms, and animals plummeted. The Christians, realizing their advantage, consequently drove hard bargains with the sellers. Even Bernáldez, the anti-Semitic curate of Los Palacios, admitted that the Jews "were forced to make disastrous sales. This happened because the Christians made very good deals and were able to obtain many luxurious homes and inheritances with very little money." In fact, it was not uncommon, he added, "to see a home exchanged for a donkey and a vineyard for a piece of woolen or cotton cloth."[7]

After the expulsion, the crown confiscated Castile's *aljamas,* Jewish cemeteries, and synagogues. Many, including Toledo's Santa María de Blanca (which still stands today), were converted into churches. Despite their imminent possession as royal property, the ghettoes were compelled to pay their taxes several years ahead so that the crown would not lose its usual revenues.

In desperation, many Jews hid gold, silver, and jewels in their clothes before leaving. It was, in fact, widely rumored that every Jew had swallowed thirty golden ducats before leaving Castile and Aragón. At the border between Andalusia and Portugal, the *alcalde* of Urena seized more than 850,000 maravedís concealed by emigrating Jews. There were similar reports of attempted smugglings at other checkpoints.

A small portion of the Jewish population, either determined to remain at all costs or possibly persuaded to do so by families eager to retain their investments, agreed to baptism. To encourage these conversions, Isabella and Ferdinand offered the new Christians exemption from the scrutiny of the Inquisition for a long "grace" period.

Besides affecting a large number of Jews, the Edict of Expulsion also affected the monarchs themselves. Several Jews held high positions at court, among them the elderly Castilian treasurer Rabbi Abraham Seneor and his son-in-law, Rabbi Meir Melamed, both of whom chose to be baptized. Later it was rumored that the aged rabbi had been forced to convert—that "he did what he did to save the lives of many people and not of his own desire."[8] Allegedly Isabella had insisted that the two men become Christians because she depended so heavily on their fiscal expertise. Determined to allow no exceptions from the expulsion, the queen, it was said, had threatened to destroy their brethren if the two did not convert.

The expulsion also created difficulties for Isaac Abravanel, the monarchs' financier. Reportedly either Ferdinand or his courtiers attempted to kidnap Abravanel's infant grandson and convert him to Christianity in order to force his parents and the elderly Abravanels to do the same. However, Abravanel, having learned about the plot before it could be effected, spirited his grandson out of the country into Portugal and soon left for Italy himself.

Just how many Jews actually converted to Christianity remains controversial. But the new converts seem to have been a tiny minority. Like Abravanel, most Spanish Jews stuck stubbornly to their faith and resolved to leave the twin kingdoms in search of a better life.

The mass exodus of the Jewish population startled the leaders and intellectuals of Western Europe, although few expressed sympathy or welcomed the new exiles. One of the few who did was Bartolomeo Senarega of Genoa, who observed that "This affair, at first sight praiseworthy, since it concerned the glory of our religion, is seen to contain some cruelty, if we consider that they [the Jews] were not beasts, but men created by God."[9] One of the few leaders who did open his doors to the Jews was the Turkish Sultan Bayezid II, who was said to have "marveled greatly at expelling the Jews from Spain, since this was to expel its wealth."[10]

Two decades after the expulsion, Machiavelli would observe that "in the name of religion," Ferdinand would "resort to a pious cruelty, despoiling the Marranos [Spanish Jews] and driving them from his kingdom. There could be nothing more pitiful or unusual than this."[11] Many Castilians themselves subsequently argued that the sovereigns' expulsion of the Jews and Spain's concomitant loss of skilled fiduciary and business leaders, was responsible for that kingdom's eventual economic decline.

In the last sad gesture of solidarity, members of the Jewish community reached out to help each other. The rich, Bernáldez noted, helped the poor obtain passage and "gave much charity" to those with the fewest resources.[12] Because both France and England refused to accept the Jews, many migrated to Portugal. Considerably smaller groups sailed to North Africa, especially Morocco and the kingdom of Fez. Still others boarded ships bound for Italy, Greece, and Turkey, the last of which received them warmly and remained hospitable for centuries.

By late May or early June large groups of Jewish families, their mules laden with household goods, food, and clothing, began the long march to Spain's borders and ports. In Andalusia, the docks of Sevilla and Cádiz were filled with anxious men, women, and children awaiting passage to foreign lands. A long, gray line of sorrowful humanity, trailed by its *fardage* of plodding mules and oxen, inched its way through the scorching heat of the Extremaduran countryside toward Portugal. At the Aragonese ports of Barcelona and Valencia once-proud Jewish moneylenders and financiers, reduced to a few parcels of clothes and household furnishings, huddled with their families on docks where ships would take them across the Mediterranean. They left, Bernáldez observed, "by the roads and fields with so much labor and ill-fortune, some collapsing, others getting up, some dying, others giving birth, others falling ill, so that there was no Christian who was not sorry for them . . . the rabbis were encouraging them and urging the women and boys sing and beat drums and tambourines to cheer the people."[13]

Through it all, the rabbis assured their exiled flock that God would take care of his people. As it happened, the July 1 deadline had been postponed until August 2—the day before Columbus's famed first voyage and one that coincided with the biblical account of Moses and the Jews at the Red Sea. In a messianic fervor stirred by twelve years of Inquisition, some Jews believed that the seas would part when they arrived at the coast. Although no such miracles occurred, the rabbis insisted that the expulsion had a mystical parallel to their ancient exodus from Egypt. And with the fervor of a long-martyred people, the disenfranchised Jewish population continued to pray for a miracle.

Initially, of course, the Sephardim, as Jews of Spanish origin are still called today, had not envisioned what lay ahead. Many had set out from Spain fired with faith in the protection of the Almighty, optimistically urging their crying infants, infirm parents, pregnant wives, and ailing relatives aboard ships that would scatter them to far corners of the known world. Historically, the late fifteenth century's dispersion of Western Europe's largest Jewish population would become known as the diaspora—the largest scattering of the Jews since the Roman destruction of the second Temple in Jerusalem in A.D. 70.

The more fortunate of the Sephardim established new communities in Turkey, Italy, Greece, and North Africa, where they retained their customs and *Ladino* dialect. But many ships carrying Jews to foreign lands were seized by pirates who took whatever wealth the exiles still had. Others, having safely made the journey to North Africa's Barbary coast, Fez, and Tlemcen, fell prey to marauding bands of robbers and thieves.

The rumor that the Jews had either brought money with them or had swallowed gold coins was a problem. Jews were routinely slaughtered and their bellies ripped open with swords to extract anticipated caches of golden coins. A small remnant of those who escaped, having been repeatedly beaten and robbed, having witnessed their wives and daughters raped or murdered, eventually returned to Castile and Aragón and opted for baptism, believing that even the dread eye of the Inquisition was preferable to living in foreign lands.

No doubt the human suffering witnessed in Castile and Aragón in the months before the Jewish exodus caused the queen sharp pangs of conscience and, perhaps, even moments of outright regret. But these were subsumed by a greater duty—Isabella's commitment to make Castile one nation united by the purity of the Christian faith. By 1492 neither the scimitar of the Moors nor the purse of the Jews would stand in her way any longer.

CHAPTER FIFTY

A New Order, A New World

Winter 1492, when the monarchs met with Moslem leaders at Santa Fe and assigned deputies to govern the occupied territories, marked the first time in their eighteen-year reign that Castile was at peace. They appointed Talavera the first Archbishop of Granada and ordered him to teach the Moors about Christianity. And they provided boats to transport Moslems who wanted to leave Castile and Aragón for North Africa. That spring the gardens of Andalusia and the *tala*-scarred land of Granada began to bloom anew. Peasants tilled the soil and planted new crops. Castilian blacksmiths forged scythes and plows instead of swords and bullets. Millers ground wheat into flour that was baked into bread solely for civilian consumption. Shepherds drove thousands of sheep south from Old Castile to Andalusia without fear of Moslem attack.

By this time, Isabella and Ferdinand were already beginning to think of their twin kingdoms as a united "Spain" as did many foreigners. Although the courts of Castile and Aragón would not be officially linked until the 1520 reign of Charles V, the idea of a new Spanish identity had taken root and was now accelerated by the conquest of Granada.

Reassured that the peninsula's resources were finally redirected toward peace, the queen now focused her attention on her family. To Isabella's consternation, there was little she could do with the Princess Isabel, who, since her widowhood in the summer of 1491, had become increasingly devout and refused to marry again. The princess, as her mother subsequently wrote Talavera, "remains determined not to marry and my Lord the King promised a year ago not to force her into it."[1]

Isabella also fretted about fourteen-year-old Prince Juan, who, she believed, needed rigorous training in the rudiments of kingship. Specifically, she feared that the opulence and luxury the prince enjoyed as a child might lead him and his high-born companions into lives of self-indulgence with "little sacrifice and little glory."[2] No doubt these anxieties were stirred by the recent example of Boabdil's fall and stories about his pampered youth. Prince Juan, Isabella now resolved, must be raised with the classical ideals and knowledge now sweeping through Western Europe.

Thus in April she asked the Italian humanist Pietro Martire to serve as Prince Juan's personal tutor and to establish a school for his companions. As Isabella suspected, Prince Juan's peers, "educated in freedom and luxury," were initially unwilling to adopt the Italian scholar's standards. Like adolescent boys in any era, they preferred contests of physical prowess to academic ones.

But Isabella was adamant. Her son and his companions would not only become erudite classicists, but the new learning that marked the Renaissance would become a signature of her court. Such a movement had, in fact, already begun. Under the tutelage of Alessandro Geraldino, Isabella's daughters were becoming accomplished Latinists. Beatriz Galindo, "La Latina," had long since become a familiar figure at Isabella's court, and in 1491 she married one of Isabella's secretaries, Francisco of Madrid. Consequently, many of the queen's *doncellas* or ladies in waiting now began to study the classics, poetry, mathematics, and literature.

In 1492 the first collection of Spanish lyrical poetry, or *cancioneros,* was published. By then Isabella was gathering paintings from the Flemish school of the northern Renaissance, including Van Eyck and Van der Veyden, which, in turn, inspired her own court painters Juan de Flandes and Michael Zittow to develop a new Hispano-Flemish style. The queen also amassed a large library of hand-copied and printed books, among them copies of Cicero and Aristotle, Nebriga's first Castilian grammar book, and Castilian translations of Vergil and Boccaccio.

In such an atmosphere, Prince Juan, "upon whom the eyes of the nation were naturally turned,"[3] dutifully complied to Martire's instruction. Suddenly it became as fashionable to be educated as to be a warrior, and by September 1492 youths were virtually beating down the doors to Martire's home for instruction in the classics.

By the early sixteenth century Spanish courtiers were expected to be as accomplished in Latin and the classics as in the martial arts. "While it was a most rare occurrence to meet with a person of illustrious birth before the present reign who had even studied Latin in his youth, there were now to be seen numbers every day who sought to shed the luster of letters of the martial glory inherited from their ancestors," observed one courtier.[4] Eventually, even the Dutch scholar-philosopher Desiderius Erasmus would praise the Spanish court for its miraculous transformation. "Liberal studies were brought in the course of a few years in Spain to so flourishing a condition as might not only excite the admiration but serve as a model to the most cultivated nations of Europe," he noted.[5]

By the summer of 1492 there were other, less pleasant signs that the medieval chivalric tradition was fading in lieu of a new order. On July 2, after a long illness, Pope Innocent VIII died. By August 11 Isabella and Ferdinand's old advocate, the opportunistic Rodrigo Borgia, was elected pope and took the title of Alexander VI.

Soon even this news was eclipsed by the death of several of the monarchs' beloved warriors. On August 27, less than three weeks after the Jews had been driven from Spain and Columbus sailed from Palos, the most celebrated warrior of the Moorish war, the forty-nine-year-old Rodrigo Ponce de Leon, Duke of Cádiz, died. With his death faded a legendary era of lance and sword, of heroism and courtly grace, of unequaled personal mettle that had inspired virtually every major victory of the war. Cádiz's gallantry, his bravery, and his utter dedication to the king and queen had epitomized the medieval concept of vassalage and personal fidelity that was fast disappearing in a cooler age of gunpowder artillery and the bureaucratic nation-state. When news of Cádiz's death reached Isabella and Ferdinand in Zaragoza, they grieved and donned mourning clothes.

A week earlier the gallant fifty-eight-year-old Medina Sidonia, as if still rivaling his old enemy for the monarchs' favor, had also passed away. To Isabella and Ferdinand, those two deaths, coming so close together, signaled not only the loss of two of the most valiant warriors of the Holy War, but the passage of an era. In their place would come a new breed of more sanguine courtiers in whom political proficiency would count more than ancestral traditions.

Half a world away, unknown to Isabella and Ferdinand, there were even more remarkable signs of a changing world order. After thirty-three days at sea, on October 11, two hours before midnight Columbus peered into the darkness of the ocean from the *Santa María* and saw a light flickering from the west. "It looked like a little wax candle bobbing up and down. It had the same appearance as a light or torch belonging to fishermen or travelers who alternately raised and lowered it. . . . I am the first to admit that I was so eager to find land that I did not trust my own sense," the explorer would write in his log.[6] To confirm the vision Columbus called two witnesses to his side. The first, Pedro Gutierrez, a representative of King Ferdinand, saw the light for a moment, but the second sailor saw nothing.

Four and a half hours later, at 2:30 A.M. on October 12, another sailor named Rodrigo de Triana stationed at the prow of the *Pinta* sighted the white glow of two beaches connected by a dark curve of grassy land. "*Tierra! Tierra!*" he bellowed joyously. At his announcement, the *Pinta*'s captain, Martin Alonso Pinzón fired a single blank shot from a *lombarda* announcing the historic event. The *Pinta* then slowed its course and waited for Columbus's approach on the *Santa María*.

After Columbus confirmed Triana's observation, the explorer ordered the crew of his fleet to lower all sails except the mainmasts. Then, fearing rocky shoals around the new land, Columbus ordered the three ships to tack offshore for the next two and a half hours.

Columbus's expedition had sailed to Watlings Island, known today as San Salvador, at the center of the Bahama Islands. In the gradually brightening light of dawn the explorer and his crew gazed with wonder on a lush stretch of tropical forest rimmed by glittering sand beaches. Cautiously, Columbus ordered the fleet to patrol the waters and take soundings to find an opening where they could safely anchor. Finally, after rounding what is known today as Gardiner's Reef, Columbus's fleet anchored in a shallow bay five fathoms deep.

On shore naked people "not at all black" stared curiously at the Spaniards.[7] Columbus and a small entourage then manned a small boat armed with artillery and the royal banners of Castile and sailed toward shore. Soon they were joined by other boats from the *Niña* and the *Pinta* with their respective captains, Martin Alonso Pinzón and his brother Vicente Yáñez Pinzón, who held aloft banners with painted green crosses topped by crowns depicting *F* for Ferdinand and *I* for Isabella.

Once having reached shore, the Castilians fell to their knees and thanked the Almighty. Then Columbus rose and named the island San Salvador in honor of Isabella and Ferdinand and for the divine protection that had enabled him and his men to make the journey unharmed. To Columbus and his crew there was no doubt that they had reached an outer island of the famed Cipangu, or Marco Polo's Japan, the alleged gateway to the Orient.

It would not be until five months later, in March 1493, that Isabella and Ferdinand learned of Columbus's historic landing. Still, despite the pomp and honors the delighted monarchs heaped upon Columbus, no one, not even the most learned scholars of Europe, would understand that instead of a passageway to the Orient, the explorer had discovered a chain of tropical islands off the continents of North and South America. Indeed, a New World gleaming with wealth and possibilities had been found.

By the end of 1492 the twenty-two-year-old French king Charles VIII was suffering from fears of eternal hellfire. Nine years earlier, as his father, Louis XI, lay dying at Plessis Castle, his confessor had convinced the old French king to return Roussillon and Cerdagne to Ferdinand. Nevertheless, the French regent Anne de Beaujeu had stubbornly retained those provinces.

In 1492 Ferdinand once again petitioned France, hoping to settle the business at last. This time, according the French historian Philipe de Commynes, the wily Ferdinand bribed two prelates in Charles's court to convince him that his continued possession of Roussillon and Cerdagne was a canonical sin. He also begged the pope to demand that Charles return the two provinces on pain of excommunication.

Consequently, the French priests sharply reminded Charles that his father had ceded the property on his deathbed to Ferdinand. Although King Juan II of Aragón had not fulfilled his promise to pay the contested 300,000 ducats owed France, the prelates reminded Charles that the sum had been used by Ferdinand and Isabella to finance the Moorish war. To thus demand the return of money used for such a holy purpose was unthinkable. Should Charles die without returning Roussillon and Cerdagne, his soul might well remain in perpetual purgatory.

The young French king was shaken by these pronouncements; so, it was said, was his older sister, Anne de Beaujeu. Moreover, Charles was far more interested in acquiring the kingdom of Naples, which he now claimed through his Anjou ancestry, than retaining Cerdagne and Roussillon. In his fantasies, the short, homely French king pictured himself a military genius who would not only rule Naples but Constantinople and Jerusalem as well.

To act on these appetites would, however, require cooperation from several rulers whom Charles had already offended. Among them was Henry VII, who bitterly resented Charles for his support of the English pretender, Perkin Warbeck. Equally daunting was Charles's enmity with Maximilian, heir to the Holy Roman Empire, whose daughter Margaret had been betrothed to Charles from infancy. But in 1492 the French king abruptly jilted that girl for Anne of Brittany in order to restore that duchy to the French crown. The widowed Maximilian, who had planned to marry Anne of Brittany himself, was doubly enraged.

Surrounded with enemies, Charles was thus compelled to appease other European powers. He began with England, where, in 1492, he signed the treaty of Etaples and agreed to desist from supporting all pretenders to the English crown. Nevertheless, Charles knew that if he attempted to invade Naples, Ferdinand and Isabella, who were allied to Maximilian, would quickly appear at the foot of the Pyrenean provinces of Cerdagne and Roussillon with thousands of soldiers fresh from the Moorish war. With the shrewd timing that would eventually make Ferdinand the most admired and despised monarch in Western Europe, the Spanish king had selected 1492 to demand their return.

By the terms of the treaty of Barcelona, as the resultant pact was called, France agreed to return Roussillon and Cerdagne at no expense to Aragón. At the same time Ferdinand and Isabella promised that they would not ally themselves to any nation hostile to France. The two countries also pledged to come to each other's defense as a first priority, with the exception of their protection of the Holy See. Secretly, Ferdinand and Isabella also agreed not to marry their children to the kings of England, Germany, or any other enemies of France.

By early December 1492, Charles VIII had instructed his French ambassadors to witness the signature of the treaty in Barcelona. To celebrate the occasion the city had been festooned in silken banners. Catalonian nobles, prelates, and Barcelonian dignitaries greeted the ambassadors at the city gates and musicians serenaded them. As a symbol of friendship, Isabella and Ferdinand presented the ambassadors with jewels, gold, and silver. Then the French envoys were treated to a glittering series of banquets, bullfights, and fiestas.

At noon on the cloudy day of December 7 as Ferdinand emerged from Barcelona's tribunal in the *Casa de Deputación* and walked down a flight of stairs toward the Plaza of the Kings, a man darted from a corner and thrust a dagger into the back of the king's neck.

"St. Mary preserve us! Treason! Treason!"[8] Ferdinand called out as blood began to gush from a deep wound. The would-be assassin, a sixty-three-year-old peasant named Juan de Canamas, was immediately seized by Ferdinand's attendants and stabbed in three places. Despite his injury, the king ordered his defenders to desist and to preserve the assailant's life so his motive could be examined.

Fortunately, the heavy gold collar or chain the king wore around his neck had partially deflected Canamas's knife. The resultant wound was, nevertheless, very serious, being some four inches deep and six wide. When Isabella learned about Ferdinand's injury, she rushed to his side. Some weeks later she wrote her confessor Talavera that "The wound was so large—so Doctor Guadalupe says, for I hadn't the heart to behold it—so wide and deep that four fingers' lengths would not equal its depth and its width was a thing of which my heart trembles to tell . . . and it was one of the griefs I felt to see the King suffer what I deserved, without himself deserving the sacrifice he made, it seemed, for me—it quite destroyed me."[9]

In those first moments the queen feared that the Catalonians, who had so bitterly opposed Ferdinand's reign in his youth, had secretly fomented a plot to assassinate him. Then she worried that the attack was provoked by the newly arrived French ambassadors. Finally Isabella, fearing other assassins might attempt to murder her children, ordered galley ships to be readied in Barcelona harbor to spirit the *Infantes* and key members of the court out of the city. The queen then attached herself to Ferdinand's side as his private-duty nurse. For the next ten days she nursed him back to health, sleeping and eating so little that her attendants became worried about her own well-being.

With news of the assassination attempt, the panicked Barcelonians had rushed into the streets. "Treason! Treason! They have murdered the King! The King is dead!" they wailed, convinced that the French, the Navarrese, or the Catalonians had attempted to murder the king. Before long anguished crowds of citizens also gathered outside the royal palace, lamenting that Ferdinand had been slain and calling for the assassin's death. Though bleeding and faint, Ferdinand attempted to raise himself to the window to reassure the citizenry that he was still alive, but his doctors insisted he remain in bed.

At first Ferdinand seemed to improve but then he developed a high fever. A medical examination revealed that the assailant's dagger had severed part of the king's shoulder bone. Ultimately, in what must have been an excruciating operation without benefit of anesthesia, court doctors removed the loose bone fragment. But shortly thereafter Ferdinand again ran a high fever and became critically ill.

Immediately after Ferdinand's injury, Isabella had prostrated herself before the Almighty to pray for her husband's recovery. In addition, the queen had ordered Barcelona's priests, prelates, and monks to pray for the king. Now, as Ferdinand's life hung in balance, all of Barcelona was hushed. The churches were filled from morning to night. City officials ceased their work. Special masses were held around the clock. Processions of monks and prelates marched through the streets with chants and prayers to the Almighty. Scores of citizens promised to make pilgrimages and give alms if Ferdinand survived.

By the end of December, Ferdinand's crisis had passed and he began to recover. In gratitude, some Barcelonians walked barefoot through the streets to begin their promised pilgrimages. Others were seen crawling on their knees to nearby churches and shrines to fulfill their promises to God.

But Ferdinand's brush with death wreaked an even more profound, if less public, change in Isabella. Although she was already a pious Catholic, she now began to suffer pangs of conscience about her own spiritual status. Thus, on December 30, after Ferdinand's recovery was assured, Isabella wrote her old confessor Talavera:

> Very pious and very revered Father: Since we see that kings, like other men, are exposed to mortal accidents, it is a reason why they should be prepared for death. And I say this, although I have never doubted it, and have reflected on it for a long time; for

grandeur and prosperity made me think of it all the more, and fear
to reach the end of life without sufficient preparation. But the distance is great from the firm belief to . . . concrete experience.
And since the King my Lord has seen death near at hand, the experience was more real and more lasting than if I myself had been
at the point of death. . . . Indeed then, before I touch death
again . . . I should like to be in other dispositions than those in
which I find myself at this moment and particularly as to my deficits. Inform yourself of all the cases where it seems to you there
can be restitution and satisfaction of the interested persons, and
how this may be effected; send me a memorandum of it—it will
be the greatest peace in the world for me to have it. And having
it, and knowing my debts, I shall labor to pay them.[10]

The attempted assassination left Isabella with scars that cut as deeply into her spirit
as the sword had penetrated Ferdinand's body. Henceforth the queen would
become even more conscious of her sins and penitent about the omissions she may
have committed in her rise to power as Queen of Castile. Perhaps the rash acts of
Isabella's youth and young adulthood—her complicity in poisoning public opinion
about La Beltraneja's legitimacy, her arrogation of the throne in 1474 and that
girl's relegation to a Portuguese monastery—had pricked her conscience. Perhaps
too, the Inquisition and the decision to expel the Jews weighed heavily upon the
queen, even though she publicly maintained that such decisions were executed for
the good of Christian Spain. But Isabella would never allude to any of these acts
as sins. Instead she would demand that Talavera monitor her behavior still more
closely in the future.

"I don't know how we shall thank God for so great a grace—many virtues
would not suffice to do it. And what shall I do who have none? Please God,
henceforth I shall serve Him as I ought. Your prayers and your counsels will aid
me in this, as they always have helped me."[11]

By then Isabella's conscience had already been tested in the disposition of
Ferdinand's assailant Canamas. Her husband's would-be assassain was one of the
serf class whom, ironically, Ferdinand had recently freed from the tyranny of the
Catalonian aristocrats. It immediately became apparent that Canamas was a *loco
imaginativo y malicioso*—a crazed, malevolent-spirited man—for at the public
examination he claimed that the devil had insisted that he was the rightful heir to
the Aragonese crown and thus justified in his attempt upon Ferdinand's life.
Although the king initially pleaded clemency for his assailant, the Barcelonian
nobility were so mortified that a native had injured the king that they insisted upon
killing him.

To underscore the heinousness of the crime, Canamas's punishment was to be
conducted by the most pitiless methods of the day. First he was to be placed in a
cart and displayed throughout the city. Then he was to have the hand that had
struck the king cut off. Afterward he was to be methodically mutilated, first by
having one nipple plucked off with a red-hot tongs, then an eye, then the other
hand, and then finally his feet. After his members were severed, the nobility

recommended that "they stone him and burn him and cast the ashes to the wind."[12]

Isabella, appalled by the harshness of the punishment, demanded that Canamas be strangled before his punishment was fulfilled. In the shadow of Ferdinand's injury, in her growing awareness of the transience of all life, she could not allow such cruelties to continue. Shortly before Canamas's execution she sent the peasant a confessor to absolve him of his sins. And when she learned that the peasant refused to confess, Isabella prayed for Canamas's soul herself.

By early January 1493, the king was sufficiently recovered for the festivities and peace talks to resume. On January 19 the historic alliance was signed simultaneously by Charles VIII in France and Ferdinand and Isabella in Barcelona. With his signature, Ferdinand had at last vindicated his father's humiliation at failing to retrieve his Catalonian possessions from France. Now, for the first time in thirty years, Ferdinand ruled over a reunited kingdom whose key defensive provinces, the "buffer zones" of Cerdagne and Roussillon, were to be restored. He had fulfilled his father's tremulous praise of him as "savior of the country."

Isabella also must have glowed with pleasure but of a different hue. No longer would the French-held provinces of Roussillon and Cerdagne be a source of marital contention. No longer would Ferdinand resent the years that Isabella insisted he put aside the Pyrenean provinces in favor of the Holy War.

Weeks after the treaty of Barcelona was signed, Talavera received reports about the festivities. Having been newly ordered by Isabella to monitor her behavior, the archbishop responded with a scathing letter in which he criticized the queen for what he perceived as the excessive opulence of the court. Among Talavera's condemnations was the richness of the court's dress, the practice of mixing the sexes at the royal banquet, dancing, and the bullfight. He wrote:

> I do not condemn the gifts and the favors, though to be good and
> proper they should be moderate. Nor the hours of supping and
> lunching at Your Highnesses table and with Your
> Highnesses . . . nor the expenses of coats and new dresses al-
> though whosoever overdid it does not escape blame.
>   But what in my view offended God . . . was the dances,
> especially by one who should not have danced. . . . And fur-
> thermore the license of French knights mingling with Castilian
> ladies at supper, and each one taking whomsoever he would by
> the rein. . . . Oh, how inspired the French will be by Castilian
> decorum and gravity! . . . And what shall I say of the bullfights,
> which indisputably are a spectacle condemned?
>   God knows how open I keep my eyes to watch the ground
> your *chopines* [thick soled shoes] tread.[13]

Isabella wrote back a hasty defense.

> I should not wish to appear to excuse myself. But because it
> seems to me that they reported more than actually happened, I
> will tell what took place. If they said there that I danced, I did

not: it did not even enter my thought. As for taking the reins of
the ladies, I did not know it was done until I read your
letter. . . . Having the French sup at table is a very common
thing; they do it continually (and will not take the example from
here). Each time the principal dignitaries eat with the Kings here,
the others eat at tables in the hall of ladies and knights . . .
never the ladies alone.

The men's clothes, she admitted, were very costly. "I did not order it but hindered
it all I could and admonished them not to do it. As for the bulls . . . that is not
a question for me alone."[14]

As queen, wife, and woman, Isabella thus attempted to rationalize the
necessity for certain "sinful" practices within her court. The difference between
Talavera's impeccable Christian standards and the world of political expediency
where Isabella was forced to dwell presented irreconcilable dualities. The queen's
solution would be to vacillate between the two, first swinging one way, then the
other, like the pendulum of a primitive church clock that tried to keep pace with
the swift passage of time. At the dawn of a secular Renaissance the struggle
between humanism and religious piety would perpetually challenge Isabella.

CHAPTER FIFTY-ONE

Descubrimiento

In March 1493 news of Columbus's discovery flooded over Isabella and Ferdinand like sunshine following a squall. Stormy weather had, in fact, forced the returning explorer to land in Portugal rather than Spain. Thus it was that Columbus wrote the king and queen about his remarkable discovery from Lisbon on March 4. Shortly thereafter Columbus wrote to his friends at court, Gabriel Sánchez and Luís Santángel. The letter to Isabella and Ferdinand has been lost, but the one to Santángel was preserved and reflects the explorer's enthusiasm for the islands he discovered in the "sea of India," in reality, the Caribbean.

Thirty three days after my departure from Cádiz . . . I discovered many islands, inhabited by innumerable people. Of these I took possession in the name of our fortunate monarch, with public proclamation and colors flying, no one offering any resistance.

I named the first of these islands San Salvador, thus bestowing upon it the name of our Holy Savior, under whose protection I made the discovery . . . the second Santa María de la Concepción, the third Fernandina, the fourth Isabella, the fifth Juana. In the same manner I named the rest. Arriving at the one last mentioned I sailed along its coast, toward the West, discovering so great an extent of land that I could not imagine it to be an island but the continent of Cathay.

These islands are of a beautiful appearance and . . . adorned with a great variety of exceedingly lofty trees, which . . . never lose their foliage for I saw them as verdant and flourishing as they exist in Spain in the month of May, some covered with flowers, others loaded with fruit . . . although it was . . . November when I visited this delightful region.[1]

Columbus's triumph had come after many months of travail. From Palos, the navigator had sailed his tiny fleet to the Castilian-owned Canary Islands, where other Spaniards had enslaved the aboriginal Guanches. Columbus had chosen to depart from the civilized world from those islands for he knew he could not sail directly across the Ocean Sea due to North Atlantic headwinds. The Canaries, in contrast, located four degrees north of the Tropic of Cancer, enjoyed northeastern trade winds that would propel him across the sea. In addition, the 1480 treaty of Alcaçovas stipulated that the seven-island Canary chain was the southernmost point for those sailing under the Spanish flag. And a 1492 state-of-the-art map by Martin Behaim had placed the legendary Cipangu on the same latitude as the Canaries.

Several days out from Palos, Columbus had even more compelling reasons to anchor at the Canaries. The *Niña,* the smallest and lightest ship in his fleet, traveled faster than either the *Pinta* or the *Santa María,* and to hold it back the ship's pilot was constantly forced to "shorten" his sails. To prepare the *Niña* for the strong winds and high waves of the Atlantic, Columbus planned to have the caravel remasted and rerigged in the Canaries.

On the sixth day of the voyage, however, the *Pinta*'s large outboard rudder loosened from its socket. Even after its captain, Martin Alonso Pinzón, secured it, the problem recurred. Consequently, Columbus considered leaving the *Pinta* in the Canaries and chartering a sturdier vessel. He and his pilots then sailed the *Santa Maria* and *Niña* into the port of San Sebastian on the island of Gomera to search for another boat while the *Pinta* stopped at Las Palmas on Grand Canary Island for repairs.

In 1492 the lushly wooded, mountainous island of Gomera was the most civilized of the Canary settlements and was governed by the Herrera y Peraza family. Years earlier, Queen Isabella had married off a beautiful green-eyed brunette named Beatriz de Bobadilla, cousin and namesake of Isabella's best friend, to Gomera's governor Peraza to remove her from Ferdinand's roving eye. In the intervening years, Peraza had been killed and Beatriz, or Doña Beatriz de Peraza y Bobadilla, as the lovely widow was called, had become the island's regent-governor for her son Guillen.

When Columbus arrived, Doña Beatriz was absent but expected to return shortly on a forty-ton vessel from the island of Lanzarote. For nine days Columbus waited, hoping to charter that boat and make the young widow's acquaintance. Finally, exasperated, the navigator ordered the *Santa María* and the *Niña* to sail for Grand Canary Island. On September 1, the newly reinstated fleet reappeared in Gomera to pay their respects to the widow who had, by then, returned home.

Doña Beatriz entertained Columbus and his captains lavishly in the castle at San Sebastian. Legend has it that the future discoverer stared into the jade-green eyes of his lovely hostess and promptly fell in love. At forty-one Columbus was still an attractive man, whose charisma and vulnerability inevitably drew women to his side.

To aid Columbus, Beatriz provided him and his crew with the best Gomera had to offer—salt, wine, molasses, honey, and other supplies—enough, Columbus noted in his ship's log, for a twenty-eight-day voyage. In addition, Beatriz graciously urged his sailors to collect wood from Somera's dense forests and water from its sparkling streams.

Whatever amorous exchanges may have passed between Columbus and Peraza's widow must, of necessity, have been brief. No doubt, the memory of another woman's voice was echoing in the future explorer's ears—the voice of Queen Isabella who had finally granted him permission to explore the Ocean Sea. The queen's grant was the opportunity of a lifetime—indeed, of the millennia— and there was no time to waste. Before dawn on the morning of September 6, Columbus and his small fleet set sail.

At 3:00 A.M. on September 8 a northeasterly wind freshened and filled the fleet's white sails with their scarlet crosses like great birds that sped across the Atlantic. The only intimation of trouble was a rumor that a Portuguese squadron lurked near Hierro, the last outpost of the Canaries, waiting to apprehend Columbus.

"There could be some truth in it," Columbus mused in this ship's log, "for King John [João] must be angry that I went over to Castile."[2] But by the next morning, when Columbus's expedition passed Hierro and headed for the open Atlantic, the Portuguese threat had not materialized.

Although the boats traveled at speeds ranging from 60 to 174 miles a day, the sight of a seemingly endless watery expanse frightened the sailors and fed their most primitive fears. "This day we completely lost sight of land, and many men sighed and wept for fear they would not see it again for a long time," Columbus reported on that same September 9. "I comforted them with great promises of lands and riches."[3]

Serendipity and the explorer's keen seamanship had much to do with the seemingly invisible hand that guided the ships. By a quirk of fate, Columbus's westerly route along the twenty-eighth parallel of latitude coincided exactly with the northeasterly trade winds, which, at that time, veered far enough north to give him an initial thrust across the Atlantic.

Columbus navigated on this first journey by "dead reckoning," plotting estimated distances on a chart with the help of a compass, rather than by celestial navigation, as is often thought. By his calculations Cipangu was 760 leagues west of the Canaries, or some 3,000 nautical miles. Although the crew was familiar with Columbus's estimates, the admiral feared that if the journey proved unduly long, the sailors would grow restive, perhaps even mutinous. To prevent that, Columbus kept two sets of calculations—the first, a private one that recorded the true distances traveled, and the second, a public one that deliberately underestimated the mileage.

For ten days the trade winds pushed the fleet so steadily across the Atlantic that by September 19 they had traveled 1,261 nautical miles. On the twentieth the winds ceased and Columbus changed course. But the next day the wind was even weaker, and the fleet was suddenly immersed in a seemingly endless expanse of yellowish-green weed, the so-called Sea of Sargasso, part of the western Atlantic extending from the Bahamas into the gulf stream. The vast gulfweed sea and light winds unnerved the sailors, who were convinced that their boats would become permanently entangled.

Although Columbus repeatedly reassured them, he was already worrying about another phenomenon. On the night of September 13 the compass needle had veered a full point to the northeast, a "mistake" that Columbus initially blamed on his men's poor steering. But after much scolding and several nocturnal sightings of the North Star to confirm "true north," Columbus noticed that the compass needle continued to deviate.

By September 17, the sailors had grown "frightened and downcast and . . . would not say why."[4] Already anxious, they now began to ponder the superstitious rumors that surrounded the voyage—tales that they might fall off the end of the earth, or plummet into an abyss, or witness a supernatural rotation of the globe. Vainly, Columbus tried to soothe his sailors with his theory that the North Star rather than the compass had moved—a celestial deviation that has since been confirmed by modern astronomers. Ultimately, the explorer privately surmised what would later become a navigational truism—that a mathematical compensation must be made for the discrepancy between the "true north" of the Arctic Pole and "magnetic" north, which lies close to Greenland.

By September 24, the sailors were so worried that they began to debunk Columbus and his theory. The explorer reported in his log he was having "serious trouble with the crew." "The more God shows the men manifest signs that we are near land, the more their impatience . . . increases and the more indignant they become against me . . . complaining that they will never be able to return home. They have said it is insanity and suicidal on their part to risk their lives following the madness of a foreigner."[5]

Furthermore, Columbus added, the men said that "because my proposition has been contradicted by so many wise and lettered men who considered it vain and foolish, they may be excused for whatever might be done in the matter." Moreover, Columbus was troubled by a disgruntled group of seamen from Palos, who, he noticed, "stick together" and seemed to speak as if in a single voice. Most worrisome of all was the attitude of the Palos shipowner and captain of the *Pinta*. "I know that Martin Alonso [Pinzón] cannot be trusted . . . [for] . . . he wants the rewards and honors of this enterprise for himself."[6]

By the beginning of October the situation was no better. Even Columbus's pilots, perplexed by the deviating compass needle, were "agitated and confused." There were, however, many distractions that kept the sailors amused, sightings of ringtail doves and terns, porpoises rising majestically through the waves, schools of fish to be netted and cooked, the rotation of four-hour watches of the crew, the cabin boys' endless turning of the *ampolleta*, or half-hour glass, to keep track of time—and most intriguing of all, the prospect of being the first to sight land. To encourage that discovery Isabella and Ferdinand had, in fact, promised the winner a reward of 10,000 maravedís.

But by October 1 it had been three weeks since the sailors had seen land—longer than any record known to European sailors of the fifteenth century. Would it not be better to turn back now while they still had food and water, Columbus's men argued, rather than to drift slowly through a perpetual sea until such irreplaceable provisions as wood and fresh water ran out? This time it was

Peralonso Niño, pilot of the *Santa María,* who calmed the sailors. By his impromptu estimates, Columbus's expedition had traveled 578 leagues, which suggested that the voyage was more than two-thirds complete.

On October 4 petrels and other seabirds appeared around the ships—a sure sign to Columbus and his men that they were near land. The land in question, according to Columbus, was the outer islands surrounding Cipangu, or Japan. Nevertheless, the *Pinta*'s captain mistrusted Columbus's navigation and on October 6 urged him to change direction and sail southwest by west to explore those islands and stop in Japan. Columbus, worried about the limits of his crew's patience, refused Pinzón's request, claiming his first priority was to reach the mainland. "My decision," he noted, "has not pleased the men, for they continue to murmur and complain."[7]

Had Columbus followed Pinzón's request to change direction sooner he would have landed in Florida near modern-day Cape Canaveral and discovered the North American continent. Decades later, in a series of sixteenth-century lawsuits brought by Pinzón's family to claim the lands discovered during Columbus's first voyage, plaintiffs and defenders accused the other's ancestor of cowardice. Each contested that the other mariner had balked at this critical point in the voyage but was ultimately persuaded to continue by the other for a few more days.

On October 7 some members of the *Niña* were convinced that they saw land. Yet because Columbus had strictly prohibited false sightings and threatened the forfeiture of the reward, no one dared call out "Tierra!" until he was sure. Still, the thin outline on the distant horizon was so tantalizing that Columbus's fleet sailed straight ahead for nearly seventy miles before realizing it was a mirage.

At sunset Columbus, puzzling over the thick flock of birds that flew in a southwesterly direction, ordered the expedition to follow them. From his Portuguese sailing days, he recalled stories about how such birds often led sailors to uncharted lands. Eventually his hunch would prove correct, for unwittingly the fleet had crossed the autumnal Atlantic flyway, a migratory pattern followed by North American birds past Bermuda to the West Indies.

On the night of October 9–10 the sounds of migrating birds filled the air above the taut sails of the three ships. "We must be very close to landfall, thank God," Columbus mused. By morning the trade winds had freshened to a lusty seven and one-half knots but the sailors, having lost confidence in Columbus's underestimations, "grumbled and complained of the long voyage." Columbus reproached his crew for their "lack of spirit" and reminded them that "for better or worse they had to complete the enterprise on which the Catholic Sovereigns had sent them."[8] He also reminded his sailors of the honors that would soon be theirs. Moreover, he underscored his own determination to see the voyage through to completion. "I had started out to find the Indies and would continue until I had accomplished that mission, with the help of Our Lord."[9]

By October 11 signs of land were unmistakable—flocks of seabirds, green reeds, floating land plants, and a carved wooden stick—objects that, the explorer noted, "made the crew breathe easier . . . even become cheerful."[10] Riches—primitive and civilized—were on everyone's mind, not only the legendary gold of Cipangu but the real possibility of collecting 10,000 maravedís as the first sailor to sight land. As a result, nearly all of the 120 men on Columbus's expedition scrutinized the horizon that day and well into the night.

* * *

"I now believe that the light I saw earlier was a sign from God and that it was truly the first positive indication of land," Columbus would later write about his observation on that night.[11] Four and a half hours later, with Rodrigo de Triana's shout of "Tierra" and the historic retort of the Pinta's *lombarda,* Columbus's hunch was affirmed.

Once assured of *descubrimiento,* or discovery, the sailors' attitudes toward Columbus changed dramatically. At dawn, when the admiral and his men went ashore to claim San Salvador for Isabella and Ferdinand, the sailors (or so his son Fernando claimed two decades later) begged Columbus's pardon "for the injuries that through fear and little faith they had done him."[12]

"No sooner had we concluded the formalities of taking possession of the island than people began to come to the beach, all naked as the mothers that bore them," Columbus observed.[13] Before long the explorer learned that those natives called their island *Guanahani,* after the iguanas that dwelt there. The aborigines, he wrote, were tall, well-proportioned people with handsome faces and skin the color of Canary Islanders or of "sunburned peasants" in contrast to the black-skinned Negroes of Africa: their hair was not kinky, but "straight and coarse like horsehair."[14] Centuries later, anthropologists noted that the San Salvadorans, like all the people Columbus met on his first voyage, were Taino Indians whose ancestors came from South America in the fourteenth century. Observing them to be peaceful people, Columbus presented them with red sailors' caps and glass Venetian beads. The Indians, in turn, regarded the Castilians as "men from heaven" and offered them food and drink.

Privately, however, Columbus's attitude toward the Indians was immediately exploitative, epitomizing the European attitude toward the natives in the centuries to come. "I want the natives to develop a friendly attitude toward us because they are a people who can be made free and converted to our Holy Faith more by love than by force," he mused.[15] To preserve that positive first impression, Columbus instructed his men to take nothing without giving something in return.

Columbus was also struck with the natives' gentleness. "I cannot get over the fact of how docile these people are," he wrote on October 13. "They have so little to give but will give it all for whatever we give them, if only broken pieces of glass and crockery."[16] He was also intrigued with the gold the Indians wore in their noses—a confirmation, he believed, that they had reached the Orient with its legendary rich caches of gold. But, to the explorer's frustration, the Indians could not seem to explain where the gold originated, nor did it seem to be mined locally.

Nevertheless, the natives were so acquiescent and so readily mimicked the Castilians that Columbus was sure they would make "good servants." He also believed they could easily be converted to Christianity "for they seem to have no religion."[17] Before long he had commandeered six Indians with the intention of teaching them Spanish and using them as guides and interpreters.

By the time the boats left San Salvador on October 14, the Spaniards were already using those six captives as guides. On the fifteenth, Columbus and his expedition arrived at Santa María de la Concepción, or Rum Cay as it is known today, which, the captives said, was rich with gold. The night of their arrival, however, one of the Indians escaped, and the next day another jumped overboard onto a native canoe.

Later, when another Indian paddled a canoe near the *Santa María* with an offer to trade, the Spanish sailors captured him. But Columbus had learned valuable political lessons in the Portuguese and Spanish courts. First, the explorer presented the frightened native with a red cap, glass beads, and falcon bells, which he placed on the captive's ears. Then he set the delighted Indian free, hoping he would believe "that the men who had fled had done us some harm and that was why we were carrying them along with us. Thus I . . . gave him all the . . . articles in order that the people might hold us in such esteem that on some other occasion when Your Highnesses send men back here they will be well treated."[18]

But Columbus no longer trusted his native prisoners. When the San Salvadorans directed Columbus to still another island where the people wore gold, he grew skeptical. "I do not know if this is another ruse of theirs or not, for I am beginning to believe that all they want to do is escape and they will tell me anything I want to hear."[19]

The gold on this new island, which Columbus christened Fernandina, or Long Island, never did materialize. However, it was there that Columbus and his sailors first observed natives sleeping in *hamacas*, woven nets of cloth slung from two trees or posts. Before long Columbus's crew adopted the hammocks for their own slumber aboard the crowded decks of the *Niña*, *Pinta*, and *Santa María*, a tradition still retained in many navies.

By October 19 Columbus and his crew had reached Saomete, or Isabella, today known as Crooked Island, where the natives insisted a king lived who had "a lot of gold." By then Columbus was increasingly disillusioned. "I do not hold much stock in what they tell me, for I have been fooled before," he scrawled in his log.[20] Nevertheless, the Castilians explored the densely thicketed northwest cape of Crooked Island, the Cabo de Isleo. For the first time they saw parrots whose flocks were so thick as to "darken the sun" and a "thousand" fruit-bearing trees, but still no signs of the promised gold.[21]

Now the aborigines insisted on traveling to the large island of "Colba," or Cuba, which they claimed was an important navigational crossroads with an abundance of gold and spices. Nearby was still another gold-rich island called Bohio, or modern Haiti. Columbus, convinced he was grazing the outer islands of the Orient, accordingly set sail for Cuba because "I am sure Cuba and Japan are one and the same."[22]

On October 28 the Spaniards anchored at the harbor of the Bahia de Baray in Cuba where the scenery overwhelmed them. "I have never seen anything so beautiful. The country around the river is full of trees, beautiful and green and different from ours, each with flowers and . . . fruit. There are many birds of all sizes that sing very sweetly, and there are many palms different from those in Guinea or Spain," observed Columbus.[23] In honor of Prince Juan, he named the island Juana.

Despite the absence of the promised gold, Columbus was convinced that Cuba was near the Chinese mainland. He thus decided to sail for the city of Quinsay, or modern Hankow, then the legendary home of Marco Polo's Great Khan. The expedition arrived at Cuba's Puerto Gibara on November 1. The natives then suggested Columbus could travel inland through the valley of the Cacoyugin to meet their leader who, the explorer assumed, would be the Great Khan himself. Before long a Castilian named Rodrigo de Jerez was dispatched to the alleged Chinese ruler with a set of official papers, Old World spices, and Venetian glass. To circumvent the language differences, he was accompanied by two Indian guides and a *converso* interpreter, Luís de Torres.

At least as important as gold was the hope of finding the fabled spices of the Indies. Before long, Columbus's erstwhile rival Pinzón appeared with "some bright reddish things like nuts"—creole pepper.[24] Pinzón also presented Columbus with objects he believed to be cinammon nuts but were, in reality, another unnamed product. In time, the crew would discover still other crops—sweet potatoes, beans, a masticlike resin from gumbo-limbo trees, and wild cotton.

By November 5 Columbus's envoys had returned with disappointing news. After traveling upland to the modern town of Holguin, the Spaniards arrived at a crude village of palm-thatched huts and were presented to a tribal leader. From the poverty of the village and the absence of jade, pearls, and silks, the Spaniards soon realized the Indian leader was not the Great Khan.

Ultimately the most extraordinary Cuban discovery was *tabaco*, or tobacco, which the natives, Columbus observed, smoked in "a charred, hollow wood." By the time Columbus left Cuba on November 12 he noted that the natives were

> very trusting, and not only believe . . . there is a God in Heaven and . . . we come from Heaven. They learn very quickly any prayer we tell them to say and . . . make the sign of the cross. Therefore, Your Highnesses must resolve to make them Christians. I believe that if this effort commences in a short time a multitude of peoples will be converted to our Holy Faith and Spain acquire great domains and riches . . .

Still, such expressions of Christian piety did not stop Columbus from seizing five young men in a boat or kidnapping seven young women and three children. "I did so," Columbus explained, in reference to the women, "so that the men I had taken would conduct themselves better in Spain than they might have otherwise, because of having women from their own country there with them."[25]

By mid-November half of Columbus's four goals for the expedition had been fulfilled—the discovery of new lands and an assessment of the pagan population as potential converts. The other two goals—the rich spice trade and the fabled gold of the Orient—still eluded him.

For a week the expedition skirted other mountainous islands of the Lesser Antilles as Columbus searched for Babeque, or Great Iguana Island.

On Wednesday, November 21, the wind shifted. As the *Niña* and *Santa María* sailed southeast, the *Pinta* suddenly changed direction. Columbus reported:

> This day, Martin Alonso Pinzón sailed away with the caravel *Pinta* without my will or command. It was through perfidy. I think he believes that an Indian I had placed on the *Pinta* could lead him to much gold, so he departed without warning and with-

out the excuse of bad weather, but because he wished to do so.
He has done and said many other [similar] things to me.[26]

That night was clear, and Columbus could still see the *Pinta* at a distance of twelve miles. He even signaled it with a light. But Pinzón refused to turn back. This was the most dramatic example yet of the hostility between the two mariners, each of whom needed the other to launch the expedition, but who now vowed to win glory for himself.

On the twenty-fourth, the *Niña* and *Santa María* landed at the Cuban provinces' flat island of Puerto Cayo Moa and skirted the harbor of Cabo Campana, or Cape Bell. By December 5 Columbus had sighted the easternmost point of Cuba and, thinking it to be an extremity of the Eurasian continent, named it Alpha and Omega. Because the winds prevented him from reaching Babeque, the explorer sailed instead toward Bohio, or Haiti. The captive Indians, however, trembled when they realized Columbus's intent for they believed the native Haitians were one-eyed, dog-faced monsters who ate human flesh.

Nevertheless, on Thursday, December 6, the *Santa María* and *Niña* skirted the coast of Haiti, sighting Tortuga and finally, at sunset, entering a harbor Columbus dubbed Puerto de San Nicolas, in honor of that saint's feast day. In contrast to the San Salvadorans' warm greeting, the Haitians fled when they saw the foreign boats. By that time Columbus's desire to find gold for Ferdinand and Isabella had become an obsession. "I hope to God that I can have some good trade in gold before I return to Spain," he scribbled rather desperately in his log that night.[27] Ostensibly his motive for finding the gold was religious, for in a subsequent entry he wrote that he had petitioned the monarchs "to see that all the profits of this, my enterprise, should be spent on the conquest of Jerusalem."[28]

The following day, Columbus sailed west past Cape Saint Mole and Port à l'Écu, anchoring in a harbor called Puerto de la Concepción, or Moustique Bay, where heavy winds and rain detained the expedition for five days. On December 12 Columbus nailed a cross at the entrance to the harbor and christened Haiti Española in honor of the Castilian crown. Later, thanks to Martire's Latinization of that name, the island would be known as Hispaniola.

During the dedication ceremony the natives fled and the Spaniards captured only one young girl. In the interests of establishing friendly relations, Columbus again decided to turn the frightened girl back, but not before dressing her in sailor clothes and regaling her with glass beads, hawk bells, and brass rings. Apparently the scheme worked, for on the thirteenth when Columbus sent a nine-man expedition into the village, they were greeted by the natives who offered them fish and manioc bread. And when an Indian from the *Santa María* told the Haitians that Columbus wanted a parrot, the natives brought the sailors a whole flock of the gaily colored birds.

But Columbus, restless with gold fever, set sail again. On December 14 the *Niña* and *Santa María* followed a north/northeast course toward Tortuga and, on the sixteenth, encountering a solitary Indian canoeing in the turbulent waters, hoisted him aboard. When the Europeans set him ashore at what would later be called Haiti's Port de Paix, the Haitian agreed to act as their ambassador. Ultimately the Spaniards were introduced to the young Haitian king, whose advisors gave them directions to Babeque. The next day a *cacique,* the Indian term for "high governor," appeared and traded a piece of gold leaf with the sailors. To Columbus's intense frustration, although he was now seeing larger collections of gold among the Indians, his search for its source still seemed futile.

Still, the explorer was heartened by the natural subservience of the natives, who, he noted for Isabella and Ferdinand's benefit, "are suitable to be governed and made to work and sow and do everything else that shall be necessary . . . to observe our customs."[29] But in 1492, seduction, rather than enslavement, was Columbus's preferred approach. Tuesday, December 18, was the Spanish feast day for Santa María de la O, or Saint Mary of the Conception, and thus the fleet was decorated with banners and guns. Columbus invited the cacique and his men aboard the *Santa María* to taste European food and for their amusement ordered the *lombardas* to be fired. During that meeting, an old Indian had so convinced Columbus that gold could be found to the east that the explorer set sail that same night.

On December 20, after passing Cape Haitien, the expedition landed in a harbor called La Mar de Santo Tomas, modern Acul Bay. Here, as at the previous Haitian village, the Spaniards were welcomed by natives who, convinced "that I and all my people came from Heaven," brought them white bread and water in gourds and clay pitchers.[30]

The natives treated the Spaniards so generously that Columbus wrote "I already consider them to be Christians and subjects of the Sovereigns of Castile."[31] Of souls to be converted to Christianity and slaves to work willingly in future Spanish colonies, Columbus had few doubts. Yet by December 21 the failure to find gold was beginning to unravel his nerves and perhaps even his judgment. On the twenty-second Columbus set sail again. But strong easterly winds forced him to anchor near the mouth of the Bay of Acul. A messenger arrived from Guacanagari, the cacique of all of northeastern Haiti, inviting him to visit. With the invitation had come a rich gift—an embroidered cotton belt at whose center was a mask with ears, tongue, and nose of hammered gold.

Pondering the valuable gift and sensing he was at last close to the source of the region's gold, Columbus dispatched his ambassadors. Another chief soon appeared, announcing that "in this isle Española there is a great quantity of gold and that people from other places come here to buy it . . ."[32] Thereafter more than 1,000 people visited the *Santa María* in canoes bringing gifts—seeds, spices, fish, earthen water jugs. Another five hundred or so, lacking boats, swam to Columbus's caravel, insisting that the Spaniards accept their presents. "Your Highnesses may believe that in all the world there cannot be better or more gentle people," wrote Columbus. "You will soon make them Christians and will teach them the good customs of your realms. . . ."[33]

On December 23 Columbus's men returned from their meeting with Guacanagari with an invitation for the admiral and his fleet to sail to the harbor. The Spaniards had returned with several Indians, one of whom promised to show Columbus where gold could be mined on Hispaniola.

Enticed, Columbus sailed before sunrise on December 24 from Acul Bay to Punta Santa, also known as Cape Haitien. That night the *Santa María* and *Niña* anchored about three miles out in the bay, which, men from the first expedition assured Columbus, was free from rocky shoals. Soon after the 11:00 P.M. watch, Columbus entrusted the *Santa María* to its owner and an officer of the watch, Juan de la Cosa, and retired to his cabin. Shortly after midnight, Christmas Day, Columbus was awakened abruptly by a sudden jolt.

Apparently la Cosa had been so tired that he had left the steering of the *Santa María* in the hands of a young boy, who did not realize that the ship was slowly slipping onto a coral reef. When the rudder ran aground and the boy yelled for help, Columbus sprang onto the deck and summoned his men. The admiral then ordered la Cosa to raise the rowboat and haul in the anchor, but instead, the mariner and his friends piled into the boat and headed for the *Niña*, a mile and a half windward. Once they arrived at the *Niña*, its appalled captain, Vicente Yáñez Pinzón, refused to allow the deserters to board.

The tide, meanwhile, was relentlessly pushing the *Santa María* onto the coral shelf. By then the ship already listed to one side. Hoping to lighten its weight, Columbus ordered the main mast cut. But it was too late: The coral reef had burst or ripped apart the seams of the boat, which began to fill with water. Panicked, Columbus ordered the crew to take refuge on the *Niña*. The men spent Christmas Day grimly unloading the supplies stored on the *Santa María*.

To console Columbus, Guacanagarí sent a "weeping" relative and men to assist in the task of stripping the shipwreck. On December 26 the cacique himself arrived to pay the disheartened Columbus a visit on the *Niña* and to offer his services.

Columbus hosted Guacanagari to a meal aboard ship, and later the cacique honored him on the shore with a dinner of shrimp, game, and bread. He also presented the explorer with gold-trimmed masks and jewelry. To amuse the Indians, Columbus then ordered the crew of the *Niña* to shoot holes in the *Santa María*'s hull.

Not all the forty men from the *Santa María* could be accommodated on the smaller *Niña*. The only solution, Columbus decided, was to leave some in a settlement on Haiti. The turn of events, he rationalized, must have been ordained by the Almighty. "It was," Columbus wrote that day, "Our Lord [who] caused me to run aground at this place so that I might establish a settlement here."[34]

The resultant fort, built on the eastern end of Caracol Bay from the wooden hull and beams of the *Santa María*, was called Navidad, or Nativity, to commemorate the day the shipwreck occurred. Within that towered and moated stronghold, the sailors stored European seeds, wine, biscuits, guns, and other supplies from the *Santa María*. Thirty-nine men chosen from both the *Niña* and the *Santa María* were left behind in Fort Navidad under the command of Diego de Harana, the fleet's marshall and cousin of Columbus's mistress, and two other officers. Most of the men, or so Columbus claimed, had begged to remain behind to establish the first Spanish settlement in the Indies.

On January 4, 1493, after leaving the men under the protection of Guacanagari and the Almighty, Columbus departed on the *Niña*. But despite the Haitian cacique's talk of gold, the explorer set his course directly for Spain.

On the eve of his departure Columbus wrote:

> If I were certain that the *Pinta* would reach Spain in safety with
> Martin Alonso Pinzón, I would not hesitate to continue the explo-

ration. But because I do not know if this will happen, and since
Pinzón would be able to lie to the Sovereigns to avoid the punishment he deserves for leaving me without permission . . . I feel
confident that Our Lord will give me good weather and everything
will be remedied.[35]

On January 6, as the *Niña* sailed beyond Isle Cabra, Columbus directed a sailor to
climb to the top of the mast to look for shoals. To the man's astonishment, he
sighted the *Pinta*. Because the water was too shallow for the two boats to anchor,
they were forced to sail thirty miles to the closest Haitian harbor at the Monte
Cristi peninsula. Pinzón then boarded the *Niña* and apologized, claiming that "he
had become separated against his will." Privately Columbus observed that he
"gave many reasons for his departure, but they are all false. Pinzón acted with
greed and arrogance that night when he sailed off and left me . . ."[36]

Adding to Columbus's disgust was the realization that Pinzón had found the
elusive gold mines in both Monte Cristi and in the "Cibao," the Haitian interior.
Pinzón's crew purchased great stores of the metal and loaded it onto the *Pinta*.
Pinzón heard about Columbus's shipwreck from the Indians a few days after the
incident. Thus on January 6 he was presumably traveling downwind to rescue the
admiral.

From the first Pinzón had resented the foreigner whose seamanship was less
than his own, but who nevertheless held a royal charter from Isabella and
Ferdinand that guaranteed ennoblement for his heirs. Conversely, Columbus
loathed the crude, uneducated mariner, who not only had the good luck to sight
land from his boat first, but had even found some of the Indies' fabled gold.

Yet to return to Spain alone in a tiny caravel in the dead of winter was,
Columbus knew, foolhardy. Probably that was why the explorer grimly held his
temper until he and Pinzón returned to Spain. "I am going to ignore these actions,"
the admiral vowed, "in order to prevent Satan from hindering this voyage, as he
has done until now."[37]

CHAPTER FIFTY-TWO

Crosswinds

The trip home from the Caribbean began with favorable winds and a bright sky. Instinctively Columbus had chosen a northeasterly course that brought him into the Bermuda latitude. From there the explorer caught sturdy westerlies that sped him across the Atlantic at an average speed of one hundred miles a day.

Europe, meanwhile, was suffering one of the worst winters of the century. Violent winds, harsh storms, and icy temperatures lashed over the oceans, making sea travel extremely perilous. Twenty-five ships were lost in Flanders alone and countless others trapped in harbors from Lisbon to Genoa because of the violent winds.

Lulled by the soft breezes and warm temperatures of the Caribbean, Columbus remained ignorant of the harsh North Atlantic weather. On January 6, the day he met Pinzón and nearly a week after his departure from northern Haiti, Columbus observed that "the breeze is as mild and sweet as in Sevilla in April or May, and the sea, God be given many thanks, is very calm all the time."[1]

The explorer's first inkling of the violent storms that wracked Europe would not come until February 12 when he crossed into the northern latitudes near the Azores. Heavy seas and driving winds suddenly inundated both ships, swirling them through turbulent waters. "If the caravel had not been very sound and well equipped," wrote Columbus, "I fear we would have been lost."[2]

The storm raged for three days, throwing waves so high that at times they crested over the decks of the ships, despite the crews' efforts to avoid each cascading swell. To save the boats required the vigilance and energies of all hands working feverishly for several sleepless days. On the night of February 13–14 violent crosswinds confounded every effort to keep the caravels on course. As the winds reached hurricane levels, the *Niña* and the *Pinta* were separated. In that murky, desperate night Columbus and Pinzón lighted signal fires to follow each other. But it was no use. By morning the two ships had been blown in separate directions, and each was alone in a gray, swirling sea. Ironically, the winds that had brought the two rivals together again in the Caribbean had now blown them so far apart that the ships would not find each other again until Castile.

That night Columbus and his crew prayed to the Almighty as never before. Their terror was so extreme they even tried bribery. Three lotteries were held aboard ship to select sailors for a pilgrimage if the *Niña* survived. Lacking paper, the sailors used chick peas for lots, the "winning" pea being cross-hatched with a knife. By some coincidence, or perhaps a sailor's sleight-of-hand, Columbus won two of the three lotteries. Nevertheless, the bad weather intensified, and because "all were resigned to being lost," Columbus and his terrified crew vowed collectively to visit the first shrine of the Virgin they found on land.[3]

Privately, Columbus worried that the news of his great discovery would never find its way back to Spain. "It seems to me that the great desire I have to bring this wonderful news to Your Highnesses and to show that I have been proven truthful in what I have said and volunteered to discover, causes me to fear greatly that I will not succeed in doing so. It seems to me that even a gnat can disturb and impede it," he wrote.[5]

Later that night, as if in answer to Columbus's prayers, the sky began to clear, and at dawn on February 15 a sailor sighted land. For two days the relieved sailors debated their location, some insisting they were near Madeira, others that they had reached Lisbon.

By Monday, February 18, Columbus's suspicion that they had reached the Portuguese-held Azores was confirmed. The explorer's worst fear had come true: The *Niña* would have to seek help from the country that had twice rejected him and already regarded his voyage with suspicion. But Columbus had no choice: His crew was faint with hunger and exhaustion, the *Niña* needed new provisions, and the explorer himself had gone sleepless for four nights. Furthermore, he was in terrible pain. "My legs," he noted, "have become cramped from exposure to the cold and water and from having so little food"—an arthritic condition that would plague Columbus for the rest of his life.[5]

Once the badly battered *Niña* anchored at the tiny island of Santa Maria, Columbus sent three crew members ashore to find food and announce their historic journey. By dusk, representatives from Santa Maria's deputy governor, João de Castanheira, arrived with chicken, bread, and other provisions. Columbus's men had not returned, they explained, because the deputy-governor had decided to host the sailors overnight for "the great pleasure he was having hearing about their voyage."[6] The next morning Castanheira promised to return with them and additional supplies.

By then, Columbus had learned that the *Niña* was anchored close to a tiny chapel built to the Virgin. Believing it an ideal moment to fulfill their third vow, Columbus dispatched half his crew to the chapel at dawn on February 20, while he and the rest of the men remained aboard ship. Once ashore, the mariners removed all their clothes except their shirts. Thus garbed as penitents they entered the chapel. As the sailors knelt in prayer a horseback posse rode toward the shrine and seized the Spaniards.

Distrusting the fantastic story Columbus's men had told about their return from the Indies, Castanheira suspected that the *Niña* had just returned from poaching in Portuguese West Guinea. Thus he had clapped half the crew in jail.

Ludicrous though the arrest was, Castanheira's assumption was not completely unfounded. The Azores were, in fact, a favorite port of call for sailors returning from Portuguese-held West Africa, and occasionally Spanish sailors who made illegal trading missions to Guinea were apprehended there. Castanheira thus assumed the sailors' story about a journey to the Indies was a ruse told to protect their ship after the storm.

By 11:00 A.M. Columbus, growing anxious at his men's failure to return, gave orders for the *Niña* to sail toward Santa Maria's main harbor of Punta Frades. A group of armed men that included Castanheira immediately rowed toward the ship and demanded the right to board. When Columbus refused, Castanheira demanded to see his papers. Sensing that if he boarded the Portuguese boat Castanheira would take him prisoner, Columbus displayed his passport and credentials over the *Niña*'s railings. He then haughtily informed the Portuguese official that he was "Your Highnesses' Admiral of the Ocean Sea and Viceroy of the Indies which now belong to Your Highnesses." He also reminded Castanheira that the sovereigns "felt much love and friendship for the King of Portugal."[7] If Castanheira did not release his sailors, Columbus threatened, he would return to Spain to demand justice. After more angry words Columbus sailed the *Niña* toward the Azorean island of San Miguel.

The next day Columbus returned to Santa Maria where, to his surprise, a priest, a notary, and five of his sailors appeared in the *Niña*'s rowboat. The officials stayed overnight on the *Niña* to examine Columbus's papers and his cargo of Indians, birds, and plants. Finally they granted the exasperated explorer rights of entry. Shortly thereafter, the rest of Columbus's crew was released from jail.

But Columbus was thoroughly disgusted with Santa Maria and his first reception on European land. On February 24, after obtaining fresh water and rocks for ballast, he ordered the *Niña* to sail for Palos.

Initially, the winds favored Columbus's speedy return to Castile. But on February 26 a storm once again surrounded the *Niña* and built to such a pitch that by the twenty-eighth Columbus could no longer keep the caravel on course. Daily the situation worsened. On March 2 the winds ripped apart nearly all the sails. Erratic wind and sea currents threw the *Niña* against the waves, and once again Columbus's sailors believed they were going to die. Again they held a lottery, and, as before, Columbus drew the winning pea. This time the terrified crew vowed that if they reached land, they would spend their first Saturday night ashore eating only bread and water.

By March 4 the winds swelled to cyclone force and "appeared to raise the ship in the air with the water from the sky and the lightning in every direction." But at nightfall there was a reprieve: At 7:00 P.M., just after the evening watch had begun, land was sighted directly ahead. Columbus, fearing the *Niña* would be dashed on the rocks by the strong offshore winds, raised the remaining mainsail and tacked all night with "infinite labor and fright."[8] At sunrise on Monday, March 4, Columbus gazed with horror at the Portuguese peninsula known as the Rock of Sintra, a high-cliffed promontory lying just north of the Tagus River and the city of Lisbon.

With his boat now badly crippled, Columbus again had no alternative—he had to enter the Tagus to repair the *Niña* and seek new supplies. On the riverbanks, Portuguese fishermen gaped at the sight of the battered caravel traveling upstream in the wake of the violent storm. They were so astonished, Columbus reported, that many spent the morning praying for the crew. Finally the *Niña* anchored at Restello, or Bellem as it is known today, four miles south of Lisbon.

Since sunrise Columbus had been considering a way to avoid a repetition of the treatment he had received in the Azores. To avoid accusations that he had sailed illegally to West Africa or otherwise violated the treaty of Alcaçovas, Columbus hastily dispatched a letter to King João asking permission to enter the port of Lisbon. "His Highness should know," the admiral added pointedly, "that I did not come from Guinea but from the Indies."[9] Moreover, the letter announced that Isabella and Ferdinand had given Columbus permission to enter Portuguese harbors to seek help if necessary.

That same day he attached a postscript to his own letter to Isabella and Ferdinand announcing his great discovery and explaining why he had landed in Portugal. "After having written this and being in the Sea of Castile, there rose upon me so great a wind from the S and SE that I had to ease the ships. But today, which was the greatest wonder in the world, I made this harbor of Lisbon . . ."[10]

Coincidentally, a Portuguese warship was anchored near the *Niña*. Before long the ship's master, the explorer Bartholomew Dias, who discovered Africa's southernmost tip in 1488, boarded the *Niña* and demanded that Columbus return with him to his captain, Álvaro Damão. But Columbus refused, declaring he would leave only by force. Then after reviewing Columbus's papers, the Portuguese explorer retreated. Some hours later Damão appeared "with great ceremony, complete with drums, trumpets and pipes, making a great display to pay his respects to the new Admiral and offering to do everything I ordered him to do."[11]

By then, word had spread about Columbus's historic discovery and the *Niña* became choked with visitors. On March 8 a royal messenger arrived with an invitation from King João requesting Columbus's visit and offering to have the *Niña* repaired and his sailors provisioned at the expense of the Portuguese crown. It would have been an insult for Columbus to refuse João's largesse. Thus, "in order to avoid suspicion, although I did not want to go," he consented.[12]

Instinctively Columbus feared a trap. Specifically, he feared that João had ulterior motives for his kindnesses and may have been prepared to accuse the explorer of some violation—of crossing illegally, perhaps, into Portuguese territory, or even of stealing a copy of Toscanelli's map, which the crown kept under lock and key. As it turned out, Columbus's fears were groundless. On March 9, after a thirty-mile mule ride to Valle do Paraíso, Columbus was greeted warmly by the Portuguese king at the monastery of Santa Maria das Virtudes.

The king, Columbus recalled, "received me with great honor and showed me much respect, asking me to sit down and talking very freely with me." He also hastened to assure Columbus that he would order "everything done which would be of use to Your Highnesses and to your service, even more fully than if it were for his service."[13] Still, beneath the veneer of warmth, Columbus sensed the king was suspicious.

> He indicated that he was greatly pleased that the voyage had been accomplished successfully, although he understood that in the capitulation between the Sovereigns and himself the conquest belonged to him. I told him that I had not seen the capitulation and did not know anything other than that the Sovereigns had commanded me not to go to La Mina nor to any part of Guinea and that this had been proclaimed in all of the ports of Andalusia before I started on the voyage. The King graciously responded that he was certain that there would be no need for mediators in this matter.[14]

Two days later Columbus left the Portuguese court, carrying with him King João's greetings to Isabella and Ferdinand. On the road from Alhandra a royal messenger intercepted Columbus with another offer from King João: permission to travel overland from Portugal to Castile with all expenses paid by the crown for lodgings, meals, beasts, and attendants.

Ultimately, Columbus declined. King João's prickly attitude worried him; thus he preferred to sail home. On March 11, the newly restored *Niña* set sail for Castile, and by the fifteenth, a Friday—always a lucky day for Columbus—the explorer crossed the bar of Saltes and slipped into the harbor of Palos. A crowd stared at the tiny caravel in disbelief as it anchored. Then, as if in one massive reflex, the flock of men rushed toward the *Niña*.

Once the news spread about Columbus's discovery, the citizens of Palos thronged to the caravel. Mesmerized by the Indians, the strange plants, birds, and foods from the Indies and by the sailors' stories, the enraptured citizenry followed Columbus to church for a thanksgiving service. To announce the historic landing, all the church bells of Palos were rung. In the ensuing confusion Columbus and his crewmen were carried through the streets and caught up in a dizzying round of *bodas y banquetes*, celebrations and festivities.

Ironically, Pinzón had landed in Galicia several days before Columbus reached Palos. Filled with dreams of glory, that captain informed the king and queen from his northern anchorage that he planned to visit them in Barcelona. To his surprise, Isabella and Ferdinand wrote back forbidding him to travel to them "save in the company of the Admiral, with whom he had sailed on that voyage of discovery."[15] Pinzón, chagrined by the monarchs' cold reply in his moment of glory, "went home to Palos a sick man."[16] By some accounts, he arrived on March 15 just a few hours after Columbus; by others he arrived a few days later. In any case, he appeared after Columbus's victorious return. This final humiliation, according to Columbus's son, was more than Pinzón could stand, and a "few days after his arrival he died of grief."[17]

There are contradictory reports about Columbus's reaction to Pinzón's last illness. Some historians maintain that Columbus did not learn about Pinzón's

March 20 death until he had left Palos; others, that Columbus stayed at Pinzón's home during the last days of his rival's life. Whatever the truth was, the last entry in Columbus's log suggests that even at the height of his glory, in the triumphal march he now planned to Barcelona to meet the king and queen, he could not forget those who had ridiculed him.

> His Divine Majesty does all good things, and everything is good except sin and nothing can be imagined or planned without His consent. This voyage has miraculously proven this to be so, as can be learned . . . by the remarkable miracles which have occurred during the voyage and for me who has been in the court of Your Highnesses for such a long time with opposition and against the advice of so many of the principal persons of your household, who were all against me and treated this undertaking as a folly.[18]

As Columbus anticipated, his discovery of what he believed to be the East Indies would silence old enemies in Isabella and Ferdinand's court, just as it had broken Pinzón. But before long, Columbus would learn about the crosswinds of jealousy that inevitably surround an extraordinary accomplishment and may blow stronger than the gales that impeded his first passage home.

To Isabella and Ferdinand, Columbus's discovery of the "Indies" was not only a miracle but a confirmation of God's will that they were his chosen shepherds. With the receipt of Columbus's announcement, the monarchs replied: "We have seen your letters and we have taken much pleasure in learning whereof you write, and that God gave so good a result to your labors, and well guided you in what you commenced, whereof He will be well served and we also, and our realms receive so much advantage . . ."[19]

It was imperative that the gains of Columbus's *descubrimiento,* or discovery, be consolidated by a return voyage. Isabella and Ferdinand wrote:

> As we will that . . . which you have commenced with the aid of God be continued . . . we wish you to come soon and . . . hasten your coming as much as possible so that everything may be seen to, and as you see that the summer is with us and we must not . . . miss the time to return, see whether something could not already be prepared in Seville or in other places for your return to the lands you have discovered.[20]

The uneasy political atmosphere of 1493 probably contributed to the urgent tone of this letter. No doubt the monarchs were alarmed to learn that Columbus had been forced to land in Portugal. They were also worried about France's imperialist ambitions. Although Roussillon and Cerdagne had been restored to Aragón, Charles VIII was clearly planning to invade Naples. In response, Isabella and Ferdinand had secretly renewed Catherine's marriage treaty to Prince Arthur of England. The papal states—Milan, Florence, Naples, and the Holy See itself—

were divided into squabbling factions that threatened to thrust the Italian peninsula—and Christianity itself—into war.

Columbus's *descubrimiento* thus came at a fortuitous time, less than a year after Isabella and Ferdinand had conquered Granada. As such, those two triumphs had established Castile as Europe's premier Christian nation—a kingdom that not only defeated the pagan within its borders but now claimed the heathens of the Indies as well. From that perspective Columbus's discovery was Ferdinand and Isabella's apogee, a masterstroke whose implications would reverberate through Europe and profoundly change its political configuration even before its true significance—the discovery of the American continents—was known.

But more voyages, more explorations, and more settlements were necessary if the newly discovered lands were to remain securely in Castilian hands. After Easter, in compliance with the monarchs' orders, Columbus thus set out from Sevilla and traveled to Barcelona with seamen, servants, and six Indians.

The procession caused an immediate sensation. As the entourage traveled north, peasants and merchants crowded the roads to catch a glimpse of the explorer, his Indians, and his strange assortment of aromatic herbs, plants, and birds. The Indians were scantily dressed, their bodies painted and decorated with fish bones, crude collars, bracelets, and gold ornaments, their exotic appearance enhanced by cages full of squawking parrots. After the smirks and hurts of a lifetime, Columbus was not one to shrink from celebrityhood; thus he paraded proudly past the admiring crowds.

On April 20 the admiral arrived in Barcelona, where he was formally greeted by the city fathers and *grandees* of Isabella and Ferdinand's court. The next day Columbus crossed the stone-paved courtyard between Barcelona's royal palace and the Church of Santa Clara. Nobles and *hidalgos* clothed in brocade and velvet applauded as he walked toward Isabella and Ferdinand, who were seated on raised thrones beneath a golden canopy. As Columbus approached the dais and prostrated himself before the king and queen, they "rose from their thrones as if he were a great lord, and would not let him kiss their hands."[21] Later, inside the great hall of the palace, Isabella and Ferdinand paid Columbus an even greater honor: They insisted that a chair be brought for the explorer to be seated next to them and Prince Juan.

Afterward, the monarchs plied Columbus with questions, stared at the Indians, and examined his trays of gold bars, cotton pods, and exotic herbs. For an hour or so Columbus talked enthusiastically about his explorations, and from time to time he gazed up at the king and queen. Isabella was clearly entranced by the explorer's tales and descriptions of the gentle Indians, moved as a woman as well as a queen by his exploits and dangerous journey home.

Then the music of *Te Deum* sung by the royal chorus wafted through the air and the court fell to their knees. Tears of joy and thanksgiving rolled down the faces of the king, the queen, and the explorer. In that emotional moment, there seemed little doubt that Columbus's magnificent discovery, the capstone of Isabella and Ferdinand's long efforts to create a Christian universe, had been graced by God.

For weeks, Columbus was the center of attraction at the Castilian court. The navigator spent hours describing his discoveries to Isabella and Ferdinand. He was seen regularly hunting with Ferdinand, an honor usually reserved for the king's closest kin. Banquets, fiestas, and religious services were held in the explorer's honor. At one memorable feast in Cardinal Mendoza's home, Columbus was seated next to his host and paid the singular honor of having his food served in a covered dish and tasted for poison. In 1493, the Italian humanist Martire, who had not even noticed Columbus's 1492 departure, panegyrized him as "having given light to the hidden half of the world."[22]

Isabella and Ferdinand immediately bestowed titles, gifts, and special privileges upon the explorer. By late April, the king and queen dubbed Columbus Admiral of the Ocean Sea and proclaimed that henceforth the explorer would be known as Don Cristobal Colón. On May 20 they issued letters granting Columbus a new coat of arms within which he had the singular distinction of displaying the royal symbols of a golden Castilian castle and a purple lion.

Eight days later the sovereigns confirmed the Capitulations of 1492—the original documents that granted Columbus hereditary rights to all discovered lands and a share in their profits. In hopes that "with His help you will find and discover other islands,"[23] Isabella and Ferdinand also honored Columbus with the title of *Capitan general de la Armada,* or Captain General of the Fleet.

That title was meant to establish Columbus's authority over all aspects of the second voyage, whose primary goal was to convert the Indians. To carry out that task, twelve priests were named to the expedition, among them the young Bartolomé de Las Casas, who would eventually become Columbus's first chronicler and the famed historian of the Indies.

The conversions, Isabella and Ferdinand warned Columbus, had to be accomplished with gentleness and not by force. Columbus was

> to treat the said Indians very well and lovingly and to abstain
> from doing them any injury, arranging that both peoples hold
> much conversation and intimacy, each serving the others to the
> best of their ability. Moreover, the said Admiral is to present them
> with . . . merchandise of their Highnesses that he is carrying for
> barter and honor them much and, if any person . . . should mal-
> treat the said Indians in any manner whatsoever, the said Admiral,
> as Viceroy and Governor of Their Highnesses, is to punish them
> severely. . . . [24]

The second object of the new voyage was the establishment of a licensed trading post, which was to include not only spices, plants, and artifacts but gold. All goods exchanged with the Indians were to be supervised by the Castilian crown and regulated through *alcaldes* and clerks. Through that system all gold was to remain the property of the crown, except one-eighth, which was to go to the admiral.

In preparation for the second voyage, Isabella and Ferdinand appointed Juan Rodríguez de Fonseca, Archdeacon of Sevilla, to help Columbus assemble a fleet of seventeen boats and collect provisions, arms, seeds, tools, and other essentials. Selecting the men for the second voyage was the most difficult task of all for the Castilians, excited by "the fame of gold and the other wonders of that land," had thrown themselves at Columbus's feet from the day of his arrival in Palos.[25] "So many offered themselves," the explorer's sons would later recall, "that it was necessary to restrict the number of those who might go thither."[26]

The same might have been said about those who flocked around the Indians in Barcelona. To the courtiers of Isabella and Ferdinand's court, the aborigines were a source of wonder and amusement to be alternately fed, clothed, teased, educated, and petted. Moreover, it was widely rumored that the male Indians had been secretly introduced to several Barcelona prostitutes.

That initial contact, according to one historical theory, precipitated the spread of syphilis, which seems to have appeared in Western Europe in the late 1490s. Another theory suggests that the sailors of Columbus's first journey brought the disease home. The debate has never been settled. Some epidemiologists maintain that syphilis was already endemic to Europe, having been contracted from the East via Italy, and that the sailors on Columbus's first and second journeys actually spread it to the West Indians. In any case, the prudish Isabella and Ferdinand would not have approved of the Europeans' sexual contact with the "gentle savages" under their care in Barcelona. Nor could Columbus, for he was intent upon having the Indians baptized as soon as possible to demonstrate their spiritual malleability.

In fact, shortly after Columbus's arrival King Ferdinand, Prince Juan, and several other *grandees* volunteered to serve as sponsors for the Indians' baptismal ceremony. Afterward one Indian was chosen to remain with the Castilian court in the service of Prince Juan. The rest were sent to Sevilla to receive religious instruction as missionaries who would return with Columbus on his second voyage.

Isabella and Ferdinand lost no time in proclaiming Columbus's discovery to the rest of the European world. The first person they notified was the new pope, Rodrigo Borgia, now known as Alexander VI. As the highest spiritual authority in Christendom, it was Pope Alexander's duty to establish a nation's rights to hitherto unclaimed heathen lands. By early April 1493 the Castilian monarchs, fearing that Portugal would try to claim those lands for itself, had forwarded a copy of Columbus's letter to the pope. There were good reasons for Isabella and Ferdinand's anxieties. Weeks before Columbus had appeared in Barcelona, one of their Portuguese ambassadors informed them that João was quietly outfitting an expedition to explore the "Indies" himself. To discourage the project, the alarmed sovereigns dispatched another ambassador, Lope de Herrera, to the Portuguese court. Ostensibly, Herrera's mission was to thank King João for his gracious reception of Columbus in Lisbon. Yet during his visit he asked King João to order his subjects to respect Castile's discoveries in the Indies.

Initially João complied and agreed to a sixty-day postponement. In return, the king dispatched his own ambassador to Isabella and Ferdinand to propose that Castile and Portugal divide the globe. By that arrangement Portugal would retain all lands beneath the Canaries and Castile, all those above it. Once again Isabella and Ferdinand turned to the pope for assistance. On May 3 Alexander thus issued a bull granting Isabella and Ferdinand territorial rights to all lands they discovered in the Western Ocean.

But before the end of that month, King João sent a second ambassador to remind Isabella and Ferdinand about the Treaty of Alcaçovas. According to that treaty and a subsequent papal bull, Portugal was entitled to all lands west of Africa and south of the Canaries. Although the Portuguese messenger was polite, Isabella and Ferdinand quickly grasped his meaning.

Nevertheless, at that very moment, two Castilian ambassadors, the Archbishop of Toledo and Diego López, Count of Haro, were traveling to the Holy See, presumably to express Isabella and Ferdinand's allegiance to the new pope. But on June 19 Haro chided Alexander for corrupt practices, the flagrant use of benefices as bribes, and his stubborn protection of heretics and Moors from the Spanish Inquisition. As a parting salvo, he warned Alexander that papal hostility to Ferdinand's cousin King Ferrante of Naples made the promise of Spanish aid to the Holy See doubtful.

That same day another Castilian ambassador, Bernardino de Carvajal, preached a sermon in Rome comparing the Canary Islands to conquests of "other unknown islands toward the Indians . . . [that] may be fully regarded as the most precious things in the whole world, and it is expected that they will shortly be prepared for Christ by royal messengers."[27] The implications of Carvajal's sermon, which was subsequently printed in Rome, were clear: Castile now stood at the head of a new Christian empire, whose domains were not only European but extended into the distant lands of the Ocean Sea. Alexander, fearing Isabella and Ferdinand's wrath and their threatened loss of support, thus obliged with two new bulls; the first, *Eximiae Devotionis,* reaffirmed the king and queen's rights to the Indies, and a second, *Inter Caetera,* established a *raya,* or line of demarcation, between Castilian and Portuguese discovery rights. This bull stated:

> In these unknown lands where Christopher Columbus has stepped,
> lives a people, naked, vegetarian, who believe in one God and ask
> but to be taught to believe in Jesus Christ. All these islands and
> territories, abounding in gold, spices and treasure, situated west
> and south of a line that runs from the North to the South Pole, a
> hundred leagues west of the Isles of the Azores and Cape Verde,
> are allocated to the Catholic Kings . . . [28]

This bull infuriated the Portuguese ambassadors who arrived in Spain in August 1493. King João, they insisted, planned to discover lands of his own "which were profitable and richer than the others" that he believed lay between Africa and the Orient. Clearly, Isabella and Ferdinand were stymied. It was an admittedly impossible task to fix property lines equitably upon a section of the globe whose watery expanse was uncertain. Yet to leave it unclaimed seemed equally naive.

On September 26 Alexander issued still another bull, *Dudum Siquidem,* extending the Spanish sovereigns' rights "to all islands and mainlands, whatso-ever, found and to be found . . . in sailing or traveling toward the west or south, whether they be in regions, occidental or meridional and oriental and of India."[29] All previous grants made to the disputed territories "whether to kings, princes, infantes, religious or military orders"[30] were null and void.

A day earlier, to the sounds of blaring trumpets and cannon salutes, Columbus sailed from the port of Cádiz into the Atlantic at the head of a gaily decorated and emblazoned seventeen-vessel fleet to begin his second voyage to the Indies. Shortly thereafter two Castilian ambassadors, Pedro de Ayala and Garcí López de Carbajal, traveled to Lisbon to notify King João about his departure and the new papal bull.

King João was enraged by the news. Obviously Alexander VI favored Isabella and Ferdinand without any regard to the difficulties *Dudum Siquidem* presented to Portugal. With half the globe still uncharted, the possibilities for Spanish supremacy now seemed unlimited. It was entirely possible that Columbus might discover lands off the African coast that would threaten Portuguese properties. Even worse, he might sail far enough west to claim the entire Asian peninsula for Castile, thereby choking Portugal out of claims to the rich spice and gold trade of the Orient it might have gained by circling Africa.

To placate João, Isabella and Ferdinand had instructed their ambassadors to suggest that the disagreement be referred to arbitration at the Holy See or another common arena. But João would not consider more papal intervention. Caustically he referred to the emissary as "a mere abortion, having neither head nor foot"[31]—a reference to Carbajal's dullness and Ayala's lameness. Then, with obvious malicious intent, he "accidentally" brought the Castilian ambassadors before a well-drilled and mounted battalion of Portuguese cavalry.

Despite a subsequent flurry of alarmed ambassadorial reports from Lisbon, Isabella and Ferdinand decided to do nothing. Although their political links had been weakened two years earlier by Prince Afonso's death and their daughter's widowhood, they were not eager for another Castilian-Portuguese war. Nor, apparently, was João. Finally, after brooding about it for months, the Portuguese king agreed to a meeting with Castile.

On June 7, 1494, representatives from the two kingdoms convened in Tordesillas. In the now-famous *Casa de Tratado de Tordesillas,* or meeting house of the treaty of Tordesillas, Castilian and Portuguese emissaries agreed to move the line of demarcation 370 leagues west of the Cape Verde Islands. Regardless of who discovered land, all shores west of that meridian would belong to Castile; to their east all lands would belong to Portugal.

This treaty was one of João's last accomplishments. A year later he was stricken with dropsy, or uremia, and on October 25, 1495, at forty years of age, he died. But João left Portugal with a rich inheritance. Six years after the treaty of Tordesillas, the Portuguese commander Pedro Álvares Cabral landed on the shores of a rich, densely forested continental expanse that would become known as Brazil.

CHAPTER FIFTY-THREE

Los Reyes Católicos

While plans to convert Columbus's Indians preoccupied Isabella in the spring of 1493, they were merely a prelude to her reformation of Castilian Christianity. The assassination attempt upon Ferdinand had so magnified the queen's awareness of her own mortality that she was increasingly anxious to perfect herself, her subjects, and the Spanish church.

To accomplish that goal Isabella initially turned inward. After Talavera's 1492 appointment as Archbishop of Granada, the queen searched for a new confessor—someone pious, but wise enough to counsel her on the political and spiritual issues that confounded her conscience. The post had been difficult to fill. Few men were devout enough to disdain the worldly temptations that inevitably accompanied that office, fewer still strong enough to resist flattering the queen.

With such restrictions, it was inevitable that Isabella would bind herself to another religious fundamentalist, this time a fifty-four-year-old ascetic Franciscan monk named Francisco Jiménez de Cisneros. Born to impoverished *hidalgo* parents, the youthful Cisneros had studied in Salamanca and Rome and returned to Castile during King Enrique's reign to become a monk.

By the mid-fifteenth century the Franciscan order was divided into two branches—the "conventuals" who owned property and indulged freely in secular pleasures, and the smaller, more orthodox "observatines" who rigorously obeyed the Franciscan vows of poverty, chastity, and obedience.

Cisneros belonged to the latter group, among which he was considered an extremist. Habitually the young monk slept on the ground with a piece of wood for his pillow. He wore no underclothes, only a hair shirt next to his skin. His meals were often bread and water. His self-flagellations were a daily exercise. For several years Cisneros sought spiritual ecstasy by living alone on green herbs and water in the thick chestnut forests of the convent of Our Lady at Castanar. But while the monk shunned the world, the church would not allow him to live as a recluse for long and eventually transferred him to the Convent of Salzeda, over which he was appointed guardian.

By the late 1480s Cisneros's fanatic reputation was already so legendary among the Castilians that soldiers at the siege of Málaga had dubbed their *lombardas* his "seven sisters." In 1492 Cardinal Mendoza, an old admirer of Cisneros's who once predicted that a man "so extraordinary would not long be buried in the shades of a convent," determined to fulfill that prophecy by introducing him to court.[1]

Isabella was immediately impressed with Cisneros, but when she asked him to become her confessor, the gaunt Franciscan hesitated. Although Cisneros had no spiritual objection to serving the queen, he feared the opulence of the royal court would corrupt his vows. Finally he agreed to accept the position with the understanding that when he was not needed for court duties he would be able to return to his own monastery.

The queen reluctantly consented. Despite subsequent criticisms from Ferdinand and her courtiers, Isabella never regretted her choice; Cisneros would hold her accountable to the strictest standard of religious conscience. Moreover, he helped her reform the Spanish Catholic church.

That opportunity first presented itself when, in 1494, Cisneros was appointed the provincial, or regional head, of the Franciscans. Henceforth, the monk began to live an even more divided existence. Between appearances at court, Cisneros, barefoot and dressed in coarse cotton robes, begged his food as alms and traveled highways by foot to inspect the Franciscan monasteries. Behind the mendicant trailed his mule Bentillo, burdened with parcels of books.

In the two and a half centuries since St. Francis founded his mendicant order, the vows of poverty, chastity, and obedience had gradually been disregarded in many Spanish Franciscan monasteries. By the late fifteenth century many owned large estates and tracts of land. Others had built lavish shrines and chapels with funds donated by the wealthy who were eager to buy themselves a place in heaven. Instead of eating coarse fare, the monks enjoyed white flour, choice meats, and the finest wines, and their meals were often shared with their richly clad *barraganas,* or legalized concubines.

Early in her reign, Isabella sent ambassadors to Rome and into the monasteries themselves to protest these excesses, but the corruptions had continued. Finally, in March 1493, Pope Alexander issued the first of a series of bulls granting the monarchs permission to name prelates to reform "all the monasteries and convents of any order within her realm."[2] The following year, when Cisneros was named the Franciscan provincial, that movement began in earnest.

To conduct the reform, Cisneros followed a set pattern. For several days he visited a monastery to examine its activities, account books, and records of possessions. Afterward he called a meeting and ordered the monasteries to rid itself of their worldly holdings. Simultaneously, he forbade the refectories from serving rich foods and prohibited the monks from dressing in costly clothes. All *barraganas* were ordered to leave. And so could any monk unwilling to follow the tenets of St. Francis.

This uncompromising attitude soon made Cisneros hated and feared. In Toledo, when the brotherhood of one Franciscan order protested the reforms, Cisneros had them locked out of the monastery. The monks staged a protest, holding the cross aloft and chanting *In exitu Israel* (Israel in exile) to an astounded crowd of onlookers. But in the end Cisneros had his way. On June 18, 1494, Alexander VI issued a papal brief and a bull establishing the Franciscan reform movement.

The queen adopted a different approach. Like Cisneros she visited the convents, but instead of railing at the sisters, she attempted to change their behavior by her own example. As a devout Catholic, Isabella became a member of the "third order," as the groups of secular women pledged either temporarily or permanently to religious life, were called. During her visits to the convents, Isabella appeared in modest clothes, accompanied by only a few attendants, a rosary, a book of hours, her spindles and needles. Daily Isabella prayed with the nuns, ate at their tables, sewed, spun, and talked with them about the true spirit of Christianity and the value of religious commitment. By doing so the queen anticipated the appearance of another zealous reformer, St. Teresa of Ávila, whose writings would complete the spiritual transformation of the convents ninety years later.

Simultaneous with these reforms, Isabella was waging a parallel campaign for Christianity in newly conquered Granada. Although the 1492 treaty promised that the Moors could preserve their mosques and retain their religion, the Spanish sovereigns hoped to convert them. But to wrench the Crescent out of Moorish hands and forcibly replace it with the Cross so soon after the war might easily prompt a rebellion.

As an alternative, Isabella and Ferdinand began an education campaign directed at Moorish youth to gradually familiarize them with the Castilian language and Christianity. To head the program, the monarchs appointed the soft-spoken but uncompromising Talavera, Archbishop of Granada.

As spiritual leader of the Moorish province, Talavera's motto was "What is done for fear and by force cannot long endure, while what is done for love and charity is enduring."[3] In that spirit he studied Arabic and even established an Arabic grammar school for the Christian clergy. To pique the interests of the Moors, he translated parts of the Catholic canon into Arabic. Knowing that the Moslems abhorred Castilian music, he allowed Arabic instruments to be played at church.

To encourage conversions, Talavera insisted that the Inquisition be barred from the kingdom of Granada for forty years. But despite these efforts, the conversions proceeded slowly. Doubtless, many Moors who seriously considered baptism were unnerved by the presence of the *elches,* former Moslems who once endorsed Catholicism and later rejected it. As "relapsed" Christians, that population was a negative example to the young Moors whom Talavera hoped to convert. Had they lived in other Castilian provinces, the *elches* would have been subject to the harsh scrutiny of the Inquisition, but as Granadian citizens they lived in a state of political immunity.

By 1494 the tyranny of the Spanish Inquisition had become so pervasive that Pope Alexander VI was besieged with complaints. Ironically, the expulsion of the Jews had done little to stem the tide of tribunals, *auto-da-fes,* and condemnations by the Spanish Inquisition, the victims of which appealed to Rome with increasing urgency.

Torquemada's favorite suspects continued to be *conversos* and their ancestors, many of whom were burned in effigy. In 1493 the deceased grandfather of Segovia's *converso* bishop, Juan Arías Dávila, became one of Torquemada's victims. But the elderly bishop, refusing to tolerate his grandfather's denunciation, exhumed his bones to save them from the fires of the Inquisition. Then the prelate traveled to Rome to seek redress for his grievances.

That same year the Inquisition accused the Bishop of Aranda's deceased grandfather of "judaizing." Like Arías, Aranda traveled to Rome to appeal his case personally to the pope. Although the case dragged on for years and Aranda's grandfather was eventually condemned, the pope treated the two bishops well. In the early 1490s they served as papal legates for Alexander and, once ensconced in his favor, attacked Torquemada and his pitiless practices. In 1494 the pope, already disgusted by the flood of complaints he continued to receive from Castile and Aragón, reached a startling decision: He would, he told the Spanish bishops, strip Torquemada of his powers as Grand Inquisitor. However, Torquemada's demotion was to be gradual, conducted in incremental steps consistent with Alexander's masterful diplomacy. Fearful of incurring Isabella and Ferdinand's wrath, the pope couched Torquemada's demotion in terms of his advanced age and failing health. In his papal brief of June 23, Alexander noted that he cherished the seventy-four-year-old Torquemada "for his great labors in the exaltation of the Faith" but out of concern for his gout, was appointing several assistants to aid him with his duties.[4]

In reality, Alexander's appointees were not "assistants" at all but could operate freely without Torquemada. Four months later the pope would name still another "assistant," Sánchez de la Fuente, Bishop of Ávila, to serve as Judge of Appeal for Castile and Aragón. Through that appointment, all inquisitional condemnations could be appealed to the Bishop of Ávila. Thus was Torquemada quietly deposed as the highest authority in the Spanish Inquisition.

At the same time Alexander was stripping Torquemada of his powers, another champion of the church was loosening his grasp on Castile. In 1494, after a lifetime of service to the crown, Cardinal Mendoza's health began to fail. The prelate, founder of the College of Santa Cruz in Valladolid and long considered the "most splendid and brightest light of the Mendoza household," had been stricken with kidney disease.[5] Mendoza's illness was a terrible blow to the queen, who had depended heavily on his counsel for years. In June the cardinal made his will and named Isabella his executor. Then, the sixty-seven-year-old Mendoza began to consider his successor. Long before his death on January 11, 1495, he recommended Cisneros.

As queen, vested with the singular power to appoint ecclesiastics in Castile,

Isabella was not compelled to follow Mendoza's recommendation. But ultimately she did appoint Cisneros his successor. That choice was admittedly unorthodox, for the position was usually reserved for men from high-born families, but Cisneros's religious fervor and reformist zeal had convinced the queen that he was eminently qualified. Moreover, Isabella was convinced that once Cisneros became Archbishop of Toledo, he would reform all the monasteries in Castile.

Ferdinand vehemently opposed Cisneros's appointment. For many years the king had assumed that the archbishopric of Toledo would go to his illegitimate son, Alfonso, Archbishop of Zaragoza. Still, Isabella was resolute. It was, she reminded Ferdinand, her royal prerogative to make all ecclesiastical appointments in Castile.

What was left unsaid was even more powerful: Tolerant as Isabella had been of Ferdinand's infidelities, she could not countenance placing his bastard son at the head of the Castilian church.

In April 1495, when Isabella returned to Madrid, she received confirmation of Cisneros's appointment from Pope Alexander and called the confessor to her side. Then without revealing its contents, the Queen handed Cisneros the papal appointment. "See," she said, "what it is that the Roman Pontiff wants."[6] When the Franciscan's eyes fell upon the parchment, he grew white and dropped the paper.

"There must be some mistake in this; it cannot be intended for me," the confessor muttered, and rushed from the queen's chambers.[7] After several hours Isabella sent two *grandees* to Cisneros's convent, only to discover that the monk had left the city. Ten miles north of Madrid Isabella's messengers overtook Cisneros, who was walking rapidly through the hot noonday sun along the road to Ocaña. Eventually they convinced him to return to court for another meeting. But Isabella could not seem to change Cisneros's mind.

The Franciscan insisted that he had planned "to pass the remainder of his days in the quiet practice of his monastic duties; and it was too late now to call him into public life, and impose a charge of such heavy responsibility on him, for which he had neither capacity nor inclination."[8] For six months Cisneros continued to refuse the offer while Isabella appealed to the pope. Finally, after Alexander sent a second bull ordering the monk to assume the archbishopric of Toledo, Cisneros relented.

Although he had been coerced into the apostolic seat of power, Cisneros assumed it with authority. Moreover, his reputation for incorruptibility became legendary when it was discovered that beneath the gorgeously jeweled robes he wore in the cathedral, he continued to wear a hair shirt. Although he was ordered to live in the cardinal's palace, Cisneros had the large curtained bed removed from his chamber so he could continue to sleep on wooden planks. At table, he maintained an ascetic diet, despite the variety of fine meats, cheeses, and pastries served to his companions. Within a few months Cisneros had dismantled the elegant trappings of Mendoza's old palace. The exquisite tapestries, the golden tableware, the silver candelabras and velvet curtains, all, Cisneros ordered, should be given away. In their place would come a new asceticism more suited to his Franciscan vows.

In Rome Alexander, bejeweled, heavy with rich foods and wines, a stone's throw from the home of his mistress, Giulia Farnese, and preoccupied with the lives of his three illegitimate children, became nearly apoplectic when he received reports about Cisneros's austerity. It was not fitting to the archbishopric, Alexander chided the Franciscan, to live so meanly, for it dishonored the grandeur of the church.

Cisneros bristled at Alexander's words but, being sworn to obedience, was compelled to comply with the papal edict. Before long the gilded dishes, silverware, candelabras, and tapestries had reappeared. Yet Cisneros's capitulation was superficial: Beneath his robes the archbishop continued to wear a hair shirt. Although his table groaned with rich boards of game, pastries, and sweetmeats for his guests, Cisneros maintained a regimen of fasts and coarse food. At night, beneath the luxuriously curtained and canopied bed, the Archbishop of Toledo pulled out a rude pallet for his customary rest.

Alexander's warnings to Cisneros reflected a crisis of credibility within the papacy itself that would explode into the sixteenth-century Protestant Reformation. But the opulence and nepotism that then epitomized the Catholic church had not yet come to a head. A more immediate danger now faced the papacy: Charles VIII's dynastic ambitions for the kingdom of Naples.

Despite his arrogance, Charles was clever enough to disguise his ambitions under the more legitimate claim of a Holy Crusade to wrest Constantinople and Jersusalem from the Turks. By 1492 Charles had fashioned a peace with England and, in 1493, with Hapsburg Germany. Thus shielded by his allies and crusader pretensions, Charles believed that few European princes would object—even Ferdinand and Isabella, who, by the treaty of Barcelona, were pledged to friendship.

But the Castilian monarchs had agreed to that treaty merely out of expedience, a vehicle through which to obtain Roussillon and Cerdagne. Clearly, they never expected their friendship with the French to last, for within two months of the treaty they resumed secret negotiations with England for a marriage between Catherine and Prince Arthur.

Ferdinand and Isabella began to make wary preparations for a new war. In 1494 they issued a *pragmática,* or royal command that no one, save priests and women, could ride mules in Castile and Aragón. Thus all able-bodied men were required to maintain horses, which, in the event of a sudden war with France, could be quickly summoned onto the battlefield. As an additional incentive they issued a second *pragmática* barring any individual from wearing expensive silks or clothes trimmed in silver and gold if the head of the household did not own a horse. Not only did those restrictions goad ambitious citizens into buying horses, but they discouraged frivolous dress and the waste of Castile's gold and silver reserves. That same summer the monarchs also assembled a navy in Galicia and Guipúzcoa.

Affairs in Italy, meanwhile, had grown so unstable that Charles soon found a way to further his ambitions. In January 1494 Ferdinand's first cousin, the seventy-year-old Neapolitan king Ferrante, died and the scepter passed to his son Alfonso. Almost immediately that new king, who was considerably more timid than his father, made peace with Pope Alexander and sealed that friendship by marrying his daughter to Alexander's youngest son, Jofre.

When, on May 8, Alfonso was crowned by another of the pope's sons, Charles VIII, his Milanese ally Lodovico il Moro, and the pope's rival Cardinal Guilano hotly protested. That was just the opportunity Charles had been waiting for to achieve the pope's downfall and gain a foothold on Naples. Thus he threatened to withdraw benefices from his cardinals if they continued to support Alexander. He also urged Cardinal Guilano to call a Council of Cardinals to protest Alexander's bribes, many of which were said to have resulted in his 1492 election to the papacy.

Charles's accusations were based on fact. Indeed, as an Italian contemporary observed, Alexander's "simonical election was the secret terror of his whole life."[9] Above all, Alexander VI dreaded "the use that might be made of this blot in his title to the Papacy, by the Cardinals of the opposition and his other enemies to bring about his downfall, in view of the universal feeling of the crying need of reform of the Church." Emboldened by support from his Italian allies, Charles VIII thus coolly announced in June 1494 that he would order an army to Italy on behalf of the Crusade. Along the way he planned to seize Naples, "to possess himself of the Italian peninsula between the new French state and the continent . . . to make the Papacy again dependent upon France and himself master of Europe."[10]

Isabella and Ferdinand were appalled. Fearing for the safety of his Sicilian kingdom, Ferdinand immediately dispatched his envoy, Alfonso de Silva, *clavero* of Calatrava, to the French court. In a meeting at the Rhône port town of Vienne, the Castilian ambassador praised Charles for his expedition against the infidel and assured him of Ferdinand's assistance. But in the next breath, the ambassador chastised Charles for waging war on any European prince for the shame it shed upon Christianity.

Specifically, de Silva insisted, Naples was a fief of the church and as such should be left free. Charles stared at de Silva in disbelief. Beside him the president of the Paris parliament haughtily retorted that the French king had a legitimate claim to the kingdom of Naples and had every intention of taking it to strengthen his position against the infidel. As the Frenchman finished, Charles rose abruptly from his chair and left the chambers.

A second conversation between the king and de Silva merely widened the breach. Once again de Silva reiterated that the church and its fiefs had to be protected. But Charles asserted that the treaty clause protecting the Holy See was meaningless, a formulaic addition that appeared routinely in all the treaties of Christendom. For the rest of de Silva's visit, Charles refused to talk with him. He even posted a guard at his door to keep the Castilian ambassador away.

By the mid-1490s, the French army was among the best equipped and disciplined militias of Western Europe. In addition to the usual *espingardas* and *lombardas,* it had a formidable collection of highly efficient culverins, falconets, and eight-foot bronze cannons. The Italian city-states, in contrast, seldom maintained armies of their own. To settle their disputes, those kingdoms routinely hired *condottiere,* or heavily armed professional soldiers. Because money, rather than patriotism, was the decisive factor in their allegiances these *condotierre* avoided bloodshed whenever possible. As a result, sham battles were common and many disputes were settled without a single casualty.

Thus it was with relatively few practical or spiritual constraints that Charles VIII arrived in the border country of Savoy on September 5, 1494, with 32,000 men. For years the fanatic Dominican preacher Savonarola had been railing against the excesses of his fellow Florentines. In a Lenten sermon that year he had even prophesied the coming of a messianic figure who would conquer the Italian peninsula without shedding a drop of blood. To the Savoyians, terrified by the shining French cannons, Charles VIII personified that savior and thus their children greeted him with flags and banners. The French king was given a similarly warm reception in Tuscany. Buoyed by his reception, Charles thus sent Alexander the menacing message that he intended to visit Rome by Christmas. On October 26, as Charles advanced southward, Pietro de Medici, the despotic ruler of Florence, abdicated his throne. Five days later Savonarola triumphantly exclaimed that "the prophecies are on the eve of their fulfillment, retribution is beginning; God is the leader of this host."[11] On November 9 the citizens of Pisa hailed Charles as their liberator from Florentine oppression and, on the seventeenth, when the French king entered Florence itself, the city was festooned with banners.

Gradually the pope was being trapped. Daily, French boats appeared upon the Tiber and arrived at the Roman seaport of Ostia to provision the French army. Twice Charles sent envoys demanding that Alexander refute his support for Alfonso as King of Naples; twice the pope refused. On November 22 Charles sent the pope a manifesto declaring that he needed free passage through Italy to overthrow the Turks and rescue Jerusalem. To underscore his demands, the king threatened to call a council in which, he intimated, he would have Alexander deposed.

On December 10 the Neapolitan army made an unsuccessful attempt to defend Rome. In addition, advancing French forces choked off food supplies to the Eternal City. The frightened pope now vainly sought help from Venice. Alexander also continued to appeal to Isabella and Ferdinand who, by then, were preparing a new army for his defense. Simultaneously, Ferdinand opened communications with Ludovico Sforza in Milan and urged an alliance between him and the alarmed Venetians.

In gratitude, Alexander granted Isabella, Ferdinand, and their successors *tercias,* or two-ninths, of the church tithes. He issued new bulls of crusade, granting them one-tenth of the ecclesiastical rents to defend the Holy See. Finally, he honored the monarchs with the title of *Los Reyes Católicos,* or the "Catholic Kings," to commemorate their defense of the church.

Despite those honors, Ferdinand sent one last embassy to Charles before declaring full-scale war. Alexander, meanwhile, surrounded by enemies and fearing he would be deposed, grew increasingly frightened. Already, within the cavernous gilded and magnificently frescoed Vatican apartments, Alexander's personal possessions had been packed in anticipation of sudden flight. His most coveted treasures—golden tiaras, jeweled chalices, relics—had been stored away in the nearby Roman Castle of Sant'Angelo.

Nevertheless, the usually decisive Alexander was overcome with fear. "At one moment he wanted to defend himself, the next to come to terms; then, again, he thought of leaving the city," wrote a contemporary.[12] Exacerbating Alexander's anxieties were a stream of letters from Charles threatening Rome with invasion if the pope did not grant him Naples. Before long, three French forces had surrounded the Eternal City, and on Christmas Day 1494, the terrified pope granted Charles VIII permission to enter. On the twenty-seventh he even agreed to let the French king quarter his army on the left bank of Rome. Then the Vicar of Christ shut himself up in the Vatican.

At 3:00 P.M. on December 31 Charles and his army marched triumphantly into the city. By twilight the old Via Lata (now the Corso) was lighted with torches to illuminate the procession, which included battalions of Swiss and German mercenaries and thousands of French infantrymen and light cavalry. Among them rode the French king, "the flower of French chivalry," garbed in silk mantles and gilded armor, and surrounded by a cadre of several hundred bodyguards. The grim parade climaxed with the thundering arrival of thirty-six bronze cannons agleam in the torchlight and pulled in carts by horses.

The French show of strength so terrified the Romans that they buried their valuables. Soon they were forced into the streets by French soldiers who moved into their homes to "burn the wood and eat and drink everything they can find without paying a penny."[13] Before long the citizens began to riot. "The discontent of the people is at its height, the requisitions are fearful, the murders innumerable, one hears nothing but moaning and weeping," wrote the Manutan envoy Brognolo. "In all the memory of man the Church has never been in such evil plight."[14] It soon became obvious that Rome could not long provision Charles's soldiers.

Charles immediately initiated efforts to depose the pope, who by then had fled from the Vatican with six cardinals through a tunnel to the Castle of Sant'Angelo. But ultimately, those threats never materialized for Alexander had bribed one of Charles's allies, the cardinal Ascanio Sforza, to cast the decisive vote in his favor. Moreover, Charles knew that deposing the pope would be the ultimate inflammatory act. Doubtless, the princes of Western Europe would protest and send forces to protect the beleaguered pope. Even his own citizens held the Holy See in such high regard that they would not likely tolerate Charles's actions. Nevertheless, Charles continued to threaten the pope. Twice, when the French army appeared with artillery to batter the Castle of Sant'Angelo, the pope's defenders displayed the shrines of Sts. Peter and Paul and the veil of St. Veronica over the top of the ramparts. Perhaps frightened with visions of hellfire, Charles's army retreated hastily.

Finally, on January 15, 1495, Alexander and Charles came to an agreement by which "our Holy Father shall remain the King's good father and the King shall remain a good and devoted son of Our Holy Father."[15] By that pact, Charles was granted free passage through Italy and his cardinals received amnesty for their disobedience. In return, Charles agreed to concede Alexander's election to the papacy and restore Rome to the Holy See.

On January 18 Alexander and the French king signed the formal treaty. The next day Charles entered the Consistory, or College of Cardinals, to acknowledge

Alexander as the true Vicar of Christ. In return, Alexander granted the French king two cardinalships but still refused to grant him his fondest wish: the investiture of Naples.

By month's end, tensions between the Roman citizens and the soldiers were so brittle and food supplies so low that Charles recalled his troops. On January 28, without Alexander's blessing, Charles set out for Naples. Practically speaking, the pope's permission was no longer necessary. Twelve miles out of Rome, in Marino, Charles's messengers announced that Alfonso had abdicated the throne of Naples and left it to his young son, Ferrantino. Charles now had merely to draw the Italian boot onto the bottom of his own foot to be declared King of Naples.

At this point Ferdinand finally stepped in. As his army advanced toward Velletri, his ambassadors Juan de Albion and Antonio de Fonseca intercepted Charles. In a dramatic encounter, the two Spaniards chastised the French king for his unseemly behavior to the pope and his illegal invasion of Naples. Then they offered him an ultimatum: Either submit to arbitration or concede that the treaty of Barcelona was broken.

Charles responded acrimoniously, accusing Ferdinand of deliberately tricking him with the clause protecting the pope. "The issue, then, must be left to God—arms must decide it," replied the usually cool-headed Fonseca.[16] With those words, the Spanish ambassador tore up the original treaty of Barcelona before Charles and his court. In reality, Fonseca had not acted rashly. Ferdinand had, in fact, orchestrated the scene weeks earlier in Spain. Now he was now free to wage war on France.

The French king continued his march southward, finally arriving in Naples on February 22, where he was welcomed by the frightened populace. When news of the bloodless invasion reached Alexander in Rome, he bitterly noted that "the French came in with wooden spears and found they had nothing to do but the quartermaster's work of marking the doors with chalk."[17]

This insult to the Italian peninsula and the Catholic church would not remain unchallenged for long. Ambassadors from other European kingdoms crisscrossed the continent between the courts of Spain, Austria, Germany, Venice and Milan, uniting in an unprecedented alliance. By March 31 a Holy League had been formed to preserve the dignity of the Chair of St. Peter and to defend Christendom against the Turks and all others who sought to dominate it.

CHAPTER FIFTY-FOUR

Ambivalent Alliances

The League of Venice was Isabella and Ferdinand's first foray into international defense, a pact designed to advance their goal of crushing France and establishing a Spanish hegemony in Western Europe. But unlike the Portuguese and Granada wars, the Italian conflict was Ferdinand's domain, one in which Isabella would play only a peripheral role. After years of placing Castilian interests above Aragonese ones, now Ferdinand could finally devote himself fully to the protection of his paternal inheritances.

Such a split in the king and queen's interests was neither surprising nor a sign of disaffection. By 1496 Isabella and Ferdinand were in their mid-forties, their power was at its height, and they were finally able to pursue individual interests. As the years passed, Ferdinand increasingly directed his energies across Europe, toward the Holy Roman Empire, England, and especially Italy. In contrast, Isabella turned inward to the domestic problems of Castile—to ecclesiastical reform, conversions of the Moors, and the political alliances that grew out of the League of Venice and would eventually result in marriages for her children.

Charles VIII's 1494 invasion of the Italian peninsula had prompted Isabella and Ferdinand to prepare for war. That autumn Ferdinand had gathered a fleet of tall-masted warships in the Cantabrian Sea and in December named the Count of Trevino, Calceran de Requesens, as its commander. At Isabella's suggestion he also appointed the Granada veteran, Gonzalo Fernández de Córdoba, general of the Spanish infantry. He then signaled his Sicilian viceroy to fortify that island kingdom and await the arrival of Spanish troops.

But artillery and armadas were only the first step in Isabella and Ferdinand's plans. The Granada war had long since taught the monarchs that strategic alliances could break the destructive momentum of even the most determined enemy. Consequently Ferdinand dispatched another Granada war hero, Garcilasso de la Vega, to Venice as his ambassador. At night, high above Venice's lapping canals in the ducal palace, Vega and his brother held secret meetings with other European ambassadors to discuss Charles's invasion. The two Castilians immediately found a sympathetic audience. No one, not even Charles's erstwhile ally, Lodovico il Moro of Milan, condoned the French king's actions.

Like Isabella and Ferdinand they agreed that Charles had behaved so cruelly toward the pope "that the Turks would not have treated him worse."[1] Increasingly, even such wealthy city-states as Venice, located east of the Italian boot in the northern Adriatic, fretted over Charles's imperialistic ambitions. And in the German Hapsburg states, Maximilian fumed over Charles's assumption of his title as Holy Roman Emperor.

The culmination of these complaints was the League of Venice. Officially its purpose was to unite Venice, Milan, Germany, Spain, and the pope in a twenty-five-year pact to protect the Holy See and its fiefs; unofficially it was designed to oust Charles from Italy. According to the terms of the League treaty, signed in the bedchamber of the ducal palace at Venice on March 31, 1495, the alliance had been created "for the conservation of all the princes and states in Italy, even of those who are now dispossessed of their dominions."[2]

With the announcement of the League of Venice, Charles became infuriated, especially because the treaty had been signed while his ambassador, Philipe de Commynes, was living in Venice. Meanwhile, the citizens of the Italian peninsula rejoiced. In small towns and cities alike the populations sang *Te Deums;* religious processions and fiestas choked village streets; and in Venice the city fathers ordered a magnificent display of fireworks to celebrate the league.

By the terms of the agreement, league members promised to create a large army of 34,000 cavaliers and 20,000 infantrymen. Venetian galleys were to attack the French off the coast of Naples. Lodovico il Moro promised to expel the French from Asti in northwest Italy. In addition, Ferdinand vowed to reestablish his Aragonese cousin Ferrantino to the Neapolitan throne. To menace Charles directly, Maximilian and Ferdinand planned jointly to invade France's southern borders.

In Naples, meanwhile, an infuriated Charles and his army ravaged the countryside for food, women, and riches. As a final insult, he ordered his soldiers to strip the city of its ancient marble sculptures, bronze doors, and other treasures and load them onto ships bound for France. Then, on May 12, Charles had himself coronated Emperor of Naples and strutted through the streets in crimson, ermine-trimmed robes grasping the scepter and globe in his bejeweled hands.

Four days later Gonzalo Fernández de Córdoba landed in the adjacent province of Cantabria with 3,000 men. Charles fled with 9,000 troops, leaving behind the other half of his army. Near Fornovo on the banks of the Taro River he engaged in a bitter clash against league soldiers who were unable to block his retreat.

Next Charles rode toward Milan where, on October 10, after coaxing Lodovico il Moro away from the league, he escaped unharmed across the Alps. He reached Grenoble on October 27, where he abandoned the cause altogether and with it, the French army he had left behind. Instead, Charles devoted himself to merriment, wine, sport, and gluttony that made him oblivious to the plight of his stranded countrymen.

Meanwhile, Gonzalo Fernández de Córdoba and the admiral Requesens descended on the Italian kingdom from different directions. Although the Spanish forces were relatively small—600 lancers, 3,000 footsoldiers, and a 3,500-man fleet—Ferdinand and Isabella had ensured they were well-equipped and well trained. Even so, they were no match for the French, who, had they been consistently supported by Charles, might well have proved a superior force. Under de Córdoba's command, the Spaniards chased the French from St. Agatha but were defeated at Seminara. Shortly thereafter, the French general D'Aubigny fell ill and was unable to maintain his advantage. By January 1496 de Córdoba had reconquered Naples.

The war dragged on for another seven months—in the seas surrounding Naples, in the mountains of southern Calabria (the "foot" of Italy's boot), and on the northwestern borders of Upper Calabria. On July 21, 1496, de Córdoba wrung a final victory from the French at Atella. With the enemy on its knees, de Córdoba, or the "Great Captain" as Ferdinand and Isabella dubbed him, demanded that the French evacuate Naples unless they received reinforcements within thirty days.

Predictably, Charles failed to succor his men. The French thus were forced to retreat to the Neapolitan coast near Baia and Pozzuolo, where they prepared to board ships for home. Simultaneously, a virulent epidemic swept through the French camp; within a few days the Neapolitan shores were strewn with dead and dying men. Of the 5,000 French soldiers who fought against de Córdoba, only 500 would return home.

Three days before de Córdoba's victory at Atella, Henry VII of England had joined the League of Venice. The wary English king had penned his signature most reluctantly upon that document and only after months of entreaty from Isabella and Ferdinand. Ultimately the Spanish sovereigns had changed Henry's mind through a relentless letter-writing campaign, underscored by visits from their ambassador, the lame but ingratiating doctor of civil and canon law, Dr. Rodrigo González de Puebla.

In 1495 Henry had declined Ferdinand's invitation to join the League of Venice because of dynastic threats to his throne. While Henry had been crowned at Westminster a decade earlier, he was still menaced by two pretenders, Lambert Simnel and Perkin Warbeck. By 1495 the more serious of these was Warbeck, the alleged Duke of York, who claimed to be the son of the deceased Edward IV and who ultimately sought sanctuary from the Emperor Maximilian. In reaction, Henry backed away from all alliances involving the Hapsburg ruler.

Moreover, Charles's invasion of Italy meant very little to England. If anything, King Henry VII may have perceived the French siege as a welcome distraction deterring the rival kingdoms of Western Europe from becoming further involved in the Warbeck affair. In addition, Henry had remained on good terms with Charles since the 1492 Treaty of Etaples and had no intention of jeopardizing that relationship.

But Isabella and Ferdinand were resolved to break that alliance. To entice Henry, they preyed upon his conscience, delineating the grave danger Charles posed to Alexander VI. "The Pope," Isabella and Ferdinand wrote Henry in February 1495, "is in great difficulties on account of the wars in Italy. He has asked for assistance from Spain and intends to write to the other Christian Princes on the same subject. . . . Henry is bound to do what every Christian, but much more a Christian Prince, is obliged to do."[3]

Henry feigned surprise at Alexander's precarious position. With calculated credulity, he wrote Isabella and Ferdinand in July that there was "no more zealous Christian in the world, and no one more disposed to aid the Holy See than he," but he could not believe that the pope was really in danger. After all, Henry argued, communications between the papacy and England were intact. Thus "it would show a great want of respect in the Pope to England if he required her assistance and yet would not even send her a letter."[4]

Henry's reluctance to join the league further jeopardized the security of his throne. In retaliation, Maximilian, vowing to strengthen his support for Warbeck, provided the pretender with a fleet of fourteen ships, which attempted to land in Kent, England, in early summer 1495. But the citizens of Kent repulsed Warbeck's attack and after three hundred of his soldiers were "all railed in ropes, like a team of horses in a cart," the pretender escaped to Ireland.[5]

When it became obvious that appeals to Henry's Christian devotion would not work, Isabella and Ferdinand tried other enticements. The most obvious was the proposed marriage between their daughter Catherine and Henry's son Arthur. In late July, Isabella and Ferdinand wrote Puebla instructing him to inform Henry that "they are not disinclined to the marriage, but . . . desire, first that a reconciliation should take place between Henry and the King of the Romans."[6]

Of even more immediate concern was the imminent marriage between the twin monarchs' second daughter, Princess Juana, and Maximilian's son, the Archduke Philip, or Philip the Handsome, as he was widely known. As Isabella and Ferdinand reminded Puebla in that same letter, "their intention to marry one of their daughters to a son of Maximilian and another to a son of Henry will be the best security that the treaty between Henry and Maximilian will be fulfilled."[7]

That part of Isabella and Ferdinand's prediction came true. Six months before Princess Juana's marriage, Philip ended the quarrel between his father and Henry by dropping his support for the Warbeck pretender and proposing a treaty to renew commercial trade between England and Flanders. To show his appreciation to the Castilian monarchs, Henry joined the League of Venice on July 18, 1496. Yet the English king's conciliation was limited, for while he agreed to defend the pope, he refused to fight against Charles.

Isabella, who received this news while Ferdinand was battling the French in a new offensive in Catalonia, was not discouraged. In an August letter she wrote Puebla that news of Henry's agreement "has given us much satisfaction." But "as we find that the conditions are not quite equal . . . I desire that you should at any rate manage to gain little by little for us in this matter." The quickest way to do so, Isabella observed, was for Puebla to "treat for the marriage of our children; for it appears that there is not at present any King in the world who has a daughter to whom he can marry his son except ours . . ."[8]

Just three days before writing that letter, on August 22, Isabella had waved good-bye to her second daughter, the Princess Juana, as she set sail for Flanders to marry the Archduke Philip. The wedding had been anticipated for months and was the first of a twin marriage pact arranged by Isabella, Ferdinand, and Maximilian. Significantly, the pact had been signed the same day as the treaty of Venice: By its terms Princess Juana would wed Archduke Philip and a few months later her brother, Prince Juan, was to marry Maximilian's daughter, Princess Margaret. In view of that double exchange, the Hapsburg emperor and the Castilian monarchs had agreed there would be no dowries for the brides.

Nevertheless, it was with considerable expense and an enormous procession of attendants, *fardage,* and armed escorts that Isabella and Princess Juana arrived at the Laredo harbor on the Cantabrian coast in late August 1496. Ever mindful of their image as Europe's ascendant nation, the king and queen had prepared a majestic 130-boat fleet to accompany Juana on her nuptial journey north to Flanders. Some months later that same fleet was to return with Princess Margaret, who would then become Prince Juan's bride.

Elaborate precautions had been taken to ensure Juana's safety. On the chance that the Spanish fleet might encounter the French on the high seas, Isabella and Ferdinand ordered seven warships loaded with *lombardas* and falconets to accompany the bridal armada. In addition, the fleet included caravels and carracks containing the princess's possessions—trunkloads of dresses, shoes, household furniture, tapestries, and jewels. There was also a 1,500-man force of footsoldiers, archers, and sailors commanded by Ferdinand's cousin, Don Fadrique Enríquez, *Almirante* of Castile.

Princess Juana was a beautiful young woman, slim, with a high forehead, a long nose, and deepset eyes. Her coloring remains a matter of historical conjecture. From portraits some historians believe she had dark auburn hair. Others maintain that she was darker than her three blond and red-haired sisters because of Isabella's nickname for her, "*mi suegra,*" or "my mother-in-law" suggesting her strong resemblance to her deceased, brunette grandmother Juana Enríquez.

From childhood Juana had been the most brilliant of Isabella and Ferdinand's children. Besides being an accomplished Latin scholar, the princess played the monochord, the clavichord, and the guitar and danced with considerable agility. Unfortunately, the girl's natural gifts were counterbalanced by a difficult temperament that is suggested in her pouting portraits. Certainly by the time of her marriage, Juana was known for her sulks, temper tantrums, and insistence upon having her way—faults that, on at least one occasion, she would later blame upon Isabella's rigorous training.

Yet the queen had attempted to raise Juana to competent womanhood as she had the rest of her daughters. According to legend, the princess always preferred Ferdinand to Isabella. Nevertheless, it fell to Isabella to assume responsibility for the final details of Juana's departure for Flanders. In spring 1496 the king, queen, and court had traveled to the northern Astorgan village of Almazan to see Juana off together. But in early summer the French attacked Perpignan again and in mid-July Ferdinand was obliged to leave for Catalonia.

Despite months of preparation, there was still much that Isabella had to assemble for the voyage—provisions like hardtack, dried cod, casks of wine, chickens, dried pork, 200 cattle, 2,000 eggs, and thick containers of candle tallow, not to mention sea chests, packing cases, tapestries, and furniture for Juana's trousseau. In addition, the queen spent days instructing Juana's *dueñas*, ladies in waiting, cupbearers, chamberlains, and other personnel about how to aid Princess Juana and conduct themselves at the Flemish court.

By August 20 all was in readiness. But just as the bridal party filed onto the caravels and carracks at Laredo, violent storms churned the seas in the Bay of Biscay. Understandably, the bad weather did little to lighten Juana's moods or soothe Isabella's anxieties. For two days the anxious queen remained on board ship with Juana until the weather cleared. Finally, just before the ships were to depart, Isabella kissed Princess Juana good-bye and disembarked.

On shore, as Juana's carrack shrank from the shoreline, the queen burst into tears. Her tears were not simply those of a mother parting from a cherished daughter. Although Juana was leaving her homeland for a distant country and a man she had never met, the sullen princess had not even turned around to wave good-bye.

Perhaps the tragic outcome of the Princess Isabel's marriage to the Portuguese prince intensified Isabella's concerns about Juana. In addition, the queen worried about all kinds of hidden dangers—fretting one day, for instance, that Juana would be swallowed up by giant whirlpools in the English Channel and the next, that she would be captured by pirates. Unlikely though these concerns were, they may have been intuitive manifestations of Isabella's fears about her daughter's emotional health.

As she watched the royal fleet slowly sail into a dark, rising sea, Isabella may have mused that a good husband was all that Juana needed. If Archduke Philip proved as worthy as he was said to be handsome, Juana might at last find happiness.

Weeks went by before Isabella heard anything about Juana. The young bride's sea journey to Flanders had been marred by delays. After an initially favorable start, a *temporale,* or autumnal storm, blew the Spanish fleet off course and forced it to seek a safe anchorage in Portsmouth, England. In the tiny English cottage where Juana was temporarily quartered, the princess received a steady stream of curious guests until the weather improved. Thereafter the armada crossed the Channel and, by September 15, finally landed safely at Vlissingen, Flanders. The only mishap on the last leg of the voyage had been the shipwreck of a Genoese carrack that contained most of Juana's trousseau and jewels.

The silence from abroad disturbed Isabella. Already unnerved by Juana's departure, the queen became increasingly anxious about returning to Burgos on September 22. No doubt her edginess was exacerbated by news that her own mother, the queen dowager Isabel, who had lingered incoherently in the castle at Arévalo for a quarter of a century, had just died. The loss of a mother who barely knew her coupled with that of an estranged daughter could not help but upset Isabella. In public, however, the queen carefully maintained her composure. She dutifully gave instructions for her mother to be buried in the Carthusian monastery of Miraflores near Burgos, a Gothic three-arched church ornamented by Renaissance masters where her father, Juan II, was already entombed.

The only hint of the queen's inner turmoil was a request she made shortly after her return to Burgos. For nearly a month Isabella kept a group of sailors "constantly by her side to ask them questions about the winds that might have delayed her daughter."[9] And to her intimates, Isabella lamented the political circumstances that compelled her to send Juana to "remote Flanders" at a time when the seas were turning wintry.

As the days following Princess Juana's departure stretched into weeks, Isabella repeatedly wrote her daughter to inquire after her health, the Flemish court, and her marriage. Finally, in October, Isabella received notices from the Flemish court that the Spanish fleet had reached its destination. Curiously, though, not a word arrived from Juana. The princess seemed to be living in a world of her own, oblivious to her duties as a daughter of the Spanish monarchs. Juana's neglect of anyone outside the Flemish court was so pervasive that she even failed to answer letters from Henry VII, who had seen to Juana's comfort when the Spanish fleet had been forced to land at Portsmouth. His letters inquiring about her arrival in Flanders had also gone unanswered.

Finally, in late winter 1497, after Henry had failed to receive a reply to his third letter, he complained through Puebla to Isabella and Ferdinand. To the monarchs the criticism was doubly painful, for they were now receiving disturbing reports of their own about Juana. From the archduke's court at Antwerp, Juana's attendants reported that while the princess seemed happily married, she had begun to neglect her devotional duties.

Whatever political advantage Isabella and Ferdinand had originally hoped to gain by Juana's marriage to Philip now stood in serious doubt. Yet at that very moment Maximilian's daughter—Philip's sister—Margaret was expected to arrive from Flanders to become Prince Juan's bride.

CHAPTER FIFTY-FIVE

The First Knife of Sorrow

I t was during that same tense period before Juana's departure for Flanders that Columbus reappeared in Castile from his second voyage. After three years in the Indies the proud explorer had returned to Cádiz on June 11, 1496, white-haired, wrinkled, and no longer young.

The *almirante* had lingered in the Lesser Antilles so long before sailing home that Isabella and Ferdinand had written worriedly to his provisioner, the Archdeacon Fonseca, "that God may have disposed of the Admiral of the Indies" in some untoward way.[1] Delighted to learn of Columbus's safe arrival, the monarchs invited him to visit them in northern Castile in autumn 1496. The solicitous tone of their letter reflected concern over reports of his poor health and rumors that relations between the Spaniards and Indians had deteriorated into open warfare.

The reports had come from priests and *grandees* who had accompanied Columbus on the second voyage, among them a Benedictine monk, Fray Bernardo Buil, and Columbus's erstwhile lieutenant, Mosen Pedro Margarit. Months earlier, both men had returned from the Indies to complain that Columbus was mismanaging affairs there by being inconsistent and overly harsh. They also said Columbus had usurped royal authority by appointing his brother Bartholomew as *adelantado* of Hispaniola.

Columbus's first efforts at colonization there were fraught with difficulty. Six months into the expedition, the humid Caribbean climate had rotted the provisions so thoroughly that Columbus was compelled to send his deputy, Antonio de la Torre, to Spain to replenish food and medicines. The twelve caravels under Torre's command had arrived in Cádiz in early 1494 with a scant 30,000 ducats of gold, tropical birds, and the strange spices of the Indies: "cinnamon enough, but white like bad ginger, pepper in shells like beans, very strong but not with the flavor of that of the Levant; wood said to be sandalwood, but white."[2] Torre brought Columbus's letter to the king and queen describing his discoveries and proposing a caravel shuttle that would transport cattle and provisions to the Indies on a regular basis. On the return trip, Columbus had proposed that Indian cannibals be transported to Spain as slaves.

Through the explorer's correspondence, Isabella and Ferdinand learned of the massacre that had occurred at Fort Navidad after Columbus returned to Spain from his first voyage. The fort had been burned to the ground and all forty-two men left behind from the *Santa María* shipwreck had been killed, victims, or so Columbus was informed, of Indian hostilities resulting from the sailors' greed for gold and native women. Already, the monarchs were beginning to suspect that the gold-rich paradise Columbus had so enthusiastically described to them was less than perfect. Nevertheless, on April 13 they wrote a congratulatory letter, assuring him that "Their Highnesses give many thanks to God for this and they regard as a very signal service of the Admiral all that he has done and is doing herein. . . ."[3]

During his second journey Columbus had traveled widely and suffered keenly. Initially the *almirante* had sailed south of his original destination, following man-o'-war birds until he discovered a broad arc of islands now known as the Lesser Antilles—Dominica, Guadeloupe, and the Leeward, the Windward and the Virgin Islands. The lush abundance of that island chain simultaneously bewitched and horrified Columbus and his crew. Upon that verdant archipelago Columbus and his men first tasted pineapple, gazed upon "purple herons," or flamingos, and admired the Indians' cotton rugs. But there too, they first encountered disquieting evidence of cannibals who had fled their huts when the Europeans arrived, leaving behind gory remnants of human limbs and frightened women who were forced to breed babies for food. And to the explorer's ongoing frustration, the anticipated gold was nowhere to be found.

Had Columbus continued his journey south he would have eventually reached Venezuela. But by early November 1494 Columbus became worried about the men he had left behind in Navidad nearly a year earlier. Consequently, he followed the curved sweep of the island chain in a northwesterly loop, skirting Montserrat, Nevis, St. Kitts, St. Croix, and others until he reached Puerto Rico. Later, back in Hispaniola, after learning what had happened at Navidad, Columbus established two settlements that became the base for his gold-searching expeditions—Isabela, named in honor of the queen on the island's north shore, and San Tomás, in its fertile, thickly forested interior.

By the time the land was cleared and the rude forts erected, Columbus had fallen ill. Sickness had, in fact, begun to sweep through the Spanish population, the result, it was said, of hard physical labor and a diet of decaying European provisions supplemented with native fruits, cassava bread, and yams. Virtually every week a new group of colonists became ill. Consequently, at times only half the population could till the soil and search for gold. Moreover, signs of Indian hostility were appearing—thefts and a threatened invasion by a Haitian cacique.

Nevertheless, Columbus still believed that the Europeans had a distinct advantage. Specifically, he was impressed with "how cowardly were the Indians and how they feared to be eaten by horses."[4] Genuine amity between the aborigines and the Spaniards was something Columbus never considered, or if he did, just as quickly dismissed. Despite the Castilian monarchs' plea to treat the Indians gently, he now governed them sternly, convinced force would hold them better than love. All Indian thieves, he ordered, would have their hands cut off. Then, on April 24, 1494, entrusting Hispaniola to his young brother Don Diego and several deputies, among them the Benedictine monk Fray Bernardo Buil, Columbus sailed to Cuba.

For all the explorer's virtues, that autocratic streak was his fatal flaw, a trait that won him the resentment of his peers and eroded his efficiency as a colonial administrator. It was, in fact, the other face of that same visionary rigidity that enabled Columbus to cross the Ocean Sea where no European had dared to venture. Perhaps the most glaring example of that tyranny occurred during his exploration of Cuba. Despite a frustrating and ultimately unsatisfactory search for gold that lasted nearly seven weeks, the *almirante* was so certain that the island was part of the Asian mainland that he forced his soldiers to swear it was a peninsula of the Malay continent.

Columbus's intransigence may have arisen out of his frustration over the baffling lands he had discovered. This, coupled with his extreme exhaustion, seems to have stretched his nerves to their limits. By late summer Columbus was reporting that for a week at a time he seldom got more than three hours of sleep. The conditions of the voyage—scanty provisions of "rotting biscuit" and fresh water, constant danger from shoals and sandbars, disgruntled subjects and the sly treachery of the "innocent savage"—gradually unraveled the *almirante*'s usual composure. "I am on the same ration as the others," Columbus noted in his log. "May it please God that this be for his service and that of Your Highnesses. Were it only for myself I would no longer bear such pains and dangers, for not a day passes that we do not look death in the face."[5] After leaving Cuba and reaching Mona Island near Puerto Rico, Columbus became critically ill. For weeks he was so ravaged by high fevers, delirium, and coma that his sailors believed him dying and headed for Hispaniola.

In the explorer's absence, Hispaniola had degenerated into a state of near anarchy. Before his departure for Cuba the *almirante* had ordered Mosen Pedro Margarit and an expedition of nearly 400 restless adventurers to explore the island's interior for gold. Lacking sufficient provisions, the *almirante* had instructed Margarit to live off the land as best he could by trading falcon bells and Venetian beads for food. The disgruntled Spaniards had not only followed Columbus's instructions but also stripped the island's interior of gold, exhausted its food supply, and raped its women. Then in a final act of defiance, Margarit, Fray Buil, and their followers seized three caravels and sailed for Spain.

Only after the *Niña* limped into the port of Isabela on September 29, would Columbus recover sufficiently from his illness to grasp the implications of Margarit's behavior. The arthritis that plagued the *almirante* on his first passage home through the Azores was exacerbated by his recent sickness and he was now in constant pain.

Good news, nevertheless, awaited Columbus in Hispaniola. His brother Bartholomew had recently arrived from Spain with a letter from Isabella and Ferdinand congratulating him on his discoveries. It was the first time the brothers had seen each other in years, for during Columbus's 1492 voyage Bartholomew was in France, petitioning Charles VIII for support of his brother's *empresa*. When Bartholomew learned of Columbus's 1493 return to Palos, he left immediately for Spain but arrived too late to sail on the second voyage. As brother to the new *almirante*, Bartholomew was promptly made a *caballero* by Isabella and Ferdinand with the attendant privileges of that rank. In January 1494 he brought Columbus's sons, thirteen-year-old Diego and six-year-old Fernando, to serve as pages to Prince Juan. And in April he left for the Indies with three caravels laden with supplies.

Although Columbus was still weak from his illness, he soon appointed Bartholomew his *adelantado*, or interior governor of Hispaniola. But Bartholomew's task, like Columbus's own, was nearly impossible. The white man's appearance on Hispaniola had created dissension among the Indians, and although Bartholomew was intelligent and probably more even-handed than Columbus, the natives no longer trusted their rulers. The *almirante*, as his son would later write, "found the island in a pitiful state, with most of the Christians committing innumerable outrages for which they were mortally hated by the Indians, who refused to obey them. The kings and caciques of the island were united in refusing to serve the Christians . . ."[6]

By autumn 1494 Torre had returned from Spain with new provisions and another letter from the monarchs dated August 16. Again, Isabella and Ferdinand praised Columbus for his exploits. Yet they refused to agree to his suggestions to establish a Caribbean slave trade, probably because they were unsure about the spiritual states of friendly Indians. Although blacks, the Canary Island aborigines, and any prisoner of war were often made into slaves in fifteenth-century Spain, the monarchs were so confused about the Indians' conversion potential that they would eventually consult theologians. Instead, they asked in that August 1494 letter for more details about the newly discovered islands and the climate. Clearly, Isabella and Ferdinand were concerned. Two months earlier they had signed the treaty of Tordesillas and were still uncertain about the implications of the line of demarcation. Now they wanted Columbus to return to Spain for a cooperative expedition with the Portuguese to establish geographical points of reference in the Atlantic. "If it be difficult for you to come and if it would make some inconveniences for what you are about," the monarchs wrote, could not his brother or another skilled cartographer be sent to Spain instead?[7]

The *almirante*, either through Olympian pride or misinterpretation of Isabella and Ferdinand's solicitous tone, disregarded both requests. Reluctant to leave Hispaniola himself or to send Bartholomew back to Castile, Columbus essentially refused to help the king and queen settle the demarcation issue.

Above all, Columbus was obsessed with his failure to discover the promised gold mines of the Indies. "Sailors," he wrote Isabella and Ferdinand some years later, "are people who are fond of making money and of returning home, and under the spur of these two feelings are apt to venture all. . . ."[8]

One way to recoup at least part of the crown's investment, he still believed, was to create an Indian slave trade. Despite the monarchs' frank disapproval, Columbus ordered the colonists to drive 1,500 Indian captives to the town of Isabela for inspection as potential slaves. From that assemblage, 500 of the healthiest men, women, and children were selected, herded onto four caravels under de la Torre's command, and dispatched to Castile. The rest were left to become the property of the colonists.

Conditions aboard ship were abysmal: Men, women, and children were packed together in the steerage compartment like cattle. Unaccustomed to the meager provisions of hardtack and terrified by the high waves and violent winds of the northern latitudes, nearly half the Indians died by the time Torre's expedition reached Madeira. When the remaining natives arrived in Sevilla in early spring 1495, Isabella and Ferdinand assumed they were prisoners of war and hence eligible to be enslaved. Consequently, on April 12 they authorized Fonseca to proceed with the sale. Immediately curious crowds of Andalusians flocked to the marketplace, among them the chronicler Bernáldez, who duly noted that they were "naked as they were born, with no more embarrassment than wild beasts. . . ."[9]

Four days later, however, Isabella and Ferdinand learned of the Indians' civilian status in Hispaniola and immediately retracted their permission. "The sale of slaves must be absolutely suspended and payment for them not made until we have had time to consult with informed persons, with theologians and canonists, as to whether in good conscience, it is permitted to continue with this affair," they commanded.[10]

But it was too late. By the time the royal edict arrived in Sevilla, the Indians had been sold to Andalusian owners. Ultimately, as Bernáldez observed, the venture proved "very unprofitable" for within a few months most of them had died.

Meanwhile, in Hispaniola relations between the Europeans and Indians continued to disintegrate. The Indians were divided among themselves, some working reluctantly for the Europeans in their search for gold, others remaining openly hostile. By early 1495 tensions ran so high between the Spaniards and the Indians that a cacique named Guatiguana gathered an army to drive out the Spanish. In March Columbus decided to settle the issue finally. On the twenty-seventh of that month, he assembled a force of 200 infantry and 20 horse and stormed the naked natives with gunfire, lance, and sword. After the battle, many Indians were taken prisoner and Guatiguana manacled and imprisoned.

Two months later, nature or the Almighty—as the contemporary historian Las Casas would maintain—wreaked revenge upon the Spaniards. In June, while the Indians were still recovering from the recent assault, an unseasonable hurricane swept over the island, toppling trees and huts and destroying three of the Spaniards' four remaining caravels. The only ship to survive was the apparently indestructible Niña.

By then Columbus had issued new orders. To encourage the search for gold, the almirante commanded all Indians over the age of fourteen to pay tribute with monthly quotas of gold amounting to a hawk's bell of gold dust or comparable wealth in cotton. The Spanish settlers tagged those who fulfilled the order with a brass or copper token; those who failed were hunted with hounds, flogged, imprisoned, or put to death.

Then, quite unexpectedly, in October four caravels arrived from Spain. From one of them emerged Juan Aguado, a chamberlain to Queen Isabella who had accompanied Columbus on his first voyage and now reappeared with fresh supplies and a royal letter. The monarchs, having been besieged with complaints from Margarit, Fray Buil, and other deserters, had dispatched Aguado to investigate. As Bernáldez writes, "there were many murmurs about Columbus" at court for he had "neither found gold as been expected . . . and there was much discord over the justice he rendered upon others . . . the costs were very high and the return very little."[11] In short, Columbus's reputation was in question. To many at court he was no longer the *Almirante* of the Ocean Seas, the discoverer of an eastern passage to the Orient. Instead, he was "*Almirante* of the Mosquitos," explorer of a strange group of insect-infested islands that yielded inferior spices, strange fauna, and useless Indians.

How many of these sentiments the king and queen shared is not clear. Their letter was a brief request for Columbus to reduce the men on the royal payroll in Hispaniola to 500. But Aguado's subsequent actions revealed that the king and queen had sent him expressly to redress grievances on the island. Before long the chamberlain was issuing his own orders, recording complaints, imprisoning miscreants, and, in general, behaving as if he were *adelantado* of Hispaniola.

Chastened, Columbus cooperated, treating the queen's chamberlain with solicitude. Given the awkwardness of the situation, the explorer must have been anxious to leave. Yet, not until March 1496, when the new caravel the *India* was built in Hispaniola, could Columbus sail for Cádiz. Even then, the proud *almirante* could not admit defeat. He was leaving, he announced, to vindicate himself in Castile because "many spiteful envious men were giving the Sovereigns false accounts of what was happening in the Indies."[12]

Behind him Columbus left a lusterless colony, torn by strife and suspicion that had yielded little gold, few successful conversions, and a disgruntled group of Spanish adventurers. So vast was the discrepancy between Columbus's expectations for a thriving gold-trading, Christian colony and the reality, that he had little choice but to reenter the port of Cádiz with a new humility.

Inevitably, reports about Columbus's illness and fears that he had perished on the return trip home stirred Isabella and Ferdinand's sympathies. Moreover, the explorer appeared before them in Burgos's square-towered palace of El Cordón in late October or early November 1496 as a penitent, rather than as the proud discoverer of a "new world." Instead of gold-threaded doublets, velvet mantles, and others signs of rank as *almirante,* Columbus presented himself to Isabella and Ferdinand in a brown Franciscan robe signifying his membership in the Third Order.

Once again the monarchs greeted him warmly and expressed a lively interest in his discoveries. And once again Columbus displayed another round of Indians, masks, golden necklaces, belts, trees, herbs, and birds. He also showed them gold dust in its "natural state" and nuggets "fine or large as beans and chick peas and some the size of pigeon eggs."[13]

This time too, Columbus regaled them with stories about the Indians— conjectures about the slaughter of his men at Navidad, encounters with the cannibals, and the difficult circumstances at Hispaniola. But beneath the monarchs' smiles and nods were questions. Clearly, Isabella was disturbed by Columbus's enthusiasm for making slaves out of the Indians. Furthermore, despite the presentation of gold nuggets, the *almirante*'s assurances that the Indies contained rich gold deposits beneath its grassy surfaces was not yet proven. Yet the monarchs—and particularly Isabella—did not seem discouraged. The queen, Columbus would later write to Juana de la Torre, Prince Juan's nurse and sister to his assistant Antonio de la Torre, had been blessed by God "with the spirit of intelligence and grandeur in everything she did as a dear and beloved daughter." Moreover, she "knew and spoke little about the difficulties and costs."[14]

Isabella and Ferdinand assured Columbus that they would continue to support his explorations for the greater glory of the church, regardless of his ability to discover more gold. They did, however, insist that he abandon his idea of establishing a slave trade. Isabella, believing that the Indians had souls, insisted that they should not be made into chattel. Superficially Columbus agreed, although secretly he still cherished the idea. Five years later, in fact, he would give several Indians to his friends as slaves. But in the autumn of 1496 Columbus was not in a position to argue. To his relief, the king and queen had agreed to a third voyage, one that would take him below the equator to explore the late King João's suspicions that unchartered lands lay directly across the ocean from Africa.

Preparations for this *rumbo austral,* or southern voyage, would take months. In fact, nearly a year would pass before six ships could be rigged and outfitted for Columbus's third journey. There were several reasons for the delay. By early 1497 the king and queen remained preoccupied with the Italian question; simultaneously a border war with France was raging in Roussillon. Most important of all, in winter 1497 the monarchs were anxiously awaiting news of another sea journey— the imminent arrival from Flanders of Princess Margaret, destined to become Prince Juan's bride.

Throughout January, Isabella and Ferdinand waited anxiously for the Spanish fleet, but high winds and winter storms had delayed its return. By the first week in February the discouraged sovereigns planned to travel southwest of Burgos to the city of Soria. In anticipation, the court left for that city on the first Saturday in February, two days before the king and queen.

All the while Columbus's fertile mind was working overtime; from messages delivered to the king and queen Columbus knew the general direction and route of the Castilian fleet and made his own predictions about its return. That same Saturday the *almirante* wrote Isabella and Ferdinand, explaining the winds and inevitable decisions the Spanish captains would make from their last reported destination near the Isle of Wight. "If the fleet started then, it will reach the Island of Huict [Wight] on Thursday or Friday, and if it does not stop there it will enter Laredo next Monday, or all the sailor's calculations will prove to be false," he wrote.[15] Columbus was correct; on that Monday one vessel from the royal fleet finally sailed into Laredo.

Not until the following August did Isabella send Columbus a note of appreciation.

> I saw your letter and opinion on the voyage of the Archduchess,
> my very dear and beloved daughter and it is very good and as of a
> learned man who has much experience of the matters of the sea. I

am grateful to you and hold it a special obligation and service, both for your timeliness in sending it . . . as for having tendered it with the true goodwill and affection which have always been known in you; and so believe that all is received as coming from a special and faithful servant of mine.[16]

On March 8, 1497, the seventeen-year-old Princess Margaret finally arrived at the Cantabrian seaport town of Santander. The crossing had been the most terrifying experience in her life for as the Spanish fleet sailed south through the English Channel to the Bay of Biscay, violent storms overtook them, wrecking part of the fleet. To cheer herself, the droll and eminently pragmatic princess penned an epitaph about herself and sewed it to her waistband, thinking that if she was drowned her body would thus be identified. In French she had written:

> *Here lies Margaret, gentle damsel*
> *Although she had two husbands, she died unwed.*[17]

In reality Margaret had not been married but rather twice engaged—once to the French dauphin and, more recently, to Prince Juan. Shortly after Margaret's birth, Maximilian and Louis XI had betrothed her to Charles VIII. As was often the custom with infant betrothals among royalty, foreign princesses were brought to their future homes as children to become familiar with their adopted country. Thus when Margaret was seven or eight she had traveled to Paris where she was reared at the French court by Charles's regent, Anne de Beaujeu. When relations between the Holy Roman Empire and France deteriorated in the late 1480s, the engagement was broken.

Nevertheless, the Parisian years had left their imprint on the witty princess whose bright smiles, cheerful manner, and stylish clothes belied a serious intelligence. King Ferdinand and Prince Juan met Princess Margaret for the first time near Laredo in the Valley of Toranzo. The seventeen-year-old princess, mounted on horseback and outfitted in a long gold-cloth dress, golden earrings, and a French hood, was dazzlingly beautiful. Juan was infatuated and begged his parents for a speedy marriage.

The king and queen, as Isabella revealed in a subsequent letter to Columbus, were nearly as delighted as their son with their new daughter-in-law. So too was the court. "If you could see her, you would believe that you were contemplating Venus herself," wrote Martire.[18] Indeed, everyone, even the most jaded courtiers, were fascinated with the romanticism of the beautiful young couple who were soon to participate in the most glamorous wedding of the century. Despite this wave of popular sentiment, Isabella and Ferdinand insisted that in all decency the wedding be postponed until after Lent and Easter.

To honor her daughter-in-law Isabella gifted Margaret generously—with fist-size diamonds and emeralds, dozens of pearls, gold necklaces, Ferdinand's diamond-arrow bracelet, and even the famed ruby and pearl necklace the king had given Isabella on the eve of their marriage. In addition, Margaret was regaled with elaborate furnishings, prized Flemish tapestries, gold-covered quilts, belts, silver serving dishes, ornate beds, and gilded horse harnesses. On the occasion of his marriage, Juan was to receive the rents from a dozen towns—among them Alhama, Salamanca, Toro, and Loja.

On April 3, the wedding was held with great pomp at the Palace of El Cordón in Burgos. That day the queen, whose neck was said to have sparkled with jewels, received the bridal party inside the royal palace with a brilliant cortege of attendants and ladies in waiting. The center of attention was, of course, the blond bride, radiant with happiness and covered with gems.

For days afterward Burgos gave itself over to *cañas,* jousts, bullfights, and banquets. The brilliance of the wedding had not only mesmerized the entire kingdom, but was one of Isabella and Ferdinand's proudest moments, the realization of their lifelong dream to establish a Spanish dynasty. Through this fairy-tale marriage, the twin crowns of Castile and Aragón would now be linked to the Holy Roman Empire, thus surrounding France and making Spain the most powerful kingdom in Europe.

Perhaps that was why, in the subsequent raptures of love that kept the young prince and princess sequestered in their palatial apartment for days on end, Isabella said nothing. Martire wrote worriedly in June 1497:

> Our Prince is becoming pallid, consumed with passion. The doc-
> tors and the King himself beg the Queen to intervene and separate
> the newlyweds. They ask her to seek a respite in the incessant
> acts of love and they warn of the dangers that these will incur.
> Again and again they call her attention to the paleness of her son's
> face and his fatigued manner, adding that the sickness is attacking
> his marrow and weakening his very being.[19]

Despite these pleas, Isabella refused to intervene. Admittedly the prince was frail and had a worrisome health history, but marriage, the queen maintained, was a holy sacrament. "Man," Isabella told Ferdinand and the worried chorus of doctors, "does not have the power to tear asunder those whom God has joined together."[20]

For the moment, at least, Isabella's words seemed sensible. Toward the end of the summer the prince had recovered sufficiently so that he and Margaret could travel to Salamanca where they would be feted with still more celebrations.

By June of that year Isabella and Ferdinand were also busy with preparations for still another marriage, this time between the new Portuguese King Manuel and their widowed daughter, the Princess Isabel. Ever since the untimely death of Isabel's first husband, Prince Afonso, the princess had lived quietly in prayer and contemplation, dressing in the habit of the sisters of Poor Clares and begging her parents' permission to become a nun. When Isabella and Ferdinand refused, the princess had declared her intention to remain single.

Years earlier, during the brief time she had lived at the Portuguese court, Princess Isabel had attracted the attention of Manuel, future king and her husband's young uncle. Still smitten with the memory of Isabel's golden beauty and gentle disposition, the twenty-six-year-old Manuel asked for her hand after his 1495 coronation.

The widowed princess, however, was adamant in her refusal to marry for a second time, despite her parents' pleas. From their perspective it made no sense for the twenty-seven-year-old woman to while away her days in perpetual grief and retreat into a convent. Over time, the princess's self-imposed solitude and introspection had wreaked a profound transformation in her docile nature. She had fallen under the spell of fanatic priests like Cisneros; like them, she had become a fierce defender of the Christian faith and developed a profound intolerance for heretics.

In 1496 the princess finally agreed to marry King Manuel. But she imposed one condition: The Jews, who had sought sanctuary in Portugal after their 1492 explusion from Spain, were to be exiled anew. At first Manuel had hesitated, for he valued the Jews for their skills and financial services to the crown. Yet ultimately he conceded. Thus on September 13, 1497, Isabella, Ferdinand and the princess traveled from Medina del Campo to the border town of Valencia de Alcántara for the quiet marriage ceremony, on the thirtieth. The celebrations lasted for several days after which Isabella, drained by the excitement, took to her bed.

On October 4 a messenger arrived from Salamanca. Prince Juan, the envoy reported, was dangerously ill. Without hesitation, Ferdinand mounted a horse and rode rapidly to Salamanca.

A week earlier Prince Juan and Princess Margaret had entered Salamanca to a crowd of applauding onlookers and a fanfare of trumpets and drums. The streets of that venerable university city were decorated with banners, and women waved from the balconies as the handsome young couple rode through the cobblestoned streets followed by packs of excited children.

A day or two later the prince began to suffer from a fever that was so high his doctors feared for his life. The messenger had been sent to the king and queen in Alcántara then. When Ferdinand reached Prince Juan's bedside and beheld the seriousness of his son's condition, he tried to rouse the youth's spirits by assuring him of his recovery. But Isabella's "angel," as she used to call Prince Juan, sensed that this illness was to be his last. With sweet-tempered stoicism, the nineteen-year-old prince urged his father to entrust him to God because his death was inevitable. He even cited examples from the ancients that death was an escape from the invariable disappointments of life. Ferdinand was shocked by these words of "ancient wisdom from his young son."[21] Some hours later Juan confided to his father that Margaret was pregnant, and expressed the hope that if she bore a son the crowns of Castile and Aragón would remain entwined. Then, at midnight on October 6, 1497, in the arms of his old tutor Fray Diego Deza and with his dog Bruto whimpering at his bedside, Prince Juan died.

Ferdinand was numbed. For several days he had been so concerned about Isabella's overwrought nerves that he had hidden the truth from her in hopes that their son would recover. As the prince's condition had worsened, he had written Isabella letters, first speaking of his improvement and then of his deteriorating health. But with Prince Juan's death, the king had no choice. On October 9 he rode grimly to Alcántara to break the news to the anxious queen. "God giveth and God taketh away," she murmured pathetically.[22]

The death of Prince Juan, as Bernáldez would later observe, "was the first knife of sorrow to run through the soul of the Queen"—a sorrow from which neither Isabella nor the crowns of Castile and Aragón would recover.[23]

CHAPTER FIFTY-SIX

Mortifications

P rince Juan's death plunged Spain into the deepest despair. According to the historian Commynes, "The kings [sovereigns] . . . manifested such extreme grief over this that no one could believe it, and this was especially true of the Queen, who was expected to die rather than to live . . . I have never heard of greater mourning than was observed in all their kingdoms."[1]

After their son's death, Ferdinand and Isabella changed their festive wedding clothes for black *ropas de luto,* or black mourning clothes. Following their example, the Spanish court, which traditionally had worn white serge for mourning, now adopted the custom of wearing black sackcloth instead. Tolling church bells and royal messengers announced the prince's death to the citizenry. Hundreds of mourning Castilians marched behind darkly clad prelates and courtiers as Juan's coffin was slowly transported along the highway from Salamanca to Ávila, through its Market of Small Animals, and finally into the cathedral. After the funeral ceremony, the procession continued out past Ávila's gates for a few miles to Juan's final resting place at the Convento de Santo Tomás. There, for the last time, a white-faced Isabella and Ferdinand bade farewell to their only son.

For forty days all offices in Castile and Aragón remained closed. Throughout Spain the cities were draped with black banners. Solemn processions filed through the streets of every hamlet and village, and churches held memorial masses in the dead prince's honor. Noted poets and writers penned panegyrics and romances to the fallen prince. Around such touching memorials too, grew the legend that the beloved Prince Juan had died of love. But even the hopeful fruits of that love epitomized by Princess Margaret's pregnancy were doomed to end in sorrow. By late winter 1497 or early 1498 the grieving young woman aborted a stillborn girl, an "unformed mass of flesh worthy of grief."[2] With that sad miscarriage, the male line of the twin crowns of Castile and Aragón ceased. Nevertheless, Margaret continued to live at Isabella and Ferdinand's court for nearly two years where she was treated as a daughter and gifted with jewels and tapestries before her return to Flanders in late 1499.

After Juan's death, Isabella and Ferdinand tried to proceed with the affairs of the kingdom in their usual manner. In public they displayed a grave dignity, bearing the blow "with as much patience and no less courage than the many victories they won against their enemies."[3] But the effort was accomplished with difficulty, for during those public occasions the king and queen exchanged glances to chart each other's emotional stability. To those who knew Isabella and Ferdinand well, it was obvious that the light that once flickered in their spirits had been permanently extinguished.

Isabella, especially, was crushed by Juan's death. As a devout Catholic, the queen tried to accept the loss as the will of God and, hence, to be stoically endured. Officially, she and Ferdinand even promoted that attitude in their public documents. In response to condolences from Salamanca's city fathers, the king and queen wrote on November 14 that "we have accepted it with forbearance, bending our will to that of God, as is correct, because that is always best."[4] But despite her best efforts, Isabella never accommodated to the loss. Henceforth the queen would live "virtuously but without pleasure," permanently hollowed out by grief.[5] Even in the last years of her life Isabella still mourned for her son as if he had recently passed away. And, as if embracing the last remains of Prince Juan, she kept his dog Bruto by her side.

Beyond the emotional anguish of losing a child were its tragic implications for Spain. Had Juan lived, Spain would have remained intact in the hands of the Trastámara dynasty, preeminent among the nations of Western Europe, ruler of the vast wealth and resources of the New World. Now, lacking a male heir, the union of the crowns of Castile and Aragón was likely to be severed as it had been before Isabella and Ferdinand's marriage. The Castilian throne would fall to one of the monarchs' daughters and the inheritance of Aragón would remain undecided.

The news of Prince Juan's death had shocked the crowned heads of Western Europe. But when the Archduke Philip of Flanders learned about it, he immediately had himself and the Archduchess Juana declared the "Princes of Castile." Isabella and Ferdinand were appalled by the archduke's effrontery and must have wondered at Juana's role in it, especially since their daughter had not written her parents even one letter since her marriage. In reaction, the worried Spanish sovereigns ordered their *comendador,* Sancho de Lodoño, to Brussels to rebuke Philip.

At the same time they summoned the newly wed King Manuel and Queen Isabel from Portugal. Years earlier, before Prince Juan's birth, Isabella and Ferdinand's oldest daughter had been declared heir of Castile. Now, through the vicissitudes of fate, she was to inherit the throne again. Moreover, Queen Isabel was now pregnant, again kindling the king and queen's hopes that their grandchild would one day inherit the twin thrones of Castile and Aragón.

Dutifully, the young Portuguese monarchs left Lisbon in early spring 1498 and arrived at the monastery of Guadalupe on April 7 during *Santa Semana,* or Holy Week, where they remained through Easter. From the moment of their arrival the royal couple were greeted warmly and feted with celebrations as they progressed toward Toledo.

Isabella and Ferdinand received Isabel and Manuel with affection, not only as their daughter and son-in-law and sovereigns of a friendly nation, but as their future heirs. Aside from her daughter's swollen belly, Isabella did not find the new Portuguese queen greatly changed. To her consternation, the queen noted that the beautiful young Isabel was nearly as anxious and gloomy as she had been before she had wed. Although the young woman had a normal pregnancy, she was strangely convinced that she would not survive the birth. There was, in any case, little time to dwell on morbid thoughts. The *Cortes* had already been summoned. On Sunday, April 29, King Manuel and Queen Isabel were thus sworn heirs to the Castilian throne in the cathedral at Toledo by the *procuradores,* prelates, and *grandees.* By June 2 the new Castilian heirs, Isabella, Ferdinand, and their court traveled to Zaragoza where the Aragonese *Cortes* had been summoned for a similar purpose.

The Aragonese, however, were not nearly as compliant. They were, in fact, violently opposed to the idea of declaring Isabel and Manuel as heirs because of Aragonese adherence to Salic law. As usual, the Aragonese continued to remain fiercely independent of their sovereigns. Now they regarded King Ferdinand's appeal that they swear Isabel heir to the throne an infringement of their basic rights.

Inheritance of the crown of Aragón, the Zaragozan *procuradores* insisted, had to be passed directly through the male line. They recalled that in the thirteenth century, when Pedro IV passed the succession on to his daughters, Aragón had been plunged into civil war. Furthermore, Ferdinand's own father, Juan II, had expressly ordered the crown to be transmitted through the male line. If Ferdinand had no sons—which was indeed the king's current situation—the crown could be inherited by a son of Ferdinand's daughter. Since the Queen of Portugal was nearing the end of her pregnancy, the *procuradores* thus suggested postponing any decision until after the birth.

Ferdinand and Isabella, who had all too recently witnessed the perils of childbearing with their daughter-in-law Margaret, were not appeased. Instead, the king sharply reminded his *procuradores* that Aragón had no law expressly forbidding female inheritance, for as early as the twelfth century women had ruled the kingdom. Additionally, to insist on male inheritance in the wake of Prince Juan's death was to deliberately sever the union of the twin crowns and hence weaken the Spanish hegemony Ferdinand and Isabella had established in Western Europe during their twenty-four-year reign.

But the *Cortes* was intractable. Isabella, who had been privy to the rancorous debate, finally exclaimed that "It would be better to reduce the country by arms at once, than endure this insolence of the *Cortes.*"[6] The uncharacteristic outburst from a queen who had always favored reason over force stunned the *procuradores.* In the ensuing silence, an Aragonese representative reminded the queen that his peers were only acting as "good and loyal subjects, who, as they were accustomed to keep their oaths, considered well before they took them."[7] Chastened, Isabella said no more but listened silently to the heated arguments that raged on both sides.

Ultimately fate intervened. On August 23, the Portuguese queen delivered a baby boy. But whatever joy Isabella felt at the birth of her first grandchild was immediately clouded by her daughter's alarming postpartum condition. An hour after the child was born, the Spanish monarchs' oldest daughter died in her mother's arms.

The queen retired to her bed for nearly a month, wracked with inconsolable grief. The "second knife" had been turned within the queen, and with it, the first symptoms of a languishing malady. Nevertheless, the inheritance of the twin crowns seemed to have been ensured and the Aragonese Salic precedent preserved.

To establish his future role, the little prince, named Miguel for his birth on that saint's feast day, was publicly whisked through the streets of Zaragoza in an embroidered litter chair with his nurse. On September 22, the infant was presented to the four estates of the *Casa de Diputación* by his guardians, Ferdinand and Isabella, and sworn as the heir to the Aragonese throne.

But the cost had been incalculable. Princess Isabel's death swept cruelly over Isabella and Ferdinand, a malevolent wind that blew inexorably and inexplicably over Spain at its brightest moment.

In the midst of the tragic events of 1497–98, dramatic changes were sweeping over the rest of Western Europe. On June 15, 1497, Pope Alexander VI's favorite son Giovanni, Duke of Gandia, was murdered in Rome and his body thrown into the Tiber. The pope wept bitterly and shut himself in his apartments for four days, neither eating nor sleeping. When the Holy Father finally did appear at the Consistory on the nineteenth, he announced he loved the Duke of Gandia "more than anyone else in the world" and would give seven tiaras to recall him to life. "God has done this in punishment for our sins," the pope lamented, "for the Duke has done nothing to deserve this mysterious and terrible death."[8] In penitence, Alexander announced that he intended to "amend" his life and reform the church.

Initially the pope seemed sincere. That summer he formed a commission designed to remove simony and other corruptions from the church. But after an initial effort his interest flagged. Historically, Alexander's rise was founded on bribery and nepotism, and now the sixty-six-year-old pope was hopelessly immersed in a secular world in which "the advancement of his children [was his] . . . one aim."[9] Other recent events—Alexander's annulment of his daughter Lucrezia Borgia's first marriage and a Turkish attack on the Venetian-held port of Lepanto—took priority. As a result, the first draft of the papal Bull of Reform was shelved and forgotten.

But the papal states were on the brink of still another transformation. After Ferrante's death on October 7, 1496, the Neapolitan throne eventually passed to his nephew, Federico, whose sovereignty was duly recognized by Venice and the pope. Then on April 8, 1498, when Charles died from a head injury, the French crown devolved upon his cousin, the Duke of Orleans, known as Louis XII. Almost immediately Louis proclaimed himself King of Jerusalem and, through blood links to the Visconti and the Angevins, claimed title as the Duke of Milan and King of Naples.

Ferdinand quickly realized that Louis intended to invade Italy. Yet the thirty-six-year-old French king glossed over his ambitions with a veneer of friendship. At the very hour of Charles VIII's death Louis had, in fact, sent messages to Isabella and Ferdinand asking to renew his "friendship and brotherhood following the old traditions of the King of Castile and France."[10] By then, the League of Venice had been dissolved. Consequently, Louis was able to fashion a treaty with Spain on August 5 that left Italy free of all previous political entanglements. Before long, the shrewd new French king had convinced Henry VII of England, the Archduke Philip of Flanders, and even the Venetian Doge that he had rights to the duchy of Milan.

Most important of all, Louis managed to court favor with the pope by extending privileges to his son Cesare Borgia, who was eager to trade clerical orders for a secular duchy. To do so Louis had worked out an exchange. Shortly after his coronation, Louis asked the pope for an annulment from his marriage so that he could wed his predecessor's wife, Anne of Brittany. In return, Louis proposed to ennoble Cesare Borgia as the Duke of Valentinois and arrange his marriage to a French princess.

Alarmed, Ferdinand, Maximilian, and Manuel of Portugal established a Council of Reform to dethrone the pope for accepting bribes. On November 27, 1498, the Portuguese ambassadors chastised the pope for nepotism, simony, and his French alliance. Less than three weeks later Ferdinand's ambassador, Garcilasso de la Vega, accused Alexander of acquiring the papacy through unethical measures and interfering in the Spanish church.

A bitter argument ensued. The pope retaliated by declaring that Ferdinand and Isabella had acquired the Castilian throne illegally and had been punished by the death of Prince Juan. In response, Vega retorted that the Almighty had humbled Alexander with the loss of his favorite son, the Duke of Gandia.

Rancor over the purity of the church and the rights of the crown to appoint its own bishops had been building between the Spanish monarchs and the pope for years. By 1496 Alexander had received so many complaints from Castilian monasteries about Cisneros's reforms that he dispatched the general of the Franciscans, Jorge da Costa, to investigate. That free-living, conventual prelate became so alarmed by Cisneros's austere measures that he complained directly to Isabella. How, da Costa asked the queen, could she have raised a man of humble birth like Cisneros whose "sanctity was a mere cloak to hide his ambition" to the highest church office in the land?[11] And how could she allow Cisneros to wreak such devastating reforms in the monasteries? For the sake of her own salvation, the Franciscan general railed, Isabella should force Cisneros to resign.

Isabella listened to da Costa's harangue in silence. When he finished she asked coolly "if he was in his senses and knew whom he was thus addressing." "Yes," he retorted, "I am in my senses, and know very well whom I am speaking to;—the queen of Castile, a mere handful of dust, like myself!"[12]

Isabella was not easily intimidated. She had, after all, entrusted not only her soul to Cisneros as her confessor but the state of the Spanish church. Nor did she flinch when, some months later, da Costa convinced the pope to send a band of conventuals to supervise Cisneros's reforms. When Cisneros overrode their objections, Alexander issued a brief on November 9 ordering the Spanish sovereigns to desist from all reforms of the Franciscan monasteries "because of the constant disagreements and complaints" received in Rome.[13] A thorough papal investigation would follow.

In response, the queen stiffened her support for Cisneros and urged her Roman ambassador to convince the pope of the urgency of monastic reform. Isabella's timing could not have been more brilliant, for it coincided with the death of Alexander's son. On June 23, 1497, Alexander issued a new brief granting Cisneros full power to proceed.

In the ensuing years, the archbishop swept through the Franciscan monasteries zealously, reducing the monks and their life-style to the elemental piety that had inspired their twelfth-century founder. Subsequently, Cisneros would purify the other monastic orders in Spain—among them the Augustinians, Dominicans, and Carmelites. Thereafter, he turned his attention to the secular clergy to cleanse them of nepotism, corruption, and sexual debauchery.

Ironically, Cisneros's efforts, initially so bitterly resented by the Castilian clergy, would fortify Spanish Catholicism against the Protestant Reformation that would threaten the church in sixteenth-century Europe.

Despite that ecclesiastic victory, Isabella and Ferdinand remained anxious. To the Catholic sovereigns, as they were widely known, Pope Alexander's fondness for France, Princess Juana's failure to write her parents, and the Archduke Philip's initial assumption of the title as heir to the Spanish throne were worrisome signs of a new international disequilibrium. To ascertain the facts, Isabella and Ferdinand dispatched two ambassadors to England and Brussels in the early summer of 1498. By June 2, the two emissaries, Sancho de Lodoño and Fray Tomás de Matienzo, subprior of the Convent of Santa Cruz, had arrived at Henry's court in London.

A year earlier, the long-debated marriage agreement between Arthur and Catherine had finally been signed, and thus Henry was now a trusted ally. As Isabella and Ferdinand anticipated, the English king was sympathetic to the Spanish ambassadors' request that he support their demand for reformation of the papacy. Should Alexander refuse to cooperate, Henry agreed that the Spanish monarchs "have not only a right to do what they say, but also to convoke a council [of reform] if necessary."[14]

In a July 18 letter the ambassadors noted that Henry remained euphoric about the marriage alliance that would unite Catherine and Arthur. The visit was so successful, in fact, that by the time Lodoño and Matienzo left for Brussels, Henry agreed to issue a new "treaty of friendships and alliance with the Catholic Kings" which would bind "them and their successor to last for ever."[15]

From England, the Spanish ambassadors sailed to Brussels on July 31, where their task as goodwill ambassadors would become considerably more difficult. Earlier, from English reports, Matienzo had informed Isabella that the Archduchess Juana was pregnant. Now they confirmed that she was "very handsome and stout. Her pregnancy is well advanced."[16]

Gradually, however, Matienzo's reports became darker as he learned of the young woman's frightened attitude toward members of the Flemish court. At first, Juana had bristled at Matienzo's arrival and coldly announced her resentment of the subprior's attempts to serve as her confessor. When Matienzo asked if she had any messages for her parents, the archduchess flatly stated that she did not. Nor, the prelate observed, did Juana express any interest in the king and queen's welfare or anyone else in Spain. In addition to her curious detachment, the ambassadors found that the archduchess's religious habits had grown inconsistent. The truth, as Lodoño and Matienzo would only dimly understand during their six-month stay in Flanders, was that marriage to Archduke Philip had upset Juana's fragile mental balance. Within the first few months of her marriage, Juana had not only fallen madly in love but allowed herself to be psychologically abused. From a twentieth-century perspective it seems that *Felipe El Hermoso,* or Philip the Handsome, as the Spaniards called him, held Juana in a vicious cycle of affection, abuse, and intimidation from which she was constitutionally unable to escape.

At first, Juana's happiness had seemed assured. As Philip's sobriquet, "The Handsome," implied, the twenty-year-old bridegroom was very attractive—six feet two inches tall, well built, blond with blue-gray eyes and a proud carriage. Personally, however, the archduke was considerably less appealing, for by temperament he was mercurial, narcissistic, and arrogant.

Perhaps Philip's childhood had exacerbated those characteristics. As the only son of Charles the Bold's daughter, Mary of Burgundy, and the Hapsburg heir, Maximilian, Philip had grown up in a politically turbulent atmosphere. His mother had died in a riding accident when Philip was only five. Thereafter he had inherited her remaining Burgundian domains, the Netherlands, and the twin duchies of Brussels and Flanders.

Shortly after Mary's death, Maximilian resolved to claim the rights of regency over his young son, but the Flemish and Belgian nobles had bitterly protested. Consequently, the young Philip was separated from his father and raised by the Flemish court in a jingoistic atmosphere with little respect for what would become his other adult inheritance, the Austro-Hungarian Empire. Philip's sympathies were thus always closer to France than to Germany, and the resultant tensions bred an uneasy relationship between him and his father.

In fact, it was probably in an attempt to educate his son to his German responsibilities that Maximilian had called the archduke to preside over the Reichstag parliament in Lindau, Germany, in the fall of 1496 just before Princess Juana arrived in Flanders. But with her arrival, Philip left immediately for the lace-manufacturing town of Lierre, Belgium, where on October 18, 1496, he first met his Spanish bride.

Disregarding formalities, he pushed aside the shocked servants of Juana's court and walked boldly into Juana's chambers at the Hotel de Berthout-Mechelen. The archduke was so pleased by the Princess's beauty and she, in turn, so taken with her handsome bridegroom that Philip demanded an immediate marriage. Scandalized, members of Juana's court insisted that decorum must be preserved. A peevish Philip was thus forced to sit through a formal presentation of the Spanish nobles and prelates who had accompanied the princess.

Immediately afterward the archduke—or by some versions of the story Juana herself—summoned the Castilian chaplain Diego Villaescusa, Dean of Jaén, to officiate over a hurried nuptial ceremony. That very night, in a room overlooking the River Nethe, Juana's marriage to Philip was consummated. The next day the enamoured couple was married again in a formal ceremony at the collegial church of St. Gommaire. Shortly thereafter, they left for Brussels.

At first, the new archduchess was overcome with happiness. Moreover, she was dazzled by the Burgundian court, whose festive customs and careless opulence made her Spanish childhood seem dour and mean in comparison. To the nearly seventeen-year-old princess and her entourage, wool-rich Flanders was the very epitome of a corrupt society. Men and women drank beer and ale freely together in taverns. Sweethearts held hands and kissed openly on the streets. Women had license to behave as freely as men. Illicit literature circulated freely in the shops and the royal court, free from the scrutiny of the Spanish Inquisition. Even heretical books imported from England and Switzerland were easy to obtain. The northern countryside itself, with its lush forests, canals, beech trees and sturdy oaks, its fat geese and cows and strange vegetables, like cauliflower and cabbage, seemed to bespeak new earthy appetites.

After Philip and Juana's wedding, the entire country was given over to raucous celebrations and few, if any, ecclesiastical ones. The ornate gilded walls of the Burgundian palaces with their gold and silver ornaments, rich tableware, and Turkish rugs far exceeded the splendor of the Spanish castles where Juana once dwelt. The cumulative effect of the hearty Flemish cuisine of fattened beef, rich cheeses, and succulent pastries combined with Philip's lusty sexual appetites soon awakened the archduchess's sybaritic appetites.

To Philip, however, Juana was little more than a carnal plaything, and before long he set about systematically stripping the new archduchess of her Spanish staff. Pitilessly, Philip substituted Flemish attendants for Juana's personal servants and ordered many of the Spaniards back to Castile. Only Juana's former *mayordomo*, Rodrigo Manrique, was allowed to stay as the Spanish ambassador to the Flemish court. The faithful few from the archduchess's homeland who refused to return to Spain, such as Doña Marina Manuel and Doña Ana de Beaumonte, were no longer permitted to reside at the Flemish court and their allowances were taken. In compliance with Philip's anti-Spanish policy, the ambassadors Matienzo and Lodoño were both refused food at the Flemish court. Consequently they wrote Isabella and Ferdinand to send money immediately.

Isolated from her peers, simultaneously smitten and intimidated by her ruthless husband, the newly impregnated Juana was not even capable of commanding her own household. Essentially, she had been rendered helpless for all purposes but sex. When Matienzo asked the archduchess about her failure to complain about Philip's refusal to pay her attendants decent wages, Juana countered that she had attempted to do so: but finally she had given up because she learned that if she complained "the only consequence would be to cause injury to her."[17] Exactly what she meant—whether it was physical abuse, deprivation, or psychological cruelty—was unclear.

Equally pathetic was Juana's confession that she felt guilty about not writing her mother. But, she added, she was "so oppressed that she could not think of her mother and how far she was separated from her forever, without shedding tears."[18] Furthermore, and probably more to the point, the archduchess confessed that she was so afraid and suspicious of Philip that she dared not write Isabella at all, for fear her letters would be seized. Exacerbating Juana's reluctance was her sense that she no longer led a proper Christian life. After she "improved" her behavior, Juana told Matienzo, who by then served as her confessor, she would write the queen.

On November 16 the archduchess delivered a baby girl who was christened Eleanor in Brussels' Church of Saint Gudule. In anticipation of that birth, Juana had mustered enough courage to ask for the traditional parliamentary grant of 60,000 florins. But by mid-January 1499 it was apparent even to Matienzo that the archduchess's request was to be denied, for the grant had been paid directly into the archduke's exchequer and spent on "favors."

Isabella had received Matienzo's letters in late 1498 and early 1499, a time when she was already broken from the tragic deaths of Prince Juan, his stillborn child, and Princess Isabel. Their tone would have startled even the most callous mother, let alone a woman as deeply invested in her children as Isabella.

Matienzo did his best to fight for the archduchess's rights. He encouraged Juana consistently to charm Philip and his courtiers and win them to her side. But ultimately Matienzo was forced to conclude that there was "no remedy" for Philip's cruelties toward Juana, and in March 1499 he sadly returned to Spain.[19] For all the ambassador's encouragement, Juana remained powerless to extricate herself from Philip's domination and sexual magnetism. By June 1499 the Archduchess Juana was still hopelessly in love and newly pregnant with a second child.

CHAPTER FIFTY-SEVEN

Doubtful Dynasties

A restless spirit stalked Christianity in the last months of the fifteenth century. During a visit to Granada that lasted from July to November 1499, Isabella and Ferdinand grew impatient with the slow pace of the conversions. To speed the process the queen ordered Cisneros to remain there to assist Talavera while the rest of the court traveled to Sevilla.

The zealous reformer set to work immediately. In contrast to Talavera's gentle proselytizing, Cisneros called together Granada's most influential *alfaquis* and preached fiery sermons to them about the supremacy of Christianity. In his zeal, the formerly incorruptible Franciscan even bribed those who attended his sermons with gifts. By December, so many Moslems clamored for conversion that Cisneros was forced to baptize them en masse by sprinkling holy water over the heads of the crowd.

Yet the initial conversion of an estimated 3,000 Moors left Cisneros unsatisfied. With flagrant disregard for the terms of the 1492 Granada treaty, the Franciscan transformed Granada's mosques into churches and ordered their newly installed bells to ring day and night. From church altars and streets, the inexhaustible *alfaqui campanero*, or "prophet of the bells," as the Moors called Cisneros, preached the necessity for citywide conversion.

Then, in a final apocalyptic burst, Cisneros ordered his agents to remove thousands of beautifully embossed, hand-painted Arabic manuscripts from the libraries of Granada and pile them in the city's *plaza mayor* for a public bonfire. By so doing, the Franciscan intended to destroy the written records of nearly eight hundred years of Moorish culture and, with it, the Arabs' last ties to Islam.

Paradoxically, the Franciscan was a bibliophile whose respect for knowledge had inspired him to found Castile's University of Alcalá. Yet bigotry and fanaticism hobbled his highest instincts. With sanguine satisfaction the gaunt reformer watched thick yellow smoke spiral in billowy puffs above the city as priceless hand-copied manuscripts of the Koran and scientific, horticultural, and theological texts from the classical world went up in flames. From thousands of those ancient manuscripts, Cisneros deemed only three hundred medical texts worthy of preservation for his university library.

The Moors protested bitterly and, in a feverish attempt to preserve some remnants of their cultural heritage, hid a few books and exported others to the North African Berber coast. But Cisneros's literary *auto-da-fe* had been too brutal a declaration of cultural annihilation to be accepted passively.

On December 18 the embers of that resentment burst into flames. That day Cisneros sent three servants into the narrow streets of the crowded Moorish Albaicín quarter to proselytize. Before long the Christians and a Moorish *elche* had quarreled, and in the ensuing conflict two of Cisneros's servants were killed. The Moors then ran to their homes for arms and barricaded themselves in the Albaicín.

The following night a murderous band of Moslems stormed Cisneros's palace, but when servants begged the Franciscan to flee he grimly stood his ground. "God forbid I should think of my own safety, when so many of the faithful are perilling theirs!" the monk replied. "No, I will stand to my post, and await there, if Heaven wills it, the crown of martyrdom."[1]

Isabella and Ferdinand, who were then in Sevilla, learned about the rebellion indirectly. Actually, Cisneros had dispatched an Ethiopian messenger to the monarchs in Sevilla, but the man had stopped at a highway inn and become drunk. Thus days went by before the Spanish monarchs learned what was occurring, and meanwhile they had become irritated with Cisneros's silence. Ferdinand, especially, was convinced that the Franciscan had mishandled the affair, and maintained that if Isabella had promoted his illegitimate son, the Archbishop of Zaragoza, to the Toledan archbishopric, the revolt would never have occurred.

"So we are like to pay dear for our Archbishop, whose rashness has lost us in a few hours what we have been years in acquiring,"[2] Ferdinand observed tartly to the queen. Isabella, it was said, stubbornly defended Cisneros, but she, perhaps more than anyone else, was painfully aware that until her confessor's arrival in late 1499, Granada had been a peaceful city.

The tranquility Granada enjoyed in that brief "golden age" of the 1490s was, in fact, testimony to Isabella and Ferdinand's appointment of competent Mudéjar administrators to supervise the defeated Moslem kingdom. By employing local men, the monarchs had exercised a shrewd diplomacy that Niccolo Machiavelli would outline some fifteen years later in *The Prince*. The best way to govern alien territory, as that Italian statesman later observed, was "by setting up a government composed of a few men who will keep it friendly to you."[3]

One of those "friendly" men was the Count of Tendilla, the gregarious captain-general of the Granada kingdom and *alcaide* of the Alhambra, who had rushed into the narrow streets of the Albaicín at the height of the conflict to talk with the Moors. Before him went a small company of armed guards who had to fight off bellowing crowds and drive them into their homes as Tendilla entered the

Moorish quarter. But the Moslems would not be appeased. When Tendilla sent a messenger with a peace proposal, the Moors stoned him.

Thereafter, the gentle Archbishop Talavera wended his way through the angry Moorish crowds preceded only by his chaplain, who held a crucifix aloft. Then, "with words of hope and appeasement," Talavera preached forgiveness to the Moors.[4] His speech was so moving that many Moors fell to their knees in repentance and kissed the hem of Talavera's gown. Now Tendilla ventured again into the Albaicín and was greeted with cheers. Spontaneously, the Count of Tendilla threw his bonnet into the crowd to signal his good will. In the ensuing reconciliation he and Talavera convinced the Moors to give up their arms. No one, Tendilla assured the Moslems that day, would be punished except those guilty of murder. Nor would there be any more forced conversions. To assure the rebels of his sincerity, Tendilla even placed his wife and young children in the Albaicín as guarantees.

Despite these efforts, Ferdinand blamed Tendilla as well as Cisneros, "I am not surprised by the archbishop of Toledo who never saw a Muslim or knew them, but by you and the *corregidor* who have known them for so long," he wrote Tendilla.[5] Meanwhile, Isabella penned an urgent letter to Cisneros demanding an explanation. In response, her confessor galloped to Sevilla and threw himself at the feet of the king and queen. The blame, the Franciscan admitted, was indeed his for he had executed his plans without permission from the monarchs. If he had erred, it was due to his overzealousness for the Christian faith. Yet he was convinced that the treasonous behavior of the Granada Moors must be suppressed before it sparked a full-scale rebellion.

Initially, Isabella and Ferdinand dismissed the Franciscan's advice, for by the treaty of 1492 they had promised to respect Moorish customs and Islam. But by the end of January 1500, the sovereigns had to concede that Cisneros's strong-arm techniques had yielded startling results: He had already converted over 50,000 souls. Force clearly worked better than Talavera's patient proselytizing. Now rationalizing that the Granadian revolt had annulled the terms of the 1492 treaty, Isabella and Ferdinand agreed to pardon the Moors only if they converted or were exiled. Technically, the Spanish sovereigns still were not compelling the Moors to be baptized; pragmatically, of course, the Moors had no other choice. By midwinter more Moors were baptized and peace descended over Granada again.

Even Talavera conceded, "Jiménes [Cisneros] had achieved greater triumphs than even Ferdinand and Isabella, since they had conquered only the soil, while he had gained the souls of Granada!"[6]

Meanwhile, frightened Moorish peasants who lived in the neighboring Alpujarra Mountains clung tenaciously to their faith and prepared for a revolt. In late January after Cisneros had forcibly converted the Moors of craggy Huécar, angry Arab mountaineers gathered in battalions, stoned two priests to death, and stormed nearby Castilian fortresses. Then they appealed to Moslems in North Africa, who sent soldiers by boat to burn Castilian towns on the southern coast. Once again the Sultan of Egypt threatened Isabella and Ferdinand with letters.

The Moslems' counterattacks, so reminiscent of their raids on Castilian property before the Granada war, could no longer be ignored. Initially, Isabella and Ferdinand dispatched the Count of Tendilla, the Great Captain, and a small army to Huécar to quell the uprising. So frightened were the citizens of Ronda by this new military presence that they begged Isabella and Ferdinand for leniency. And on February 18 the queen assured them that "neither you, nor your wives nor children nor grandchildren would be forced to become Christian against your will."[7]

But revolt was in the air and in late February there were Moorish protests in Alhendin and Lanjaron. In exasperation, Ferdinand donned armor himself, and by March 8 his army had crushed the rebellious towns and punished the miscreants.

Ultimately, the Castilian monarchs were obliged to employ Cisneros's repressive methods to put down the unrest. Throughout their reign, in their dealings with the Moors, the *conversos*, and the Jews, the Spanish sovereigns had consistently acted out the belief that they must "never permit a disorder to prevent a war." To do so, as Machiavelli later wrote, was useless, for war was seldom avoided "but only deferred to one's own disadvantage."[8]

To Isabella and Ferdinand that "disorder" was Islam. To destroy it they now demanded that the Moors of Granada either convert or pay heavy fines of 50,000 ducats. Consequently, thousands of Moslems were baptized as Christians and reconciled as faithful subjects of the king and queen, a continuation of Castile's century-old practice of forced conversions of the Jews. Yet the monarchs had learned nothing from the earlier *converso* experience. Conversion from one religion to another would never be sincere unless it emanated spontaneously from the spirit. Once again, beneath the ritualistic obedience to the Christian faith beat rebellious Moslem hearts.

Beyond the snowcapped Alpujarras, Louis XII of France was wrestling with similar resistance. In July 1499 the French army had crossed the Alps and, at Venice's encouragement, invaded the city-state of Milan. Within a month the Milanese duke Lodovico il Moro had fled to the mountains of the German Tyrol and on October 6 Louis XII entered Milan. As he anticipated, Pope Alexander had supported the invasion for reasons no purer than the worldly gain that would accrue to him and his family. In September 1499 Alexander's son Cesare Borgia, the new Duke of Valentinois, had already stormed the northern Italian province of Romagna with French reinforcements on behalf of the Holy See.

But Louis, who considered his Milanese victory only the first step in a larger scheme to seize Naples, had committed two tactical errors. First, by assisting the pope and allowing his son to take the Romagna, Louis had offended Venice and alarmed the rest of the Peninsula. Second, Louis's invasion had alerted the kings of Spain, Portugal, and the Holy Roman Empire to his imperialistic intentions. Much shrewder than his predecessor, Louis quickly realized his blunder. To appease his potential enemies, the French king then offered Ferdinand half of the kingdom of Naples. Weeks later Ferdinand gingerly accepted the bribe. Privately he despised Louis and considered himself the rightful heir to the Neapolitan crown. Yet he knew that Louis's proposed invasion would place French soldiers perilously close to his beloved Sicily. That thought was so distasteful that ultimately Ferdinand agreed to oust his Trastámara kinsman Federico from the Neapolitan throne and divide Naples with Louis.

Even so, Ferdinand moved cautiously. By the end of 1499 he and Isabella had gathered an army in Málaga purportedly to protect Venice and its domains from a new Turkish threat. In May 1500, a Spanish militia consisting of 60 boats, 600 cavalry, and 4,000 infantry commanded by the Great Captain set sail for Sicily.

Another challenge to the twin crowns of Castile and Aragón now appeared within the royal family itself. During the early morning hours of February 25, 1500, at a ball in Ghent's Prinsenhof palace, the Archduchess Juana went into early labor and delivered a baby boy. Ten days later the infant was christened Charles, heir to the Holy Roman Empire and the Duke of Luxembourg.

When Isabella heard the news she murmured to Ferdinand the scriptural phrase "the lot falls on Matthias," referring to the fact that her grandson had been born on that saint's birthday.[9] Intuitively, though, in a parallel to the Bible story, Isabella's comment suggested that Charles, rather than the Portuguese prince Miguel, would become heir to the thrones of Castile and Aragón. This belief seemed to have two sources: first, the wellsprings of the queen's private anguish—anxiety for the small, frail Spanish heir who had been entrusted to her since birth, and second, from something even more disquieting: an intuitive sense that the ascendant star that once carried Isabella to the monarchy, enabled her to conquer the Moors, and permitted Columbus to discover the Indies, had peaked.

On July 20, Isabella's worst fears were confirmed. Five days after she and her court returned to Granada, twenty-three-month-old Miguel sickened and died. Had the child lived, the history of Spain and Portugal would have been intertwined on three continents—in Europe, Africa, and the Americas—forming an empire second to none in the sixteenth century. But Miguel's death permanently severed those ties.

Isabella and Ferdinand were inconsolable. It was, wrote the chronicler Bernáldez, the third knife of sorrow that would pierce the queen. Nevertheless, the monarchs, recognizing the importance of preserving an image of royal dignity and strength, disguised their sorrows in public "with smiling and serene appearances."[10]

The Spanish throne would now be inherited by Juana's son, the foreign-born infant later known as Charles V of the Holy Roman Empire. Numbed with sorrow, fearful of the future, Isabella and Ferdinand thus summoned the Archduke and Archduchess of Flanders to Castile.

This time it was the Archduke Philip who hesitated being sworn the official heir of Castile and Aragón. Months went by before he replied. By 1500 the arrogant young ruler had begun to tire of Juana. Although he still gloated over the idea of becoming heir to the Spanish crown, his advisors warned him to adopt a cool approach. The Netherlands were, after all, the crossroads of Europe, strategically wedged between France and Germany and, hence, vulnerable to their wars. Should Philip have to lean toward Spain or France, his Flemish courtiers clearly preferred the latter.

Because of Philip's ongoing friendship with Louis XII, his mistreatment of Juana, and his taste for licentiousness, he dreaded visiting his wife's homeland. Perhaps that was why the impolitic young archduke did not even dignify the Spanish monarchs' summons with a reply. Finally, an exasperated Isabella and

Ferdinand ordered Bishop Juan de Fonseca to Brussels to force an answer from Philip.

To coax the archduke to Spain, Fonseca was assisted by Gutierre Gómez de Fuensalida, a veteran ambassador of the German states, who countered Philip's excuses to avoid the trip. As a compromise, Philip offered to send his favorite, the Archbishop Besançon, to become acquainted with Castilian customs. Upon Besançon's return, Philip promised that he and Juana would visit Spain.

Privately, Juana disapproved of the compromise and longed to return home immediately. Hence when Philip asked her to sign a document granting Besançon ambassadorial powers, Juana balked. After a bitter argument during which the archduke threatened to refuse to visit Spain at all, Juana tearfully conceded and signed the paper. Whether Isabella and Ferdinand understood Juana's reluctant complicity in Besançon's visit is not known; but clearly they tried to impress the Flemish archbishop by entertaining him lavishly and even dangling a fat ecclesiastic position before him in return for his favor. The sovereigns were so successful in winning Besançon's goodwill that when he returned to Flanders, they congratulated themselves on their success.

In Flanders, meanwhile, Philip had honed his sadistic treatment of Juana into a high art through a combination of sexuality, tenderness, and intimidation. By the time Besançon returned to Flanders in June 1501, the archduke had a new excuse for delaying a trip to Spain: Juana was pregnant and about to deliver their third child.

Physically and psychologically, the archduke was an irresponsible man. At twenty-two Philip was at the peak of his manly vigor, and like the fleet stags and boars he chased through the Flemish woods, he gallivanted merrily through the countryside for weeks on end to hunt, play tennis, and cavort with mistresses. Juana, meanwhile, was confined to Flemish castles with her two children, a virtual prisoner in Philip's court.

When he demanded that the archduchess, then in her eighth month of pregnancy, travel with their children from Bruges to meet him at Torremonde, Juana complied against her doctors' orders. By the time the archduchess reached Ghent, her son Charles was running a high fever. Juana herself was so exhausted that she wrote Philip she could travel no farther. Instead of sympathy, the archduke reacted by ranting about Juana's incessant insubordination.

Even in private Philip did not bother to pretend to respect his wife. When he insisted that Juana sign a contract betrothing the infant Charles to Louis XII's daughter, Princess Claude, Juana had protested. "Your signature and seal were not demanded because there was any real need for them," Philip said. "In this case I can assure all and sundry that you will do as I desire. Your cooperation was requested purely to save your honor."[11]

On July 15, 1501, the unhappy archduchess gave birth to a third child, a baby girl who was christened Isabel in Brussels. The name was a poignant choice for Juana, a pathetic evocation of her strong mother and Spanish queen, the *mujer varonile,* who ruled Castile with a conviction that the archduchess must have envied.

The only bright spot in the dark year 1500 was the marriage of Isabella and Ferdinand's third daughter María. With Prince Miguel's death, the last link between Spain and Portugal had been severed and King Manuel left heirless. Like Henry VII, the thirty-one-year-old Portuguese king was menaced by pretenders: Thus his marriage to a new bride, particularly to a Spanish princess, had become a matter of political expediency.

On April 22 Isabella, Ferdinand, and Manuel formalized that agreement. The fifteen-year-old bride was the sunniest and least remarkable of Isabella's daughters, but also the luckiest. Through her uneventful marriage to the Portuguese heir, María would provide her mother with at least a modicum of happiness. Yet there was one obstacle to the marriage—the biblical prohibition against marrying the sister of a deceased wife. As a result, it was necessary to obtain a papal dispensation from Alexander, a request Isabella and Ferdinand were loath to make because of his confused loyalties.

On August 24, after protracted negotiations with Spanish ambassadors, the pope signed the dispensation. In exchange, Alexander had exacted a price: the award of a Valencian archbishopric for his nephew, Luis Borgia.

On September 23, after a week of festivities in newly Christianized Granada, Isabella and Ferdinand accompanied María and her entourage as far as Sante Fe and kissed her good-bye. By October 20 the bride and her cortege had crossed the Portuguese border at Moura, and ten days later she was married to King Manuel at Alcaçer do Sal. By early November Isabella and Ferdinand received the first notices of María's happy wedding. After two unsuccessful unions, Ferdinand and Isabella had finally linked one of their daughters to the Portuguese crown. Subsequently María would birth eight children, the eldest of whom, João, would one day wear the Portuguese crown.

But whatever joy Isabella gained from the announcement of María's marriage was overshadowed that same month by the arrival of two worrisome visitors— Besançon from Flanders and Columbus from the New World. The Admiral of the Ocean Seas, it was reported, had just arrived in Cádiz, wraithlike, arthritic, and in chains.

CHAPTER FIFTY-EIGHT

Lands of Vanity and Deceit

That Columbus had been recalled to Spain for mismanagement of Hispaniola came as no surprise to members of Isabella's court. But that the *Almirante* of the Ocean Seas had arrived home manacled like a common prisoner was shocking. Added to this humiliation, Columbus had been stripped of his rightful share of gold before he left the New World. Thus when the explorer arrived in Spain in late November 1500, he was penniless and forced to rely on the charity of his friends. By December 12 Isabella and Ferdinand had sent Columbus 2,000 ducats, ordered him released from chains, and requested his appearance at court.

Five days later Columbus and his brothers Bartholomew and Diego appeared at the Alhambra. As the explorer walked past the lacy arabesques and arches of the inner courtyard and approached Isabella and Ferdinand, tears welled up in his eyes and he knelt sobbing before them. Isabella, it is said, was so moved by Columbus's aged appearance and the hardships he had suffered that she wept too. With kindly voices, she and Ferdinand ordered Columbus to rise from his knees and speak his mind.

Eight years earlier, in 1492, when the monarchs had conquered Granada, they had ordered a poem by Francisco de Icaza to be cut into the marble entranceway of the Alhambra:

> *Give him alms, woman,*
> *for there is nothing in life, nothing*
> *so sad as to be blind in Granada.*

Perhaps they were thinking of those words as they listened to the fallen explorer. From their perspective Columbus was indeed blind, not so much from his tears of grief but from the temperamental perversity that had repeatedly marred his personal relationships and undercut the genius of his achievements.

Nevertheless, Isabella and Ferdinand listened carefully and sympathetically to the explorer's account. Afterward they assured the admiral that his services had been so remarkable to the crown that they could not allow him to be mistreated. To prove their sincerity, they ordered that Columbus's income and all his rights in Spain be restored immediately. According to the explorer's son Fernando, the monarchs also promised "to see to it that the guilty parties were punished and he [Columbus] . . . given satisfaction for his wrongs."[1]

Icaza's poem had linked women with charity, and perhaps it was fitting that Columbus sought special solace from Isabella. Despite the events that brought him home from Hispaniola in disgrace, there was an unspoken link between the explorer and the queen, the memory of a bold act against convention that gave Europe a New World. As a contemporary observed, Isabella "more than the King ever favored and defended him and so the Admiral trusted especially in her."[2]

In spite of that bond, Columbus was so anxious about his future that he repeatedly asked Isabella and Ferdinand to formalize their promises in a letter. Yet, it would not be for over a year, and then not until the eve of Columbus's departure from Granada, that the monarchs would formalize their commitment on paper. Exactly what caused the delay has never been fully explained. Perhaps it was a reflection of the monarchs' pressing concerns at home and in Italy as well as the difficult circumstances of Columbus's last voyage. On March 14, 1502, they wrote:

> Be assured that your imprisonment was very displeasing to us as
> we made clear to you and to all others, for as soon as we learned
> of it we caused you to be set free. You know the favor with
> which we have always treated you, and now we are even more
> resolved to honor and treat you well. All that we have granted
> you shall be preserved intact according to the privileges that you
> have received from us, and you and your heirs shall enjoy them,
> as is just without any contravention."[3]

Although Columbus longed to take revenge on his enemies, he was left to languish in the cool patios and by the sparkling fountains of the Alhambra during his first winter home. Isabella and Ferdinand were preoccupied with other, far more urgent projects—discussions with Philip's Flemish ambassador Besançon, the strategic movements of the Spanish fleet, and the imminent marriage of Catherine to Prince Arthur.

By May 24, 1501, an exasperated Columbus wrote Fray Gaspar from Granada that "Here there is always something going on which puts all other matters in the background. The Lady Princess [Catherine] departed in the name of Our Lord, and it is believed that now something will be done about the Indies."[4]

But again Columbus was mistaken. Not until September 3 would Isabella and Ferdinand make any major decisions about the Indies, and when they finally did, Columbus was bitterly disappointed. On that date the Spanish sovereigns appointed the *comendador* of Lares, Don Nicolás de Ovando, governor and *alcalde mayor,* or supreme justice, of the Indies. As a concession, Columbus was allowed to send an agent on Ovando's expedition to collect his share of the trade and gold profits from the New World.

The events that prompted Isabella and Ferdinand to strip Columbus of jurisdiction over the lands he had discovered began with high hopes. After more than a year's preparation, Columbus had left Sanlúcar de Barrameda with six ships on May 40, 1498, for his third voyage. Isabella and Ferdinand financed the journey for two purposes—to discover if there were lands opposite Africa in the Atlantic or lands south of the Antilles. Although the monarchs, their court, and the rest of Western Europe had long since accepted the notion that Columbus had discovered a "new world" in the Indies that was believed close to Asia, the navigator and other mariners suspected that an unknown continent lay beneath those new islands. That notion had been inspired in part by the late King João's hunch about a "mainland in the south," which if discovered might, by Aristotle's theory of similar properties in countries of similar latitudes, contain rich veins of gold as in Africa's West Coast.

From Sanlúcar de Barrameda, Columbus proceeded to the Canaries where he picked up fresh cheeses and other supplies. This time he did not stop to see the lady governor, Doña Beatriz de Peraza y Bobadilla, who had recently remarried. At Gomera, the six-boat expedition was divided into two groups. Three of the ships commanded by Columbus's trusted captains Alonso Sánchez de Carvajal, Pedro de Harana, brother of Columbus's former mistress, and Giovanni Antonio Colombo, Columbus's Genoese cousin, sailed directly to Hispaniola.

Unlike the colonists of the earlier voyages, many of the new settlers were released convicts. As rumors spread about the high disease and death rate in the Indies, young adventurers had lost their enthusiasm, making the search for manpower increasingly difficult. Thus it was that in 1497 Isabella and Ferdinand had agreed to pardon all criminals, except heretics and murderers, after a year or two of colonial service.

In truth, after Columbus's second journey, the New World came to be regarded as a fraud, an exotic, but ultimately useless island chain that returned little to the Royal Exchequer except strange fruits and herbs, sickly natives, little gold, and debts. Even Columbus's sons, Diego and Fernando, who served as pages in Isabella's court after Prince Juan's death, were now openly scorned as "mosquitoes of the man who found lands of vanity and deceit, which are the tomb and misery of the Castilians."[5]

By June 21, 1498, the three remaining ships under Columbus's command had reached the Cape Verde Islands. But on July 13 the winds died. The three ships were becalmed under a blazing sun for eight days while the casks containing the crew's fresh water supply burst their hoops.

Finally, "an east-southeast wind arose and gave a prosperous blaste to his sails," propelling the ships steadily across the southern Atlantic.[6] On July 31 Columbus changed course, and that noon a crew member sighted a three-hilled island the explorer named Trinidad. To Columbus the sight of the three hills was a confirmation of divine will, for during the voyage he had continuously invoked the Holy Trinity. The next day, as Columbus sailed along Trinidad's southern coast seeking to replenish his fresh water supply, he caught sight of the continent of South America. Today that low-lying coastline in the delta of the Orinoco River is known as Venezuela's Punta Bombeador. But in 1498 Columbus, mistaking it for a detached body of land, named it Isla Sancta, or Holy Island. When the explorer moored at Trinidad's Erin Point he was less than ten miles from continental South America: yet, for all his brilliance, he failed to understand its significance. The *almirante* would repeat his mistake on August 4 when he sailed north, threaded the three-channeled *Boca del Dragón,* or Dragon's Mouth, and entered the Gulf of Paria at the top of the Venezuelan mainland. There, because the rest of the continent stretches so far below the Paria peninsula, Columbus mistook the headlands for an archipelago.

For a week the Castilians drifted south to the bottom of the peninsula, where they met natives, traded European goods for Indian gold, attended local banquets, and kidnapped several aborigines. To his delight, Columbus observed that the Indian women wore beaded necklaces interspersed with pearls, which, the natives said, came from the Caribbean side of the peninsula. In fifteenth-century Europe, pearls were nearly as valuable as gold, and the prospect of returning to Spain with such treasures so excited Columbus that he determined to sail north of the peninsula before proceeding to Hispaniola.

Pearls thus became Columbus's newest obsession, blinding him to other potentially important discoveries. As the Spanish caravels sailed west, the brackish waters of the gulf turned increasingly fresh, a sure sign of an estuarial tide that must have emanated from a great river. Such a river, as most fifteenth-century geographers and cartographers knew, could flow only from the mouth of a large mainland, but Columbus was not convinced. Even when a reconnoitering boat reported four river channels that were actually part of the Rio Grande, the explorer stubbornly dismissed the theory that he was skirting a mainland, largely because he still did not see the outline of an extensive continental shore before him.

Pearls and a prompt return to Hispaniola were all that Columbus could think about. It was remarkable, in fact, that Columbus could think clearly at all because he was needed so urgently to steer the boats through the shoaly waters of the Paria Gulf that he had not slept in days. Instead of exploring the estuarial waters of the Orinoco River and thus discovering South America, Columbus ordered the fleet to sail back through the *Boca del Dragón* and head west.

By August 13, as the fleet progressed toward the legendary "pearl coast" in modern eastern Panama, the sailors sighted dozens of other islands, among them Tobago, Los Failes, and Margarita, named for Prince Juan's new bride. At nightfall on August 14, Columbus's eyes were so bloodshot from sleep deprivation that he was nearly blind. Finally he retired. But by the time Columbus rose the next morning, the winds and currents were already carrying his fleet away from the pearl fisheries south of Margarita toward Hispaniola.

One of the great mysteries of Columbus's third voyage was why he refused to change course and tack back to the Pearl Coast. He subsequently wrote Isabella and Ferdinand that he feared the shoals surrounding those islands and did not want to risk a shipwreck. Besides, he and his crew were exhausted and his eyes alarmingly bloodshot "from lack of sleep and the necessity of watching for the constantly changing winds and currents."[7]

Yet by August 13 or 14 Columbus finally became convinced that the land he had just explored was a continent. According to his son Fernando, Columbus reached this conclusion after mulling over the

> great size of the *Golfo de las Perlas* [Gulf of Pearls] and of the rivers issuing from it, because all the water in that sea was sweet, because Esdras in Chapter 8 of his fourth book [an apocryphal work in the Greek version of the Hebrew bible] says that of the seven parts of this sphere only one is covered with water, and also because all the Indians in the Cannibal Islands had told them that to the south there lay a very large continent.[8]

But the continent Columbus had in mind was not King João's uncharted landmass opposite Africa: It was, the explorer believed to his dying day, other lands that lay south of the "Chinese" province of Mangi, or Cuba. By the seventeenth, after Columbus sailed another hundred miles north without sighting any islands, he worked his theory into an even more startling conclusion—he had discovered the Garden of Eden. Recalling that the Holy Scriptures stated that in the Garden a spring flowed from the Tree of Life that gave birth to four large rivers—the Ganges, Tigris, Euphrates, and Nile—he now believed that the river flowing into the Gulf of Paria was somehow related. "I never read or heard that so much fresh water could mix with salt water and penetrate so far into it and in this, there is also some help from the soft temperance [of the climate] and if it does not flow from Paradise the marvel is greater still," Columbus observed.[9] He found additional support for his theory from the sudden dearth of islands in his southern approach to Hispaniola. That absence, Columbus concluded, meant he had just grazed the edge of the Terrestrial Paradise "because all men say that it's at the end of the Orient, and that's where we are."[10]

Paradoxically, as Columbus was formulating this fantastic theory, his nautical pragmatism enabled him to plot a course through the treacherous currents of the southern Caribbean. By August 20 he had arrived at Baeta Island, where his brother Bartholomew, who had been officially appointed Hispaniola's *adelantado*, or governor in 1497 by Isabella and Ferdinand, had sailed to greet him. Things had not gone well in Hispaniola in Columbus's absence. In July 1496, a few months after his departure, Bartholomew received a letter notifying him that Isabella and Ferdinand agreed to accept Indian slaves if they were genuine prisoners of war. The monarchs also ordered Bartholomew to dismantle the fort at Isabela and establish a new settlement on Hispaniola's southern coast called Santo Domingo.

The colonists, however, remained disgruntled, perpetually hungry for European provisions, ill with tropical diseases and syphilis, and, most of all, frustrated by their inability to find gold. During Bartholomew's visit to the island's southwestern peninsula, Francisco Roldán, the chief justice, gathered a group of malcontents and rebelled.

Like all rabble-rousers, Roldán shrewdly capitalized on the settlers' complaints, promising them that Columbus's critics in Spain would soon remove the explorer from authority and appoint a new governor in his place. Then, to win the Indians to his side, Roldán promised the caciques that if he were to become governor, there would be no more monthly quotas in gold or cotton.

Upon discovering the rebellion, Bartholomew made immediate efforts to suppress it. By the time Columbus arrived at Hispaniola, his brother had burned Indian villages, captured their rebellious Indian leader Guarionex, and contained Roldán's men in an area between the old capital of Isabela and the new one of Santo Domingo. But Roldán was a clever man. Before retreating to the southwestern peninsula, or the Xaragua, he had established himself as champion of the Indians and common settlers against the Castilian elite.

Thus Hispaniola was only superficially at peace when Columbus arrived on August 30, 1498. By sheer bad luck, the three ships in his advance fleet had already sailed there and landed in the Xaragua. Ignorant of Roldán's rebellion, the fleet officers had invited him aboard, and before long the revolutionary had encouraged the crew of ex-convicts to desert. Thus refortified, the rebels marched boldly into crown-held lands to attack the fortress of Concepción that stood northwest of Santo Domingo. After a series of bitter and ultimately unsatisfactory negotiations with Bartholomew, Roldán retreated again to the fertile valleys of the Xaragua.

By then, Columbus was becoming frantic about Hispaniola's lack of gold. In an effort to compensate Isabella and Ferdinand for their investment, he dispatched five ships to Spain on October 18 filled with slaves and brazilwood, which, he believed, could turn a handsome profit. "From here, we can send as many slaves as can be sold . . . 4000 [slaves] which would certainly be worth twenty million and 4,000 hundredweight of brazilwood worth as much . . ."[11]

In that same correspondence the *almirante* asked for missionaries, both to reform the Christians and to convert the Indians, as well as new able-bodied men to subdue Roldán and a judge who could administer justice and restore Hispaniola to peace. Columbus also enthusiastically described his discovery of a "terrestrial paradise" at the end of the Orient. Unlike his purposeful and confident letters of 1492 to 1494, however, now his communications were disjointed. Their distracted tone, coupled with his allusions to Hispaniola's civil disorder, alarmed Isabella and Ferdinand. The qualities that make a good explorer—a strong inner vision, an autocratic command of the crew, imagination, and enough compassion to prevent a mutiny, were not, the king and queen were beginning to understand, the same ones needed for a strong viceroy.

For all his intransigence, Columbus was not consistent. While this quality is perhaps essential to the mutable conditions at sea, it does not work well on land, and especially not when dealing with treacherous personalities such as Roldán. So by late autumn 1498, when Roldán's faction refused to make peace, Columbus foolishly conceded by offering the rebels free passage home. When the *almirante* failed to fulfill that promise, Roldán demanded reinstatement of his former position and the rights to land in the Xaragua. Columbus, weary of rebellion and "eager to put an end to this wretched business," gave in.[12]

Henceforth, the settlers established an exploitative land system known as *repartimientos* (later called *encomiendas*), which would establish the pattern for subsequent colonization in North and South America and the surrounding islands. By that system, each settler was given a generous plot of land and entitled to exploit the Indians who lived on it solely for his own profit. In October 1499 Columbus sent Isabella and Ferdinand a letter describing the *repartimiento* as the best system for keeping peace on Hispaniola. He also reiterated his request that they send a judge to help him govern the island.

While Columbus's exploratory abilities were being compromised by his administrative duties as viceroy, his discoveries stirred the imaginations of other mariners. Among them were veterans of his second voyage, Alonso de Hojeda, the cartographer Juan de la Cosa, and a Florentine sailor living in Sevilla named Amerigo Vespucci. In 1498, after the caravels had returned to Spain from Hispaniola, Hojeda somehow obtained a copy of Columbus's map of the Paria peninsula. Then he wheedled a license from Juan Fonseca, who, by then, had quarreled bitterly with Columbus and was still the royal purveyor for all New World expeditions, to explore that region. By the summer of 1499, Hojeda and his crew had reached the Venezuelan mainland, farmed the rich pearl fisheries of the southern Caribbean, and sighted other islands, among them Aruba and Curaçao.

On September 5 Hojeda's fleet had even landed in Hispaniola, where his sailors brazenly began to cut firewood for the expedition home. Roldán, who guarded his territory jealously, resolved to capture Hojeda, but after several futile attempts, that explorer escaped to the Bahamas. Hojeda's expedition, which returned with a rich cargo of pearls and a written account that Vespucci had cunningly predated in order to conceal the fact that they had used a stolen map, would become an eternal source of humiliation to Columbus. Not only did Hojeda's discovery of the Caribbean's pearl fisheries surpass Columbus's seven-year effort to strike gold, but Vespucci's name was permanently affixed to the continents of the New World.

The same year there were two other important voyages. The first was headed by Peralonso Niño, one of Columbus's former pilots, who subsequently returned to Spain with a rich cargo of pearls from Margarita. The second was commanded by Vicente Yáñez Pinzón, brother of Columbus's deceased rival, who discovered the mouth of the Amazon River.

The cumulative success of these expeditions, coupled with Columbus's anxious reports from Hispaniola, forced Isabella and Ferdinand to conclude that the explorer had woefully mismanaged his opportunities in the New World. By 1499 Ferdinand was preoccupied with affairs in Italy and deeply resented the poor financial return from the New World explorations. Even Isabella was losing patience and adamantly disapproved of the influx of slaves Columbus sent to Spain. Moreover, she was disappointed by the meager numbers of Indian converts reported by her Christian missionaries.

By March 1499 Isabella and Ferdinand finally dispatched one of their trusted courtiers to Hispaniola to serve as a judge. Francisco de Bobadilla—the second one, coincidentally, so named who would affect Columbus's life—was widely respected as an honest and decent man. He was, wrote Bernáldez, "a great gentleman and loved by all."[13] At Columbus's suggestion, the monarchs had instructed Bobadilla to conduct an inquiry into the rebellion against the *almirante* and punish the miscreants. But by May they decided to expand his original duties. On the twenty-first they appointed Bobadilla the governor and chief magistrate of Hispaniola, with full license to send any "gentlemen and other persons" back to

Spain for trial.[14] By so doing, the king and queen granted Bobadilla permission to restore order on the island regardless of a person's rank or station.

The order suggests that Isabella and Ferdinand were suspicious not only of Roldán and other crown rebels but even about Columbus. As seasoned administrators, they had not forgotten the enmities Columbus had incurred with many under his command—Pinzón, Fray Buil, Margarit, Fonseca, and now Roldán. Moreover, Columbus's stubborn insistence on sending slaves to Andalusia smacked of insubordination.

Yet Isabella and Ferdinand hesitated before finally sending Bobadilla to Hispaniola. But when, in the winter of 1499, two caravels arrived from Hispaniola loaded with disgruntled ex-settlers and slaves, the monarchs lost all patience. The situation, they now agreed, demanded an investigation. Ironically, the same fleet that would carry Bobadilla to Hispaniola was returning the twenty-one surviving Indian slaves Columbus had exported to Castile in 1498.

When Bobadilla arrived in Santo Domingo on April 23, 1500, Columbus was at the inland fortress of Concepción. As the Castilian official entered the harbor, he saw seven corpses dangling from gallows. Horrified, Bobadilla soon demanded that Columbus's brother Diego surrender all his prisoners and submit to his authority.

Then, after Bobadilla subdued the citizens of Santo Domingo with promises of lower taxes and permission to seek gold, he imprisoned Diego and seized Columbus's home. When the *almirante* finally returned to Santo Domingo, he encountered one of Bobadilla's agents, who showed him the royal letters attesting to the new governor's authority.

At first, Columbus feigned skepticism. Then he exploded with rage and refused to submit. Months later he privately admitted that he deliberately tried to obstruct Bobadilla's authority. "I published by word of mouth and by letters that Bobadilla could not use his provisions because mine were stronger," Columbus admitted in a letter to his court friend, Juana de la Torre.[15] In Castile, Martire later verified reports that Bobadilla had intercepted letters written by Columbus to Bartholomew, advising him to prepare armed men to "defend him against any affront in case the Governor intended to attack him by violence."[16]

Finally, on September 15, Bobadilla and Columbus met face to face. When the official informed the *almirante* of his position as the new governor of Hispaniola, Columbus retorted that his was the higher authority and that Bobadilla should "respect" his letters. Furthermore, he was governor by virtue of his discoveries, an authority that could not be removed even by the king and queen.

Bobadilla then coolly ordered Columbus and his brother Diego placed in jail and manacled. Afterward he urged the *almirante* to have his other brother, Bartholomew, who was then in the Xaragua, surrender. Still, the colonists either so respected or were so terrified of Columbus that no one wanted to put the explorer's feet in chains. Finally, Columbus's cook agreed to do so "with as saucy a front as if he were serving him a new and precious dish."[17] Meanwhile, Bobadilla gathered testimony against Columbus and his brothers and ordered them returned to Spain for a formal investigation.

The condition of the white-haired admiral who had discovered lands beyond the Ocean Sea was so pitiful that as soon as he boarded *La Gorda* for the return trip to Castile, its captain volunteered to unshackle him. Characteristically, Columbus disdained the offer. He informed the captain that he had been chained in the name of the crown and would be unshackled only by the king and queen. "If I had stolen the Indies," he wrote bitterly to Juana de la Torre, ". . . and given them to the Moors, I could not meet with more enmity in Spain."[18] Knowing she was close to the queen, Columbus had written Juana in the hopes that she would plead for royal mercy.

From Isabella and Ferdinand's perspective in civilized Castile, Columbus's administration in Hispaniola was nevertheless a dismal failure. Perhaps, given the inequities in weaponry, technology, and sophistication, coupled with the Europeans' greed for gold, any contact between the Indians and Spanish adventurers and missionaries was bound to end in bloodshed, as the subsequent history of the Americas would demonstrate. Moreover, Columbus's foreign origin, his haughtiness and rigidity, combined with his dazzling discoveries made him a natural target for envy both within the court and in Hispaniola.

Clearly, Columbus's talents were ultimately with the sea, not on its shores. Columbus was a brilliant dreamer, an obsessed visionary, who pressed on against all human and natural odds to fulfill his goal. He was not a calculating diplomat meant to scrape against the razor-sharp jealousies and vendettas of more earthbound men, but an ethereal genius whose gifts would enable mankind to gaze upon a New World.

On the long trip home Columbus pondered the injustice of the opinions against him. To Juana de la Torre he complained:

> They judge me as a governor who had gone to Sicily or to a city
> or town under a regular government, where the laws can be ob-
> served in toto without fear of losing all, and I am suffering grave
> injury. I should be judged as a captain who went from Spain to
> the Indies to conquer a people numerous and warlike, whose man-
> ners and religion are very different from ours, who live in sierras
> and mountains, without fixed settlements, and where by divine
> will I have placed under the sovereignty of the King and Queen
> our lords, an Other World, whereby Spain, which was reckoned
> poor, is become the richest of countries. . . .[19]

Ultimately, it would be by the yardstick of his extraordinary accomplishments on the seas, not by his blunders on land, that posterity would judge Columbus. Additionally, his brilliance as a discoverer would inspire Isabella and Ferdinand to fund a fourth journey in May 1502, this time to search for a passageway to the Indian Ocean southwest of Cuba and Jamaica. While the king and queen underwrote the new expedition at a cost of 10,000 pesos of gold, they strictly forbade the admiral from visiting Hispaniola on his outbound journey. On the return trip to Castile he was allowed to stop at that island only "if it appears to be necessary."[20]

Despite his title as *Almirantazgo*, or Viceroy, of the Indies and the continent to its south, Columbus was thus stripped of the privilege of governing the lands he had discovered. Like the queen he loved and served, Columbus was destined to have the work of a lifetime benefit a new generation of strangers.

CHAPTER FIFTY-NINE

An English Wedding

By the spring of 1501 Isabella could no longer delay Catherine's marriage. The wedding pact with Henry VII had stipulated that the Spanish sovereigns' youngest daughter travel to England as soon as Prince Arthur reached his fourteenth birthday so that he and Catherine could be wed. Even that rule, however, had been waived by a papal dispensation and thus, as early as 1498, when Arthur was only twelve, Henry had urged Catherine's journey to England.

Repeatedly the English king wrote about the "great preparations" he had made to receive Catherine. In March 1500 he peevishly observed that he "should still be uncertain whether, and when the Princess of Wales will come to England."[1] Nevertheless, the grief-stricken Isabella, dressed in perpetual black, bereft of all her children save Catherine, clung to the princess in Granada.

By fifteen years of age, the poised, blue-eyed, auburn-haired Catherine, the "baby"of the royal family, shared not only a striking physical resemblance to the queen but also a temperamental similarity. Like Isabella, Catherine was intelligent, fair-minded, and reflective. These traits, enhanced by her steady disposition, dignified carriage, and careful education, made the princess a source of pride and solace to her mother. Moreover, Catherine had grown to young womanhood during the tragic series of deaths that stripped the royal family of its heirs, and quite naturally, those sorrows had drawn her closer to the queen.

Intellectually, both mother and daughter knew that separation was inevitable, that by virtue of royal birth European princesses were obliged to mix their blood with foreign kings for political advantage. Catherine, like all her sisters, had been schooled to that duty from birth. Indeed, she had been addressed as the Princess of Wales since she was old enough to understand, and although the marriage agreement had ebbed and flowed in the churning tides of Spanish/ English relations of the 1490s, the pact was finalized on October 1, 1497, with a proxy marriage ceremony at Bewdley, England.

The following summer Henry's wife, Elizabeth of York, daughter of Edward IV, told the Spanish ambassador, Dr. Rodrigo González de Puebla, that Catherine "should always speak French with the Princess Margaret, who is now in Spain, in order to learn the language and to be able to converse in it when she comes to England." This is necessary, she added, "because these ladies do not understand Latin and much less Spanish." In addition, they urged that the Princess of Wales learn to drink wine, because "the water of England is not drinkable, and even if it were, the climate would not allow the drinking of it."[2]

In preparation too, Catherine's future husband, the reed-thin Prince Arthur, had written her love letters in Latin, probably at the direction of his tutors, noting that "the delay respecting her coming is very grievous" and begging her to sail to England as soon as possible.[3]

King Henry was even more anxious, if for no other reason than for the prestige the wedding would bring England. In August 1498 he told Puebla that "he and the Queen are more satisfied with this marriage than they would have been with any great dominions they might have gained with the daughter of another Prince, even if they were twice or three times as great as the whole property of the Duke of Bourbon."[4] A year later, in anticipation of the marriage, Henry and the Spanish sovereigns signed a treaty guaranteeing free trade between their countries and "a true friendship and alliance for all future times" between them and their heirs.[5]

Despite these protracted correspondences, Catherine's departure was a traumatic wrench to the queen who, broken by the tragedies that had marred her other children's lives, was very anxious about her last daughter's nuptials. Politically, at least until 1499, there were well-founded reasons for those anxieties. The two pretenders to Henry's throne, Perkin Warbeck and Lambert Simnel, were still alive. While both men were imprisoned in the Tower of London, they were not put to death until November of that year. There were still other compelling reasons to hasten the marriage, the most important being the Archduke Philip's overtures to Henry for a marriage between his sister Princess Margaret and Prince Arthur.

Even so, Isabella delayed Catherine's departure for another year. Once Catherine's journey was postponed because of concerns about the queen's health; another time the trip was canceled because of an outbreak of plague in northern Castile through which the princess had to travel before sailing for England. And in 1500 the rebellion of the Alpujarran Moors made the roads north of Granada again unsafe for travel.

Consequently, Catherine remained in Granada with Isabella and Ferdinand through the winter of 1501. She witnessed Columbus's humiliating return home in chains. That same winter her parents were preparing for two new wars—a campaign to crush a new Moorish rebellion west of Granada in the Sierra Bermejas and a dispatch of soldiers to Italy to defend the Venetian possessions of Corfu and Cephalonia against the Turks.

These efforts cost the nearly fifty-year-old Isabella and Ferdinand much in terms of personal energy and national resources. Once again, despite Isabella's gradually declining vitality, she conscientiously assembled men, artillery, and provisions for these battles; once again Ferdinand drilled troops, conferred with his generals, drained the royal coffers and finally pawned some of Isabella's jewels to defray the costs of war.

Even those expenditures, however, could not prevent Moorish retaliations. In a small town in the Sierra Bermejas near Ronda, they slaughtered some of Castile's most seasoned and beloved warriors—among them the Great Captain's older brother, Alonso de Aguilar, and the military engineer *El Artillero,* Francisco Ramirez.

In late March 1501 Ferdinand marched again to Ronda with a large army. The appearance of the king and his helmeted pikemen terrified the Moors, who, fearing another large-scale war, agreed to a permanent surrender. By May Ferdinand gave them two options: convert or be exiled. Most of the citizens, unable to scrape together ten doblas of gold for the fare to Africa, were thus compelled to become Christians. With peace reestablished, Ferdinand finally returned to the Alhambra on May 15 to celebrate Catherine's long-delayed departure.

There was still enough gold in the royal coffers to send Catherine to England with half her dowry—100,000 Castilian gold ducats, or English crowns, which was to be paid on her wedding day. Another 50,000 had been promised six months later, and the remaining 50,000 were in silver plate and jewels that would remain in Catherine's possession for a year. Isabella was so anxious about her daughter's reception in a foreign land that she urged Henry VII to treat Catherine kindly and not to squander money unnecessarily on wedding celebrations. As she wrote Puebla on March 23:

> I am told that the king, my brother, has ordered great prepara-
> tions to be made and that much money will be spent upon her
> reception and her wedding.
> I am pleased to hear it, because it shows the magnificent gran-
> deur of my brother and because demonstrations of joy at the re-
> ception of my daughter are naturally agreeable to me.
> Nevertheless, it would be more in accordance with my feelings
> and with the wishes of my Lord [King Ferdinand] if the expenses
> were moderate. We do not wish that our daughter should be the
> cause of any loss to England, neither in money, nor in any other
> respect. On the contrary we desire that she should be the source
> of all kinds of happiness. . . . We, therefore beg the King, our
> brother, to moderate the expenses. Rejoicings may be held, but
> we ardently implore him that the substantial part of the festival
> should be his love; that the Princess would be treated by him and
> by the Queen as their true daughter and by the Prince of Wales as
> we feel sure he will treat her. Say this to the King of England.[6]

On May 21, less than a month later, having done everything possible to ensure Catherine's happiness, Isabella and Ferdinand bade their daughter farewell from the Alhambra with festivities, garlands, and musical fanfares. For the next two months the bride, accompanied by the Count of Cabra, the Archbishop of Santiago, the Bishop of Majorca, knights, *letrados*, archers, and a household staff of fifty-five attendants, traveled the dust-filled roads of Castile, arriving at the port of La Coruña on July 5.

Like her older sister, Princess Juana, Catherine was accompanied by several trusted servants, as well as *doncellas,* cup-bearers, almoners, cooks, and other attendants. Only a few were to stay permanently in England, but to soothe Isabella and Ferdinand's fears, Henry VII promised that he would "not treat the Spanish servants as badly as they have been treated in Flanders" and would instead provide for them handsomely.[7] Although such earnestness was rare among monarchs, Henry knew about the poor treatment of Juana's servants in Flanders through ambassadorial reports, his own previous attempts to communicate with Juana, and Isabella's frank acknowledgment of the situation.

Finally, on August 17, after more delays due to Catherine's illness and bad weather, the royal fleet weighed anchor. Four days later all but one of the ships limped into the port of Laredo with ripped sails, lost rigging, and leaks in the hull. Violent storms in the Bay of Biscay had played havoc with Catherine's bridal fleet in much the same way they had with Princess Juana's armada five years earlier.

To the superstitious and to those who lived long enough to witness the tragedy that would end Catherine's life in England, the storm might have been considered a warning. But neither Isabella nor Ferdinand, nor the savants of the early Renaissance, indulged in such superstitions. However, in England, Henry VII was so worried about the delay that he sent a skilled Devonshire pilot, Stephen Brett, to Spain to guide the fleet through the treacherous Bay of Biscay past the rocky shoals of Brittany in the English Channel.

Finally, on the sun-drenched Saturday afternoon of October 2, Catherine arrived in Plymouth, England, where gaily dressed citizens and squires crowded the quays for their first glimpse of the Spanish princess. From the town, a great clamor of bells broke over the shore when sailors cast the first line at the dock.

With dignity, her reddish-gold hair blazing in the autumn sun, Catherine stood on the deck of her caravel flanked by the Count of Cabra, the Archbishop of Santiago, and the Bishop of Majorca. The girl's beauty, her sturdy figure, perhaps even something of her personal fortitude immediately excited the crowd. It was the beginning of England's love affair with the fair-skinned woman who would marry first Prince Arthur and, later, his younger brother, the future Henry VIII, who would ultimately attempt to have his marriage to Catherine annulled so that he could wed Anne Boleyn.

But for the moment, the Spanish princess was in every way her mother's daughter—pretty, personable, and filled with optimism. So she remained during the grand reception she was given as she progressed into the rose-festooned and bannered streets of London, through the lavish wedding to the slight blond prince who was a head shorter than she at St. Paul's Cathedral on November 14.

Even the sometimes sardonic Sir Thomas More, who scoffed at the "hunch-backed, undersized barefoot Pygmies from Ethiopia," as he dubbed the Spaniards of Catherine's entourage, was impressed with the bearing of the princess. "Ah but the lady! take but my word for it, she thrilled the hearts of everyone; she possesses all those qualities that make for beauty in a very charming young girl. Everywhere she receives the highest of praises but even that is inadequate. I do hope this highly publicized union will prove a happy omen for England."[8]

After the wedding, an exuberant Henry wrote Isabella and Ferdinand that

> although the friendship between the houses of England and Spain
> has been most sincere and intimate before this time, it will hence-
> forth be much more intimate and indissoluble. Great and cordial
> rejoicings have taken place. The whole people have taken part in
> them. . . . Though they cannot now see the gentle face of their
> beloved daughter they may be sure that she has found a second
> father who will ever watch over her happiness, and never permit
> her to want anything . . .[9]

Subsequently, a storm of controversy would break over the contention that the
fifteen-year-old Prince Arthur had not consummated his marriage to Catherine at
the time of the marriage. Nevertheless on November 30 the elegant young prince
communicated to Isabella and Ferdinand through their ambassador that he "had
never felt so much joy in his life as when he beheld the sweet face of his bride.
No woman in the world could be more agreeable to him."[10]

For Isabella, news that her daughter had arrived safely in England and been
married to an enthusiastic Prince Arthur was doubtless a comfort, a recompense of
sorts for the emotional void the queen felt, an emptiness that was unlikely to be
filled by the imminent arrival of the Archduchess Juana and her husband the
Archduke Philip.

CHAPTER SIXTY

Primogenita Sucesora

Isabella and Ferdinand exerted great efforts to welcome Juana and Philip as the new heirs of Castile and Aragón. In January 1502, the Marquis of Denia, the Constable of Castile, the Duke of Najara, and a virtual army of courtiers waited patiently for the archduke and archduchess at the border town of Fuenterrabia. When on the twenty-ninth, their caravan was finally sighted, musicians greeted them with a joyous fanfare. As the royal couple proceeded through the towns of northern Castile, they were feted with a seemingly dizzying series of banquets, fiestas, and fireworks.

In Isabella and Ferdinand's eagerness to impress the archduke, whom they knew from discussions with Besançon and their own ambassadors, loathed the formal solemnity of the Spanish court, the monarchs now lifted the 1494 *pragmática,* or royal decree, that prohibited ordinary citizens from wearing silks, brightly colored clothes, and gold-trimmed fabrics. Now instead they encouraged everyone to "dress as splendidly as possible; those who order new clothes choosing light colors as a better indication of happiness, and those who according to law are permitted to wear silk doublets being allowed to don coats of the same."[1]

Even so, the task of favorably impressing the archduke would be difficult, for Philip, Juana, and their retinue of two hundred people, half of whom were knights of the Burgundian Order of Golden Fleece, had first traveled through France where they had been lavishly entertained by Louis XII.

In a carefully choreographed effort to maintain Philip's loyalty, French escorts had ushered the archduke and archduchess from the Belgian border to Paris, where they were feted for three days and where, in the crush of the crowds, several commoners were killed. There too, by Louis's arrangement, Philip naively took his place in the French parliament as a peer, or servant of the crown. Addressing the assembly, he affirmed his duty as "good neighbor, humble cousin and obedient vassal."[2] Meanwhile Juana, in sullen disapproval of Philip's allegiance, visited old Spanish friends, including the Count of Cabra and his family, who were on their way back to Spain from Catherine's wedding.

By Tuesday, December 7, the enormous Flemish baggage train loaded with clothes, tapestries, porcelains, and kitchen utensils had rolled to a slushy halt at the Loire Valley hillside castle of Blois. In the torchlight of the late winter afternoon, Juana was whisked away to the chambers of Anne of France, Duchess of Bourbon, while Philip was ushered through a first-floor gallery into the throne room to meet King Louis. Three times Philip bowed in reverence to the forty-year-old French king, who returned his obeisance with an amused series of counterbows until finally the two men embraced.

Somewhat later, when Juana, who was anxious to avoid kissing Louis and signifying her allegiance, was presented to the king, she made a deep curtsy. Louis, sensing her reluctance and hoping to avoid embarrassment, quickly rose from his throne, raised Juana, and kissed her on the cheek.

For a week the young couple were entertained in the opulent splendor of Louis's favorite castle, which, with its gigantic silver candelabras, spiral staircases, satin wallpaper, and golden dishes subsequently gave Blois the reputation of being the "Versailles" of the Renaissance. Every morning after mass Philip disappeared for the day to hawk, hunt, joust, or play tennis. The evenings were whiled away with banquets, cards, masques, and dances—few of which included Juana.

Instead, the archduchess seems to have been deliberately cloistered with the ladies of the court, the most memorable of whom were the Duchess of Bourbon and the queen herself, the plain but utterly self-possessed Anne of Brittany, former wife of Charles VII and ex-fiancée to Philip's own father, Maximilian. Despite her circumstances, Juana was determined to maintain her integrity as the proud *Infanta* of Castile rather than a Flemish vassal of France. But inevitably she was subjected to humiliations—among them a forced bow to Queen Anne from a shove by the Duchess of Bourbon that sent Juana helplessly to her knees, and an unwanted introduction to the wailing two-year-old Princess Claude who was already unofficially bethrothed against her wishes to her own son Charles.

On December 13 Louis and Philip swore to uphold the treaty of Trent, an agreement already secretly effected between the archduke's father, Maximilian, and the French king that past October. By its terms, Maximilian agreed to honor Louis's investiture in Milan in exchange for protection against the Turks. Now at Blois, Philip sealed that treaty with his promise to marry his son Charles to Louis's daughter, Claude.

Simultaneously, the Archduchess Juana found herself in still another compromising position. At the conclusion of a morning church service, one of Queen Anne's ladies gave Juana some gold coins to present as an offering for the queen. When the archduchess refused to accept them because of the subservience they implied, the queen rose from her seat and stormed out of the chapel. The archduchess, determined to preserve her integrity as an independent Spanish princess, deliberately stalled for another fifteen minutes in the church. Meanwhile,

Queen Anne and her cortege waited impatiently in the church vestibule for, by the dictates of court etiquette, they could leave the chapel only when their guest followed. But Juana, rebellious by nature and never more so than when she felt threatened, swept past the queen and proceeded coolly to her private apartment. That night when she appeared at the royal banquet, she was carefully dressed in Spanish brocades and velvets, rather than in a Flemish costume.

No doubt, Philip was furious with his wife's behavior. On December 15, to avoid further embarrassment, the Flemish court abruptly left Blois. From there, in driving rain, the archduke and archduchess proceeded south to Amboise, Tours, and finally crossed the edge of the Pyrenees foothills into the Navarre. Finding the heavy Flemish wagons and carts ill-equipped for the snowy passes, the royal party were assisted by teams of Vizcayan pack mules that, at Isabella and Ferdinand's orders, stood ready to transport the Flemish baggage into Castile. On January 26, 1502, in the midst of an icy storm that blew across the foothills from the nearby Bay of Biscay, Juana and Philip crossed the Bidassoa River and entered Spain.

A chilled cortege of officials sent by Isabella and Ferdinand, headed by the Marquis of Denia, rushed forward to kiss the archduke and archduchess's hands and hurry them to the warm shelter of a nearby castle. But comfort, Isabella and Ferdinand knew, was not enough to satisfy the appetites of the sensual archduke; there must also be excitement, challenge, and above all, merriment. For months before Philip and Juana's arrival the Spanish monarchs had thus designed the couple's route to Toledo with an eye to gaiety.

The morning after their arrival, Philip was introduced to the Spanish sport of *cañas*, the long reed spears used as mock lances by knights on the tilting field. In Vitoria, the city fathers staged an elaborate bullfight that amused Philip with the skill and prowess of its agile *matadors*. At Miranda de Ebro the Flemish party was greeted by the thundering hooves from a hundred horses whose riders were dressed dramatically in crimson Moorish capes. At Burgos the royal couple were escorted under a gold brocade canopy to the Gothic cathedral and, for ten days thereafter, the archduke was hustled from hunts and tourneys to bullfights in rapid succession.

Initially, Philip was so favorably impressed that he even agreed to accompany Juana to the Carthusian monastery of Miraflores where her maternal grandparents and uncle, Prince Alfonso, were buried. But as little time as possible was spent in the "overly long" religious devotions of Catholic Spain; thus Philip and Juana quickly proceeded on to fiestas in Valladolid. Fortunately they arrived during the season of the biannual wool *feria* at nearby Medina del Campo. To distract the young archduke, the Spanish courtiers disguised him with a wig and invited him to wander through the food, animal, and fabric exhibits accompanied by a few Flemish attendants. Later the royal couple toured Segovia and arrived in Madrid during *Santa Semana,* where they learned that Isabella and Ferdinand had left Sevilla and were heading for Toledo.

That city was, of course, what Philip had been anticipating all along—the place where he and Juana would be sworn by the *Cortes* as heirs of Castile. But just after the archduke and Juana left Madrid on April 28 and reached the tiny village of Olías, Philip contracted measles. Ferdinand raced there with his physicians. From a second-story gallery, Juana bounded down the stairs and threw herself joyfully into her father's arms. Delighted, Ferdinand stepped back to regard the daughter he had not seen nor heard from in nearly six years. Smiling affectionately, he called her "my little mother." Then, with Juana on his arm, Ferdinand entered Philip's bedroom.

For a moment, the fifty-year-old, balding king and the young, still pale and scab-covered archduke scrutinized each other. From his sickbed Philip removed his bonnet as a sign of deference and attempted to kiss Ferdinand's hand. The king rebuffed his son-in-law's show of humility. Within minutes the archduke was thoroughly disarmed by Ferdinand's affectionate concern, which fit poorly with the villainous portrait Louis XII had painted of the monarch. To Ferdinand, the archduke's illness was a fortuitous stroke, a temporary incapacity that allowed the king to become acquainted with Philip during a rare period of vulnerability. And for a while, at least, Ferdinand's ploy seemed to work, for Philip soon warmed to his father-in-law.

By May 7, the archduke was well enough to dress himself in gorgeous purple satin and velvets and travel to Toledo. The city had gone wild with anticipation. In a dazzling display of pageantry an entourage of Spanish noblemen, preceded by green-coated royal falconers, all of whom had one gray sleeve, accompanied the archduke and archduchess along the dirt highway that led to the Tagus River. A mile or so out of Toledo the cortege was joined by other city officials, all of whom were dressed in bright crimsons for the occasion.

As they approached the city they met Ferdinand, flanked by the French and Venetian ambassadors, prelates, and *grandees*. Philip dismounted at the king's arrival, but Ferdinand waved him back onto his horse.

Later, as the royal couple approached the massive granite Toledo cathedral, the clergy appeared carrying an enormous gold cross. Simultaneously, all the church bells in the city chimed. In the ensuing cacophony, punctuated by cannon salutes, Philip and Juana fell to their knees to be blessed by Archbishop Cisneros. After a high mass, the royal couple and their cortege proceeded to the palace of the Marquis of Villena where Isabella, garbed in a plain black woolen dress, awaited them in a large sitting room. By her side sat her good friend Beatriz, the Marquesa of Moya, and one of Ferdinand's illegitimate daughters, who then resided at court. While Isabella had long resented Ferdinand's affairs, she had always treated his illegitimate offspring with respect.

As custom demanded, both Philip and Juana knelt at the queen's feet, but Isabella had warned the archduke's attendants beforehand that such displays of humility were unnecessary. Like Ferdinand, Isabella wanted to win her estranged daughter and arrogant son-in-law to a new affection and keep them in Spain long enough to learn its customs. Isabella thus embraced them both with motherly affection.

After a suitable exchange of pleasantries, Isabella took Juana by her hand and retired with her for an hour to a separate chamber. What transpired between mother and daughter in their first few minutes alone together remains a mystery—perhaps a gentle probe into the kind of life the young woman was leading in Flanders. In retrospect, the queen might well have spared herself the pain, for in the ensuing months the results of Juana's unhappy marriage would become painfully obvious. But for a brief time, the joy of having Juana by her side after the long separation reinvigorated the queen, whose health had gradually been failing since Prince Juan's death.

If the archduchess was preoccupied with anything in April 1502, it was with Philip. The archduke's contentment had become her sole purpose in life, and his elegant, Burgundian high-toned court and stylish costumes made her stark, somber Spanish homeland seem hopelessly dull and provincial in comparison. Juana was, as Martire observed, *semblante ensombrecido unicamente piensa en el esposo,* completely overshadowed by her husband and had lost all sense of her own identity.

Not long after Juana and Philip's arrival a courtier arrived with tragic news. In England Prince Arthur had died, leaving the sixteen-year-old Catherine a widow. Although Catherine's *dueña,* Doña Elvira Manuel, would later insist that the Spanish princess's marriage to the young—and probably consumptive—boy prince was never consummated, Catherine's widowhood would leave her stranded and impoverished in England. At first, there was talk that Catherine might return to Castile. Yet Henry, who had already received 100,000 crowns of Catherine's dowry, had no intention of returning it. Moreover, within ten months of Arthur's death his mother, Elizabeth of York, died in childbirth. Shortly thereafter, the newly widowed Henry VII expressed his wish to marry Catherine. But Isabella was adamantly opposed to the idea. In fact, seven years would go by before she would become the bride of Arthur's younger brother, the future Henry VIII.

Prince Arthur's death cast a pall over the festivities in Toledo, celebrations that had cost the aristocracy and commoners of Spain great effort despite the Flemish court's increasingly disdainful attitude toward them. Now the Spanish court was obliged to exchange their bright new clothes for *ropas de luto,* and on May 12, Philip and Juana accompanied the king and queen to San Juan de los Reyes in Toledo for a requiem mass for Prince Arthur.

Still another death, that of Ferdinand's uncle Enrique of Aragón, delayed the convocation of the *Cortes* a second time. Thus it was not until May 22 that Philip and Juana were finally sworn the Prince and Princess of Asturias. As spring turned to summer in Toledo, the archduke had become openly bored. To make time pass quickly, Ferdinand filled Philip's days with amusements—jousts, hunts, riding lessons in the short-stirrup Moorish style, *al la jineta,* even a mock battle with his *grandees* in imitation of the conquest of Granada.

Meanwhile, Isabella showed the archduke her strict weekly program of administrative duties—the regularly scheduled meetings on Thursdays and Saturdays to sign petitions and documents, the Tuesday cabinet meetings, the Wednesday conferences with the royal auditor, the Fridays devoted to the financial matters of Castile. To the carefree archduke such a schedule, coupled with the daily round of chapel devotions, seemed tortuous, a dreary track of joyless duties that oppressed him nearly as much as the lean and beerless Castilian diet and the stark landscape of windswept sierras and dry ravines.

Gradually, the archduke had come to hate Spain and everything about it—its mountainous climate, dry air, and erstwhile rivers that disappeared in summer, the intricate Mudéjar architecture, the poverty from years of the Holy War, the dark clothes and the ubiquitous domination of the church. Now he began to long for the joys of the Low Countries with their boisterous hunts, free-flowing beer, lush croplands, loose women, and careless cities. The archduke's courtiers were unhappy and, in the withering heat that descended on Old Castile in summer, talked of little else than returning home.

Meanwhile, by mid-July Ferdinand had traveled to Aragón to prepare the *Cortes* to swear Juana and the archduke heirs to the kingdom. This time whatever resistance the Aragonese felt about recognizing Juana as queen proprietress of the kingdom was muted, perhaps because of Ferdinand's advance warnings and the *procuradores'* memory of the tragic events that followed their bitter opposition to Princess Isabel and King Manuel as their heirs. By the time Juana and Philip left Castile, Ferdinand had received assurances that the *Cortes* would support these new Aragonese heirs. Superficially, there were striking parallels to the visit made by the Portuguese king and queen to Zaragoza four years earlier. And by September 1502, when the archduke and archduchess rode there to meet the *Cortes*, Juana, like her sister before her, was pregnant.

This time, however, Queen Isabella could not accompany the young couple. She had become ill again with one of her inexplicable fevers and was too weak to make the journey. By then Philip was seething with negative emotions—disgust with the Spanish life-style, disinterest in his moody wife, and most recently panic because the sudden death of his favorite, Besançon, left him without trusted counsel.

Nevertheless, the four *brazos* of the Aragonese *Cortes*—Aragón, Catalonia, Sicily, and Valencia—convened at Zaragoza and in its opening address welcomed "the princess Juana, true and lawful heir to the crown, to whom, in default of male heirs, the useage and law of the land require the oath of allegiance."[3] On October 27 the *procuradores* swore fealty to Juana as *primogenita sucesora,* or heir presumptive to the Aragonese crown, and recognized the Archduke Philip as her husband. They did, however, qualify their oath with one stipulation: Should Isabella die and Ferdinand remarry, any male child of his would take precedence in inheriting the Aragonese crown.

The next day Ferdinand received a message that Isabella was seriously ill. Entrusting the *Cortes* to Philip and Juana, he left for Toledo. At that moment the *Cortes* was debating the possibility of raising money for a war against France, a discussion that Philip, as temporary leader of that assembly, found impossible to endure. The archduke, who was never long on self-control, tolerated his role for barely a week. Then he left Zaragoza abruptly, delegating the *Cortes* to his wife. Within a few days he appeared before the king and queen, who, by then, had returned to Madrid, and announced his decision to leave Spain by himself as soon as possible. He had, he claimed, pressing business to attend to in Flanders.

In Zaragoza, the Marquis of Villena informed Juana about Philip's plans and communicated her parents' request that she do everything possible to detain him. Then Juana received the archduke's cool confirmation of his departure and plans to do so by traveling overland through France. His idea was clearly insulting, for less than three months earlier France and Spain had declared war over the division of Naples.

Juana, unnerved by the proposed departure and journey through France, abruptly left Zaragoza and hurried to Madrid to beg her husband to reconsider. Her appeals were echoed by those of the still weak Isabella, who as diplomatically as possible tried to show Philip the cruelty of forcing Juana to travel through a hostile country in the last trimester of pregnancy.

But the archduke, as Isabella ruefully perceived, was considerably less gallant toward his wife than toward errant knights on the tilting field. As Juana could not travel, the young man retorted, she should remain with her parents until her delivery, after which time he would send for her from Flanders. Nothing Isabella or Juana could say would move the archduke. He was, Martire grimly observed, "as hard as a diamond."[4]

Nor could Ferdinand dissuade Philip. Instead, the archduke arrogantly proposed that he travel through France and meet with Louis, this time as a mediator for the Spanish king. To Ferdinand, Isabella, and the courtiers and prelates of Castile, Philip's journey was a despicable act, resounding with not only personal selfishness but even treason. The *procuradores* of the *Cortes* in Toledo vehemently opposed his plan, arguing that any safe conduct granted by Louis was likely to be unreliable. Moreover, as heir to the crowns of Castile and Aragón, Philip's proposed journey through France was most unwise. It was, they maintained, an unnecessary embarrassment, a deliberate perversion of national opinion.

Undaunted by such criticisms from the men who had sworn him heir to Castile just six months earlier, Philip blithely continued preparations for his journey. Nothing seemed to shake him from his decision, including the plea that he wait until after Christmas. Instead, the determined archduke and his disgruntled attendants left Madrid on December 19, 1502, and headed for Perpignan to await Louis's safe conduct.

Isabella and Ferdinand's inability to console Juana added to their distress. With Philip's departure, the archduchess became profoundly depressed and wept piteously for days on end. When she finally ceased, she often refused to speak or respond to those around her. To the worried queen her daughter's withdrawal from her surroundings was an ominous, but familiar pattern. It reminded Isabella of her youth in rural Arévalo when her own mother, the queen widow, sobbed incessantly after the death of her husband.

CHAPTER SIXTY-ONE

Juana *La Loca*

erdinand did his best to heal the wounds caused by Philip's break with Spain. Shortly after the archduke's departure, the king reconsidered his son-in-law's offer to negotiate a treaty with Louis and decided to accept it. By then, the Spanish monarchs had nothing to lose, for Philip had already defied them by his plans to travel through France. Now, if Ferdinand could urge Philip to negotiate a peace treaty on Spain's behalf, he would turn the archduke's intransigence to the country's advantage. Even if Philip's efforts failed, Ferdinand would, at least, have cast Philip in the role of a Spanish advocate against Louis.

But as an intermediary Philip would need careful instructions—not only documents granting him ambassadorial powers, but private instructions ordering him to avoid any terms detrimental to Spain. A few days after Philip's departure, a royal messenger thus galloped toward Perpignan to deliver two sets of sealed letters from Ferdinand.

Philip was flattered by the breathless arrival of Fray Bernardo Buil, abbot of San Miguel de Cuxa, and even more so when he read Ferdinand's instructions, which were carefully worded to appeal to the young man's vanity. In Philip's eyes, his Spanish visit had been a personal triumph: He had been sworn heir to Castile and Aragón and managed to leave those despicable kingdoms shortly thereafter.

The fact that the archduke had violated the wishes of the very people who had granted him that authority meant little; neither did his in-laws' disapproval, nor the *Cortes'* criticisms, nor his abandonment of his wife. All that mattered was the fact that he was now legally heir to Castile and Aragón and canonically the *primogenita sucesora*'s husband. A decade later, Machiavelli would articulate that attitude in his description of Renaissance princes who, in their struggle for survival, "learn to be other than good" for to do otherwise "is sure to come to ruin."[1] In the archduke's amoral worldview, good and evil were idealistic concepts best left to priests, prelates, and such provincially pious leaders as Isabella and Ferdinand. That Philip misjudged the sovereigns' character, that he underestimated the profound personal commitment with which Isabella and Ferdinand ruled Spain, was a reflection of his own misguided view, one that would significantly limit his impact on Europe's political canvas.

But in December 1502 Philip gazed with puerile satisfaction upon his immediate prospects. Temporarily liberated from Juana and her parents, the archduke was free to frolic through France, hobnob with its king, even dangle his newly won ambassadorial powers before Louis as a political equal. By late February or early March 1503 Louis's safe conduct arrived. The archduke crossed the Spanish border and promptly headed for the French court, which then was in Lyons, the capital city of Provence.

Isabella and Ferdinand, meanwhile, had become increasingly alarmed about Juana's reaction to Philip's departure. Those who attended the archduchess agreed that her reaction was abnormal: She ate little, cried constantly, and when she talked at all, lamented that the separation would tempt Philip into infidelities.

Isabella repeatedly tried to comfort her daughter, explaining that while the separation was inevitable, whatever infidelities Philip committed were inconsequential to the future of their marriage. In those discussions, Isabella revealed the trials she had endured in her own union to Ferdinand—the king's repeated absences for war, his periodic excursions to Aragón, and especially her jealousy over his mistresses and his illegitimate children. These were, she assured her daughter, jealousies that she had overcome only with great difficulty and over a long period of time. In a subsequent letter of 1506, Juana would recall these conversations thus: "I am not the only one in whom this passion has been seen, but the queen my lady, to whom God give glory, as excellent and select a person as any in the world, but time cured her highness, as with the pleasure of God it will do me."[2]

Despite Isabella's ministrations, Juana was irreconcilable and clung stubbornly to her anxieties, a pattern that the Queen prayed would end when she gave birth. Gradually, that hope became a refrain repeated by members of the court. Even the usually skeptical Martire expressed the hope that Juana's spirits would improve once the labor pains began, "that is if she should have a happy delivery and should not die due to the disorder of her mind."[3]

Because of the ongoing French threat in Naples and Catalonia, Ferdinand was compelled to leave his wife and daughter in Castile in late January 1503 and return to Aragón. To distract the archduchess, and perhaps to marshal spiritual and emotional support for Isabella during Ferdinand's absence, the court then moved to Alcalá de Henares. But even as a guest in Cisneros's archbishoprical palace, Juana remained sunk in a depression from which it became increasingly difficult to rouse her, save by mentioning Philip's name. The queen's efforts to restore Juana to health so exhausted her that her attendants grew alarmed about her own fragile condition. "Cruel fruit for its tree, unfortunate grain for its earth, this daughter is to her mother!" Martire wrote bitterly about Juana.[4]

Finally, on March 10, the archduchess went into labor and, with surprisingly little pain, was delivered of her fourth child, a boy named Fernando for his Spanish grandfather. To Isabella's relief, the infant was robust and well formed. His baptism at Alcalá de Henares was celebrated joyously, and the presiding prelate, the Bishop of Málaga, praised Juana excessively as a *cristianisima,* or female Christ, whose virtues would take fifty days and nights to extol.

But neither the birth of her second son nor the attendant court festivities lightened Juana's mood. In fact, the archduchess showed so little maternal interest in the newborn that he was wholly entrusted to the care of his wet nurse, Isabel de Carvajal. As before, Juana was focused exclusively on her reunification with Philip. Almost immediately after the delivery she began to propose that she return to Flanders. The archduchess sobbed and raved daily, demanding that Isabella prepare her promptly for an overland journey through France.

Between meetings with the *Cortes,* which was still in session, the queen visited her daughter. Daily she listened to the agitated young woman and finally, weighing Juana's demands against her concerns about the war with France, suggested a sea journey to Flanders instead. As always in stressful periods, Isabella drove herself hard, applying herself conscientiously to the affairs of government, the *Cortes,* the myriad administrative details of the crown, and the provisioning of men and arms for Ferdinand's war with France.

Juana, meanwhile, continued to drain her mother emotionally and distract her from her governmental duties. To compensate, Isabella worked far into the night. "Her Highness [Isabella] . . . is in grand tribulation and much worn with Madame Princess,"[5] noted the Queen's secretary Conchillos anxiously, after learning that Isabella had not eaten her dinner one evening until after midnight.

In mid-June, after a particularly anguished session with Juana, Isabella fell ill with a fever and complained of sharp pains in her side. On Sunday, June 18, the queen's physicians, Nicolás de Soto and Julian Gutierrez y Fernand Álvarez, bled her and purged her with the juice from cassia pods. The next morning Isabella felt well enough to minister to Juana again, but by the time the queen returned to her own chambers at noon, her color was so bad that her servants put her back to bed. By evening they feared for her life. From Aragón, meanwhile, Ferdinand dispatched a stream of inquiries to Isabella's doctors about her health. Their reply of June 22 described the Archduchess Juana's emotional status and its effect upon Isabella thus:

> We believe that the Queen's life is endangered by her contact with
> Madame Princess who staged scenes every day despite whatever
> our Lord had commanded us to do [that is, allow Isabella to rest].
> And this is not so much because Our Highness stands in awe of
> the Princess's disposition which gives her so much sorrow but
> because of something even more strange: for she [Juana] sleeps
> badly, eats little and at times nothing at all, she is very sad and
> weak. Sometimes she does not talk and at other times seems car-
> ried away, her illness is progressing. . . . Reason and persua-
> sion do not relieve her, nor does anything else. . . . she cries a
> great deal . . . and all these worries fall heavily upon the
> Queen, Our Ladyship. We believe that all this distresses the

Queen who gives all the counsel and hope of her prudential
Realm. We pray humbly that the fire that consumes her Highness
[Juana] disappears. Her life and condition has long affected the
life and health of our Queen and Ladyship. From Alcalá, Tuesday,
June 22, at 7 P.M. in the afternoon. The doctor Soto. The doctor
Julian.[6]

Throughout that summer Isabella repeatedly took to her bed with mysterious
fevers. There was no question that the queen's health was failing, and the strain of
caring for Juana probably accelerated her decline. Between fevers, though,
Isabella rallied and applied her herself energetically to the affairs of Castile. By
that time Louis was threatening to invade Aragón from two sides. With a flash of
her old spirit, Isabella gathered a new army of men and munitions. During those
months Isabella not only gifted the churches and monasteries with alms, but also
fasted and prayed for Ferdinand, her children, and the greater glory of Spain.

By August Isabella had dismissed the *Cortes* and ordered the court to Segovia
from where, or so she told Juana, plans could more easily be made for her
departure for Laredo. In reality, Isabella was stalling, hoping that her daughter's
mental condition would improve before she returned to Philip's court.

There were also political reasons behind the delay. Despite Philip's excuse that
he had to leave Spain in late 1502 because of pressing business in Flanders, by
summer 1503 the archduke still had not returned to his homeland. By detaining
Juana, Isabella and Ferdinand may well have been using their daughter as
collateral against their son-in-law's political indiscretions in France.

By early September, perhaps at the suggestion of the queen's doctors, Juana
moved to La Mota, the grim, battlemented castle high above Medina del Campo's
windswept plains of wheat and grazing sheep where Ferdinand and Isabella had
often lived. Within that deep-moated fortress, the archduchess established a
separate residence under the watchful eyes of Isabella's trusted prelate, Juan de
Fonseca, Bishop of Córdoba, and other household attendants.

Once free from her mother's scrutiny, Juana began feverish preparations for
her departure from Spain by an overland route through France. Her scheme could
not have been more irrational, for by then Louis was actively waging war on
Spanish borders. Nevertheless, the archduchess insisted that her carts be transferred from Fuenterrabia to Bayonne in preparation for her journey.

In mid-November Juana received a letter from Philip announcing his arrival in
Flanders and urging her to rejoin him as quickly as possible. In that communica-
tion he further advised the archduchess that he had obtained a safeguard from
Louis in the event that she preferred to travel overland.

When Isabella learned about Juana's plans, she ordered Fonseca to dissuade
the archduchess from her trip, at least until Ferdinand's return from Aragón. The
request came from a defeated woman, desperately trying to save her daughter not
only from domination by her cruel husband but from the baffling abyss of
psychosis. For months, the queen had pondered her inability to soothe Juana and
to impart a self-protective independence to her so that she could rule Spain as a
competent *primogenita señora* without Philip's intervention. Now Isabella
clutched at every excuse, every opportunity to marshal the forces of anyone who

could influence the archduchess to conduct herself properly with Philip. From childhood Juana preferred Ferdinand to Isabella; now perhaps she would listen to the king again.

To Isabella's relief, Juana agreed to delay her trip until her father's return. But the archduchess's longing for her husband was more than her tortured psyche could bear. One chill November night, a barefoot and half-dressed Juana strolled through the heavy wooden doors of La Mota and bolted for the gate. The guards, already alerted to the archduchess's bizarre behavior, promptly lowered the gate but by then she refused to reenter the castle.

Before long, several members of court appeared to calm the raving archduchess, among them her confessor Talavera, her Flemish attendant Madame Aloin, and finally Fonseca. But Juana was intractable. Nor, despite her flimsy garments, did she seem bothered by the cool air. In fact, she angrily rejected her attendants' offers to cover her with a shawl or a cape. Then, the archduchess clung stubbornly to the iron bars of La Mota's grill, hurling obscene insults at Fonseca and his assistants until dawn. For thirty-six hours Juana remained there, until finally, weak with hunger and cold, she was coaxed into the kitchen of a guard hut.

By that time, the citizens of nearby Medina del Campo were buzzing with rumors. As it happened the biannual wool fair was again in progress, and the morning after the archduchess's outburst, peasants and merchants had arrived at La Mota to deliver supplies and goods. To their astonishment, the nearly naked princess stood tight-lipped and hollow-eyed, alternately clinging grimly to the gates and pacing back and forth between the ramparts.

Even after Juana allowed herself to be escorted into the guard's kitchen, she refused to enter the castle, despite the pleas of a great crowd of courtiers and prelates, including such trusted counselors as Talavera, Cisneros, and Fonseca. Nor did the letters from her mother in Segovia have an impact on the princess. Finally Isabella rose from her sickbed and rode to Medina del Campo. By then, of course, Juana's reputation had been ruined. *Juana La Loca,* or Joanna the Mad, the peasants had begun to call her—a sobriquet by which she would be known for the rest of her life and into the twentieth century.

The incident is often cited as the first evidence of a neurotic depression or even a psychosis that was said to have plagued Juana for the rest of her life, a disorder that bore a striking resemblance to the one her grandmother, Isabel of Portugal, suffered at a similar age. A more detailed description of Juana's symptoms has not been preserved. Historians thus have debated whether Juana's illness was an inherited psychological disorder such as schizophrenia, due perhaps to the inbreeding of the peninsula's royal families, or the exaggerated reaction of a weak woman forcibly separated from her beloved mate.

At the very least, Juana was probably what modern psychologists and psychiatrists term neurotic. Perhaps her separation from Philip strained an already fragile disposition to its limits. On the other hand, Juana's abject depression, nearly catatonic withdrawals from reality, refusal to eat and sleep, self-destructive obsession with a man who abused her, and frenzied, half-naked display to the peasants of Castile suggest something more serious than frustrated love and a passing depression.

* * *

Juana's wild-eyed appearance at Medina del Campo confirmed Isabella's worst fears. Upon seeing her mother, the archduchess hurled vicious, even obscene, insults at the queen. "She spoke to me very rudely, with such contempt and lack of respect that if I had not been aware of her mental condition, I would not have tolerated it in any way," Isabella wrote to her Flemish ambassador, Fuensalida.[7]

The queen recognized that Juana's public display meant no one would ever regard her as sane again. Consequently, Isabella attempted to soothe her ranting daughter with soft words and promises. Eventually she even coaxed the archduchess into La Mota with pledges that after Ferdinand's return, all haste would be made to return her to Flanders by sea. "Yo la metí," "I put her in," Isabella grimly reported to Fuensalida.[8]

It would not be until March 1, 1504, that Juana finally set out for Laredo, accompanied by an entourage of Spanish nobles and Flemish attendants. This time, bad weather in the Cantabrian Sea delayed the fleet until mid-May when it finally set sail from Spain, arriving nine days later in the Bay of Blankenburg near Bruges.

But even the flurry of preparations in Medina del Campo for the return voyage to Flanders did not prevent a renewal of Juana's outbursts. In a letter addressed to Philip announcing Juana's imminent return, Isabella warned her son-in-law to treat his wife with the utmost solicitude so as to keep her calm. In another letter she asked the archduke to confer full authority upon Juana's Flemish attendants, Monsieur Melu and Madame Aloin, "from the moment the princess leaves us until she reaches his side, to curb her and to restrain her from doing the things that her passion can lead her to do, and to keep her from doing anything that will bring danger or dishonor to her person."[9]

Juana's madness caused Isabella and Ferdinand profound anguish, even more than the untimely deaths of their two oldest children. The archduchess's departure left them chilled and vulnerable, menaced by a sense of impending annihilation they had not experienced since the Moorish war—emotions that must have been underscored by Juana's abandonment of her son Fernando to be raised in Spain by his grandparents.

Now Isabella and Ferdinand had ample reasons to fear that after their deaths Juana would forsake Spain in the same way she had just cast aside her own flesh and blood. In that case, the leadership of the twin crowns of Castile and Aragón would devolve upon their despised son-in-law, the Archduke Philip. Such a possibility, the king and queen resolved, must be carefully avoided.

Philip's behavior in France was at least as destructive to Isabella and Ferdinand's peace of mind as was their daughter Juana's public tantrums. The archduke had arrived in Lyons and, in his new capacity as the Spanish heir, immediately began negotiations with Louis, the papal legate, and Fray Buil over the disposition of Naples.

By early April 1503 the archduke had agreed to a pact whereby Ferdinand would relinquish all his claims to Naples through the Trastámara line in favor of his grandson Charles. Concomitantly, Louis was to surrender his rights to the Neapolitan kingdom in favor of his daughter, Claude. Since the two heirs were still infants, Naples would be ruled by two regents—the first a governor named by Louis to oversee the French share, and the second either Philip himself or another governor named by Ferdinand. The disputed province of Calabria, however, the "high heel" of Italy's "boot," was to be governed by Louis's appointed agent and by the Archduke Philip himself. With Charles V and Princess Claude's marriage, the Italian kingdom and its provinces would thus be united under the crowns of Spain, Hapsburg Germany, and France.

Buil, who had accompanied the archduke to Lyons, disputed the treaty for it deliberately excluded Ferdinand from jurisdiction over Calabria in favor of Philip; moreover, the pact granted Louis a free hand in naming a cogovernor. When the bishop pointed out that inequity, the archduke shrugged, obviously indifferent to the accusation that he had crushed Ferdinand's rights under the heel of France.

Finally, Buil notified Ferdinand. At the same time, he urged Louis and Philip to wait ten days before signing the treaty so that its long-term effects could be contemplated carefully. But Buil's pleas were futile. The proposed pact gave France and Flanders so many advantages that neither man was willing to wait. On April 5 they signed the treaty of Lyons.

From Barcelona, an enraged Ferdinand notified Henry VII and Maximilian that he had not agreed to the treaty. He also dispatched a messenger to Philip, criticizing the pact and ordering the archduke to follow his orders. But by then the treaty of Lyons had been signed, and both Philip and Louis considered it valid.

For years both Louis and Ferdinand had believed their claims to the Neapolitan monarchy were legitimate. Because neither king was eager to engage in a full-scale war, they had signed the treaty of Granada in 1500 agreeing to remove King Federico from the throne and divide Naples between themselves. At first, all went according to plan. When Louis's army invaded Naples in July 1501, the rest of Western Europe assumed that the Spaniards would defend Ferdinand's kinsman, Federico. To their astonishment, Ferdinand's deputies calmly divided the kingdom with France and coerced the frightened Neapolitan king into relinquishing his throne.

That Louis and Ferdinand had forced Federico's abdication typified the political ruthlessness of the age. Admittedly, the Neapolitan king's misjudgments had contributed to his dethronement, for after Louis invaded Milan in 1500, Federico had appealed to the Turkish Sultan Bayezid for help. Although he received little more than promises, Federico's invitation shocked the kings of Western Europe and gave Ferdinand and Louis a good excuse to depose him.

By April 1502, leaders of the French and Spanish armies were still quarreling over the boundaries established in the treaty of Granada. In July—just as Juana and Philip were being sworn heirs to Castile—Louis XII himself arrived in Naples to proclaim war against the Spaniards. By then the Spanish army, led by Gonzalo Fernández de Córdoba, the Great Captain, was severely reduced for Ferdinand had not sent him reinforcements. Hence, shortly after Louis declared war on Spain, de Córdoba ordered most of his army to the fortified city of Barletta in Apulia on the Adriatic. There, buttressed against invasion from the French, de Córdoba expected to receive new supplies from Spain or, if not, to order his soldiers to retreat onto boats from the Spanish fleet then skirting the Italian coast.

Through fall and into the winter of 1503 the French army penetrated into the

Apulian heel and gradually separated the Great Captain from the rest of the Neapolitan countryside. But as de Córdoba's nickname implied, he was a consummate tactician. When, in late February, the French Duke of Nemours arrived beneath Barletta's battlements with 4,000 soldiers and requested a pitched battle, de Córdoba rejected the challenge.

On February 22, after waiting several days for the Spanish soldiers to appear, Nemours retreated. Soon after, with a rush of men and munitions in the Moorish guerilla style, de Córdoba's men fell on the French from the rear. The Spanish army then overwhelmed the French at Castellaneta and Ruvo and obtained rich plunder—clothes, jewels, money, and most important, nearly a thousand French horses.

Thus was the state of the Neapolitan war in March 1503 when Philip met with Louis in France. Filled with confidence in the so-called treaty of Lyons, Louis promptly canceled orders to dispatch new troops to Naples and instructed his generals to desist from all future battles. Philip dispatched a similar message to the Great Captain.

But de Córdoba, who had not received such orders from King Ferdinand, continued the war. Later, when asked why he had ignored Philip's orders, he stated that "he knew no authority but that of his own sovereigns, and that he felt bound to prosecute the war with all his ability, till he received their commands to the contrary."[10]

Thus, on April 28, after de Córdoba received reinforcements from Hapsburg Germany and from fellow Spaniards at nearby Taranto, he ordered his men to march upon the French camp at Cerignola sixteen miles inland from Barletta. By the time the Spaniards arrived, it was nearly sunset. The French impulsively advanced through the fennel, canebreaks, and vineyards of the Neapolitan countryside toward their enemies. To their horror, fire burst from the Spanish arquebuses. In less than two hours 3,000 French soldiers had been killed, among them General Nemours.

With that victory, the Spaniards had conquered most of Naples. Heartened, de Córdoba then pushed on toward the city itself, capital of the duchy. The Neapolitans, having been ruled by four kings in nine years, docilely opened their gates, and on May 14 the Great Captain triumphantly entered the city.

When Louis heard about the French defeat at Cerignola and de Córdoba's occupation of the city of Naples, he exploded. Then he vented the full force of his ire upon Philip, whom he accused of having deliberately duped him in order to aid Spain. The archduke had, of course, done nothing of the sort. It was, he told the French king, simply "one of Ferdinand's old tricks."[11]

Philip's insistence on ignoring Ferdinand's orders had backfired, ruining the archduke's credibility in the eyes of the French king. Moreover, to the other crowned heads of Europe he now seemed a laughingstock—an inexperienced but pompous leader whose greedy ambitions had been crushed by Ferdinand's seasoned political acumen. Had the Spanish king set out deliberately to humiliate his ungrateful son-in-law, he could not have chosen a better way.

To avenge himself against Spain, Louis raised three armies in the summer of 1503—a militia from Genoa, another to invade Aragón at Fuenterrabia on the

Cantabrian coast, and a third in the province of Roussillon. Ultimately all three armies were defeated. The soldiers who crossed the Pyrenean foothills at Fuenterrabia were repulsed by Ferdinand's allies in Navarre long before they reached the Spanish border. In October Ferdinand and an army of 60,000 men assembled by Isabella beat the French back from Genoa to the old French border. Meanwhile, the French fleet dispatched from Marseilles was wracked by storms and forced to return to port.

On August 18 the seventy-two-year-old Pope Alexander VI died. Louis, having lost one ally and eager to gain another through the election of a French pope, thus ordered Cesare Borgia, now the French Duke of Valentinois, and his army to camp outside Rome to sway that election. When the cardinals protested, Borgia retreated and the Consistory elected an Italian pope, Pius III, who lived less than a month after his coronation.

Louis's final defeat came on December 28, when the Great Captain crushed the French again in a battle at Gaeta on Italy's west coast. By January 30, 1504, Louis reluctantly conceded that Naples "was lost beyond the hope of recovery."[12] The French king and Ferdinand then agreed to a three-year treaty that permanently excluded France from Naples, which henceforth was to be subsumed into the kingdom of Aragón.

The Spanish victory underscored Philip's blunder at Lyons and once again made him the laughingstock of Western Europe. Under other circumstances and earlier in their lives, Ferdinand and Isabella might have considered the Neapolitan triumph as divine retribution for the archduke's behavior toward Spain. But in 1504 one troubling detail stood in their way: Their daughter and heir Juana was madly, indeed insanely, in love with the handsome archduke.

CHAPTER SIXTY-TWO

Las Sombras

Juana's departure from Medina del Campo on March 1, 1504, exhausted Isabella physically and spiritually. The worried king, hoping that a change of scenery would revive his wife, took Isabella to the hermitage of La Mejorada near Olmedo to spend *Santa Semana*, the Holy Week before Easter. There, with an opportunity to rest in the greening countryside that surrounds the stone monastery and with meditation and prayers in its old Mudéjar church, it was hoped that Isabella would recover her strength.

But the press of worldly events continued to intrude. On March 31, just before leaving La Mejorada, Isabella and Ferdinand ratified the three-year treaty with France signifying the end of the Neapolitan war. Despite that victory, the Spanish sovereigns' triumph was short-lived and quickly replaced by new fears about a rebellion among the Neapolitan nobles. To protect Naples Ferdinand ordered the Great Captain to maintain his army at full force. Yet, as the Aragonese treasury lacked funds, Ferdinand failed to send de Córdoba back pay for the soldiers. Before long 4,500 frustrated men rose in rebellion and stormed the Neapolitan countryside, taking in plunder what they had not received in wages. De Córdoba, just recovering from a serious illness, had the rebellion's ringleaders executed and dismissed hundreds of others.

Isabella and Ferdinand, meanwhile, grew increasingly impatient with the Great Captain's failure to write about the conditions in Italy. After receiving reports about de Córdoba's illness, Isabella and Ferdinand wrote again, congratulating the warrior on his recovery and inquiring about events in Naples. Still no reply came, only a series of disquieting reports that Spanish soldiers were "sacking towns, rioting and behaving scandalously" in the newly conquered Neapolitan kingdom.

Silence and waiting were, in fact, to plague Isabella and Ferdinand throughout the spring of 1504, casting a shadow over virtually every aspect of their dynastic future. In June 1503 Catherine and Prince Henry had finally become betrothed, but because of the princess's previous marriage to Henry's brother, Arthur, the young couple needed a papal dispensation. But by spring of 1504 the newest pope, Julius II, had still not issued that dispensation despite the Spanish ambassador's repeated entreaties.

Another frustration was the silence surrounding Columbus's fourth journey. In October 1502 the *almirante* had touched on the isthmus of Panama, and that winter in the mosquito-infested river valleys of the Veragua and Belen he had discovered caches of pure gold whose quality far surpassed the gold of the Antilles. But the price Columbus paid for those discoveries was steep: Not only did he fall ill with malaria, but shipworms attacked his boats. It was only with difficulty that the *almirante*'s badly leaking fleet finally reached Jamaica in late June 1503. Several weeks later Columbus wrote Isabella and Ferdinand announcing his discovery of the fabled gold mines of Cathay. However, it would be eight months before Columbus and his men would be rescued. Consequently the king and queen would not receive his letter until late summer 1504.

In the spring of 1504, time also passed slowly for Princess Juana. High winds had delayed her departure for Flanders. After Easter, Isabella and Ferdinand returned to Medina del Campo, but on May 20, after learning that the archduchess had sailed for Bruges, they returned to La Mejorada to pray for her safety and reconciliation with Philip.

Initially, their prayers seemed to be answered, for Juana arrived in the Blankenburg harbor near Bruges within nine days. Moreover, the archduke, humbled by his blunder with Naples, chastised by Louis's and Ferdinand's ambassadors at the French court, and mindful of Isabella's warnings about Juana's emotional state, had arrived at the harbor to meet his wife.

Unfortunately, by the time Juana arrived in Belgium, her illness had entered a new phase. Her suspicions about Philip's infidelities had reached such a pitch that she ordered her female attendants to leave the boat before her. Only then, assured that all sexual competition was removed, would Juana step onto the dock to gaze into her husband's eyes. The archduke greeted her tenderly, and the first days of their reconciliation were rapturous.

But the couple's passion was destined to be short-lived. No sooner had the newly united couple arrived in Brussels and settled in the Burgundian palace than their relationship cooled. As earlier, the archduke treated Juana with indifference and the archduchess, convinced his callousness was due to his infidelities, scrutinized the female Flemish courtiers suspiciously. Finally Juana confronted a lady-in-waiting whose long golden tresses Philip had openly admired and, in a public scene, attacked the young woman and ripped out clumps of her hair. Then the archduchess ordered her servants to cut off all her rival's hair.

When Philip learned about Juana's assault, he chastised her publicly and vowed to ignore her until she reformed her behavior. But the archduchess refused to repent. Consequently Philip did not speak to his wife for days. Rejected by the man she so desperately loved, Juana became despondent and took to her bed.

Philip, finding little reason to remain in Brussels, left abruptly for Holland. The episode created a stir in the Burgundian palace, and before long exaggerated versions of the story had spread through the other courts of Europe.

By August, some of those reports had reached Isabella and Ferdinand, who had both fallen ill with fevers at La Mota. During these illnesses, the royal doctors had ordered the monarchs to live in separate apartments at the castle. Despite her physicians' assurances to the contrary, the queen became convinced that "because the King did not come to her as he always did in health" he was critically ill, perhaps even at death's door.[1]

Paradoxically, the fifty-three-year-old queen was considerably more debilitated than Ferdinand, who was soon fully recovered. In contrast, Isabella languished, growing paler every day, until it became obvious, even to her, that she was suffering from a serious disease that was slowly draining her of life.

The news about Juana's public tantrum and the resultant court scandal did little to improve the queen's health. The incident had, as Isabella and Ferdinand wrote their Flemish ambassador Fuensalida with typical understatement, "caused us much suffering."[2] They were even more humiliated when they received Philip's messenger, Martin de Moxica, whose diary described their daughter's crazed behavior at the Flemish court in agonizing detail. This time neither Isabella nor Ferdinand could refute that Juana's psychological state, even if distorted by Moxica's Flemish bias, had contributed to the archduke and archduchess's disaffection.

By late November still more distressing accounts of Juana's outrageous behavior trickled into the Spanish court, reports that Isabella probably never heard because of her rapidly failing health. In early autumn the archduke and archduchess had clashed over Juana's refusal to retire the Moorish slaves employed in her personal service. Philip, it was said, objected to them because they were sickly, incompetent, and superstitious. Above all, he objected to their peculiar attentions to Juana's person, their constant bathing and perfuming of her body, their continual washing of her hair, and their application of ointments, all of which he believed detrimental to the archduchess's health.

Juana, fearing she would once again be surrounded by Flemish attendants, clung to the Moorish slaves as a vestige of her Spanish identity. After a violent argument, the archduke stormed out of the castle and disappeared for a five-day hunting trip. From the road he sent Juana letters begging her to comply, but when he returned the slaves were still in his wife's service. "Madame, I am exceedingly put out to find these slaves still in your company," he announced. "Throw them out of here at once or I shall refuse to sleep in your room as long as they continue to be present."[3]

Instantly Juana relented. But the next morning the archduchess called for one of the Moors again. In vain Philip rallied their young children, Eleanor, Charles, and Isabella, behind him to appeal to Juana's reason. When that failed, he locked the archduchess in her room. To spite him, Juana went on a hunger strike.

One night when the archduke returned to his apartments, which were directly beneath those of his wife, she pounded relentlessly on the floor with a rock. When that failed to bring Philip upstairs, she stabbed violently at the floorboards with a knife. "Senõr, talk to me. I want to know if you are there!" Juana bellowed through the floor until dawn.[4] That morning when a steely-eyed Philip appeared before her, Juana vowed she would "let myself die before I ever again do anything you want!"[5]

Had Juana and Philip's relationship flowered, had the archduke initially ingratiated himself to Isabella and Ferdinand as an ally of Spain, the twin crowns of Castile and Aragón might well have passed peacefully into his hands, regardless of Juana's psychological state. The precedent for leadership by a king-consort had been established centuries earlier, usually because of a queen's inability to bear arms. But Philip, with his French ties and hatred of everything Spanish, was unequivocally alienated from his in-laws.

By September Isabella's deteriorating health brought the question of her succession to a crisis. That month, the queen's decline became a matter of public record in Spain as well as in the other courts of Western Europe. Her courtiers buzzed with speculations about who would inherit the throne, whether Juana and Philip would be called to Spain before Isabella's death, and whether Castile would be overrun with Flemish courtiers. As Isabella's condition worsened, as she began to have trouble breathing, and as her body swelled with retained water, even she understood that death was imminent. Legend has it that Isabella remained in the castle at La Mota until her death. Yet some modern historians believe that she spent her last days in a small palace within the nearby town of Medina del Campo. But wherever Isabella dwelt, her illness so alarmed the Castilian citizenry that they made daily visits to the churches of Spain to pray for her recovery.

Since the first months of 1504 some of the most superstitious had, in fact, been convinced that the queen's life was doomed. That spring a violent earthquake had rocked Andalusia, destroying crops and houses and leveling the town of Carmona, one of Isabella's private possessions. Then a hurricane ripped through southern Spain, bringing with it high winds, floods, and the plague. *La sombra de la muerte,* the shadow of death, they predicted, now hovered over the queen and would fold its dark wings around her before the year had ended.

But even to skeptics, the enlightened Renaissance men of Isabella's court, it was obvious that the queen was suffering from a fatal disease. On October 3 Martire anxiously wrote the Count of Tendilla:

> Ay, Spain is buried! The doctors have given up all hope about the recovered health of the Queen. The illness has extended into her veins and little by little is terminating in dropsy. The fever has not disappeared and seems to be in her very marrow. Day and night she has an insatiable thirst and loathes food. The deadly tumor is between her skin and her flesh. We live with the somber faces of the King and the most intimate courtiers.[6]

By the laws of inheritance, Castile and Aragón were to fall to Juana and, by extension, her husband, the Archduke Philip. For Isabella, that eventuality was distasteful for she could not accept the prospect of Philip's authority over her beloved Castile. Yet the dying queen knew that Juana's psychological deterioration would eventually force Philip to assume full responsibility.

Through the haze of her sufferings Isabella pondered the dilemma: Clearly, she could not leave the Castilian throne to Ferdinand, who, despite his years of loyal service to the kingdom, was legally barred from governing the kingdom after her death. At the same time, she recoiled from the idea of leaving the kingdom to her delusional daughter and brutish son-in-law.

Henceforth, the future of Castile and the salvation of her soul, rather than the preservation of her body, would become Isabella's overriding obsession. Even Columbus's imminent arrival in Spain, preceded by a letter announcing his discovery of "Chinese" gold, would not distract her from the hard task ahead.

With her waning strength, Isabella gave alms to the churches and monasteries of Castile, particularly those she had neglected during more vibrant periods in her life. On good days courtiers, counselors, prelates, and confessors visited the queen at her bedside to conduct the affairs of government. She met with Italian ambassadors who provided her with details about the Neapolitan war and de Córdoba's heroic exploits. One of them, a distinguished Italian officer named Prospero Colonna, confided in Ferdinand that he had come to Castile "to behold the woman who from her sickbed ruled the world."[7] Other dignitaries arrived bearing gifts, jeweled gold crosses, even a stone from Jerusalem's Church of the Holy Sepulcher. On bad days, or when Isabella was too exhausted to talk, the counselors and ambassadors left her alone.

Through the failing autumn light that penetrated the glazed windows of her bedroom, Isabella carefully considered how to dispose of her kingdom and worldly possessions. Finally, on October 12, exactly twelve years after Columbus's discovery of the Antilles, the ashen queen signed her last will and testament. The document, some twenty-eight pages in typeset, covered nearly every aspect of the Castilian kingdom and its future government. Within it Isabella assigned gifts and pensions to those who had been her loyal servants and grown old in her attendance, among them her childhood friend Beatriz de Bobadilla, her husband, Andrés Cabrera, and the papal ambassador Garcilasso de la Vega.

The queen also made generous provisions to the poor, orphans, widows and almhouses. Many of her household goods were to be distributed to convents and hospitals. All debts incurred under her reign were to be satisfied within a year. Any superfluous offices in her household or by her privilege were revoked so that the money or land could revert to the crown. Furthermore, the queen instructed her executors, Ferdinand and Cisneros, that Castile must never give up Gibraltar because of its strategic importance in defending Spain from Moslem North Africa.

After death, Isabella ordered that her remains be taken to Granada and placed in a simple tomb in the Franciscan monastery at the Alhambra. Her funeral was to be conducted with a minimum of expense and the money that would otherwise have been spent, used to ransom Christian captives in North Africa and dower a dozen poor girls.

Isabella's one personal request was to be buried next to Ferdinand, and ultimately she left the final choice of a site to him. "Should the King, my lord, prefer a sepulcher in some other place, then my will is that my body be transported there and laid by his side that the union we have enjoyed in this world and through the mercy of God may hope again for our souls in heaven, may be represented by our bodies in the earth."[8]

Knowing that Ferdinand would be dispossessed of the Castilian crown and its privileges, Isabella made every effort to ensure his comfort after her death. The king was thus to receive half the net profits from the Indies and 10 million maravedís a year, based on the *alcabalas,* or taxes, from Castile's military orders. It was, Isabella wrote with tenderness, "less than I could wish and far less than he deserves considering the eminent services he has rendered the state."[9] In still another sign of her profound attachment, Isabella left Ferdinand her jewels "so that, seeing them, he may be reminded of the singular love I always bore him while living, and that I am waiting for him in a better world; by which remembrance he may be encouraged to live the more justly and holy in this."[10]

As anticipated, Isabella left the inheritance of the Castilian crown to her "dearly beloved daughter" Juana, Archduchess of Austria and Duchess of Burgundy "who was heir and Queen Proprietress of these my said realms, lands and lordships, whom God has allowed me to name head of the kingdom." [11] In that capacity, Isabella instructed her daughter and son-in-law to conduct themselves as Christian rulers who should use "much care in honoring the obligations of God and the Holy Church."[12] Above all, she urged Juana and her husband to obey Ferdinand with the love that was "due to him beyond every other parent, for his eminent virtues."[13]

Isabella overlooked few details or provisions for Castile's future. To prevent the appointment of Flemish nobles to high positions in Castile, Isabella ordered Juana to keep the kingdom Spanish and to name only natives as officers, prelates, and judges. With similar firmness, Isabella instructed her daughter to consult the *Cortes* on all legislative matters. To ignore it, she observed, would be political folly for it represented the national consensus of the towns.

Then, with startling insight, Isabella addressed the probable scenario of events in the years following her death. The Castilian crown was to pass to Juana immediately upon her death. However, if for any reason her daughter was either absent from Castile or "being present should prove unwilling or unable to govern," Ferdinand was to be named regent until their grandson Charles turned twenty.[14] With characteristic tact Isabella explained that she had made this decision "by the consideration of the magnanimity and illustrious qualities of the king my lord, as well as his large experience and the great profit which will redound to the state from his wise and beneficent rule."[15]

Three days after Isabella's will was completed, her health grew worse. "You ask me respecting the state of the queen's health," Martire wrote. "We sit sorrowful in the palace all day long, tremblingly waiting the hour when religion and virtue shall quit the earth with her."[16] For a brief time the queen rallied anew, signing documents, listening to thorny administrative problems, giving alms to the poor. Outside high winds and severe rainstorms whipped across the Castilian *Meseta,* bending olive and cork trees, flooding villages and pastures where the merino sheep, driven north by shepherds from their summer in Andalusia, now huddled against stone walls for shelter.

On November 7 Columbus arrived in Spain at the harbor of Sanlúcar de Barrameda. Neither Isabella nor Ferdinand acknowledged the *almirante*'s arrival from his fourth and last voyage, despite the piteous tone of his last communication. "Until now," he had written from Jamaica before his rescue, "I have always taken pity on my fellow man; today, may heaven have mercy on me, may the earth cry for me, as I wait for death alone, sick and racked with pain." [17]

But such words could no longer stir the sympathies of the queen, for by November Isabella's own vitality was ebbing rapidly. The mysterious New World, with all its raw and frustrating potential, needed the energies of a younger, more vibrant monarch. In her last hours Isabella concentrated nearly all her energy on the immediate future of continental Castile: A profusion of governmental details still loomed over the queen, who, with customary conscientiousness, was determined to settle them before she died.

On November 23, just three days before her death, Isabella added a codicil to her will. Among the amendments were provisions for a recodification of the laws. Early in Isabella's reign the jurist Montalvo had attempted to clarify Castile's contradictory laws in his eight-volume tome, the *Ordenanzas Reales de Castilla,* but twenty years later there were still so many contradictions that she ordered a new version.

In addition, the plight of the New World Indians weighed heavily on Isabella's conscience. By 1504 the *repartimiento* system had become so badly abused in the West Indies that the Indians were little more than slaves. While most of the abuses had been carefully hidden from the queen, she instinctively distrusted the *repartimientos.* Furthermore, the slavery issue disturbed her for, like many prelates in her council, she believed that the "red men" had souls. Thus, with the convoluted spiritual bias of the early Renaissance, she believed the Indians should not be enslaved. Isabella consequently pleaded that her successors redouble their efforts to win the Indians to Christianity "without any injury to them or their subjects, but command that they are treated well . . ." [18]

Finally, Isabella pondered the perpetuity of the *alcabala,* or sales tax, the principal means of crown revenue established in the *Cortes* of 1480, which, she feared, could not be legally sustained after her death. To address the problem, the queen named a commission to study it and if necessary, find other ways to collect funds for Castile. With the feeble scrawl of the infirm, Isabella signed the codicil *Yo La Reina* for the last time in her life, and sank wearily onto her pillows.

But while Isabella's signature was fainter than on earlier documents still preserved in the General Archives of the Kingdom at Simancas, her spirit burned bright. When Ferdinand, Beatriz de Bobadilla, and other beloved courtiers gathered around her bedside, Isabella begged them not to grieve. "Do not weep for me, nor waste your time in fruitless recovery," she implored, "but pray rather for my soul." [19]

A few days later the queen confessed and, with the modesty that characterized her life, asked that her feet be covered when she received the Sacrament of Extreme Unction. By nightfall on November 25, it was obvious that Isabella was dying. A storm raged outside against the turrets and ramparts of the royal houses of Medina del Campo. Inside the queen's bedroom, by the light of wax torches, Ferdinand, Cisneros, Beatriz, and a few other courtiers spent the night gazing at the fading queen, who had lapsed into unconsciousness.

By morning Isabella was ashen-colored, her eyes closed, her breathing labored and irregular. Between eleven and twelve noon she stirred, gasped gently, and died. Castile had lost its greatest queen and Western Europe its purest Christian inspiration.

Martire wrote later that day to inform Talavera:

> My hand falls powerless by my side for the very sorrow. The world has lost its noblest ornament; a loss to be deplored not only by Spain, which she has so long carried forward in the career of glory, but by every nation in Christendom; for she was the mirror of every virtue, the shield of the innocent, and an avenging sword to the wicked. I know none of her sex, in ancient or modern times, who in my judgment is at all worthy to be named with this incomparable woman.[20]

In an adjacent room a somber Ferdinand dictated a letter to the officials of the Castilian kingdom, informing them of Isabella's death.

> On this day, Our Lord has taken away Her Serene Highness Queen Isabella, my dear and beloved wife, and although her death is the greatest suffering that I could ever have in this life, on one hand the pain of it and what I have lost upon losing her as well as all these kingdoms burns my heart. On the other hand, seeing that she died as a saint and a Catholic as she had lived her life, I hope that Our Lord has her in his glory and that for her it is a better and more eternal kingdom than the ones she had on earth, because Our Lord wanted it this way. We must accept His will and thank him for everything He does.[21]

That evening Ferdinand appeared at a hastily erected stand in Toledo's *plaza mayor* with Cisneros and the rest of the court. After a trumpet fanfare the Duke of Alba climbed the stairs of the wooden platform, raised Queen Isabella's banner three times, and announced "Castile, Castile for our Sovereign Lady, Queen Juana."[22] Then, in view of Juana's absence, Ferdinand publicly assumed the title of regent, or governor, of Castile and received homage from the *grandees*.

As Isabella had requested, her unembalmed body was wrapped in a coarse Franciscan robe. The next morning Ferdinand and a mournful cortege dressed in black robes followed the dark-draped litter that carried Isabella's coffin south to Granada.

The storm that had lashed Medina del Campo so ferociously during Isabella's last hours now blew into a ferocious gale. For three weeks, as the funeral procession picked its way south through the queen's childhood home of Arévalo, through the cathedral city of Toledo, through Toro, Jaén, and Íllora, the skies were filled with rain and storm clouds obscured the heavens. Rivers overflowed, bridges washed away, and dry plains became small seas, making the journey with its precious coffin even more difficult.

To poets and writers it seemed that the heavens above the Iberian peninsula had emptied themselves in sorrow. "I never encountered such perils in all of my hazardous journey to Egypt," Martire observed of that trip south to Andalusia.[23]

Finally on December 18, Isabella's mourners reached Granada. As the cortege and its casket climbed the hill to the Alhambra, past the valley where the Duke of Cádiz, Rodrigo Ponce de León, once so gallantly bowed to Isabella after a Moorish victory, the sun broke through the clouds. But to the mourners, to Ferdinand, indeed to all of Castile, the return of good weather was irrelevant. All eyes, all thoughts were on the queen, as her casket was draped in black velvet and consigned to the Franciscan monastery where it would rest for seventeen years before its final removal to the new Royal Chapel of the as-yet-unbuilt Cathedral of Granada where her effigy would be immortalized in white marble.

Spain would never recover from Isabella's death. She was Hispania's greatest queen, and introduced its Golden Age of art and literature, which would flower for more than a century after her death. Among its fruit would be the painters Juan de Borgona, Antonio Moro, and El Greco, the architects Rodrigo Gil de Homtanon and Diego de Siloe, and the writers Cervantes, Lope de Vega, and Calderon.

Isabella's spirit still resides in the shadowy solemnity of Spain's Mudéjar churches and Gothic cathedrals, in the echoing steps of its stone castles and quiet cloisters, in the pensive strum of guitars and the musical pageants known as the *zarzuelas,* in the customs and languages of the Caribbean and South America, and most of all in the tenacious Spanish character, which, despite poverty, religious repression, and bitter wars, remains hopeful, even optimistic about its future.

Epilogue

I n the years immediately after Isabella's death, the Castilian kingdom was once again split in two, this time by the clause in the queen's will that left the disposition of the crown contingent upon Juana's ability to rule. By January 1505 the *Cortes* swore its allegiance to Juana and Philip, but in the next breath, declaring the archduchess incompetent to rule, it assigned the Castilian crown to Ferdinand as regent.

In Flanders, Philip protested bitterly. Secretly, he pandered to the long-frustrated ambitions of Castilian nobles, such as the Marquis of Villena and the Duke of Najara, promising them more freedom and wealth than they had enjoyed under Isabella if they would foment a rebellion against Ferdinand.

In contrast, the Archduchess Juana, either out of perversity toward Philip or a sense of her own incompetence, enthusiastically endorsed Ferdinand's regency. In what was perhaps the last courageous act of her life, Juana even penned a letter in support of the *Cortes*. As usual, however, the archduchess was surrounded by Philip's spies, who seized the letter, imprisoned its courier, and confined Juana to her apartments.

Meanwhile, Philip attempted to capitalize on all of Ferdinand's political weaknesses at home and abroad. Knowing that the Great Captain's relationship with Ferdinand was strained, Philip wrote offering to help him secure peace in Naples with reinforcements in exchange for rights to its government. Simultaneously, Philip encouraged Louis to distract Ferdinand on two fronts—in Naples and on the ever-vulnerable border of Roussillon.

Although most of the Castilian citizenry supported Ferdinand in the months immediately following Isabella's death, the old embers of aristocratic discontent suppressed during Isabella's thirty-year reign now flared anew. Ferdinand, the nobles began to grumble among themselves, should return to Aragón and leave Castile to Juana and her husband. Although disillusioned with the fickle *grandees* who once fought and feasted so loyally by his side, the fifty-two-year-old Ferdinand nevertheless determined to retain the regency.

In 1504 it was Ferdinand, of course, who felt Isabella's death most keenly. Her memory glowed within him like a shrine—in thoughts about her tender loyalty, her intelligence, her piety, and most recently, the strong aversion she developed to Philip's administration of Castile. Like Isabella, Ferdinand vowed to do anything he could to prevent that eventuality in Aragón—even if that meant acting in a manner that seemed initially dishonorable to the queen's memory.

Intuitively, Ferdinand realized that Louis must have feared Philip's ascendancy nearly as much as he did, for if the archduke inherited Castile, he would eventually become master over a vast empire—not only Flanders, Burgundy, and the Holy Roman Empire, but Spain and its New World properties. Such an empire would dwarf France in scope and wealth and also surround it physically.

Thus Ferdinand schemed to win Louis's friendship: He proposed that he marry the French king's niece, a beautiful eighteen-year-old named Germaine de Foix of the royal house of the Navarre. If Germaine ultimately produced a son for Ferdinand, that newborn would inherit Aragón instead of Charles. Moreover, by the terms of Ferdinand's agreement with Louis, the new baby would also inherit the kingdom of Naples.

Thus on March 18, 1506, the Aragonese king married Germaine de Foix in Dueñas, the same hillside village north of Valladolid where Isabella and Ferdinand had once lived as newlyweds. The Castilian citizenry regarded Ferdinand's marriage with contempt. Their beloved Queen Isabella had been dead little more than a year. They believed the marriage dishonored her memory, for it reversed Ferdinand and Isabella's lifetime efforts to unite their twin crowns against France. And why, they murmured, was the wedding effected in the very town where the twin sovereigns spent their first year of married life?

Nevertheless, the marriage did put Philip on the defensive. Before long he proposed a compromise whereby he, Juana, and Ferdinand would rule Castile as coregents. Through that ploy the archduke and archduchess landed at La Coruña on April 28, 1506. Significantly, Philip arrived with a formidable army of 3,000 German soldiers who were soon joined by 6,000 Castilians who opposed the "old Catalan," as they now derisively termed Ferdinand. Despite the archduke's pugnacious intentions, he avoided a meeting with Ferdinand and deliberately followed a circuitous route to the Castilian interior. Finally, buttressed by a large army, Philip met Ferdinand at Puebla de Senabria at the southeast border of Galicia.

In contrast to the archduke's elegant clothes, Ferdinand arrived in a simple black mantle and informal hat, accompanied by a few men on mules "with love in his heart and peace in his hands."[1] But the Aragonese king was not allowed to meet with his daughter Juana. Equally pathetic was the king's friendly greeting to some of his old subjects—among them the Duke of Najara and the warrior-diplomat Garcilasso de la Vega. "I congratulate you, Garcilasso, you have grown wonderfully lusty since we last met," Ferdinand remarked wryly when he embraced the warrior and felt the armor beneath his rich garments.[2]

By June Ferdinand was a defeated man. His declining popularity and the alliance of some of the Castilian nobles with Philip had come as a terrible shock. As a result he retreated completely, deciding instead to concentrate his energies upon his Aragonese and Neapolitan holdings. From his perspective, the Castilian kingdom was fraught with tensions and so divided by the jealousies of the Flemish and Castilian nobles that civil disruption was inevitable. At fifty-four Ferdinand had no heart to fight again for the Castilian crown or its inheritance by a Spanish heir; he was too weary—and too embittered—to defend Isabella's last wishes any longer.

In an act that has perplexed historians for generations, the wily king agreed to concede Castile to his "beloved children," Philip and Juana. On June 27 Ferdinand swore an oath to that effect in a solemn ceremony. The next day he did something even more uncharacteristic: He signed a paper that not only attested to Juana's incapacity but assigned the full authority of Castile to Philip. However, almost immediately afterward he claimed that he had been coerced by the presence of Philip's army and declared the agreement invalid. Under ordinary circumstances, Ferdinand explained, he would never agree "that his daughter should be deprived of her liberty or rights as hereditary proprietress of this kingdom."[3]

Then, on July 5, Ferdinand bid farewell to the *grandees*. The following September, after a brief sojourn in Aragón, Ferdinand, his new wife, and his court set sail for Naples.

To leave Castile in the hands of the Archduke Philip was exactly what the dying Isabella had tried to avoid. But fate, or perhaps a man-made plot, was to intervene. By July 12 Philip and Juana were sworn the new King and Queen of Castile by the *Cortes* at Valladolid. Then, with flagrant disregard for Isabella's will, Philip appointed dozens of Flemish aristocrats to high posts in the Castilian court and removed many of the Spaniards, among them the Marqués and Marquesa of Moya, who were summarily evicted from Segovia. Outraged, many Castilian nobles protested, regretting their support of the brash Flemish archduke.

On September 25 the unthinkable occurred. The twenty-eight-year-old Philip died suddenly in Burgos, victim of a fever that appeared after an unusually strenuous game of *pelota*. Although the doctors insisted he died of natural causes, poison was naturally suspected. But by whom? By Ferdinand, who had just arrived in Naples after setting sail just three weeks earlier? By some vengeful Castilian courtier who resented the Flemish rule? Anything was possible.

Whatever the truth may have been, Castile was suddenly leaderless. In the ensuing panic, a seven-member provisional council was named to govern Castile. At its head was Cisneros, who governed with the three members of the Castilian nobility, the Duke of Najara, and two Flemish *grandees*.

With Philip's death, Juana lost her tenuous grip on reality. She immediately sank into an emotionless abyss from which she could seldom be roused. For days Juana stared blankly at the floor, refused to eat, and lived next to Philip's bier. With his death she became even more jealous of female rivalry than before and thus forbade all women, including nuns, to approach his remains.

Predictably, Juana's psychotic behavior wrought havoc with the Castilian government. When members of the provisional council pleaded with her to sign papers legitimizing their temporary authority, the archduchess refused. With similar intransigence she withdrew from all requests by the *Cortes,* counselors, and ambassadors for even rudimentary governmental decisions. "My father will attend to all this when he returns," she replied woodenly. "He is much more conversant with business than I am; I have no other duties now but to pray for the soul of my departed husband."[4]

In December, Juana demanded that Philip's casket be opened so she could touch and gaze upon her husband's decomposed body. Later that month she also resolved to transport her husband's body from Burgos to Granada. In one of the most bizarre funeral trains in European history, the grieving young queen ordered the procession to travel only at night with the excuse that "a widow who had lost the sun of her own soul should never expose herself to the light of day."[5]

Wherever she stopped to rest, she demanded that the local priests perform funeral rites over Philip's body, as if he had just died. One night, after arriving at a hermitage and discovering it was a convent of nuns, she ordered her exasperated cortege to remove the casket and retire with her to the open fields beyond the convent walls.

Meanwhile, urgent letters had been sent to Ferdinand in Italy, who, still stinging from his bitter Castilian departure, continued his trip through Naples. It would not be until July 1507 that Ferdinand and his court returned to the Valencian coast and not for another month—nearly a year after Philip's death—that he arrived in Castile. In contrast to his 1506 departure, his arrival was greeted with wild enthusiasm by the *Cortes* and the citizens, all of whom had grown disgusted with Juana's behavior.

In Tortola Ferdinand finally met Juana, whose madness had transformed her into a haggard and unkempt woman who filled him with genuine horror. With kisses and cajolery, Ferdinand eventually convinced her to retire to a small palace at Tordesillas. To console her, he ordered Philip's casket to be entombed at the nearby Mudéjar monastery of Santa Clara. Although it was not until 1510 that the *Cortes* finally confirmed his role as permanent regent for Juana and her son Charles, Ferdinand ruled Castile peacefully until his death in 1516.

The intervening years brought a series of sweeping changes to Europe and the Americas. In 1506, after a warm but ultimately noncommittal reception from Ferdinand after his fourth voyage to the New World, Columbus died. The *almirante*'s estate then fell to his sons Diego and Fernando, who spent decades in court trying to have his rights reinstated. By then, younger mariners were bringing news of startling discoveries and wealth from the Americas to Castile. In 1512 Ponce de León discovered Florida. A year later Vasco Núñez de Balboa crossed the Isthmus of Darien in Panama and gazed upon the Pacific.

In May 1509, after seven years of widowhood and a penurious existence at the English court, Isabella and Ferdinand's twenty-four-year-old daughter Catherine married the eighteen-year-old Prince Henry, who assumed the title of Henry VIII of England that June, two months after his father's death.

On May 3 of that same year Germaine de Foix gave birth to a son who lived only briefly. Her subsequent efforts to provide Ferdinand with an heir were unsuccessful, and in later years, as the king's health began to decline, he was forced to accept that the twin crowns of Castile and Aragón would fall to Juana's foreign-born son Charles.

By 1510 France and Aragón were fighting again in Italy, this time over Milan and Venice, until finally, in 1513, Ferdinand permanently routed the French from Italy. The king's proudest accomplishment, though, was conquest of the Navarre from his grandniece Catalina and its subsequent annexation to Aragón as it once was during the reign of his father.

Isabella's old confessor Cisneros would also leave his mark on Spain. Shortly after Ferdinand's return from Naples, the Franciscan reformer was elevated by Pope Julius II to cardinalship. Cisneros left two erudite monuments to posterity— the completion of the University of Alcalá in 1508 and the publication of the Complutensian Polyglot Bible in 1517, which offered translations of the Holy Scriptures from the Latin Vulgate in their original Hebrew, Chaldean, and Greek.

During his busy life, Cisneros also became Inquisitor-General of Spain and from that pinnacle instituted even more repressive measures against heretics. His religious fervor finally impelled him to conduct a crusade against the Moors of North Africa, and in 1509 he conquered the strategic seaport of Oran on the Barbary coast. With that foothold, other Spanish leaders won Algiers, Tunis, Tlemcen, and Tripoli.

By 1513 Spain thus held important properties in Italy, Africa, and the Americas. But the mighty Spanish empire, now extending to three continents and receiving rich shipments of gold and pearls from the Americas and such coveted raw goods as sugarcane from the Canaries, would fade with the sixty-three-year-old Ferdinand's death on January 22, 1516.

For nearly a year Cisneros governed Castile as regent until, on November 8, 1516, shortly after the arrival of the sixteen-year-old Duke of Luxembourg, the future Charles V, the famous Franciscan died. Thereafter, the glory that was Spain would become subsumed in the Hapsburg Empire, its management buried beneath a welter of bureaucracy that, ironically, had attempted to use Isabella's streamlined governmental formulas as its base. Although Charles visited Spain seven times and would die there, he often ruled the kingdom from afar, imperially, with the eye of a fond stranger who appreciated the kingdom for its sturdy Catholicism and its American gold, which he used to support the anti-Lutheran wars of the Holy Roman Empire.

By the late sixteenth century Spain's proudest moments were behind it. Its armada was destroyed by the English in 1588. Its emperor Charles V, having failed to suppress the Protestant Reformation, ceded his throne to his devout son Philip II who launched the Counter-Reformation. Defeated, stripped of its many possessions, its intellectual life hobbled by the expulsions and persecutions of the Inquisition, Spain slipped back into obscurity, despised as a "dark" country of religious repression, sadistic tortures, intolerance, and academic provincialism.

Yet for a magical thirty years under Isabella's leadership Castile had become the most admired and cultured nation in Western Europe, especially when viewed against the stark backdrop of its subsequent history as an impoverished Catholic nation severed from the mainstream of European intellectual life.

In that brief incandescent moment, white hot as a rack of memorial candles burning in a church chapel, Isabella's memory still glows in Spain today.

ACKNOWLEDGMENTS

While writing *Isabella of Castile: The First Renaissance Queen*, I was blessed with support and inspiration from many quarters. I worked in the Rare Book and Wertheim Study of the New York Public Library, the Biblioteca Nacional in Madrid, and the Archivo General de Simancas in northern Castile. The staffs in these institutions were very helpful and went out of their way to help me obtain obscure materials. Special thanks are due to Wayne Furman, Dominick Pilla, Isaac Gerwitz, Radames Suarez, and Stanley Kruger of the New York Public Library; to Juan Pablo Fusi Aizpúrua, director of the Biblioteca Nacional in Madrid; and to Ascensión de la Plaza and Isabel Aguirre of the Archivo General de Simancas for their interest and help in accessing archival information.

I am also indebted to several friends, among them Elaine Crane, the Honorable Stephen Crane, Joseph Pede, Diana Benzaia, and María Paz Aspe, who introduced me to scholars in the Spanish history community. My friends Robin and John Brancato, Doris Bucher, Ronni Sandroff, Maryann Brinley, Mary Alice Kellogg, Shel Secunda, Janet Gardner, Elizabeth Howell, and Peggy Schmidt cheered me on at difficult junctures. I am especially grateful to Victoria Secunda, who not only encouraged me during the lonely months of writing but offered practical suggestions about the first chapter.

In the academic community, I am grateful to Louise Mirrer-Singer and Joseph F. O'Callaghan of Fordham University, Nicholas Sanchez-Albornoz of New York University, Eugene Lyon of the St. Augustine Foundation, Benjamin Gampel of the Jewish Theological Seminary, Jane Gerber of the City University of New York, Elizabeth Del Alamo, and Danila Spielman, all of whom directed me to important research on Isabella's life.

I offer special appreciation to Janine Ronsmans, former director of the New

York Office of Spain 1992, for her practical assistance during my several research trips to Spain and for the many stimulating discussions we shared about Isabella and her era. Many thanks as well are due Charlotte Moslander of the College of New Rochelle Library and Dr. Nalaini Sriskandarajah for her professional opinion about Princess Juana.

In Spain, I am indebted to three assistants without whose efforts *Isabella of Castile* would have been a lesser book. The first is Bernardo Jose Garcia Garcia, a doctoral candidate in Spanish history at the Universidad Complutense of Madrid who valiantly obtained archival materials and photographs despite the difficulties of overseas telephone connections and foreign mails. Two wonderful Valladolid archivists, Carmen Juarez Ruíz and Nieves Asensio Rodríguez, not only obtained and translated fifteenth-century documents at Simancas but doggedly tracked down scholars and books.

Dominica Contreras, the Marquesa Lozoya of Segovia, graciously offered me the use of her library; Manuel Ballesteros Gaibrois of the Universidad Complutense of Madrid and Julio Valdeon Baruque of the University of Valladolid offered valuable advice, and Amando Represa Rodríguez, former director of the Archivo General de Simancas, helped me obtain additional source materials.

In the United States, several individuals stood so close to the book that it could not have been written without them. Above all, I wish to thank my agent, Agnes Birnbaum, whose unflagging enthusiasm and editorial suggestions were invaluable in shaping the final manuscript.

I am also grateful to my editors at St. Martin's Press. Toni Lopopolo offered constructive criticism on an early draft and was truly inspirational. Tony Clark turned the long manuscript into a shorter, more readable book with rare sensitivity and skill. Bill Thomas ushered the book through the final stages of production with care and enthusiasm.

In New York, Inma Lazáro, Joaquin Arroyo, and Anna Josuva conscientiously translated fifteenth-century manuscripts into modern English far better than my own efforts. Evelyn Mariperisena and Roberta Cores of the Tourist Office of Spain patiently helped me locate obscure towns on the map. Teresa Earenfight, a doctoral candidate at Fordham University, must have been "sent by divine inspiration," for she unfailingly obtained research, tracked down art sources, and went beyond the call of duty in her capacity as my assistant.

Finally, but hardly least, I thank my family—my daughters, who have blossomed into young women during the years the book took shape, and my parents, who always encouraged me to read as a child.

Most of all, I wish to thank my husband, Peter, who not only shared my initial enthusiasm for Isabella but carefully read the manuscript at considerable sacrifice to his leisure time and offered eloquent suggestions for improvement. For that gift of love, even a queen would be humbled.

NOTES

CHAPTER ONE

1. Lucio Marineo Siculo, *Vida y hechos de los reyes católicos* (Madrid: Ediciones Atlas, 1943), p. 155.
2. William H. Prescott, *History of the Reign of Ferdinand and Isabella the Catholic* (Philadelphia: Lippincott, 1872 [1837]), vol. 1, p. 206.
3. Fernando del Pulgar, *Crónica de los señores reyes católicos Don Fernando y Doña Isabel de Castilla y de Aragón*, BAE (Madrid: Ediciones Atlas, 1953), vol. 70, pp. 256–57.
4. Prescott, *History of the Reign of Ferdinand and Isabella.*
5. Tarsicio de Azcona, *Isabel la Católica: Estudio crítico de su vida y su reinado* (Madrid: Biblioteca de Autores Cristianos, 1964), p. 212.
6. Diego Enríquez Castillo, ed., *Crónica del Rey Don Enrique el Cuarto*, BAE (Madrid: Ediciones Atlas, 1953), vol. 70, p. 633.
7. Baldesar Castiglione, *The Book of the Courtier*, trans. Charles S. Singleton (New York: Doubleday, 1959), p. 237.
8. Ramón Menéndez Pidal, "The Catholic Kings According to Machiavelli and Castiglione," in *Spain in the Fifteenth Century, 1369–1516*, ed. Roger Highfield (London: Macmillan, 1972), p. 395.
9. Martin A. S. Hume, *Queens of Old Spain* (London: E. Grant Richardson, 1906), p. 137.

CHAPTER TWO

1. Royall Tyler, *The Emperor Charles the Fifth* (London: George Allen and Unwin, 1956), p. 251.
2. Jocelyn N. Hillgarth, *The Spanish Kingdoms, 1250–1516* (Oxford: Clarendon Press, 1978), vol. 2, p. 152.

CHAPTER THREE

1. Joceyln N. Hillgarth, *The Spanish Kingdoms, 1250–1516* (Oxford: Clarendon Press, 1978), vol. 2, p. 308.
2. Ibid., p. 314.
3. Ibid., p. 315.
4. William H. Prescott, *History of the Reign of Ferdinand and Isabella the Catholic* (Philadelphia: Lippincott, 1872 [1837]), vol. 1, p. 123.

CHAPTER FOUR

1. Tarsicio de Azcona, *Isabel la Católica: Estudio crítico de su vida y su reinado* (Madrid: Biblioteca de Autores Cristianos, 1964), p. 21.
2. Alonso de Palencia, *Crónica de Enrique IV,* ed. Antonio Paz y Melia, BAE (Madrid: Ediciones Atlas, 1973), vol. 257, p. 11; Diego Enríquez Castillo, ed., *Crónica del Rey Don Enrique el Cuarto,* BAE (Madrid: Ediciones Atlas, 1953), vol. 70, p. 100.
3. William H. Prescott, *History of the Reign of Ferdinand and Isabella the Catholic* (Philadelphia: Lippincott, 1872), vol. 1, p. 162.
4. Palencia, *Crónica de Enrique IV,* vol. 257, p. 75.
5. Diego de Valera, *Epistolas* (Madrid: Sociedad de Bibliofilos Españoles, 1878), p. 8.
6. Gaspar Gómez de la Serna, "Arévalo, en la infancia de la reina," *Clavileno* 2 (1950):27.

CHAPTER FIVE

1. Fernando del Pulgar, *Claros varones de Castilla,* ed. Robert Brian Tate (Oxford: Clarendon Press, 1971), p. 62.
2. St. Thomas Aquinas, *Basic Writings of Saint Thomas Aquinas,* ed. Anton C. Pegis (New York: Random House, 1945), pp. 879, 880–81.
3. Diego Enríquez Castillo, ed., *Crónica del Rey Don Enrique el Cuarto,* BAE (Madrid: Ediciones Atlas, 1953), vol. 70, p. 120.
4. Ibid.
5. *Memorias de Don Enrique IV de Castilla,* Colección Diplomatica de Enrique IV (Madrid: Real Academia de la Historia, 1835–1913), p. 638.
6. Alonso de Palencia, *Crónica de Enrique IV,* ed. Antonio Paz y Melia, BAE (Madrid: Ediciones Atlas, 1973), vol. 257, p. 107.
7. Tarsicio de Azcona, *Isabel la Católica: Estudio crítico de su vida y su reinado* (Madrid: Biblioteca de Autores Cristianos, 1964), p. 40.

CHAPTER SIX

1. William H. Prescott, *History of the Reign of Ferdinand and Isabella the Catholic* (Philadelphia: Lippincott, 1872 [1837]), vol. 1, p. 181.
2. William Thomas Walsh, *Isabella of Spain: The Last Crusader* (New York: Robert M. McBride Co., 1930), p. 17.
3. William D. Phillips, Jr., *Enrique IV and the Crisis of Fifteenth Century Castile, 1425–1480* (Cambridge, MA: Medieval Academy of America, 1978), p. 94.

CHAPTER SEVEN

1. Tarsicio de Azcona, *Isabel la Católica: Estudio crítico de su vida y su reinado* (Madrid: Biblioteca de Autores Cristianos, 1964), pp. 79–81.
2. William Thomas Walsh, *Isabella of Spain: The Last Crusader* (New York: Robert M. McBride Co., 1930), p. 33.

3. Azcona, *Isabel la Católica,* p. 80.
4. *Memorias de Don Enrique IV de Castilla,* Colección Diplomatica de Enrique IV (Madrid: Real Academia de la Historia, 1835–1913), pp. 326–27.
5. Azcona, *Isabel la Católica,* p. 112.
6. Diego Enríquez Castillo, ed., *Crónica del Rey Don Enrique el Cuarto,* BAE (Madrid: Ediciones Atlas, 1953), vol. 70, p. 143.
7. Azcona, *Isabel la Católica,* p. 90.
8. Alonso de Palencia, *Crónica de Enrique IV,* ed. Antonio Paz y Melia, BAE (Madrid: Ediciones Atlas, 1973), vol. 257, p. 168.
9. William H. Prescott, *History of the Reign of Ferdinand and Isabella the Catholic* (Philadelphia: Lippincott, 1872 [1837]), vol. 1, p. 182.
10. Palencia, *Crónica de Enrique IV,* vol. 257, p. 204.

CHAPTER EIGHT

1. William H. Prescott, *History of the Reign of Ferdinand and Isabella the Catholic* (Philadelphia: Lippincott, 1872 [1837]), vol. 1, p. 185.
2. Fernando Diaz-Plaja, ed., *Siglo XV: Historia de España en sus documentos* (Madrid: Ediciones Catedra, 1984), pp. 158–59.
3. Malcolm Letts, *The Travels of Leo of Rozmital,* Hakluyt Society, 2nd series, no. 108 (Cambridge: Cambridge University Press, 1957), p. 92; Alonso de Palencia, *Crónica de Enrique IV,* ed. Antonio Paz y Melia, BAE (Madrid: Ediciones Atlas, 1973), vol. 257, pp. 132–33.
4. Fernando del Pulgar, *Crónica de los señores reyes católicos Don Fernando y Doña Isabel de Castilla y de Aragón,* BAE (Madrid: Ediciones Atlas, 1953), vol. 70, pp. 230–31.
5. Tarsicio de Azcona, *Isabel la Católica: Estudio crítico de su vida y su reinado* (Madrid: Biblioteca de Autores Cristianos, 1964), p. 115.
6. Prescott, *History of the Reign of Ferdinand and Isabella,* vol. 1, p. 188.
7. Diego de Valera, *Epistolas* (Madrid: Sociedad de Bibliofilos Españoles, 1878), p. 45–6.
8. Ibid., p. 46.
9. Juan Torres Fontes, "La contratación de Guisando (Toros de Guisando)," *Anuario de Estudios Medievales* 2 (1965):404.
10. Ibid., p. 403.
11. Ibid., p. 404.

CHAPTER NINE

1. Helen Nader, *The Mendoza Family in the Spanish Renaissance, 1350 to 1550* (New Brunswick, NJ: Rutgers University Press, 1979), p. 32; Fernando del Pulgar, *Crónica de los señores reyes católicos Don Fernando y Doña Isabel de Castilla y de Aragón,* BAE (Madrid: Ediciones Atlas, 1953), vol. 70, p. 261.
2. Alonso de Palencia, *Crónica de Enrique IV,* ed. Antonio Paz y Melia, BAE (Madrid: Ediciones Atlas, 1973), vol. 257, p. 256; William H. Prescott, *History of the Reign of Ferdinand and Isabella the Catholic* (Philadelphia: Lippincott, 1872 [1837]), vol. 1, p. 189.
3. Diego de Valera, *Epistolas* (Madrid: Sociedad de Bibliofilos Españoles, 1878), pp. 47–8.
4. Pulgar, *Crónica de los señores reyes católicos,* p. 231.
5. Diego Enríquez Castillo, ed., *Crónica del Rey Don Enrique el Cuarto,* BAE (Madrid: Ediciones Atlas, 1953), vol. 70, p. 178; Agustín Millares Carlo, "Contribuciones

documentales a la historia de Madrid," *Biblioteca de Estudios Madrilenos* 13 (1971) 202.
6. Palencia, *Crónica de Enrique IV*, pp. 261–62.
7. Ibid.
8. Ibid.
9. Ibid., p. 262.
10. Valera, *Epistolas*, p. 48.
11. Pulgar, *Crónica de los señores*, p. 232.
12. *Archivo General de Simancas, Patrimonio Real*, 7-112, leg. 738.
13. Palencia, *Crónica de Enrique IV, p. 264.*
14. Ibid., p. 265.

CHAPTER 10

1. Felipe Fernández-Armesto, *Ferdinand and Isabella* (New York: Taplinger, 1975), p. 40.
2. Alonso de Palencia, *Crónica de Enrique IV*, ed. Antonio Paz y Melia, BAE (Madrid: Ediciones Atlas, 1973), vol. 257, p. 267.
3. Julio Puyol, ed., *Crónica incompleta de los Reyes Católicos, 1469–1476* (Madrid: Tipografia de Archivos, 1934), p. 70.
4. Diego Enríquez Castillo, ed., *Crónica del rey Don Enrique el Cuarto*, BAE (Madrid: Ediciones Atlas, 1953), vol. 70, p. 181.

CHAPTER ELEVEN

1. Alonso de Palencia, *Crónica de Enrique IV*, ed. Antonio Paz y Melia, BAE (Madrid: Ediciones Atlas, 1973), vol. 257, p. 270.
2. Fernando del Pulgar, *Crónica de los señores reyes católicos Don Fernando y Doña Isabel de Castilla y de Aragón*, BAE (Madrid: Ediciones Atlas, 1953), vol. 70, p. 236.
3. Diego Enríquez Castillo, ed. *Crónica del Rey Don Enrique el Cuarto*, BAE (Madrid: Ediciones Atlas, 1953), vol. 70, p. 189.
4. Palencia, *Crónica de Enrique IV*.
5. Ibid.
6. Andrés Bernáldez, *Historia de los reyes católicos Don Fernando y Doña Isabel*, BAE (Madrid: Ediciones Atlas, 1953), vol. 70, p. 574.
7. Palencia, *Crónica de Enrique IV*.
8. Castillo, ed., *Crónica del Rey Don Enrique el Cuarto*, p. 200.
9. Tarsicio de Azcona, *Isabel la Católica: Estudio crítico de su vida y su reinado* (Madrid: Biblioteca de Autores Cristianos, 1964), p. 142.

CHAPTER TWELVE

1. Tarsicio de Azcona, *Isabel la Católica: Estudio crítico de su vida y su reinado* (Madrid: Biblioteca de Autores Cristianos, 1964), p. 143.
2. Fernando Diaz-Plaja, ed., *Siglo XV: Historia de España en sus documentos* (Madrid: Ediciones Catedra, 1984), p. 163.
3. Ibid., pp. 164–66.
4. Ibid., p. 163.
5. Alonso de Palencia, *Crónica de Enrique IV*, ed. Antonio Paz y Melia, BAE (Madrid: Ediciones Atlas, 1973), vol. 257, p. 270.
6. Diego de Valera, *Epistolas* (Madrid: Sociedad de Bibliofilos Españoles, 1878), p. 49.
7. Azcona, *Isabel la Católica*, p. 145.

CHAPTER THIRTEEN

1. Alonso de Palencia, *Crónica de Enrique IV*, ed. Antonio Paz y Melia, BAE (Madrid: Ediciones Atlas, 1973), vol. 257, p. 277.
2. Manuel Danvila, "Tres documentos ineditos referentes al matrimonio de los reyes católicos—1468, 1469 y 1470," *Boletín de la Real Academia de la Historia* 40(1) (1902):278.
3. Fernando del Pulgar, *Crónica de los señores reyes católicos Don Fernando y Doña Isabel de Castilla y de Aragón*, BAE (Madrid: Ediciones Atlas, 1953), vol. 70, p. 238.
4. Ibid.
5. Ibid.
6. Diego de Valera, *Espistolas* (Madrid: Sociedad de Bibliofilos Españoles, 1878), p. 52.
7. Palencia, *Crónica de Enrique IV*, vol. 257, p. 284.
8. Ibid.
9. Ibid.
10. Valera, *Epistolas*, p. 53.
11. Palencia, *Crónica de Enrique IV*, vol. 257, p. 287.

CHAPTER FOURTEEN

1. *Memorias de Don Enrique de Castilla*, Colección Diplomatica de Enrique IV (Madrid: Real Academia de la Historia, 1835–1913), p. 605.
2. Ibid., p. 606.
3. Ibid., p. 607.
4. Ibid., p. 608.
5. Ibid.
6. Ibid., p. 609.
7. Alonso de Palencia, *Crónica de Enrique IV*, ed. Antonio Paz y Melia, BAE (Madrid: Ediciones Atlas, 1973), vol. 257, p. 288.
8. Ibid.
9. Julio Puyol, ed., *Crónica incompleta de los Reyes Católicos, 1469–1476* (Madrid: Tipografia de Archivos, 1934), pp. 87–88.
10. Fernando del Pulgar, *Crónica de los señores reyes católicos Don Fernando y Doña Isabel de Castilla y de Aragón*, BAE (Madrid: Ediciones Atlas, 1953), vol. 70, p. 256.
11. Ibid.
12. Palencia, *Crónica de Enrique IV*, vol. 257, pp. 288–89.
13. Ibid., p. 289.
14. Felipe Fernández-Armesto, *Ferdinand and Isabella* (New York: Taplinger, 1975), p. 35.
15. Palencia, *Crónica de Enrique IV*, vol. 257, p. 294.
16. *Memorias de Don Enrique IV*, pp. 610–11.
17. *Archivo General Simancas, Patrimonio Real*, PR-11-45.
18. Palencia, *Crónica de Enrique IV*, vol. 257, p. 296.
19. Ibid., p. 295.
20. Diego de Valera, *Epistolas* (Madrid: Sociedad de Bibliofilos Españoles, 1878), p. 54.
21. Palencia, *Crónica de Enrique IV*, vol. 257, p. 296.
22. Ibid., p. 297.
23. Valera, *Epistolas*, p. 54.
24. Tarsicio de Azcona, *Isabel la Católica: Estudio crítico de su vida y su reinado* (Madrid: Biblioteca de Autores Cristianos, 1964), p. 152.

CHAPTER FIFTEEN

1. Julio Puyol, ed., *Crónica incompleta de los Reyes Católicos, 1469–1476* (Madrid: Tipografia de Archivos, 1934), pp. 90–91.
2. Diego Enríquez Castillo, ed., *Crónica del Rey Don Enrique el Cuarto*, BAE (Madrid: Ediciones Atlas, 1953), vol. 70, p. 190.
3. Ibid., p. 191.
4. Ibid., p. 192.
5. Ibid., p. 193.
6. Antonio Paz y Melia, ed., *El cronista Alonso de Palencia. Su vida y sus obras: Sus Decadas y las crónicas contemporaneas* (Madrid: Hispanic Society of America, 1914), p. 101.
7. Puyol, *Crónica incompleta de los Reyes Católicos*, p. 87.
8. William H. Prescott, *History of the Reign of Ferdinand and Isabella the Catholic* (Philadelphia: Lippincott, 1872 [1837]), vol. 1, p. 215.
9. Ibid., p. 214.
10. Fernando del Pulgar, *Epistolas y Coplas de Mingo Revulgo*, ed. J. Dóminguez Bordona (Madrid: Ediciones de "La Lectura," 1929), p. 62.
11. Tarsicio de Azcona, *Isabel la Católica: Estudio crítico de su vida y su reinado* (Madrid: Biblioteca de Autores Cristianos, 1964), p. 162.
12. Ibid., p. 163.
13. Fernando del Pulgar, *Crónica de los señores reyes católicos Don Fernando y Doña Isabel de Castilla y de Aragón*, BAE (Madrid: Ediciones Atlas, 1953), vol. 70, pp. 243–44.
14. Alonso de Palencia, *Crónica de Enrique IV*, ed. Antonio Paz y Melia, BAE (Madrid: Ediciones Atlas, 1973), vol. 257, p. 303.

CHAPTER SIXTEEN

1. Alonso de Palencia, *Crónica de Enrique IV*, ed. Antionio Paz y Melia, BAE (Madrid: Ediciones Atlas, 1973), vol. 257, p. 314.
2. Jaime Vicens Vives, *Historia crítica de la vida y reinado de Fernando II de Aragón* (Zaragoza: Institución Fernando el Católico, 1962), p. 279, n. 912.
3. Palencia, *Crónica de Enrique IV*, pp. 312–13.
4. Diego Clemencin, *Elogio de la reina Católica Doña Isabela*, vol. 6, *Memorias de la Real Academia de la Historia* (Madrid: Real Academia de la Historia, 1821), pp. 99–100; Palencia, *Crónica de Enrique IV*, pp. 316–17.
5. Clemencin, *Elogio de la Reina Católica Doña Isabela*, vol. 6, p. 100.
6. Diego Enríquez Castillo, ed., *Crónica del Rey Don Enrique el Cuarto*, BAE (Madrid: Ediciones Atlas, 1953), vol. 70, p. 204.
7. Ibid.
8. Fernando del Pulgar, *Crónica de los señores reyes católicos Don Fernando y Doña Isabel de Castilla y de Aragón*, BAE (Madrid: Ediciones Atlas, 1953), vol. 70, p. 243.
9. *Memorias de Don Enrique IV de Castilla*, Coleccíon Diplomatica de Enrique IV (Madrid: Real Academia de la Historia, 1835–1913), pp. 619–21.

CHAPTER SEVENTEEN

1. Jaime Vicens Vives, *Historia crítica de la vida y reinado de Ferdinand II de Aragón* (Zaragoza: Institucíon Fernando el Católico, 1962), p. 280, n. 115.
2. Ibid., p. 287.
3. Ibid., p. 288.

4. Jeronimo Zurita, *Anales de la Corona de Aragón*, ed. Angel Canellas López (Zaragoza: Instituto Fernando el Católico, 1977), book 18, p. 662.
5. Alonso de Palencia, *Crónica de Enrique IV*, ed. Antonio Paz y Melia, BAE (Madrid: Ediciones Atlas, 1973), vol. 257, p. 318.
6. Ibid., p. 319.
7. *Memorias de Don Enrique IV de Castilla*, Coleccíon Diplomatica de Enrique IV (Madrid: Real Academia de la Historia, 1835–1913), pp. 630–32.
8. Ibid., pp. 638–39.
9. Diego Enríquez Castillo, ed., *Crónica del Rey Don Enrique el Cuarto*, BAE (Madrid: Ediciones Atlas, 1953), vol. 70, p. 204.
10. Julio Puyol, ed., *Crónica incompleta de los Reyes Católicos, 1469–1476* (Madrid: Tipografia de Archivos, 1934), pp. 95–96.
11. Fernando del Pulgar, *Crónica de los señores reyes católicos Don Fernando y Doña Isabel de Castilla y de Aragón*, BAE (Madrid: Ediciones Atlas, 1953), vol. 70, p. 244.
12. Tarsicio de Azcona, *Isabel la Católica: Estudio crítico de su vida y su reinado* (Madrid: Biblioteca de Autores Cristianos, 1964), pp. 173–74.
13. Ibid., p. 174.

CHAPTER EIGHTEEN

1. Jaime Vicens Vives, *Historia crítica de la vida y reinado de Fernando II de Aragón* (Zaragoza: Institución Fernando el Católico, 1962), p. 294.
2. Diego de Valera, *Epistolas* (Madrid: Sociedad de Bibliofilos Españoles, 1878), p. 71.
3. Luis Súarez Fernández, Juan de Mata Carriazo Arroquia, and Manuel Fernández Álvarez, *La España de los Reyes Católicos (1474–1515)*, *Historia de España*, ed. Ramón Menéndez Pidal, (Madrid: Espasa-Calpe, 1969), I, CIV.

CHAPTER NINETEEN

1. Ivan Cloulas, *The Borgias*, trans. G. Roberts (New York: Franklin Watts, 1989), p. 36.
2. Tarsicio de Azcona, *Isabel la Católica: Estudio crítico de su vida y su reinado* (Madrid: Biblioteca de Autores Cristianos, 1964), p. 178.
3. Ibid., p. 181.
4. Diego Enríquez Castillo, ed., *Crónica del Rey Don Enrique el Cuarto*, BAE (Madrid: Ediciones Atlas, 1953), vol. 70, p. 213.
5. Ibid.
6. Alonso de Palencia, *Crónica de Enrique IV*, ed. Antonio Paz y Melia, BAE (Madrid: Ediciones Atlas, 1975),vol. 258, p. 80.
7. Ibid.
8. Jaime Vicens Vives, *Historia crítica de la vida y reinado de Fernando II de Aragón* (Zaragoza: Institución Fernando el Católico, 1962), p. 334.
9. Ibid.
10. Azcona, *Isabel la Católica*, p. 186.
11. Ibid.

CHAPTER TWENTY

1. Diego de Valera, *Epistolas* (Madrid: Sociedad de Bibliofilos Españoles, 1878) p. 79.
2. Ibid., p. 78.
3. Ibid.
4. Ibid.
5. Ibid.

6. Alonso de Palencia, *Crónica de Enrique IV,* ed. Antonio Paz y Melia, BAE (Madrid: Ediciones Atlas, 1975), vol. 258, p. 94.
7. J. B. Sitges, *Enrique IV y la Excelente Señora, llamada vulgarmente Doña Juana la Beltraneja, 1425–1530* (Madrid: Rivadeneyra, 1912), p. 244.
8. Antonio Paz y Melia, ed., *El cronista Alonso de Palencia. Su vida y sus obras: Sus Decadas y las crónicas contemporaneas* (Madrid: Hispanic Society of America, 1914), pp. 129–30.
9. Julio Puyol, ed., *Crónica incompleta de los Reyes Católicos, 1469–1476* (Madrid: Tipografia de Archivos, 1934), p. 118.
10. Ibid., pp. 121–22.

CHAPTER TWENTY-ONE

1. Jaime Vicens Vives, *Historia crítica de la vida y reinado de Fernando II de Aragón* (Zaragoza: Institución Fernando el Católico, 1962), p. 343, n. 1122.
2. Ibid., p. 344.
3. Ibid.
4. Ibid.
5. Alonso de Palencia, *Crónica de Enrique IV,* ed. Antonio Paz y Melia, BAE (Madrid: Ediciones Atlas, 1975), vol. 258, p. 114.
6. Diego Enríquez Castillo, ed., *Crónica del Rey Don Enrique el Cuarto,* BAE (Madrid: Ediciones Atlas, 1953), vol. 70, p. 217.
7. Ibid., pp. 217–18.
8. Vicens Vives, *Historia,* p. 368.
9. Ibid., p. 366.
10. Castillo, *Crónica del Rey Don Enrique el Quarto,* vol. 70, p. 218.
11. Ibid.

CHAPTER TWENTY-TWO

1. Fernando del Pulgar, *Crónica de los señores reyes católicos Don Fernando y Doña Isabel de Castilla y de Aragón,* BAE (Madrid: Ediciones Atlas, 1953), vol. 70, p. 259.
2. Jeronimo Zurita, *Anales de la Corona de Aragón,* ed. Angel Canellas López (Zaragoza: Instituto Fernando el Católico, 1977), book 18, p. 745.
3. Alonso de Palencia, *Crónica de Enrique IV,* ed. Antonio Paz y Melia, BAE (Madrid: Ediciones Atlas, 1975), vol. 258, p. 126.
4. Diego Enríquez Castillo, ed., *Crónica del Rey Don Enrique el Cuarto,* BAE (Madrid: Ediciones Atlas, 1953), vol. 70, p. 220.
5. Antonio Paz y Melia, ed., *El cronista Alonso de Palencia. Su vida y sus obras: Sus Decadas y las crónicas contemporaneas* (Madrid: Hispanic Society of America, 1914), p. 166.
6. Diego de Valera, *Epistolas* (Madrid: Sociedad de Bibliofilos Españoles, 1878), p. 89.
7. Castillo, ed., *Crónica del Rey Don Enrique el Cuarto,* vol. 70, p. 220.
8. Paz y Melia, ed., *El cronista Alonso de Palencia,* pp. 164–65.
9. Palencia, *Crónica de Enrique IV,* vol. 258, p. 148.
10. Castillo, ed., *Crónica del Rey Don Enrique el Cuarto,* vol. 70, p. 220.
11. Palencia, *Crónica de Enrique IV,* vol. 258, p. 153.
12. Valera, *Epistolas,* p. 94.
13. Palencia, *Crónica de Enrique IV,* vol. 258, p. 153.
14. Valera, *Epistolas,* p. 94.
15. Palencia, *Crónica de Enrique IV,* vol. 258, p. 153.
16. Ibid.

17. Valera, *Epistolas*, p. 94.
18. Ibid.

CHAPTER TWENTY-THREE

1. Alonso de Palencia, *Crónica de Enrique IV*, ed. Antonio Paz y Melia, BAE (Madrid: Ediciones Atlas, 1975), vol. 258, p. 160–61.
2. Ibid., p. 162.
3. Ibid., p. 165.
4. Ibid.
5. Tarsicio de Azcona, *Isabel la Católica: Estudio crítico de su vida y su reinado* (Madrid: Biblioteca de Autores Cristianos, 1964), p. 211.
6. Julio Puyol, ed., *Crónica incompleta de los Reyes Católicos, 1469–1476* (Madrid: Tipografia de Archivos, 1934), p. 133.
7. Palencia, *Crónica de Enrique IV*, vol. 258, p. 167.
8. Fernando del Pulgar, *Crónica de los señores reyes católicos Don Fernando y Doña Isabel de Castilla y de Aragón*, BAE (Madrid: Ediciones Atlas, 1953), vol. 70, p. 255.
9. Ibid., p. 256.
10. Ibid.
11. Ibid.
12. Palencia, *Crónica de Enrique IV*, vol. 258, p. 168.

CHAPTER TWENTY-FOUR

1. Jaime Vicens Vives, *Historia crítica de la vida y reinado de Fernando II de Aragón* (Zaragoza: Institución Fernando el Católico, 1962), p. 404.
2. Fernando del Pulgar, *Crónica de los señores reyes católicos Don Fernando y Doña Isabel de Castilla y de Aragón*, BAE (Madrid: Ediciones Atlas, 1953), vol. 70, pp. 258–59.
3. Ibid., pp. 260–61.
4. Andrés Bernáldez, *Historia de los reyes católicos Don Fernando y Doña Isabel*, BAE (Madrid: Ediciones Atlas, 1953, vol. 70, p. 580.
5. Julio Puyol, ed., *Crónica incompleta de los Reyes Católicos, 1469–1476* (Madrid: Tipografia de Archivos, 1934), pp. 164–69.
6. Ibid., p. 169.
7. Bernáldez, *Historia de los reyes católicos*, vol. 70, p. 577.
8. Ibid.
9. Tarsicio de Azcona, *Isabel la Católica: Estudio crítico de su vida y su reinado* (Madrid: Biblioteca de Autores Cristianos, 1964), p. 239.
10. Ibid., p. 240.
11. Ibid., p. 241.
12. Vicente Rodriguez Valencia, *Isabel la Católica en la opinion de españoles y extranjeros. Siglos XV al XX* (Valladolid: Instituto de Isabel la Católica de la Historia Eclesiastica, 1970), p. 12.
13. Alonso de Palencia, *Crónica de Enrique IV*, ed. Antonio Paz y Melia, BAE (Madrid: Ediciones Atlas, 1975), vol. 258, p. 189.

CHAPTER TWENTY-FIVE

1. Fernando del Pulgar, *Crónica de los señores reyes católicos Don Fernando y Doña Isabel de Castilla y de Aragón*, BAE (Madrid: Ediciones Atlas, 1953), vol. 70, p. 273.
2. Julio Puyol, ed., *Crónica incompleta de los Reyes Católicos, 1469–1476* (Madrid: Tipografia de Archivos, 1934), p. 238.

3. Ibid., p. 239.
4. Ibid., pp. 240–41.
5. Ibid., pp. 241–42.
6. Ibid., p. 245.
7. Ibid., p. 246.
8. William H. Prescott, *History of the Reign of Ferdinand and Isabella the Catholic* (Philadelphia: Lippincott, 1872 [1837], vol. 1, p. 251; Jeronimo Zurita, *Anales de la Corona de Aragón,* ed. Angel Canellas Lopéz (Zaragoza: Instituto Fernando el Católico, 1977), book 19, p. 152.
9. Pulgar, *Crónica de los señores reyes católicos,* vol. 70, p. 273.

CHAPTER TWENTY-SIX

1. William H. Prescott, *History of the Reign of Ferdinand and Isabella the Catholic* (Philadelphia: Lippincott, 1872 [1837], vol. 1, p. 255.
2. J. B. Sitges, *Enrique IV y la Excelente Señora, llamada vulgarmente Doña Juana la Beltraneja, 1425–1530* (Madrid: Rivadeneyra, 1912), p. 311.
3. Andrés Bernáldez, *Historia de los reyes católicos Don Fernando y Doña Isabel,* BAE (Madrid: Ediciones Atlas, 1953), vol. 70, p. 587.
4. Alonso de Palencia, *Crónica de Enrique IV,* ed. Antonio Paz y Melia, BAE (Madrid: Ediciones Altas, 1975), vol. 258, p. 272.
5. Tarsicio de Azcona, *Isabel la Católica: Estudio crítico de su vida y su reinado* (Madrid: Biblioteca de Autores Cristianos, 1964), p. 249.
6. Bernáldez, *Historia de los reyes católicos,* vol. 70, p. 587.
7. Fernando del Pulgar, *Crónica de los señores reyes católicos Don Fernando y Doña Isabel de Castilla y de Aragón,* BAE (Madrid: Ediciones Atlas, 1953), vol. 70, p. 313.

CHAPTER TWENTY-SEVEN

1. Jean Hippolyte Mariejol, *The Spain of Ferdinand and Isabella,* trans. and ed. Benjamin Keen (New Brunswick, NJ: Rutgers University Press, 1961), p. 22.
2. Jocelyn N. Hillgarth, *The Spanish Kingdoms, 1250–1516* (Oxford: Clarendon Press, 1978), vol. 2, p. 363.
3. Fernando del Pulgar, *Crónica de los señores reyes católicos Don Fernando y Doña Isabel de Castilla y de Aragón,* BAE (Madrid: Ediciones Atlas, 1953), vol. 70, p. 312.
4. Ibid., p. 313.
5. Ibid.
6. Ibid.
7. Ibid.
8. Ibid., p. 317.
9. Roger Bigelow Merriman, *The Rise of the Spanish Empire in the Old World and in the New* (New York: Macmillan, 1918), vol. 2, p. 117.

CHAPTER TWENTY-EIGHT

1. Fernando del Pulgar, *Crónica de los señores reyes católicos Don Fernando y Doña Isabel de Castilla y de Aragón,* BAE (Madrid: Ediciones Atlas, 1953), vol. 70, p. 309.
2. Ibid., p. 310.
3. J. B. Sitges, *Enrique IV y la Excelente Señora, llamada vulgarmente Doña Juana la Beltraneja, 1425–1530* (Madrid: Rivadeneyra, 1912), p. 314.
4. Pulgar, *Crónica de los señores reyes católicos,* vol. 70, p. 310.
5. Ibid., p. 318.

6. Ibid., p. 283.
7. Ibid., p. 257.
8. Ibid., p. 322.
9. Ibid.
10. Ibid., p. 323.

CHAPTER TWENTY-NINE

1. Fernando del Pulgar, *Crónica de los señores reyes católicos Don Fernando y Doña Isabel de Castilla y de Aragón,* BAE (Madrid: Ediciones Atlas, 1953), vol. 70, p. 326.
2. Ibid.
3. Ibid., p. 257.
4. Ibid., pp. 324–25.
5. Ibid., p. 326.
6. Jocelyn N. Hillgarth, *The Spanish Kingdoms, 1250–1516* (Oxford: Clarendon Press, 1978), vol. 2, p. 423.
7. Pulgar, *Crónica de los señores reyes católicos,* pp. 326–27.
8. Ibid., p. 327.
9. Alonso de Palencia, *Crónica de Enrique IV,* ed. Antonio Paz y Melia, BAE (Madrid: Ediciones Atlas, 1975), vol. 267, p. 51.
10. Ibid., p. 49.
11. Ibid., p. 61.
12. Tarsicio de Azcona, *Isabel la Católica: Estudio crítico de su vida y su reinado* (Madrid: Biblioteca de Autores Cristianos, 1964), pp. 289–90.
13. Fernando del Pulgar, *Epistolas y Coplas de Mingo Revulgo,* ed. J. Dóminguez Bordona (Madrid: Ediciones de "La Lectura," 1929), pp. 53–54.
14. Andrés Bernáldez, *Historia de los reyes católicos Don Fernando y Doña Isabel,* BAE (Madrid: Ediciones Atlas, 1953), vol. 70, pp. 592–93.
15. José Camon Aznar, *Sobre la muerte del principe Don Juan* (Madrid: Real Academia de la Historia, 1963), p. 49.
16. Ibid.

CHAPTER THIRTY

1. Fernando del Pulgar, *Crónica de los señores reyes católicos Don Fernando y Doña Isabel de Castilla y de Aragón,* BAE (Madrid: Ediciones Atlas, 1953), vol. 70, p. 337.
2. Ibid.
3. Andrés Bernáldez, *Historia de los reyes católicos Don Fernando y Doña Isabel,* BAE (Madrid: Ediciones Atlas, 1953), vol. 70, p. 593.
4. Jaime Vicens Vives, *Historia crítica de la vida y reinado de Fernando II de Aragón* (Zaragoza: Institución Fernando el Católico, 1962), p. 490.
5. Ibid., p. 495.
6. Ibid., p. 494.
7. Ibid., p. 508.
8. Ibid.
9. Pulgar, *Crónica de los señores reyes católicos,* vol. 70, p. 342.
10. Jeronimo Zurita, *Anales de la Corona de Aragón,* ed. Angel Canellas López (Zaragoza: Instituto Fernando el Católico, 1977), book 20, p. 347.
11. Francisco Esteve Barba, *Alfonso Carrillo de Acuña: Autor de la unidad España* (Barcelona: Editorial Amaltea, 1943), p. 247.
12. Pulgar, *Crónica de los señores reyes católicos,* vol. 70, p. 338.
13. Ibid., p. 345.

14. Tarsicio de Azcona, *Isabel la Católica: Estudio crítico de su vida y su reinado* (Madrid: Biblioteca de Autores Cristianos, 1964), p. 295.
15. Ibid., p. 297.
16. Zurita, *Anales de la Corona de Aragón*, book 20, pp. 378–79; Azcona, *Isabel la Católica*, pp. 294–300.
17. Pulgar, *Crónica de los señores reyes católicos*, vol. 70, p. 350.
18. Ibid.
19. J. B. Sitges, *Enrique IV y la Excelente Señora, llamada vulgarmente Doña Juana la Beltraneja, 1425–1530* (Madrid: Rivadeneyra, 1912), p. 344.
20. H. V. Livermore, *A New History of Portugal*, 2nd ed. (Cambridge: Cambridge University Press, 1966), p. 122.

CHAPTER THIRTY-ONE

1. Andrés Bernáldez, *Historia de los reyes católicos Don Fernando y Doña Isabel*, BAE (Madrid: Ediciones Atlas, 1953), vol. 70, p. 653.
2. Henry Kamen, *Inquisition and Society in Spain in the Sixteenth and Seventeenth Century* (London: Weidenfeld and Nicolson, 1985), p. 12.
3. Fernando del Pulgar, *Crónica de los señores reyes católicos Don Fernando y Doña Isabel de Castilla y de Aragón*, BAE (Madrid: Ediciones Atlas, 1953), vol. 70, p. 257.
4. Fidel Fernández, *Fray Hernando de Talavera: Confesor de los reyes católicos y primer arzobispo de Granada* (Madrid: Biblioteca Nueva, 1942), p. 17.
5. Pulgar, *Crónica de los señores reyes católicos*, vol. 70, p. 359.
6. Ibid.
7. Ibid.
8. Ibid.
9. Ibid.
10. Ibid.
11. Ramón Menéndez Pidal, "The Significance of the Reign of Isabella the Catholic, According to Her Contemporaries," in *Spain in the Fifteenth Century*, ed. Roger Highfield (London: Macmillan, 1972), p. 417.
12. Pulgar, *Crónica de los señores reyes católicos*, vol. 70, p. 256.
13. Felipe Fernández-Armesto, *Ferdinand and Isabella* (New York: Taplinger, 1975), p. 108.
14. Menéndez Pidal, "Significance of the Reign of Isabella," p. 386.
15. Pulgar, *Crónica de los señores reyes católicos*, vol. 70, p. 354.
16. Ibid.
17. Ibid.
18. Townsend Miller, *The Castles and the Crown: Spain: 1451–1555* (New York: Coward-McCann, 1963), p. 110.

CHAPTER THIRTY-TWO

1. Cecil Roth, *A History of the Marranos* (Philadelphia: Jewish Publication Society of America, 1932), p. 42.
2. Ibid.
3. Fernando del Pulgar, *Crónica de los señores reyes católicos Don Fernando y Doña Isabel de Castilla y de Aragón*, BAE (Madrid: Ediciones Atlas, 1953), vol. 70, p. 331.
4. Henry Kamen, *Inquisition and Society in Spain in the Sixteenth and Seventeenth Century* (London: Weidenfeld and Nicolson, 1985), p. 42.
5. Andrés Bernáldez, *Historia de los reyes católicos Don Fernando y Doña Isabel*, BAE (Madrid: Ediciones Atlas, 1953), vol. 70, pp. 599–600.

6. Pulgar, *Crónica de los señores reyes católicos,* vol. 70, p. 432.
7. Yitzhak Baer, *History of the Jews in Christian Spain* (Philadelphia: Jewish Publication Society of America, 1961), vol. 2, p. 353.
8. William H. Prescott, *History of the Reign of Ferdinand and Isabella the Catholic* (Philadelphia: Lippincott, 1872 [1837]), vol. 1, p. 343.
9. Fernando Diaz-Plaja, *Siglo XV: Historia de España en sus documentos* (Madrid: Ediciones Catedra, 1984), p. 205.
10. Edward Peters, *Inquisition* (New York: Free Press/Macmillan, 1988), p. 55.

CHAPTER THIRTY-THREE

1. William H. Prescott, *History of the Reign of Ferdinand and Isabella the Catholic* (Philadelphia: Lippincott, 1872 [1837]), vol. 1, p. 426.
2. Alonso de Palencia, *Crónica de Enrique IV,* ed. Antonio Paz y Melia, BAE (Madrid: Ediciones Atlas, 1975), vol. 267, p. 91.
3. Fernando del Pulgar, *Crónica de los señores reyes católicos Don Fernando y Doña Isabel de Castilla y de Aragón,* BAE (Madrid: Ediciones Atlas, 1953), vol. 70, p. 371.
4. Palencia, *Crónica de Enrique IV,* vol. 267, p. 94.
5. Pulgar, *Crónica de los señores reyes católicos,* vol. 70, p. 373.

CHAPTER THIRTY-FOUR

1. Henry Kamen, *Inquisition and Society in Spain in the Sixteenth and Seventeenth Century* (London: Weidenfeld and Nicolson, 1985), p. 47.
2. Ibid., p. 48.
3. Ibid., p. 49.
4. Luis Suárez Fernández, Juan de Mata Carriazo Arroquia, and Manuel Fernández Álvarez, *La España de los Reyes Católicos (1474–1515)* (Madrid: Espasa-Calpe, 1983), vol. 2, p. 216.
5. Kamen, *Inquisition and Society in Spain,* p. 34.
6. Ibid.
7. Ibid.
8. William Thomas Walsh, *Isabella of Spain: The Last Crusader* (New York: Robert M. McBride Co., 1930), p. 261.
9. Ibid., p. 264.
10. Ibid.
11. Ibid., p. 265.
12. Ibid.
13. Pulgar, *Crónica de los señores reyes católicos,* vol. 70, p. 377.
14. Walsh, *Isabella of Spain,* p. 267.

CHAPTER THIRTY-FIVE

1. Andrés Bernáldez, *Historia de los reyes católicos Don Fernando y Doña Isabel,* BAE (Madrid: Ediciones Atlas, 1953), vol. 70, p. 610.
2. Ibid., p. 609.
3. Alonso de Palencia, *Crónica de Enrique IV,* ed. Antonio Paz y Melia, BAE (Madrid: Ediciones Atlas, 1975), vol. 267, p. 102.
4. Fernando del Pulgar, *Crónica de los señores reyes católicos Don Fernando y Doña Isabel de Castilla y de Aragón,* BAE (Madrid: Ediciones Atlas, 1953), vol. 70, p. 384.
5. Ibid.

6. Jeronimo Zurita, *Anales de la Corona de Aragón,* ed. Angel Canellas López (Zaragoza: Instituto Fernando el Católico, 1977), book 20, pp. 431–32.
7. Bernáldez, *Historia de los reyes católicos,* vol. 70, p. 610.
8. Palencia, *Crónica de Enrique IV,* vol. 267, p. 102.
9. Washington Irving, *A Chronicle of the Conquest of Granada, from the Mss. of Fray Antonio Agapida,* (New York: AMS Press, 1970, [1829]), vol. 1, p. 73.
10. William H. Prescott, *History of the Reign of Ferdinand and Isabella the Catholic* (Philadelphia: Lippincott, 1872 [1837]), vol. 1, p. 472.
11. Ibid., p. 392.
12. Ibid., p. 393.

CHAPTER THIRTY-SIX

1. Fernando del Pulgar, *Crónica de los señores reyes católicos Don Fernando y Doña Isabel de Castilla y de Aragón,* BAE (Madrid: Ediciones Atlas, 1953), vol. 70, p. 395.
2. Alonso de Palencia, *Crónica de Enrique IV,* ed. Antonio Paz y Melia, BAE (Madrid: Ediciones Atlas, 1975), vol. 267, p. 113.
3. Jeronimo Zurita, *Anales de la Corona de Aragón,* ed. Angel Canellas López (Zaragoza: Instituto Fernando el Católico, 1977), book 20, p. 464.
4. Pulgar, *Crónica de los señores reyes católicos,* vol. 70, p. 400.
5. Ibid.
6. Ibid.
7. Ibid., p. 401.
8. Luis Suárez Fernández, Juan de Mata Carriazo Arroquia, and Manuel Fernández Álvarez, *La España de los Reyes Católicos 1474–1515* (Madrid: Espasa-Calpe, 1969), vol. 1, p. 554.
9. Ibid., p. 556.
10. Palencia, *Crónica de Enrique IV,* p. 120.
11. Ibid.
12. Suárez Fernández, de Mata Carriazo Arroquia, and Fernández Álvarez, *La España de los Reyes Católicos,* p. 556.

CHAPTER THIRTY-SEVEN

1. William H. Prescott, *History of the Reign of Ferdinand and Isabella the Catholic* (Philadelphia: Lippincott, 1872 [1837]), vol. 1, p. 488.
2. Felipe Fernández-Armesto, *Ferdinand and Isabella* (New York: Taplinger, 1975), p. 60.
3. Gonzalo Fernández de Oviedo, *Libro de la camara real del principe Don Juan* (Madrid: Imprenta de la viuda e hijos de Galiano, 1870), p. 23.
4. Ruth Matilda Anderson, *Hispanic Costume, 1480–1530* (New York: Hispanic Society of America, 1979), p. 12.
5. Fernando del Pulgar, *Crónica de los señores reyes católicos Don Fernando y Doña Isabel de Castilla y de Aragón,* BAE (Madrid: Ediciones Atlas, 1953), vol. 70, p. 411.
6. Ibid.
7. Ibid., p. 413.
8. Ibid., p. 416.
9. Washington Irving, *A Chronicle of the Conquest of Granada, From the Mss. of Fray Antonio Agapida,* (New York: AMS Press, 1970 [1829]), vol. 1, p. 276.
10. Pulgar, *Crónica de los señores reyes católicos,* vol. 70, p. 419.

CHAPTER THIRTY-EIGHT

1. Jeronimo Zurita, *Anales de la Corona de Aragón,* ed. Angel Canellas López (Zaragoza: Instituto Fernando el Católico, 1977), book 20, p. 489.
2. Ibid., p. 490.
3. Fernando del Pulgar, *Crónica de los señores reyes católicos Don Fernando y Doña Isabel de Castilla y de Aragón,* BAE (Madrid: Ediciones Atlas, 1953), vol. 70, p. 427.
4. Washington Irving, *A Chronicle of the Conquest of Granada, From the Mss. of Fray Antonio Agapida,* (New York: AMS Press, 1970 [1829]), vol. 1, p. 299.
5. Pulgar, *Crónica de los señores reyes católicos,* vol. 70, p. 427.
6. William Thomas Walsh, *Isabella of Spain: The Last Crusader* (New York: Robert M. McBride Co., 1930), p. 288.
7. Pulgar, *Crónica de los señores reyes católicos,* vol. 70, p. 428.
8. Ibid.

CHAPTER THIRTY-NINE

1. William Thomas Walsh, *Isabella of Spain: The Last Crusader* (New York: Robert M. McBride Co., 1930), p. 289.
2. Gianni Granzotto, *Christopher Columbus: The Dream and the Obsession* (Garden City, NY: Doubleday, 1985), p. 69.
3. Samuel Eliot Morison, *Admiral of the Ocean Sea. A Life of Christopher Columbus* (Boston: Little, Brown, 1942), p. 45.
4. Ferdinand Columbus, *The Life of Christopher Columbus by His Son Ferdinand,* trans. and ed. Benjamin Keen (New Brunswick, NJ: Rutgers University Press, 1959), p. 10.
5. Granzotto, *Christopher Columbus,* p. 41.
6. Morison, *Admiral of the Ocean Sea,* p. 25.
7. Ibid., p. 60.
8. Columbus, *Life of Christopher Columbus,* p. 20.
9. Ibid., p. 19.
10. Ibid., p. 22.
11. Morison, *Admiral of the Ocean Sea,* p. 39.
12. Ibid., p. 70.
13. Ibid., p. 71.
14. Ibid., p. 84.
15. Columbus, *Life of Christopher Columbus,* p. 10.
16. Bartolomé de Las Casas, *History of the Indies,* trans. and ed. Andree Collard (New York: Harper & Row, 1971), p. 27.

CHAPTER FORTY

1. Ludwig Pastor, *The History of the Popes from the Close of the Middle Ages* (St. Louis: B. Herder, 1923), vol. 5, p. 242.
2. William H. Prescott, *History of the Reign of Ferdinand and Isabella the Catholic* (Philadelphia: Lippincott, 1872 [1837]), vol. 1, p. 489.
3. Andrés Bernáldez, *Historia de los reyes católicos Don Fernando y Doña Isabel,* BAE (Madrid: Ediciones Atlas, 1953), vol. 70, p. 622.
4. Prescott, *History of the Reign of Ferdinand and Isabella,* vol. 1, p. 492.
5. Luis Suárez Fernández, Juan de Mata Carriazo Arroquia, and Manuel Fernández Álvarez, *La España de los Reyes Católicos (1474–1515)* (Madrid: Espasa-Calpe, 1983), vol. 2, p. 649.
6. Fernando del Pulgar, *Crónica de los señores reyes católicos Don Fernando y Doña*

Isabel de Castilla y de Aragón, BAE (Madrid: Ediciones Atlas, 1953), vol. 70, p. 439.

7. Suarez Fernández, de Mata Carriazo Arroquia, and Fernández Álvarez, *La España de los Reyes Católicos,* p. 665.
8. Bernáldez, *Historia de los reyes católicos,* vol. 70, p. 623.
9. Pulgar, *Crónica de los señores reyes católicos,* vol. 70, p. 439.
10. Prescott, *History of the Reign of Ferdinand and Isabella,* vol. 1, p. 490.
11. Pulgar, *Crónica de los señores reyes católicos,* vol. 70, p. 440.
12. Bernáldez, *Historia de los reyes católicos,* vol. 70, p. 623.
13. Pulgar, *Crónica de los señores reyes católicos,* vol. 70, p. 441.

CHAPTER FORTY-ONE

1. Fernando del Pulgar, *Crónica de los señores reyes católicos Don Fernando y Doña Isabel de Castilla y de Aragón,* BAE (Madrid: Ediciones Atlas, 1953), vol. 70, p. 448.
2. Washington Irving, *A Chronicle of the Conquest of Granada, From the Mss. of Fray Antonio Agapida,* (New York: AMS Press, 1970 [1829]), vol. 2, p. 47.
3. Pulgar, *Crónica de los señores reyes católicos,* vol. 70, p. 459.
4. William H. Prescott, *History of the Reign of Ferdinand and Isabella the Catholic* (Philadelphia: Lippincott, 1872 [1837]), vol. 2, p. 23.
5. Pulgar, *Crónica de los señores reyes católicos,* vol. 70, p. 453.
6. William Thomas Walsh, *Isabella of Spain: The Last Crusader* (New York: Robert M. McBride Co., 1930), p. 306.
7. Pulgar, *Crónica de los señores reyes católicos,* vol. 70, p. 463.
8. Andrés Bernáldez, *Historia de los reyes católicos Don Fernando y Doña Isabel,* BAE (Madrid: Ediciones Atlas, 1953), vol. 70, p. 629.
9. Pulgar, *Crónica de los señores reyes católicos,* vol. 70, p. 470.
10. Ibid.
11. Bernáldez, *Historia de los reyes católicos,* vol. 70, p. 630.
12. Pulgar, *Crónica de los señores reyes católicos,* vol. 70, p. 471.

CHAPTER FORTY-TWO

1. Samuel Eliot Morison, *Admiral of the Ocean Sea. A Life of Christopher Columbus* (Boston: Little, Brown, 1942), p. 88.
2. Ferdinand Columbus, *The Life of Christopher Columbus by His Son Ferdinand,* trans. and ed. Benjamin Keen (New Brunswick, NJ: Rutgers University Press, 1959), p. 38.
3. Ibid., p. 39.
4. Gianni Granzotto, *Christopher Columbus: The Dream and the Obsession* (Garden City, NY: Doubleday, 1985), p. 81.
5. Morison, *Admiral of the Ocean Sea,* p. 75; Salvador de Madariaga, *Christopher Columbus, Being the Life of the Very Magnificent Lord Don Cristobal Colón* (New York: Macmillan, 1940), p. 161.
6. Christopher Columbus, *Textos y documentos completos,* 2nd ed., ed. Consuelo Varela (Madrid: Alianza Universidad, 1984), p. 12; Morison, *Admiral of the Ocean Sea,* p. 76.

CHAPTER FORTY-THREE

1. Jeronimo Zurita, *Anales de la Corona de Aragón,* ed. Angel Canellas López (Zaragoza: Instituto Fernando el Católico, 1977), book 20, p. 558.
2. Fernando del Pulgar, *Crónica de los señores reyes católicos Don Fernando y Doña*

Isabel de Castilla y de Aragón, BAE (Madrid: Ediciones Atlas, 1953), vol. 70, pp. 479–80.

3. Ruth Matilda Anderson, *Hispanic Costume, 1480–1530* (New York: Hispanic Society of America, 1979), p. 135.

4. Diego Clemencin, *Elogio de la reina Católica Doña Isabel,* vol. 6, *Memorias de la Real Academia de la Historia* (Madrid: Real Academia de la Historia, 1821), p. 364.

CHAPTER FORTY-FOUR

1. Luis Suárez Fernández, Juan de Mata Carriazo Arroquia, and Manuel Fernández Álvarez, *La España de los Reyes Católicos (1474–1515)* (Madrid: Espasa-Calpe, 1983), vol. 2, p. 757.

2. Fernando del Pulgar, *Epistolas y Coplas de Mingo Revulgo,* ed. J. Dóminguez Bordona (Madrid: Ediciones de "La Lectura," 1929), p. 45.

3. Fernando del Pulgar, *Crónica de los señores reyes católicos Don Fernando y Doña Isabel de Castilla y de Aragón,* BAE (Madrid: Ediciones Atlas, 1953), vol. 70, p. 492.

4. Ibid.

5. Ibid.

6. Alonso de Palencia, *Crónica de Enrique IV,* ed. Antonio Paz y Melia, BAE (Madrid: Ediciones Atlas, 1975), vol. 267, p. 232.

7. Pulgar, *Crónica de los señores reyes católicos,* vol. 70, p. 499.

8. Andrés Bernáldez, *Historia de los reyes católicos Don Fernando y Doña Isabel,* BAE (Madrid: Ediciones Atlas, 1953), vol. 70, p. 635.

9. Pietro Martire d'Anghiera, *Epistolarios,* ed. and trans. José López de Toro (Madrid: Imprenta Gongora, 1953), vol. 9, p. 133; William H. Prescott, *History of the Reign of Ferdinand and Isabella the Catholic* (Philadelphia: Lippincott, 1872 [1837]), vol. 2, pp. 64-65.

10. Prescott, *History of the Reign of Ferdinand and Isabella,* vol. 2, p. 68–69.

11. Martire, *Epistolarios,* vol. 9, p. 140.

12. Pulgar, *Crónica de los señores reyes católicos,* vol. 70, p. 503.

CHAPTER FORTY-FIVE

1. Fernando del Pulgar, *Crónica de los señores reyes católicos Don Fernando y Doña Isabel de Castilla y de Aragón,* BAE (Madrid: Ediciones Atlas, 1953), vol. 70, p. 504.

2. Luis Suárez Fernández, Juan de Mata Carriazo Arroquia, and Manuel Fernández Álvarez, *La España de los Reyes Católicos (1474–1515)* (Madrid: Espasa-Calpe, 1969), vol. 1, p. 781.

3. Pulgar, *Crónica de los señores reyes católicos,* vol. 70, p. 505.

4. Ibid., p. 506.

5. Ibid.

6. Ibid.

7. Ferdinand Columbus, *The Life of Christopher Columbus by His Son Ferdinand,* trans. and ed. Benjamin Keen (New Brunswick, NJ: Rutgers University Press, 1959), p. 39.

8. Ibid., pp. 39-40.

9. Ibid., p. 40.

10. Ibid.

CHAPTER FORTY-SIX

1. Rafael Sabatini, *Torquemada and the Spanish Inquisition* (Boston: Houghton Mifflin, 1924), p. 316.

2. Ibid., p. 319.
3. Ibid., p. 320.
4. Ibid., p. 316, n. 1.
5. Ibid., p. 324.
6. Ibid., p. 325.
7. Ibid., p. 325.
8. Ibid., p. 326.
9. Jocelyn N. Hillgarth, *The Spanish Kingdoms, 1250–1516* (Oxford: Clarendon Press, 1978), vol. 2, p. 446.
10. Ibid., p. 447.
11. Luis Suárez Fernández, *Documentos acerca de la Expulsión de los Judios* (Valladolid: Consejo Superior de Investigaciones Científicas, 1964), pp. 381–83.

CHAPTER FORTY-SEVEN

1. William Thomas Walsh, *Isabella of Spain: The Last Crusader* (New York: Robert M. McBride Co., 1930), p. 326.
2. Washington Irving, *A Chronicle of the Conquest of Granada, From the Mss. of Fray Antonio Agapida,* (New York: AMS Press, 1970 [1829]), vol. 2, p. 325.
3. Andrés Bernáldez, *Historia de los reyes católicos Don Fernando y Doña Isabel,* BAE (Madrid: Ediciones Atlas, 1953), vol. 70, p. 642.
4. Walsh, *Isabella of Spain,* p. 325.
5. Irving, *A Chronicle of the Conquest of Granada,* p. 379.
6. Ibid.
7. Fernando del Pulgar, *Crónica de los señores reyes católicos Don Fernando y Doña Isabel de Castilla y de Aragón,* BAE (Madrid: Ediciones Atlas, 1953), vol. 70, p. 511.
8. Luis Suárez Fernández, Juan de Mata Carriazo Arroquia, and Manuel Fernández Álvarez, *La Espāna de los Reyes Católicos (1474–1515)* (Madrid: Espasa-Calpe, 1969), vol. 1, p. 876.
9. Pulgar, *Crónica de los señores reyes católicos,* vol. 70, p., 510.
10. Jocelyn N. Hillgarth, *The Spanish Kingdoms, 1250–1516* (Oxford: Clarendon Press, 1978), vol. 2, p. 388.
11. Suárez Fernández, de Mata Carriazo Arroquia, and Fernández Álvarez, *La España de los Reyes Católicos,* pp. 845–46.
12. Hillgarth, *Spanish Kingdoms,* vol. 2, p. 388.
13. William H. Prescott, *History of the Reign of Ferdinand and Isabella the Catholic* (Philadelphia: Lippincott, 1872 [1837]), vol. 2, p. 101.

CHAPTER FORTY-EIGHT

1. Ferdinand Columbus, *The Life of Christopher Columbus by His Son Ferdinand,* trans. and ed. Benjamin Keen (New Brunswick, NJ: Rutgers University Press, 1959), pp. 40–41.
2. Ibid., p. 41.
3. Christopher Columbus, *The Log of Christopher Columbus,* trans. Robert H. Fuson (Camden, ME: International Marine Publishing Co., 1987), p. 51.
4. Columbus, *Life of Christopher Columbus,* p. 43.
5. Ibid.
6. Gianni Granzotto, *Christopher Columbus: The Dream and the Obsession* (Garden City, NY: Doubleday, 1985), p. 92.
7. John H. Parry and Robert G. Keith, eds., *New Iberian World. A Documentary History*

of the Discovery and Settlement of Latin America to the Early Seventeenth Century, vol. 2, *The Caribbean* (New York: Times Books, 1984), p. 19.

8. Ibid., p. 20.
9. Samuel Eliot Morison, *Admiral of the Ocean Sea. A Life of Christopher Columbus* (Boston: Little, Brown, 1942), p. 107.
10. Columbus, *Log of Christopher Columbus,* p. 155.

CHAPTER FORTY-NINE

1. Fernando del Pulgar, *Crónica de los señores reyes católicos Don Fernando y Doña Isabel de Castilla y de Aragón,* BAE (Madrid: Ediciones Atlas, 1953), vol. 70, p. 518.
2. Ben-Zion Netanyahu, *Don Isaac Abravanel: Statesman and Philosopher* (Philadelphia: Jewish Publication Society of America, 1953), p. 56.
3. Jacob R. Marcus, *The Jew in the Medieval World, 315–1791* (Cincinnati, OH: Sinai Press, 1938), p. 53.
4. William H. Prescott, *History of the Reign of Ferdinand and Isabella the Catholic* (Philadelphia: Lippincott, 1872 [1837]), vol. 2, p. 136.
5. Pietro Martire d'Anghiera, *Epistolarios,* ed. and trans. José López de Toro (Madrid: Imprenta Gongora, 1953), vol. 9, p. 200.
6. Fernando Diaz-Plaja, ed., *Siglo XV: Historia de España en sus documentos* (Madrid: Ediciones Catedra, 1984), pp. 303–4.
7. Andrés Bernáldez, *Historia de los reyes católicos Don Fernando y Doña Isabel,* BAE (Madrid: Ediciones Atlas, 1953), vol. 70, p. 652.
8. Yitzhak Baer, *History of the Jews in Christian Spain* (Philadelphia: Jewish Publication Society of America, 1961), vol. 2, p. 436.
9. Jocelyn N. Hillgarth, *The Spanish Kingdoms, 1250–1516* (Oxford: Clarendon Press, 1978), vol. 2, p. 452.
10. Henry Kamen, *Spain, 1469–1714. A Society of Conflict* (London: Longman, 1983), p. 42.
11. Niccolo Machiavelli, *The Prince,* trans. and ed. Daniel Donno (New York: Bantam Books, 1966), p. 77.
12. Bernáldez, *Historia de los reyes católicos,* vol. 70, p. 653.
13. Ibid.

CHAPTER FIFTY

1. Diego Clemencin, *Elogio de la reina Católica Doña Isabel,* vol. 6, *Memorias de la Real Academia de la Historia* (Madrid: Real Academia de la Historia, 1821), p. 373.
2. Pietro Martire d'Anghiera, *Epistolarios,* ed. and trans. José López de Toro (Madrid: Imprenta Gongora, 1953), vol. 9, p. 193.
3. Ibid., p. 194.
4. William H. Prescott, *History of the Reign of Ferdinand and Isabella the Catholic* (Philadelphia: Lippincott, 1872 [1837]), vol. 2, pp. 191–92.
5. Ibid.
6. Christopher Columbus, *The Log of Christopher Columbus,* trans. Robert H. Fuson (Camden, ME: International Marine Publishing Co., 1987), pp. 73–75.
7. Ibid., p. 76.
8. Andrés Bernáldez, *Historia de los reyes católicos Don Fernando y Doña Isabel,* BAE (Madrid: Ediciones Atlas, 1953), vol. 70, p. 656.
9. Clemencin, *Elogio de la reina Católica Doña Isabel,* vol. 6, p. 356; William Thomas Walsh, *Isabella of Spain: The Last Crusader* (New York: Robert M. McBride Co., 1930), p. 397.

10. Clemencin, *Elogio de la reina Católica Doña Isabel*, vol. 6, p. 355; Walsh, *Isabella of Spain*, p. 396.
11. Clemencin, *Elogio de la reina Católica Doña Isabel*, vol. 6, p. 357; Walsh, *Isabella of Spain*, p. 397.
12. Bernáldez, *Historia de los reyes católicos*, vol. 70, p. 656.
13. Clemencin, *Elogio de la reina Católica Doña Isabel*, vol. 6, pp. 364–66; Ruth Matilda Anderson, *Hispanic Costume 1480–1530* (New York: Hispanic Society of America, 1979), p. 139.
14. Clemencin, *Elogio de la reina Católica Doña Isabel*, vol. 6, pp. 374–76.

CHAPTER FIFTY-ONE

1. Christopher Columbus, *Textos y documentos completos*, 2nd ed., ed. Consuelo Varela (Madrid: Alianza Universidad, 1984), pp. 140–41; William Thomas Walsh, *Isabella of Spain: The Last Crusader* (New York: Robert M. McBride Co., 1930), pp. 399-401.
2. Christopher Columbus, *The Log of Christopher Columbus*, trans. Robert H. Fuson (Camden, ME: International Marine Publishing Co., 1987), p. 61.
3. Ibid., p. 62.
4. Salvador de Madariaga, *Christopher Columbus, Being the Life of the Very Magnificent Lord Don Cristobal Colón* (New York: Macmillan, 1940), p. 202.
5. Columbus, *Log of Christopher Columbus*, pp. 66–67.
6. Ibid., p. 67.
7. Ibid., p. 71.
8. Ibid., p. 72.
9. Ibid.
10. Ibid., p. 73.
11. Ibid., p. 75.
12. Ferdinand Columbus, *The Life of Christopher Columbus by His Son Ferdinand*, trans. and ed. Benjamin Keen (New Brunswick, NJ: Rutgers University Press, 1959), p. 60.
13. Columbus, *Log of Christopher Columbus*, p. 76.
14. Ibid.
15. Ibid.
16. Ibid., p. 78.
17. Ibid., p. 77.
18. Ibid., p. 81.
19. Ibid.
20. Ibid., p. 88.
21. Ibid., p. 89.
22. Ibid., p. 92.
23. Ibid., p. 93.
24. Ibid., p. 102.
25. Ibid., p. 107.
26. Ibid., p. 113.
27. Ibid., p. 129.
28. Ibid., p. 157.
29. Ibid., p. 138.
30. Ibid., p. 145.
31. Ibid.
32. Ibid., p. 147.
33. Ibid., p. 149.
34. Ibid., p. 155.

35. Ibid., p. 163.
36. Ibid., p. 166.
37. Ibid.

CHAPTER FIFTY-TWO

1. Christopher Columbus, *The Log of Christopher Columbus,* trans. Robert H. Fuson (Camden, ME: International Marine Publishing Co., 1987), p. 179.
2. Ibid., p. 184.
3. Ibid., p. 185.
4. Ibid.
5. Ibid., p. 187.
6. Ibid., p. 188.
7. Ibid., p. 189.
8. Ibid., p. 192.
9. Ibid., p. 194.
10. Samuel Eliot Morison, *Admiral of the Ocean Sea. A Life of Christopher Columbus* (Boston: Little, Brown, 1942), p. 340.
11. Columbus, *Log of Christopher Columbus,* p. 194.
12. Ibid., p. 195.
13. Ibid.
14. Ibid.
15. Ferdinand Columbus, *The Life of Christopher Columbus by His Son Ferdinand,* trans. and ed. Benjamin Keen (New Brunswick, NJ: Rugers University Press, 1959), p. 101.
16. Ibid.
17. Ibid.
18. Columbus, *Log of Christopher Columbus,* p. 196.
19. Salvador de Madariaga, *Christopher Columbus, Being the Life of the Very Magnificent Lord Don Cristobal Colón* (New York: Macmillan, 1940), p. 241.
20. Ibid.
21. Columbus, *Life of Christopher Columbus,* p. 101; Gianni Granzotto, *Christopher Columbus: The Dream and the Obsession* (Garden City, NY: Doubleday, 1985), p. 190.
22. Pietro Martire d'Anghiera, *Epistolarios,* ed. and trans. José López de Toro (Madrid: Imprenta Gongora, 1953), vol. 9, p. 246.
23. Columbus, *Life of Christopher Columbus,* p. 106.
24. John H. Parry and Robert G. Keith, eds., *New Iberian World. A Documentary History of the Discovery and Settlement of Latin America to the Early Seventeenth Century,* vol. 2, *The Caribbean* (New York: Times Books, 1984), p. 72.
25. Columbus, *Life of Christopher Columbus,* p. 109.
26. Ibid.
27. Morison, *Admiral of the Ocean Sea,* p. 370.
28. Ivan Cloulas, *The Borgias,* trans. Gilda Roberts (New York: Franklin Watts, 1989), pp. 78–79.
29. J. H. Parry, *The Age of Reconnaissance: Discovery, Exploration and Settlement, 1450–1650* (Berkeley: University of California Press, 1963), pp. 151–52.
30. Morison, *Admiral of the Ocean Sea,* p. 373.
31. William H. Prescott, *History of the Reign of Ferdinand and Isabella the Catholic* (Philadelphia: Lippincott, 1872 [1837]), vol. 2, p. 178.

CHAPTER FIFTY-THREE

1. William H. Prescott, *History of the Reign of Ferdinand and Isabella the Catholic* (Philadelphia: Lippincott, 1872 [1837]), vol. 2, pp. 379–80.
2. Tarsicio de Azcona, *Isabel la Católica: Estudio crítico de su vida y su reinado* (Madrid: Biblioteca de Autores Cristianos, 1964), p. 591.
3. Jocelyn N. Hillgarth, *The Spanish Kingdoms, 1250–1516* (Oxford: Clarendon Press, 1978), vol. 2, p. 472.
4. Rafael Sabatini, *Torquemada and the Spanish Inquisition* (Boston: Houghton Mifflin, 1924), p. 427.
5. Pietro Martire d'Anghiera, *Epistolarios*, ed. and trans. José López de Toro (Madrid: Imprenta Gongora, 1953), vol. 9, p. 295.
6. Alvar Gomez de Castro, *Delas Hazañas de Francisco de Cisneros*, ed. and trans., Jose Oroz Reta (Madrid: Fundacion Universitaria Espanola, 1984), p. 51.
7. Prescott, *History of the Reign of Ferdinand and Isabella*, vol. 2, p. 386.
8. Ibid., p. 387.
9. Ludwig Pastor, *The History of the Popes, from the Close of the Middle Ages* (St. Louis: B. Herder, 1923), vol. 5, p. 426.
10. Ibid., p. 433.
11. Ibid., p. 438.
12. Ibid., pp. 446–47.
13. Ivan Cloulas, *The Borgias*, trans. Gilda Roberts (New York: Franklin Watts, 1989), p. 107.
14. Pastor, *History of the Popes*, p. 454.
15. Cloulas, *The Borgias*, p. 108; Andrés Bernáldez, *Historia de los reyes católicos Don Fernando y Doña Isabel*, BAE (Madrid: Ediciones Atlas, 1953), vol. 70, p. 684.
16. Prescott, *History of the Reign of Ferdinand and Isabella*, vol. 2, p. 286.
17. Pastor, *History of the Popes*, pp. 463–64.

CHAPTER FIFTY-FOUR

1. Gustav Adolf Bergenroth, ed., *Calendar of Letters, Despatches and State Papers Relating to the Negotiations Between England and Spain Preserved in the Archives at Simancas and Elsewhere*, vol. 1, *Henry VII, 1485–1509* (London: Kraus, 1969 [1862]), p. 64.
2. Ibid., p. 55.
3. Ibid., p. 53.
4. Ibid., p. 54.
5. Michael Van Cleave Alexander, *The First of the Tudors. A Study of Henry VII and His Reign* (Totowa, NJ: Rowman and Littlefield, 1980), p. 112.
6. Bergenroth, *Calendar of Letters*, vol. 1, p. 61.
7. Ibid.
8. Ibid., p. 112.
9. Pietro Martire d'Anghiera, *Epistolarios*, ed. and trans. José López de Toro (Madrid: Imprenta Gongora, 1953), vol. 9, p. 325.

CHAPTER FIFTY-FIVE

1. Salvador de Madariaga, *Christopher Columbus, Being the Life of the Very Magnificent Lord Don Cristobal Colón* (New York: Macmillan, 1940), p. 293.
2. Samuel Eliot Morison, *Admiral of the Ocean Sea. A Life of Christopher Columbus* (Boston: Little, Brown, 1942), p. 435.

3. Christopher Columbus, *Textos y documentos completos*, 2nd ed., ed. Consuelo Varela (Madrid: Alianza Universidad, 1984), p. 149.
4. Ferdinand Columbus, *The Life of Christopher Columbus by His Son Ferdinand*, trans. and ed. Benjamin Keen (New Brunswick, NJ: Rutgers University Press, 1959), p. 128.
5. Ibid., p. 142.
6. Ibid., p. 148.
7. Morison, *Admiral of the Ocean Sea*, p. 485.
8. Christopher Columbus, *The Authentic Letters of Columbus*, ed. and trans. William Eleroy Curtis (Chicago: Field Columbian Museum, 1895), p. 125.
9. William Thomas Walsh, *Isabella of Spain: The Last Crusader* (New York: Robert M. McBride Co., 1930), p. 431.
10. Ibid.
11. Andrés Bernáldez, *Historia de los reyes católicos Don Fernando y Doña Isabel*, BAE (Madrid: Ediciones Atlas, 1953), vol. 70, p. 678.
12. Columbus, *Life of Christopher Columbus*, p. 169.
13. Ibid., p. 174.
14. Columbus, *Textos y documentos completos*, p. 264.
15. Columbus, *Authentic Letters of Columbus*, p. 125.
16. Madariaga, *Christopher Columbus*, pp. 304–5.
17. William H. Prescott, *History of the Reign of Ferdinand and Isabella the Catholic* (Philadelphia: Lippincott, 1872 [1837]), vol. 2, p. 363.
18. Pietro Martire d'Anghiera, *Epistolarios*, ed. and trans. José López de Toro (Madrid: Imprenta Gongora, 1953), vol. 9, p. 334.
19. Ibid.
20. Ibid.
21. Ibid., p. 346; José Camon Aznar, *Sobre la muerte del principe Don Juan* (Madrid: Real Academia de la Historia, 1963), p. 79.
22. Luis Suárez Fernández, Juan de Mata Carriazo Arroquia, and Manuel Fernández Álvarez, *La España de los Reyes Católicos (1474–1515)* (Madrid: Espasa-Calpe, 3rd ed., 1983), vol. 2, p. 476.
23. Bernáldez, *Historia de los reyes católicos*, vol. 70, p. 691.

CHAPTER FIFTY-SIX

1. Philippe de Commynes, *Memoirs*, ed. Samuel Kinser, trans. Isabelle Cazeaux (Columbia, SC: University of South Carolina Press, 1969), vol. 2, p. 585.
2. Pietro Martire d'Anghiera, *Epistolarios*, ed. and trans. José López de Toro (Madrid: Imprenta Gongora, 1953), vol. 9, p. 365.
3. José Camon Aznar, *Sobre la muerte del principe Don Juan* (Madrid: Real Academia de la Historia, 1963), p. 33.
4. Ibid., p. 35.
5. Andrés Bernáldez, *Historia de los reyes católicos Don Fernando y Doña Isabel*, BAE (Madrid: Ediciones Atlas, 1953), vol. 70, p. 692.
6. William H. Prescott, *History of the Reign of Ferdinand and Isabella the Catholic* (Philadelphia: Lippincott, 1872 [1837]), vol. 2, p. 363.
7. Ibid.
8. Ludwig Pastor, *The History of the Popes, from the Close of the Middle Ages* (St. Louis: B. Herder, 1923), vol. 5, p. 500.
9. Ibid., p. 513.
10. Bernáldez, *Historia de los reyes católicos*, vol. 70, p. 692.
11. Prescott, *History of the Reign of Ferdinand and Isabella*, vol. 2, pp. 393–94.

12. Ibid., p. 394.
13. Manuel de Castro, "Confesors franciscanos en la corte de los reyes católicos," *Archivo Ibero-Americano,* 2nd series, 34 (1974): 83.
14. Gustav Adolf Bergenroth, ed., *Calendar of Letters, Despatches and State Papers Relating to the Negotiations Between England and Spain Preserved in the Archives at Simancas and Elsewhere,* vol. 1, *Henry VII, 1485–1509* (London: Kraus, 1969 [1862]), p. 164.
15. Ibid., pp. 180–81.
16. Ibid., p. 181.
17. Ibid., p. 200.
18. Ibid., p. 199.
19. Ibid., p. 202.

CHAPTER FIFTY-SEVEN

1. William H. Prescott, *History of the Reign of Ferdinand and Isabella the Catholic* (Philadelphia: Lippincott, 1872 [1837]), vol. 2, p. 416.
2. Ibid., p. 419.
3. Niccolo Machiavelli, *The Prince,* trans. and ed. Daniel Donno (New York: Bantam Books, 1966), p. 24.
4. Pietro Martire d'Anghiera, *Epistolarios,* ed. and trans. José López de Toro (Madrid: Imprenta Gongora, 1953), vol. 9, pp. 405–6.
5. Helen Nader, *The Mendoza Family in the Spanish Renaissance, 1350 to 1550* (New Brunswick, NJ: Rutgers University Press, 1979), p. 157.
6. Prescott, *History of the Reign of Ferdinand and Isabella,* vol. 2, p. 423.
7. Diego Clemencin, *Elogio de la reina Católica Doña Isabel,* vol. 6, *Memorias de la Real Academia de la Historia* (Madrid: Real Academia de la Historia, 1821), p. 392.
8. Machiavelli, *The Prince,* p. 20.
9. William Thomas Walsh, *Isabella of Spain: The Last Crusader* (New York: Robert M. McBride Co., 1930), p. 448; Amarie Dennis, *Seek the Darkness. The Story of Juana la Loca,* 3rd ed. (Madrid: Sucesores de Rivadeneyra, 1956), p. 57.
10. Martire, *Epistolarios,* vol. 9, p. 411.
11. Dennis, *Seek the Darkness,* p. 60.

CHAPTER FIFTY-EIGHT

1. Ferdinand Columbus, *The Life of Christopher Columbus by His Son Ferdinand,* trans. and ed. Benjamin Keen (New Brunswick, NJ: Rutgers University Press, 1959), p. 225.
2. Samuel Eliot Morison, *Admiral of the Ocean Sea. A Life of Christopher Columbus* (Boston: Little, Brown, 1942), p. 578.
3. Columbus, *Life of Christopher Columbus,* p. 225.
4. Morison, *Admiral of the Ocean Sea,* p. 578.
5. Salvador de Madariaga, *Christopher Columbus, Being the Life of the Very Magnificent Lord Don Cristobal Colón* (New York: Macmillan, 1940), p. 342.
6. Morison, *Admiral of the Ocean Sea,* p. 525.
7. Christopher Columbus, *Textos y documentos completos,* 2nd ed., ed. Consuelo Varela (Madrid: Alianza Universidad, 1984), p. 240.
8. Columbus, *Life of Christopher Columbus,* p. 188.
9. Columbus, *Textos y documentos completos,* p. 216; Bartolomé de Las Casas, *History of the Indies,* trans. and ed. Andree Collard (New York: Harper & Row, 1971), p. 241.
10. Columbus, *Textos y documentos completos,* p. 241.
11. Ibid., p. 243.

12. Columbus, *Life of Christopher Columbus*, p. 214.
13. Madariaga, *Christopher Columbus*, p. 342.
14. Ibid., p. 343.
15. Ibid., p. 349.
16. Ibid.
17. Ibid., p. 350.
18. Columbus, *Textos y documentos completos*, p. 264.
19. Ibid., pp. 269–70.
20. Morison, *Admiral of the Ocean Sea*, pp. 582–83.

CHAPTER FIFTY-NINE

1. Gustav Adolf Bergenroth, ed., *Calendar of Letters, Despatches and State Papers Relating to the Negotiations Between England and Spain Preserved in the Archives at Simancas and Elsewhere*, vol. 1, *Henry VII, 1485–1509* (London: Kraus, 1969 [1862]), p. 217.
2. Ibid., p. 156.
3. Ibid., p. 212.
4. Ibid., p. 190.
5. Ibid., pp. 210–11.
6. Ibid., p. 253.
7. Ibid., p. 251.
8. St. Thomas More, *Selected Letters*, ed. Elizabeth Frances Rogers (New Haven: Yale University Press, 1961), pp. 2–3.
9. Bergenroth, *Calendar of Letters*, vol. 1, p. 264.
10. Ibid., p. 265.

CHAPTER SIXTY

1. Amarie Dennis, *Seek the Darkness. The Story of Juana la Loca*, 3rd ed. (Madrid: Sucesores de Rivadeneyra, 1956), p. 74.
2. Ibid., p. 68.
3. William H. Prescott, *History of the Reign of Ferdinand and Isabella the Catholic* (Philadelphia: Lippincott, 1872 [1837]), vol. 2, p. 65.
4. Pietro Martire d'Anghiera, *Epistolarios*, ed. and trans. José López de Toro (Madrid: Imprenta Gongora, 1955), vol. 10, p. 42.

CHAPTER SIXTY-ONE

1. Niccolo Machiavelli, *The Prince*, trans. and ed. Daniel Donno (New York: Bantam Books, 1966), p. 56.
2. William H. Prescott, *History of the Reign of Ferdinand and Isabella the Catholic* (Philadelphia: Lippincott, 1872 [1837]), vol. 3, p. 218.
3. Pietro Martire d'Anghiera, *Epistolarios*, ed. and trans. José López de Toro (Madrid: Imprenta Gongora, 1955), vol. 10, p. 42.
4. Ibid., p. 48.
5. Townsend Miller, *The Castles and the Crown: Spain: 1451–1555* (New York: Coward-McCann, 1963), p. 219.
6. Narciso Alonso Cortes, "Dos medicos de los reyes católicos," *Hispania* 11 (45) (1951): 617–18.
7. Luis Suárez Fernández, Juan de Mata Carriazo Arroquia, and Manuel Fernández

Álvarez, *La España de los Reyes Católicos (1474–1515)* (Madrid: Espasa-Calpe, 3rd ed., 1983), vol. 2, p. 629.

8. Ibid.
9. Amarie Dennis, *Seek the Darkness. The Story of Juana la Loca,* 3rd ed. (Madrid: Sucesores de Rivadeneyra, 1956), p. 100.
10. Prescott, *History of the Reign of Ferdinand and Isabella,* vol. 3, p. 71.
11. Ibid., p. 88, n. 1.
12. Jocelyn N. Hillgarth, *The Spanish Kingdoms, 1250–1516* (Oxford: Clarendon Press, 1978), vol. 2, p. 558.

CHAPTER SIXTY-TWO

1. Pietro Martire d'Anghiera, *Epistolarios,* ed. and trans. José López de Toro (Madrid: Imprenta Gongora, 1955), vol. 10, p. 85.
2. Luis Suárez Fernández, Juan de Mata Carriazo Arroquia, and Manuel Fernández Álvarez, *La España de los Reyes Católicos (1474–1515)* (Madrid: Espasa-Calpe, 3rd ed., 1983), vol. 2, p. 636.
3. Amarie Dennis, *Seek the Darkness. The Story of Juana la Loca,* 3rd ed. (Madrid: Sucesores de Rivadeneyra, 1956), p. 103.
4. Suárez Fernández, de Mata Carriazo Arroquia, and Fernández Álvarez, *La España de los Reyes Católicos,* vol. 2, p. 638.
5. Townsend Miller, *The Castles and the Crown: Spain: 1451–1555* (New York: Coward-McCann, 1963), p. 229.
6. Martire, *Epistolarios,* vol. 10, pp. 85–86.
7. William H. Prescott, *History of the Reign of Ferdinand and Isabella the Catholic* (Philadelphia: Lippincott, 1872 [1837]), vol. 3, p. 174.
8. Isabel I, *Testamento de Isabel la Católica y codicilio. La Testamentaria de Isabel la Católica* (Valladolid: Instituto Isabel la Católica de Historia Ecclesiastica, 1968), p. 448.
9. Ibid., pp. 451–52.
10. Ibid., p. 469.
11. Ibid., p. 458.
12. Ibid., p. 463.
13. Ibid.
14. Ibid., p. 461.
15. Ibid., pp. 461–62; Prescott, *History of the Reign of Ferdinand and Isabella,* vol. 3, p. 178.
16. Martire, *Epistolarios,* vol. 10, p. 87; Prescott, *History of the Reign of Ferdinand and Isabella,* vol. 3, p. 175.
17. Christopher Columbus, *Textos y documentos completos,* 2nd ed., ed. Consuelo Varela (Madrid: Alianza Universidad, 1984), pp. 329–30; Gianni Granzotto, *Christopher Columbus: The Dream and the Obsession* (Garden City, NY: Doubleday, 1985), p. 266.
18. Isabel I, *Testamento de Isabel la Católica,* p. 482; Prescott, *History of the Reign of Ferdinand and Isabella,* vol. 3, pp. 180–81.
19. Prescott, *History of the Reign of Ferdinand and Isabella,* vol. 3, p. 183.
20. Martire, *Epistolarios,* vol. 10, p. 90; Prescott, *History of the Reign of Ferdinand and Isabella,* vol. 3, p. 184.
21. Suárez Fernández, de Mata Carriazo Arroquia, and Fernández Alváres, *La España de los Reyes Católicos,* vol. 2, p. 640.
22. Fernando del Pulgar, *Crónica de los señores reyes católicos Don Fernando y Doña*

Isabel de Castilla y de Aragón, BAE (Madrid: Ediciones Atlas, 1953), vol. 70, p. 523.

23. Martire, *Epistolarios,* vol. 10, pp. 93–94.

EPILOGUE

1. Roger Bigelow Merriman, *The Rise of the Spanish Empire in the Old World and in the New* (New York: Macmillan, 1918), vol. 2, p. 330.

2. William H. Prescott, *History of the Reign of Ferdinand and Isabella the Catholic* (Philadelphia: Lippincott, 1872 [1837]), vol. 3, pp. 236–37.

3. Alan Lloyd, *The Spanish Centuries* (Garden City, NY: Doubleday, 1968), p. 111.

4. Prescott, *History of the Reign of Ferdinand and Isabella,* vol. 3, p. 273.

5. Ibid., p. 281.

BIBLIOGRAPHY

PRIMARY DOCUMENTARY AND NARRATIVE SOURCES

Aquinas, Saint Thomas. *Basic Writings of Saint Thomas Aquinas*. Ed. Anton C. Pegis. New York: Random House, 1945.

Archivo General de Simancas (AGS) Patrimonio Real.

Arribas Arranz, Filemón. *Documentos de los Reyes Católicos, relacionados con Valladolid*. Valladolid: Imprenta Sever-Cuesta, 1953.

Beltrán de Heredia, Vicente. *Cartulario de la Universidad de Salamanca*, vol. 3, *La Universidad en el Siglo de Oro*. Salamanca: Universidad de Salamanca, 1971.

Bergenroth, Gustav Adolf, ed. *Calendar of Letters, Despatches and State Papers Relating to the Negotiations Between England and Spain Preserved in the Archives at Simancas and Elsewhere, vol. 1, Henry VII, 1485–1509*. London: Kraus, 1969 [1862].

Bernáldez, Andrés. *Historia de los reyes católicos Don Fernando y Doña Isabel*, Biblioteca de Autores Españoles, vol. 70, pp. 567–773. Madrid: Ediciones Atlas, 1953.

Boccaccio, Giovanni. *The Decameron*. Trans. Mark Musa and Peter Bondanella. New York: New American Library, 1982.

Castiglione, Baldesar. *The Book of the Courtier*. Trans. Charles S. Singleton. New York: Doubleday, 1959.

Castillo, Diego Enríquez, ed. *Crónica del Rey Don Enrique el Cuarto*, Biblioteca de Autores Españoles, vol. 70, pp. 97–227. Madrid: Ediciones Atlas, 1953.

Clemencin, Diego. *Elogio de la reina Católica Doña Isabel*, vol. 6, *Memorias de la Real Academia de la Historia*. Madrid: Real Academia de la Historia, 1821.

Columbus, Christopher. *The Authentic Letters of Columbus*. Ed. and trans. William Eleroy Curtis. Chicago: Field Columbian Museum, 1895.

———. *Cartas de particulares a Colón y relaciones coetaneas*. Ed. Juan Gil and Consuelo Varela. Madrid: Alianza Universidad, 1984.

———. *The Log of Christopher Columbus*. Trans. Robert H. Fuson. Camden, ME: International Marine Publishing Co., 1987.

————. *Textos y documentos completos,* 2nd ed. Ed. Consuelo Varela. Madrid: Alianza Universidad, 1984.

Columbus, Ferdinand. *The Life of Christopher Columbus by His Son Ferdinand.* Trans. and ed. Benjamin Keen. New Brunswick: Rutgers University Press, 1959.

Commynes, Philippe de. *Memoirs.* 2 vols. Ed. Samuel Kinser, trans. Isabella Cazeaux. Columbia, SC: University of South Carolina Press, 1969.

Diaz-Plaja, Fernando, ed. *Siglo XV: Historia de España en sus documentos.* Madrid: Ediciones Catedra, 1984.

Gómez de Castro, Alvar. *De las hazañas de Francisco de Cisneros.* Ed. and trans. Jose Oroz Reta. Madrid: Fundacion Universitaria Española, 1984.

Gómez de Fuensalida, Gutierre. *Correspondencia de Gutierre Gómez de Fuensalida, embajador en Alemania, Flandes e Inglaterra (1469–1509).* Ed. Duque de Berwick y Alba. Madrid: 1907.

Isabel I. *Testamento de Isabel la Católica y codicilio. La Testamentaria de Isabel la Católica.* Valladolid: Instituto Isabel la Católica de Historia Eclesiastica, 1968.

Las Casas, Bartolomé de. *History of the Indies.* Trans. and ed. Andree Collard. New York: Harper & Row, 1971.

————. *A Selection of His Writings.* Trans. and ed. George Sanderlin. New York: Knopf, 1971.

Letts, Malcolm, trans. *The Travels of Leo of Rozmital.* Hakluyt Society, 2nd ser. no. 108. Cambridge: Cambridge University Press, 1957.

Luna, Álvaro de. *Crónica de Don Alvaro de Luna.* Ed. Juan de Mata Carriazo. Madrid: Espasa-Calpe, 1940.

————. *Libro de las virtuosas e clares mujeres.* Madrid: Sociedad de Bibliofilos Españoles, 1891.

Machiavelli, Niccolo. *The Prince.* Trans. and ed. Daniel Donno. New York: Bantam Books, 1966.

Mariana, Juan de. *History of the Royal Genealogy of Spain.* Trans. Thomas Richers. London: James Round, 1724.

Marineo Siculo, Lucio. *Vida y hechos de los reyes católicos.* Madrid: Ediciones Atlas, 1943.

Martire d'Anghiera, Pietro. *Epistolarios,* vols. 9–10. Ed. and trans. José López de Toro. Madrid: Imprenta Gongora, 1953, 1957.

Memorias de Don Enrique IV de Castilla. Colección Diplomatica de Enrique IV. Madrid: Real Academia de la Historia, 1835–1913.

Millares Carlo, Agustín. *Contribuciones documentales a la historia de Madrid,* vol. 13, *Biblioteca de Estudios Madrilenos.* Madrid: Instituto de Estudios Madrilenos, 1971.

More, Saint Thomas. *Selected Letters.* Ed. Elizabeth Frances Rogers. New Haven: Yale University Press, 1961.

Navarrete, Martin Fernández de, ed. *Colección de los documentos de los viajes y descubrimientos,* 2nd ed. Madrid: Imprenta Nacional, 1859.

Ochoa, Eugenio de, ed. *Epistolario Español. Colección de cartas de Españoles ilustres antiguos y modernos,* vol. 2, *Biblioteca de Autores Españoles.* Madrid: Ediciones Atlas, 1965.

Oviedo, Gonzalo Fernández de. *Libro de la camara real del principe Don Juan.* Madrid: Imprenta de la viuda é hijos de Galiano, 1870.

Palencia, Alonso de. *Crónica de Enrique IV. Biblioteca de Autores Españoles,* Vols. 257, 258, and 267. Ed. Antonio Paz y Melia. Madrid: Ediciones Atlas, 1973–1975.

Palma, Bachiller. *Divina Retribución.* Madrid: Sociedad de Bibliofilos Españoles, 1879.

Parry, John H., and Robert G. Keith, eds. *New Iberian World. A Documentary History of*

the Discovery and Settlement of Latin America to the Early Seventeenth Century, vol.
2, *The Caribbean*. New York: Times Books, 1984.

Paz y Melia, Antonio, ed. *El cronista Alonso de Palencia. Su vida y sus obras: Sus
Decadas y las crónicas contemporaneas*. Madrid: Hispanic Society of America, 1914.

Perez de Guzman, Fernan. *Generaciones, semblanzas e obras de los excelentes reyes de
España Don Enrique el Tercero e Don Juan el Segundo*, vol. 68, *Biblioteca de Autores
Españoles, 697–719*. Madrid: Ediciones Atlas, 1875.

Ponce de León, Rodrigo, Marqués de Cádiz. *Historia de los hechos de Don Rodrigo Ponce
de León, Marqués de Cádiz (1443–1488)*. Colección de Documentos Ineditos de la
Historia de España, vol. 106, pp. 145–317. Vaduz: Kraus Reprint Ltd., 1966 [1893].

Pulgar, Fernando del. *Claros varones de Castilla*. Ed. Robert Brian Tate. Oxford:
Clarendon Press, 1971.

———. *Coplas de Mingo Revulgo*. Ed. Rodrigo de Cota. Madrid: D. Antonio de Sancha,
1888.

———. *Crónica de los señores reyes católicos Don Fernando y Doña Isabel de Castilla
y de Aragón*, Biblioteca de Autores Españoles, vol. 70, pp. 229–565. Madrid:
Ediciones Atlas, 1953.

———. *Epistolas y Coplas de Mingo Revulgo*. Ed. J. Dóminguez Bordona. Madrid:
Ediciones de "La Lectura," 1929.

Puyol, Julio, ed. *Crónica incompleta de los Reyes Católicos, 1469–1476*. Madrid:
Tipografia de Archivos, 1934.

Rodriguez Valencia, Vincente. *Isabel la Católica en la opinion de españoles y extranjeros.
Siglos XV al XX*. Valladolid: Instituto de Isabel la Católica de la Historia Eclesiastica,
1970.

Rumeu de Armas, Antonio, ed. *Itinerario de los reyes católicos, 1474–1516*. Madrid:
Consejo Superior de Investigaciones Cientificas, 1974.

Suárez Fernández, Luis. *Documentos acerca de la Expulsion de los Judios*. Valladolid:
Consejo Superior de Investigaciones Científicas, 1964.

Valera, Diego de. *Epistolas*. Madrid: Sociedad de Bibliofilos Españoles, 1878.

———. *Memorial de diversas hazañas: Crónica de Enrique IV*. Ed. Juan de Mata
Carriazo. Madrid: Espasa-Calpe, 1941.

Zurita, Jeronimo. *Anales de la Corona de Aragón*. 8 vols. Ed. Angel Canellas López.
Zaragoza: Instituto Fernando el Católico, 1977.

SECONDARY WORKS

Agnado Bleye, Pedro. " 'Tanto Monta': La concordia de Segovia y la Empresa de Fernando
el Católico." *Estudios Segovianos* 1 (1949): 381–389.

Alba, Duque de. "La copa de oro de los Marqueses de Moya." *Estudios Segovianos* 1
(1949): 183–88.

Alonso Cortes, Narciso. "Dos medicos de los reyes católicos." *Hispania* 11 (45) (1951):
607–57.

Álvarez Rubiano, Pablo. "Diego Arías Dávila." *Estudios Segovianos* 1 (1949): 367–72.

Anderson, Ruth Matilda. *Hispanic Costume, 1480–1530*. New York: Hispanic Society of
America, 1979.

Ariès, Philippe. *Centuries of Childhood. A Social History of Family Life*. Trans. Robert
Baldick. London: Jonathan Cape, 1962.

———, and Georges Duby, eds. *A History of Private Life*, vol. 2, *Revelations of the
Medieval World*. Trans. Robert Goldhammer. Cambridge, MA: Harvard University/
Belknap Press, 1988.

Asenjo González, María. *Segovia: La ciudad y su tierra a fines del medievo*. Segovia: Diputación Provincial de Segovia, 1986.

Azcona, Tarsicio de. *Isabel la Católica: Estudio crítico de su vida y su reinado*. Madrid: Biblioteca de Autores Cristianos, 1964.

Baer, Yitzhak. *History of the Jews in Christian Spain*. 2 vols. Philadelphia: Jewish Publication Society of America, 1961.

Ballesteros Gaibrois, Manuel. *Isabel de Castilla, Reina Católica de España*, 2nd ed. Madrid: Editora Nacional, 1970.

———. *La Obra de Isabel la Católica*. Segovia: Diputación Provincial de Segovia, 1953.

———. *Valencia y los Reyes Católicos (1479–1493)*. 2 vols. Valencia: F. Vives Mora, 1943.

Bard, Rachel. *Navarra: The Durable Kingdom*. Reno: University of Nevada Press, 1982.

Baron, Hans. *The Crisis of the Early Italian Renaissance*. Princeton: Princeton University Press, 1966.

Beinart, Haim, *The Conversos on Trial: The Inquisition in Ciudad Real*. Jerusalem: Magnus Press Hebrew University, 1981.

Benito Ruano, Eloy. *Toledo en el siglo XV: Vida politica*. Madrid: Consejo Superior de Investigaciones Científicas, 1961.

Bentley, Jerry H. *Politics and Culture in Renaissance Naples*. Princeton: Princeton University Press, 1987.

Bernis, Carmen. "Modas moriscas en la sociedad cristiana española del siglo XV y principios del XVI." *Boletín de la Real Academia de la Historia* 144 (1959): 199–236.

———. *Trajes y modas en la España de los Reyes Católicos*,vol. 1, *Las mujeres*. Madrid: Instituto Diego Velazquez del Consejo Superior de Investigaciones Científicas, 1978.

———. *Trajes y modas en la España de los Reyes Católicos*, vol. 2, *Los hombres*. Madrid: Instituto Diego Velazquez del Consejo Superior de Investigaciones Científicas, 1979.

Bindoff, S. T. *Tudor England*. Harmondsworth: Pelican, 1950.

Bisson, Thomas N. *The Medieval Crown of Aragon. A Short History*. Oxford: Clarendon Press, 1986.

Borchsenius, Poul. *The Three Rings: The History of the Spanish Jews*. Trans. Michael Heron. London: George Allen and Unwin, 1963.

Bullough, Vern. *The Subordinate Sex*. Urbana: University of Illinois Press, 1973.

Camoëns, Luis de. *The Lusiad*. Trans. Richard Fanshawe, ed. Jeremiah D. M. Ford. Cambridge, MA: Harvard University Press, 1940.

Camon Aznar, José. *Sobre la muerte del principe Don Juan*. Madrid: Real Academia de la Historia, 1963.

Cardini, Franco. *Europe 1492: Portrait of a Continent Five Hundred Years Ago*. New York: Facts On File, 1989.

Carretero, Zamora, Juan Manuel. *Cortes, monarquía, ciudades: Las Cortes de Castilla a comienzos de la epoca moderna (1476–1515)*. Madrid: Siglo XXI, 1988.

Castro, Manuel de. "Confesors franciscanos en la corte de los reyes católicos." *Archivo Ibero-Americano*, 2nd ser., 34 (1974): 55–126.

Cepeda Adan, José. "La sociedad en la época de los Reyes Católicos." *Estudios Americanos* 2 (6) (1950): 353–74.

Chabod, Federico. *Machiavelli and the Renaissance*. Trans. David Moore. London: Bowes and Bowes, 1958.

Chaytor, H. J. *A History of Aragon and Catalonia*. London: Methuen, 1933.

Christian, William A., Jr. *Local Religion in Sixteenth-Century Spain*. Princeton: Princeton University Press, 1981.

Cleugh, James. *Chant Royal*. New York: Doubleday, 1970.

Cloulas, Ivan. *The Borgias*. Trans. Gilda Roberts. New York: Franklin Watts, 1989.

Comay, Joan. *The Diaspora Story: The Epic of the Jewish People Among the Nations.* New York: Random House, 1980.

Condert, Allison. *Alchemy: The Philosopher's Stone.* Boulder: Shambhala, 1980.

Cutter, Irving S., and Henry R. Viets. *A Short History of Midwifery.* Philadelphia: W. B. Saunders, 1964.

Danvila, Manuel. "Tres documentos ineditos referentes al matrimonio de los reyes católicos—1468, 1469 y 1470." *Boletín de la Real Academia de la Historia* 40 (1) (1902): 131–39.

Dennis, Amarie. *Seek the Darkness. The Story of Juana la Loca,* 3rd. ed. Madrid: Sucesores de Rivadeneyra, 1956.

Deyermond, Alan. *The Middle Ages.* New York: Barnes and Noble, 1971.

Deyermond, Alan, and Ian Macpherson, eds. *The Age of the Catholic Monarchs, 1474–1516: Literary Studies in Memory of Keith Whinnon.* Liverpool: Liverpool University Press, 1989.

Dumm, Demetrius. *The Theological Basis of Virginity According to St. Jerome.* Latrobe, PA: St. Vincent Archabbey, 1961.

Elliott, J. H. *Imperial Spain, 1469–1716.* Harmondsworth: Penguin, 1970 [1963].

Erasmus, Desiderius. *The Correspondence of Erasmus.* Trans. R. A. B. Mynors and D. F. S. Thomson, annotated James K. McConica. Toronto: University of Toronto Press, 1977.

Espejo, Cristobal, and Julian Paz. "Los Antiguos ferias de Medina del Campo," *Boletín de la Sociedad Castellana de Excursiones* 6 (72) (1908): 575–77.

Esteve Barba, Francisco. *Alfonso Carrillo de Acuña: Autor de la unidad España.* Barcelona: Editorial Amaltea, 1943.

Fernández, Fidel. *Fray Hernando de Talavera: Confesor de los reyes católicos y primer arzobispo de Granada.* Madrid: Biblioteca Nueva, 1942.

Fernández, Manuel. *España y los españoles en los tiempos modernos.* Salamanca: Álvarez/Universidad de Salamanca, 1979.

Fernández-Armesto, Felipe. *Ferdinand and Isabella.* New York: Taplinger, 1975.

Fernández-Domínguez Prieto, Enrique. "Zamora en la encrucijada historica de España y Portugal," *Studia Zamorensia* 3 (1982): 25–62.

Ferrandis Torres, Manuel, ed. "Una proyección geografica del pensamiento de Isabel." In *Curso de Conferencias sobre la politica Africana de los Reyes Católicos,* vol. 1, pp. 49–67. Madrid: Instituto de Estudios Africanos, 1951.

Ferrara, Orestes. *Un pleito sucesorio: Enrique IV, Isabel de Castilla y la Beltraneja.* Madrid: Ediciones La Nave, 1945.

Fildes, Valerie. *Wet Nursing: A History from Antiquity to the Present.* New York: Basil Blackwell, 1988.

Fitzmaurice-Kelly, Julia. "Women in Sixteenth-Century Spain." *Revue Hispanique* 70 (157) (1927): 557–632.

Forbes, Thomas Rogers. *The Midwife and the Witch.* New Haven: Yale University Press, 1966.

Garcia, Vicente Romano, ed. *Coplas de la Panadera.* Pamplona: Aguilar, 1963.

Garcia y Garcia de Castro, Luís. "Un humanista en la corte de los Reyes Católicos," *Santa Cruz* 7 (12) (1948–52): 52–63.

Gies, Frances and Joseph. *Life in a Medieval Castle.* New York: Thomas Y. Crowell, 1974.

———. *Marriage and the Family in the Middle Ages.* New York: Harper & Row, 1987.

———. *Women in the Middle Ages.* New York: Harper & Row, 1978.

Gil, Juan. *Mitos y utopias del descubrimiento,* vol. 1, *Colón y su tiempo.* Madrid: Alianza Universidad, 1989.

Gil Farres, Octavio. *Historia de Moneda Española.* Madrid: Apartado, 1976.

Gold, Penny Schine. *The Lady and the Virgin: Image, Attitude and Experience in Twelfth-Century France*. Chicago: University of Chicago Press, 1985.

Gómez de la Serna, Gaspar. "Arévalo, en la infancia de la reina," *Clavileno* 2 (1950): 25–31.

Goní Gaztambide, José. *Historia de la bula de la cruzada en España*.Vitoria: Editorial del Seminario, 1958.

———. "La Santa Sede y la reconquista del reino de Granada (1479–1492)." *Hispania Sacra* 4 (1951): 43–80.

Gottfried, Robert S. *The Black Death. Natural and Human Disaster in Medieval Europe.* New York: Free Press/Macmillan, 1983.

Granzotto, Gianni. *Christopher Columbus: The Dream and the Obsession.* Garden City, NY: Doubleday, 1985.

Grau, Mariano. "Así fué coronada Isabel la Católica," *Estudios Segovianos* I (1949): 20–39.

Gual Camarena, Miguel. "El Matrimonio de Fernando e Isabel (1469). Documentación valenciana." *Hispania* 16 (63) (1956): 65–80.

Hale, J. R. *War and Society in Renaissance Europe, 1450–1620.* Baltimore: John Hopkins University Press, 1985.

Haliczer, Stephen. *The Comuneros of Castile: The Forging of a Revolution, 1475–1521.* Madison: University of Wisconsin Press, 1981.

Haliczer, Stephen, ed. and trans. *Inquisition and Society in Early Modern Europe.* London: Croom Helm, 1987.

Hare, Christopher. *A Queen of Queens and the Making of Spain.* New York: Scribners, 1906.

Henisch, Bridget Ann. *Fast and Feast. Food in Medieval Society.* University Park: Pennsylvania State University Press, 1976.

Herald, Jacqueline. *Renaissance Dress in Italy, 1400–1500.* London: Bell and Hyman, 1981.

Hillgarth, Jocelyn N. *The Spanish Kingdoms, 1250–1516.* 2 vols. Oxford: Clarendon Press, 1976–78.

Hueso de Chercoles, Ricardo. "Alonso de Quintanilla, un estadista en el tiempo de los reyes católicos." *Boletín del Instituto de Estudios Asturianos* 29 (84–85) (1975): 115–44.

Huizinga, Johan. *The Waning of the Middle Ages.* London: Edward Arnold, 1924.

Hume, Martin A. S. *Queens of Old Spain.* London: E. Grant Richardson, 1906.

Irving, Washington. *A Chronicle of the Conquest of Granada From the Mss. of Fray Antonio Agapida.* 2 vols. New York: AMS Press, 1970 [1829].

———. *Tales of the Alhambra.* Madrid: GREFOL, 1981 [1832].

Kagan, Richard L. *Students and Society in Early Modern Spain.* Baltimore: Johns Hopkins University Press, 1974.

Kamen, Henry. *Inquisition and Society in Spain in the Sixteenth and Seventeenth Century.* London: Weidenfeld and Nicolson, 1985.

———. *Spain, 1469–1714. A Society of Conflict.* London: Longman, 1983.

Kayserling, M. *Christopher Columbus and the Participation of the Jews in the Spanish and Portuguese Discoveries,* 4th ed. Trans. Charles Gross. New York: Hermon Press, 1968.

Kelly-Gadol, Joan. "Did Women Have a Renaissance?" In *Becoming Visible: Women in European History,* ed. Renate Bridenthal and Claudia Koonz, pp. 139–64. Boston: Houghton Mifflin, 1977.

Kelso, Ruth. *Doctrine for a Lady of the Renaissance.* Urbana: University of Illinois Press, 1978 [1956].

Kendall, Paul Murray. *Louis XI*. New York: Norton, 1971.

Keyes, Frances Parkinson. *The Land of Stones and Saints*. Garden City, NY: Doubleday, 1957.

Labarge, Margaret Wade. *A Small Sound of the Trumpet: Women in Medieval Life*. Boston: Beacon Press, 1986.

Lacave, José Luís, ed. *Los Judios de España: Presencia Historica y Cultural*. Madrid: Graficas Monterreina, 1989.

Lacroix, Paul. *France in the Middle Ages*. New York: Frederick Ungar, 1963.

Ladero Quesada, Miguel Angel. *Castilla y la conquista del Reino de Granada*. Granada: Diputación Provincial, 1987.

————. "Notas sobre la politica confessional de los Reyes Católicos." In *Homenaje al Profesor Alarcos*, vol. 2, pp. 1–11. Valladolid: Universidad de Valladolid, 1966.

————. *El Siglo XV en Castilla. Fuentes de renta y politica fiscal*. Barcelona: Ediciones Ariel, 1982.

Lamperez y Romea, Vicente. "Los palacios de los reyes de España en la Edad Media." *Boletín de la Sociedad Castellana de Excursiones* 13 (145) (1915): 1–102.

Lavin, James D. *A History of Spanish Firearms*. London: Herbert Jenkins, 1965.

Lea, Henry Charles. *A History of the Inquisition of the Middle Ages*. 3 vols. New York: Macmillan, 1922.

Lewis, Bernard. *The Muslim Discovery of Europe*. New York: W. W. Norton, 1982.

Livermore, H. V. *A New History of Portugal*, 2nd ed. Cambridge: Cambridge University Press, 1966.

Lloyd, Alan. *The Spanish Centuries*. Garden City, NY: Doubleday, 1968.

López Alonso, Carmen. *La pobleza en la España medieval*. Madrid: Centro de Publicaciones, Ministerio de Trabajo y Seguridad Social, 1986.

Lozoya, Marques de. "El Segovia viejo: I. Exposicion de Arte Antiguo (1948)." *Estudios Segovianos* 45 (1955): 261–81.

Lunenfeld, Marvin. *Keepers of the City: The Corregidores of Isabella I of Castile (1474–1504)*. Cambridge: Cambridge University Press, 1987.

Lynch, John. *Spain under the Habsburgs*. 2 vols. New York: Oxford University Press, 1964.

Lynn, Caro. *A College Professor of the Renaissance. Lucio Marineo Siculo Among the Spanish Humanists*. Chicago: University of Chicago Press, 1937.

MacKay, Angus. *Spain in the Middle Ages: From Frontier to Empire, 1000–1500*. New York: St. Martin's Press, 1977.

McKendrick, Melveena. *Ferdinand and Isabella*. New York: Harper & Row, 1968.

Madariaga, Salvador de. *Christopher Columbus, Being the Life of the Very Magnificent Lord Don Cristobal Colón*. New York: Macmillan, 1940.

Marcus, Jacob R. *The Jew in the Medieval World, 315–1791*. Cincinnati, OH: Sinai Press, 1938.

Mariejol, Jean Hippolyte. *The Spain of Ferdinand and Isabella*. Trans. and ed. Benjamin Keen. New Brunswick, NJ: Rutgers University Press, 1961.

Martin Postigo, Maria de la Soterraina. *Los presidentes de la real cancilleria de Valladolid*. Valladolid: Instituto Cultural de Simancas, 1982.

Mattingly, Garrett. *Catherine of Aragón*. Boston: Little, Brown, 1941.

Menéndez Pidal, Ramón. "The Catholic Kings According to Machiavelli and Castiglione." In *Spain in the Fifteenth Century, 1369–1516*, ed. Roger Highfield, pp. 405–25. London: Macmillan, 1972.

————. "The Significance of the Reign of Isabella the Catholic, According to Her Contemporaries." In *Spain in the Fifteenth Century*, ed. Roger Highfield, pp. 380–404. London: Macmillan, 1972.

Menéndez Pidal de Navascues, Faustiño. *Heraldica Medieval Española*. 2 vols. Madrid: Hidalguía, 1982.

Merriman, Roger Bigelow. *The Rise of the Spanish Empire in the Old World and in the New*. 2 vols. New York: Macmillan, 1918.

Meseguer Fernández, Juan. "Franciscanismo de Isabel la Católica." *Archivo Ibero-Americano*, 2nd ser., 19 (73–74) (1959): 153–95.

———. "Isabel la Católica y los Franciscanos (1451–1476)." *Archivo Ibero-Americano*, 2nd ser., 34 (119) (1970): 1–46.

Millares Carlo, Agustín. "Contribuciones documentales a la historia de Madrid," *Biblioteca de Estudios Madrilenos* 13 (1971): 200–204.

Miller, Beth, ed. *Women in Hispanic Literature: Icons and Fallen Idols*. Berkeley: University of California Press, 1983.

Miller, Townsend. *The Castles and the Crown: Spain: 1451–1555*. New York: Coward-McCann, 1963.

———. *Henry IV of Castile, 1425–1474*. Philadelphia: Lippincott, 1972.

Moorman, John R. H. *A History of the Franciscan Order from Its Origins to the Year 1517*. Oxford: Clarendon Press, 1968.

Morales Muñiz, Maria Dolores-Carmen. "Las mercaderes del rey Alfonso XII de Castilla a la villa de Arévalo." *Anuario de Estudios Medievales* 16 (1986): 481–93.

Morena Romera, Bibiana. "Translado del rey don Fernando el Católico difunto, desde Madrigalejo a la ciudad de Granada." *Cuadernos de la Historia Contemporanea* 10 (1983): 249–64.

Morison, Samuel Eliot. *Admiral of the Ocean Sea. A Life of Christopher Columbus*. Boston: Little, Brown, 1942.

Nader, Helen. *The Mendoza Family in the Spanish Renaissance, 1350 to 1550*. New Brunswick, NJ: Rutgers University Press, 1979.

Netanyahu, Ben-Zion. *Don Isaac Abravanel: Statesman and Philosopher*. Philadelphia: Jewish Publication Society of America, 1953.

———. *The Marranos of Spain, from the Late Fourteenth Century to the Early Sixteenth Century According to Contemporary Hebrew Sources*. Millwood, NY: Kraus Reprint, 1973 [1966].

New York Public Library. *Tesoros de España. Ten Centuries of Spanish Books*. New York: New York Public Library Publications, 1985.

Nowell, Charles E. *A History of Portugal*. New York: Van Nostrand, 1952.

Numbers, Ronald L., ed. *Medicine in the New World: New Spain, New France and New England*. Knoxville: University of Tennessee Press, 1987.

O'Brien, Joseph A. *The Inquisition*. New York: Macmillan, 1973.

O'Callaghan, Joseph E. *A History of Medieval Spain*. Ithaca, NY: Cornell University Press, 1975.

Oettel, T. "Una catedrática en el siglo de Isabel la Católica." *Boletín de la Real Academia de la Historia* 107 (1935):289–360.

Ortega La Madrid, Paulino. "El emblema heraldico de la flechas de la Reina Isabel de Católica comentado por un humanisto italiano." *Publicaciones del Instituto "Tello Tellez de Menses"* 6 (1951):111–15.

Palacio Atard, Vicente. "Razón de la Inquisicion." *Santa Cruz* 7(12) (1948–52):27–40.

Pando Villarroya, José Luís de. *Colón y el viage tercero*. Madrid: Pando Ediciones, 1986.

Parry, J. H. *The Age of Reconnaissance: Discovery, Exploration and Settlement, 1450–1650*. Berkeley: University of California Press, 1963.

Parry, V. J. *A History of the Ottoman Empire to 1730*. Ed. M. A. Cook. Cambridge: Cambridge University Press, 1976.

Pastor, Ludwig. *The History of the Popes, from the Close of the Middle Ages.* 11 vols. St. Louis: B. Herder, 1912–1914.

Pearsall, Ronald. *The Alchemists.* London: Weidenfeld and Nicolson, 1976.

Pelikan, Jaroslav. *The Growth of Medieval Theology (600—1300),* vol. 3, *The Christian Tradition: A History of the Development of Doctrine.* Chicago: University of Chicago Press, 1978.

Peñalosa, Luís Felipe de. "Retratos segovianos del siglo XIX. II: Exposición de Arte Antiguo (1949)." *Estudios Segovianos* 45 (1955):283–353.

———. *Segovie: La Vaisseau de Pierre.* Trans. Marie-Loup Soungez.

Pérez, Joseph. *Isabel y Fernando. Los Reyes Católicos.* Trans. Fernando Santos Fontenla. Madrid: Nerea, 1988.

Peters, Edward. *Inquisition.* New York: Free Press/Macmillan, 1988.

Pfandl, Ludwig. *Juana la Loca.* 9th ed. Madrid: Espasa-Calpe, 1984 [1937].

Phillips, William D., Jr. *Enrique IV and the Crisis of Fifteenth Century Castile, 1425–1480.* Cambridge, MA: Medieval Academy of America, 1978.

Plunket, Ierne L. *Isabel of Castile and the Making of the Spanish Nation.* New York: Putnam, 1915.

Ponce de León y Freyre, Eduardo. *El Marques de Cádiz, 1443–1492,* 2nd ed. Madrid: Anaquel, 1949.

Prescott, William H. *History of the Reign of Ferdinand and Isabella the Catholic.* 3 vols. Philadelphia: Lippincott, 1872 [1837].

Purcell, Mary. *The Great Captain: Gonzalo Fernández de Córdoba.* New York: Doubleday, 1962.

Represa Rodriguez, Amando. "Origen y desarrollo urbano del Valladolid medieval (siglos X-XIII)." In *Historia de Valladolid,* pp. 65–86. Valladolid: Editorial Sever-Cuesta, 1980.

———. "El Valladolid de los Reyes Católicos." *Santa Cruz* 7(12) (1948–52):64–75.

Rey, Eusebio. "La Bula de Alejandro VI otorgando el título de 'Católicos' a Fernando e Isabel." *Razon y Fe* 146 (1952):59–75.

Rice, Eugene, Jr. *Saint Jerome in the Renaissance.* Baltimore: Johns Hopkins University Press, 1985.

Rodríguez Villa, Antonio. *La Reina doña Juana la Loca.* Madrid: Libreria de M. Murillo, 1892.

Rogers, Katharine. *The Troublesome Helpmate: A History of Misogyny in Literature.* Seattle: University of Washington Press, 1966.

Romeu Palazuelos, Enrique. "Beatriz de Bobadilla." In *Homenage a Elias Serra Rafols,* vol. 3, pp. 217–34. Seville: Universidad de la Laguna, 1970.

Rose, Mary Beth. *Women in the Middle Ages and the Renaissance: Literary and Historical Perspectives.* Syracuse, NY: Syracuse University Press, 1986.

Roth, Cecil. *A History of the Marranos.* Philadelphia: Jewish Publication Society of America, 1932.

Rowland, Beryl. *A Medieval Woman's Guide to Health: The First Gynecological Handbook.* Kent, OH: Kent State University Press, 1981.

Rucquoi, Adeline. *Valladolid en la edad media: el mundo abreviado.* Valladolid: Junta de Castilla y León, 1987.

Sabatini, Rafael. *Torquemada and the Spanish Inquisition.* Boston: Houghton Mifflin, 1924.

Sadoul, Jacques. *Alchemists and Gold.* Trans. Olga Sieveking. New York: G. P. Putnam's Sons, 1972.

Sánchez Canton, Francisco Javier. *Libros, Tapices y Cuadros que coleccionó Isabel la Católica.* Madrid: Consejo Superior de Investigaciones Científicas, 1950.

Sebastian de Erice, Jose. "La diplomatica de Isabel de España y sus constantes historicas." In *Curso de conferencias sobre la politica africana de los reyes católicos*, vol. 1, pp. 68–90. Madrid: Instituto de Estudios Africanos, 1951.

Shahar, Shulamith. *The Fourth Estate: A History of Women in the Middle Ages*. Trans. Chaya Galai. London: Methuen, 1984.

Shaw, Stanford. *History of the Ottoman Empire and Modern Turkey*, vol.1, *Empire of the Gazis: The Rise and Decline of the Ottoman Empire, 1280–1808*. Cambridge: Cambridge University Press, 1976.

Singer, Charles, and E. Ashworth Underwood. *A Short History of Medicine*, 2nd ed. New York: Oxford University Press, 1962.

Sitges, J. B. *Enrique IV y la Excelente Señora, llamada vulgarmente Doña Juana la Beltraneja, 1425–1530*. Madrid: Rivadeneyra, 1912.

Smith, Dennis Mack. *A History of Sicily: Medieval Sicily, 800—1713*. New York: Viking, 1968.

Spufford, Peter. *Handbook of Medieval Exchange*. London: Offices of the Royal Historical Society, 1986.

Stuard, Susan Mosher. *Women in Medieval Society*. Philadelphia: University of Pennsylvania Press, 1976.

Suárez Fernández, Luis. "Las ciudades castellanas en la época de los reyes católicos." In *Historia de Valladolid*, pp. 113–23. Valladolid: Editorial Sever-Cuesta, 1980.

———. *Fernando el Católico y Navarra. El proceso de incorporación del reino a la Corona de España*. Madrid: Ediciones Rialp, 1985.

———. *Política internacional de Isabel la Católica*. 2 vols. Valladolid: Universidad de Valladolid, 1965–1969.

———. "La política internacional en el comienzo del reinado de los Reyes Católicos." *Santa Cruz* 7(12) (1948–52):41–51.

———. "En torno al pacto del los Toros de Guisando." *Hispania* 91 (1963):3–23.

———. *Historia de España*, vol. 7, *Las Trastámaras y los reyes católicos*. Ed. Angel Montenegro Duque. Madrid: Editorial Gredos, 1985.

———, Juan de Mata Carriazo Arroquia and Manuel Fernández Álvarez. *La España de los Reyes Católicos (1474–1516)*. *Historia de España* vol. 17, Book 1, ed. Ramón Menéndez Pidal. Madrid: Espasa-Calpe, 1969.

———, and Manuel Fernández Álvarez. *La España de los Reyes Católicos (1474–1516)*. Vol. 17, book 2, ed. Ramón Menéndez Pidal. 3rd ed. Madrid: Espasa-Calpe, 1983.

Tannahill, Reay. *Food in History*. 2nd ed. New York: Crown, 1988 [1973].

Taviani, Paolo Emilio. *Christopher Columbus: The Grand Design*. Trans. William Weaver. London: Orbis, 1985.

Taylor, F. Sherwood. *The Alchemists: Founders of Modern Chemistry*. New York: Henry Schuman, 1949.

Toledo Giran, José. "La libreria de un obispo valenciano incantada por la reina doña Isabel la Católica." *Anales del Centro de Cultura Valenciana*, 2nd ser. 21(44) (1960):78–88.

Torre, Antonio de la, ed. *La Casa de Isabel la Católica*. Madrid: Consejo Superior de Investigaciones Científicas, 1954.

———. "Isabel la Católica: Corregente en la Corona de Aragón." *Anuario de Historia del Derecho Español*, 1st ser. 23(53) (1953):423–28.

———. "Maestros de los hijos de los reyes católicos." *Hispania* 16(63) (1956):256–66.

———. "Unas noticias de Beatriz de Galindo, 'La Latina.'" *Hispania* 17 (1957):255–67.

———. "Unas noticias sobre Cristobal Colón," *Hispania* 17 (1957):505–9.

———. *Los Reyes Católicos y Granada*. Madrid: Instituto Jeronimo Zurita, 1946.

———. "Viajes y transportes en tiempo de los reyes católicos," *Hispania* 16 (1954):365–410.

Torres Fontes, Juan. "La contratación de Guisando (Toros de Guisando)." *Anuario de Estudios Medievales* 2 (1965):399–428.

Trevor-Davies, R. *The Golden Century of Spain, 1501–1621.* Westport, CT: Greenwood Press, 1984 [1937].

Tyler, Royall. *The Emperor Charles the Fifth.* London: George Allen and Unwin, 1956.

Val, Maria Isabel del. *Isabel la Católica, Princesa (1468–1474).* Valladolid: Instituto Isabel la Católica de Historia Eclesiástica, 1974.

Valdeon Baruque, Julio. "Valladolid en los siglos XIV y XV." In *Historia de Valladolid,* pp. 87–112. Valladolid: Editorial Sever-Cuesta, 1980.

Valdeon Baruque, Julio, Jose Maria Salrach, and Javier Zabalo. *Feudalismo y consolidación de los pueblos hispanicos (siglos XI–XV),* vol. 4 of *Historia de España.* Ed. Manuel Tuñon de Lara. Barcelona: Editorial Labor, 1982.

Van Cleave Alexander, Michael. *The First of the Tudors. A Study of Henry VII and His Reign.* Totowa, NJ: Rowman and Littlefield, 1980.

Verd Martorell, Gabriel. *Cristobal Colón y la revelación del enigma,* 3rd ed. Palma de Mallorca: IMGESA, 1986.

Vicens Vives, Jaime. *Approaches to the History of Spain.* Trans. and ed. Joan Connelly Ullman. Berkeley: University of California Press, 1967.

———. *Fernando el Católico: Principe de Aragón, rey de Sicilia (1458–1478).* Madrid: Consejo Superior de Investigaciones Científicas, 1952.

———. *Historia crítica de la vida y reinado de Fernando II de Aragón.* Zaragoza: Institución Fernando el Católico, 1962.

Villa, Justa de la. "El matrimonio de Isabel y Valladolid." *Clavileno* 3 (1950):31–37.

Villalba Ruíz de Toledo, F. Javier. *El Cardenal Mendoza (1428–1495).* Madrid: Ediciones Rialp, 1988.

Walsh, Michael, ed. *Butler's Lives of Patron Saints.* Kent: Burns and Oates, 1987.

Walsh, William Thomas. *Isabella of Spain: The Last Crusader.* New York: Robert M. McBride Co., 1930.

Wiesner, Merry E. "Early Modern Midwifery: A Case Study." In *Women and Work in Preindustrial Europe,* ed. Barbara Hanawalt, pp. 94–113. Bloomington: University of Indiana Press, 1986.

Yerushalmi, Josef Hayim. *The Lisbon Massacre of 1506 and the Royal Image in the Shebet Yehudah.* Cincinnati: Hebrew Union College, 1976.

INDEX

NATIONAL UNIVERSITY
LIBRARY SAN DIEGO c. 1